Oslo Legal Studies

edited by

The Faculty of Law of the University of Oslo

represented by

the dean Prof. Dr. Dag Michalsen

Volume 1

Melanie Regine Hack, Ph.D.

Taking age equality seriously: The example of mandatory retirement

A comparative legal analysis between Norway and Germany in light of Council Directive 2000/78/EC

Nomos

The Deutsche Nationalbibliothek lists this publication in the Deutsche Nationalbibliografie; detailed bibliographic data are available on the Internet at http://dnb.d-nb.de

at.: Oslo, Univ., Diss., 2016

ISBN 978-3-8487-3059-9 (Print)
978-3-8452-7207-8 (ePDF)

British Library Cataloguing-in-Publication Data
A catalogue record for this book is available from the British Library.

ISBN 978-3-8487-3059-9 (Print)
978-3-8452-7207-8 (ePDF)

Library of Congress Cataloging-in-Publication Data
Hack, Melanie Regine
Taking Age Equality Seriously: The Example of Mandatory Retirement
A Comparative Legal Analysis between Norway and Germany in Light of Council Directive 2000/78/EC
Melanie Regine Hack
423 p.
Includes bibliographic references and index.

ISBN 978-3-8487-3059-9 (Print)
978-3-8452-7207-8 (ePDF)

1. Edition 2016

Alder er som at bestige et bjerg.
Man bliver nok lidt forpustet, men får en langt bedre udsigt.

Ingrid Bergman

Acknowledgements

First and foremost I express my sincere gratitude to my supervisor Prof. Stein Evju, head of the labour law research group at the Department of Private Law at University of Oslo. He has always been a 'Doktorvater'. Stein's inexhaustible knowledge and boundless support have been inspiring and motivating. Last but not least, many thanks for your patience and flexibility with this truly international project throughout my pursuit of my PhD, no matter where in the world I have been, be it Norway, Mexico, Germany, the UK or the US. I could not have imagined a better advisor and mentor than you, Stein.

I am also profoundly grateful to Prof. Dr. Beate Sjåfjell for her support, particularly leading up to my PhD midterm evaluation. I thank Prof. Colm O'Cinneide for his scientific advice as well as many fruitful discussions and suggestions during my stay as a guest researcher at University College London (UCL), Faculty of Laws.

I offer special thanks and appreciation to my thesis committee, Prof. Dr. Hans Petter Graver, Prof. Dr. Ann Numhauser-Henning and Prof. Dr. Dagmar Schiek, for their insightful comments and encouragement. I am particularly indebted to the Committee's leader, Prof. Dr. Graver, who encouraged me to publish my thesis in this new series. Likewise, I thank Faculty Dean Prof. Dr. Dag Michalsen and the head of the Department of Private Law, Prof. Dr. Guiditta Cordero Moss, for their support and for granting me the opportunity and honour to publish my thesis in the series Oslo Legal Studies.

I truly appreciate my colleagues and comrades, Dr. Terese Smith Ulseth, Marianne Jenum Hotvedt, Ph.D. and Marie Nesvik. Together we formed the first generation of the newly established research group on labour law at the Faculty of Law in 2008. Thanks to all our colleagues who joined the group over time and who contributed stimulating discussions during our regularly "arbeidsrettslunsj" meetings, creating an inspiring and enriching atmosphere. I also thank my PhD fellow, Julia Pohl, for her unconditional intellectual and practical support during my stay in Oslo.

I gratefully acknowledge the funding sources that made my Ph.D. work possible. I am particularly indebted to the Faculty of Law for funding publication and making it possible for me to hold the product of my last years' PhD journey in my hands. The Faculty supported me immensely through this journey, which literally opened up the world for me. I not only became a part of Norwegian academia and society but I was able to explore other parts of the world through several research visits, for which I am very thankful.

Furthermore, I would like to thank Det juridiske fakultets reisefond av 1973 for funding my research stays at UCL London, UK and The George Washington University Law School, USA, and E.ON Ruhrgas for supporting me with a scholarship to visit the Max Planck Institute for Social Law and Social Policy in Munich, Germany.

Special mention also goes to Bodil Silset, Siri Margrethe Vinger, Eli Knotten, Eva Modvar and Mona Østvang Ådum for their continuous support in any administrative and library research questions. Without your knowledge and expertise, we could not do the work we do.

Finally, I owe special thanks to Pål Behrens and Ida Flaatten from the Finance Sector Union Norway for giving me the opportunity to work as a consultant in a very interesting Supreme Court case on age discrimination and to put my knowledge into practical action.

I cannot possibly name all of the people across the globe who contributed their time, energy, and knowledge in support of my work. I am deeply grateful to every one of you. Without you, this journey would not have been possible. Tusen hjertelig takk.

Inhaltsverzeichnis

List of abbreviations

Abb.	Abbildung
a.D.	außer Dienst
ADEA	The Age Discrimination in Employment Act of 1967
AE	Arbeitsrechtliche Entscheidungen
AFP	avtalefestet pensjon
AG	Amtsgericht
AG	Advocate General
AGG	Allgemeines Gleichbehandlungsgesetz
a.M.	am Main
Anm.	Anmerkung
ArbG	Arbeitsgericht
ArbGG	Arbeitsgerichtsgesetz
ArbVG	Arbeitsvertragsgesetz
ARD	Arbeidsretten
Art.	Artikel
AZR	Arzt Zahnarzt Recht
ArztR	ArztRecht
Ärzte-ZV	Zulassungsverordnung für Vertragsärzte
BAG	Bundesarbeitsgericht
BAGE	Entscheidungen des Bundesarbeitsgerichts (Amtliche Sammlung)
BayBG	Bayerisches Beamtengesetz
BayHSchPG	Bayerisches Hochschulpersonalgesetz
BB (B.B.)	Betriebs Berater
BBG	Bundesbeamtengesetz
B.C.	Before Christ
Bd.	Band
BeamSTG	Beamtenstatusgesetz
BeckOK	Beck'scher Online-Kommentar
BetrVG	Betriebsverfassungsgesetz
BFOQ	bona fide occupational qualification
BGB	Bürgerliches Gesetzbuch

BGBl.	Bundesgesetzblatt
BGH	Bundesgerichtshof
BIS	Department for Business Innovation and Skills
BMC	BioMedCentral
BNotO	Bundesnotarordnung
BOLSA	Bonn Longitudinal Study on Aging
Brem.	Bremisch
BremBG	bremisches Beamtengesetz
BSG	Bundessozialgericht
BSGE	Entscheidungen des Bundessozialgerichts (Amtliche Sammlung)
Bt-Drs.	Bundestagsdrucksache
BVerfG	Bundesverfassungsgericht
BVerfGE	Bundesverfassungsgerichtsentscheidung
CCPR	Covenant on Civil and Political Rights
CEDAW	Convention on the Elimination of All Forms of Discrimination against Women
CESCR	The Committee on Economic, Social and Cultural Rights
CFREU	Charter of Fundamental Rights of the European Union
chap.	chapter
CJEU	Court of Justice of the European Union
CMAJ	Canadian Medical Association Journal
CMLR	Common Market Law Review
CRPD	Convention on the Rights of Persons with Disabilities
CSP	Center for Senior Policy
DB	Der Betrieb
Dir.	Directive
DRA	default retirement age
DStR	Deutsches Steuerrecht
DÖV	Die Öffentliche Verwaltung
EASA	European Aviation Safety Agency
EC	European Community
ECHR	Convention for the Protection of Human Rights and Fundamental Freedoms
ECR	European Court Reports
ECJ	European Court of Justice
ECSR	European Committee of Social Rights

ECtHR	European Court of Human Rights
ed.	editor
edt.	edition
Eds./eds.	Editors
EEA	European Economic Area
EEC	European Economic Community
EFTA	European Free Trade Association
e.g.	exempli gratia
EHRLR	European Human Rights Law Review
EHRR	European Human Rights Reports
EMRK	Europäische Menschenrechtskonvention
ERCL	European Review of Contract Law
ESC	European Social Charter
et al.	et alii
EuGH	Europäischer Gerichtshof
EU	European Union
EuZA	Europäische Zeitschrift für Arbeitsrecht
Eurostat	Statistical Office of the European Communities
EWS	Europäisches Wirtschafts- und Steuerrecht
EØS	Det europeiske økonomiske samarbeidsområde
Fafo	Fagforeningen
f.	folgende (Singular), German abbreviation for following page
ff.	folgende (Plural), following pages
FA	Fachanwalt Arbeitsrecht
FFS	Fellesforbundet for Sjøfolk
Fig.	Figure
fn.	footnote
FOR	forskrift
ftrl	folketrygdlov
GesR	GesundheitsRecht
GG	Grundgesetz
GKV	Gesetzliche Krankenversicherung
GKV-OrgWG	Gesetz zur Weiterentwicklung der Organisationsstrukturen in der gesetzlichen Krankenversicherung
GOR	genuine and determining occupational requirement
GP	general practitioner
GPR	Zeitschrift für das Privatrecht der Europäischen Union

GRCh	Grundrechtecharta
Grl.	Grunnloven
H.	Heft
HBG	Hessisches Beamtengesetz
HPN	Statens Helsepersonellnemnd
HH	Hamburg
hlspl.	Helsepersonellov
HM	Hartmannbund
HmbBG	Hamburgisches Beamtengesetz
HPN	Statens Helsepersonellnemnd
HR	Høyesterett
HRC	The UN Committee for Human Rights
HRG	Hochschulrahmengesetz
ibid.	ibidem
ICAO	International Civil Aviation Organisation
ICCPR	International Covenant on Civil and Political Rights
ICESCR	International Covenant on Economic, Social and Cultural Rights
ICEAFRD	International Convention on the Elimination of All Forms of Racial Discrimination
i.c.w.	in conjunction with
ILO	International Labour Organization
ILC	International longevity center – USA
Innst.	Innstilling
Innst. O.	Innstilling til Odelstinget
Innst. S.	Innstilling til Stortinget
i.R.	im Ruhestand
JAA	Joint Aviation Authorities
JAR-FCL	Joint Aviation Requirements for Flight Crew Licensing
jurisPR-ArbR	jurisPraxisReport-ArbeitsRechts
JuS	Juristische Schulung
JZ	Juristen-Zeitung
KS	Kommunens Sentralforbund
KSchG	Kündigungsschutzgesetz
KSzWR	Kölner Schrift zum Wirtschaftsrecht
LBG	Landesbeamtengesetz
LDO	Likestilling- og diskrimineringsombudet

LDN	Likestillings- og diskrimineringsnemnda
lit.	litera
Lt-Dr.	Landtags-Drucksache
LuftZO	Luftverkehrs-Zulassungs-Ordnung
LuftPersV	Verordnung über Luftfahrtpersonal
MedR	Medizinrecht
Meld. St.	Melding til stortinget
m.fl.	med flere
m.m.	med mere
Mich L Rev	Michigan Law Review
mv.	med videre
NAV	Ny Arbeids- og velferdsforvaltningen
NBG	Niedersächsisches Beamtengesetz
Nds.	Niedersachsen
NHO	Næringslivets hovedorganisasjon
NIP	Nytt i privatretten: nyhetsbrev for informasjon på det privatret
NMA	Norwegian Medical Association
No./no.	number
Nos.	numbers
NOSOCO	Nordic Social-Statistical Committee
NOU	Norges Offentlige Utredninger
NVwZ	Neue Zeitschrift für Verwaltungsrecht
NZA	Neue Zeitschrift für Arbeitsrecht
NZS	Neue Zeitschrift für Sozialrecht
NJW	Neue Juristische Wochenschrift
nr.	Nummer
NRW	Nordrhein-Westfalen
NWSA	National Women's Studies Association
NZS	Neue Zeitschrift für Sozialrecht
OECD	Organisation for Economic Co-operation and Development
OJ L	Official Journal L
OTP	obligatorisk tjenestepensjon
Ot.prp.	Odelstingsproposisjon
OVG	Oberverwaltungsgericht
OWR	Older Workers Recommendation
para./paras.	paragraph(s)
p.	page

pp.	pages
PersV	Die Personalvertretung
Plenarprot.	Plenarprotokoll
Prop.	Proposisjon
QCEA	Quaker Council for European Affairs
Qual Saf Health Care	Quality and Safety in Health Care
RabelsZ	Zeitschrift für ausländisches und internationales Privatrecht
RdA	Recht der Arbeit
RESC	Revised European Social Charter
RG	Reichsgericht
RGZ	Entscheidungen des Reichsgerichts in Zivilsachen
RTV	Rahmentarifvertrag
Rt	Norsk Rettstidende
RV	Rentenversicherung
s./S.	sentence
SAE	Sammlung arbeitsrechtlicher Entscheidungen
SAS	Scandinavian Airline Systems
SBG	Saarländisches Beamtengesetz
Sess.	Session
SGB	Sozialgesetzbuch
SGb	Die Sozialgerichtsbarkeit
SHI	Statutory Health Insurance
SoldGG	Gesetz über die Gleichbehandlung der Soldatinnen und Soldaten
SPH	Statens personalhåndbok
SPK	statens pensjonskasse
St. Prp.	Proposisjon til stortinget
St. Meld	Melding til stortinget
suppl.	Supplement
stpkl	lov om Statens pensjonskasse
SächsBG	Sächsisches Beamtengesetz
TEC	Treaty establishing the European Community
TEU	Treaty on European Union
TFEU	Treaty on the Functioning of the European Union
Tidsskr Nor Lægeforen/Tidsskr Nor Legeforen	Tidsskrift for den norske Lægeforening/Legeforening

tjml	tjenestemannslov
TVöD	Tarifvertrag für den öffentlichen Dienst
TV-L	Tarifvertrag für den öffentlichen Dienst der Länder
TzBfG	Teilzeit- und Befristungsgesetz
ThürBG	thüringisches Beamtengesetz
UDHR	Universal Declaration of Human Rights
UiO	University of Oslo
UK	United Kingdom
UN	United Nations
UN	Doc United Nations Document
UN	HRC United Nations Committee for Human Rights
univl.	universitets- og høyskoleloven.
US/USA	United States of America
v./vs.	versus
VG	Verwaltungsgericht
VGH	Hessischer Verwaltungsgerichtshof
Vol./vol.	Volume
WEA	Working Environment Act
w.f.r.	with further references
w.r.t.	with reference to
ZBR	Zeitschrift für Beamtenrecht
ZESAR	Zeitschrift für europäisches Sozial- und Arbeitsrecht
ZIAS	Zeitschrift für ausländisches und internationales Arbeits- und Sozialrecht
ZRP	Zeitschrift für Rechtspolitik
ZTR	Zeitschrift für Tarifrecht
ZvglRW	Zeitschrift für vergleichende Rechtswissenschaften

Part I

1 Introduction

1.1 Taking age equality seriously: The thesis in a nutshell

> *The fact is that when I come to think it over, I find that there are four reasons for old age being thought unhappy: First, that it withdraws us from active employments; second, that it enfeebles the body; third, that it deprives us of nearly all physical pleasures; fourth, that it is the next step to death. Of each of these reasons, if you will allow me, let us examine the force and justice separately.*
> *[...] OLD AGE WITHDRAWS US FROM ACTIVE EMPLOYMENTS. From which of them? Do you mean from those carried on by youth and bodily strength? Are there then no old men's employments to be after all conducted by the intellect, even when bodies are weak?*[1]

The thesis' title, *Taking Age Equality Seriously,* constitutes the leitmotiv for the whole analysis.

Even if multifarious meanings of the notion equality do exist,[2] it may be put forward that age equality in employment, as a starting point for this thesis, means that every individual employee (in principle) should have the same opportunity to participate fully and equally in working life, irrespective of his or her chronological age. The essential aim of age equality should be to facilitate the equal participation of all people – irrespective of their age – in society and in working life, based on equal concern and respect for the human dignity of each individual.[3] In order to achieve such substantive age equality, the existing obstacles for the participation of employees in working life have to be dismantled. A society and a working life for all ages also encompasses the goal of providing older persons with the opportunity to continue contributing to society and to provide employ-

---

1 *Cicero* (106 B.C.–43 B.C.), On Old Age The Harvard Classics, 1909–14, paras. 1-29, 13ff.

2 *Bamforth*, Nicolas/*Malik*, Maleiha/*O'Cinneide*, Colm (2008), Discrimination law: Theory and context, p. 174.

3 *Fredman*, Sandra (2003), The age of equality, in: Age as an equality issue, Fredman, Sandra/Spencer, Sarah (eds.), p. 21.

ment opportunities for all older employees who want to work. As stressed by the United Nations, 'To work towards this goal, it is necessary to remove whatever excludes or discriminates against them'.[4]

Mandatory retirement generally constitutes such an obstacle to the equal participation of older employees. It affects not only the older employee's right not to be discriminated against on the grounds of age, but also concerns his or her right to work and is above all strongly linked to the employee's human dignity per se. From the employee's perspective, exercising the right to work principally implies exercising freedom of choice as to whether his or her working life is extended or not. The termination of the employment relationship via an absolute age limit has a strong impact on the right to work, as it often, de facto, can be equalised with a termination of working life.

At present, mandatory retirement is highly debated at the national, European and international level. The reasons for this are twofold: first, from a socio-political angle, that is, in view of an increasing pressure on the financial stability of the pension systems due to the demographic change, there is a need to review the existing mandatory retirement provisions critically. Second, from a legal perspective the equality principle in terms of age and the protection against age discrimination has been considerably strengthened both in human rights law and in European Union (EU) law in the past decade. Against this background, the main focus of the thesis rests on a legal analysis of selected mandatory retirement provisions that force older employees to retire at a certain age.[5]

The thesis' key aim is to examine these provisions in terms of their compatibility with the prohibition against age discrimination as it is manifested in Council Directive 2000/78/EC.[6] In doing so, the selected provisions in Norwegian law are compared to their respective mandatory retirement provisions in German law. Norway traditionally has a strong focus on equality and rather high mandatory retirement ages, as well as an overall high participation rate for older employees in working life. Germany

4 *United Nations* (UN) (2002), Report of second world assembly on ageing, Madrid 6-12 April 2002, para. 19, p. 9, para. 28, p. 12, see moreover para. 23, p. 11.

5 The notions employee and worker are used synonymously in this thesis and encompass in principle both so-called intellectual or white-collar worker and manual or blue-collar workers.

6 Council Directive 2000/78/EC of 27 November 2000 establishing a general framework for equal treatment in employment and occupation, OJ L 303.

on the other hand, features lower participation rates and lower age limits.[7] Via a legal comparison, the thesis aims at elaborating on whether – and if so how – the selected mandatory retirement provisions in these countries comply with the prohibition against age discrimination, and if the examined legal status quo in one country might function as a role model for *de lege ferenda* amendments in the other country. The analysis is not a general study of EU law. Rather, Dir. 2000/78/EC constitutes the standard of comparison. Both countries implemented the Directive and, therefore, in principle, they are forced to comply with the Directive's requirements and the prohibition against age discrimination as concretised therein. Even though Norway was not legally bound under the Agreement on the European Economic Area (EEA agreement) to implement Dir. 2000/78/EC, it chose to do so on policy grounds.[8]

That the prohibition of age discrimination has to be taken seriously on a national level is inter alia a result of the fact that the principle of non-discrimination on the grounds of age constitutes a general principle of EU primary law.[9] It functions as a kind of instrumental goal to achieve the overarching societal goal of age equality in employment. This finds its legal manifestation in Dir. 2000/78/EC. Thereby it also has an impact on the Norwegian legal situation. However, the principle of non-discrimination on the grounds of age is not unlimited. Age discrimination may in certain circumstances be justified. This is accounted for in the various justification provisions in Dir. 2000/78/EC, which are central to this thesis.[10]

Analysing mandatory retirement provisions in light of Dir. 2000/78/EC requires to address two overarching questions. First, when is age discrimination considered to be in accordance with the Directive's justification requirements? Second, are the selected provisions on mandatory retirement in Norwegian and German law compatible with these requirements?

---

7 see in detail to labour market statistics chap. 7.

8 Agreement on the European Economic Area (EEA), OJ No L 1, 3.1.1994; see in detail chap. 11.2; see also *Hack*, Melanie R. (2010 c), Etter lek med ild, nå lek med vann: Aldersgrense, pensjonsalder, sjømenn Høyesterettsdom 18. februar 2010 (HR-2010-00303-A), Nytt i privatretten (NIP), (2), 2010, pp. 2-3; *Hack*, Melanie R. (2012 a), To be or not be be? – The Norwegian dilemma of being just politically bound to Framework Directive 2000/78/EC, Europäische Zeitschrift für Arbeitsrecht (EUZA) 2012, pp. 357 367.

9 see the landmark judgement C-144/04 (*Mangold*), Judgement of the Court 22 November 2005, ECR 2005 I-9981, para. 75; see in detail chap. 10.1.

10 see in detail chap. 10.3 and chap. 12.

As various competing and conflicting values and interests might be affected by mandatory retirement provisions, a balancing tool is needed to determine if age discrimination is justified or not. Mandatory retirement vitally reflects the fundamental conflict between the competing interests and values that are affected in relation to the justification of age discrimination. Generally speaking, it is a conflict between the interests of the older employee to be treated fairly and with dignity, on the one hand, and the various economic or security-related interests of employers, third parties or society in general on the other hand.[11] To determine how much weight should be placed on the different involved interests and values and in order to identify whether the reasons that are given for age discrimination 'are strong enough to displace the value of equality'[12] the principle of proportionality constitutes the analytical balancing tool.[13] Proportionality is an important element, for any justification analysis in cases of age discrimination as it is a fundamental part of the general principle of non-discrimination on the grounds of age.[14] A necessary prerequisite to a proportionality assessment is to identify the potential legitimate aims underlying the mandatory retirement provision in question. The central question in this regard is whether these potential legitimate aims may still be maintained to justify mandatory retirement in light of demographical and gerontopsychological findings as well as labour-market statistics. Consequently, an interdisciplinary approach is necessary in order to examine whether typically referred to justification patterns in the legal discourse on mandatory retirement may also be upheld in view of scientific findings of neighbour disciplines.[15]

When analysing mandatory retirement and its conformity with the prohibition against age discrimination as manifested in Dir. 2000/78/EC, it is, moreover, necessary to identify clearly the interrelationship between the prohibition and the concepts of age equality and ageism. By operating with chronological age as the decisive proxy, mandatory retirement age

11 *Fredman* (2003), p. 46ff.

12 ibid., p. 50.

13 similar ibid., p. 50 f.

14 see in detail to the requirements of the proportionality principle as part of the justification provisions in Dir. 2000/78/EC: chap. 10.3.5.

15 stressing the necessity of an interdisciplinary approach also *Temming*, Felipe (2008), Altersdiskriminierung im Arbeitsleben: Eine rechtsmethodische Analyse, p. 55.

limits have to be regarded as the legal manifestation of stereotypes of age and ageing – of so-called ageism. As ageism is an inherent part of mandatory retirement, the thesis therefore also sheds light on the concept of ageism.

After having examined the *de lega lata* status quo, the comparative analysis involves, as a further step towards ascertaining through a legal comparison what kind of solutions *de lege ferenda* might be most appropriate in terms of achieving and guaranteeing substantive age equality for the older employee. The examination of flexible solutions to build a smooth pathway from working life to retirement as an alternative to mandatory retirement age limits in this regard is key.

1.2 Themes and issues

1.2.1 Challenges of an ageing society

The necessity of critically assessing mandatory retirement is not only pivotal in view of the employee's protection against unjustified age discrimination, but also from the perspective of the society as a whole. It inter alia derives out of the fact that societies in Europe, including Norway and Germany, face a major challenge – the so-called demographic change. Demographic change basically means that a population's age structure changes, which, per se, does not necessarily lead to serious consequences for those societies. However, in the case of Norway and Germany, both countries are confronted with a so-called 'double demographic change'[16]; that is, the ageing of the population due to longer life expectancy, on the one hand, and the shrinking of the population on the other caused by low birth rates, which leads to an increased number of older people in relation to younger people.[17] This phenomenon is not unique to Norway and Germany, and it not only occurs Europe-wide, but also globally, as the number of people aged 60+ has been estimated to double from 11% of the world population

16 see to this aspect already and for further references *Hack*, Melanie R. (2010 a), Impact or potential of anti-discrimination legislation in light of the demographic change – Comparisons between Norway and Germany' EuZA 2010, pp. 347-359, p. 347.

17 ibid.

to 22% in 2050.[18] Remarkably, the increase will be the greatest and most rapid in developing countries where the older population has even been estimated to quadruple by 2050.[19] Furthermore, it is not a phenomenon that has to be tackled in the distant future, but rather something, which is going to change the 'face' of the European population dramatically and fundamentally in the present time, as the turning point has been estimated to be reached in 2013/2014.[20] Some even call this process a 'demographic revolution'.[21] This has also been recognised by European policymakers who even included the necessity of keeping the issue on the agenda in Art. 159 Treaty on the Functioning of the European Union (TFEU).

As a consequence of this 'revolution', the patterns of the workforce and labour markets in general are also going to change.[22] The double demographic change leads to a changed life cycle, which in turn impacts on the patterns of the work cycle. A biologically defined expansion of old age based on an earlier maturity and a later menopause faces a narrowing of the sociologically defined adult age on the grounds of a later entry into the workforce and an earlier exit from the labour force as a consequence of early retirement. The previously valid intergenerational contract between three generations has now changed to a contract between five generations.[23] The current problem concerns this generation of employees, in

18 see http://epo.de/index.php?option=com_content&view=article&id=9706:qweltalten-indexq-anteil-aelterer-menschen-weltweit-waechst-rapide&catid=99:topnews (last accessed: 17.12.2014); see also Art. 2 UN Political Declaration (2002) Second World Assembly on Ageing; UN Madrid International Plan of Action on Ageing (2002) (Madrid Plan), I. Introduction, para. 2; see in detail to the UN Madrid Plan chap. 9.7.1.4.

19 see Art. 2 Madrid Plan, I. Introduction, para. 2.

20 COM(2010) 2020, Communication from the Commission Europe 2020, A strategy for smart, sustainable and inclusive growth, p. 5, 7.

21 *Doron*, Israel (2007), Demographic, social change and equality, in: Equality law in an enlarged European Union, Meenan, Helen (ed.), p. 118.

22 ibid., p. 132.

23 In general five generations are to be found in society (age 5, 25, 45, 65, 85), whereof three generations are at work (age 25, 45, 65), see *Lehr*, Ursula (2007), Psychologie des Alterns, 11. edt., p. 43; see with regard to the problematic of 'intergenerational conflict': *Doron* (2007), p. 136 f.

that it has to care for two generations who are not yet employed and for almost two generations who are already in retirement.[24] Moreover, this middle generation is often confronted with non-solid work careers.

The intergenerational contract based on three generations, which *Bismarck* had in mind when he introduced the old-age insurance and invalidity schemes in 1889 in Germany, has moved out of balance.[25] Bismarck formulated, on 9 May 1884, in a session of the German Reichstag concerning the *Socialistengesetz*, the key aim of his social-policy concept, '*Geben Sie dem Arbeiter das Recht auf Arbeit, so lange er gesund ist, sichern Sie ihm Pflege, wenn er krank ist, sichern Sie ihm Versorgung, wenn er alt ist'*.[26] It has to be noted that the entitlement to an old-age pension was limited to those employees who had reached the age of 70 (the age limit was lowered in 1916 to 65 years of age).[27] However, only a few people ever reached the age limit of 70 years, as in 1900, the average life expectancy was 46.4 years for men and 52.5 years for women in Germany.[28]

Early retirement and the increased longevity of retirees has led to an overall elongated period of retirement.[29] Several productive years of working life might therefore be 'lost', which leads to negative effects for society as a whole and which puts the sustainability of the social security systems at risk. The increased pressure on the national social security systems is caused by a shrinking of the younger workforce, on the one hand, and an increasing number of the elderly, in particular, through the rise in the number of retirees. The threatened financial stability of the social security systems makes it even more necessary to promote age equality to encourage older people to remain part of the workforce and to unleash the full

24 *Lehr* (2007), p. 43 according to *Lehr* the generation of those in employment encompasses persons between 25 to 58 years of age. Given the renunciation from early retirement schemes and the rise in the exit age of employees, this may probably be modified.

25 see references given by *Lehr* (2007), p. 43; *Bertelsmann*, Klaus (2007), in: Rust, Ursula/Falke, Josef (eds.), AGG, § 10, para. 226; see also *Christensen*, Anna (2000), Normativa grundmönster i pensjonssystemen, in: Lovens liv, Festskrift Jörgen Dalberg-Larsen, Olsen, Henrik P. (ed.), pp. 171-193, p. 171 f.

26 Stenographische Berichte über die Verhandlungen des Reichstags, Session 1884, V, IV, Bd. I, p. 481.

27 see for further details *Lehr* (2007), p. 43.

28 see http://www.berlin-institut.org/newsletter/Newsletter_13_09_2006.html (last accessed: 17.12.2014).

29 *Fredman* (2003), p. 22; see also *Numhauser-Henning*, Ann (2010), Åldersdiskriminering og några antsällningsskydssrelaterade fråga, in: Vänbok til Ronnie Eklund. Ahlberg, Kerstin (ed.), pp. 439-473, p. 443 referring to *Christensen* (2000), pp. 171-193, see in particular p. 171 f.; see also *Hippe*, Jon M./*Midtsundstad*, Tove/*Arup Seip*, Åsmund/*Bogen*, Hanne/*Hernes*, Gudmund (2012), When I'm Sixty-Four – seniorpolitiske framtidsbilder, Fafo-rapport 2012:02, pp. 61ff.; *Fafo* (2012), Seniorpolitiske framtidsbilder, p. 2.

potential of an ageing and increasingly diverse workforce.[30] This has also been emphasised in the EU's strategy for smart, sustainable and inclusive growth – in *Europe 2020*.[31] As long-term challenges such as globalisation, pressure on resources and ageing intensify, one of the strategy's explicit aims is to create conditions for modernising labour markets with a view to raising employment levels with regard to the elder workforce and to ensure the sustainability of the social models.[32]

One of the strategy's headline targets is that at least 75 per cent of the population aged 20–64 should be employed, which explicitly encompasses the greater involvement of older workers.[33] The *Lisbon Strategy 2010* had already stipulated that working lives should be prolonged by increasing the effective average exit age from the labour market.[34] To bring population ageing into public awareness, the European year for active ageing and solidarity between generations was launched in 2012 by the EU and Norway joined in with this celebration.[35]

Modernising labour markets in light of the demographic change and creating a more inclusive working life for the older workforce makes it necessary to evaluate the status quo critically.[36] To cope with the challenges of an ageing society, working life might therefore be restructured and the organisation of work might be modernised such as for example via postponing retirement and by offering a smooth transition from one job to another and encouraging flexible working arrangements to build flexible pathways from work to retirement.[37]

30 The *Third European Demography Forum*, which took place in November 2011 pointed to the demographic dimension of the *Europe 2020* Strategy by stressing that the strategy 'can only succeed if it takes into account a rapidly changing demographic context and if it finds ways of unleashing the full potential of an ageing and increasingly diverse population' see http://ec.europa.eu/social/main.jsp?catId=88&langId=en&eventsId=284&furtherEvents=yes (last accessed: 17.12.2014).

31 COM(2010) 2020, Conclusions by the European Council EUCO 13/10 http://ec.europa.eu/eu2020/pdf/115346.pdf (last accessed: 17.12.2014).

32 COM(2010) 2020, p. 3, 16, 17.

33 ibid., p. 10.

34 see for an evaluation of the Lisbon Strategy 2010 the Commission working staff document SEC(2010) 114 final.

35 http://ec.europa.eu/social/main.jsp?langId=en&catId=89&newsId=1191&furtherNews=yes (last accessed: 17.12.2014).

36 see to this aspect *International Labour Organization* (ILO), Equality at work, 2007, p. 10.

37 see in this regard chap. 16.

The need to address the phenomenon of an ageing population has also been emphasised in the UN Proclamation on Ageing, where it is stressed in the Preamble that, 'Noting the unprecedented ageing of populations taking place throughout the world [...] Aware that a revolutionary change in the demographic structure of societies requires a fundamental change in the way in which societies organize their affairs'. It is also worth mentioning the Preamble's Art. 1 (l), where it is stated, 'To provide the immense human and material resources now urgently needed for adjustments to humanity's coming of age, which can be understood as a demographic phenomenon, but also as a social, economic and cultural one of great promise'.[38]

1.2.2 Key objective of the research: Provisions on mandatory retirement

The starting point for the thesis' analysis are the selected mandatory retirement provisions. This is why it is necessary to terminologically distinguish between the age at which the employee becomes entitled to receive a pension, which is the so-called pensionable age, and the age at which the employee is required to terminate the employment relationship, which constitutes the so-called retirement age or mandatory retirement age.[39] With regard to terminological uncertainty, which surrounds the notion of 'retirement age', a distinction also has to be made between 'pensionable age', 'state-imposed retirement age' and 'contractual or employer-imposed retirement age'.[40] Moreover, there is a functional relationship between explicit mandatory retirement provisions and other mechanisms that lead to a termination of the employment relationship on the grounds of age. Some employees may for example lose their right to protection from unfair dismissal after having reached a certain age, so that employers are able to set retirement ages, as the legislation deprives the employee who is over a certain age of protection from unfair dismissal.[41] Such provisions therefore de facto function as mandatory retirement.[42] The focus in this thesis rests on selected provisions of the former category; that is, mandatory retirement age limits that are imposed by the state as well as retirement ages that are laid down in collective agreements, in agreements at plant level or in the individual employment contract and which automa-

---

38 see also Art. 3; see in detail chap. 9.7.1.3.

39 *Ghosheh* (2008), p. 9; *European Commission* (2010), Developing anti-discrimination law in Europe, p. 52.

40 see for clarification *O'Cinneide*, Colm (2005), Age discrimination and European law, p. 41.

41 see to this aspect in general ibid., p. 41.

42 see in detail chap. 3.

tically terminate the employment relationship.[43] Three examples are selected: first, mandatory retirement for physicians imposed by law, second, mandatory retirement for pilots laid down in collective agreements and finally, mandatory retirement for university professors that is also stipulated by the state.[44] The main reason for choosing these examples has been to cover a wide range of justification arguments that come into play when discussing mandatory retirement ranging for example from security-related aspects, such as in the case of pilots, to health-related issues, as regards to physicians, or arguments such as creating academic career opportunities for younger employees, as in the case of professors.

Central to the compatibility analysis are two sets of norms: first, provisions on mandatory retirement and second, provisions that prohibit age discrimination in employment. The second category of norms is typically characterised by the fact it aims at extending the employee's protection against unjustified dismissals related to the employee's age, such as in the case of mandatory retirement. The prohibition against age discrimination in principle widens the employee's rights and protection when in employment. By contrast, provisions on compulsory retirement limit the employee's rights, almost nullifying them, as the employment relationship is generally unilaterally terminated without giving the employee any influence over the decision's outcome.

1.2.3 Employees subject to mandatory retirement

Analysing mandatory retirement entails taking a closer look at who is subject to such provisions. Mandatory retirement provisions use chronological age as the determinant to de facto determine when an employee is regarded as too old for the respective position. Thus, the employee's age constitutes the decisive benchmark. However, in view of multiple factors that have to be taken into account as regards age and ageing, chronological age alone – as in the case of mandatory retirement – does not constitute a useful instrument to distinguish between older workers and the rest of the workforce, and one has to be aware of the fact that any attempt at cate-

---

43 *Ghosheh* (2008), p. 9; see the analysis of selected examples in chap. 13 to 15.
44 see chapters 13 to 15.

gorising workers into age groups runs the risk of being ageist in itself.[45] This leads to the question as to when employees really are considered (too) old. *Lehr* put this in a nutshell by asking, '*Doch wann ist ein Mensch alt? Wenn er wie ein 58-jähriger Rentner heute, noch mehr als ein Viertel seines Lebens vor sich hat?*'[46]

Terminologically, employees facing the last part of their working life, such as those subject to compulsory retirement, are generally described as older or senior workers. The notion of the 'older employee' is typically referred to when it comes to the justification of mandatory retirement, where arguments such as the employee being 'too old' or ones where 'older employees should pave the way for their younger colleagues' come into play.[47] However, as a result of increased life expectancy and improved medical services, the threshold of so-called old age has been postponed, which calls into question what has previously been regarded as an older worker.[48] Clear distinctions between 'younger' and 'older' workers are therefore sometimes difficult to make. When an employee may be regarded as young or old depends inter alia on subjective perception.[49] Not surprisingly, a universally applicable definition of an older worker is hard to find.[50] The boundaries of what is regarded as old age are fluid, as

45 see to the different dimensions of age and the ageing process, chap. 6; see to ageism chap. 4.

46 'But when is a person too old? When he has like a today's 58-year-old pensioner more than a quarter of living in front of him?' (translation by author of *Lehr* (2007), p. 43); similar *Meenan*, Helen (2007 a), Age Discrimination: Cinderella & the Golden Bough, in: Meenan (ed.), Equality Law in an Enlarged European Union, pp. 278-312, p. 280.

47 see in detail to such justification patterns chap. 12.3.

48 similar in general *Solem*, Per E. (2007), Aldring og social deltagelse, in: Geronto-psykologi, Larsen, Lars (ed.), pp. 95 120, p. 98.

49 see in this regard in detail *von Hoff*, Konrad (2009), Das Verbot der Altersdiskriminierung aus Sicht der Rechtsvergleichung und der ökonomischen Analyse des Rechts, p. 55 f. with reference on p. 56 fn. 16 to Oswald, Frank (1991), Das persönliche Altersbild älterer Menschen, Zeitschrift für Gerontologie und Geriatrie 1991, pp. 276ff., according to which men in the age group 63 to 96 years of age declared in an interview on average the age of 72 as the start of the ageing process and were interestingly enough none of the respondents regarded himself as old.

50 *Dunkel-Benz* e.g. distinguishes between 'younger' old people or seniors (those between 40 and 60 years of age), 'new' seniors (those aged 60 to 75 years), old seniors (those between 75 and 90 years of age) and finally the very old people, *Dunkel-Benz*, Friederike (2008), Altern aus medizinischer Sicht – Vermeidbares und Unvermeidliches, NZA-Beil. 2008, p. 25: 'Wir unterscheiden: junge Alte (40

age is a result of a multitude of different factors. When it for example comes to the work sphere, the sector the employee has worked in, such as the job itself, and the employee's educational status and personal qualities have to be considered.[51] However, it cannot be neglected that significant biological and life course differences might exist between employees in their mid-twenties and those in their mid-seventies.[52] Simply claiming that age should be completely irrelevant may therefore not be a useful way forward.[53]

With a lack of a uniform definition for what constitutes an older worker, in general, employees above the age of 50 are considered to fall under this category.[54] Following the recent survey by the Norwegian Senior Policy Barometer in 2012, the average age of 57.9 – compared to the age of 55 in 2001 – has been seen as a benchmark after which employees are regarded as older.[55] However, when it comes to mandatory retirement, employees who are even younger may face an age limit, such as ballet dancers at the Norwegian Opera, who e.g., generally have to retire at the age of 41.[56]

---

bis 60 Jahre), neue Alte (60 bis 75 Jahre), Alte (75 bis 90 Jahre) und Hochbetagte (über 90 Jahre).*'*; similar *Sargeant*, who distinguishes between 'older age discrimination' and 'senior age discrimination', see *Sargeant*, Malcolm (2006), Age discrimination in employment, p. 79ff.

51 see to this aspect *Meenan* (2007 a), p. 279 who refers to Reday-Mulvey, Geneviève (2005), Working Beyond 60 Key Policies and Practices in Europe, p. 64.

52 in general *Iversen*, Thomas N./*Larsen*, Lars/*Solem*, Per E. (2009), A conceptual analysis of ageism, Nordic Psychology 2009, Vol. 61 (3), pp. 4-22, p. 7 refrring to Blaakilde, Anne L. (2002), Ord skaber alder, in: Swane, Christine E./Blaakilde, Anne L./Amstrup, Kirsten (eds), Gerontologi – livet som gammel, 2. edt., pp. 265-276; see also *Hagestad*, Gunhild O./*Uhlenberg*, Peter (2005), The social separation of old and young: A root of ageism, Journal of Social Issues, Vol. 61 Issue 2, 2005, pp. 343-360, p. 351.

53 see to this aspect in general *Iversen* et al. (2009), p. 7.

54 *ILO* (2008), Conditions of work and employment: Issues for older workers, Information Sheet No. OW-1.

55 *Norsk Seniorpolitisk Barometer* (2012 a), Yrkesaktiv befolking, 13-23 august 2012, p. 26.

56 § 3 (1) s. 2 Lov 21. august 1998 nr. 65 *om pensjonsordning for ballettdansere, sangsolister og korsangere ved Den Norske Opera & Ballett (operapensjonsloven).* Due to § 3 (1) s. 3 a prolongation of the contract is possible for three further seasons.

When using the term 'older' or 'senior' employee in this thesis, all employees are considered who are confronted with an exit from working life as a result of compulsory retirement, which might coincide with their eligibility to claim a pension – the pensionable age – or which may be higher or even lower than the general pension age.

1.3 Basic concepts: Age equality, ageism, age discrimination and mandatory retirement

Even if the terms 'age equality', 'ageism' and 'age discrimination' are often used synonymously,[57] they may be described as being of a unique nature as they are simultaneously interwoven concepts.[58]

In its most general sense, 'to discriminate' means to select between different options or to draw some type of distinction.[59] From a normative perspective, discrimination law is not concerned with prohibiting all such selections or distinctions per se; rather, it is concerned with demarcating those selections and distinctions that are regarded as invidious, e.g. those made on the basis of age or disability.[60] Age discrimination may therefore generally be described as treating someone as distinct to another person on the grounds of age.[61] Mandatory retirement provisions are an explicit example of such discrimination based on age, as they draw a distinction between persons of the particular age in question and those who are younger than the respective age limit. The relationship between mandatory

57 similar *Heikkinnen*, Satu/*Krekula*, Clary (2008), Ålderism ett fruktbart begrepp?, Sociologisk Forskning 2008, pp. 19-34, p. 21 f. who refer to the fact that in gerontological research age discrimination and ageism often are used as synonyms or as separated notions, where age discrimination primarily is related to discriminative behaviour and practices in particular in the sphere of employment; see also chap. 5.1.

58 The necessity to distinguish between ageism and age discrimination has similarly been stressed by *Ghosheh*, Naj (2008), Age discrimination and older workers: Theory and legislation in comparative context, Conditions of Work and Employment Series No. 20, ILO Conditions of Work and Employment Programme, p. 3.

59 see *Senne*, Daniela (2006), Auswirkungen des europäischen Verbots der Altersdiskriminierung auf das deutsche Arbeitsrecht, p. 24 f.; *Bamforth* et. al (2008), p. 17.

60 *Bamforth* et al. (2008), p. 18.

61 see for an analysis of the prohibition against age discrimination in Dir. 2000/78/EC: chap. 10.2.

retirement and age discrimination becomes apparent if one considers that the use of mandatory retirement actually undermines the protection afforded by employment law, which includes protection against age discrimination, once an employee has reached the age limit.[62]

The prohibition against age discrimination is deeply embedded in the overarching principle of equality, which in turn also encompasses age equality. From the perspective of the older employee being confronted with mandatory retirement, age equality in its substantive sense means that three aspects have to be acknowledged: the exercise of choice, dignity and their participation in working life.[63] Depriving the employee of his choice by establishing compulsory retirement may be characterised as a paternalistic way of determining the end of the employee's working life, which also affects the employee's human dignity.[64] However, human dignity is not limited by a calendar and does not volatise as soon as a certain chronological age laid down in a mandatory retirement provision has been reached.[65] Those who are willing to and are capable of extending their working life are excluded from making use of this opportunity merely based on the fact that they have reached a certain chronological age. Overnight, these employees are regarded as being too old to exercise their profession or participate in working life. Consequently, only the removal of the age barrier will open up a range of choices for the individual employee, maintain his dignity and ensure his participation and inclusion in working life.[66] However, it has to be acknowledged that providing mere formal equality by removing age limits as such may not be sufficient.[67] Substantive age equality in terms of opportunities can only be achieved if the employees, in reality, have a choice in genuinely materialising these choices.[68] In the employment sphere, such an approach goes hand in hand with measures to guarantee that all employees, irrespective of their age, have a real choice. Such measures – that typically may be described as

---

62 *Ghosheh* (2008), p. 10.

63 see in detail chap. 5.3.

64 similar *O'Cinneide* (2005), p. 42; see to paternalistic reasons of age discrimination *Senne* (2006), p. 33 f.; see also chap. 5.3.3.

65 *Simitis*, Spiros (1994), Altersdiskriminierung – die verdrängte Benachteiligung, Neue Juristische Wochenschrift (NJW) 1994, pp. 1453-1454, p. 1453; *Senne* (2006), p. 301.

66 in general *Fredman* (2003), p. 43 f.

67 see to this aspect *Fredman* (2003), p. 44.

68 ibid.

affirmative action measures by promoting opportunities for a certain group of employees – could for example entail strengthening the so-called work-ability of older employees, opening up flexible working times, job-sharing and, generally, the adjustment of pension schemes.[69] However, providing a real choice also encompasses giving older employees the chance not to make use of these opportunities and to choose to retire.[70]

By establishing a prohibition against age discrimination, the law additionally tries to capture a social phenomenon that is inter alia caused by the ability of humans to think in categories and to lean on generalisations – so-called stereotypes.[71] Classic examples in this regard are stereotypes towards older people, which may find their normative expression in the use of age as a decisive proxy in mandatory retirement provisions. These provisions, operating with a chronological age, typically exclude employees above a certain age from working life based on certain stereotypes related to the employee's chronological age. In consequence, these age limits are also of an ageist nature, as ageism may generally be described as the expression of stereotypes or prejudices and/or discrimination against older employees based on their chronological age or based on the perception of the respective employee as being 'old' or 'too old'.[72] Thus, in this regard, age discrimination may also be seen as being part of the broader concept of ageism.

1.4 Mandatory retirement in light of pension reforms

1.4.1 Recent developments in Norway

As the combination of an increasing number of older people and higher average pensions will lead to a dramatic increase in pension expenditure for the Norwegian National Insurance Scheme (*folketrygden*), Norway was forced to reform its pension system in 2011.[73] One of the reform's key objectives is to increase work incentives and facilitate work opportu-

69 see in this regard de lege ferenda considerations in cap. 16.2.
70 similar *Fredman* (2003), p. 44.
71 *Senne* (2006), p. 2 f.
72 see for an extensive definition *Iversen* et al., p. 15; see in detail chap. 4.
73 see to the demographic change chap. 7.

nities for retirees.[74] In doing so, the reform aims at tackling the demographic challenges and the pressure on the social security system, inter alia by age-related public expenditures, such as pensions, health care and long-term care.[75]

The *folketrygden* constitutes the general public pension system in Norway, and covers everyone who lives and works in Norway. The pensions under the *folketrygden* encompass the old-age, disability and survivors' pensions.[76] Besides that, employees have, in addition, supplementary pension schemes through the company they work in, which are financed by contributions from the individual employee and the employer: the so-called *tjenestepensjonsordninger* – occupational pension schemes.[77] Since 2006, these *tjenestepensjonsordninger* – previously being only for public-sector employees – have also been mandatory for the private sector, where businesses, under detailed rules, have to place at least 2% of the employee's pay in a contribution-based supplementary pension scheme: the so-called *obligatorisk tjenestepensjon* (OTP) – the mandatory occupational pension.[78] As an alternative, the individual business must have a benefit-based supplementary pension scheme that is of at least an equivalent level.[79] Moreover, the individual may also save for a pension through

74 see overview of the new system at: http://www.regjeringen.no/nb/dep/ad/kampanjer/pensjonsreform/no/sporsmal-og-svar.html?id=86829#02 (last accessed: 17.12.2014; The pension regulations that are now applicable are very complex and depending on the year the respective person is born. *Kjønstad* identifies four different pension regulations depending on the person's date of birth, see *Kjønstad*, Asbjørn (2012), Folketrygdens alderspensjoner. Jussens venner, 47(2), pp. 85-157, chap. 1.3., p. 88ff; see in general an overview of the main features of the new system, chap.3.3., p. 99ff.

75 see in general http://www.regjeringen.no/nb/dep/ad/kampanjer/pensjonsreform/no/sporsmal-og-svar.html?id=86829#02 (last accessed: 17.12.2014); see also in detail *Lowzow*, Andreas H. (2010), Ny alderspensjon, Institutt for offentlig retts skriftserie nr. 4 for 2010, chap. 2.3.2.3; *Kjønstad* (2012), chap. 2.2., p. 94, 96.

76 Nordic Social-Statistical Committee (*NOSOCO*) (2008), Old-age pensions in Norway, in: Old-age pension systems in the Nordic countries, pp. 95-104, p. 95.

77 ibid., p. 95.

78 Lov 21. desember 2005 nr. 124 *om obligatorisk tjenestepensjon (OTP-loven)*; see also ibid., p. 95. Besides that occupational pension schemes are to be found in the *Statens pensjonskasse* (Norwegian public service fund) such as in collective agreements, in particular in the communal sector.

79 *NOSOCO* (2008), p. 95.

individual schemes.[80] Finally, early retirement schemes exist – the so-called *avtalefestet pensjon* (AFP) – in slightly different versions for the private and public sectors.[81]

Until the enactment of the reform, a relatively high number of employees exited the labour market before the general pension age of 67, as the losses in old-age pension benefits were rather small and opportunities to combine income from work with a pension without facing financial penalties were restricted.[82] One of these options for early retirement is the AFP, a contractual early retirement scheme, which opens up early retirement at the age of 62.[83] It is widely used in the private as well as public sectors and has to be coordinated with the pension reform.[84]

The pension reform's central instrument is the introduction of flexibility (*fleksibel alderspensjon*), which makes it possible for persons between the ages of 62 and 75 to draw old-age pensions.[85] If it is drawn before the age of 67, the pension must, when the respective person attains the age of 67, be at least equal to the minimum pension level (*garantipensjon*) for those with an insurance period of 40 years.[86] Flexibility also implies freedom of choice for the individual person, who may choose the respective pension amount to draw at any time.[87] The pension can be drawn while the person in question has a full income at the same time.[88] Thus, one of the major changes brought about by the reform is that work income and a pension may be combined without leading to deductions in the pension, as was the case prior to the changes.[89] If the employee should decide to continue working – even while a pension is being drawn –, an additional pen-

80 ibid., p. 95.

81 see in detail https://www.nav.no/no/Person/Pensjon/Avtalefestet+pensjon+AFP (last accessed: 17.12.2014).

82 see for an overview of the previous applicable pension systems since the introduction of the first *alderstrygdloven* in 1936, *Kjønstad* (2012), chap. 1.2., p. 86ff.

83 see for further details https://www.nav.no/Pensjon/Avtalefestet+pensjon+(AFP); Organisation for Economic Co-operation and Development (*OECD*) (2013), Ageing and employment policies: Norway 2013, Working better with age, p. 55 f.

84 see for further details: http://www.regjeringen.no/nb/dep/ad/kampanjer/pensjonsreform/no/afp.html?id=506123 (last accessed: 17.12.2014).

85 §§ 19-4, 20-2 Lov 28. februar 1997 nr. 19 *om folketrygd (folketrygdloven eller ftrl)*; see in detail *Kjønstad* (2012), p. 96; *OECD* (2013), p. 49 f.

86 §§ 19-11, 20-15 ftrl; see in detail *Kjønstad* (2012), p. 96.

87 see in detail *Lowzow* (2010), chap. 7, 8; *Kjønstad* (2012), chap. 4.6, p. 107 f.

88 *Lowzow* (2010), chap. 7, 8. *Kjønstad* (2012), p. 96, chap. 4.6, p. 107 f.

89 *Kjønstad* (2012), p. 96, chap. 10.7, p. 152 f., critical p. 153.

sion entitlement may be earned, up to and including the year in which the respective person reaches the age of 75.[90] This applies even if the person has already started drawing the pension, which therefore creates incentives for retirees to re-enter the labour market. Pensions that are drawn with effect from 2011 onwards are subject to a life-expectancy adjustment (*levealdersjustering*).[91] A life-expectancy adjustment means that the pension will be adjusted to the life expectancy of the respective cohort. Provided that the life expectancy of the population continues to increase, the age adjustment will ensure that the pension remains sustainable. If life expectancy increases between cohorts, the age adjustment causes the younger cohorts to have a lower retirement fund at a given age of withdrawal. Continuing to work for longer and to postpone the withdrawal of the pension may compensate for this, so that an employee born in 1983 e.g. would have needed to work until the age of 71, according to general estimations from the Norwegian Labour and Welfare Service (NAV).[92] When it comes to the calculation of the pension, all of the years of contributions to the *folketrygden* count – the so-called *alleårsregel*.[93] As a result of a new pension-calculating mechanism, the annual pension amount will be higher, the longer the deferral of the pension drawing is.[94] Central to the new pension system therefore are inter alia improved economic incentives for employees to extend their working life.[95] One of the reform's key aspects thus is that younger cohorts are expected to work beyond 70 and up to 75 years of age to achieve a 'full' pension. The paradox is that some employees may have to end their employment relationship due to mandatory retirement age limits that are e.g. set at the age of 70. Therefore, also in this regard, existing mandatory retirement provisions have to be reviewed critically to cope with the reform's aims and for

---

90 *Lowzow* (2010), chap. 7, 8; *Kjønstad* (2012), p. 96, chap. 4.6, p. 107 f.

91 see §§ 19-6 (1), 20-12 (1) ftrl; *Kjønstad* (2012), chap. 2.4., p. 95 f., chap. 7, p. 131 f., critical in particular chap. 10.3, p. 149 f.

92 see for an overview: https://www.nav.no/Pensjon/Alderspensjon/Levealdersjusteri ng (last accessed: 17.12.2014); see also *Kjønstad* (2012), p. 101 under reference to Ot.prp. nr. 37 for 2008–2009, *Om lov om endringer i folketrygdloven (ny alderspensjon)*, p. 72.

93 *Kjønstad* (2012), chap. 2.4., p. 95 f., chap. 10.5, p. 151 f.

94 *OECD* (2013), p. 49.

95 *Lowzow* (2010), chap. 2.3.2.3; *Kjønstad* (2012), in general chap. 2.3, p. 94. *Kjønstad* is critical if these incentives may de facto encourage employees to continue working, see chap. 10.6, p. 152.

those provisions not to run counter to those aims. A further major shortcoming, as criticised in a recent report by the Organisation for Economic Co-operation and Development (OECD), however, is that only about 40% of new pensioners, mainly those working in the private sector, are substantially affected by the new regulations so far.[96]

1.4.2 Recent developments in Germany

Germany has also gone through several pension 'reforms' in the past.[97] These reforms basically aimed at guaranteeing the financing of the state pension insurance in the long run, despite the ageing of the German society, without, at the same time, burdening future generations with too many increases in pension contributions.[98] If one compares recent discussions on pensions with the discussions that took place 10 or 20 years ago, one aspect becomes apparent: while previous reforms aimed at tackling the demographic developments, inter alia by reducing the supposed remarkable increase in contribution payments to a level that was acceptable for the contributors to the pension system, recent discussions also primarily concentrate on whether the future benefit level (*Leistungsniveau*) of the pension scheme will be entirely sufficient to secure a standard of living and guarantee an income in old age that is free of poverty.[99] The recent reform discussion is therefore coined by the notion of *Altersarmut* – poverty in old age.[100]

In general, the German pension system consists of three pillars, whereof the first pillar encompasses the mandatory state pension insurance (*gesetzliche Rentenversicherung*).[101] The second pillar covers voluntary Occupa-

96 *OECD* (2013), p. 51.

97 see for an overview of past and recent pension reforms *Rische*, Herbert/*Thiede*, Rheinhold (2013), Die Zukunft der gesetzlichen Rentenversicherung, Neue Zeitschrift für Sozialrecht (NZS) 2013, pp. 601-605, p. 601ff.

98 ibid., p. 601.

99 ibid.

100 ibid.

101 see overview given at *OECD* (2011), Pensions at a glance 2011: Retirement-income systems in OECD countries, Germany.

tional Pension Insurance (*betriebliche Altersvorsorge*)[102] and the third pillar finally is based on private insurance, with the so-called *Riester-Rente* as its most prominent form.[103] The most recent and fundamental legal adjustment concerns the gradual increase of the general pension age (the so-called *Regelaltersgrenze*)[104] from the age of 65 to the age of 67 starting in 2012 and lasting until 2029.[105]

Early drawing of a pension is possible for long-term insured persons at the age of 63.[106] Predrawing of a pension due to unemployment or after part-time employment prior to retirement (*Altersteilzeit*) may be claimed after the age of 60 has been reached.[107] Women may claim early pensions at the age of 60.[108] Early drawing of the state pension leads to deductions of 0.3% for each month of early drawing.[109] In the case of early drawing before the *Regelaltersgrenze*, limitations as regards additional income apply. On the contrary, after having reached the *Regelaltersgrenze*, no restrictions whatsoever exist as regards potential further income (*Hinzuverdienst*).[110]

Furthermore, in the German context, it is crucial to be aware of the distinction between the *Pension*, on the one hand, which describes the pension that civil servants (*Beamte*) in the public sector are entitled to, and the

---

102 see in detail *Rengier*, Bernhard (2012), Teil H. Betriebliche Altersversorgung, § 36 Grundlagen, paras. 1-186, in: Moll, Wilhelm (ed.) Münchener Anwaltshandbuch Arbeitsrecht, 3. edt. 2012; see also *Schwintowski*, Hans-Peter (2009), § 43 Betriebliche Altersvorsorge, para. 1, in: Beckmann, Roland M./Matusche-Beckmann, Annemarie, Versicherungsrechts-Handbuch, 2. edt. 2009.

103 *Kreikebohm*, Ralf (2013 a), in: Sozialgesetzbuch VI, Kreikebohm, Ralf (ed.), 4. edt. 2013, Einleitung, IV. Die Rentenreform 2001, para. 47.

104 In German terminology there is often not a clear distinction made between pensionable age and mandatory retirement age as it is in most cases generally referred to the notion '*Altersgrenze*'; see as regards '*Regelaltersgrenze*' § 35 of the Social Code Book VI (SGB VI).

105 see §§ 35, 235 SGB VI. The age limit in § 35 SGB VI has been raised to 67 according to the *Gesetz zur Anpassung der Regelaltersgrenze an die demografische Entwicklung und zur Stärkung der Finanzierungsgrundlagen der gesetzlichen Rentenversicherung* (*RV-Altersanpassungsgesetz vom 20.04.2007*, BGBl. 2007, I, p. 554ff.); see to this aspect *Groß*, Daniela (2010), Die Rechtfertigung einer Altersdiskriminierung auf der Grundlage der Richtlinie 2000/78/EG, p. 27.

106 § 36 s. 2 SGB VI.

107 *Rengier* (2012), § 38 Ansprüche nach dem Betriebsrentengesetz, para. 98.

108 ibid.

109 ibid, para. 99; see also § 77 SGB VI.

110 see in general to limits of further income (*Hinzuverdienstgrenzen*) § 34 SGB VI relevant for those retiring earlier; see also *Kreikebohm*, Ralf (2013 b), in: Beck'scher Online-Kommentar Sozialrecht, BeckOK SGB VI, Rolfs, Christian/ Giesen, Richard/ Kreikebohm, Ralf/Udsching, Peter (eds.), E. Hinzuverdienstgrenzen (§ 34), § 35, para. 5.

Rente, which circumscribes the pension that other public-sector employees (*öffentliche Angestellte*) such as private-sector employees are entitled to. Despite these differentiations in this thesis, the English notion of a 'pension' is broadly used to describe both pension types.

One further important development concerns recent legal amendments coming into force in July 2014 relating to § 41 of the Social Code Book VI (Sozialgesetzbuch SGB VI), which was supplemented by a new statutory regulation. The section now states that if a clause in an employment contract lays down the terms for the termination of the employment contract on reaching the general pension age, it is now possible for the parties to the employment contract to postpone the termination date, if necessary, even several times. In short, this means that the provision now explicitly allows for temporary extensions of the employment relationship beyond the pension age.[111] This new regulation thus also explicitly calls for extending the working lives of older employees.

1.5 Structure of the thesis

After having highlighted the central themes and issues of the thesis in the introductory chapters, part I goes into more detail regarding both the chosen approaches (interdisciplinary and comparative) and the respective methodological aspects. The concepts of mandatory retirement, ageism and age equality are explained and, in view of the chosen interdisciplinary approach, the gerontopsychological findings, data on the labour-market situation as well as the demographical findings are also presented in part I. The subject covered in part II is the manifestation of the prohibition against age discrimination in human rights law and EU law. Moreover, an overview is provided on the manifestation of the prohibition against age discrimination at the national level in both Norwegian and German law. The selected examples of the mandatory retirement provisions in Norwegian and German law are finally examined in part III in terms of their compatibility with the prohibition against age discrimination and the relevant justification provisions as concretised in Dir. 2000/78/EC therein.

111 see chap.11.5.1 and 16.2.3 for further details, in particular regarding the potential problems arising from the new regulation.

Possible *de lege ferenda* solutions both as regards to mandatory retirement in general and as regards to the selected mandatory retirement provisions in particular are finally discussed in part IV of the thesis.

2 Perspectives and methodology

2.1 Interdisciplinary approach

Analysing mandatory retirement and its compatibility with the prohibition against age discrimination in Dir. 2000/78/EC is a very complex topic that requires an interdisciplinary approach. Empirical findings from neighbouring disciplines are therefore of vital importance for the legal analysis, as they may contribute to rebutting some of the often-used arguments to justify and maintain mandatory retirement age limits.[112] Consequently, from a normative perspective, the examined selected legal provisions on mandatory retirement cannot be discussed in isolation from their broader context. It is therefore crucial to contextualise the analysis of mandatory retirement by also examining any relevant neighbouring disciplines on employment law to get an idea of the whole picture.[113] Moreover, taking such a broad intersectional, interdisciplinary approach is necessary, indispensable and fundamental in order to cope with the unique feature of the prohibition of age discrimination in employment, and to understand and interpret it properly.[114] In sum, following such a multiaxial approach contributes to a more comprehensive and holistic understanding of the legal analysis of mandatory retirement.

While the situation of older employees, in particular concerning the legitimacy of mandatory retirement, has already been discussed for many years in gerontology, demography and economics, the fire has only been

112 see to the typically used justification patterns chap. 12.3.

113 similar *Deflem*, Mathieu (2008), Sociology of law: Visions of scholarly tradition, p. 151 who emphasises: 'Law cannot simply be viewed as exogenous to the realm of organizations. Instead, law is endogenous to the social realm it seeks to regulate.'

114 similar *Lüderitz*, Martin (2005), Altersdiskriminierung durch Altersgrenzen, pp. 26-33; *Senne* (2006), p. 20, pp. 24-87; *Temming* (2008), p. 15 f., pp. 41-61; *Rothermund*, Klaus/*Temming*, Felipe (2010), Diskriminierung aufgrund des Alters, p. 13.

fuelled on the normative side of the debate since the last decade.[115] In particular, the implementation of Dir. 2000/78/EC and the manifestation of the prohibition of non-discrimination on the grounds of age has contributed considerably to the development that the need to evaluate mandatory retirement from a contextual perspective also came to the forefront of discussions in employment law, which can be illustrated in particular in judgements of the Court of Justice of the European Union (CJEU).[116]

This was for example highlighted in the *Rosenbladt* case before the CJEU. The referring German *ArbG Hamburg* had doubts concerning the compatibility of a clause on the automatic termination of employment contracts based upon having reached a specific fixed age (in this case 65)[117] with the prohibition of age discrimination as manifested in Dir. 2000/78/EC and whether the provision could be maintained 'regardless of the economic, social and demographic situation and of the situation actually prevailing on the employment market'.[118] Also in Norwegian case law concerning the justification of age limits, some courts have begun to take particular consideration of the economic, gerontological or socio-demographic factors. Interestingly enough, especially the courts of lower instance in both Germany and Norway seem to be placing these aspects increasingly on the agenda. One example constitutes the decision concerning mandatory retirement determined at the plant level – the *Gjensidige* case.[119]

---

115 see already in 1984 critical analysis by *Schröder*, Ulrich (1984), Altersbedingte Kündigungen und Altersgrenzen im Individualarbeitsrecht; and later *Fredman* (2003), pp. 21-69; *Lüderitz* (2005); *Temming* (2008), p. 602ff.

116 see e.g. the argumentation of the referring Court in *Rosenbladt*: Case C-45/09 (*Rosenbladt*), Judgement of 12 October 2010, European Court Reports (ECR) 2010 I-09391, para. 27, 28; see also questions by the referring Court in Joined Cases C-159/10 and C-160/10 (*Fuchs* and *Köhler*), Judgement of July 2011, ECR 2011 I-06919, in particular para. 2.

117 The mandatory retirement age limit was laid down in a collective agreement for employees in the commercial cleaning sector, see § 19 (8) of *Allgemeingültiger Rahmentarifvertrag für die gewerblichen Beschäftigten in der Gebäudereinigung* (RTV).

118 C-45/09 (*Rosenbladt*), paras. 27, 28.

119 TOSLO-2009-143503, where the Oslo District Court declared the mandatory retirement provision being a violation of the prohibition against age discrimination. The Norwegian Supreme Court however finally ruled that the mandatory retirement was in conformity with the prohibition against age discrimination Gjensidige-saken Rt. 2011 s. 964 (*Gjensidige*).

2.2 Comparative approach: Why and how

2.2.1 Why choose a comparative approach?

The reason for choosing a legal comparison as a central approach for the thesis is that an analysis of different 'legal cultures' may contribute to revealing the discrepancies and inconsistencies of legal norms in their national legal context.[120] Legal comparison entails being willing to cross the borders of national law 'with the express purpose of undertaking a comparative analysis deliberately piercing the normative façade in order to uncover the historical, political and economic background of the regulations in question'.[121] Thus, looking via legal comparison 'out of the cave', to use *Plato*'s allegory, contributes to stimulating the critical discourse and to raising awareness about potentially unsolved problems of the law.[122] In doing so, comparative law offers the possibility and provides – after having assessed the respective *de lega lata* status quo – a basis for an evaluation of how the law might be altered *de lege ferenda* to offer a 'better solution'[123] for the legal problem in question.

---

120 in this regard *de Cruz*, Peter (2007), Comparative law in a changing world, 3. edt. p. 11.

121 *Simitis*, Spiros (1994), Denationalizing labour law: The case of age discrimination, 15 Comparative Labor Law & Policy Journal (1994), pp. 321-339, p. 323.

122 *Yntema*, Hessel E. (1956), Comparative legal research: some remarks on 'looking out of the cave', 54 Michigan Law Review (Mich L Rev), pp. 899-928, p. 899, 901; see also *de Cruz* (2007), p. 11; similar also *Brand*, Oliver (2003), Grundfragen der Rechtsvergleichung, Juristische Schulung (JuS) 2003, pp. 1082-1091, p. 1084; *Pound*, Roscoe (1954), Some thoughts about comparative law, in: Festschrift Ernst Rabel I (1954), pp. 7-16, p. 9.

123 *Zweigert*, Konrad F./*Kötz*, Hein (1998), Comparative law, 3 edt., p. 10 f., see in particular p. 15 where they point to the fact that 'The primary aim of comparative law, as of all sciences is knowledge. […] Comparative law is an 'école de vérité' which extends and enriches the 'supply of solutions' (Zotelmann) and offers the scholar of critical capacity the opportunity of finding the 'better solution' for his time and place.'

2.2.2 Why choose a legal comparison between Norway and Germany?

The key legal question as regards both Norway and Germany is whether the selected provisions are in conformity with the prohibition against age discrimination as concretised in Dir. 2000/78/EC. When it comes to the implementation of Dir. 2000/78/EC, the non-EU member takes an exceptional position, as Norway was legally not obliged to implement the Directive.[124] This makes it particularly interesting to compare Norway to the EU member Germany and to see if and how both differ when it comes to examining the selected provision's conformity with the prohibition against age discrimination. From a Norwegian perspective, this is even more interesting, as the majority of CJEU cases that had a strong impact on the outcome of the *Høyestrett*'s cases on mandatory retirement were based on references for preliminary rulings brought to the CJEU by German courts. Examples are *Rosenbladt* and *Prigge*, which played a considerable role in the Norwegian *Høyesterett* cases of *Gjensidige* and *CHC*.[125]

Based on these aspects, it might also be fruitful to analyse whether the arguments and legitimate aims, and the national situation that has been referred to in the justification analysis of the German mandatory retirement age limits might be transferred to the Norwegian situation. However, the CJEU's analysis is also critically assessed in this thesis, so that ultimately the analysis of the Norwegian and German provisions might differ from the Court's judgement.

From a German perspective, it is interesting to determine whether Norway might function as a role model when it comes to mandatory retirement and older employees in employment. One reason for this is that Norway, when compared to Germany, has a relatively high exit age for older employees from the work sphere and a generally higher participation rate for older employees in working life.[126] Moreover, at first glance, Norway seems to operate with mandatory age limits that are set at a higher age than for the respective applicable German counterparts.

---

124 see to this aspect chap. 11.2

125 C-45/09 (*Rosenbladt*); C-447/09 (*Prigge*), Judgement of 13 September 2011, ECR 2011 I-8003; Rt. 2011 s. 964 (*Gjensidige*); Rt. 2012 s. 219 (*CHC*); see to this aspect analysis by *Hack* (2012 a), pp. 357ff.

126 see to this aspect chap. 7.

2.2.3 How to undertake a legal comparative analysis: The chosen method of comparison

There are several distinguishable approaches with which to carry out a legal comparative analysis.[127] In principle, the legal comparison of the problem under investigation may extend over the systematic context and structures of an entire legal system (a macrocomparison) or it may concentrate on particular problems or conflicts of interest and the solutions offered by the national systems (a microcomparison or a horizontal legal comparison).[128] Microcomparison aims at uncovering the different solutions to the same social problem. It is concerned with specific legal institutions or problems and examines the rules that are used to solve current problems or certain conflicts of interest.[129] As the key subject of this research constitutes selected mandatory retirement provisions and their compatibility with the prohibition against age discrimination, or in other words, as the thesis' core concern is a specific legal problem, it is meaningful to conduct the legal comparison on the micro level.

On the micro level, the key method is that of comparative functionalism.[130] This method takes as a starting point that the underlying principle of all comparative law is that of functionality.[131] It claims that in law, only that may fruitfully be compared, which, in principle, is comparable; that

---

127 *Frankenberg* distinguishes between 'Encyclopedic Comparison', 'Constructive Comparison', 'Comparative Historical Reconstruction', 'Juxtaposition-plus' and 'Comparative Functionalism', *Frankenberg*, Günter (1985), Critical comparisons: Re-thinking comparative law, Harvard International Law Journal, Vol. 26 No. 2, pp. 411-455, pp. 427 f.; others distinguish between 'functional comparative law', 'sociological comparative law' and 'economic analysis of law', see the references given by *Grossfeld*, Bernhard (1990), The strength and weakness of comparative law, p. 9, 70 w.f.r. in fn. 62- 64; see also to the different types of comparative studies already *Hug*, Walther (1932), History of comparative law, Harvard Law Review, Vol. 45 Issue 6, 1932, pp. 1027-1070, p. 1027 f.

128 *Zweigert/Kötz* (1998), p. 4, 5; see for an overview *Eichenhofer*, Eberhard (1997), Einführung in die Sozialrechtsvergleichung, NZS 1997, pp. 97-102, p. 98 f, 100 f.

129 ibid.

130 see to an overview of the proponents of the functional method: *Michaels*, Ralf (2006), The functional method of comparative law, in: The Oxford Handbook of Comparative Law, pp. 339-382, p. 340, fn. 1.

131 *Zweigert/Kötz* (1998), p. 34; *Kötz*, Hein (1999), Comparative law in Germany today, Revue internationale de droit compare, Vol. 51 No. 4, 1999, pp. 753-758, p. 755.

is, when it fulfils the same function and addresses the same conflict.[132] This proposition is based on the assumption that every society is confronted with substantially the same problems, which are solved in different ways, but nevertheless often lead to the same or at least very similar results.[133] This is referred to as the *praesumptio similitudinis*.[134]

The process of comparison may, according to the understanding of the functional approach laid down in this thesis, be divided into three main steps.

First, the working hypothesis[135] of any comparative examination has to be formulated 'in purely functional terms'.[136] This means that the key problem has to be formulated and identified in a manner that is free of any national understanding and terminology of the law to secure objectivity to the greatest possible extent. The initial point and lynchpin[137] of any (functional) comparative analysis therefore always constitutes a certain social problem, the so-called *tertium comparationis*.[138] The overarching social problem that both societies are faced with is that of an ageing population. The focus in this analysis rests on ageing in employment as a societal problem and as the *tertium comparationis* that is exemplified by the situation of older employees facing mandatory retirement.

---

132 *Zweigert/Kötz* (1998), p. 34.

133 ibid., p. 39, 40.

134 ibid., p. 40; critical to this approach inter alia *von Benda-Beckmann*, Keebet (1979), Einige Bemerkungen über die Beziehung zwischen Rechtssoziologie und Rechtsvergleichung, Zeitschrift für vergleichende Rechtswissenschaft 78 (1979), pp. 51-67, p. 56 f.

135 see the terminology used by *Zweigert/Kötz* (1998), p. 34.

136 *Zweigert/Kötz* (1998), p. 34.

137 *Eichenhofer* (1997), p. 98 uses the expression 'Angelpunkt' and refers in this regard to *Zweigert/Kötz* by quoting 'Angelpunkt jeder Rechtsvergleichung ist stets das konkrete Sachproblem'.

138 see for a discussion *Michaels* (2006), p. 367ff.; *Eichenhofer* uses the term '*pre-legal problem*' ('*vorrechtliches Problem*') to describe the initial question, *Eichenhofer* (1997), p. 99.

Second, the ways in which the examined legal systems resolve the identified key social problem from step one have to be described with regard to each legal system separately. Thus, the presentation of the examined countries follows a holistic approach, encompassing both 'law in the books'[139] and 'law in action'.[140]

Finally, what is ascertained in the second step is compared and evaluated from a purely functional perspective. After juxtaposing the Norwegian and German legal situation, the real process of comparison begins, which involves adopting different perspectives to shed light on and examine the different solutions given by the analysed systems.[141] The country of departure for this final comparison and evaluation of the offered solutions is Norway. In the presentation of the solutions given by the domestic as well as the compared 'foreign' legal system, it is essential to be aware of the natives' spears.[142] This means that to guarantee objectivity, the process of comparison in the functional sense requires that the solutions given by the national legal system must be freed from the context of the national system, and before the real comparative evaluation can take place, they have to be set in the context of all the solutions from the other examined jurisdictions.[143] Thus, following the principle of functionality encompasses cutting loose the solutions given by the different jurisdictions from their conceptual context and stripping them of 'their national doctrinal overtones so that they may be seen purely in the light of their function, as an attempt to satisfy a particular legal need'.[144] When it comes to assessing why different legal solutions are given in the countries' analyses, it is the comparatist's task to find out why these differences might exist, which also involves taking the social reality into consideration and, in this regard, 'comparative law has much to gain from an interdisciplinary

---

139 *Pound*, Roscoe (1910), Law in the books and law in action, American Law Review, Vol. 44, 1910, p. 11ff.

140 ibid.

141 see in general *Zweigert/Kötz* (1998), p. 43.

142 'Rechtsvergleicher sind es gewohnt, in fremde Dickichte einzudringen, und darauf gefaßt, daß unter jedem Busch ein Eingeborener mit Pfeilen lauert', *Rabel*, Ernst, (1951) Deutsches und Amerikanisches Recht, Rabels Zeitschrift für ausländisches und internationals Privatrecht, 1951, Vol. 16 H. 3, pp. 340-359, p. 340.

143 *Zweigert/Kötz* (1998), p. 43, 44.

144 ibid., p. 44, see also p. 10.

approach'.[145] Functionalism may thus be used in its entirety as a socio-legal approach. This means that in principle, an interdisciplinary approach is beyond doubt part of a legal comparative analysis in the functional sense. Nevertheless, the interdisciplinary approach is addressed here in a separate chapter and not in a subchapter relating to the functional approach. This is not done to neglect the holistic understanding of functionalism, but is rather a means through which to accentuate the interdisciplinary approach in a separate chapter, as the approach warrants specific attention. According to the understanding of the author, explicitly and separately addressing the interdisciplinary approach in a legal analysis of mandatory retirement is necessary in order to cope with the existing shortcomings in the legal discussion in this field, which particularly fail to take into account the scientific findings of related disciplines. It is argued here that in taking age equality seriously, an interdisciplinary perspective is obligatory, which, moreover, needs to be addressed explicitly. Furthermore, given the key claim of taking age equality seriously, it is important to emphasise that in any critical assessment of the compatibility of the selected mandatory retirement provisions with the prohibition against age discrimination, an interdisciplinary approach is inherent to any justification analysis. To conclude, irrespective of whether a legal comparative analysis is applied or not, the interdisciplinary approach is already a quintessential aspect of a thorough justification analysis.

Despite its benefits, comparative functionalism has to be confronted with the question regarding to what extent the given solutions can be extracted from their conceptual national context to reach 'pure' functionality.[146] The problem is that the comparatist faces difficulties in not seeing foreign jurisdictions through preconceptions derived from his own legal

---

145 *Kötz* (1999), p. 756; see also *Zweigert/Kötz* (1998), p. 44 reffering to p. 10 f.

146 *Frankenberg* (1985), p. 440; see to the critic of comparative functionalism also: *De Coninck,* Julie (2010), The functional method of comparative law, Quo vadis? RabelsZ 74, 2010, p. 351-359; *Henry*, Hagen (1997), Kulturfremdes Recht erkennen. Warum? Wie?, Zeitschrift für Rechtsvergleichung 1997 Vol. 38 H 2, pp. 45-55, see to the critic p. 53ff.; *Brand*, Oliver (2007), Conceptual comparisons: Towards a coherent methodology of comparative legal studies, Brooklyn Journal of international law, Vol. 32 Issue 2, 2007, pp. 405-466, pp. 412ff., 415ff.; see also *Husa*, Jaakko (2003), Farewell to functionalism of methodological tolerance?, RabelsZ 419, 2003, Bd. 67 H. 3, pp. 419- 447 who advocates a 'moderate version of functionalism' (p. 421) by accepting its inborn limitations, see for an overview of critics and challenges to functionalism, pp. 434ff., 443ff.; *Schmidt*,

system.[147] The desired objectivity is therefore challenged by the subjectivity of the observer in question.[148] Nevertheless, one has to take into consideration the fact that the comparatist, with regard to the foreign legal system, enjoys, as a non-domestic scholar, the privilege of possessing an unbiased mind and thus may be able to see things with fresh eyes – an advantage and possible productive and inspiring process that should be utilised.[149] Notwithstanding its critics, the functional method is the preferable one in this study, since it offers a clear structured approach through which to analyse different solutions to a problem that is common for the countries under comparison. The challenge in the process of comparison undoubtedly is to attempt to always be aware of the risk of subjectivity and thereby the limitations of comparative law, or as *Zweigert* and *Kötz* formulated it, 'One must never allow one's vision to be clouded by the concepts of one's own national system; always in comparative law one must focus on the concrete problem'.[150] This means, in relation to this work, being aware of the difficulty of viewing – from the author's perspective – the 'foreign' Norwegian legal system through a purely neutral lens, since it may have a German 'colouration'.

Folke (1981), The need for a multi-axial method in comparative law, Festschrift für Konrad Zweigert zum siebzigsten Geburtstag, pp. 525-536, see to the critic in particular, p. 528 f., 532 f.

147 see *Frankenberg* (1985), who claims that 'Comparison has to be self-reflective. The comparatist has to reflect upon herself as a subject of and to law. Instead of pretending to the posture of a neutral, objective, and disinterested observer, the comparatist has to regard herself as being involved [...].' To tackle what he calls 'ethnocentrism' the comparatist should due to *Frankenberg* examine and disentangle the cultural ties that bind him to the domestic legal system, see p. 443, 444; see to the challenges of the comparative method in general *Grossfeld* (1990), p. 9.

148 Also the leading exponents of the functional approach *Zweigert* and *Kötz* are at least to some extent aware of this problem, see *Zweigert/Kötz* (1998), p. 35.

149 *Fahlbeck*, Reinhold (2003), Comparative labor law – Quo vadis? Comparative Labour Law & Policy Journal, Vol. 25:7 (2003-2004), pp. 7-20, p. 13; see also *Frankenberg* (1985), p. 445; *Summers*, Clyde W. (1982), Employee participation in Sweden and the United States: Some comparisons from an American perspective, 1 Arbetsrättsliga Uppsatser 49 (1982), pp. 49-80, p. 49.

150 *Zweigert/Kötz* (1998), p. 35.

2.2.4 The standard of comparison: Dir. 2000/78/EC

Not only are selected mandatory retirement provisions in Norway compared to the respective German provisions, they are also analysed as regards their conformity with Dir. 2000/78/EC. Therefore, the common standard of comparison for the compatibility analysis is Dir. 2000/78/EC, which has influenced the Norwegian as well as the German anti-discrimination legislation.

The prohibition against discrimination on the grounds of age is manifested in both countries.[151] Any direct or indirect age discrimination may be justified in line with Dir. 2000/78/EC requirements only under certain justification criteria.[152] The core element of any justification of age discrimination thereby constitutes the proportionality principle.[153] Even if the proportionality principle is – in contrast to Germany – a rather foreign concept in the Norwegian context, it is now explicitly laid down in § 13-3 (1), (2) *arbeidsmiljøloven* (Working Environment Act (WEA)).[154] Consequently, the general proportionality principle, which is laid down and concretised in Dir. 2000/78/EC, constitutes the common principle for both countries under examination. Moreover, when applying and interpreting

---

151 § 13-1 WEA in Norway and §§ 1, 7 Allgemeines Gleichbehandlungsgesetz (AGG) in Germany; see analysis chap. 11.

152 see § 13-3 WEA, §§ 8, 10 AGG.

153 see chap. 10.3.5; In EU law the proportionality principle already is known from the field of gender equality. See with regard to the equal treatment for men and women and the infringement of Art. 119 EC Treaty the criteria for the objective justification of indirect discrimination on grounds of gender C- 96/80, (*Jenkins*), Judgement of 31 March 1981, 1981, I-00911; C- 170/84 (*Bilka*), Judgement of 13 May 1986, ECR 1986, I- 01607, para. 8, 37 and tenor/operative part; see in general *Ellis* (1999), The principle of proportionality in the laws of Europe; *Tridimas*, Takis (2006), The general principles of EU law, in particular chap. 3 p. 136ff.; such as *Knill*, Christoph/*Becker*, Florian (2003), Divergenz trotz Diffusion?, Rechtsvergleichende Aspekte des Verhältnismäßigkeitsprinzips in Deutschland, Großbritannien und der Europäischen Union, Die Verwaltung Vol. 36 No. 4, 2003, pp. 447-481; *Baker*, Aaron (2008), Proportionality and employment discrimination in the UK, Industrial Law Journal Vol. 37, pp. 305-328, p. 305ff.

154 In German law it is implied in §§ 8, 10 AGG.

the justification requirements in Dir. 2000/78/EC, the jurisdiction of the CJEU plays a central role in both countries.[155] In determining the scope of any derogation from a fundamental right such as the principle of non-discrimination on the grounds of age, the principle of proportionality as one of the general principles of Community law must be observed, as the CJEU pointed out in *Mangold*. The proportionality principle in turn requires that derogations from this individual right remain within the limits of what is appropriate and necessary in order to achieve the aim in view and that the principle of non-discrimination be reconciled as far as possible with the requirements and those of the aim pursued by the provision in question.[156] As regards the thesis' key question, the proportionality test functions as an instrument with which to determine if the selected provisions on mandatory retirement in Norway and Germany may be justified or not and thus if they are compatible with Dir. 2000/78/EC requirements or not.

2.3 Linguistic and terminological challenges

As a comparative study, the thesis involves examining several legal systems and studying the legal material in the respective languages. Since the thesis is written in English, the linguistic and terminological challenges have to be addressed. If one takes as a starting point that law lives in and through language, the question arises as to what the consequences might be if the law is transferred into another language.[157] In this regard, particular attention has to be paid to the fact that legal terminology is full of 'linguistic traps and potential minefields of misunderstanding, which vary from country to country'.[158] Consequently, any effort of translation runs

---

155 see as regards the Norwegian context e.g. the following cases of the Norwegian Supreme Court (*Høyesterett)* judgements: Rt. 2010 s. 202 (*Kystlink*), Rt. 2011 s. 609 (*SAS*), Rt. 2011 s. 964 (*Gjensidige*), Rt. 2012 s. 219 (*CHC*); see in detail chap. 11.

156 C-144/04 (*Mangold)*, para. 65 w.r.t. settled case-law in gender equality law Case C-476/99 *Lommers* [2002] ECR I-2891, para. 39, which in turn refers to C-222/84 (*Johnston*), ECR 1986, I-01651, para. 38; C-273/97 (*Sirdar*), ECR 1999 I-07403, para. 26; C-285/98 (*Kreil*), ECR 2000 I-00069, para. 23

157 *Grossfeld* (1990), p. 101.

158 *de Cruz* (2007), p. 220 f.; see also references given by *Grossfeld* (1990), p. 85, fn. 1.

the risk of ignoring the inherent conceptual differences between the various languages.[159] Keeping this in mind, language is inevitably an important parameter in a comparative legal analysis,[160] or, in other words, 'Legal linguistics is an essential concomitant of comparative law, one which does not make it any easier'.[161] In this study, an attempt is made to be aware of the linguistic and terminological traps and minefields. To avoid any misunderstanding/misinterpretation, the original legal term is used where necessary and its meaning is explained.

2.4 The legal system in Norway and Germany: Methodological and institutional overview

Conducting a comparative analysis involves differentiating between the national sources of law[162] and the methods of interpretation of the legal provisions that are used in the national context. Even if both countries in principle may be viewed as belonging to different legal families,[163] legislation constitutes the primary source of employment law in both countries.

As regards the parent legal families or major legal systems, in general, common law has to be distinguished from the civil law legal family. It has to be noted that Germany belongs to the second group, which is often divided into countries employing the Roman legal tradition (such as the French legal tradition) and countries employing the German legal tradition, while the Norwegian system – being part of the Nordic legal family – is rather difficult to assign to either the common or the civil law tradition. *Zweigert/Kötz* favour attributing the Nordic laws to the civil laws. They allocate the Scandinavian legal systems to 'a special "Nordic" legal group within the Civil Law'.[164]

---

159 see in detail *de Cruz* (2007), p. 220.

160 ibid.

161 *Grossfeld* (1990), p. 101.

162 see with regard to the problem of how to define the notion ‚sources of law', *de Cruz* (2007), p. 28.

163 Similar with regard to the distinctive features between the Swedish and the German legal system, *Rönnmar*, Mia (2004), Arbetsledningsrätt och arbetsskyldighet, p. 35.

164 *Zweigert/Kötz* (1998), p. 285.

Due to the German positivistic tradition, statutes play a key role as a source of German employment and labour law.[165] There is no code or piece of comprehensive legislation in the field. Legislation is spread over a number of different acts.[166]

In Norway, labour and employment legislation is rather comprehensive with the WEA as the central piece of legislation. Nevertheless, anti-discrimination legislation consists of several acts.[167] Besides the statutes, col-

---

165 In general collective labour law concerns collective agreements, their enforcement and legal effect, and industrial relations law, while individual labour law is concerned with the employer and the individual employee. Besides that one may distinguish between worker protection laws and procedural law, see for a general overview and as regards the German system in particular *Foster*, Nigel/*Sule*, Satish (2010), German legal system, 4. edt. p. 579. In order to simplify matters this thesis uses the notion labour law as generic term.

166 *Foster*, Nigel/*Sule*, Satish (2002), German legal system and laws, 3.edt. p. 527; *Foster*/*Sule* (2010), German legal system and laws, 4 edt. p. 581; *Brox*, Hans/ *Rüthers*, Bernd/*Henssler*, Martin (2007), Arbeitsrecht, 17. ed., para. 114. However there is an ongoing debate in Germany to codify labour law in one single act, the so-called *Arbeitsvertragsgesetz*, see among others: *Merten*, Sonja (2008), Das Arbeitsvertragsgesetz und das AGG, Beilage zum Fachanwalt Arbeitsrecht (FA) 2008, pp. 173-176; *Bauer*, Jobst-Hubertus (2009), Der Professorenentwurf zum ArbVG - Kein Danaergeschenk, sondern sinnvolle Diskussionsgrundlage!, Arbeitsrechtliche Entscheidungen (AE) 2009, pp. 14-15; *Iannone*, Enrico (2009), Die Kodifizierung des Arbeitsvertragsrechts - ein Jahrhundertprojekt ohne Erfolgsaussicht?.

167 These are at present: *Lov om arbeidsmiljø, arbeidstid og stillingsvern mv. (arbeidsmiljøloven) av* 17. juni 2005 nr. 62 (The Working Environment Act (WEA)); *Lov om forbud mot diskriminering på grunn av seksuell orientering, kjønnsidentitet og kjønnsuttrykk (diskrimineringsloven om seksuell orientering) av* 21. juni 2013 nr. 58; *Lov om likestilling mellom kjønnene (likestillingsloven) av* 21. juni 2013 nr. 59 (the Gender Equality Act); *Lov om forbud mot diskriminering på grunn av etnisitet, religion og livssyn (diskrimineringsloven om etnisitet) av* 21. juni 2013 nr. 60 (the Act on Prohibition of Discrimination on the basis of ethnicity, religion etc. - the Discrimination Act); *Lov om forbud mot diskriminering på grunn av nedsatt funksjonsevne (diskriminerings- og tilgjengelighetsloven) av* 21. juni 2013 nr. 61 (Act on Prohibition of Discrimination on the basis of disability - Discrimination and Accessibility Act) and the provisions on non-discrimination in the housing acts: *Lov om eierseksjoner (eierseksjonsloven) av* 23. mai 1997 nr. 31 (The Property Unit Ownership Act); *Lov om husleieavtaler (husleieloven) av* 26. mars 1999 nr. 17 (The Tenancy Act); *Lov om bustadbyggjelag (bustadbyggjelagslova) av* 06. juni 2003 nr. 38 (The Residential Building Association Act); *Lov om burettslag (burettslagslova) av* 06. juni 2003 nr. 39 (The Housing Association Act).

lective agreements play a central role in the German context and, traditionally, they play an even more central role in the Norwegian context. However the situation is different when it comes to provisions on mandatory retirement. While such provisions in Germany traditionally have been included in collective agreements and agreements on plant level (*Betriebsvereinbarung*), collective agreements play a rather minor role in this regard – if at all –in Norway. There, such provisions are hardly to be found in national collective agreements or agreements at enterprise level in the private sector. However, one example, where provisions on mandatory retirement are to be found in collective agreements both in Norway and in Germany concerns pilots.[168]

The prevailing methods of interpretation of the legal provisions are basically the same in both Norway and Germany, such as for example teleological interpretation, with its search for the *ratio legis* of the provision in question. However, it has to be noted that in Norway, the legal background material, that is to say the preparatory work (*lovforarbeider*) of the legislation in question, is an important source for the interpretation of a legal provision, as it may provide useful guidance for interpretation. In contrast to Norway, preparatory works of legislation are, in the German context, of rather minor relevance. They are often not as comprehensive and detailed as their Norwegian counterparts are.[169]

Relevant Norwegian preparatory work is, for example, reports from committees or commissions, which are appointed to evaluate the need for new legislation and to make proposals. Their reports are usually published in the publication series *Norges offentlige utredninger* (Official Norwegian Reports, NOU). The NOU is submitted for public consulation among various bodies and institutions for their opinion (hearing) and the responsible ministry then prepares a bill on legislation – proposisjon i lovsak (Prop. L, previously called *Odelstingsproposisjon* (Ot.prp.)) – including analyses, explanations and motivations of the proposals concerned with its underlying motives, which the government presents to the Storting (parliament) as a bill. An Ot.prp. and a so-called *Innstilling* (Innst.) of one of the parliament's special commitees (*fagkomite*) are further part of the relevant preparatory work.[170]

---

168 see in detail analysis in chap. 15.

169 see to this aspect from a Swedish perspective: *Rönnmar* (2004), p. 35.

170 see for an overview https://www.stortinget.no/no/Stortinget-og-demokratiet/Arbeidet/Lovarbeidet/ (last accessed: 17.12.2014).

Following *Eckhoff*'s interpretation of the concept of sources of law, several categories of sources of law, in general, can be distinguished between in Norway: statute law and regulations; preparatory work (background material to the legislation); case law, in particular that of the Supreme Court; the practice of other authorities; private practices; general opinions of justice; and finally, 'real', or value considerations pertaining to the fairness and appropriatness of the outcome.[171]

The primary sources of German labour law are the Constitution, ordinary legislation, collective agreements, works council agreements and the individual labour contract.[172]

Furthermore, in contrast to civil law countries such as Germany, precedents play an important role as a source of law in the Norwegian legal system. Once a legal precedent exits, it has to be considered and thus may have a decisive impact on the outcome of a later case. Therefore, the 'picture' of the legal sources changes fundamentally, once a precedent is available for the legal question to be analysed.[173] This is true for decisions of the Supreme Court of Norway (*Norges Høyesterett*), which inter alia has to deal with questions of individual employment law, and the decisions of the Labour Court of Norway (*Arbeidsretten*) with regard to the field of collective labour law.

In principle, the ordinary courts consist of three instances: the District Courts (*tingrett*) in the first instance, the Courts of Appeal (*lagmannsrett*) in the second instance and, finally, in the third instance, the Supreme Court. These courts are supplemented by a special court for resolving disputes in the field of collective labour law – the Labour Court.

On the contrary, it is rather questionable as to whether the decisions of the labour courts constitute a formal source of labour law in Germany.[174] The 'doctrine of precedent' – as it is commonly known in common law countries – is, in principle, unknown in the German legal system and does not generally exist. According to the Basic Law (*Grundgesetz* – GG), one of

---

171 *Eckhoff,* Torstein/*Helgesen,* Jan E. (2001), Rettskildelære, 5.edt., p. 23; see for translation *Bertnes*, Pål A (1993), Sources to legal information in Norway, International Journal of Legal Information, Vol. 21, pp. 154-166, p. 156; see moreover *Aarbakke*, Magnus/*Helgesen*, Jan (1982), Sources of law in Norway, in: The sources of law. A comparative empirical study, National systems of sources of law, Kourilsky, Chantal /Rácz, Attila/Schäffer, Heinz (eds.), pp. 189-225, p. 189 f.; see for a short description in general and with regard to labour law in particular, see *Jakhelln*, Henning (2007), Oversikt over arbeidsretten, 4. edt., p. 80ff.

172 *Weiss*, Manfred/*Schmidt*, Marlene (2008), Labour law and industrial relations in Germany, p. 38ff.; *Brox* et al. (2007), para. 116ff., p. 43ff.; see in detail also: *Thüsing*, Gregor (2014) in: Henssler, Martin/Willemsen, Heinz J./Kalb, Heinz-Jürgen (eds.), Arbeitsrecht Kommentar, 6. edt. 2014, Vor § 611.

173 see to this aspect *Andenœs*, Mads H. (1997), Rettsskildelære, p. 41; and in detail: *Eckhoff*/*Helgesen* (2001), p. 155ff, in particular p. 159.

174 see *Brox* et al. (2007), para. 116.

the fundamental constitutional principles is that the judiciary is only bound by law and justice.[175] Consequently, in German law, it is often the case that decisions by a court only have the force of law for the parties involved in the particular dispute.[176] The judiciary is not bound by previous court decisions and may decide independently from these decisions. This means that even for a lower court, such as the *Amtsgericht* (AG), which is the lowest German court, a binding effect with regard to decisions made by the highest courts does not exist.[177] Notwithstanding this 'independence' of the judiciary from the doctrine of precedent, examining the practical reality reveals, however, a slightly different picture, as the decisions of the superior courts de facto often have a decisive influence on the decisions of the lower courts.[178] Although the overwhelming consensus in Germany is that court decisions are not a formal source of law, it cannot be denied that they play an important role in the development of the law.[179] This is particularly true with regard to labour law. As no comprehensive legislation exists in this area of law, it is essential to look at how labour law is applied in case law to concretise the principles of labour law, to specify general clauses and terms and to fill the gaps in the legislation that have been left open to the legislator.[180] This applies in particular with regard to the decisions of the Federal Labour Court (*Bundesarbeitsgericht* – BAG).[181] In labour law, judge-made law plays an important

175 Art. 20 (3) i.c.w. Art. 1(3); Art. 97 (1) GG.

176 *Robbers*, Gerhard (1998), An introduction to German law, p. 20, 21.

177 As a consequence an AG may reach a different conclusion on the very same point of law than for example the *Bundesgerichtshof* (BGH) - the highest civil court in Germany - in a previous decision, see ibid., p. 20.

178 *Robbers* (1998), p. 20, 21 who stresses the quasi-normative force of the head-notes containing the *ratio decedendi* (*Leitsatz*) as they are formulated in cases of the superior courts.

179 ibid., p. 19.

180 *Foster/Sule* (2002), p. 527; *Foster/Sule* (2010), p. 581 f.; *Weiss/Schmidt* (2008), p. 39, 40; *Gamillscheg* (1964), Die Grundrechte im Arbeitsrecht, Archiv für civilistische Praxis, vol. 164, pp. 385-445, pp. 388ff.; see in detail also critical analysis by *Söllner*, Alfred (1985), Zur Verfassungs- und Gesetzestreue im Arbeitsrecht, Recht der Arbeit (RdA), 1985, pp. 328-337, pp. 328ff., who finally concludes that court decisions do not constitute a normative source of law '*Der Richterspruch ist – auch im Arbeitsrecht – keine normative Rechtsquelle*' (p. 337).

181 *Foster/Sule* (2002), p. 527; *Foster/Sule* (2010), p. 581.

role.[182] The BAG and the lower labour law courts[183] have contributed considerably to the development of this field of law.[184] Especially in the field of labour law, the BAG de facto 'has become at least as important as the legislator'.[185] In consequence, labour law can be characterised as the area of German law that features 'the closest similarity to common law'.[186] Or, as *Gamillscheg* put it in a nutshell more than five decades ago, '*Der Richter ist der eigentliche Herr des Arbeitsrechts'*.[187]

The following study considers these mentioned differentiations with regard to the legal method and sources of labour and employment law. Consequently, in the analysis of the Norwegian legal situation, court decisions are considered – in contrast to the analysis of the German law – to a greater extent and to as comprehensive an extent as possible. Most of the relevant cited Norwegian court decisions can primarily be accessed via the online database *Lovdata*.[188] The cited German court decisions are merely exemplary in character. Here, the analysis is limited to selected case law

---

182 *Gamillscheg* (1964), pp. 388ff.; *Weiss/Schmidt* (2008), p. 39, 40.

183 Court of first instance is the *Arbeitsgericht* (ArbG), followed by the *Landesarbeitsgericht* as Court of Appeal (*Berufungs- und Beschwerdeinstanz*). The Appelate Court (*Revisionsgericht*) and thus Court of ultimate resort is the *Bundesarbeitsgericht.* A direct review (*Sprungrevision*) from *Arbeitsgericht* to *Bundesarbeitsgericht* may be possible, see for an overview *Weiss/Schmidt* (2008), p. 149ff.

184 This inter alia based on the fact that due to the § 45 IV of the Act on Court Procedure in Labour Law Matters (*Arbeitsgerichtsgesetz*, ArbGG), the BAG may in questions of substantial relevance decide to develop law further, *Weiss/Schmidt* (2008), p. 39, 40.

185 ibid., p. 39.

186 *Foster/Sule* (2002), p. 527; *Foster/Sule* (2010), p. 581; However as stressed by *Weiss/Schmidt* keeping in mind the principle of separation of legislative and judicial powers as laid down in the Constitution (Art. 20 III GG) the debate remains more or less academic, *Weiss/Schmidt* (2008), p. 39, 40.; see moreover to the role of judge-made law in German labour law *Brox* et al. (2007), para. 117ff., p. 43ff.

187 'A judge is the actual master of labour law', translation by author of *Gamillscheg* (1964), p. 388.

188 www.lovdata.no; The list of cited cases does not claim to be exhaustive.

that is most suitable for the illustration of the legal discourse.[189] This is primarily case law which is analysed and discussed in the literature and, in particular, in the commentary literature.[190]

However, regardless of what kinds of legal sources are used and how they are applied in the national context – that is to say, besides the aspects which result from the national legal system and its prevailing doctrines – it has to be noted that for the comparative analysis and its search for the 'best solution', the arguments as to why a national legal solution should or should not be preferred, should, in the end (as a rule), only be purely objective in nature (*Sachargumente*).[191] Thus, the comparative analysis finally forces the revelation of objective arguments that argue for the preferred solution.[192] Here again, the merit of the comparative method in the purely functional sense becomes visible.

3 The concept of mandatory retirement

3.1 Mandatory retirement versus pensionable age

In general, 'mandatory retirement' or 'compulsory retirement' – being the thesis' key research objective – are formulations that are used synonymously in this thesis to generally describe age limits that are to be distinguished from the notion of 'pensionable age' or 'pension age'. The pension age describes the age at which individuals become entitled to a (state) pension, which in principle has to be distinguished from the age at which employees retire from work.[193] Furthermore, a distinction has to be made to age-based limitations in dismissal protection legislation. The exit age from the workforce may coincide with the pension age, but this is not

189 Considering the enormous German case law in the area of labour and employment law, an exhaustive analysis can hardly be achieved. Only the BAG for example closed in the year 2013 2.650 cases, whereof 679 had to deal with the termination of employment, see http://www.bundesarbeitsgericht.de/statistik.html (last accessed: 17.12.2014).

190 Relevant sources are www.beckonline.de and www.juris.de (last accessed: 17.12.2014).

191 *Eichenhofer* (1997), p. 99.

192 ibid.

193 *O'Cinneide* (2005), p. 41; *Evju*, Stein (2006), Aldersdiskriminering, likebehandling og pensjonsalder, arbeidsrett Vol. 3 nr. 3 2006, pp. 137–161, p. 156.

always necessarily the case. The term 'mandatory retirement' generally describes the automatic termination of the employment relationship after the employee has reached a particular chronological age and where the employee is obliged to retire.[194] One example in this regard is to be found in the Norwegian context in the *aldersgrenseloven*, where such an obligation is explicitly manifested in § 2 (4).[195] Sometimes, pensionable age and mandatory retirement age are interlinked by law.[196] Mandatory retirement age limits may be lower, equivalent to the pensionable age or even higher.

The general pensionable age in Norway for the last four decades has been set at 67. As a consequence of the 2011 pension reform, the general pension age has been lowered to 62 years of age.[197] This applies in general for private- as well as for public-sector employees. Despite the reform, the age of 67 is often correspondingly set as the mandatory age limit in collective agreements, in agreements at the plant level or it may be individually agreed upon in the employment contract.

In Germany, the formerly applicable pensionable age of 65 is due to increase according to a recent reform in 2012 in a stepwise manner up to 67 years of age.[198] The pensionable age for public servants is supposed to increase correspondingly. In Germany, mandatory retirement age limits may also be laid down in collective agreements, plant agreements (*Betriebsvereinbarung*) or in the individual employment contract.[199] Compulsory retirement age limits, e.g. in collective agreements, are typically

---

194 *Ghosheh* (2008), p. 9; see in general as regards provisions in Norwegian law that entail an obligation to retire: *Jakhelln*, Henning (2000), Åremålskontrakter, særskilte aldersgrenser og retrettstillinger, in: Arbeidsrettslige studier bind II, (originally published in Institutt for offentlig retts skriftserie nr. 5/1986), pp. 756-828, p. 772 f.

195 see § 2 Lov 21. desember 1956 nr. 1 *om aldersgrenser for offentlige tjenestemenn m.fl. (aldersgrenselov)*.

196 *European Commission* (2010), p. 52.

197 see §§ 19-4, 20-2 ftrl; Originally the general pensionable age was set at 70 years of age from 1937 and was lowered to 67 in 1973 and in 2011 to 62 years of age, see *Kjønstad* (2012), p. 85; see also chap. 1.4.1.

198 § 235 SGB VI i.c.w. § 35 SGB VI; see to the recent pension reform in Germany chap. 1.4.2.

199 extensive analysis by *Temming* (2008), p. 335ff., critical to the legal competence of the parties to the plant agreement to lay down mandatory retirement provisions, p. 356ff., see p. 364 f. as regards age limits in individual employment contracts, p. 364 f.

set at the age of 65.[200] For about 100 years, the age of 65 has been the general age limit that has been commonly used in Germany.[201] As it corresponds in principle to the pensionable age, it is supposed to increase in line with the amendments in § 35 SGB VI.[202]

3.2 General versus special mandatory retirement age limits

Moreover, one has to differentiate between general and special mandatory retirement age limits (*særaldersgrenser*). Some professions stipulate special mandatory retirement age limits that are typically lower than the general age limit. These age limits are 'special' insofar as they are often related to certain types of professions and the particular requirements that come with these, such as a high degree of mental and physical fitness. Classic examples are age limits for pilots, police officers or professions in medical and health care.[203]

The public sector generally operates with a general 70-year age limit in § 2 *aldersgrenselov.*[204]

At the regional level, the legal situation is rather fragmented with various applicable regulations.[205] In general, the mandatory retirement age limits shall correspond to the age limits set at state/governmental level.[206] The specific age limits are laid down in *rundskriv 10 a, 10 b* and correlate to the age limits in the state/governmental sector.[207] According to the *Hovedtariffavtalen*

---

200 see e.g. § 33 (1) *Tarifvertrag für den öffentlichen Dienst* (TVöD).

201 *Temming/Rothermund* (2010), p. 60.

202 see to this aspect *Groß* (2010), p. 27.

203 Further examples constitute the mandatory age limits for ballet dancers (age of 41) and members of the chorus (age of 56) such as soloists (age of 52) of the Norwegian Opera & Ballet, see § 2 and § 3 (1) Lov 21. august 1998 nr. 65 *om pensjonsordning for ballettdansere, sangsolister og korsangere ved Den Norske Opera & Ballett (operapensjonsloven).* Mandatory retirement age limits for physicians and for pilots are analysed in detail in chap. 13 and 15.

204 see chap. 14.2

205 see overview in '*Aldersgrenser i norsk lovgivning*', in: http://www.seniorpolitikk.no/fakta/arbeid/aldersgrenser-i-norsk-lovgivning (last accessed: 17.12.2014)

206 § 2 (2) FOR 1997-04-22 nr 374 (*Forskrift om pensjonsordninger for kommunalt eller fylkeskommunalt ansatte*) w.r.t. *aldersgrenseloven.*

207 see http://www.seniorpolitikk.no/fakta/arbeid/aldersgrenser-i-norsk-lovgivning.

for kommunene, the age limits that are applicable in the municipalities shall be consistent with the respective provisions in the *aldersgrenseloven*.[208] This, in principle, implies that the respective age limits may be subject to collective bargaining.[209]

In the private sector in Norway, § 15-13 a (1) s. 1 WEA, which is commonly referred to as the 70-*årsgrense* (70-year age limit) is of central relevance.[210] According to this provision, the employment relationship may be terminated after the employee has reached the age of 70, without the need for an objective reason for the dismissal, as otherwise required due to § 15-7 WEA. Strictly speaking, the *70-årsgrense* therefore does not constitute an age limit that compulsorily terminates the employment relationship; rather, it regulates the scope of dismissal protection.[211] Consequently, one may characterise the 70-*årsgrense* as an indirect general age limit.[212] It has to be noted moreover that § 15-13 a (1) s. 2 WEA explicitly opens up for the determination of lower age limits in for example collective agreements or plant agreements, as long as they are objectively justi-

---

208 *Hovedtariffavtalen for kommunene*, chap. 2.1.3, 2.4.1

209 see http://www.seniorpolitikk.no/fakta/arbeid/aldersgrenser-i-norsk-lovgivning.

210 With amendments coming into force July 1st 2015 (lov 24 apr 2015 nr. 21), the age limit has been raised by to years to 72 years of age according to § 15-13 a (1) aml. Despite the amendment, the 72-years age limit in § 15-13 a (1) aml is still under debate. A recently designated committee (*aldersgrenseutvalg*) shall evaluate whether the age limit should be further raised up to 75 years of age or entirely abolished, see to the Committee's mandate: https://www.regjeringen.no/no/aktuelt/nytt-utvalg-skal-se-pa-tilpasninger-i-arbeidslivet-med-sikte-pa-okt-aldersgrense/id2439416/ (last accessed: 22.02.2016) The committee's final recommendations are expected by December 2016. Throughout the thesis the 70-years age limit in the version applicable until 1st of July 2015 is referred to.

211 According to § 15-13 a (2) WEA the employment relationship is not automatically terminated at the age of 70, the employer rather has to give notice about the dismissal 6 month in advance.

212 A similar provision is to be found in § 5-12 (1) Lov 21. juni 2013 nr. 102 *om stillingsvern mv. for arbeidstakere på skip (skipsarbeidsloven)*; see to the previous regulation in § 19 no. 1 (6) Lov 5. mai 1975 nr. 18 *Sjømannslov (Opphevet),* which has been subject to the first case before the *Høyesterett* concerning Norway's relationship to Dir. 2000/78/EC and its prohibition against age discrimination: case Rt. 2010 s. 202 (*Kystlink*); see for further details: *Hack* (2012 a), p. 360ff; *Hack* (2010 c), Etter lek med ild, nå lek med vann: Aldersgrense, pensjonsalder, sjømenn Høyesterettsdom 18. februar 2010 (HR-2010-00303-A), Nytt i privatretten: nyhetsbrev for informasjon på det privatret (NIP) 2010 (2), pp. 2-3.

fied and not disproportionate, according to the exception regulation to age discrimination contained in § 13-3 (2) WEA.[213] Often, general mandatory retirement age limits are therefore set at the age of 67 in collective agreements or plant agreements in line with the pensionable age.[214] As regards special mandatory retirement age limits, several examples of *særaldersgrenser* are to be found in the public sector in Norway.[215] They may be set at 60, 63 or 65.[216]

Professions that are encompassed by these 'special' age limits are, according to the *aldersgrenselov,* characterised by extraordinary physical or mental pressure on the employee, so that the profession's exercise until the age of 70 in general is irresponsible (§ 2 (1) s. 2 (a) *aldersgrenselov*). Moreover, those professions are encompassed that make special demands on the employee's physical and mental capabilities that are, under normal circumstances, already weakened before having reached the age of 70, so that the profession may not be practised in a responsible manner (§ 2 (1) s. 2 (b) *aldersgrenselov*). Allocated to the first category are e.g. nurses, cleaners or industrial workers. Police officers or ambulance men belong to the second category, for example.

In general, Germany does not have a codified general applicable age limit to determine that the employment relationship of private-sector employees terminates after having reached retirement age.[217] By contrast, the public sector operates with a general mandatory retirement age limit for for example civil servants, judges or soldiers.[218] However, mandatory retirement age limits are manifested in for example collective agreements. Some argue that the widespread use of such general age limits in Germany

213 Also the age for lower age limits has been increased by lov 24 apr 2015 nr. 21 up to 70 years of age, see § 15-13 a (3) aml. The legal requirements for such lower age limits have been tightened. They may only be determined provided they have been made familiar to the employees, they have been applied consistently by the employer and finally the employee is entitled to satisfying occupational pensions. Throughout the thesis the age limit in the version applicable until 1st of July 2015 is referred to.

214 On example in this regard constitutes the *Gjensidige* case: Rt. 2011 s. 964 (*Gjensidige*).

215 see the overview given in https://www.regjeringen.no/contentassets/d718daa9e5ff4655b69a5febc63cea1c/aldersgrensene_i_staten.pdf (last accessed: 17.12.2014); *Fornyings-, administrasjons- og kirkedepartementet* (2013), Statens Personalhåndbook, chap. 5.2.1., Aldersgrensene i staten, p. 128.

216 see § 2 (2) *aldersgrenselov*.

217 *Senne* (2006), p. 294, 298; *Bertelsmann* (2007), § 10, para. 230.

218 see in detail *Temming* (2008), p. 318; see also *Bertelsmann* (2007), § 10, para. 239.

may be characterised as being the cost for a relatively high level of protection for older employees via the German dismissal legislation and so-called *Unkündbarkeitsklauseln* (non-termination clauses).[219]

Besides this, special age limits are also to be found in Germany. Examples are age limits for notaries[220] or midwives,[221] which both have to retire at the age of 70, while, for example, chimney sweepers[222] already have to retire at the age of 65. Further examples include pilots.[223] Up until 2008, physicians e.g. were forced to retire at the age of 68. Interestingly enough, this age limit was abolished in 2008.[224]

In addition, age limits for authorised experts (*Sachverständige*) have been subject to the case law of the highest courts in Germany and may no longer be justifiably maintained, according to recent judgements.[225]

3.3 Absolute versus relative mandatory retirement age limits

Furthermore, one has to distinguish absolute from relative mandatory retirement provisions. In contrast to absolute age limits, relative age limits allow for a prolongation of the employment relationship beyond the age limit in question. However, these 'relative' age limits generally also allow for an extension only up to a certain age and do not generally provide for an unlimited opportunity to extend working life. In the end, these alleged

---

219 *Temming/Rothermund* (2010), p. 60.

220 § 47 Nr. 1 i.c.w. § 48 (a) *Bundesnotarordnung* (BNotO); see in this regard judgement of the German Supreme Court in BVerfG, Beschluss vom 21. Juni 1989 – 1 BvR 32/87 –, BVerfGE 80, 257-268.

221 see judgement of the German Supreme Court: BVerfG, Beschluss vom 16. Juni 1959 – 1 BvR 71/57 –, BVerfGE 9, 338-354 (*Altersgrenze für Hebammen*).

222 § 9 *Schornsteinfegergesetz*; see judgement of the German Supreme Court BVerfG, Beschluss vom 30. April 1952 – 1 BvR 14/52, 1 BvR 25/52, 1 BvR 167/52 –, BVerfGE 1, 264-28 (*Bezirksschornsteinfeger*).

223 see chap. 15.

224 see in detail chap. 13.

225 BVerwG, Urteil vom 01. Februar 2012 – 8 C 24/11 –, BVerwGE 141, 385-393; BVerfG, Stattgebender Kammerbeschluss vom 24. Oktober 2011 – 1 BvR 1103/11 –, juris; pro maintenance of age limit for public authorised experts (*öffentlich bestellte Sachverständige*): BVerfG, Kammerbeschluss vom 16. November 1990 – 1 BvR 1280/90 –, juris and arguing for maintaining age limits for *Prüfingenieure for Baustatistik*: BVerfG, Beschluss vom 04. Mai 1983 – 1 BvL 46/80, 1 BvL 47/80 –, BVerfGE 64, 72-86 (*Prüfingenieur*).

'relative' age limits are thus also absolute. Relative and absolute mandatory retirement provisions are to be found in Norway as well as in Germany.[226]

4 Mandatory retirement and the concept of ageism

We don't all grow white or black, but we all grow old.[227]

4.1 Introduction

Common to the different types of mandatory retirement provisions is that they operate with chronological age as the decisive proxy to determine whether the employee has to exit working life or not. In this regard, mandatory retirement provisions constitute a clear example of ageism, as they are an expression of negative stereotypes, prejudices and discrimination against older employees solely on the basis of their chronological age. Or as *Bytheway* put it, 'ageism legitimates the use of chronological age to mark out classes of people who are systematically denied resources and opportunities that others enjoy, and who suffer the consequences of such denigration, ranging from well-meaning patronage to unambiguous vilification'.[228] As ageism is thus immanent to any form of age discrimination, it is essential to shed further light on this concept.

---

226 see as regards relative age limits in Norway e.g.: § 3 *aldersgrenselov*; § 3 (1) s. 3 *operapensjonslov*. *Lüderitz* discusses such relative age limits as an alternative (*milderes Mittel*) to an absolute age limit, see *Lüderitz* (2005), p. 111. *Lüderitz* uses the term mandatory retirement and pension age synonymously. Similar *von Hoff* (2009), p. 290; and as regards absolute age limits *e.g:* § 3 (1) s. 3 *aldersgrenselov*; § 3 (1) s. 3 *operapensjonslov*. Examples of both relative and absolute mandatory retirement age limits are further discussed in chap. 13-15.

227 *Butler*, Robert N. (1969), Age-ism: Another form of bigotry, in: The Gerontologist 1969, pp. 243-246, p. 246.

228 *Bytheway*, Bill (1995), Ageism, p. 14, developed from Bytheway, Bill/Johnson, J. (1990), On defining ageism, Critical Social policy, 1990, pp. 27-39.

4.2 Defining ageism

The notion of 'ageism' was initially coined by the psychiatrist *Robert Butler* in 1969, who defined ageism as 'prejudice by one age group toward other age groups'.[229] A few years later, in 1973, *Butler* and *Lewis* suggested a more extensive definition, 'Ageism can be seen as a process of systematic stereotyping and discrimination against people because they are old, just as racism and sexism accomplish this for color and gender'.[230]

This definition became the 'classic' definition of ageism – some theorists even call it the 'ultimate definition'.[231] Like in the classic version, ageism is often compared to other 'isms' such as sexism and racism.[232] However, regarding ageism as equivalent to or 'just the same as' sexism and racism fails to take into account the unique nature of ageism.[233] The uniqueness of ageism is based on its pervasive as well as dynamic character.[234] It is pervasive to the extent that probably everyone is affected at some point in their life whether within or outside the context of employ-

---

229 *Butler* (1969), p. 243 who does in his definition not clearly distinguish between age discrimination and ageism; *Butler* was involved in a controversy concerning the use of a high-rise block in Washington D.C. Due to a proposal of local authorities it should be used as a public housing for people, many of whom would be poor, black and old. When being asked by a reporter of the Washington Post whether the negativism against this project was a function of racism, he said that it rather constituted a function of ageism, see for the history of ageism: *Bytheway*, Bill (2005), Ageism, in: The Cambridge handbook on age and ageing, Johnson, Malcolm L. et al. (edt.), pp. 338-345, p. 338 f.

230 quoted from *Oswick*, Cliff/*Rosenthal*, Patrice (2001), Towards a relevant theory of age discrimination in employment, in: Noon, Mike/Ogbonna, Emmanuel (eds), Equality, Diversity and Disadvantage in Employment, 2001, p. 156-171, p. 157; see also *Bytheway* (2005), p. 338.

231 see for an overview *Iversen* et al. (2009), p. 7.

232 This reference to sexism and racism is almost universal in the literature concerning ageism, see for an overview to this aspect *Iversen* et al. (2009), p. 7.

233 *Oswick*/*Rosenthal* (2001), p. 156; see in detail also *Iversen* et al. (2009), p. 7, 8. *Iversen* et al. refer moreover to the fact that prejudicing and stereotyping of the elderly often occurs unnoticed and unchallenged by the public and that no social sanctions against those people exist who express negative prejudices or stereotypes against elderly people. Rather on the contrary to express a certain form of negativity towards older people seems to be commonly accepted, which is due to *Iversen* et al. in strong contrast to the reactions of society to remarks of racist or sexist character.

234 *Oswick*/*Rosenthal* (2001), p. 156, 165.

ment.[235] By contrast, not everyone will similarly be directly exposed to either racism or sexism.[236] It can be described as dynamic, as ageing constitutes an ongoing process of change, while in contrast to that, the way in which individuals are affected – with rare exceptions – by sexism and racism is rather characterised by a certain degree of continuity throughout the life cycle.[237] The authors *Oswick* and *Rosenthal* put the unique feature of ageism into a nutshell by stating, 'Someone who is born a woman does not slowly become a man or vice versa, equally a black person does not gradually become white, but a young person will gradually become an old person. Or as Bytheway succinctly puts it: "No one is born old"'[238]

Ageism should thus be treated separately instead of treating it as equivalent or by comparing it directly with racism and sexism.[239] Nevertheless, the phenomenon of ageism cannot be examined in isolation. It is rather crucial to be aware of its interplay and intersection or interaction with other 'isms'.[240] A typical example constitutes the situation of older female

---

235 ibid., p. 156 who also on p. 165 refer to the aspect that the fact that everybody is affected by ageism during lifetime gives this 'atypical' form of discrimination 'an air of legitimacy'. This argumentation is also used in the so-called 'fair innings-argument' to justify mandatory retirement, see in detail chap. 12.3.3.

236 ibid., p. 156.

237 *Bytheway* (1995), p. 10.

238 *Oswick/Rosenthal* (2001), p. 156 quoting *Bytheway*, Bill (1995), Ageism, p. 10.

239 Research on ageism lived until recently a rather shadowy existence compared to research on sexism and racism, see to this aspect *Iversen* et al. (2009), p. 5, 7 f.; see also *Nelson*, Todd D. (2005), Ageism: Prejudice Against Our feared Future Self, Journal of Social, Vol. 61, No. 2, pp. 207-221 who illustrated this aspect by comparing search results in the database Psychinfo. According to his search just 294 articles could be found related to ageism while 3111 dealt with racism and 1385 with sexism, see p. 207 f.

240 see to this aspect among others: *Arber*, Sara/ *Ginn*, Jay (1991), Gender and Later Life; *Calasanti*, Toni M./ *Slevin*, Kathleen F. (2006), Introduction: Age Matters, in: Age Matters: Re-aligning Feminist Thinking, Calasanti/Slevin (eds.), pp. 1-20; *Calasanti,* Toni M./*Slevin,* Kathleen F. / *King*, Neal (2006), Ageism and feminism: From 'Et Cetera' to Center, NWSA Journal (now: Feminist Formations), Vol. 18, No. 1, pp. 13-30; *Calasanti*, Toni M. (2008), A feminist confronts ageism, Journal of Ageing Studies 2008, Vol. 22 (2), pp. 157-162, p. 155 f.; focusing on the concept of intersectionality inter alia *Krekula*, Clary/*Närvänen*, Anna-Liisa/*Näsman*, Elisabet (2005), Ålder i intersektionell analys, Kvinnovetenskaplig tidskrift 2-3.05, pp. 81-94; with regard to the concept of intersectionality in feminist theory, see *Lykke*, Nina (2005), Nya perspektiv på intersektionalitet. Problem och möjligheter, Kvinnovetenskaplig tidskrift 2-3.05, pp. 7-17; *Søndergaard*, Dorte M. (2005), Making sense of gender, age, power and

employees in the workplace, where the 'gender dimensions of ageism'[241] or 'gendered ageism'[242] come into play. This is because (older) women are especially vulnerable to discrimination on the grounds of both age and gender – so-called multiple discrimination.[243]

Moreover, several of the existing definitions of ageism may be criticised as being more or less diffuse, unclear and often too simplified to cope with the concept's complexity.[244] *Iversen* et al. therefore offer a conceptual clarification of ageism by proposing a reformulation of the definition of ageism to address the phenomenon's complexity:

> Ageism is defined as negative or positive stereotypes, prejudice and/or discrimination against (or to the advantage of) elderly people on the basis of their chronological age or on the basis of a perception of them as being 'old' or 'elderly'. Ageism can be implicit or explicit and can be expressed on a micro-, meso- or macro-level.[245]

Even if this reformulation contributes to more conceptual clarity, it may nevertheless be criticised for still – like previous definitions – focusing on the social exclusion and discrimination of older people (discriminatees)

---

disciplinary position: Intersecting discourses in the academy, Feminism and psychology 2005 Vol. 15 No. (2), pp. 189-208; from the perspective of medical care for example: *Sheehan*, Myles N. (2003), disabilities and ageing, Theoretical Medicine and Bioethics, 2003, Vol. 24: 6, pp. 525-533, p. 526; see to the distinction between additive and intersectional discrimination chap. 10.2.2.3

241 see in detail *Duncan*, Colin/*Loretto*, Wendy (2004), Never the right age? Gender and age-based discrimination in employment, Gender, Work and Organization. Vol. 11 No. 1 January 2004, pp. 96-115, 98ff.

242 *Meenan,* Helen (2007 c), Age discrimination in Europe: Late bloomer or wallflower?, Nordisk Tidsskrift for Menneskerrettigheter 2007 Nr. 02, p. 114.

243 see chap. 10.2.2.3.

244 *Iversen* et al. (2009), p. 5, 6.; *Iversen* et al. have critically reviewed 27 different versions of ageism, see p. 8ff, see in particular Table 1, pp. 8-11. According to their critic the definitions may e.g. often themselves invite to stereotyping when it is only referred to age through the word old and by using the term elderly it is suggested that elderly people are different from the other people, see p. 7, 8; *Simone de Beauvoir* similarly describes the differentness between the young and the old in her observation that older people are often treated by society as if *'they belong to an entirely different species'*, as if the elderly person is 'another being', *de Beauvoir*, Simone (1972), *Coming of Age*, translated by Patrick O' Brian, ed. 1996, p. 3.

245 *Iversen* et al. (2009), p. 15; see also for an alternative theory of ageism *Oswick*/*Rosenthal* (2001), pp. 156-171.

through primarily younger people (discriminators).[246] Yet the fluid character of the ageing process makes a clear demarcation between discriminator and discriminatee based on the factor of age rather difficult.[247] People of all ages may take on the role of discriminators and, vice versa, may be discriminatees. Even the determination of one age group as such is problematic due to the difficulty of choosing the right reference figures – shall it be, for example, the chronological age, biological age or the psychological age?[248] Moreover, if chronological age is to be the reference element, what age should then be decisive? Where should one draw the line? Thus, ageism also differs from the other 'isms', as a clear assignment to one specific group is not possible. Keeping the highlighted difficulties in mind, this study is therefore based on a broad understanding of ageism that encompasses all ages.[249] Even if this analysis primarily concentrates on ageism towards older employees, it has to be accounted for that the examined provisions on mandatory retirement may also have ageist effects as regards younger employees.

4.3 Intermediate conclusion

To sum up, ageism may in general affect people of all ages, from the young to the very old, in different forms and on different levels and in interaction with other 'isms'. Correspondingly, age-discrimination legislation should address all ages to avoid being ageist in itself. People of all ages should in principle benefit from protection against age discrimination to an equal extent.[250] Hence, neither in Norwegian nor in German anti-discrimination legislation does delineation into a particular age band exist. The protection against age discrimination in employment is, at the outset, guaranteed for employees of all ages. However, in the Norwegian context,

---

246 similar already *Oswick/Rosenthal* (2001), p. 157 with further references.

247 similar *Heikkinnen/Krekula* (2008), p. 26, 27; *Oswick/Rosenthal* (2001), p. 164.

248 see to the different forms of ageing, chap. 6.2.

249 *Iversen* et al. primarily focus on ageism towards older people, which they regard as being qualitatively different as ageism towards young people, see *Iversen* et al. (2009), p. 4 f., 19.

250 similar *Fredman* (2003), p. 24 who also refers to the aspect that discrimination policies and legislation that solely focus on older people are running the risk of disregarding questions of inter-generational equity.

this 'protection' is modified by two aspects: first, by (absolute) mandatory retirement provisions that are to be found in several professions and second, by the *70-årsgrense* in § 15-13 a WEA.[251]

Considering the fact that more than four decades ago the notion of ageism came to the fore, one might legitimately ask if ageism might finally have been overcome.[252] From a normative perspective, considering the still-prevailing stereotypes as expressed in the use of chronological age limits in mandatory retirement provisions, this question simply has to be answered in the negative. Rather, it is the case that the image of older people in today's society is still dominated by the myth of ageing as an expression of decline and loss of physical and mental skills.[253] Age stereotypes, which serve to maintain early retirement schemes and mandatory retirement provisions, still prevail. These negative images of age and ageing also have impacts on the 'self-image' (*Selbstbild*) of older people.[254] Several studies have revealed a discrepancy between the self-image and the public image (*Selbstbild und Fremdbild*) – a discrepancy between what older people want to do and are capable of doing and what the environment expects them to do.[255] Similarly, a discrepancy often exists between the attitude of employers towards older employees, between the operational requirements and expectations, on the one hand, and the real capabilities and potential of older workers on the other hand.[256] *Butler* put

251 see as regards an example for the German context also the highly debated § 622 II 2 of the *Bürgerlerliches Gesetzbuch* (BGB) in its previously valid version that did not take into account the period of employment completed before the employee reaches the age of 25 for calculating the notice period in dismissals. This provision was subject to C-555/07 (*Kücükdeveci*), Judgement of 19 January 2010, ECR 2010, 2010 I-00365.

252 *Lehr*, Ursula (2007), p. 199.

253 ibid., p. 199, 200.

254 see in detail *Lehr* (2007), p. 201 and *Temming* (2008), p. 21.

255 *Lehr* refers for example to a series of studies, which showed that it is mainly the attitude of other people which will force many to age-appropriate behaviours, but not so much their own desires or the decline of skills, see *Lehr* (2007), p. 202 f.

256 *Lehr* refers e.g. to experiments with false application documents in which all job-related details have been kept constant and where only the age data varied, which demonstrated that with increasing age, a poorer rated health status is expected, such as reduced job commitment, lower performance motivation, increased resistance to technological change and less flexibility and decreasing willingness to undertake advanced training, see *Lehr* (2007), p. 211 f. who inter alia refers to Craft et al. (1979), Simulated management perceptions, hiring decisions and age, Aging and Work 2, p. 95-102.

this discrepancy already in 1969 into a nutshell, 'We have chosen mandatory retirement from the workforce and thus removed the elderly from the mainstream of life. Age-ism is manifested in the taunting remarks about 'old fogeys', [...] in age discrimination in employment independent of individual competence'.[257]

To disprove these stereotypes that mandatory retirement provisions seem to be deeply founded in, it is essential to take a closer look at recent gerontological findings on the ageing process, which could inter alia unmask the myth of ageing as a mere process of a decline in capabilities.[258] This is done in chap. 6 which forms, together with chap. 7 and 8, the interdisciplinary approach to the analysis of mandatory retirement. However, before going into this, the thesis further explores the concept of age equality, and its relationship to mandatory retirement and the prohibition against age discrimination.

5 Mandatory retirement and the concept of age equality

5.1 Age equality and age discrimination

From a semantic point of view, the terms 'non-discrimination' and 'equality' may be considered the same. However, some authors have argued that when it comes to anti-discrimination law, the mere prohibition of discrimination might have less aspiring aims than the potentially broader concept underlying equality law regimes.[259] It has been argued that the notion of discrimination is primarily focused on a particular form of action, while the term equality, on the contrary, rather describes an ideal.[260] The term 'equal treatment' could therefore be characterised as being the positive

---

257 *Butler* (1969), p. 244; see a discussion of the often referred to decline of capabilities/work performance with age in light of current gerontopsychological research findings chap. 6.3.5.

258 see chap. 6.

259 see to this aspect in detail with further references *Schiek*, Dagmar/*Waddington*, Lisa/*Bell*, Mark (2007), Introductory chapter, A comparative perspective on non-discrimination law, in: Cases, materials and text on national, supranational and international non-discrimination law, Schiek, Dagmar/Waddington, Lisa/Bell, Mark (eds.), pp. 25-32, p. 26.

260 ibid.

noun for anti- or non-discrimination.[261] In line with this, equality has also been characterised as being the 'flip side'[262] of discrimination. The initial point for this thesis, however, is that the prohibition against age discrimination in Dir. 2000/78/EC has to be regarded as being part of the general overarching principle of equality, which in turn encompasses age equality.

5.2 Age equality among whom?

Even though it is a part of the general concept of equality, the unique nature of 'age' equality as compared to, for example, gender equality has to be accounted for.[263] Its most central characteristic is that 'age does not define a fixed delineated group'.[264] From a gerontological point of view, age and ageing as such prove to be inter- and intraindividually different.[265] Not surprisingly, it is rather difficult to determine the boundaries between a certain age group that is subject to discrimination and those who are not discriminated against. As all individuals during their lifecycle have been young and may be getting old, the fundamental opposition between 'self' and 'other' is not as stark as it typically is for other forms of discrimination such as discrimination on the grounds of race or gender.[266] Actually, from the employee's perspective, there are often several conflicts of interest involved, such as the interests of younger employees versus the interests of older employees and vice versa.[267] Moreover, in the same alleged age 'group' there may also be different interests involved. Whether, for example, a certain chronological age of the employee – such as a manda-

---

261 ibid.; similar *Bayefsky*, Anne (1990), The principle of equality or non-discrimination in international law, Vol. 11 No.1-2 (1990), pp. 1-34 who argues that non-discrimination and equality are positive and negative statements of the same principle, see in detail p. 1.

262 *Howard*, Erica (2010), The EU Race Directive, p. 109.

263 The most profound analysis of age equality is provided by *Fredman* (2003), The age of equality, in: Age as an equality issue, Fredman/Spencer (eds.), pp. 21-69, which most of the subsequent scientific articles concerned with equality in general and age quality in particular are build upon.

264 *Fredman* (2003), p. 37.

265 see chap. 6.4.

266 *Fredman* (2003), p. 21; *Fredman*, Sandra (2011), Discrimination law, 2. edt., p. 101.

267 *Fredman* (2011), p. 101.

tory retirement age that distinguishes between those being of that age or older and those who are younger – should function as a parameter to determine a certain age group is therefore rather questionable.[268]

While the Framework Directive as well as the Norwegian WEA and the German AGG refer to discrimination between any age groups, the prohibition against age discrimination, as manifested in the American legislation, in the Age Discrimination in Employment Act of 1967 (ADEA), has restricted its scope of applicability, as it only encompasses employees above the age of 40.[269] However, also in the US example, it may be difficult to demarcate a boundary for different age groups between those who are above the age of 40.

5.3 Age equality of what?

One of the most famous phrases in defining the concept of equality is the often referred to formula given by *Aristotle* that 'things (and persons) that are alike should be treated alike, while things that are unalike should be treated unalike in proportion to their unalikeness'.[270] Despite its famousness, one has to be aware of the fact that this formula is only intended to achieve formal equality. It has been particularly criticised for not requiring more than 'equality as consistency'.[271] It is not very clear when it comes to identifying the persons that should be treated alike.[272] This is especially problematic as regards the parameter of age, where the question arises: 'are two people of different ages "alike" in the relevant sense? And if they are, should they always be treated alike?'[273] In some situations, treating different people alike may even worsen the suffered disadvantage. Being a merely relative principle, requiring only that people be treated consistently, the *Aristotelian* formula lacks a proper differentiation between dis-

---

268 see chap. 6.4.

269 see to this aspect among others: *Fredman* (2011), p. 101; *Hahn*, Oliver (2006), Auswirkungen der europäischen Regelungen zur Altersdiskriminierung im deutschen Arbeitsrecht, p. 67ff. and extensive analysis as regards the ADEAs personal scope at *Fenske*, Antje (1998), Das Verbot der Altersdiskriminierung im US-amerikanischen Arbeitsrecht, p. 31ff., p. 50.

270 *Schiek* et al. (2007), p. 27 who refer to Aristotle, Ethica Nichomacea 1131a-6 (translation W. Ross, 1925).

271 *Fredman* (2003), p. 38 f.; *Fredman* (2011), p. 8ff; see to the critics also *Schiek* et al. (2007), p. 27; *Ellis*, Evelyn/*Watson*, Philippa (2012), EU anti-discrimination law, 2. edt., p. 5.

272 *Schiek* et al. (2007), p. 26; *Ellis*/*Watson* (2012), p. 5.

273 *Fredman* (2003), p. 39.

crimination that is invidious and discrimination that might be appropriate.[274] *Fredman* illustrates the formula's deficits by using the example of flexible retirement, which could be a useful contribution to extending the working life of older employees.[275] If the employer were to apply the *Aristotelian* principle here and were to accordingly deny all employees of any age to make use of this option, an older employee would not be able to prove the case that the refusal to allow for flexible retirement constitutes a breach of the principle to treat likes alike.[276] This is due to the fact that equality in the sense of consistency does not give the employee a right to flexible working, as it only requires an employer to treat employees consistently regardless of their age.[277] The ideal of equality is thus reduced to a formal requirement that lacks equality in a true substantive sense.[278] The term 'equality' should not be understood as treating all people the same.[279] According to a more pluralist approach to equality, substantive equality should rather be based on difference and people should be treated differently according to their needs.[280] In a pluralist sense, the aim would therefore be 'to create a society where differences and diversity between groups and individuals are considered an asset and everyone is treated with the same respect'.[281] Assimilation is thus not what is intended by the concept of equality. Rather, it has to be acknowledged that different people (and so different employees) have different needs, which makes it, in turn, necessary for the achievement of genuine equality to remove any barriers or disadvantages that certain groups may face. From the perspective of older employees, achieving age equality in its true and substantive sense therefore entails the eradication of age discrimination and ageism as it may be

---

274 ibid., p. 38 f.; *Schiek* et al. (2007), p. 26 f.

275 *Fredman* (2003), p. 39.

276 ibid.

277 ibid.

278 *Schiek* et al. (2007), p. 26, 27; see the critics of the terminological distinction between formal and substantive equality: *McColgan* (2014), Discrimination, equality and the law, p. 22 and *Smith*, Nicholas (2007), A critique of recent approaches to discrimination law, New Zealand Law Review, 2007, pp. 499-525, p. 503 f., 506ff.

279 see in this regard also *Gosepath*, Stefan (2007), Equality, in: Stanford Encyclopedia of Philosophy, available at: http://plato.stanford.edu/entries/equality/.

280 *Howard* (2010), p. 128 referring to Bacik (1997: 119-120).

281 see for further details *Howard* (2010), p. 128 referring to proponents of a pluralistic approach.

manifested, for example, in existing mandatory retirement provisions.[282] However, being a rational concept, age equality may only be achieved in social reality by using a medium of comparison.[283] The quest to take age equality seriously therefore needs further clarification by asking, 'Equality of What?'[284]

5.3.1 Equality of opportunities versus equality of results

In general, equality in its substantive sense comprises equality of results and equality of opportunities.[285] When asking 'equality of what?' one has therefore necessarily to distinguish between these sub-concepts. Equality of opportunity as regards age means that all individuals regardless of their age are, as a starting point, provided with the same opportunity to participate in society to a full and equal extent, which especially concerns decisions that affect their situation.[286] Equality of results focuses on the contrary, as the notion implies, on the results that should be equal. The pri-

282 One further example of accomplishing for genuine age equality could be measures of 'positive action', see in this regard ibid., p. 2; That a mere formal approach to equality is not sufficient has in particular been acknowledged in the Universal Declaration of Human Rights (UDHR) such as the various UN Conventions on equality, which aim at achieving de facto substantive equality. Common to the different UN conventions is that they understand equality as a right that is necessary to achieve substantive equality, see to this aspect *Schiek* et al. (2007), p. 28; see in detail as regards human rights law, chap. 9.

283 *Schiek* et al. (2007), p. 28.

284 ibid., quoting the heading of one of the chapters of *Sen*, Amartya (1992), Inequality, Re-examined.

285 Substantive equality is a multifaceted concept that furthermore comprises equality in relation to substantive rights and equal respect, see *Barnard*, Catherine/ *Hepple*, Bob (2000), Substantive Equality', The Cambridge Law Journal, Vol. 59 Issue 03, pp. 562-585, pp. 564ff. discussing in turn concepts of substantive equality developed by *Fredman*, Sandra (1999), A critical review of the concept of equality in U.K. anti-discrimination law, Independent review of the enforcement of U.K. anti-discrimination legislation, Working Paper No. 3, Cambridge Centre for Public Law and Judge Institute of Management Studies, 1999, paras. 3.7-3.19; see in general *Schiek* et al. (2007), p. 28.

286 see also recital (9) of Dir. 2000/78/EC: 'Employment and occupation are key elements in guaranteeing equal opportunities for all and contribute strongly to the full participation of citizens in economic, cultural and social life and to realising their potential.'

mary concern of equality of results is to achieve a fairer distribution of benefits.[287] An example for equality of outcome in terms of age could be the representation of age groups in employment that reflect their proportions in the population, which could be achieved by preferential treatment or so-called positive discrimination of the respective underrepresented group, such as, for example, by making use of quota rules.[288] Central for this thesis is equality understood as equality of opportunity, which means equality in terms of the situation of older employees, in that all employees, irrespective of their age, should, in principle, be provided with the same opportunity to participate fully and equally in working life.

However, as the initially outlined description of the challenges of an ageing society implies, the impetus that lies at the bottom of claims to foster age equality in employment and to prolong working lifes of older employees is to a great extent fuelled by utilitarian considerations.[289] From a utilitarian perspective the achievement of age equality should first and foremost not be realized for the sake of the individual but for societal reasons. For utilitarians, since everyone counts as one and no one as more than one according to its founder *Bentham*, the interests of all members of society should be treated equally without considering an individual's personal or material situation.[290] In essence, as *Sen* formulated it the 'utilitarian formula requires the maximization of the sum-total of the utilities of all people taken together, and that is, in an obvious sense not particularly egalitarian.'[291] However, the utilitarian approach may nevertheless be interpreted as egalitarian insofar as it in its objective function adds exactly

287 see in detail to equality of results and its different meanings *Fredman*, Sandra (2011), Discrimination Law. 2. edt., p. 14ff.

288 see for the differentiation of positive discrimination, contributing to equality of results and positive action measures, that might aim at equality of results or at equality of opportunity, *Howard* (2010), pp. 116 f., 120ff.

289 similar *Fredman* (2003), p. 23, who also points to the fact that the challenges of an ageing society have tended to eclipse issues that concern younger people, including children.

290 see as regards utilitarianism as a conception of distributive equality and for references to Bentham: http://plato.stanford.edu/entries/equality/#Uti (last accessed at: 17.12.2014)

291 *Sen* (1992), Inequality re-examined, p. 13 refering in fn. 4 to his earlier book on equality: On economic Inequality 1973).

the same weight to the utilities of all people, which in combination with the maximizing format ensures that the same value is attached to everyone's utility in the maximizing exercise.[292] According to *Sen*

> The egalitarian foundation is, thus, quite central to the entire utilitarian exercise. Indeed, it is precisely this egalitarian feature that relates to the foundational principle of utilitarianism of 'giving equal weight to the equal interests of all the parties (Hare 1981: 26), or to 'always assign the same weight to all individuals' interests (Harsanyi 1982: 47).[293]

From the perspective of the society as a whole, the longer an employee may stay active in employment the better. Given the financial pressure on social security systems there is undoubtedly a societal need to encourage older employees to extend their working lifes. For the stability of the pension system it is thus a financial necessity that is in the interest of the greatest number of individuals. In the discussion of the legitimacy of mandatory retirement provisions weight is therefore also to be add on interests of the society at large. In an utilitarian sense encouraging older employees to extend their working lifes by abolishing mandatory retirement also serves societal interests.

However, the problem that occurs with the utilitarian concept of equality is that for utilitarians, restrictions on interests that are grounded on morals or justice cannot be admitted.[294] One may thus conclude that as long as utilitarianism lacks a concept of justice and fair distribution, it does not comply with the aim of treating all as equals.[295] Or as *Rawls* put it 'Utilitarianism does not take seriously the distinctions between persons.'[296] In other words: by neglecting the separateness of individuals utilitarianism does not provide an interpretation of moral equality understood as equal respect for each individual person.[297] Having these limitations of the utilitarian concept in mind it is crucial as stressed by *Fredman* that utilitarian considerations

> …do not obscure the concerns with individual justice and social equity which should underpin the move to eliminate age discrimination. A reversal of labour market conditions or a change in the demographic pressures to a situa-

292 *Sen* (1992), p. 14.
293 ibid., p. 14 with further references in particular in fn. 5.
294 see http://plato.stanford.edu/entries/equality/ (last accessed at 17.12.2014).
295 ibid.
296 *Rawls*, John (1971), A theory of justice, p. 27; see to the critics also ibid.
297 similar http://plato.stanford.edu/entries/equality/ (last accessed at 17.12.2014).

> tion which is again unfavourable to older people, should not themselves be sufficient to trump the claims of individuals. Nor should the focus be entirely on older people.[298]

Basing fairer distribution primarily on results, may as rightly stressed by *Fredman* not be unproblematic. To highlight the limitations of an approach that is primarily based on identical treatment, it is quintessential to put an emphasis on results.[299] But, as pointed out by *Fredman* to avoid collapsing into utilitarianism the distributive aim must be linked to a strong notion of individual rights.[300] Thus, so *Fredman* 'the emphasis on results should imply a right to equivalent quality of life so far as possible; without having to trade off one individual's rights against those of another.'[301] It is therefore important to also consider individual rights-based arguments in the analysis of the concept of age equality like discussing age in equality as a question of choice for the individual or as an aim of dignity.[302] This is essential, as solely applying a utilitarian concept of equality would finally negate a dignity-based approach with its focus on the individual.

5.3.2 Age equality in employment as a question of choice

According to the understanding laid down in this thesis, age equality in the sense of providing the same opportunities for older workers also implies that every employee should be provided with a choice. Equality of opportunity cannot be realised in the employment context without, at the same time, giving the employee, regardless of his age, a real choice in choosing from an equal set of alternatives and thus contributing to a satisfying working life. This means that, in principle, the employee in question should have the freedom of choice as to whether he also wants to continue to work beyond the retirement age. This genuine choice also has to do with the protection of the employee's dignity, self-esteem and self-fulfil-

---

298 *Fredman* (2003), p. 43, who also points to the fact that the challenges of an ageing society have tended to eclipse issues that concern younger people, including children.

299 ibid., p. 23.

300 ibid., p. 43.

301 ibid., p. 43.

302 similar ibid., p. 43.

ment in working life.[303] It simply enables the employee to de facto make use of his right to work regardless of his age. Any equal treatment on the grounds of age would be unsubstantial, as long as obstacles exist related to the prohibited characteristic age that would hinder the genuine exercise of choice.[304] Nevertheless, as long as a real choice exists, equality of results is not required.[305]

Moreover, equality in its substantive sense also comprises of equality as regards substantive rights such as freedom of profession.[306] Thus, part of the exercise of choice in the employment sphere is also the freedom to choose an occupation and the right to engage in work, which should also be guaranteed regardless of the employee's age.[307]

5.3.3 Age equality in employment as a question of dignity

A further aim of age equality is to ensure that the employee in question is treated with equal dignity.[308] Dignity is a value that regularly appears in discussions on substantive equality. *Fredman* is an example in this regard – she stresses that dignity may constitute one of the aims of equality.[309] While there is no controversy regarding the fact that the protection of human dignity constitutes a central aim of human rights generally, it has to be acknowledged that the meaning of dignity per se is also difficult to grasp. The relationship between dignity and the concept of equality is contested.[310] Critics of *Fredman's* approach of identifying dignity as one of the aims underlying substantive equality argue about how 'the meaning of dignity is "difficult to pin down"'.[311] The argument has been made 'that "dignity" is something that is attributed to people because of something

303 similar *Fredman* (2011), p. 105.
304 *Fredman* (2003), p. 43.
305 ibid.
306 *Schiek* et al. (2007), p. 28.
307 The freedom to choose an occupation and right to engage in work is e.g. manifested in Art. 15 Charter of Fundamental Rights of the European Union (CFREU), see also chap. 10.1
308 see *Fredman* (2003), p. 44 f.
309 elaborately ibid., p. 44 f.
310 see the critics *McColgan* (2014), p. 23 f., 24; see also *Smith* (2007), pp. 512ff.
311 see the critics *McColgan* (2014), p. 23, who quotes *Feldman*, David, Human dignity as a legal value: Part 1, Public Law (1999), pp. 682-702 p. 682.

else' and that '"dignity" cannot replace "rationality" (or any other core human attribute) as a foundation for equality, because rationality is (a candidate for) the foundation of human dignity.'[312] For *Smith* therefore, respect for human dignity in general constitutes an even more abstract notion than the concept of equality.[313] Basically, he criticises how those theorists concerned with substantive equality who refer to the impairment of dignity as the essence of discrimination are not able to demonstrate to what degree the reference to dignity contributes to more clarity and concretisation of the concept of equality.[314]

However, as rightly put forward by *Feldman*, 'some rights seem to have a particularly prominent role in upholding human dignity'.[315] Among these is the right to be free of discriminatory treatment, as discrimination constitutes a major assault on dignity.[316] Considering dignity as an aim of substantive equality is not to be understood as putting into question that dignity is one of the foundations and key aims of human rights in general. Rather, it gives the concept of equality a needed substantive boost/underpinning. Depriving an employee of his right to work by establishing mandatory retirement provisions and thus excluding the employee from working life is – according to the understanding laid down here – an assault on the individual's dignity. Despite its critics, the approach taken by *Fredman* is, therefore, also to be followed in this work. In line with her, it can thus be ascertained that dignity constitutes one aim of equality. Moreover, a dignity-based approach with its focus on the individual is pivotal in avoiding the concept of age equality being too firmly rooted in utilitarian considerations focusing only on societal needs.

That equality of rights of the elderly is strongly related to the dignity principle is recognised both in human rights law and in EU primary law.[317] It is important to note that dignity in every respect constitutes an irreducible minimum, aiming at enhancing rather than reducing the status

---

312 *Smith* (2007), p. 514.

313 ibid., p. 513 f. in particular p. 522.

314 ibid., p. 523; in this regard also *McColgan* (2014), p. 23 f.

315 *Feldman*, David (1999), Human dignity as a legal value: Part 1, Public Law (1999), pp. 682-702 p. 695; see also *McColgan* (2014), p. 23 f.

316 ibid.

317 see chap. 9 and 10; Art. 25 CFREU e.g. explicitly stresses that 'The Union recognises and respects the rights of the elderly to lead a life of dignity and independence and to participate in social and cultural life.' See in general the manifesta-

of the individual employee.[318] In the working sphere, equality based on dignity also means that every employee should be treated with equal respect irrespective of his merits or capabilities.[319] Being also a somewhat opaque and malleable concept, dignity, on the other hand, has served in particular in case law as an argument to maintain mandatory retirement.[320] It has been argued that the abolishment of mandatory retirement would undermine the dignity of the employee in question, as the older employee would then be 'subject to degrading personal appraisal instead of the less intrusive mechanism of automatic retirement'.[321] However, using dignity as an argument to maintain mandatory retirement runs contrary to its key aim, as it is rather paternalistic, degrading and an affront to the employee's dignity to attach per se stereotypical and stigmatic views of capability to certain age groups.[322]

5.3.4 Age equality in employment as a question of participation and social inclusion

Equality in its substantive sense also encompasses the participation and inclusion of all groups in society such as regards all aspects of social life.[323] This also entails the employment sphere and the participation and social inclusion of older workers.[324]

---

tion of the human dignity principle in Art. 1 CFREU; As regards EU secondary law Dir. 2000/78/EC bases e.g. the protection against age-related harassment in Art. 2 No. 3 on the dignity of the person.

318 *Fredman* (2003), p. 45.

319 ibid.

320 ibid.; see to the use of the dignity-argument as a potential legitimate aim to justify age discrimination chap. 12.3.2.1.

321 *Fredman* (2003), p. 45.

322 similar ibid.; *O'Cinneide* (2005), p. 42; see to the use of the capability-argument as a potential legitimate aim to justify age discrimination, chap. 12.3.2.1.

323 *Young*, Iris (1990), Justice and the politics of difference, p. 158, 173.

324 The participation of the elderly in social and cultural life is, in addition to the dignity principle, also reflected in Art. 25 CFREU; see moreover recital 8, 9 Dir. 2000/78/EC; Particular emphasis is furthermore put on the need to ensure full participation and social inclusion of older employees in human rights soft law, see in detail chap. 9.7.1.

5.4 Limitations to the concept of age equality

The achievement of genuine age equality in employment through for example the abolishment of mandatory retirement cannot be provided in an unlimited fashion. One has to be aware of the fact that basically not all distinctions based on age are of a discriminatory character.[325] As *Fredman* put it, 'The crucial challenge is therefore to demarcate valid from invalid distinctions'.[326] This is why the Framework Directive opens up for the justification of so-called direct age discrimination in its Art. 6 No. 1. The demarcation of valid from invalid differentiations based on age – that is, justified from unjustified differentiations – is, in this thesis, carried out by using the proportionality principle as a measurement tool. The question regarding which of the involved interests may displace age equality is assessed in detail in chap. 12.3, where the typically referred to justification patterns in cases of mandatory retirement are examined critically.

5.5 Intermediate conclusion

Equality is a vague and multifaceted concept that is contested. Consequently, a 'pluralism of equalities' exists.[327] In line with *Fredman*, *Barnard* and *Hepple*, it can be concluded that aiming for formal equality is not enough and that a substantive approach is required.[328] Moreover, in a pluralist sense, diversity and difference should be valued. Even though utilitarian considerations beyond a doubt play a role in discussions on the legitimacy of mandatory retirement, they cannot trump considerations based on the individual. In keeping with *Fredman*, it is argued here that a rich understanding of the concept of age equality should be advocated.[329]

Following *Fredman's* extensive analysis on the concept of age equality, it can be concluded that 'the function of equality is to enhance dignity, autonomy and participation of all age groups.'[330] As was stressed initially,

---

325 *Fredman* (2003), p. 37.

326 ibid.

327 see the conclusion in *McCrudden*, Christopher (2003), Theorising European equality law, in: Equality in diversity, The new equality directives, Costello, Cathryn/Barry, Ellis (eds.), 2003, pp. 1-38, p. 38.

328 *Fredman* (2003), p. 39; *Barnard/Hepple* (2000), pp. 564ff.

329 *Fredman* (2003), p. 46.

330 ibid., p. 69.

participating in working life throughout one's whole life is crucial if one is to take age equality seriously. From an age-equality perspective, in its substantive sense, this involves two steps: first, the realisation of equality of opportunity and second, the substantiation of it. In the first instance, the employee should get the opportunity to participate in working life. This implies, as initially stressed under reference to *Fredman,* dismantling the existing obstacles such as mandatory retirement that deny any opportunity to participate in working life.[331] Once this step is completed, de facto participation has to be realised. Such a realisation or substantiation may then be established through positive measures. With its focus on mandatory retirement, in chapters 12 to 15, the analysis herein mainly concentrates on the first step.

The US President *Johnson* put the claim for a substantive equality concept concisely in his famous speech at Howard University in 1965 by stating: 'Thus it is not enough just to open the gates of opportunity. All our citizens must have the ability to walk through those gates.'[332]

If one transfers Johnson's concept to the discussion on age equality in employment, the remaining key question then is whether and how– after a critical review of the existing obstacles and their potential abolishment – participation might be realised. This is then a question of a thorough analysis of *de lege ferenda* measures.

6 Mandatory retirement from a gerontological perspective

> *Indeed Cephalus, I replied, I enjoy talking with the very old, for we should ask them, as we might ask those who have travelled a road that we too will probably have to follow, what kind of road it is, whether rough and difficult or smooth and easy. And I'd gladly find out from you what you think about this, as you have reached the point in life the poets call 'the threshold of old age'. Is it a difficult time? What is your report about it?*[333]

---

331 see chap. 1.1 above.

332 The speech is available at: http://www.lbjlib.utexas.edu/johnson/archives.hom/speeches.hom/650604.asp (last accessed at: 17.12.2014)

333 *Plato*, Republic, book I, 328 e, translation G.M.A. Grube, 1992; *Plato* refers concerning 'the treshold of old age' to Homer, Ilias 22.60, 24.487; Odyssey 25.246, 348, 23.212.

6.1 Introduction

An often-used argument to maintain and justify mandatory retirement and to dismiss older employees on the grounds of their age is their supposed physical and mental decline and its supposed impact on their work performance.[334] The core of this argumentation affects the stability of mental capacities and the ability of the individual employee to adapt to changes and demands in the working environment. To gauge the legitimacy of such argumentation, it is necessary to take a closer look at the scientific research findings on gerontopsychology, which is concerned with ageing from its psychological dimension.[335]

In general, gerontology encompasses all the sciences that deal with questions of ageing and later life, such as sociology, psychology and the biology of ageing.[336] The term 'gerontology' has to be distinguished from the notion of 'geronting', which describes the self-regulatory process through which the individual inter alia reacts to processes of biological ageing (so-called senescing) and the process of changing social roles due to societal norms (so-called eldering).[337]

6.2 The many faces of age and ageing

Before going into the gerontopsychological research findings, the many faces of age, or rather the 'dimensions of age'[338] have to be accounted for. In general, we can distinguish between chronological, biological, psychological and social age.[339] Chronological or calendaric age may be defined as 'the elapsed time in days, months and years since birth',[340] while an

---

334 The typical used justification patterns are examined in detail in chap. 12.3.

335 This has also been stressed among others by *Temming* (2008), p. 15 f., 42ff.; see also already *Senne* (2006), pp. 35-43.

336 see *Stuart-Hamilton*, Ian (2006), The psychology of ageing, 4· edt., p. 269.

337 see for further details *Schwall*, Alexander R. (2012), Defining age and using age-relevant constructs, in: The Oxford Handbook of Work and Aging, Hedge, Jerry W./Borman, Walter, C. (eds.), chap. 10, pp. 169-186, p. 172.

338 *Schroots* Johannes J. F. /*Birren*, James E. (1988), The nature of time: implications for research on aging, Comprehensive Gerontology C, 2: 1–29 use the notion 'concepts of time' instead of concepts or dimensions of age.

339 *Settersten,* Richard A. Jr./*Mayer,* Karl U. (1997), The Measurement of Age, Age Structuring, and the Life Course, Annual Review of Sociology, 1997, Vol. 23, pp. 233-261, p. 239, 240; *Ilmarinen*, Juhani (2011), Research Challenges for older workers, in: Older workers in a sustainable society, Ennals, Richard/ Salomon, Robert (eds.), pp. 15-18, p. 18.

340 *Schroots/Birren* (1988), p. 5.

individual's biological age constitutes his/her current position with regard to his/her potential lifespan.[341] Correspondingly, the biological age of an individual may be younger or older than his/her chronological age.[342] From a biological perspective, ageing can be characterised as a steadily proceeding, generally irreversible reduction of physiological functions and cellular structures, which is accompanied by an increasing susceptibility of the organism for disease and which, in the end, inescapably leads to death.[343]

Moreover, so-called true ageing processes may be distinguished from 'non-ageing processes'. *Evans* identifies three causes for 'non-ageing' processes: selective survival, cohort differences and finally differential challenges that young and old people are confronted with. True ageing may be divided into primary and secondary ageing. Primary ageing is a result of the interaction between extrinsic factors in one's lifestyle and environment with intrinsic, genetically determined factors. By contrast, secondary ageing describes the individual's capability to adapt to the consequences of loss of adaptabilities.[344] The environmental impact on the ageing process becomes apparent by examining the geographical differences in life expectancy. In the western district of *Indre vest* in Oslo, for example, the life expectancy for women is around 83 years, and for men it is around 78–80 years, while, by contrast, the lowest recorded life expectancy for women is to be found in the eastern district of *Indre øst,* with an average age of 78.1 for women and 71.6 for men.[345]

Social age is defined by the roles and habits of an individual in relation to other members of society of which he/she is a part.[346] Thus, an individual may be older or younger depending on the extent to which he or she demonstrates age-graded behaviour, which is expected of the individual

---

341 see to the distinction *Birren* James E ./*Cunningham*, Walter R. (1985), Research on the psychology of aging: principles, concepts and theory, in: Handbook of Aging and Psychology, Birren James E./Schaie, Warner K. (eds.), pp. 3–34, p. 8; *Schroots/Birren* (1988), p. 5 f.; *Settersten/Mayer* (1997), p. 239, 240.

342 *Birren/Cunningham* (1985), p. 8; *Settersten/Mayer* (1997), p. 239, 240.

343 *Lehr* (2007), p. 47 referring in this regard to Schachtschabel, D.O. (2004), Humanbiologie des Alterns, in: Kruse, A./Martin, M. (eds.), Enzyklopädie der Gerontologie, pp. 167-181, p. 167.

344 see in detail *Evans*, John G. (2003), Age discrimination: Implications of the ageing process, in: Age as an equality issue, Fredman/Spencer (eds.), p. 11ff.; similar *Solem* (2007), p. 95, 96.

345 *Dybendal*, Kirsten E./*Skiri*, Halvard (2005), Klare geografiske forskjeller i levealder mellom bydeler i Oslo, in: samfunnspeilet 2005 vol. 6., pp. 18-27, p. 20.

346 *Settersten/Mayer* (1997), p. 239, 240; It has to be noted that social age to wide extent is gender-based on the impact of women's reproductive roles on the picture of their working lives, see *Meenan* (2007 a), p. 279 referring to Arber/Ginn (eds.) (1995), Connecting Gender and Ageing: A Sociologial Approach, pp. 5-11; see also *Solem* (2007), p. 95, 96.

by the particular society or culture he/she belongs to.[347] Finally, a third dimension – psychological age – is distinguishable, which is defined by the age-related behavioural capacities of individuals to adapt to changing environmental demands.[348] Some also describe this ability as the dimension of functional age or they take this concept even further as 'occupational functional age'.[349] For the evaluation of the typically referred to justification patterns to maintain mandatory retirement, the psychological or occupational functional-age dimension seems to be the most interesting category as it is closely related to the competence of the individual employee in a particular occupation.

Moreover, it has to be noted that the group of people who are above the age of 60, especially the group of those who are over 80, is generally characterised by a high proportion of women.[350] The ageing process therefore cannot be seen as 'gender neutral'.[351] Consequently, some refer to this phenomenon as the 'feminisation' of the ageing process, since the ageing society unquestionably – at least for those above 75 years of age – constitutes a female society.[352]

---

347 *Settersten/Mayer* (1997), p. 239, 240.

348 *Schroots/Birren* (1988), p. 13 refrring to Birren (1959), Principles of research on ageing, in: Birren (ed.), Handbook of ageing and the individual, pp. 3-42.

349 *Schroots/Birren* (1988), p. 6 who review 'functional age' as a different type of age and define it – under reference to Birren (1969), The concept of functional age, theoretical background, Human development 1969: 12, 214-215 – as a 'a dimension on which individuals could be younger or older than their chronological years in their ability to adapt to their environments'. The functional age dimension has been criticized inter alia by *Salthouse* who claimed that the concept has several different meanings and that as a consequence three categories should be introduced: the 'occupational functional age', the 'biomedical functional age' and the 'structural organization of human functioning', see in detail *Salthouse*, T. A., (1986). Functional age: Examination of a concept, in: Birren, J. E./Robinson, P. K./Livingston, J. (eds.), Age, Health, & Employment, pp. 78-92.

350 *Lehr* (2007), p. 39; see in general *UN* (2002), Gender dimensions of ageing.

351 *Doron* (2007), p. 119.

352 *Lehr* (2007), p. 39 referring to Tews, H. P. (1993), Neue und alte Aspekte des Strukturwandels des Alters, in: Naegele, G./Tews, H. P. (eds), Lebenslagen im Strukturwandel des Alters (p. 15-42), p. 10; see also in general *UN* (2002), Gender dimensions of ageing.

6.3 Key findings and developments in gerontopsychological research

An array of theories has dealt with the process of ageing.[353] The long-disproved deficit model of ageing was especially inspired by biological theories of ageing, which constitutes the classical exponent of the early period of empirical gerontopsychological research.[354] It has been followed by exponents who regard ageing as a process of success that could, according to some, be achieved by disengagement from social life, while others have referred to activity in old age as the most successful way of ageing.[355] The continuity theory tried to solve the contradiction between disengagement and activity by advocating continuity as the key to successful ageing.[356] Further theories postulated the growth of maturity and wisdom in old age.[357] Recent studies finally stressed individual differences in the ageing process and the multiple factors that are involved.[358]

6.3.1 Ageing as a process of decline

In this model, particular stress is placed on the decline of physiological and psychological capabilities, an assumption that implicitly or explicitly had an impact on the first gerontopsychological studies that were concerned with the relationship between intelligence, the ability to react and memory, on the one hand, and age on the other.[359] A classic example is the first *Wechsler–Bellevue Intelligence Scale* of 1939; intelligence tests in which a maximum intellectual capacity was recorded in the third decade of life and a significant decline in intellectual performance was recorded from the middle of the fifth decade of life.[360] This intelligence curve became so popular that it might have significantly contributed to the gen-

---

353 see for an extensive overview *Schroots*, Johannes J. F. (1996), Theoretical developments in the psychology of aging, The Gerontologist 1996, Vol. 36 No. 6, pp. 742-748; The following chapters are based on an overview of existing literature and thus do not represent own research findings.

354 see chap. 6.3.1.

355 see chap. 6.3.2.

356 see chap. 6.3.3.

357 see chap. 6.3.4.

358 see chap. 6.3.5

359 *Lehr* (2007), p. 47.

360 see description and analysis at *Lehr* (2007), p. 50ff.

eral deficit model of ageing, such as the still-prevailing negative stereotypes and generalisations about ageing.[361] Various explanations were put forward for the decline in cognitive capacities. Inter alia, the question was raised as to whether people with a higher degree of intelligence possess better possibilities for compensating for the ageing process and thus of successfully continuing in their professional career.[362] To an increasing extent, scientists became finally became aware of the various factors and the complexity of the ageing process, such as the role of education and social status. The deficit model has been particularly criticised for its scientific method, as it was based on cross-sectional studies. These studies compared the cognitive abilities of more or less representative samples of specific birth cohorts and showed, in relation to the comparability of education, a significant lack of research.[363] Based on the fact that the 'older' age groups consisted of comparatively less people with a background in middle and high school than the 'younger' age groups, the ascertained performance decline could not primarily be explained by the age of the probands, but was also largely due to a large extend by their different educational levels.[364] This was demonstrated in several studies in the years 1950 to 1970, where age differences in the test performances diminished when younger and older probands were compared who had received the same 'duration of schooling'.[365] Later in 1996 researchers have noted that better education is associated with a significantly slower deterioration of intellectual performance with age.[366] The decline in intellectual-performance capacity with age can thus by no means be regarded as universal, but rather depends on several determinants, such as education.[367] In partic-

361 *Lehr* (2007), p. 51.
362 ibid.
363 ibid.
364 see in detail ibid., p. 84.
365 see for an overview of the respective studies: ibid., p. 52, 84ff. *Lehr* refers moreover to the fact that the adulterated results of cross-sectional studies about intelligence become visible, if one takes into consideration that the average duration of schooling (in the US were most of this studies were conducted) in the year 1975 for the at that time 65-years-olds was 9 years in contrast to 12,3 years for the 25-year-olds.
366 *Lehr* (2007), p. 84 with further references.
367 see elaborately to this aspect: *Lehr* (2007), pp. 84 f. who e.g. refers to the finding that a clear link between the duration of school attendance and cognitive performance in old age could be demonstrated in several longitudinal studies.

ular, recent longitudinal studies concerned inter alia with the interaction of ageing and intellectual capacity were finally able to unmask the myth of the deficit model where ageing is considered merely as a process of decline.[368]

6.3.2 Ageing as a process of success

In contrast to the deficit models of ageing, there are theories that understand ageing primarily as a process of success with the central focus on 'adding life to the years'.[369] The subjectively coined concept of successful ageing relies on the assumption that the transition to old age causes a destabilisation of the interior and exterior situation.[370] In this context, satisfaction with life is considered an indicator for a successful adaptation to the process of ageing.[371] However, with regard to the question regarding which way of ageing is considered to be 'the most successful', that is, guaranteeing a 'maximum of happiness and satisfaction',[372] two contrasting approaches exist: the activity theory, on the one hand, and the disengagement theory on the other.[373] According to the exponents of the activity theory, older people should be kept involved and active in the community, maintain an active lifestyle and attitudes and perpetuate social contacts as far and for as long as possible.[374] By contrast, the disengagement theory holds that older people lose many of their social contacts with others in the social systems they belong to and prefer social isolation and an

---

368 see in detail in chap. 6.3.5.
369 *Havighurst,* Robert J. (1961), Successful aging, The Gerontologist (March 1961) 1 (1), pp. 8-13, p. 8.
370 ibid., p. 8.
371 *Havighurst* (1961). pp. 8-13; see in general overview given at *Lehr* (2007), p. 56.
372 ibid., p. 8.
373 ibid.; see also for an overview *Solem* (2007), p. 106.
374 ibid., p. 8.

inevitable withdrawal from society in preparation for death.[375] Ageing successfully means, according to this approach, accepting and desiring a process of disengagement from active life.[376]

6.3.3 Ageing as a process of continuity

To solve the antipode between activity and disengagement, *Atchley* regarded ageing as a process of continuity. The central premise of his 'continuity theory' is that middle-aged older people make adaptive choices in an attempt to preserve and maintain existing internal and external structures.[377] Older people seem to prefer to accomplish this aim by using continuity, e.g. by using familiar strategies in familiar arenas of their social world.[378] Thus, continuity is used as an adaptive strategy to deal with changes resulting from normal ageing.[379]

6.3.4 Ageing as a process of growth in wisdom and maturity

In opposition to the deficit models of ageing, there are theories that postulate the growth of maturity and wisdom in old age.[380] The so-called theory of gerotranscendens belongs to this category of theories.[381] One of its exponents, *Tornstam*, postulates, on the one hand, the existence of an intrinsic drive; the shift from a materialistic and rational life perspective to

---

375 see the classic definition given by *Cumming*, Elaine/*Henry*, W.E. (1961) (eds), Growing old: The process of disengagement, p. 14; see also *Cumming*, Elaine/ *Dean*, Lois R./*Newell*, David S./*McCaffrey*, Isabel (1960) Disengagement – A tentative theory of aging, Sociometry, vol. 23, No. 1, 1960, pp. 23-35; *Hochschild*, Arlie R. (1975), Disengagement theory: A critique and proposal, American Sociological Review, Vol. 40, No. 5, 1975, pp. 553-569.

376 *Havighurst* (1961), p. 8; see to the disengagement and activity theory and their critics in overview given by *Senne* (2006), p. 41 f.

377 *Atchley*, Robert C. (1989), A continuity theory of normal aging, The Gerontologist (1989) 29 (2), pp. 183-190, p. 183; see also *Atchley*, Robert C. (1971), Retirement and leisure participation: Continuity or crisis?, The Gerontologist 11(1): 13–17.

378 *Atchley* (1989), p. 183.

379 ibid.

380 see overview given by *Lehr* (2007), p. 66.

381 see overview given by ibid., p. 69.

a cosmic and transcendent view of life.[382] While he, on the other hand, also emphasises the age-related need for solitude, without claiming that there is a clear relationship between 'gerotranscendens' and a reduction in social participation.[383] The theory of gerotranscendens has the use of an inner model of explanation in common with the disengagement theory; namely, that some changes in interests and activities are related to age-related changes in needs.[384] Due to *Tornstam,* gerotranscendence may be regarded as 'the final stage in a possible natural progression towards maturation and wisdom'.[385] However, the central proposition of this theory that the expected process of growth primarily takes place at the higher and advanced ages cannot yet be sufficiently confirmed.[386]

6.3.5 Recent studies: The decline of capabilities with age – a myth?

Focal points of gerontopsychological research in recent decades have been stability and change with regard to intelligence, memory, personality and the social situation of the elderly person in employment, family and society. The results of this research demonstrate a significant correction of earlier assumptions that ageing constitutes a process of decline. Rather, recent research indicates a high degree of consistency in terms of functions and reactions in the transition from middle to old age and that a multitude of determinants interacts in the process of ageing. In terms of the exposure of the myth of the deficit model of ageing, longitudinal gerontological research has made a particularly strong contribution to the field.[387] Empirical studies have demonstrated that the most important mental capabilities exhibit stability until the middle of the eighth decade of life and that the general assumption that intelligence and memory function decline

---

382 see overview given at *Tornstam*, Lars (2003), gerontranscendence from young old age to old age, online publication from The Social Policy Group Uppsala, in detail *Tornstam*, Lars (1989), Gero-transcendence: A reformulation of the disengagement theory, Aging 1, 1989, pp. 55-63; see also later elaborately *Tornstam*, Lars (2005), Gerotranscendence: A developmental theory of positive ageing.

383 *Tornstam* (1989).

384 see to this aspect in detail *Solem* (2007), p. 105.

385 http://www.soc.uu.se/forskning/forskningsprojekt/gerotranscendence/ (last accessed: 17.12.2014).

386 *Lehr* (2007), p. 69.

387 see in detail ibid., p. 76.

with age could not be attested.[388] In the Bonn Longitudinal Study on Ageing (BOLSA), for example, a deterioration in the intellectual-performance capability was initially observed after individuals entered into their ninth decade of life.[389] Similarly, in the longitudinal study in Gothenburg, the general assumption of a decline in intelligence and memory function could not be confirmed.[390] Common to these and comparable studies is that they were able to demonstrate a strong interindividual variability.[391] Moreover, it has to be noted that the measured intelligence was characterised by a high degree of complexity.[392]

Two main components of intelligence have to be differentiated: fluid and crystalline intelligence. Crystallised intelligence encompasses general knowledge, expertise, vocabulary and language comprehension. Its counterpart, so-called fluid intelligence, comprises of abilities such as problem solving or reasoning and dealing with new situations.[393] When it comes to

388 see for further details overview given at ibid., p. 76 f; see also *Schaie*, Warner K. (2005), What can we learn from longitudinal studies of adult development? Research in Human Development, 2, pp. 133-158.

389 *Rott*, Christoph/*Thomae*, Hans (1991), Coping in longitudinal perspective: Findings from the Bonn Longitudinal Study on Aging, Journal of Cross-Cultural Gerontology, vol. 6, Issue 1, pp. 23-40; see also *Lehr*, Ursula/*Minnemann*, Elisabeth (1987), Veränderung von Quantität und Qualität sozialer Kontakte vom 7. zum 9. Lebensjahrzehnt, in: Formen seelischen Alterns. Lehr, Ursula/Thomae, Hans (eds.), pp. 80 91, pp. 80-91; *Lehr* (2007), p. 77.

390 *Steen*, B./*Djurfeldt*, H. (1993), The gerontological and geriatric population studies in Gothenburg/Sweden, Zeitschrift für Gerontologie 26, pp. 163-169.

391 see in detail *Lehr* (2007), 24, p. 77 f. who inter alia refers to the so-called Baltimore-study and the Duke-studies. Both stated a high degree of variability between individuals as regards the process of ageing. Knowing that the person in question was of 65, 70 or 75 years of age proved to be just a poor indicator for the health and functional status, the intellectual achievements, social integration and the successful adaptation to changes in the social environment, see Shock, N. W. et al. (1984), Normal human aging, the Baltimore Longitudinal Study of Aging, NIH Publication No. 84 – 2450, p. 207 f.; *Busse*, E.W./*Maddox*, G.L. (eds.) (1985), The Duke longitudinal studies on normal aging: 1955-1980, p. 138.

392 *Lehr* (2007), p. 76 f.

393 ibid., p. 78ff, p. 79 Abb. 16 referring to Horn J. L./Catell, R. B. (1966), Age differences in primary mental ability factors, Journal of Gerontology 21, pp. 210-220.

the ageing process, research was able to demonstrate that fluid intelligence might decrease in old age, while, on the contrary, crystallised intelligence seems not be affected by the ageing process.[394]

Critical studies further concluded that there may be no or at least only a weak relationship between age and productivity.[395] In various studies on the relationship of the impact of ageing on work performance, no effects or only negligible effects could be demonstrated.[396] However, as pointed out by *Schwall*, the question still needs to be addressed as to whether the absence of a statistical relationship is a result of a true absence of a relationship between ageing and work performance or whether some change processes due to ageing may be compensated for by gains in expertise and crystallised intelligence.[397] Thus, potential age-related performance losses might be compensated for by the fact that older employees may often possess greater job commitment, a better overview, experience, expert knowledge and knowledge about social connections/affiliations, such as increased tolerance in developing alternative modes of action strategies to save energy in the sense of efficient decision-making and performance.[398] Especially the cognitive and physiological decline observed in laboratory studies had no effect in most professional fields, as the age-sensitive abilities were not critical to the final job performance.[399] In addition, it has been stressed that there are many work activities and occupational roles that depend more on experience and practice.[400] In line with that, it has further been highlighted that an older employee's motivation to work,

394 ibid., p. 78.

395 see overview given at *Lehr* (2007), p. 214; see also *Ng*, Thomas, W. H./*Feldman*, Daniel C. (2008), The relationship of age to ten dimensions of job performance, Journal of Applied Psychology, vol . 93(2), 2008, pp. 392-423 who could not demonstrate a remarkable relation between age and core task permformances, creativity and performance in training programmes.

396 see in detail *Lehr* (2007), pp. 76ff. and *Schwall* (2012), p. 170.

397 *Schwall* (2012), p. 170.

398 see for further examples *Lehr* (2007), p. 216; The promotion of such positive aspects of the ageing process was an integral aspect of the *UN International Plan of Action on Ageing in 2002*, where it was inter alia stated that older persons should be viewed as attractive, diverse and creative individuals who make vital contributions. In particular a realistic portrait of the skills and abilities of older workers should be promoted by correcting negative and damaging stereotypes about older workers, see *Madrid Plan* 2002, para. 28, 112; see chap. 9.7.1.1.

399 see in detail *Lehr* (2007), p. 214.

400 ibid.

higher satisfaction with the job and a higher commitment to work have to be accounted for.[401] It has been argued that even if older employees might take more time to adapt to new demands, they are generally very familiar with job-related demands due to their rich working experience and so are able to adjust to new demands.[402] Consequently, they are able to compensate for any potential age-related losses. It could not be scientifically proven that older employees were any less accurate, durable or reliable in their job performance than their younger colleagues were.[403] Quite the contrary, chronological age as such does not constitute a decisive determinant for the job-performance capability.[404] Remarkably, even within the same age group, significant differences in performances could be observed[405]

Similarly, in a Finnish longitudinal study, the relationship between consistency and a change in job performance, on the one hand, and lifestyle on the other hand was examined. The results of this study indicate that the professional capacity has to be assessed differently and in its relation to the non-professional behaviour and characteristics of the individual worker in question.[406] Interestingly enough, Finnish studies were also able to demonstrate that the functional variations are often greater between workers of the same age than between workers of different ages, which also indicates a 'need for individual solutions to work and age'.[407] During the ageing process, already existing differences between individuals may even increase.[408] Through being aware of these disparities, in 2004, the

401 ibid. p. 214 referring to Schooler, C. et al. (1998), Aging and work: an overview, in: Schaie, K. W./Schooler, C. (eds.), Impact of work on older adults, pp. 1-19, p. 13.

402 ibid.

403 *Lehr* (2007), p. 215 f . referring to Stagner, R. (1985), Aging in industry, in: Birren/Schaie (eds), Handbook of psychology of aging, 2. edt., pp. 789-817.

404 ibid., p. 214, 216.

405 ibid., p. 216.

406 *Seitsamo*, Jorma/*Ilmarinen*, Juhani, (1997), Life style, aging and work ability among active Finnish workers in 1981-1992, Scand. Journal of Work and Environmental Health 23, Suppl.1, pp. 20-26; see also for an overview *Lehr* (2007), p. 217 f ; see to moreover to Finnish studies on workability, chap. 16.

407 *Meenan* (2007 a), p. 282 f., who refers in this regard to Ilmarinen, Juhani (2001), Ageing Workers in Finland and in the European Union: Their situation and the Promotion of Their working Ability employability and employment, Vol. 2 No. 4, Geneva Papers on Risk and Insurance, pp. 623-641.

408 see to this aspect *Solem* (2007), p. 96.

European Commission recommended a personalised approach to increase the participation of older workers in active employment and to postpone their exit from the workforce.[409]

6.4 Intermediate conclusion

Recent research findings have shown that no monocausal explanation is available for the ageing process. Quite the contrary, a number of different factors of an e.g. genetic, biological, physiological, psychological and ecological nature interact and are part of a rather complicated reciprocal causal network of multidimensional determinants.[410] The conditions for the ageing process are thus characterised by their complexity. To cope with this complexity, *Lehr* suggests taking into consideration several interacting indicators – the 'correlates of psycho-physical wellbeing and longevity'.[411] This implies that several factors are to be considered and thus none of the theories can give sufficient explanations for the ageing process. Rather, it is necessary to take a differentiated approach to the process of ageing. The widespread idea that old age is inevitably connected with a general decline in the ability to work cannot be maintained.[412] Besides the different factors that influence the ageing process, one has therefore to be aware of the inter- and intraindividual variability with regard to intellectual and physical capabilities.[413] This variability also has a strong impact on the job performance of the individual employee. With regard to job-performance capability in later life, one may thus conclude

409 COM(2004) 146 final, Communciation Increasing the employment of older workers and delaying the exit from the labour market, p. 10, 14.

410 *Lehr*, Ursula (2008), Living in an aging world: a challenge for the individual and the society, HUM ONTOGENET 2(2), 2008, pp. 41-49, p. 47; *Lehr*, Ursula (1982), Socio-psychological correlates of longevity, Annual Review of gerontology and geriatrics 3, pp. 102-147.

411 ibid.

412 *Schröder* (1984), p. 44 f. with further references in fn. 34.

413 *Lehr* (2007), p. 77; see also *Senne* (2006), p. 45; *Temming* (2008), 48ff.; The UN Principles for Older Persons of 1991 put these findings in a nutshell by emphasising in the Preamble the need to unmask the still prevailing myth of ageing as a process of decline by stressing that the 'tremendous diversity in the situation of older persons, not only between countries but within countries and between individuals' has to be appreciated and that one should be 'Aware of the scientific research disproving many stereotypes about inevitable and irreversible declines

by saying that ageing is an individual process of change, which is characterised by its inter- and intraindividual variability, which is determined by a range of factors and thus is determined more by multicausality than by monocausality. In short, ageing is a process that is characterised by its complexity.

7 Mandatory retirement, the labour-market situation and demographical findings

> *When discussing and constructing the legal concept of 'equality' one cannot ignore the social context, in general, and the demographic context, in particular.*[414]

7.1 Introduction

Following an interdisciplinary approach in the legal analysis of mandatory retirement also entails an examination of the demographics and the labour-market situation,[415] which demonstrates that, in this regard, the Pulitzer prize-winning gerontologist *Butler* was also more than right, foreshadowing in 1969 how 'ageing is the great sleeper of American life'.[416] By contextualising mandatory retirement, the legal analysis is connected to the changing realities in the labour market and in demographics.[417] Law and the concept of age equality cannot be viewed in isolation; rather, they may be characterised as being 'both an active participant as well as a passive mirror and observant'[418] of social reality. This is even truer if one looks at the ageing population and the ageing workforce that pose a contextual challenge to the legal conceptualisation and implementation of age equal-

---

with age [...].', see Preamble of the *UN Principles for Older Persons* of 16 December of 1991; see also UN Political Declaration to the Second World Assembly on Ageing, Art. 6, Art. 10.

414 *Doron*, (2007), p. 117, see also p. 141.

415 see to the necessity to take an interdisciplinary approach already chap. 2.1 and chap. 2.2.3.

416 *Butler* (1969), p. 245. *Butler* won in 1976 for his book 'Why survive? Being old in America', published in 1975, the Pulitzer Prize for General Non-Fiction.

417 similar *Doron* (2007), p. 140.

418 ibid.

ity.[419] In order to connect the legal discourse on age equality and mandatory retirement to social reality, it is therefore necessary to underpin the connection with empirical social and demographic data.[420]

7.2 Employment and unemployment rates of older workers

When it comes to employment rates[421] over the past decade in Norway, the overall employment rate for the 50–64 age group stood at 74.5% in 2011, a number that is well above the OECD average of 61.2%.[422] The overall employment rate, for example, for the 55–64 age group, was at 70.5% in Norway in 2011, while it was 59.9% in Germany.[423] Compared to other OECD countries, this places Norway among the best performers in the OECD area.[424] Taking a closer look at sub-groups, the employment rates for the 55–59 and 60–64 age groups have even increased over the past decade in Norway.[425] However, this increase was less than the OECD average.[426] In the 65–69 age group, the employment rate was 25.6% in Norway in 2011, which is above the OECD average of 18.5% and well above the German average of approximately 11%.[427] The employment rate for this age group increased by 3.3% in the OECD area from 2001 to 2011, with a growth rate of 3.6 % in Norway, while it increased by nearly 5% in the case of Germany.[428]

---

419 ibid., p. 141.

420 As stressed by *Doron* the effectiveness of the concept of 'equality' and 'non-discrimination' as active social and legal instruments 'might rest upon their ability to be sensitive to the diverse and complex interactions between the law and the sociodemographic changes.', ibid., p. 141.

421 Due to the OECD definition 'Employment rate represent persons in employment as a percentage of the population of working age (15- 64 years).', see http://stats.oecd.org/glossary/detail.asp?ID=785 (last accessed: 17.12.2014).

422 *OECD* (2013), p. 34. Remarkably, in 2001, the rate was already 74.1% and was relatively stable over the next decade, in comparison to an increase of 5.6 percentage points in the OECD area during the same period.

423 *OECD* (2012), Employment Outlook 2012, Statistical Annex Table C

424 *OECD* (2013), p. 34, p. 36 Figure 2.2, Panel A.

425 ibid., p. 34, p. 36 Figure 2.2., Panel B.

426 ibid.

427 ibid. The German data are not specified directly in concrete numbers in the OECD-report but may be read out of Figure 2.2, Panel B.

428 ibid.

In 2011, Norway recorded an overall low unemployment rate[429] of 3.3%; the unemployment rate for the 55–64 age group even stood at 1.3%, which is the lowest among OECD countries.[430] It is remarkable that the unemployment rate for the 55–64 age group in the last decade has been very stable.[431] However, it has to be acknowledged that the Norwegian labour market is, as pointed out by the OECD, marked by high disability rates for older people that constitute many pathways to retirement being available.[432]

Current OECD data reveal that in 2011, Germany had an overall unemployment rate of 6.5% among those aged 55 to 64.[433] Even if from the national perspective this is a considerable amelioration compared to the situation in 1994 when the unemployment rate in Germany was at 11.6%,[434] the rate is five times higher than in the case of Norway.

7.3 The labour-force participation of older workers

Remarkably, Norway is one of the few OECD countries where participation rates, according to a recent 2013 OECD survey, remain relatively high up to the age of 62.[435] This is particularly noteworthy for men, but women also record relatively high participation rates beyond the age of 60.[436] Nevertheless, as pointed out in the OECD study, growth over the past decade has been lower than in most other OECD countries.[437]

---

429 According to the definition of the OECD 'Unemployment rates represent unemployed persons as a percentage of the labour force (the total number of people employed plus unemployed).', see http://stats.oecd.org/glossary/detail.asp?ID=2795 (last accessed: 17.12.2014).

430 *OECD* (2013), p. 37, Figure 2.3, Panel A.

431 *OECD* (2012), Employment Outlook 2012, Statistical Annex Table C.

432 *OECD* (2013), p. 37, 60ff.

433 *OECD* (2012), Employment Outlook 2012, Statistical Annex Table C. For reasons of compatibility the age group 55 to 64 years of age has been chosen.

434 *OECD* (2009), Employment Outlook 2009, Statistical Annex Table C.

435 *OECD* (2013), p. 33.

436 ibid., p. 34, p. 35 Figure 2.1.

437 Interestingly enough, Denmark, France and the Netherlands all have male participation rates just as high for 50-year-olds; however, exit from the labour market begins in these countries earlier than in Norway, *OECD* (2013), p. 33.

With regard to Norway, OECD data from 2011 reveal a labour-force participation rate[438] of 70.5% in the 55–64-year-old age group, which has been steadily increasing when compared to the figure of 64.8% in 1995.[439] According to data from Norwegian statistics as regards employees between 67 and 74 years of age, a labour-force participation rate of 11.6% (males: 15.8% and females 7.9%) has been registered in 2014.[440] In all cases, the data remained stable with merely a few variations over the past few years.[441]

The OECD study of 2013 also took a closer look at labour dynamics for older workers in Norway – as the OECD did not evaluate Germany in detail, comparable data are not valuable in this regard. One of its key findings is that the mobility among older workers in Norway is low. The so-called retention rate, that is, the rate at which firms retain older workers in their workforce, is high after the age of 60. The retention rate increased considerably and was at 65.2% in 2010, which is 11% higher than in 2005.[442] If one compares this with the OECD average of 42.2% in 2010, it becomes clear from the study that Norwegian employees tend to benefit more from stable jobs than their counterparts do in all other OECD countries except Iceland.[443]

However, while retention rates for older employees are relatively high in Norway, the aggregate share of new hires of older workers is, by contrast, rather low, at 4.9% for people aged 50–64 in 2011. [444] As pointed out by the OECD, not only is the hiring rate low, but also the gap is high between the hiring rates of those in the 25–49 age group compared to those in the group aged 50–64.[445] The fact that relatively few older employees are switching jobs may imply (according to the OECD study) that these workers are locked into their current jobs.[446] Once registered as inactive, only a few older workers in Norway go back to work, which seems, according to the OECD, to be a common trend across European countries.[447]

---

438 'The labour force participation rate is defined as the ratio of the labour force to the working age population, expressed in percentages.', definition from OECD glossary of statistical terms, see http://stats.oecd.org/glossary/detail.asp?ID=2008 (last accessed: 17.12.2014).

439 *OECD* (2012), Employment Outlook 2012, Statistical Annex Table C.

440 see *Statistisk sentralbyrå* (2014), Arbeidskraftundersøkelsen, 3. kvartal 2014, tabell. 9, which shows the *arbeidsstyrken* in this age group. The *arbeidsstyrken* is defined as the sum of the employed and unemployed, meaning people who offer their labor in the labor market.

441 see in particular with regard to the development of the labour force participation of male and female employees since 1989 up to 2004 the survey of *Lohne*, Ylva L./*Næsheim*, Helge N. (2006), Eldre i arbeidslivet, p. 9, Tabell 3.1.

442 *OECD* (2013), p. 39 f.

443 ibid., p. 39, p. 41 Figure 2.6.

444 ibid., p. 40, p. 42 first panel of Figure 2.7.

445 ibid., p. 40.

446 ibid., p. 41.

447 ibid., p. 41, p. 42 Figure 2.7.

In Germany, the labour-force participation of older workers (those aged 55 to 64) increased considerably from 40.6% in 1994 to 52.1% in 2005 and finally to 64.0% in 2011.[448]

Remarkably, there has been a significant increase in female labour-force participation for women aged 55 to 64 in the past few years. In Norway, the labour-force participation of the women aged 55 to 64 years increased from 49.2% in 1979 to 61.6% in 2000 and to 66.9% in 2011.[449] While the male labour-force participation in this age group has remained more or less static over the years (around 75%), the influx of female workers has led to the female labour-force participation rate nearly reaching equivalence with that of the male labour-force participation rate.[450] The labour-force participation of women in this age group increased in Germany from 28.4% in 1979 to 33.5% in 2000 and it went up to 56.7% in 2011.[451]

7.4 The exit age from the labour market

In Norway the average exit age from the labour force was relatively constant and above the estimated EU-27 average of 61.5 it was 63.3 in 2001 and 63.2 in 2009.[452] Employees in Germany withdrew from the labour market at average age of 62.4 in 2010 compared to 60.6 in 2001.[453] In both countries workers left the labour market before the traditional stan-

448 *OECD* (2009), Employment Outlook 2009, Statistical Annex Table C; *OECD* (2012), Employment Outlook 2012, Statistical Annex Table C;

449 *OECD* (1996), Employment Outlook 1996, Statistical Annex, p. 189 Table B (the labour force participation of men in 1979 for the age group 55 to 64 years was 82%, see p. 188 Table B); *OECD* (2012), Employment Outlook 2012, Statistical Annex Table C.

450 *OECD* (2009), Employment Outlook 2009, Statistical Annex Table C; *OECD* (2012), Employment Outlook 2012, Statistical Annex Table C. The labour force participation of men in 2000 for the age group 55 to 64 years was 74.4% and 73.9% in 2011.

451 *OECD* (1996), Employment Outlook 1996, Statistical Annex, p. 189 Table B (the labour force participation of men in 1979 for the age group 55 to 64 years was 66.9%, p. 188 Table B). The available data for male labour force participation in 2011 reveal for the age group 55 to 64 years a labour force participation of 71.7%, an increase from 52.4% in 2000 (53.9% in 1995), see *OECD* (2012), Employment Outlook 2012, Statistical Annex Table C.

452 *Eurostat* (2013), Average exit age from the labour force –annual data. Data for 2010 were not yet available in case of Norway.

453 ibid.

dard pensioneligibility age of 67 in case of Norway and 65 in case of Germany.[454] As pointed out by the OECD if life expectancy continues to increase, as most population projections demonstrate – including Norway and Germany a significant increase in the effective retirement age is necessary to maintain control of the cost of pensions.[455]

7.5 The demographic challenge in Norway and Germany

The concept of demographic change generally describes a population's age structure adjusting to changes in living conditions.[456] In consequence, changes in a society's age composition are the result of social shifts.[457] Both Norway and Germany are facing similar future challenges in this regard. In general, constant low fertility rates – in particular in the case of Germany – and changes such as an increasing longevity are the driving forces of both demographic challenges. Taking a glance at the statistics concerning population by age and sex in 1910, in 2010 and the estimated number of persons that there will be in 2050/2060, the impact of the demographic changes becomes obvious, as the former population pyramid steadily transforms to a mushroom shape.[458]

As life expectancy is also estimated to increase, Norway will be confronted with a steadily ageing population in the long run.[459] Despite comparatively high fertility rates, Norway will also be affected by the demographic change.[460] The demographic data are unambiguous: the number of

---

454 see for an overview *OECD* (2011), Trends in retirement and in working at older ages, in: Pensions at a glance 2011: Retirement-income Systems in OECD and G20 Countries, p. 41, 43 Figure 2.3.

455 *OECD* (2011), p. 47.

456 *Linz*, Kathrin/*Stula*, Sabrina (2010), Demographic change in Europe, Working paper no. 4 of the Observatory for Sociopolitical Developments in Europe, p. 2.

457 ibid.

458 see figures in *Statistics Norway* (2009), Population projections, National and regional figures, 2009-2060; *Statistisches Bundesamt* (2009), Bevölkerung Deutschlands bis 2060, 12. koordinierte Bevölkerungsvorausberechnung, p. 15; Schaubild 3; see to this aspect also *Lehr*, Ursula (2009), in: Online-Handbook Demography, Population Ageing, Berlin Institute for Population and Development (ed.), available at: http://www.berlin-institut.org/?id=573 (last accessed at: 17.12.2014).

459 *OECD* (2013), p. 28.

460 ibid. p. 28 w.r.t. Norwegian Ministry of Finance.

citizens living in Norway and those in the 55–75 age group will increase sharply in the years to come.[461] Already in the short run, over the next 15 years, this group will increase by over 300,000 people, and in the long term, there will be 1.3 million people in this age bracket by 2030.[462] This implies that approximately every fourth citizen in Norway will be a senior citizen in 20 years' time.[463] Notably, the core group of seniors alone, those between 60 and 70 years, is estimated to cover more than 700,000 people.[464] The number of people who will be 67 or over will rise dramatically from 617,000 in 2009 to approximately 1.6 million in 2060.[465]

As regards Germany, the impact of demographic change is even more apparent, as approximately every third citizen is estimated to be 65 years of age or older in 2060, which is 34% of the population.[466] In 2060, those being 70 will twice outnumber the number of babies being born.[467] In 2008, about 4 million citizens were 80 or older, which is estimated to increase up to 10 million in 2050, and which will decrease to approximately 9 million in 2060.[468] In 2060, approximately 14% of the population, that is, every seventh citizen, will thus be 80 years of age or older.[469]

As a consequence of demographic change, the patterns of the workforce are also going to change. Both countries are undoubtedly moving towards an increasingly 'greying' workforce. As pointed out by the OECD, a general broad indicator of the increasing economic burden that an ageing society may place on the working-age population is given by the so-called old-age dependency ratio.[470] According to the OECD, it describes the ratio of the population aged 65 and above to the population aged 20–64.[471] In the case of Norway, this ratio is expected to almost double from 32.7% in 2011 to 62.2% in 2050, which is in line with the average rise for the

461 see http://ec.europa.eu/social/main.jsp?langId=en&catId=89&newsId=1191&furtherNews=yes (accessed at: 17.12.2014)
462 ibid.
463 ibid.
464 ibid.
465 *Statistics Norway* (2009), Population projections, National and regional figures, 2009-2060.
466 *Statistisches Bundesamt* (2009), p. 5.
467 ibid.
468 ibid.
469 ibid.
470 *OECD* (2013), p. 28.
471 ibid.

OECD area as a whole.[472] However, the increase in Norway seems to be less dramatic than that estimated for the EU-21 countries, where the ratio is projected to increase from 37.1% in 2011 to 76.1% in 2050.[473] The German old-age dependency ratio – people older than 65 years per 100 persons aged 15 to 64 – was at 31.2% in 2011 and will rise to 39.3% in 2025 and to 55.8% in 2050.[474]

As stressed by the OECD in its country study on Norway, one has to acknowledge – despite the fact that it is sometimes argued that the consequences of ageing could be counterbalanced by policies to encourage greater immigration, higher fertility or faster productivity growth – that these developments might indeed help, but that they need to go hand in hand with attempts to mobilise available labour reserves to sustain economic growth.[475] Thus, in light of the outlined demographic prospects, there is also a real pressure to boost the employability of older people further in Norway.[476] Keeping in mind that active life expectancy – that is, the expected healthy life-years remaining at the age of 50 – is 25 years for men and 26 for women in Norway, there is, according to the OECD's analysis, still room for improving the labour prospects for the oldest cohorts well beyond the current level, despite the fact that the employment rates for the older age groups are already relatively high in Norway.[477] Given its strong potential compared to other EU countries such as Germany, Norway seems to be better positioned than many others are to tackle the demographic challenge.[478] Nevertheless, as emphasised by the OECD, further changes in incentives, attitudes and employability are prerequisites to realise that potential. [479] A central part of this is also to reassess existing mandatory retirement provisions critically.

472 ibid. Figure 1.1.

473 ibid.

474 Lehr (2009); Eurostat (2012), Old age dependency ratio, available at: http://epp.eurostat.ec.europa.eu/tgm/table.do?tab=table&init=1&plugin=1&language=en&pcode=tsdde510 (last accessed: 27.12.2014).

475 *OECD* (2013), p. 29.

476 ibid.

477 ibid.

478 ibid.

479 ibid.

8 Implications of the gerontological, demographical and statistical findings of the labour market for the analysis of mandatory retirement

Both from the perspective of demography and gerontology, the maintenance of mandatory retirement seems more than doubtful. The demographic data demonstrate that the demographic change poses an extra challenge to the Norwegian and German welfare systems. However, in particular as regards Norway, positive development is nevertheless possible if the existing labour-force potential is used to tackle this challenge.[480] Making use of this potential implies necessarily to de facto enable older employees to extend their working life and for them to get the real opportunity to do so. To unleash this potential, mandatory retirement age limits function as a barrier for further development. Thus, these obstacles need to be scrutinised and opportunities for continued employment after the 'mandatory retirement age' should be considered.[481]

Similarly, the gerontopsychological findings have demonstrated that it is essential to move beyond a static stereotypical view of older workers. Even though the deficit model of ageing has been disproved both empirically and theoretically,[482] employment law and, in particular, the judiciary – in Norway as well as in Germany – still rely on this model of ageing and seem, predominantly, to be reluctant to integrate new research on gerontology and medicine.[483] Nevertheless, fortunately there are other examples in case law where recent gerontopsychological findings are explicitly referred to, such as demography and the situation in the labour market. Interestingly enough, particularly the courts of first instance seem to recognise the necessity of considering recent gerontological findings in the

480 *OECD* (2013), p. 29; similar the European Commission stresses: 'Europe needs to make full use of its labour potential to face the challenges of an ageing population and rising global competition' COM(2010) 2020.

481 Already in 1984 *Schröder* came to a similar conclusion, see *Schröder* (1984), p. 43.

482 see for detailed overview: *Lehr* (2007), p. 76ff.

483 In the Norwegian context this reluctance becomes visible in particular in the following judgments: Rt. 2010 s. 202 (*Kystlink*); Rt. 2011 s. 964 (*Gjensidige*); Rt. 2012 s. 219 (*CHC*); For the German context see the examples of case law given by *Rothermund/Temming* (2010), p. 13 fn. 8, p. 14 fn. 10.

evaluation of age limits.[484] This tendency may be illustrated in the German context by the reference to a preliminary ruling from the ArbG *Hamburg* in *Rosenbladt*.[485]

The employers contributed to a significant extent to the maintenance of the myth of ageing as process of decline. Studies concerning the employer's expectations towards older employees still reveal a multitude of stereotypes and prejudices, which primarily concern a supposed decrease in average labour productivity between 40 and 50 years, such as general physical and mental performance losses.[486] Experiments with false application documents in which all job-related details have been kept constant and where only the age data varied, demonstrated, for example, that with increasing age, poorer rated health status is expected, such as reduced job commitment, lower performance motivation and an increased resistance to technological change, such as less flexibility and a decreasing willingness to undertake advanced training.[487] Thus, a discrepancy still exists between the attitudes and behaviours of the employers towards older employees, on the one hand, and the real capabilities and potential of older employees on the other.[488]

Fixed age limits or mandatory retirement, which are primarily based on the generalised assumption that the professional activity (mental and physical capability) of all, or even the majority of workers decreases with age, without taking into consideration the de facto job-performance capacity of the individual employee, may, from a legal point of view, hardly be maintained in light of the mentioned variability in ageing in later life.[489] Or, to say it in the words of *Meenan*, they constitute 'blunt tools' with which to manage younger and older employees.[490] It is very difficult to determine – in view of these findings – a justifiable fixed age limit for mandatory

484 see in the Norwegian context the argumenatation of the court in TSTVG-2005-75777 Stavanger District Court, (*Statoil*); see for a discussion of the case: *Kruge*, Geir J. (2007), Diskriminering på grunn av alder – særlig om aldersgrenser, Status og kommentar, Arbeidsrett 2007, pp. 237-252, in particular p. 241ff.; see also the dissenting vote in Rt. 2010 s. 202 (*Kystlink*), para. 90.

485 see question referred to by the ArbG Hamburg in Case C-45/09 (*Rosenbladt*); see for the German context also in detail: *Rothermund*/*Temming* (2010), p. 14.

486 see to this aspect *Lehr* (2007), p. 211 f . referring to Craft et al. (1979), Simulated management perceptions, hiring decisions and age, Aging and Work 2, pp. 95-102; see also *Kadefors*, Roland/*Hanse*, Jan J. (2012), Employers' attitudes toward older workers and obstacles and opportunities for the older unemployed to reenter working life, in: Nordic journal of working life studies vol. 2 , No. 3 August 2012, pp. 29-47, p. 34ff., p. 45.

487 *Lehr* (2007), p. 211 f. with further references.

488 ibid. p. 212.

489 similar *Fredman* (2003), p. 45; *O'Cinneide* (2005), p. 6, 42; *Temming* (2008), p. 58 f.

490 *Meenan* (2007 a), p. 312; similar *O'Cinneide* (2005), p. 42.

retirement.[491] Should it be 63, 65, 68 or 70?[492] Perpetuating mandatory retirement in employment in principle contradicts the scientific findings and contributes to the retention of the myth of ageing being a mere process of a decline in capabilities.[493]

Norway and Germany might benefit in two ways from critically reviewing mandatory retirement: first, it would help to reduce the impact of demographic change and second, it would help to address the current and future lack of professionals. In doing so, it would benefit society as a whole as well as the employers and the individual employees.

491 similar *Schröder* (1984), p. 57.

492 Examples are to be found in Norway in § 2 (1), (2) *aldersgrenselov*.

493 see for an analysis of the justification of selected age limits chap.13 to 15.

Part II

9 Prohibition against age discrimination in human rights law

9.1 Introduction

This chapter briefly examines from a legal positivistic angle to what extent the right to age equality and protection against age discrimination is recognised as a universal right under human rights law.[494] To go into human rights law is particularly necessary, as human rights instruments had, and still have an important impact on the development of the prohibition against age discrimination on the EU level.[495] Today's anti-discrimination law is characterised by a matrix of different applicable and interrelated sources of law, which are located at the international, European and national level. Additionally, this complex structure of anti-discrimination legislation demands a further elaboration on the foundation of the prohibition against age discrimination in human rights law. Moreover, the different legal instruments have in common that they also influence the understanding and interpretation of provisions on equality and non-discrimination at the national level.[496]

The complexity also becomes apparent by looking at Dir. 2000/78/EC itself. It explicitly points to human rights law inter alia in its recital 4 by stressing that the right of all persons to equality before the law and protection against discrimination constitutes a universal right that is recognised

---

494 see to this aspect from a general perspective *McCrudden*, Christopher/*Prechal*, Sacha (2009), The concepts of equality and non-discrimination in Europe, p. 2.

495 similar *Polloczek*, Tobias (2008), Altersdiskriminierung im Licht des Europarechts, p. 41; *Polloczek* rightly stresses that the impact of human rights law on the development of the prohibition on age discrimination in EU law also results from the fact that EU Member States already are bound by human rights treaties; see in general to the impact of public international law on EU employment and labour law already *Schiek*, Dagmar (2005), Europäisches Arbeitsrecht, 2. edt., p. 45ff.

496 see with regard to the terminological distinction between principle of equality and the prohibition of discrimination, *Giegerich*, Thomas (2007), in: Rust, Ursula/Falke, Josef (eds.), AGG, Einleitung, para. 20-23; see also for the distinction between equality and non-discrimination chap. 5.1.

in human rights law.[497] Recital 4 is a clear indicator that human rights law functioned as a central point of reference for the EC legislator when establishing the anti-discrimination framework on the EU level.[498] Given the fact that with the coming into force of the Lisbon Treaty, the principle of non-discrimination on the grounds of age got its explicit 'authoritative foundation', and when considering the intended accession of the EU to the Convention for the Protection of Human Rights and Fundamental Freedoms (ECHR)[499], which might considerably strengthen the protection of human rights in Europe, the legal situation becomes even more complex.[500] Even if the EU is not yet directly and formally a contracting party to any of the human rights treaties, it is nevertheless indirectly closely bound to them.[501] One example in this regard is that many of the provisions of the Charter of Fundamental Rights of the European Union (CFREU) are based on the ECHR and the European Social Charter (ESC) in its revised form.[502]

A further example of the interplay between human rights law and EU law constitutes the ECHR and the case law of the European Court of Human Rights (ECtHR), which have a strong and increasing impact on the CJEU.[503] Prior to the Lisbon Treaty and the CFREU coming into force, the CJEU was strongly guided by the ECHR when deciding on fundamental rights issues. The

---

497 recital 4 Dir. 2000/78/EC; see also recitals 1, 5, 6.

498 *Hahn* (2006), p. 49; *Däubler*, Martin (2008), in: Däubler, Wolfgang/Bertzbach, Martin (eds.) (2008), Allgemeines Gleichbehandlungsgesetz, 2.edt., Einleitung, para. 138 and 146.

499 European Convention on Human Rights (Convention for the Protection of Human Rights and Fundamental Freedoms, ECHR) 1950, CETS No. 5.

500 see Art. 6 No. 2 TEU Treaty on European Union (TEU), 2009, OJ C 83/13, Consolidated version, 2012, OJ C 326/13; see for an analysis of the manifestation of the prohibition of age discrimination in EU primary and secondary law chap. 10.

501 *Mikkola*, Matti (2010), Social human rights of Europe, p. 52.

502 Charter of Fundamental Rights of the European Union (CFREU), 2000, OJ C 364/01; European Social Charter (ESC) 1961, CETS No. 35; European Social Charter (revised – RESC)1996, CETS No. 163; see ibid., p. 52; In general further human rights treaties where non-discrimination clauses and the rights of the elderly are embodied are to be found in the Inter-American systems (e.g. the American Convention on Human Rights), and in the African system (e.g. in Art. 2 of the African Charter on Human and Peoples' Rights), see in detail *Rodriguez-Pinzon*, Diego/*Martin*, Claudia (2003), The international status of the rights of Elderly Persons, American University International Law Review 18, No. 4, 2003, pp. 915-1008, pp. 993ff., 1004ff.

503 *McCrudden*/*Prechal* (2009), p. 2 who also point out that the impact also takes place the other way around as the ECtHR seeks inspiration in EU law and jurisprudence; see also *Däubler* (2008), para. 187.

ECHR is often ultimately referred to as being 'an authoritative source of equality and non-discrimination law'[504] for the national law of the member states of the EU as well as for EEA member states. It has to be kept in mind that the EU's accession to the ECHR does not necessarily hinder the EU from providing for protection in some areas, even going beyond those of the ECHR.[505] As regards for example the ESC, both the Preamble of the Treaty on European Union (TEU) and Art. 151 (1) Treaty on the Functioning of the Union (TFEU) explicitly refer to the ESC and the fundamental social rights manifested therein.[506]

Moreover, as explicitly laid down in Art. 53 CFREU, the level of protection provided for by the EU shall not be less than what is determined in international law and by international agreements to which the Union or all the member states are part of. It is also stressed in the TEU that the EU is founded on the values of respect for human dignity, equality and respect for human rights.[507] As stated in Art. 6 No. 3 TEU, it is furthermore the obligation of the EU to 'respect fundamental rights', as guaranteed by the ECHR and 'the constitutional traditions common to the Member States' as general principles of EU law.[508] For the development of the concept of age equality and non-discrimination on the grounds of age in the European legal context, human rights thus constitute a central legal source alongside the legal development in EU law and the constitutional traditions of the EU member states.[509]

Common to the human rights instruments that are going to be presented is that they all have provisions on non-discrimination. However, age is not explicitly listed as a protected ground. This is, in general, due to the fact that the protection against age discrimination rather belongs to the younger generation of discrimination grounds that are put on the agenda as a concern in human rights law. While the need to protect older employees against age discrimination has already been addressed in soft law, it still needs *de lege ferenda* to be manifested explicitly in hard law. From a *de*

504 *McCrudden/Prechal* (2009), p. 2.

505 see *Däubler* (2008), para. 187.

506 Treaty on the Functioning of the European Union (TFEU), 2009, OJ C 83/47.

507 see Art. 2 TEU, Art. 6 No. 1 TEU; see also Preamble to TEU, such as Art. 3 No. 3 TEU and Art. 21 TEU; see to the role of human rights also *Novitz*, Tonia/*Syrpris*, Philip (2010), Giving with the one hand and taking with the other: Protection of worker's human rights in the European Union, in: Fenwick, Colin/Novitz, Tonia (eds.), Human rights at work, pp. 463-483, p. 469.

508 see also for further details *Novitz/Syrpris* (2010), p. 469.

509 see to this aspect also *McCrudden/Prechal* (2009), p. 2; see for an overview of the manifestation of the prohibition of age discrimination in EU law and on national level chap. 10 and 11.

lege lata viewpoint, the key underlying question in this regard is, as *Chen* put it already in 1987 (which is also the initial point for this chapter), 'How, then, has the world community responded to the challenge of aging as a new human rights concern?'[510] Or, in other words, to what extent do these human rights instruments actually offer protection against age discrimination and mandatory retirement? The answer to this question is decisive for this analysis, as the more the prohibition of non-discrimination on the grounds of age is also manifested in human rights law, the more important it is to take age equality seriously. Part of this chapter furthermore concerns an examination of the manifestation of the right to work in human rights law, as it also is affected when it comes to mandatory retirement.

9.2 Charter of the United Nations

The Charter of the UN signed in June 1945 already stresses in its Preamble the equal rights of men and women, and due to the Charter's Art. 1 No. 3, one of the purposes of the UN is the promotion and encouragement of the respect for human rights and fundamental freedoms for all 'without distinction as to race, sex, language, or religion'.[511] Furthermore, the Charter makes clear in Art. 55 of chapter IX that the promotion of full employment (Art. 55 (a)) and 'universal respect for, and observance of, human rights and fundamental freedoms for all without distinction as to race, sex, language, or religion' (Art. 55 (c)) constitute basic premises for the creation of conditions of stability and wellbeing. However, Art. 55 (c) is silent about distinctions due to age and it is thus questionable as to whether age discrimination is permissible under the Charter.[512] Looking at the Charter itself is not very fruitful for any further interpretation in this regard. As the intention of the framers of the Charter was not to spell out the contents in the Charter itself, it remains more for the subsequent

---

510 *Chen*, Chung-Lu (1987), Aging: A new human rights concern – A policy-oriented perspective, Proceedings of the American Society of International Law, American Society of International Law, Vol. 81, 1987, pp. 169–175, p. 171.

511 Charter of the UN, signed 26 June 1945 and coming into force 24 October 1945.

512 *Lee*, Luke T. (1987), Remark to "Aging: A new human rights concern", in: Proceedings of the American Society of International Law, American Society of International Law, Vol. 81, 1987, pp. 169–175, p. 166.

human rights instruments, such as the 1948 Universal Declaration of Human Rights (UDHR), to fill in the lacunae left by the Charter.[513] Therefore, the next logical step is to evaluate whether the UDHR entails protection against age discrimination.[514]

9.3 Universal Declaration of Human Rights

Art. 1 s. 1 UDHR states that 'All human beings are born free and equal in dignity and rights'.[515] In general, the right to equality manifested therein might be interpreted broadly as also encompassing the right to age equality. However, it has to be noted that the UDHR in itself is not a legally binding treaty of human rights law; rather, it has a recommendatory character. Nevertheless, it is recognised in the literature that the UDHR contributed to the formation of international customary law in terms of the human rights guaranteed therein.[516]

As emphasised by *Lee,* human rights impose not only a moral, but also a legal obligation upon the states, which means that only if the rights of the elderly are built upon a solid legal base, may these rights be exercised effectively. Human rights are inherent in human beings and exist whether or not they are manifested in positive law. Despite criticisms from the positivists, *Lee* argues that, even from a positivist standpoint, human rights do have binding legal force. Such binding force stems from the UN Charter, where Art. 56 may be interpreted as the acceptance of an international legal obligation to fulfil the purposes set forth in Art. 55.[517]

---

513 ibid., p. 166 f.

514 ibid., p. 167, who raises this question in terms of the rights of the elderly.

515 The UDHR was adopted by the UN on 10 December 1948. After Second World War the UDHR laid down for the first time on international level a prohibition against discrimination and equality rights. Both preamble and Art. 1 UDHR clearly build upon the formulation of the Declarations of Human Rights in 1776 and 1789, see for an historical overview: *König*, Doris/*Peters*, Anne (2006), Das Diskriminierungsverbot, in: EMRK/GG Konkordanzkommentar zum europäischen und deutschen Grundrechtsschutz, Grote, Rainer/Marauhn, Thilo (eds.), chap. 21, p. 1117, 1118, para. 1-3; *Schraepler*, Ernst (1985), Die Entwicklung nach dem Zweiten Weltkrieg bis 1970, in: Hartung, Fritz/Commichau, Gerhard (eds.), Die Entwicklung der Menschen- und Bürgerrechte von 1776 bis zur Gegenwart, 5. edt. pp. 33- 40, p. 33 f.; in particular p. 35.

516 see to this aspect in detail *Polloczek* (2008), p. 42.

517 see the discussion by *Lee* (1987), p. 165 f.; Art. 56 of the UN Charter states: 'All Members pledge themselves to take joint and separate action in co-operation with the Organization for the achievement of the purposes set forth in Article 55. '

With regard to age equality and non-discrimination, Art. 2 UDHR is of particular relevance.[518] It states in its first sentence that everyone is entitled to all the rights and freedoms laid down in the Declaration 'without distinction of any kind, such as race, colour, sex, language, religion, political or other opinion, national or social origin, property, birth or other status'. This non-discrimination provision has even acquired the status of *jus cogens*.[519] The right to non-discrimination in Art. 2 UDHR is accessory, as it is related to the exercise of other rights and freedoms laid down in the UDHR. Age is not among the grounds that are listed in Art. 2 UDHR. However, the use of the wording 'such as' and 'other status' indicates that the list of protected grounds of discrimination is not exhaustive and is of a rather exemplary character. It is thus questionable as to whether age may be subsumed under this notion.[520] The majority of states and some authors deny such an interpretation.[521] This restrictive understanding may be contrasted with the view that the drafters of the UDHR might consciously have avoided a closed formulation of Art. 2 UDHR to be 'open' for legal developments *de lege ferenda*.[522] It has to be kept in mind that at the point of enactment of the UDHR, neither demographic change nor the vulnerable situation of older workers had been an issue of legal debate.[523]

Despite the uncertainties concerning Art. 2 UDHR, it has to be noted that further protection against discrimination is generally provided for in Art. 7 UDHR. It states, 'All are equal before the law and are entitled without any discrimination to equal protection of the law. All are entitled to equal protection against any discrimination in violation of this Declaration and against any incitement to such discrimination'.

---

518 *Polloczek* (2008), refers on p. 42 moreover to the aims of the UN Charter, in particular to Art. 1 (3), Art. 13 (1) (b), Art. 55 (c).

519 see in general to the doctrine of *jus cogens* and human rights law, *Rehman*, Javaid (2010), International human rights law, 2. edt., p. 25 f.

520 similar *Lee* (1987), p. 167 who raises this question just from the perspective of the elderly; see also *Polloczek* (2008), p. 43; see generally *Rehman* (2010), p. 22 f.

521 see to this aspect in detail *Polloczek* (2008), p. 43; see generally *Rehman* (2010), p. 22 f.

522 see to this aspect also *Polloczek* (2008), p. 43.

523 Also in the United States – a pioneer in discrimination legislation – the legal protection against age discrimination came first two decades after the UDHR on the agenda with the enactment of the ADEA in 1967.

The question has been raised as to whether this provision may be regarded as an autonomous prohibition against discrimination or rather as a general principle of equality.[524] The answer to this question depends on the importance that is attached to the Article's s. 2. If s. 2 is regarded as a reference back to Art. 2 s. 1, it might be regarded as an autonomous prohibition against discrimination. On the contrary, one might also argue that this reference is limited to the specific protection guaranteed in s. 2, while s. 1 stipulates the general principle of equality, postulating equality beyond the grounds of discrimination prohibited by Art. 2 s. 1. Given the explicit separation of both sentences in Art. 7, one might ultimately argue for the general principle of equality being manifested in s. 1.[525] If so, one might further argue *a majore ad minus* that protection against age discrimination is generally encompassed by Art. 7 s. 1.

From the perspective of the older worker facing mandatory retirement, essential employment rights are moreover guaranteed under Art. 23 UDHR, including the right to work and the free choice of employment (Art. 23 (1)), as any forced exit from the labour force constitutes an obstacle to the exercise of these universal rights.[526] As Art. 23 just speaks of 'everyone', all employees, regardless of their age, are encompassed by this provision.

9.4 The International Covenant on Civil and Political Rights and the International Covenant on Economic, Social and Cultural Rights

The UDHR was finally codified into two covenants, the International Covenant on Civil and Political Rights (ICCPR) and the International Covenant on Economic, Social and Cultural Rights (ICESCR).[527]

From a multiple discrimination angle, it is also worth looking at the International Convention on the Elimination of All Forms of Racial Discrimination (ICEAFRD), Convention on the Elimination of All Forms of Discrimination against Women (CEDAW) and the Convention on the Rights of Persons with Disabilities (CRPD). From the perspective of migrant older workers, it is

---

524 see to this question *Giegerich* (2007), para. 32; *Polloczek* (2008), p. 42, fn. 141.

525 *Giegerich* (2007), para. 32.

526 see moreover as regards the right to equal pay for equal work without any discrimination Art. 23 (2).

527 Both Covenants were adopted by the UN General Assembly on 16 December 1966. ICCPR came into force March 23, 1976. The ICESCR came into force 16 January 1976.

noteworthy to look at the International Convention on the Protection of the Rights of All Migrant Workers and Members of Their Families of 1990, where age is explicitly manifested in Art. 7 as a prohibited ground of discrimination.[528]

9.4.1 Protection against age discrimination in the ICESCR and ICCPR

Also Art. 2 No. 1 ICCPR and Art. 2 (2) ICESCR entail an accessory prohibition against discrimination.[529] By contrast, Art. 26 ICCPR entails a so-called independent or non-accessory prohibition against discrimination, which means that one may refer to Art. 26 ICCPR to challenge discrimination, regardless of whether or not there is a nexus to civil and political rights laid down in the Covenant.[530] In its General Comment No. 18, the Human Rights Committee (HRC) clarified the relationship between Art. 2 and Art. 26 ICCPR and stated that Art. 26 ICCPR does not merely duplicate the guarantee already laid down in Art. 2, but provides, in itself, an autonomous right.[531] Art. 26 ICCPR lays down a general principle of equality and a positive obligation for the legislator to combat discrimination.[532] Common to Art. 2, Art. 26 ICCPR and Art. 2 No. 2 ICESCR, as in Art. 2 UDHR, is the use of the formulation 'such as' and 'other status'. Age as a protected ground is not expressly listed.

In contrast to the ICCPR with its Art. 26, the ICESCR does not contain a general principle of equality that might cover age. In its General Comment No. 6 of 1995, the Committee on Economic, Social and Cultural Rights (CESCR) evaluated the economic, social and cultural rights of older persons.[533] In doing so, it dealt with discrimination on the grounds of age and discussed the question as to whether it is prohibited by the ICE-

---

528 see for a general analysis of the features of multiple discrimination, chap. 10.2.2.3.

529 Further equality provisions are e.g. to be found in Art. 27 ICCPR (minority rights) and in Art. 3 ICESCR (equal right of men and women) such as Art. 7 (a) (ii) (equal renumeration for equal work between women and men), Art. 7 (c) ICESCR (equal opportunity to be promoted in employment), Art. 10 (3).

530 see for further details *Nowak*, Manfred (2005), U.N. Covenant on Civil and Political Rights: CCPR Commentary, CCPR Commentary, Art. 26, para. 12.

531 CCPR, General Comment No. 18: Non-discrimination, 10 November 1989, para. 12.

532 *König/Peters* (2006), p. 1123, para. 9.

533 CESCR, General Comment No. 6: The economic, social and cultural rights of older persons, 08 December 1995.

SCR.[534] The Committee emphasised that the omission of age as an explicit prohibited grounds of discrimination in Art. 2 No. 2 may not be understood as an intentional exclusion, but rather that it is due to the fact that at the time of the adoption of the ICESCR – and thus unlike today – demographic ageing was not yet regarded as an evident or urgent problem.[535] However, this lack of awareness is, according to the Committee's view, not decisive, as 'other status' may be interpreted as also being applicable to age.[536] Even if, according to the Committee, this does not yet lead to the conclusion that a comprehensive protection against age discrimination is provided by the ICESCR, it at least underlines that 'the range of matters in relation to which such discrimination can be accepted is very limited'.[537] It is remarkable that the CESCR also stresses that in the few areas where age discrimination is still tolerated, such as in the case of mandatory retirement ages, a clear trend is observable towards the abolishment of such age barriers.[538] In light of this tendency, the Committee expresses the view that state parties to the ICESCR 'should seek to expedite this trend to the greatest extent possible'.[539] Similarly, the CESCR has pointed out in its General Comment No. 20 of 2009 that the nature of discrimination changes due to different contexts and evolves over time, which makes a 'flexible approach' to the notion of 'other status' necessary.[540] It has also been emphasised that additional grounds falling under the expression 'other status' are commonly recognised and characterised by the fact that they 'reflect the experience of social groups that are vulnerable and have suffered and continue to suffer marginalization'.[541] With reference to its General Comment No. 6, the CESCR acknowledges again that age is a prohibited ground of discrimination and highlights inter alia the need to address discrimination against unemployed older persons who are seeking work.[542] Both General Comments illustrate that the protection against age

534 ibid., para. 11.
535 ibid.
536 ibid.
537 ibid., para. 12.
538 ibid., para. 12.
539 ibid., para. 12.
540 CESCR, General Comment No. 20: Non-Discrimination in Economic, Social and Cultural Rights (Art. 2, para. 2), 2 July 2009, para. 27 referring to para. 15.
541 ibid. Besides that, it is stressed that intersectional discrimination may be encompassed.
542 ibid., para. 29 referring to CESCR General Comment No. 6.

discrimination is encompassed by the ICESCR. They moreover demonstrate the Committee's awareness of the vulnerable situation of older employees, in particular, those confronted with compulsory retirement.

Moreover, the UN HRC has repeatedly recognised in its case law that age falls under the notion of 'other status' in Art. 26 s. 2 ICCPR.[543]

The first case on age discrimination and mandatory retirement, *Love v. Australia*, concerned the compulsory retirement of pilots on having reached the age of 60. The HRC concluded in this case that age is basically encompassed by the ICCPR and is to be subsumed under the notion of 'other status'.[544] The HRC acknowledged that mandatory retirement systems may also have a protective function, as they limit the lifelong working time and may be supplemented by comprehensive social security schemes to secure the workers' subsistence.[545] Moreover, it referred to the fact that mandatory retirement legislation may be based upon employment policy reasons.[546] Further reference was made by the HRC to the international safety standards laid down by the International Civil Aviation Organisation (ICAO). It considered these standards to be widely accepted both on the national and international level and, most importantly, at the same time these provided for a mandatory retirement at 60 for pilots. It recognised the aim of maximising the safety of the passengers, crew and persons that otherwise might be affected by flight travel as a legitimate aim under the ICCPR and thus ultimately found that the compulsory retirement age was reasonable and objective and did not constitute a breach of Art. 26 ICCPR.[547] In *Love v. Australia*, the HRC followed the line established in its first case on age discrimination: *Schmitz-de-Jong v. Netherlands*.[548] This case concerned the refusal of a senior citizen partner's pass to a 44-year-old woman. The pass was only provided to partners of 60 years of age and older.[549] The claimant argued that the refusal constituted age discrimination in breach of Art. 26 ICCPR.[550] The HRC found that the age limitation in question on granting only partners who had reached the age of 60

543 UN HRC, 28 April 2003, Communication No. 983/2001, *Love et al v. Australia*, UN. Doc. CCPR/C/77/D/983/2001, para. 8.2; UN HRC, 20. July 1998, Communication No. 895/1999, *Alejandro Marín Gómez* v. *Spain* UN. Doc. CCPR/C/73/D/895/1999 (1998), para. 9.2; UN HCR, 24. October 2011, Communications Nos. 1757, 1765/2008, *Albareda and others v. Uruguay,* UN. Doc. CCPR/C/103/D/1637/2007, para. 9.2; see also UN HCR, 27 March 2006, *Hinostoza Solís v Peru Communication, No. 1016/2001,* UN. Doc CCPR/C/86/D/1016/2001 (2006), para. 6.3; see to the case law also *Nowak* (2005), Article 26, para. 47; *Joseph*, Sarah/*Schultz*, Jenny/*Castan*, Melissa (2004), The International Covenant on Civil and Political Rights, 2. ed., p. 690, [23.24], p. 714 f., *Joseph*, Sarah/*Castan*, Melissa (2013), The International Covenant on Civil and Political Rights, 3. ed., ICCPR, p. 792 f.

544 UN HRC, *Love v. Australia*. para. 8.2.

545 ibid., para. 8.2.

546 ibid.

547 ibid., para. 8.2., 8.3 and para. 4.12; see to the discussion of the justification of mandatory retirement for pilots in detail, chap. 15.3.3.

548 UN HRC, 09 August 2001, Communication No. 855/1999, *Schmitz de Jong* v. *Netherlands*, CCPR/C/72/D/855/1999.

549 ibid., para. 7.2.

550 ibid., paras. 1, 4.2.

years the right to obtain an entitlement to various rate reductions as a partner to a pensioner over the age of 65 years constituted an objective criterion of differentiation and the application of this differentiation was not unreasonable.[551] A breach of any article of the Covenant could not be ascertained.[552]

In addition, in *Albareda and others v. Uruguay*, the HRC had to deal with age discrimination, this time with the mandatory retirement of specific public servants over the age of 60 years.[553] As referred to by the government, the *ratio legis* of the disputed provision was to avoid the negative consequences of the age-related loss of reflexes and memory.[554] To maintain the effectiveness of staff performing the duties of a first secretary, it therefore introduced the contested compulsory retirement at the age of 60.[555] Interestingly enough, the HRC did not find this reasoning irrational.[556] However, the government failed to explain to a sufficient extent why age could affect the capability performance of one administrative category of civil servants but not of another. Based on these grounds, the HRC finally found a violation of Art. 26 in conjunction with Art. 2 ICCPR.[557]

9.4.2 The right to work and free choice of employment in the ICESCR and ICCPR

In addition, it has to be noted that according to Art. 6 ICESCR, the state parties to the Covenant recognise the right to work, which encompasses the right of every employee to 'the opportunity to gain his living by work which he freely chooses or accepts, and will take appropriate steps to safeguard this right'.[558] According to Art. 6 No. 2 ICESCR, the full realisation of this right shall be ensured by several measures taken by the state party to the ICESCR to achieve 'full and productive employment under conditions safeguarding fundamental political and economic freedoms to the individual'. Remarkably, the CESCR recalled General Comment No. 6

551 para. 7.2.
552 para. 8.
553 UN HRC, Albareda and others v. Uruguay .
554 ibid., paras. 6, 9.3.
555 ibid., paras. 6, 9.3.
556 ibid., para. 9.3; critical to the HRCs reasoning: *Joseph /Castan* (2013), p. 793, para. 23.64.
557 UN HRC, *Albareda and others* v. *Uruguay,* paras. 9.4, 10.
558 Art. 6 No. 1 ICESCR; see for an analysis of the right to work CESCR, General Comment No. 18: Right to work, 24 November 2005; see also *Joseph*, Sarah (2010), UN Covenants and Labour Rights, in: Fenwick, Colin/Novitz, Tonia (eds.), Human Rights at work: Perspectives on Law and Regulation, pp. 331ff, pp. 337ff.

and also placed particular emphasis, as regards the right to work, on the necessity of taking measures to prevent discrimination on the grounds of age in employment and occupation.[559]

Besides this, Art. 7 ICESCR lays down that equal rights, particularly in terms of equal pay and access to employment, are recognised by the state parties to the ICESCR. Moreover, of particular importance from the perspective of older workers is Art. 7 (c), which guarantees the 'Equal opportunity for everyone to be promoted in his employment to an appropriate higher level, subject to no considerations other than those of seniority and competence'. A narrower right to work is laid down in Art. 25 (c) ICCPR, according to which, in conjunction with Art. 2, every citizen shall have the equal right and opportunity to work in the public service.[560]

Art. 25 (c) has to be distinguished from Art. 6 ICESCR, as Art. 25 (c) entails neither a guarantee for an actual public-service job nor the obligation that governments are required to ensure that many such jobs are available.[561] Rather, it guarantees each adult citizen a right to be free from unfair exclusion or removal from an available government position. By contrast, Art. 6 ICESCR stipulates that states should take steps to maximise gainful employment among its adult population in the public and private sectors. In *Hinostoza Solís v. Peru Communication,*[562] the HRC applied the reasoning in *Love v. Australia*, para. 8.2. – that a distinction based on age which is not based on reasonable and objective criteria may amount to discrimination on the grounds of 'other status' under the clause in question, or to a denial of equal protection of the law within the meaning of Art. 26 s. 1 – also to Art. 25 (c) in conjunction with Art. 2 No. 1 ICCPR. The complaint concerned a public servant who was made redundant during a restructuring of the public service. The dismissals were based on age and time in service. The complainant's employment was terminated as he was over 60 years of age and had only served for 11 years. He claimed that his termination constituted discrimination in violation of Art. 25 (c) ICCPR. The HRC finally found in para. 6.4 'that the age limit [...] for continued post occupancy was an objective distinguishing criterion and that its implementation in the context of a general plan for the restructuring of the civil service was not unreasonable'. Consequently, no violation could be ascertained. Art. 25 has been interpreted similarly to Art. 26 ICCPR as regards the non-discrimination provision.[563] Nevertheless, the approaches to the justification differed somewhat, which can be illustrated by the fact that four HRC members dissented and stated that the HRC's reasoning departed from that given in *Love v. Australia*. While the HRC in *Love v. Australia* assessed whether the mandatory retirement age in question was reasonable, it seems to assume in *Hinostoza Solís v. Peru Communication* that using age as a criterion with which to choose redundancies was per se reasonable. By contrast, the dissenters argued that the state had failed to demonstrate that age constituted an objective criterion upon which the dismissal decisions had been based.[564]

---

559 CESCR, General Comment No. 18, para 16 referring to CESCR General Comment No. 6, para. 22, para. 24.

560 see for further analysis and references *Joseph* (2010), pp. 347 f.

561 *Joseph* (2010), p. 347 f.

562 UN HRC, *Hinostoza Solís v Peru Communication*, para. 6.3.

563 *Joseph* (2010), p. 356 f. referring to para 6.4.

564 see to this aspect ibid., p. 357.

9.5 International Labour Organization instruments

On the level of the International Labour Organization (ILO), three conventions are of particular relevance: the Discrimination (Employment and Occupation) Convention (ILO No. 111),[565] the Employment Policy Convention (ILO No. 122)[566] and finally, the Termination of Employment at the Initiative of the Employer Convention (ILO No. 158).[567]

In addition, ILO Convention No. 156 on Equal Opportunities and Equal Treatment for Men and Women Workers: Workers with Family Responsibilities of 1981 implicitly deals in its Art. 7 with the issue of discrimination against workers who are taking care of older persons and of older workers who entered working life at a later a point in life.[568]

9.5.1 The Discrimination (Employment and Occupation) Convention (ILO No. 111) and Employment Policy Convention (ILO No. 122)

Convention No. 111 defines discrimination in its Art. 1 No. 1 (a) as any distinction, exclusion or preference that is based on the grounds of race, colour, sex, religion, political opinion, national extraction or social origin and that has the effect of nullifying or impairing equality of opportunity or treatment in employment or occupation.[569] This definition neither refers explicitly to age as a ground of discrimination nor entails an open formulation such as 'other status', which would open it up for a broad interpretation.[570] Thus, solely based on this provision, a prohibition of age discrimi-

565 ILO Convention No. 111 concerning Discrimination in Respect of Employment and Occupation, adopted in 1958, entered into force in 1960.

566 ILO Convention No. 122 concerning Employment Policy, adopted in 1964, entered into force in 1966.

567 ILO Convention No. 158 concerning Termination of Employment at the Initiative of the Employer, adopted in 1982, entry into force 1985.

568 see for an overview of the fundamental rights in ILO Conventions and their corresponding articles in the ESC and the ICESCR: *Mikkola* (2010), chap. 2.1.1, Fig. 15, p. 49.

569 see also Premable of ILO no.111 Convention's reference to equal opportunity and that discrimination constitutes a violation of the rights expressed by the UDHR.

570 similar *Polloczek* (2008), p. 43; see also Art. 5, which lays down that special measures of protection or assistance shall not constitute discrimination (Art. 5 No. 1), explicitly mentions age as a legitimate reason for special protection or assistance (Art. 5 Nr. 2).

nation cannot be derived from Convention No. 111.[571] Nonetheless, it has to be noted that Art. 1 No. 1 (b) of Convention No. 111 also offers member states the possibility of being able to add other grounds of discrimination for their domestic purposes, provided that representative employers and workers' organisations, and other appropriate bodies, have been consulted prior to that.[572]

The Employment Policy Convention (ILO No. 122) in its Art. 1 calls on the member states to declare and pursue an active employment policy established for the promotion of full, productive and freely chosen employment. This is further concretised in Art. 1 No. 2 (c), pursuant to which this policy shall aim at guaranteeing the freedom of choice of employment and 'the fullest possible opportunity for each worker to qualify for, and to use his skills and endowments in, a job for which he is well suited, irrespective of race, colour, sex, religion, political opinion, national extraction or social origin'.[573] What has been said for ILO Convention No. 111 also applies for ILO Convention No. 122: age is notably absent in Art. 1 No. 2 (c). To close the gap in the protection against age discrimination, which was, in particular, caused by the omission of age in the definition of discrimination in Art. 1 No. 1 (a) ILO Convention No. 111, the ILO finally adopted recommendation 162, the so-called Older Workers Recommendation (OWR) of 1980.[574]

9.5.2 Termination of Employment at the Initiative of the Employer Convention (ILO No. 158) and recommendation No. 166 of 1982

What is also worth looking at is the Termination of Employment at the Initiative of the Employer Convention No. 158 that determines in its Art. 5 valid reasons for the termination of the employment relationship. While for example race, sex or religion is explicitly mentioned as an invalid reason, Convention ILO No. 158 does not go into age. A formulation such as

---

571 similar *Ghosheh* (2008), p. 14; *Polloczek* (2008), p. 44.

572 see also *Ghosheh* (2008), p. 14.

573 Art. 1 No. 2 (c) ILO No. 122.

574 R162 – Older Workers Recommendation, 1980 (No. 162) Recommendation concerning Older Workers, Adoption: Geneva, 66th ILC session (23 June 1980), Status: Instrument with interim status; Even if designed for the protection of older workers the OWR does not itself define 'older workers' but leaves it to the Member States to do so, see para. 2.

'other status' is missing. However, the first sentence of Art. 5 begins with the formulation that the following listed reasons 'inter alia' shall not constitute valid reasons to terminate the employment relationship. Based on this formulation, one might argue that the list of unlawful reasons is of exemplary character. Nevertheless, this seems to be rather weak in terms of also being able to subsume age. However, this Convention was finally supplemented by recommendation No. 166 of 1982[575] concerning the termination of employment at the initiative of the employer. Recommendation No. 166 solved this uncertainty. It clarifies that in addition to the grounds referred to in Art. 5 ILO Convention No. 158, 'age, subject to national law and practice regarding retirement' shall not constitute a valid reason for termination.[576] Thus, according to Art. 5 ILO No. 158 read in conjunction with recommendation No. 166, age per se cannot be regarded as a valid reason for termination.

9.6 Council of Europe Human Rights instruments

Besides the universal human rights systems, several regional human rights treaties embody non-discrimination clauses and particular rights for the elderly. In the context of the Council of Europe, two treaties are of particular relevance: the ECHR and the ESC.

---

575 R166 – Termination of Employment Recommendation, 1982 (No. 166), Recommendation concerning Termination of Employment at the Initiative of the Employer, adopted Geneva, 68th ILC session (22 June 1982), Status: No conclusions.

576 ibid., II. Standards of general application, para. 5 (a).

9.6.1 The European Convention on Human Rights and Fundamental Freedoms

The key non-discrimination provision in the ECHR is Art. 14.[577] According to this Article, the enjoyment of the rights and freedoms laid down in the Convention shall be guaranteed 'without discrimination on any grounds such as sex, race, colour, language, religion, political or other opinion, national or social origin, association with a national minority, property, birth or other status'. The Article's de facto impact is first and foremost limited, as Art. 14 ECHR is also accessory in nature.

Based on its accessoriness, some even call Art. 14 ECHR 'parasitic'.[578] The ECtHR has increasingly eased the requirement of a nexus between the asserted discrimination and one of the rights or freedoms guaranteed in the ECHR in its case law.[579] Even if the requirement to establish a connection between substantive Convention provisions and Art. 14 ECHR was rather strictly interpreted by the ECtHR, the Court finally opened up for a more flexible interpretation in the *Belgian Linguistic* case.[580] In any case, Art. 14 ECHR does not presuppose a breach of the provision in question, so that it is at least, in this regard, autonomous.[581]

Similar to the analysed non-discrimination clauses on the UN level, age is not explicitly listed as a protected ground in Art. 14. ECHR. However, the list is non-exhaustive.[582] There are no indications that the drafters from the ECHR have intentionally omitted age. Quite the contrary, the reason why

---

577 see for an overview of social rights under the ECHR, *Mikkola* (2010), chap. 2.3, Fig. 25, p. 82 and with regard to Art. 14 ECHR chap. 2.3.4, p. 91 f.; see for an overview of background and drafting history of Art. 14 ECHR *König/Peters* (2006), p. 1120 f., 1126 f., para. 5 f., 15ff; *van Dijk*, Pieter/*van Hoof*, Fried/ *van Rijn*, Arjen/*Zwaak*, Leo (eds.) (2006), Theory and Practice of the European Convention on Human Rights, 4 edt., chap. 1, p. 27.

578 see *McColgan*, Aileen (2003), Principles of equality and protection from discrimination in international human rights law, European Human Rights Law Review (E.H.R.L.R), 2003, Issue 2, pp.157-175, p. 159, 163.

579 see for an overview: *König/Peters* (2006), p. 1132 f., para. 30 f., p. 1126, para. 18; *Gerards*, Janneke (2004), The Application of Article 14 ECHR by the European Court of Human Rights, in: Niessen/Chopin (eds.), The development of legal instruments to combat racism in a diverse Europe, p. 5ff.

580 see in detail *De Schutter*, Olivier (2005), The prohibition of discrimination under European human rights law, p. 21 referring in fn. 44 to the relevant case law.

581 to this aspect *Danisi*, Carmelo (2011), How far can the European Court of Human Rights go in the fight against discrimination? Defining new standards in its nondiscrimination jurisprudence, International Journal of Constitutional Law, 2011: 9, pp. 793-807, p. 794.

582 see *Engel* case, ECHR 23 November 1976, Series A, Vol. 22, para. 72; see discussion in *Temming* (2008), p. 73ff.

age is not explicitly included might simply have been due to a lack of awareness.[583] Several judgements of the ECtHR clearly allow for the conclusion that age may be subsumed under the category of 'other status' in Art. 14 ECHR.[584] However, a nexus to other substantive Convention rights still has to be established.[585] In particular, when it comes to age discrimination in employment and the analysis of mandatory retirement, this seems to be somewhat problematic, as at first glance, hardly any of the other Convention rights could be affected here.[586]

In view of a more flexible approach as established in *Belgian Linguistic*, a nexus might possibly be established to Art. 8 – the right to respect for private and family life. The reason for that is that even if originally the historic function of Art. 8 has been to protect private and family life from excessive intrusions, the ECtHR progressively stated that self-determination or autonomy of the individual also constitutes an essential principle underlying Art. 8.[587] Self-determination or autonomy also plays an essential role when it comes to the older employee facing mandatory retirement. Moreover, in a discussion of mandatory retirement, Art. 11 ECHR protecting the right to freedom of assembly and association might also be affected, as compulsory retirement provisions may also be laid down in collective agreements. However, this does not make it any easier from the perspective of the individual employee to establish the required nexus.

---

583 similar *Schokkenbroek*, Jeroen (2004), A new European standard against discrimination: Negotiating Protocol No. 12 to the European Convention on Human Rights, in: Niessen, Jan /Isabelle Chopin (eds.), The development of legal instruments to combat racism in a diverse Europe, 2004, p. 63.

584 see for an overview *Temming* (2008), p. 73 f. referring among others to the following cases: European Commission on Human Rights, *Nelson* v. *United Kingdom,* 13 October 1986, No, 11077/84; Committee of Ministers: *X* v. *United Kingdom*, 12. October 1978 respective 12 June 1979, No. 7215/75; ECtHR: *Dudgeon* v. *United Kingdom*, Judgement of 22 October 1981, Series A, No. 45; (1982) EHRR 149 ; see also references to case- law given by *European Union Agency for Fundamental Rights/European Court of Human Rights – Council of Europe* (2011), Handbook on European non-discrimination law, p. 102 f., where it is referred to ECtHR, Schitzgebel v. Switzerland (No. 15762/07), 10 June 2010; ECtHR, Tv.UK [GC] (No. 24724/94), 16. December 1999; ECtHR V.v.UK [GC] (No. 24888/94), 16 December 1999; ECtHR, D.G. v. Ireland (No. 39474/98), 16 May 2002; ECtHR Boumar v. Blegim (No. 9106/80), 29 February 1988.

585 *van Hoof* (2006), in: van Dijk et. al. (2006), chap. 30, p. 989.

586 similar *van Hoof* (2006), chap. 30, p. 990, who stresses that Art. 14 ECHR cannot be invoked in several important areas of social life, such as the employment sphere.

587 see to this aspect in general and referring to case-law of the ECtHR *De Hert*, Paul/*Mantovani*, Eugenio (2011), Specific human rights of older persons?, E.H.R.L.R, 2011 Issue 4, pp. 398-418, p. 407, 408, fn. 78.

Not surprisingly, inter alia due to its accessory character, some have criticised that Art. 14 ECHR has a limited scope, offers rather weak protection and that the Convention's achievements in terms of equality issues may rather be described as unremarkable.[588] The solution for filling the gap caused by the limitations in Art. 14 ECHR and to overcome its shortcomings was finally seen in the drafting of Protocol No. 12 in 2000, which entered into force in 2005.[589] The Protocol embodies in Art. 1 (a) a general prohibition of discrimination, which constitutes an autonomous and free-standing guarantee.[590]

The Protocol is controversial and a number of states have not ratified it.[591] Some are apprehensive concerning a general non-accessory prohibition against discrimination, which, according to critics, is imprecise and too far-reaching. Others fear that the Protocol might be interpreted to such an extent that the signature states might be obliged to enact laws against discrimination that are applicable also in relation to private parties.[592]

The list of discrimination grounds does not explicitly include age, but is open-ended (other status). Given the underlying aim behind Protocol No. 12 to overcome the limitations of Art. 14 ECHR, the question arises as to why the list of discrimination grounds has not been extended to also cover at least those grounds which have already been regarded as falling under

---

588 see e.g. *Däubler* (2008), para. 183, who stresses that the Convention's deficits are apparent considering the fact that e.g. the free choice of employment is not guaranteed therein; see to the accessory character of Art. 14 ECHR also *Gerards* (2004), p. 7ff.

589 The Protocol was opened for signature on 4 November 2000 and came into force 1 April 2005, see for an overview of legal background and drafting history: *Schokkenbroek* (2004), p. 61ff.; *König/Peters* (2006), p. 1122, para. 7; *Mikkola* points out, that Protocol No. 12 will increase significantly the overlapping of the provisions of the two European key instruments – the ECHR and the ESC –, see *Mikkola* (2010), p. 92 ; see also *Meenan*, Helen (2007 b), Reflecting on age discrimination and rights of the elderly in the European Union and the Council of Europe, 14 MJ 1 (2007 b), p. 42, 43 who discusses the limitations of Protocol No. 12, see pp. 47ff., 80.

590 *Schokkenbroek* (2004), p. 73; *De Schutter* (2005), p. 24; critical to Art. 1 *Däubler* (2008), para. 186.

591 Both Norway and Germany signed but have until now not ratified Protocol No. 12. It is not decided yet whether Norway should ratify Protocol No. 12, see NOU 2011: 18, *Struktur for likestilling*, vedlegg 1, p. 188 and for a detailed discussion NOU 2009:14, pp. 293-301; see for the current status: http://conventions.coe.int/Treaty/Commun/ChercheSig.asp?NT=177&CM=10&DF=07/06/2010&CL=ENG (last accessed: 17.12.2014).

592 see for an overview of the critics: *König/Peters* (2006), p. 1122, para. 7.

the notion of 'other status' in Art. 14 ECHR, such as age. According to the Explanatory Report to Protocol No. 12, it was considered preferable to have a list of non-discrimination grounds identical to that of Art. 14 ECHR.[593] Thus, the drafters also refrained from extending the list to encompass e.g. sexual orientation or age.[594] This was not due to a lack of awareness that such grounds also play an important role in today's societies as compared to the time when Art. 14 ECHR was drafted, but such an inclusion was considered as unnecessary from a legal point of view based on the open-ended character of the list of non-discrimination grounds and because of the fact that an inclusion of additional discrimination grounds might lead to 'unwarranted *a contrario* interpretations as regards discrimination based on grounds not so included'.[595] By maintaining the existing catalogue, openness to further development as regards potential – at present not yet debated – discrimination grounds should be guaranteed. However, as noted previously, the ECtHR has already applied Art. 14 ECHR in its case law in relation to discrimination grounds that are not explicitly listed in this provision.[596] Since the listed grounds of discrimination correspond to those mentioned in Art. 14 ECHR, one can conclude that also with regard to Art. 1 of Protocol No. 12, discrimination on the grounds of age is encompassed by the notion of 'other status'.[597]

593 *Council of Europe*, Explanatory Report to Protocol No. 12 to the Convention for the Protection of Human Rights and Fundamental Freedoms (ETS No. 177), para. 20 available at: http://conventions.coe.int/Treaty/en/Reports/Html/177.htm (last accessed: 17.12.20140); see also *Mowbray*, Alastair (2004), European Convention on Human Rights, Article 14 prohibition of discrimination, p. 621, para. 20.

594 ibid.

595 ibid.

596 ibid.

597 *Polloczek* (2008), p. 53.

9.6.2 The European Social Charter

In contrast to other human rights treaties, the ESC of 1961 does not contain a separate non-discrimination provision.[598] Originally, a non-discrimination clause was only to be found in the Preamble to the ESC. However, Art. 1 (2) on the right to work – viewed in the context of the Preamble para. 4 – has been the platform for the development in case law of far-reaching protection against discrimination on different grounds of discrimination.[599] According to the interpretation of the European Committee of Social Rights (ECSR), Art. 1 (2) therefore imposes an obligation upon states 'to eliminate all forms of discrimination in employment', whatever the legal nature of the respective professional relationship.[600] This interpretation follows first from the requirement that the right of the worker to earn his living shall, according to Art. 1 (2), be protected 'effectively' and second, from the wording of para. 4 of the Preamble, which states that the enjoyment of the Charter's social rights should be guaranteed 'without discrimination on grounds of race, colour, sex, religion, political opinion, national extraction or social origin'.[601] In particular, the development in EU anti-discrimination law has had an impact on the ECSR's case law. In line with that, age as a protected ground of discrimination has not been an issue in its case law before the coming into force of Dir. 2000/78/EC.

---

598 see to this aspect in detail *Scheinin*, Martin/*Krause*, Catarina (2000), The right not to be discriminated against: The case of social security, in: Orlin, Theodore S./Scheinin, Martin (eds.), The jurisprudence of human rights law: A comparative interpretive approach, 2000, pp. 253-286, p. 268 f.

599 see in general *Samuel*, Lenia (2002), Fundamental social rights, case law of the European Social Charter, 2. edt., p. 18 referring to. Conclusion I, p. 15; see also *Gomien*, Donna/*Harris*, David/*Zwaak*, Leo (1996), Law and Practice of the European Cnvention on Human Rights and the European Social Charter, p. 383 referring to Conclusions III, p. 8 and Conclusion I, p. 15.

600 ECSR, *Fellesforbundet for Sjøfolk* (FFFS) v. *Norway,* Complaint No. 74/2011, Decision on the Merits 2 July 2013, para. 104 referring to *Syndicat national des Professions du tourisme* v. *France*, Complaint No. 6/1999, decision on the merits of 10 October 2000, para. 24 and *Quaker Council for European Affairs (QCEA)* v. *Greece*, Complaint No. 8/2000, decision on the merits of 25 April 2001, para. 20; see also *Gomien* et al. (1996), p. 383 referring to Conclusions III, p. 8 and Conclusion I, p. 15.

601 see Art. 1 (2) in conjunction with the Preamble, para. 4; see in this regard also *Fellesforbundet for Sjøfolk* (FFFS) v. *Norway*, para. 104; *Gomien* et al. (1996), p. 383.

Since then, the Committee has consistently emphasised that under Art. 1 (2), domestic legislation has to prohibit discrimination in employment that also encompasses discrimination on the grounds of age.[602] Both direct and indirect discrimination has to be prohibited.[603] According to the Committee, discriminatory acts and provisions that are prohibited by Art. 1 (2) may apply to all aspects of employment, including dismissals.[604]

The adoption of the so-called Revised European Social Charter (RESC) in 1996 led to the inclusion of Art. E in part V.[605] It contains an accessory and open-ended (other status) prohibition against discrimination.

Its accessory nature again has to do with Art. 1 (2).

As age is not among the explicitly listed grounds, the open-ended character of Art. E raises the question as to whether it might be interpreted as covering age as a non-discrimination ground.[606]

In general, the list of explicit enumerated discrimination grounds in RESC is much wider than the original non-discrimination clause that is manifested in the Preamble to the ESC of 1961. Art. E also lists 'language', not only political, but also 'other opinion', 'health', 'association with a national minority' and 'birth or other status'. It is even wider than Art. 14 ECHR – on which it has been based – as Art. 14 ECHR does not contain 'health' as a listed ground of non-discrimination.[607] It is questionable whether age as a ground of discrimination was intentionally omitted by the drafters and whether its inclusion into the list of grounds was in any way subject to debates in the drafting process to RESC.[608] The wording of Art. E at least indicates that the contracting parties to the ESC deliberately

---

602 *Fellesforbundet for Sjøfolk* (FFFS) v. *Norway*, para. 105 w.r.t. Conclusions XVIII-1; Conclusions 2006, Norway; Conclusions 2008, Lithunania, Conclusions 2008, Netherlands; see for further details also *De Schutter* (2005), p. 29 fn. 70 w.r.t. Conclusions 2002, pp. 22-28 (France), p. 30, fn. 75 and Conclusions 2002 (Italy), p. 75.

603 *Fellesforbundet for Sjøfolk* (FFFS) v. *Norway*, para. 105 w.r.t. *Autism-Europe* v. *France*, Complanit no. 13/2002, decision on the merits of 4 November 2003, para. 52.

604 ibid., para. 106 w.r.t. Conclusions XVI-1, Austria; Conclusions 2008, Azerbaijan.

605 see in general Explanatory report to the RESC, para. 135-137, available at: http://conventions.coe.int/Treaty/EN/Reports/HTML/163.htm (last accessed: 17.12.2014).

606 see in detail *Polloczek* (2008), p. 55.

607 see also Explanatory report to RESC, para. 136.

608 see in general ibid., paras. 135-137.

refrained from determining an exclusive list of discrimination grounds.[609] The Explanatory Report to the RESC only mentions that the requirement of a certain age for access to some forms of education might be an objective and reasonable justification for discrimination.[610] The question of whether or not age is encompassed has to date gained little to no attention in the literature.[611] However, Art. E has to be read as also encompassing age.[612] In any case, the more decisive provision in terms of protection against discrimination constitutes, according to the ECSR Art. 1 (2). It has to be noted that as stressed by the ECSR in matters concerning discrimination in employment, it is not necessary to combine Art. 1 (2) with Art. E.[613] The reason for this is that Art. 1 (2) alone prohibits discrimination, according to the ECSR.[614]

Being a kind of additional regulation to Art. 1 (2), the right to protection in cases of termination of employment is further generally manifested in Art. 24. The ECSR made it clear that the cases are generally excluded from the scope of Art. 24 where a statute sets a mandatory retirement age so that the employment relationship automatically ceases through the operation of the law. The reason for this is that 'termination of employment' in the sense of Art. 24 only means termination at the initiative of the employer. This has to be distinguished from 'situations where an employee may be dismissed at the initiative of the employer solely on the ground of the former having reached the pensionable age',[615] as these situations are considered to be contrary to the Charter, unless the termination may properly be justified with reference to one of the valid grounds that are explicitly established by Art. 24.[616] In this regard, only two types of

609 see to the non-exhaustive character of Art. E: ibid., para. 136; see also for further references *Polloczek* (2008), p. 5.

610 Explanatory report to RESC, para. 136.

611 see for further details *Polloczek* (2008), p. 55.

612 see in this regard also *Mikkola* (2010), p. 539; *Meenan* (2007 b), p. 72 referring to frequently asked questions, 2, available at: http://www.coe.int/t/dghl/monitoring/socialcharter/Presentation/NonDiscrimination_en.asp (last accessed: 17.12.2014).

613 *Fellesforbundet for Sjøfolk* (FFFS) v. Norway, para. 51.

614 ibid., para. 51.

615 ibid., para. 85 referring to Conclusions 2012, General Introduction and para. 86.

616 ibid., para. 85 referring to Conclusions 2012, General Introduction and para. 86.

grounds are considered to be valid: first, those that are related to the employee's capacity or conduct and second, those that are based on the operational requirements of the enterprise; that is, on economic reasons.[617]

As emphasised by the ECSR, it is the aim and purpose of the ESC as a human rights protection instrument 'to protect rights not merely theoretically, but also in fact'.[618] Provisions that for example according to their wording do not amount to a mandatory retirement age of a certain group of workers, may de facto often be applied as such.[619] This was the case in *Fellesforbundet for Sjøfolk* (FFFS) *v. Norway*, which concerned the dismissal of a seafarer who had reached the age of 62 and who de facto was subject to compulsory retirement. The background of the case is the so-called *Kystlink* judgement of the Norwegian *Høyesterett*.[620] In essence, the complaint concerned the question of whether a lower age limit set out in national legislation for a certain category of employees as regards abolishing dismissal protection amounts to discriminatory treatment on the grounds of age that is contrary to either Art. 24 or Art. 1 (2), or to both.[621] In its analysis, the ECSR assessed the age limit's conformity with Art. 24 and Art. 1 (2) ESC. It, in particular, recalled that a dismissal on the grounds of age would not constitute a valid reason for termination of the employment relationship, unless the termination could be proven to be within the context of national law, objectively and reasonably justified by a legitimate aim.[622] A legitimate aim may be a legitimate employment policy, labour-market objectives or the operational requirements of the undertaking, establishment or service and the means of achieving the aim in question have to be appropriate and necessary.[623] The ECSR concluded that the age limit was not based on objective grounds, as the Norwegian government had failed to submit sufficient evidence that the age limit served the recruitment of younger seamen to the seaman profession.[624] Furthermore, it could not be demonstrated that the referred to aims could

---

617 ibid., para. 85 referring to Conclusions 2012, General Introduction and para. 86.

618 ibid., para. 113 referring to International Commission of Jurists v. Portugal, Complaint No. 1/1998, decision on the merits of 9 September 1999, para. 32.

619 ibid., para. 113.

620 Rt. 2010 s. 202 (*Kystlink*).

621 *Fellesforbundet for Sjøfolk* (FFFS) v. Norway, para. 50.

622 ibid., para. 84 referring to Conclusions 2008, Lithuania.

623 ibid., para. 84 referring to Conclusions 2008, Lithuania.

624 ibid., para. 97.

have been achieved by less intrusive means.[625] The ECSR finally concluded that the age limit in question disproportionally affected the rights of the seamen within its scope of application and that no valid reasons, as stipulated by Art. 24, were required in the Seamen's Act for the termination of employment.[626] The ECSR held

> ...that the contested provision enables dismissal directly on grounds of age and does therefore not effectively guarantee the seamen's right to protection in cases of termination of employment. This is the situation irrespective of whether the seaman in question will be entitled to pension following the termination of his employment relationship.[627]

Ultimately, the ECSR also concluded on the same grounds that the difference in treatment constituted discrimination that was contrary to the right to non-discrimination in employment as guaranteed by Art. 1 (2).[628] The ECSR particularly stressed that elderly people cannot be excluded from the effective protection of the right to earn their living in an occupation that had been freely entered into.[629] In sum, the ECSR applied a stricter justification analysis than the *Høyesterett* did in the underlying *Kystlink* case.

9.7 Protection against age discrimination in human rights soft law

9.7.1 UN soft law mechanisms

The lacunae left by the open wording in Art. 2, 7 UDHR, Art. 2 No. 1, Art. 26 ICCPR and Art. 2 (2) ICESCR might be filled by looking at UN soft law. It may offer an important source for the recognition of the right to be protected against discrimination on the grounds of age as a universal right.

---

625 ibid., para. 97.
626 ibid., para. 97.
627 ibid., para. 99.
628 ibid., para. 117.
629 ibid., para. 115.

9.7.1.1 International Plan of Action on Ageing

A strong impact on the increased worldwide awareness of the situation of older people led to the first World Assembly on Ageing, which was held in the summer of 1982 in Vienna.[630] The Assembly adopted the so-called International Plan of Action on Ageing (the Vienna Plan).[631] It encompasses several recommendations to assist and protect older people. A major aim was to encourage the member states to consider the special needs of the elderly and to facilitate the participation of older people in society to the greatest possible extent, which explicitly included the employment sphere.[632] These recommendations envisage e.g., that measures should be taken or encouraged by the nation-states to guarantee a smooth and gradual transition from active employment to the phase of retirement.[633] Interestingly enough, the myth of ageing as a process of decline is explicitly addressed, as it is recommended that government policies should reject stereotypical concepts related to the capabilities and needs of older people, in particular the concept that advanced age equals incapacity.[634] It was stressed that the right of older employees to work should be based on their ability to perform the work in question rather than on their chronological age.[635]

9.7.1.2 UN Principles for Older Persons

In 1991, the UN Principles for Older Persons were adopted by the UN General Assembly.[636] The Preamble highlights that the enormous diversity in the life situations of older persons – which exits not only between countries, but also but within countries and between individuals as such – should be acknowledged and addressed through different policy mea-

---

630 see overview given at http://www.un.org/en/globalissues/ageing/ (last accessed: 17.12.2014).

631 The Vienna International Plan of Action on Aging was adopted by the World Assembly on Aging held in Vienna, Austria from 26 July to 6 August 1982, General Assembly Resolution A/RES/37/51, 6 August 1982.

632 Vienna Plan, Recommendation 37.

633 ibid., Recommendation 40.

634 ibid., Recommendation 37 (d).

635 ibid.

636 UN General Assembly, 16. December 1991, A/RES/46/91.

sures.[637] Remarkably, it is stressed that one should be 'aware of the scientific research disproving many stereotypes about inevitable and irreversible declines with age'.[638] Moreover, it is pointed out that worldwide life expectancy has increased and health conditions have improved.[639] It is therefore called for that older people, who are actively capable of participating and willing to participate in society, which includes the employment sphere, should be provided with the opportunities to do so.[640] Crucial in protecting older employees facing mandatory retirement from age-based discrimination are the principles of independence, participation, self-fulfilment and dignity.[641] As regards the principle of independence, particular emphasis is placed on three aspects that are crucial from the perspective of the older employee: first, older persons should be provided with the opportunity to work or to have access to alternative income-generating opportunities, second, older persons should be enabled to de facto participate in the decision-making process about when and at what pace withdrawal from the labour force should take place and third, this is finally supplemented by the objective that older persons should gain access to appropriate educational and training programmes.[642] The principle of independence thus clearly addresses what is essential in the achievement of substantive age equality for older employees and is central to the analysis of mandatory retirement. It aims first at providing the de facto opportunity to work. Second, it facilitates access to education and training, which is essential in terms of lifelong learning and strengthening the employee's workability. Finally, it enhances active participation by determining the conditions regarding the older employee's exit from the workforce. The essential role of active involvement and the social inclusion of older persons in society and the necessity that older persons share their expertise and skills with younger generations is referred to in the principle of participation.[643] Both principles strongly reflect the interrelationship between non-discrimination and the right to work. They clarify that this should be a question of employee participation and an expression of the

637 ibid., preamble.
638 ibid.
639 ibid.
640 ibid.
641 see in detail *Cotter* (2008), p. 52 f; *Rodriguez-Pinzon/Martin* (2003), p. 948.
642 UN Principles for Older Persons, principle of independence, no. 2 - 4.
643 ibid., principle of participation, see no. 7.

employee's choice to extend or not to extend his or her working life. Providing this opportunity constitutes the exact opposite to existing compulsory retirement provisions, which are often neither open to flexible transition to retirement nor to codetermination by the employee. Being able to pursue such opportunities contributes, as highlighted by the principle of self-fulfilment, to how older persons may fully develop their potential.[644] Moreover, what is central to this is that they get access to educational resources.[645] Finally, in respect of the principle of dignity, it is expressed that older persons should be treated fairly, irrespective of their age, gender, racial or ethnic background, disability or any other status, and that they should be valued independently of their respective economic contributions.[646]

9.7.1.3 Proclamation on Ageing

Moreover, elderly issues are addressed in the UN Proclamation on Ageing of 1992.[647] The proclamation urges the international community to make the immense human and material resources available in order to tackle humanity's coming of age.[648] It admonishes the states so that they will enhance the view of the elderly as being contributors to their societies rather than them being viewed as a burden, and posits that all generations should cooperate in creating a balance between traditions, on the one hand, and innovation on the other.[649] It reminds the international community, in particular, to give adequate support to older women for their

644 ibid., principle of self-fulfillment, no. 15.
645 ibid., no. 16.
646 ibid., principle of dignity, no. 18; Interestingly enough, the aspect of multiple discrimination is - albeit implicit – referred to in this formulation see to the aspect of multiple discrimination, chap. 10.2.2.3.
647 UN, Proclamation on Ageing, General Assembly, 16. October 1992, A/RES/47/5 (1992).
648 ibid, para. 1 (l); see also the preamble.
649 ibid., para. 2 (d), (f), (l).

'largely unrecognized contributions to the economy and the well-being of society'.[650] In recognising humanity's demographic coming of age, it declared the year of 1999 as the International Year of Older Persons.[651]

9.7.1.4 Madrid International Plan of Action on Ageing

Finally, in 2002, the UN Second World Assembly on Ageing was held, where a Political Declaration and the Madrid International Plan of Action on Ageing (the Madrid Plan) were developed and adopted.[652] The Madrid Plan was created to respond to the opportunities and challenges that come with population ageing as one of the 21st century's key challenges and to promote the development of a society for all ages.[653] The ageing population is even characterised as 'a universal force that has the power to shape the future as much as globalization'.[654] The Plan explicitly calls for recognising the contributions that older persons can make to society and for embracing the potential that rests in the ageing population as a fruitful basis for future development.[655] It particularly stresses the importance of promoting and protecting human rights and fundamental freedoms, including the right to development, and the necessity of implementing ageing in global agendas as being essential for the creation of an inclusive society for all ages.[656] One of the key aims is therefore to create a society where older persons may realise their potential and 'participate fully and without discrimination on the basis of equality'.[657] To ensure that older persons are treated with respect, it is fundamental to combat age-based discrimina-

650 ibid., para. 2 (d), (f), (l).

651 ibid., para 3.; The years unifying theme was 'Towards a society for all ages'. The four facets of the underlying conceptual framework included the situation of older people, life-long development of the individual, multigenerational relationships and development and the demograpic change, see http://www.un.org/ecosocdev/geninfo/ageing/ageing-e.htm. (last accessed: 17.12.2014).

652 UN International Plan of Action on Ageing (The Madrid Plan), 12. April 2002, see overview given at: http://undesadspd.org/Ageing/Resources/MadridInternationalPlanofActiononAgeing.aspx (last accessed: 17.12.2014).

653 Political Declaration to UN Second World Assembly on Ageing, Art. 1.

654 Madrid Plan, para. 15.

655 ibid., para. 15.

656 ibid., para. 13; Moreover, the Plan reaffirms the principles and recommendations set out in the UN principles for Older Persons, see Art. 3 Political Declaration.

657 Madrid Plan, para .13; Political Declaration Art. 2, 5.

tion and to promote the dignity of older persons, according to the Plan.[658] This may be achieved by nurturing and strengthening intergenerational solidarity through an equitable and reciprocal relationship between and among generations.[659] To realise these issues, the Plan gives an extensive list of recommendations that, in principle, reaffirm the UN Principles for Older Persons and even go beyond them.

The recommendations for action are organised according to three priority areas: first, older persons and development, second, advancing health and wellbeing into old age and finally, ensuring enabling and supportive environments.[660]

The Madrid Plan advocates flexible approaches for the transition from work to retirement and endorses that older employees are provided with the opportunity to extend their working career. Of vital importance in terms of older employees is the priority chapter about 'Older persons and development'.[661] It explicitly addresses the active participation of older persons in society and aims at recognising the social, cultural, economic and political contributions that older people may make.[662] An essential element in this regard constitutes the issue of work and the ageing workforce.[663] The key objective here is to provide employment opportunities for all older persons. Older employees who want to work should be enabled to continue income-generating work for as long as they wish to do so and for as long as they are able to perform the work productively.[664] Both the empowerment of older people and the promotion of their full participation are referred to as fundamental elements for active ageing.[665] Providing the opportunity to work thereby goes hand in hand with a further central objective as regards equality of opportunity throughout working life; namely, having access to knowledge, education and training.[666] This is supplemented by the objective of fully utilising the potential and expertise of persons of all ages and of recognising the benefits of

658 Madrid Plan, para .13.
659 ibid., para .13, see also para. 42 f., 44; Political Declaration, Art. 16.
660 see Madrid Plan, I. Introduction, para. 14; Art. 1 Political Declaration.
661 Madrid Plan, II. Recommendations for action, A. Priority direction I: Older persons and development, paras. 16ff.
662 ibid., para 16, 19ff., 21; Art. 5 Political Declaration.
663 Madrid Plan, paras. 23-27.
664 ibid., para. 23, 28; Political Declaration, Art. 12.
665 Political Declaration, Art. 12.
666 Madrid Plan, para. 35ff., 40ff.

increased experience with age and of maintaining an ageing workforce.[667] It is, in particular, stressed that a favourable attitude among employers concerning the productive capacity of older employees should be promoted as being conducive to their continued employment, and that awareness of their worth in the labour market, which encompasses the employee's self-awareness, should be facilitated.[668] The Madrid Plan further emphasises that a realistic portrait of the skills and abilities of older workers should be promoted, so that any damaging stereotypes about older employees or job candidates might be corrected.[669] In this regard, the Political Declaration stresses that if ageing is embraced as an achievement and if the potential of older persons were acknowledged, relying on the human skills, experiences and resources of older people would be naturally recognised in a positive light as an asset in the growth of mature, fully integrated human societies.[670] It is furthermore stressed that policies to extend older workers' employability, such as flexible work and retirement arrangements, and adaptive working environments, such as vocational rehabilitation for older persons with disabilities, are essential to address potential labour shortages that may result from demographic transformation.[671] Older workers should be encouraged to willingly defer full retirement and continue to be employed, whether in the form of part-time or full-time employment.[672] The specific needs of older employees should be accounted for in human resource practices and policies to facilitate retention and the productive fulfilment of older employees in the workforce.[673] This entails appropriate adjustments to the workplace environment and working conditions, where needed, to maintain older workers' work ability and to ensure that older employees de facto possess the relevant skills, health and capacity to remain in employment also in their later years.[674] By promoting the recruitment of older persons and preventing the occurrence of disadvantages experienced by older workers, age barriers in the formal labour market should be eliminated and disincentives to work

667 ibid., para. 23, 41.
668 ibid., para. 21 (i); see also para. 112, where the need to foster a positive image of ageing is emphasised.
669 ibid., para. 28 (m), see in this regard also explicitly para. 113.
670 Political Declaration, Art. 6, Art. 10.
671 Madrid Plan, para. 24, 28 (c).
672 ibid., para. 27.
673 ibid., para. 27.
674 ibid., para. 27, 28 (c), (k).

beyond pension age should be removed.[675] In doing so, the application of the 'principle of flexible retirement policies and practices'[676] plays a key role, while at the same time, already acquired pension rights should be maintained.[677] In the application of such flexible solutions, both the needs of the employee as well as the employer should be accounted for.[678] Such a flexible approach runs contrary to the practice of using mandatory retirement age limits and forcing older employees to exit the workforce. In short, in the Madrid Plan, the UN once more calls into question the still-prevailing practices of using mandatory retirement. The aspects that have been pointed out in the Plan should also be kept in mind in the assessment of compulsory retirement on the national level. Besides this, it is noteworthy that particular emphasis is also placed on gender equality and the vulnerable situation of older women in working life, who often, as they age, face difficulties and are confronted with misleading and negative stereotypes.[679] Moreover, the potential interrelationship of old age and disability is addressed.[680]

9.7.2 ILO soft law mechanisms

When it comes to protection against age discrimination, the Older workers recommendation (OWR) may be regarded as the most relevant ILO instrument.[681] Even if the OWR 'merely' constitutes soft law, it may nonetheless function as an instrument to close the gap that exists with regard to the lack of explicit codification of the protection against discrimination on the grounds of age in the above-mentioned ILO Conventions.[682] Detailed policy recommendations are provided that in turn may have an impact on

---

675 ibid., para. 28 (g), (h).

676 ibid., para. 28 (g).

677 ibid., para. 28 (g), (h), (j).

678 ibid., para. 28 (h), see also lit. (l) and (n).

679 see e.g. Madrid Plan, para. 8, 12 (f), 22 (c), 25, 28 (d), 40. (d), 112; Political Declaration, Art. 5, Art. 8.

680 Madrid Plan, para. 87 also in this regard the vulnerable situation of older women is stressed.

681 similar *Ghosheh* (2008), p. 14.

682 see to the soft law status also: *Meenan*, Helen (2005), The future of ageing and the role of age discrimination in the global debate, The Journal of International Aging, Law & Policy, Vol. I, 2005, p. 10; *Polloczek* (2008), p. 44.

the development of national policies and legislation.[683] The desire to close the gap in the protection against age discrimination becomes especially apparent with regard to the Preamble of the OWR, which stresses that in view of the lack of protection in the existing legal instruments, there is a need to supplement these 'with standards on equality of opportunity and treatment for older workers, on their protection in employment and on preparation for and access to retirement'.[684]

The OWR stipulates that the employment problems of older workers should be dealt with in view of a contextualised and well-balanced strategy for full employment, where employment problems are not shifted from one population group to another.[685] It is further noteworthy that it calls on member states to promote equality of opportunity and treatment for workers of all ages and to take measures to prevent the discrimination of older workers in employment and occupation.[686] In addition, the OWR requires that older workers should enjoy equality of opportunity and treatment irrespective of their age and thus without age discrimination in several aspects of working life, such as getting access to employment of their choice by taking into account the personal skills, experience and qualifications of the worker in question.[687] Moreover, the OWR calls for measures aimed at the improvement of working conditions and environments at all stages of the working cycle, which also encompasses special measures 'to enable older workers to continue in employment under satisfactory conditions'.[688] Such measures might for example include adapting a job and its content to workers,[689] a gradual reduction in working time for older employees who request it,[690] measures to ensure that the decision to retire is voluntary[691] and finally, making the age for qualifying for retirement flexible.[692] It is remarkable that the OWR clearly refrains from suggesting that older workers should terminate working life in line with existing regimes on compulsory retirement, but instead stresses the importance of

---

683 *Ghosheh* (2008), p. 14.
684 OWR, preamble.
685 ibid., para 2.
686 ibid., para. 3.
687 ibid., para. 5 (b).
688 ibid., para. 11.
689 ibid., para. 13 (c).
690 ibid., para. 14 (b).
691 ibid., para. 21 (a).
692 bid., para. 21 (b).

addressing issues such as age discrimination, which might affect the workers' ability to work and to prolong their working career.[693] In particular, paragraph 5 (b) (i) expresses one of the key aims; namely, to ensure a smooth transition to retirement based on the employee's voluntary decision to terminate his working career.[694] Age limits concerning access to employment may only be set in exceptional cases based on special requirements related to certain types of employment.[695] In chap. IV, the OWR finally lays down the requirements that should be fulfilled regarding the process of 'Preparation for and Access to Retirement'.[696] It opens up in particular for the extension of working life, as it stipulates that older workers who are fit for work should be able to postpone retirement beyond the normal pension age.[697]

9.7.3 Council of Europe soft law mechanisms

On several occasions, the Parliamentary Assembly of the Council of Europe has directly addressed issues related to the challenges of ageing populations, demographic change in general and as regards age discrimination against older employees in particular.

The Parliamentary Assembly of the Council of Europe stressed in its Resolution 1793 (2011) on *Promoting active ageing – capitalising on older people's working potential* that even if age discrimination might often be unconscious, it ultimately 'undermines older people's dignity, their human rights and self-esteem and is a huge waste of talent'. The Assembly considers ageism as a harmful prejudice that leads to widespread lack of respect for the elderly such as for example in the workplace, where older employees are subject to unequal treatment.[698] In addition, the Assembly particularly notes

---

693 similar *Ghosheh* (2008), p. 14.

694 OWR, para. 5 (b) (i).

695 ibid.

696 see for further details OWR, chap. IV paras. 20-30.

697 OWR., para. 29; OWR, para. 30 stresses the need to establish retirement preparation programmes to prepare the workers for the transition to retirement.

698 Resolution 1793 (2011), para. 1.

> ... that many working-age individuals, who could work and actively contribute to society, are either unemployed or 'inactive', in particular in the 50 plus age group. Globalisation and increased competition are having an impact on the work environment and on the quality of work available to older workers, who also face a number of obstacles to remaining in or re-entering the employment market.[699]

As regards age discrimination, the Parliamentary Assembly explicitly encouraged the Council of Europe member states to give consideration, as appropriate, first to adopting legislation to prohibit age discrimination, removing barriers to the labour market and empowering older persons 'to enter, remain in or return to the labour market, in accordance with their capabilities and willingness to work'[700] and second, to implementing programmes that aim at redirecting 'both employees' and employers' attitudes towards a more positive assessment of active ageing and facilitating an efficient information and process among employer organisations and trade unions, with regard to employment initiatives for an ageing workforce'.[701] In view of flexible work arrangements, the Parliamentary Assembly moreover encouraged the member states to promote policies aiming at improving the quality of flexible work arrangements for older employees that enable them to move to less demanding jobs and opt for a restructuring of their work through 'part-time work, teamwork, job-sharing, task rotation and redefinition of tasks between team members'.[702] Moreover, these flexible work arrangements should include the facilitation of phased retirement.[703] In terms of training, reskilling and lifelong learning, the Assembly for example. invokes the adoption of a life course approach and the need to take preventive measures aiming at enhancing the employability of employees as they age.[704]

Also in Recommendation 1796 (2007) entitled *The situation of elderly persons in Europe,* the Parliamentary Assembly inter alia acknowledged that a person's age can no longer be viewed as an indicator of health. In

699 ibid., para. 3.

700 ibid., paras. 6.1, 6.1.1.

701 ibid., paras. 6.1, 6.1.2.

702 ibid., paras. 6.3, 6.3.1

703 ibid., paras. 6.3, 6.3.2 and 6.3.3. see for a discussion of flexible work arrangements as *de lege ferenda* options chap. 16.

704 ibid., paras. 6.4., 6.4.1, see also paras. 6.4.2 and. 6.4.3.

view of this, it states that, 'there is a pressing need to change approaches and stereotypes related to ageing and to adjust policies accordingly, notably with regard to the compulsory retirement age'.[705]

Having said this, the Assembly also explicitly refers in this context to one of the UN Madrid Plan conclusions on giving older persons the opportunity to stay in satisfying and productive employment for as long as they wish to do so and are capable of doing so.[706] The Assembly ascertains that older people are still too often subject to discrimination in the employment sphere.[707]

Ultimately, already in Resolution 1502 (2006) on *Demographic challenges for social cohesion,* the Parliamentary Assembly reminded the Council of Europe member states to

> … promote active ageing by giving those who are still in good health, and who express a willingness to do so, the chance to work longer, and by giving more attention to the number of years worked, rather than age on entering retirement, in other words, more flexibility.[708]

9.8 Intermediate conclusion

Of the analysed key human rights treaties, two types of provisions on non-discrimination could be identified: first, those which are non-accessory or autonomous prohibitions[709] and second, accessory prohibitions.[710] Some of the provisions are closed; others are open-ended.[711] In the majority of the analysed open-ended provisions, it has been recognised that age falls under the notion of 'other status'. With the exception of ESC and RESC, the analysed instruments do have a 'universal' scope of application, as they are formulated explicitly to protect 'everyone', which also includes

705 Recommendation 1796 (2007), para. 4.

706 ibid., para. 5; see already to the UN Madrid Plan chap. 9.7.1.4. above.

707 Recommendation 1796 (2007), para. 6.

708 Resolution 1502 (2006) Demographic challenges for social cohesion, para. 8.3.3.

709 Art. 26 ICCPR; Art. 1 ILO Convention No. 111.

710 Art. 2 UDHR; Art. 2 Nr. 1 and Art. 3 ICCPR, Art. 2 Nr. 2 ICESCR; Art. 14 ECHR; Art. E RESC.

711 closed list of discrimination grounds: Art. 1 (a) ILO Convention No. 111; non-exhaustive list: Art. 2 UDHR, Art. 2 (1), 26 ICCPR, Art. 2 (2) ICESCR, Art. 14 ECHR, Art. E RESC.

every employee, irrespective of his/her chronological age.[712] Besides this, one might argue that age equality, in principle, is also part of the general principle of equality as for example manifested in Art. 7 UDHR. The examined hard law provisions on non-discrimination may thus at least constitute 'a helpful tool'[713] together with the analysed soft law instruments in the fight for age equality.[714] This is even truer if these non-discrimination provisions may be read in conjunction with the right to work and free choice of employment, as both universal rights are essential for the full realisation of age equality for older employees.

However, when it comes to the legal enforceability of the analysed provisions, it has to be kept in mind that an employee might only make use of these provisions if they are directly applicable (self-executing).[715] In principle, two questions have to be addressed in this regard: first, whether the provision in question is justiciable at all and second, whether it is directly applicable in national law. If the state is obliged by human rights law to guarantee the protection of individuals against age discrimination, this in turn leads to the question as to whether the protection should also be applicable in horizontal relations between private parties. In case the provision in question has to be interpreted as also establishing subjective rights for individuals, an individual might rely directly on the prohibition against age discrimination in a legal dispute.[716] As age discrimination may not only appear in employment relations with a public employer, but also with regard to private employers, furthermore, the question has to be addressed as to whether private parties are also bound by the prohibition against age discrimination as manifested in human rights law, the so-called third-party applicability or horizontal effect.[717] Both the self-executing nature and

---

712 similar *Chen* (1987), p. 171, 172.

713 *Cotter* (2008), p. 39, who argues that Art. 2 UDHR constitutes a 'helpful tool' in fighting for age equality.

714 *Lee* e.g. points out that to fill in the gaps left by Art. 2 UDHR the Vienna International Plan of Action on Aging functions as an authoritative interpretation, which establishes aging as a human rights concern even from a positivistic angle, see *Lee* (1987), p. 167.

715 see *Polloczek* (2008), p. 39.

716 see in detail *Polloczek* (2008), p. 40, 41.

717 see in detail to the terminological distinction between horizontal effect and third-party applicability: *Nowak*, Manfred (2005), CCPR Commentary, Article 2, para. 20: 'The term "horizontal effects" ("*Horizontalwirkung*") is to be understood in the broad sense of effects that human rights produce on the horizontal level

third-party applicability of the examined prohibitions against discrimination in human rights law have been subject to debate.[718] However, the answer to the questions related to this aspect requires a thorough analysis that is not part of this thesis.

As pointed out by *Chen*, the fact that the analysed human rights instruments are silent on the question of compulsory retirement based on having reached a certain chronological age does not imply that such practices per se are justified.[719] On the contrary, the fact that the prohibition against age discrimination may be subsumed in the various non-discrimination clauses, together with the analysed soft law, leads to the conclusion that mandatory retirement should in fact be outlawed.[720] Moreover, denying a person the exercise of the right to work due to mandatory retirement affects human dignity. *Chen* put this in a nutshell by stating, 'To deny or restrict a person's opportunity to work and to participate in other value processes, purely on the basis of an arbitrary chronological age limit, is not compatible with the overriding policy of human dignity'.[721]

The lack of an explicit protection against age discrimination might be 'cured' by the analysed soft law instruments. Despite their soft law status, these instruments such as for example the UN Madrid Plan or the OWR illustrate par excellence what has to be done by the member states to 'take age equality seriously' to achieve substantive age equality: older employees shall, without being discriminated against on the grounds of their age,

---

between private parties, i.e. not on the vertical level between the individual and the State. In contrast to the term third-party effects" ("*Drittwirkung*") […] horizontal effects are thus not limited to the repercussions that basic rights have on the structuring of relationships under private law; rather they compromise the obligation of State parties to take additional measures …[…] for the protection of human rights against interference by private parties.'

718 arguing for a self-executing nature of the prohibition against discrimination as manifested in e.g. Art. 2 (2) and Art. 3 ICESCR and the ILO conventions e.g. *Rudolf*, Beate (2007), § 2, in: Gleichbehandlungsrecht, Rudolf, Beate/Mahlmann, Matthias (eds.), para. 38, p. 71 w.f.r; see to the critics of the self-executing nature of the ESC e.g. overview given by *Polloczek* (2008), p. 55; see also *Nowak* (2005), Art. 26 CCPR, paras. 57-59; see as regards Protocol No. 12: *Rudolf* (2007), § 2, paras. 32-35, p. 70 f. w.f.r.; see also *Polloczek* (2008), p. 54; and in detail *Mowbray* (2004), Article 14, p. 622, paras. 24-28; *De Schutter* (2005), p. 25.

719 *Chen* (1987), p. 171 f.

720 ibid.

721 *Chen* (1987), p. 170.

enjoy equality of opportunity and treatment in working life. Flexible approaches should be preferred to absolute age limits to enable the older worker to have a smooth transition towards retirement.[722] Older employees should get the opportunity to exercise their right to work without being discriminated against on the grounds of age. It remains to be seen whether the analysed soft law mechanisms may in this regard function as an effective tool in the fight for age equality and, in the long run, pave the way to effective and comprehensive protection against age discrimination. *De lege lata*, one might conclude that the UN via the soft law mechanisms should at least send a clear signal that they want to strengthen legal protection around the rights of older employees to realise the 'vision of equality for persons of all ages'.[723] This may, in the end, also lead to a spillover effect with regard to the explicit implementation of protection against age discrimination in hard law. As stressed by *Kofi Annan* in his foreword to the Madrid Plan, the real test will be the implementation of the Plan and in recognising the urgent need to take the issue of an ageing population and the demographic transformation as one of the central challenges of the 21st century seriously.[724]

9.9 De lege ferenda: The need for their 'own' human rights instrument

Soft law might be regarded as a catalyst in strengthening protection against age discrimination and towards substantive protection *de lege ferenda* of the rights of the elderly, in particular of older employees. However, the examined soft law instruments have been criticised for failing to demand the development of a specific instrument that would offer the elderly sufficient protection as one of the fastest growing and most vulnerable groups in society.[725] As it is not legally enforceable, the OWR's practical impact for example has been criticised as being too weak to increase

722 see to this aspect *de lege ferenda* considerations in chap. 16.

723 Art. 19 Political Declaration.

724 *Annan*. Kofi A., Foreword to UN Madrid Plan and the Political Declaration, 2002. It has to be noted that the primary responsibility for providing leadership on ageing matters and on the implementation of the Madrid Plan rests upon the national governments, see Madrid Plan, para. 116; Art. 17 Political Declaration.

725 *Rodriguez-Pinzon/Martin* (2003), p. 950; similar *Mégret*, Frédéric (2011), The human rights of older persons: A growing challenge, Human Rights Law Review 11:1 (2011), pp. 37-66, p. 48, 49; *Lee* (1987), p. 168.

age equality and to contribute significantly to the de facto protection of older workers.[726] Some claim, therefore, that more has to be done inside as well as outside the sphere of the UN to sufficiently combat age discrimination.[727] In general, it has to be ascertained that there is a need for raising awareness and providing more information about the situation of older people in order to increase their active participation in society and to achieve age equality. Some argue that this may also encompass coordination of the several existing international treaties which cover all forms of discrimination 'in order to give the older generation the ultimate respect it deserves'.[728] In contrast to other vulnerable groups such as women, which have already been subject to specific human rights treaties, no such instrument of human rights law exists that is tailored specifically to the particular needs of the older population.[729]

Discrimination against children might be an important point of reference in the analysis of the rights of the elderly as a vulnerable group, as so far this is the only group defined on the basis of age.[730]

726 *Heemskerk* (2009), p. 23; some authors therefore deny deriving a prohibition against age discrimination from the OWR, see *Polloczek* (2008), p. 44.

727 *Cotter* (2008), p. 76.

728 ibid.

729 *Rodriguez-Pinzon/Martin* (2003), p. 946; see also *Doron*, Israel (2005), From national to international elder law, The Journal of International Aging, Law & policy, 2005, Vol. I, pp. 43-67, p. 58; see in this regard also CESCR, General comment No. 6, 1995, para. 13.

730 *Rodriguez-Pinzon/Martin* (2003), p. 946.

Therefore, several authors call for a treaty that is designed specifically for this group.[731] It is necessary to identify older persons clearly, including older employees as a disadvantaged group that requires more substantive protection. The major lacuna in human rights law caused by the absence of a specific charter of rights for the older population has been criticised as being, in part, an expression of inactivity and the lack of awareness for international action to promote the rights of the elderly.[732] Even if the examined UN soft law instruments rang the bell, there is still a decisive step missing towards a charter that bears obligatory legal validity. Besides its obligatory legal status as hard law, such a document would also be of great educational, symbolic and political value and would finally put the rights, interests and needs of the elderly on the worldwide agenda.[733]

---

731 see e.g. the debate concerning the establishment of so called 'elder law', which is a reaction to the lack of an explicit human rights framework for the elderly, see in this regard extensively *Mégret* Frédéric (2011), The human rights of older persons: A growing challenge, Human Rights Law Review. 11:1, 2011, pp. 37-66; *Van Bueren*, Geraldine (2009), The protection of the human rights of older persons in Europe: A legal perspective; see also *Doron* (2005); in favor of the creation of a transnational human rights agreement for older people: *Tang*, Kwong-Leung/*Lee*, Jik-Joen (2006), Global social justice for older people: The case for an international convention on the rights of older people, British Journal of Social Work, Vol. 36, pp. 1135–1150, in particular p. 1143 f.; supporting an international convention also: UN Expert Group (2009), Report of the expert group meeting, "Rights of older persons", pp. 18-20; The Advisory Committee of the UN Human Rights Council delivered in 2010 a working document – the so-called *Chung*-report named after the rapporteur *Chinsung Chung*–- that defended according to its title 'The necessity of a human rights approach and effective United Nations mechanism for the human rights of the older person', see Working Paper, A/HRC/AC/4/CRP; *Meenan*, Helen (2009), Reflecting on age discrimination in the European Union – the search for clarity and food for thought, ERA Forum (2009) 10, pp. 107-124, p. 109; see also for a critical review of the ongoing debate: *Doron*, Israel/*Apter*, Itai (2010), The debate around the need for an international convention on the rights of older persons, The Gerontologist Vol. 50 Issue 4, 2010, pp. 586-593, see for an overview of counterarguments p. 589ff. and finally advocating a international convention for the rights of older persons, in particular p. 592; already in 2002 *Butler* proposed on behalf of the International Longevity Center – USA a "Declaration of the Rights of Older Persons", see *Butler*, Robert N. (2002), Declaration of the rights of older persons, The Gerontologist 2002 vol. 42 Issue 2, pp. 152-153.

732 *Doron* (2005), p. 67.

733 ibid.

Given the challenges resulting from demographic change, there is reason for hope that *de lege ferenda* the necessity for such a specific human rights instrument for the elderly is acknowledged.[734]

10 Prohibition against age discrimination in EU primary and secondary law

10.1 EU primary law

The prohibition against age discrimination is an explicit part of both EU primary and secondary law. It was acknowledged as a general principle of EU law for the first time in the famous and highly debated *Mangold* judgement, where the CJEU stated: 'The principle of non-discrimination on grounds of age must thus be regarded as a general principle of Community law'.[735]

With its emphasis on strengthening the protection against age discrimination by declaring it a general principle of EU law, one might even describe *Mangold* as the *kopernikanische Wende*[736] in age discrimination law.[737] Fundamental to the process of the strengthening has been the enactment of the Lisbon Treaty, which led, with the enactment of the CFREU on 1 December 2009, to the principle's explicit manifestation in EU primary law. It is now laid down in Art. 6 No. 1 TEU in conjunction with Art. 21 No. 1 CFREU.[738]

---

734 similar already *Chen* (1987), p. 170.

735 C-144/04 (*Mangold)*, para. 75; see to an extensive and thorough analysis of the Mangold judgement *Temming* (2008), pp. 375ff.

736 This as been discussed by *Streinz*, Rudolf/*Herrmann,* Christoph (2007), Der Fall Mangold - eine "kopernikanische Wende im Europarecht"?, RdA 2007, pp. 165-169.

737 The judgement has been subject to a multitude of analyses in literature, see among others the extensive analysis by *Evju* (2006), pp. 137ff; *Temming* (2008), pp. 375ff.; *O'Cinneide*, Colm/*Tobler*, Christina (2012), The Evolution and Impact of the case-law of the Court of Justice of the European Union on Directives 2000/43/EC and 2000/78/EC, pp. 15ff.

738 see to the general principle of equality Art. 20 CFREU.

In general, on the level of EU primary law, the principles of non-discrimination and equality have been either explicitly or implicitly manifested. Besides the CFREU, several articles of both the TEU and the TFEU make references in this regard.[739] This is for example already emphasised in Art. 2 TEU, which states:

> The Union is founded on the values of respect for human dignity, freedom, democracy, equality, the rule of law and respect for human rights, including the rights of persons belonging to minorities. These values are common to the Member States in a society in which pluralism, non-discrimination, tolerance, justice, solidarity and equality between women and men prevail.[740]

Ultimately, the TEU refers in its Art. 3 No. 3 TEU to the 'European social market economy'. One of the EU's central aims as laid down in Art. 3 Nr. 3 TEU and supplemented in the TFEU's employment chapter in articles 145–150 is a highly competitive social market economy that aims at full employment and social progress. In doing so, one of the EU's central aims is to combat social exclusion and discrimination and promote social justice and protection, equality between women and men and solidarity between generations.

The crucial role of both the *Mangold* decision as well as the Lisbon Treaty has been emphasised by the CJEU in *Kücükdeveci*, where the Court again specifically acknowledged the existence of a principle of non-discrimination on the grounds of age, which must be regarded as a general principle of EU law.[741] Moreover, the Court pointed out in *Kücükdeveci* that it also has to be noted that Art. 6 No. 1 TEU provides that the CFREU is to have the same legal value as the Treaties and that under Art. 21 Nr. 1 of the Charter any discrimination based on age shall be prohibited.[742]

One might argue that with the coming into force of the Lisbon Treaty and the enactment of the CFREU, a process of constitutionalisation has been taking place in the EU. This might thus also lead to a constitutional underpinning of the idea of age equality and might thus impact the inter-

---

739 see for an overview *Numhauser-Henning*, Ann (2011), Var står diskrimineringsretten i dag?, in: Festkrift till Boel Flodgren/Lindell-Frantz, Eva/Moberg, Krister/Nyström, Birgitta/Olsson, Katarina (eds.), pp. 289-307, pp. 292-297.

740 It is moreover also explicitly referred to equality in the preamble to the TEU.

741 C-555/07 (*Kücükdeveci*), Judgement of the Court of 19 January 2010, ECR 2010, I-365, para. 21, 22 referring to C-144/04 (*Mangold*), para. 75 and C-43/75 (*Defrenne*), Judgement of 8 April 1976, ECR 1976, 455, para. 54.

742 C-555/07 (*Kücükdeveci*), para. 22.

pretation of the prohibition against age discrimination as concretised in Dir. 2000/78/EC. At least the approach to EU equality law has increasingly become a rights-based approach.[743] Moreover, what is important in this context is the intended EU accession to the ECHR. The EU shall, due to Art. 6 No. 2 TEU, accede to the ECHR. According to Art. 6 No. 3 TEU inter alia the fundamental rights, as guaranteed by the ECHR, shall constitute general principles of the EU law. The key question is whether the accession to the ECHR has any considerable impact on the interpretation of the prohibition against age discrimination.[744] *De lege lata* one may ascertain that the level of protection provided for by EU law is higher than the level currently provided by Art. 14 ECHR and Art. 1 of the Additional Protocol No. 12.[745] As long as this remains the case, the accession to the ECHR will probably have no considerable impact on the prohibition against age discrimination in EU law. In any case, the high level of protection applicable in the EU shall, according to Art. 53, remain unaffected.

Furthermore, what needs to be considered is the prohibition's relationship to other CFREU rights. What is essential in the context of mandatory retirement is, in particular, the right to work as manifested in Art. 15 CFREU and the right of social partners to collective bargaining, as guaranteed in Art. 28 CFREU.

Art. 15 lays down the 'Freedom to choose an occupation and right to engage in work'. According to Art. 15 No. 1 CFREU, 'Everyone has the right to engage in work and to pursue a freely chosen or accepted occupation,' and pursuant to Art. 15 No. 2, every EU citizen 'has the freedom to seek employment, to work, to exercise the right of establishment and to provide services in any Member State'. Art. 28 CFREU inter lia states that 'Workers and employers, or their respective organisations, have, in accordance with Community law and national laws and practices, the right to negotiate and conclude collective agreements at the appropriate levels'. In a discussion on the rights of older employees, one might also examine Art. 25 CFREU, according to which the EU 'recognises and respects the rights of the elderly to lead a life of dignity and independence and to participate in social and cultural life'. However, 'work life' is not explicitly mentioned in Art. 25 CFREU.

---

743 see to this aspect in detail *Meenan* (2009), p. 109; arguing for a fundamental rights based approach also already *Temming* (2008), pp. 419 in view of the *Mangold* judgement.

744 *Obwexer*, Walter (2012), Auswirkungen des Beitritts der EU zur EMRK auf das Verbot der Altersdiskriminierung, in: Altersdiskriminierung, Wachter, Gustav (ed.), pp. 13-28, p. 15; similar also *Hanau*, Peter (2010), Die Europäische Grundrechtscharta - Schein und Wirklichkeit im Arbeitsrecht, NZA 2010, pp. 1-6, p. 6; see for an analysis of the ECHR already chap. 9.6.1. above.

745 see analysis by *Obwexer* (2012), p. 28

What also has be considered in this regard is the aspect of human dignity, which is generally protected via Art. 1 CFREU. The right to collective bargaining comes particularly into play in cases where the mandatory retirement provision is manifested in a collective agreement and is thus the result of collective bargaining. Here, the interests of the social partners in their right to manifest for example age limits via collective bargaining procedures, have to weighed against the employee's interests not be discriminated against on the grounds of age and to exercise his right to work. A classic example of these competing interests is to be found in compulsory retirement provisions for pilots that are typically laid down in collective agreements, as further assessed in chap. 15.

To conclude *de lege lata*, the CFREU gives more impetus to the assertion of the prohibition of age discrimination in secondary law and ultimately contributes, together with Dir. 2000/78/EC, to a strengthening of the protection against age discrimination.[746] It finally has to be kept in mind that the realisation of the Charter's basic rights functions through the medium of EU secondary law. In terms of the realisation of the prohibition against age discrimination, Dir. 2000/78/EC thus is essential, as it concretises the prohibition in EU primary law or, as the CJEU made it clear in *Kücükdeveci*, 'Directive 2000/78 gives specific expression to that principle'.[747]

10.2 Secondary law: Prohibition against age discrimination in Dir. 2000/78/EC

The adoption of the Amsterdam Treaty in 1997 led to the manifestion of Art. 13 TEC, which authorised the European Community to take measures against discrimination on the grounds of 'sex, racial or ethnic origin, religion or belief, disability, age or sexual orientation'. With the coming into force of Council Directive 2000/78/EC the prohibition against age discrimination became an explicit part of EU secondary law. As clearly set out already in its Art. 1, the Directive aims at laying down a general framework to combat discrimination on the grounds of religion or belief,

---

746 similar *Hanau* (2010), p. 3.

747 C-555/07 (*Kücükdeveci*), para. 21; see also C-476/11 (*Kristensen*), Judgement of the Court of 26 September 2013, ECR 00000, I-00000, para. 19 and 32, 37; see to the aspect of concretisation also *Obwexer* (2012), p. 14, *Schlachter* (2014), p. 18.

disability, age or sexual orientation as regards employment and occupation, with a view to implementing the principle of equal treatment in the member states.

10.2.1 Material and personal scope of Dir. 2000/78/EC

The material scope of Dir. 2000/78/EC is manifested in Art. 3, which sets out the Directive's *rationae materiae* and specifies the areas identified in its Art. 1.[748] As regards its personal and material scope, it is basically applicable to all persons, as regards both the public and private sectors, including public bodies, inter alia in relation to:

> (a) conditions for access to employment, to self-employment or to occupation, including selection criteria and recruitment conditions, whatever the branch of activity and at all levels of the professional hierarchy, including promotion [749]

as well as

> (c) employment and working conditions, including dismissals and pay[750]
> Member states may, according to Art. 3 No. 4. provide that the Directive, in so far as it relates to discrimination on the grounds of disability and age, shall not be applicable to the armed forces.[751]
> In general, the Directive aims at protecting workers of all ages and does not focus primarily on older workers.[752]

---

748 COM(1999) 565 final, Proposal for a Council Directive(2000/C 177 E/07) establishing a general framework for equal treatment in employment and occupation, OJ C 177 E/42, p. 9.

749 Art. 3 No. 1 (a).

750 Art. 3 No. 1 (c).

751 see to this exception in detail *Lüderitz* (2005), p. 55.

752 see recital 8, 11, 12 and 25 such as Art. 6 No. 1 s. 2 (a) and (b) Dir. 2000/78/EC. agreeing: *Kummer*, Pierre (2003), Umsetzungsanforderungen der neuen arbeitsrechtlichen Antidiskriminierungsrichtlinie (RL 2000/78/EG), p. 68; *Linsenmaier*, Wolfgang (2003), Das Verbot der Diskriminierung wegen des Alters, RDA 2003, Sonderbeilage Heft 5, pp. 22-33, p. 22, 25; *Schlachter*, Monika (2003), Altersgrenzen angesichts des gemeinschaftsrechtlichen Verbots der Altersdiskriminierung, in: Altersgrenzen und Alterssicherung im Arbeitsrecht, Gedenkschrift für Wolfgang Blomeyer. Rheinhard Richardi, and Hermann Reichold (eds.), pp. 355 373, p. 357; after an extensive analysis also agreeing *Senne* (2006), p. 139ff., in particular p. 142; agreeing also *Polloczek* (2008), p. 88. It has also been stressed both in literature and by the CJEU that Art. 2 Dir. 2000/78/EC prohibits due to a

The Directive's open approach is in stark contrast to the prohibition against age discrimination as manifested in the US ADEA with its limited scope of protection that merely only covers employees above the age of 40.[753]

Encompassed by the notion of age is, moreover, not only chronological age that is for example. used in provisions on mandatory retirement, but also age discrimination that occurs without directly using age as a proxy, for example in cases of so-called indirect age discrimination or age-based harassment.[754]

Compared to other anti-discrimination directives that are also based on Art. 13 EC such as for example the Anti-racism Directive[755], the material scope of Dir. 2000/78/EC is rather limited. It merely covers employment and occupation, while for example the Anti-racism Directive covers, in addition to employment and occupation, social protection – including social security and healthcare – social advantages, education and finally, access to and the supply of goods and services that are available to the public, including housing.[756] In this context, it is important to notice the European Commission's proposal for a new directive based on Art. 13 EC, which will extend the scope of the prohibition against age discrimination covering areas outside the labour market by complementing the existing legal framework of the EC and by establishing 'a uniform minimum level of protection within the European Union'.[757] The new Directive will be applicable outside the labour market in the areas of 'social protection,

broad understanding differences based on absolute such as on relative age, see to this aspect AG *Sharpston*, in: C-427/06 (*Bartsch*), para. 96ff, 103ff. and in detail *Groß* 2010), p. 36 f.

753 critical to the ADEA's limited scope inter alia: *Woodruff*, Bryan B. (1997-1998), Unprotected until forty: The limited scope of the Age Dsicrimination in Employment Act of 1967, Indiana Law Journal Vol. 73, 1997-1998, pp. 1295-1312; critical to upper age limits in the application of age discrimination laws also *Fredman* (2003), p. 24.

754 see *Meenan* (2007 a), p. 279, 283, 302.

755 Council Directive 2000/43/EC of 29 June 2000 implementing the principle of equal treatment between persons irrespective of racial or ethnic origin.

756 Art. 3 No. 1 (e)-(h) Council Directive 2000/43/EC of 29 June 2000 implementing the principle of equal treatment between persons irrespective of racial or ethnic origin, OJ L 180.

757 COM(2008) 426 final, Proposal for a Council Directive on implementing the principle of equal treatment between persons irrespective of religion or belief, disability, age or sexual orientation, 2008/0140 (CNS), p. 1.

including social security and healthcare; social advantages; education; access to and supply of goods and services which are available to the public, including housing'.[758]

Under reference to the Employment Guidelines for 2000 agreed by the European Council in 1999, the Dir. 2000/78/EC inter alia reiterates that particular emphasis has to be placed on the need to pay special attention to supporting older employees in order to increase their participation in the labour force.[759] It is, moreover, clearly stressed that discrimination based on age may undermine the achievement of the objectives of the EC Treaty, among others, the attainment of a high level of employment.[760] To maintain these objectives, any direct or indirect discrimination on the grounds of age as regards the areas of employment and occupation should be prohibited throughout the Community as explicitly stated in the Directive's foreword.[761] In particular, recital 9 is noteworthy, which succinctly emphasises that, 'Employment and occupation are key elements in guaranteeing equal opportunities for all and contribute strongly to the full participation of citizens in economic, cultural and social life and to realising their potential'.[762]

It has to be kept in mind that the prohibition against age discrimination, as manifested in EU law, in principle does not claim the achievement of substantive equality.[763] By critically examining the legitimacy of unequal treatment on the grounds of age in light of its justification provisions, it generally aims at achieving formal equality and not equality of results.[764]

758 COM(2008) 426 final, p. 14, 18, 19 (proposal for recital 9 and proposal for Art. 3 (1)).
759 recital 8 Dir. 2000/78/EC referring to Employment Guidelines for 2000 agreed by the European Council at Helsinki on 10 and 11 December 1999.
760 recital 11 Dir. 2000/78/EC.
761 recital 12 Dir. 2000/78/EC.
762 recital 9 Dir. 2000/78/EC.
763 see to this aspect in detail: *Hahn* (2006), p. 77.
764 ibid.

10.2.2 Forms of age discrimination prohibited by Dir. 2000/78/EC

In general, discrimination may occur in the form of direct or indirect age discrimination.[765] Besides this, one has to pay attention to so-called multiple discrimination, were age plus other grounds of discrimination may be involved.[766] In addition, age-based harassment and mobbing, the instruction to discriminate on the grounds of age and discrimination by association, as well as as discrimination based on assumed characteristics, also have to be acknowledged and accounted for.[767]

10.2.2.1 Direct age discrimination

As explicitly stated in Art. 2 No. 1 in conjunction with Art. 1, the concept of discrimination in terms of age entails that for the Directive's purpose to put into effect the principle of equal treatment in order to combat discrimination inter alia on the grounds of age, the principle of equal treatment implies that direct as well as indirect discrimination based on any of the grounds listed in Art. 1, including age, shall be prohibited. According to the Directive's wording in Art. 2 No. 2 (a), direct age discrimination takes places where one person, on the grounds of her age, is treated less favourably than another is, has been or would have been treated in a comparable situation. This so-called comparator approach entails that the claimant has to refer to a real or hypothetical 'comparator'.[768] As using the subjunctive in the wording of Art. 2 No. 2 (a) indicates, the provision in question may already be of direct discriminatory character, in cases where

---

765 *Fredman* (2003), pp. 55ff., 58ff.; *Hepple*, Bob (2003), Age discrimination in employment: Implementing the Framework Directive 2000/78/EC, in: Age as an equality issue, Fredman/Spencer (eds.), pp. 71-96, p. 82ff.; see also to indirect discrimination elaborately: *Tobler*, Christa (2005), Indirect discrimination.

766 see in detail chap. 10.2.1.3.

767 see for example to the different forms of unwanted conduct in the sense of mobbing and harassment: COM (1999) 565 final, p. 9; see to the aspect of harassment as a form of discrimination also *Senne* (2006), p. 170; critical *Hahn* (2006), p. 103; see in general to the aspect of mobbing and its relevance for different age groups: *Senne* (2006), p. 172ff.; The instruction to discriminate shall according to the Directive constitute a form of discrimination, see Art. 2 No. 4 i.c.w. Art. 2 No. 1 Art. 1 Dir. 2000/78/EC; see for a detailed analysis *Hahn* (2006), p. 107, with further references in fn. 456; see also *Senne* (2006), p. 174 f.

768 *O'Cinneide* (2005), p. 20.

de facto a less favourable treatment has not yet taken place compared to another person, as long as it can be shown that the other person 'would have been treated' more favourably. Accordingly, it is sufficient to refer to a hypothetical comparator.[769]

However, it has to be accounted for that the concept of direct discrimination is deeply entrenched with the *Aristotelian* equality principle or, in other words, it is embedded in the consistency principle, meaning that basic fairness requires consistent treatment.[770] As a result, it features the same weakness as the consistency principle.[771] It lacks the necessary substantive corroboration, as it is merely a relative principle.[772] One of its key deficits in this is that a comparator has to be identified.[773] This proves to be a rather difficult task for several reasons: first, on the grounds of the unique feature of age discrimination, which is related to the fluid nature of a person's age, second, based on the difficulties in determining 'age groups' and finally, due to the inter- and intraindividual differences that might already exist among persons of a similar chronological age.[774] In essence, the following questions arise: 'How much of an age difference is necessary? Must it be a person much younger or older or will any age difference suffice?'[775]

On the grounds of the demonstrated weakness of the comparator approach, it has been argued that we should move away from it. Instead of using the Directive's definition, it has been suggested that legislation should manifest simply that it constitutes discrimination to subject a person to a detriment based on her age. In doing so, it would be superfluous to have to identify a specific comparator.[776]

---

769 *Högenauer*, Nikolaus (2002), Die europäischen Richtlinien gegen Diskriminierung im Arbeitsrecht, p. 94.

770 see to the *Aristotelian* principle already chap. 5.3 above.

771 *Fredman* (2003), pp. 38, 39. 55.

772 ibid.

773 ibid.

774 similar *Fredman* (2003), p. 55; *O'Cinneide* (2005), p. 20 f.; see also *Hahn* (2006), p. 98 f.

775 *Fredman* (2003), p. 55 f.

776 ibid., p. 56; *Hepple* (2003), p. 82; similar *O'Cinneide* (2005), p. 20 who inter alia suggests to use several hypothetical comparators in combination to make it easier for the courts to identify whether age was the causative factor and to clarify to what extend the treatment in question would vary with age.

10.2.2.2 Indirect age discrimination

Direct age discrimination has to be distinguished from indirect age discrimination as laid down in Art. 2 No. 2 (b) in conjunction with Art. 2 No. 1, Art. 1 Dir. 2000/78/EC. According to this provision, indirect age discrimination exists in situations where an apparently neutral provision, criterion or practice would put persons of a particular age at a particular disadvantage compared with other persons, unless, according to Art. 2 No. 2 (b) (i), the provision, criterion or practice in question is objectively justified in line with the proportionality principle.[777] An example of what might constitute an indirectly discriminatory criterion or practice could be the requirement for a job to have several years of job experience or seniority, to possess decision-making capabilities, know-how and emotional maturity. While these requirements might be indirectly discriminatory in particular for younger employees, requiring, by contrast, a high degree of mobility such as a high level of physical fitness – as for example in professions such as airline pilots – or certain computer skills, might more likely be a case of indirect age discrimination as regards older employees.[778] However, this should not negate the fact that older employees may also possess these skills. Given the inter- and intraindividual variability of the ageing process that causes the fluidity and diversity of age groups, difficulties also arise in the case of indirect age-discrimination cases.[779] This is particularly true as regards the wording of Art. 2 No. 2 (b), with its formulation that persons of a 'particular age' may be subject to the disadvantage. As in the case of direct age discrimination, the comparator problem needs to be solved in order to demonstrate the disadvantage.[780]

---

777 see in general extensive analysis by *Tobler*, Christina (2008), Limits and potential of the concept of indirect discrimination; such as *Forshaw*, Simon/*Pilgerstorfer*, Marcus (2008), Direct and indirect discrimination: Is there something in between?, Industrial Law Journal Vol. 37, 2008, pp. 347-364; *Hepple* (2003), p. 83 f.

778 *Hepple* (2003), p. 83; *O'Cinneide* (2005), p. 19ff, in particular p. 25 f.; *Polloczek* (2008), p. 89.

779 similar *O'Cinneide* (2005), p. 26 f.

780 see examples given by *O'Cinneide* (2005), p. 26, 27 who points out that case-law concerning gender discrimination might function as a guidance in defining relevant groups; critical to the ambiguous wording in Art. 2 No. 2 (b) also *Hepple* (2003), p. 83 f.

10.2.2.3 Age discrimination plus X: The case of multiple discrimination

Age discrimination may also occur together with other grounds of discrimination.[781] Of the prohibited discrimination grounds, age has a great, if not yet the greatest potential to interact with other grounds.[782] Age and the ageing process are inescapable and unquestionably related to our core identity, as age cannot be changed like for example one's religion or even gender.[783] Each individual employee thus unavoidably has several different characteristics such as age, race, gender and disability, so that cases of multiple discrimination are likely to occur.[784] In general, multiple discrimination can therefore be defined as discrimination that is based on two or more grounds of discrimination.[785]

As regards age discrimination in employment, multiple discrimination may occur in situations where for example younger black workers are treated differently to older black workers. Moreover, a significant correlation might exist between age and disability, as with increasing age, the older employee, more likely might become disabled or already disabled employees grow older and may then be subject to multiple discrimination. From the perspective of the older employee, an example would be that of an older female employee having problems with her back and who faces difficulties in finding a job. In this example, a combination of age, gender and disability could be identified.[786]

781 *Sargeant* (2006), p. 6; similar *Meenan* (2007 c), p. 114.

782 similar *Meenan* (2007 a), p. 279; *Schmidt*, Marlene (2008), Germany, in: The law on age discrimination in the EU, Sargeant, Malcolm (ed.), pp. 29-54, p. 26, 27; see examples of multiple discrimination in old age given in *Age reference Group on Equality and Human Rights* (2005), Age and... multiple discrimination in older people - A Discussion Paper, p. 3, 4.

783 *Meenan* (2007 a), p. 279.

784 ibid., p. 279; see also *Schmidt* (2008), p. 26 f.

785 *Gerards*, Janneke (2007), Multiple Discrimination, Cases, materials and text on national, supranational and international non-discrimination law. Schiek, Dagmar/Waddington, Lisa/Bell, Mark (eds.), chap. 1.5, pp. 170-179, p. 171.

786 see examples given at *Age reference Group on equality and Human Rights* (2005), p. 21; *Sargeant* (2006), p. 160ff., 170ff.; *Meenan* (2007 a), p. 282; *Gerards* (2007), p. 171; see for a detailed analysis of the correlation of age and disability *Sargeant* (2005), Disability and age-multiple potential for discrimination, International Journal of the Sociology of Law, Vol. 33, Issue 1, 2005, pp. 17-33.

Two subcategories of multiple discrimination are to be distinguished: the first category is often referred to as additive, cumulative or compound discrimination.[787] It describes the situation where the person who claims to be discriminated against can be assigned to two or more separate groups, which are all subject to discrimination legislation.[788] This case is characterised by the occurrence of grounds of discrimination.[789]

A classic example is that of a police department that uses, in its application procedure, both a written test, which might disproportionally affect applicants of a different ethnic or national origin, and a minimum height requirement, which might adversely affect female applicants.[790]

The second category is predominantly described as intersectional discrimination.[791] In contrast to additive discrimination, it is characterised by the fact that in this case, it may be neither effective nor useful to break down the alleged multiple discrimination into its component parts. Quite the contrary, 'It is where the sum of the parts is something more than the constituent elements'.[792] It is the unique combination of grounds of discrimination that is characteristic for this sub-category.[793] Based on this intertwining, some argue that age-based discrimination is based upon similar prejudices to other forms of discrimination and that consequently, it should be treated in a similar manner.[794] This viewpoint is fortified by the fact that all grounds of discrimination are based upon the general principle of equal treatment. Interestingly enough, the Framework Directive also explicitly refers to this aspect in recital 3 - even though it refers to it in

787 *Makkonen*, Timo (2002), Multiple, compound and intersectional discrimination, Bringing the experience of the most marginalized to the fore, p. 10; *Hannett*, Sarah (2003), Equality at the intersections: The legislative and judicial failure to tackle multiple discrimination, Oxford Journal of Legal Studies, Vol. 23 No. 1, 2003, pp. 65-86, p. 68; *Sargeant* (2006), p. 160ff.; *Gerards* (2007), p. 171.

788 *Sargeant* (2006), p. 160ff.

789 *Gerards* (2007), p. 171.

790 see *Shoben*, Elaine W. (1980), Compound discrimination: The interaction of race and sex in employment discrimination, New York University Law Review, Vol. 55, Issue 5, 1980, pp. 793-837, p. 794 f.

791 *Hannett* (2003), p. 68; *Sargeant* (2006), p. 160ff.; see also *Solanke*, Iyiola (2009), Stigma: A limiting principle allowing multiple-consciousness in anti-discrimination law?, in: European Union Non-discrimination law, Schiek, Dagmar/Chege, Victoria (eds.) non-discrimination law, 2009, pp. 115-130, p. 123.

792 *Sargeant* (2006), p. 160.

793 *Gerards* (2007), p. 171.

794 *Sargeant* (2006), p. 6.

terms of gender equality.[795] As stressed in recital 3 Dir. 2000/78/EC, 'women are often the victims of multiple discrimination'. As regards the employment sphere, a typical example for intersectional discrimination thus constitutes the discrimination of an older women, who would be discriminated against not so much because of being a woman or an older employee, but because of being both; namely, an older woman.[796] Some have therefore coined the interaction of age and gender discrimination a 'double jeopardy'.[797] Besides the employment sphere, the interaction or combination of age-based and gender-related discrimination often occurs in the field of social services. One of the problems that arises in this regard concerns the aspect that age discrimination is, due to the restricted scope of Dir. 2000/78/EC, limited to the employment and occupation sphere. *De lege ferenda* this problem might be solved by the coming into force of a new Council directive applicable outside the employment sphere, as proposed in COM (2008) 426 final.[798] Finally, it has to be noted that it is rather difficult within the existing European legal framework to address

795 see also Dir. 2000/43/EC, Preamble, recital 14.

796 see for further examples *Gerards* (2007), p. 171; *Makkonen* (2002), p. 10; see in general to the intersection of gender and other grounds: *Schiek*, Dagmar (2009) Multiple discrimination in EU law opportunities for legal responses to intersectional gender discrimination?, Part I executive summary, European Network of Legal Experts in the field of Gender Equality. pp. 1-26; *Meenan*, Helen (2006) Thinking outside the box: age and other grounds, Contemporary Issues in Law, 8 (1), pp. 80-96; see moreover *Nielsen*, Ruth (2009), Is European Union equality law capable of addressing multiple and intersectional discrimination yet? Precautions against, neglecting intersectional cases, in: Schiek, Dagmar/Chege, Victoria (eds.) European Union non-discrimination law, 2009, pp. 31-51, p. 42; see to the aspect of 'gendered ageism', chap. 4.2; see to multiple discrimination as regards e.g. age and ethnicity or race *Sargeant* (2006), p. 168 f; *Meenan* (2007 a), p. 282; similar *Fredman*, Sandra (2005), Double trouble: multiple discrimination and EU law, in: European Anti-Discrimination Law Review, 2005 Issue No. 2, pp. 13-18, p. 13, 17.

797 *Itzin*, Chaterine/*Phillipson*, Chris, Gendered ageism: A double jeopardy for women in organizations, in: Itzin, Janet/Newman, Catherine (eds.), Gender, Culture and Organizational Change, pp. 84-94, p. 82; *Duncan*/*Loretto* (2004), p. 98ff; *Macnicol*, John (2006), Age discrimination: An historical and contemporary analysis, p. 25 referring to Sontag, Susan (1978), The double standard of Aging, in: Carver, Vida/Liddiard, Penny (eds.), An ageing population, pp. 72-80; see as regards the aspect of double jeopardy in case of older people of an ethnic minority: *Stuart-Hamilton* (2006), p. 174.

798 COM(2008) 426 final.

cases of multiple discrimination due to the application of different legislation, different justification standards and problematic issues as regards enforceability of multiple discrimination claims.[799]

The complexities become even more apparent if different legal enforcement mechanisms also exist that are provided separately for the different grounds. Difficulties may further arise in cases where different exception provisions exist with regard to the various grounds of discrimination. In a case of discrimination against e.g. an elderly disabled employee, the applicable exception provision might be the exception clause in Art. 6 No. 1 for age or the rather narrowly defined exception for disability in Art. 2 No. 2 (b) i, ii Dir. 2000/78/EC. While in a case of additive discrimination, this problem might be solved by assessing each ground and its respective justification separately, in a case of intersectional discrimination, such a solution might be a rather difficult task, as both grounds are intertwined.[800] The question of what standard of justification should apply becomes even more complex in a case where one form of discrimination is direct discrimination and the other is indirect. Moreover, strongly interrelated to this and almost inherent to multiple discrimination is the problem of finding an appropriate comparator that is especially difficult to establish in cases of intersectional discrimination.[801]

10.2.3 Mandatory retirement: An example of direct age discrimination

Mandatory retirement provisions that stipulate the termination of an employment relationship when the employee has reached a certain chronological age basically treat those employees who have reached this age limit less favourably on the grounds of age than for example employees who are younger than the employee subject to the provision is. It is questionable whether the comparator in this regard should be an employee much younger than the employee subject to the age limit should or whether any age difference would be sufficient, meaning that a person

---

799 see to differences in personal and material scope of EU non-discrimination legislation in detail inter alia as regards the the fact that Dir. 2000/78/EC only contains a closed list of grounds of discrimination as manifested in its Art. 1. As a result it may be difficult to subsume cases of intersectional discrimination *Gerards* (2007), p. 172; see also *Fredman*, (2005), p. 16 f.; *Meenan* (2008), p. 14; critical also: *Schmidt* (2008), p. 26, 27.

800 similar *Gerards* (2007), p. 173.

801 see already above chap. 10.2.2.1; see *Hannett* (2003), p. 81ff., in particular p. 82, 83; *Gerards* (2007), p. 173 f.; *Monaghan*, Karon (2011), Multiple and intersectional discrimination, in: European Anti-Discrimination Law Review, Issue No. 13, 2011, pp. 20-32, p. 25 and examples at p. 20, 32.

being just one day younger may also be a sufficient comparator.[802] Depending on the chosen comparator, different results may be achieved.[803] *O'Cinneide* put this problematic into a nutshell by asking:

> If a court or tribunal is hearing a claim of direct age discrimination brought by a sixty-three year old nearing retirement, should the appropriate comparator be sixty-one, fifty-five, twenty-one, or any other age? A sixty-three year old employee nearing retirement may be in a wholly different position to a sixty-one year old in many key respects, and both may be in a different position to a fifty-five year old.[804]

Despite these difficulties, however, it may be generally ascertained that those employees having reached the chronological age in question and thus being subject to compulsory retirement are treated differently based on their age than those not being forced to retire compulsorily. To conclude, mandatory retirement provisions therefore constitute a case of direct age discrimination as laid down in Art. 2 No. 2 (a) in conjunction with Art. 1 Dir. 2000/78/EC.[805]

10.3 Justifying direct age discrimination: The system of exception and justification provisions in Dir. 2000/78/EC

Even if the prohibition against age discrimination is essential to achieve an age-diverse workforce where older workers are integrated, differences in treatment based on age may nevertheless be justified under certain circumstances.[806] For this reason, as stressed in recital 25, it is essential to differentiate between, on the one hand, a difference in treatment which is justified, in particular by legitimate employment policy, labour-market and vocational training objectives and, on the other hand, discrimination which must be prohibited.

---

802 see to the comparator problematic already chap. 10.2.2.1 above.

803 *O'Cinneide* (2005), p. 20.

804 ibid., p. 20.

805 same conclusion inter alia to be found in *Lüderitz* (2005), p. 51; *Temming* (2008), p. 602 f.; *Groß* (2010), p. 100.

806 recital 25 Dir. 2000/78/EC.

The Directive's exception and justification provisions that are pivotal in terms of analysing cases of direct age discrimination as regards their compatibility with the prohibition against age discrimination are Art. 2 No. 5, Art. 4 No. 1 and Art. 6 No. 1 Dir. 2000/78/EC. Moreover, Art. 7 No. 1 Dir. 2000/78/EC on positive measures needs to be considered.

10.3.1 Exception according to Art. 2 No. 5 Dir. 2000/78/EC

According to Art. 2 No. 5, the Directive allows for measures laid down by national law that are necessary in a democratic society for public security reasons, to maintain public order and prevent criminal offences, as well as to protect the health and rights and freedoms of others.

At first glance, Art. 2 No. 5 may be characterised more as an exception to the Directive's scope rather than as a justification provision.[807] In this context, the subject under debate has been whether Art. 2 No. 5 generally allows for age-related distinctions to maintain the employee's operational capacities as regards professions that make high demands on the employee's physical constitution as for example in the police or emergency services.[808] According to this view, any further justification assessment on a case-by-case basis as required for example by Art. 4 No. 1 would be obsolete.[809] However, the provision's wording already militates against such a generalised understanding. As formulated by Art. 2 No. 5, the measure has to be 'necessary', which has to be interpreted strictly to the extent that the measure has to be suitable, necessary and proportional in the narrow sense; in short, the proportionality test has to be fulfilled.[810]

807 viewing Art. 2 No. 5 both as an exception and justification provision e.g. *Schlachter* (2014), p. 29 referring to *Schlachter* (2003), p. 356 f.; examining Art. 2 No. 5 as an exception provision e.g. *Lüderitz* (2005), p. 53ff.; *Senne* (2006), p. 160 f.; *Hahn* (2006), p. 92 f.; *Polloczek* (2008), p. 81, 83 f.; *Groß* (2010), p. 38.

808 see to these professional categories recital 13 Dir. 2000/78/EC.

809 see arguments by *Schlachter* (2003), p. 356 f.

810 arguing for a strict understanding also *Polloczek* (2008), p. 84; advocating a proportionality assessment, but requiring only the measure's necessity and suitability: *Schmidt*, Marlene/*Senne*, Daniela (2002), Das gemeinschaftsrechtliche Verbot der Altersdiskriminierung und seine Bedeutung für das deutsche Arbeitsrecht, RdA 2002, pp. 80-89, p. 82; *Lüderitz* (2005), p. 54; *Hahn* (2006), p. 92 f; *Senne* (2006), p. 161.

In addition, according to the CJEU's view, Art. 2 No. 5 has to be read as establishing an exception to the principle of non-discrimination that has to be interpreted strictly.[811]

The central counterargument against a generalised approach is that if Art. 2 No. 5 is not interpreted strictly, the rather restrictive justification requirements in Art. 4 No. 1 that require a proportional measure could be disregarded and undermined.[812] Any blanket application of Art. 2 No. 5 on age-based measures related to physically demanding jobs in the fields covered by this provision would thus imply that the measure in question would never be assessed in terms of proportionality.[813] Following a strict interpretation of Art. 2 No. 5 thus entails that any measure assessed under Art. 2 No. 5 needs to pass the proportionality test, so that in principle, the same proportionality standard has to be fulfilled as for example in Art. 4 No. 1 or Art. 6. No. 1.[814]

Moreover, it has been debated as to whether the provision's term 'measures laid down by national law' is solely directed at the member states or whether it also allows for the partners of a collective or plant agreement to lay down such measures.[815] This question arises in particular in cases of mandatory retirement age limits for pilots that are typically laid down in collective agreements and where Art. 2 No. 5 might inter alia be invoked in terms of public security reasons.[816]

---

811 C-341/09 (*Petersen*), para. 60; C-447/09 (*Prigge*), para. 56; *Schlachter* (2014), p. 29 f. interprets the CJEU's approach to the extent that the Court examines Art. 2 No. 5 as a justification provision.

812 *Hahn* (2006), p. 92.

813 similar *Polloczek* (2008), p. 83 f.

814 see to the proportionality requirements in detail chap. 10.3.5.; see for an assessment of Art. 2 No. 5 as regards the selected examples on mandatory retirement chap. 10.3.3.2 and 15.3.3.2.

815 see in this regard CJEU in C-447/09 (*Prigge*), Judgement 13 September 2011, ECR 2011 I-8003, para. 61ff. arguing that Member States may authorise through rules the social partners to adopt measures in the meaning of Art. 2 No. 5 Dir. 2000/78/EC; arguing that only governmental measures are encompassed: *Linsenmaier* (2003), p. 26; arguing for a wider scope including measures in collective agreements among others: *Schlachter* (2003), p. 357 and recently *Schlachter* (2014), p. 30; see to this debate in general also *Polloczek* (2008), p. 83 and *Hahn* (2006), p. 92.

816 see for an analysis chap. 15.3.

10.3.2 Justification according to Art. 4 No. 1 Dir. 2000/78/EC

According to Art. 4 No. 1, member states may, notwithstanding Art. 2 No. 1 and No. 2 provide, that a difference in treatment that is based on a characteristic related to any of the grounds referred to in Art. 1, such as age, shall not constitute discrimination where, due to the nature of the particular position or of the context in which the occupational activities are carried out, the characteristic in question constitutes a genuine and determining occupational requirement, provided that the objective is legitimate and the requirement is proportionate.

Art. 4 No. 1 in principle refers to both Art. 2 No. 1 and No. 2. However, given the fact that the 'justification requirements' are already an inherent part of indirect discrimination as defined in Art. 2 No. 2 (b), any justification according to Art. 4 No. 1 may, systematically, only be relevant in cases of direct discrimination.[817] The overwhelming view in the literature regarding Art. 2 No. 2 (b) is as a legal definition of indirect discrimination and not as a justification provision in its own right.[818] However, the question of the provision's legal classification will be left unanswered in this thesis, which solely deals with the justification cases regarding direct age discrimination.

To justify age discrimination, three requirements have to be fulfilled according to Art. 4 No. 1: first, age has to be a genuine and determining occupational requirement (GOR), second, the objective underlying the differential treatment has to be legitimate and finally, the GOR has to be proportionate.[819] These requirements have to be interpreted narrowly, and such a justification may only take place under very few circumstances, as an employee's capabilities and qualifications rather than his age should be the decisive factor in determining the proper exercising of a job.[820] The employee's age may thus only be referred to as a GOR as long as the age is strongly linked in such a manner to the exercise of the profession that an employee being of a different age could not similarly perform the job-

---

817 see to this aspect *Temming* (2008), p. 505; *Schlachter* (2014) p. 30; see in general to indirect (age) discrimination above chap. 10.2.2.2.

818 see to the discussion whether Art. 2 No. 2 (b) constitutes a justification provision *Groß* (2010), p. 43, who finally denies this; see also *Schlachter* (2014), p. 28 f. who calls it a '*tatbestandsauschließende Rechtfertigung*'.

819 *O'Cinneide* (2005), p. 34; *Hahn* (2006), p. 112 f.; *Schlachter* (2014) p. 31.

820 see in general recital 23 Dir. 2000/78/EC; arguing for a narrow interpretation also: *Hahn* (2006), p. 113; *Groß* (2010), p. 66; *Schlachter* (2014), p. 30 referring as regards gender discrimination to Schlachter (1993), Wege zur Gleichberechtigung – Eine rechtsvergleichende Untersuchung des Arbeitsrechts der Bundesrepublik und der Vereinigten Staaten, p. 135 f.

related tasks.[821] It seems to be rather difficult to see many circumstances where such a blunt and general characteristic such as age would qualify as a GOR.[822] In general, age is a poor indicator or proxy for an employee's de facto capabilities in respect of his mental and physical fitness, so that normally, it can hardly be used a substitute for a 'real' GOR.[823] However, there might be situations where age functions as a proxy for another quality or characteristic that in turn might constitute a GOR. There may be circumstances where an individual assessment of the employee might be impracticable and thus where age discrimination might be necessary.[824] A typical situation where this occurs has been subject to debate in the justification of mandatory retirement for pilots, as discussed in chap. 15.3. Further examples where age might be a GOR concerns jobs in film and theatre, in executive positions of an organisation or association where the members are of a certain age.[825]

When interpreting Art. 4 No. 1 Dir. 2000/78/EC, it is often referred to other legal systems, which have a similar regulation.[826] One example constitutes the US approach manifested in § 623 (f) (1) Alt. 1 of the ADEA of 1964, which states that age discrimination may be justified, provided that age is a 'bona fide occupational qualification reasonably necessary to the normal operation of that

821 see to this aspect *Hahn* (2006), p. 113ff.; *Groß* (2010), p. 66; *Schlachter* (2014), p. 30 referring as regards gender discrimination to Schlachter (1993), Wege zur Gleichberechtigung, p. 135 f.

822 *O'Cinneide* (2005), p. 34; similar also *Lüderitz* (2005), p. 84. *Lüderitz* uses the term *'Pensionsgrenze'* but in the sense of mandatory retirement; *Groß* (2010), p. 66.

823 *O'Cinneide* (2005), p. 34 f.

824 see to the discussion of this aspect ibid., p. 13 f., 34 f.

825 see examples discussed by *Groß* (2010), p. 67ff., who is critical as regards using age as a GOR, which is part of a certain corporate concept or philosophy, such as e.g. a fashion company that focuses primarily on fashion for the young and hires only young employees, see discussion on p. 68 f.; similar already *Lüderitz* (2005), p. 83; *Hahn* (2006); p. 114 f.; see also recently *Schlachter,* Monika (2014), Gutachten, Das Verbot der Altersdiskriminierung und der Gestaltungsspielraum der Tarifvertragsvertragsparteien, Hugo Sinzheimer Institut (HIS)-Schriftenreihe, Band 10, 2014, p. 30 referring to *Schmidt/Senne* (2002), p. 83 who considered age to be a potential GOR as regards roles in theatre like that of the 'juvenile lover'.

826 *Sodan*, Helge (2009), Vertrags(zahn)ärzte und ihre Patienten im Spannungsfeld von Sozial-, Verfassungsrecht und Europarecht, Eine kritische Analyse unter besonderer Berücksichtigung der Arztwahlfreiheit der Versicherten, p. 67.

particular business or enterprise'; a so-called bona fide occupational qualification (BFOQ) defence.[827] Classic examples where age has been recognised as a BFOQ are mandatory retirement ages for firefighters, police officers, air traffic controllers and bus drivers.[828]

10.3.3 Justification according to Art. 6 No. 1 Dir. 2000/78/EC

The most relevant justification provision constitutes Art. 6 No. 1 2000/78/EC, being established for age discrimination cases only. Differences in treatment on the grounds of age may be justified due to Art. 6 No. 1 s. 1 Dir. 2000/78/EC. It states that, notwithstanding Art. 2 (2), differential treatments based on age shall not constitute age discrimination, 'if, within the context of national law, they are objectively and reasonably justified by a legitimate aim, including legitimate employment policy, labour market and vocational training objectives, and if the means of achieving that aim are appropriate and necessary'.[829] In Art. 6 No. 1 s. 2 (a)–(c), several examples of legitimate aims and justifiable differences of treatment on the grounds of age are listed. It states:

> Such differences of treatment may include, among others:
> (a) the setting of special conditions on access to employment and vocational training, employment and occupation, including dismissal and remuneration conditions, for young people, older workers and persons with caring responsibilities in order to promote their vocational integration or ensure their protection;
> (b) the fixing of minimum conditions of age, professional experience or seniority in service for access to employment or to certain advantages linked to employment;
> (c) the fixing of a maximum age for recruitment which is based on the training requirements of the post in question or the need for a reasonable period of employment before retirement.

---

827 see in detail and examples given at *Sodan* (2009), p. 67; see also *Groß* (2010), p. 65 f.; see for a comparative analysis of the ADEA and the Directive also *Hahn* (2006), p. 115ff.; see for a detailed analysis of the BFOQ-defense and examples of US case law *Fenske* (1998), pp. 150ff.

828 see examples given at *Sodan* (2009), p. 67; see also *Groß* (2010), p. 65 f.

829 As with Art. 4 No. 1, Art. 6 No. 1 in principle also refers to both indirect and direct discrimination.

The list is of a rather exemplary character.[830] Additionally, these examples do not per se justify age discrimination but need to fulfil the proportionality test as stipulated by Art. 6 No. 1 s. 1.[831] Therefore, the crucial factor for standard retirement ages, which are not explicitly mentioned in Art. 6 No. 1 s. 2, is whether they are compatible with the justification requirements in respect of the proportionality test as laid down in Art. 6 No. 1 s. 1.[832] As stressed in recital 25, the prohibition of age discrimination also has to be seen in relation to the aims that are set out in the Employment Guidelines such as encouraging diversity in the workforce. Among others, legitimate aims may therefore include the support of older employees with the aim of increasing their ratio in the labour force and enhancing their employability and workability, in particular through vocational training.[833]

It has to be noted that the prohibition against age discrimination is the only discrimination ground, which in the case of direct discrimination, also opens it up for justification. One might therefore argue that age discrimination is the least protected ground and that due to that, a hierarchy of discrimination grounds exists with for example age on the bottom and gender on the top in terms of the protected grounds.[834] However, according to the view held in this thesis, all discrimination grounds are to be traced back to the general principle of equality, which militates against any ranking of grounds of discrimination. This is in line with the Directive's purpose, according to which inter alia age-based discrimination should be combated as regards employment and occupation 'with a view

---

830 This is indicated by the use of the phrase 'among others' in Art. 6 No. 1 s. 2; see also *Lüderitz* (2005), p. 88; Opinion of AG *Trstenjak* delivered on 28 April 2010 in: C-45/09 (*Rosenbladt*), ECR 2010 I-09391, paras. 80-83.

831 see in detail *Groß* (2010), p. 71; *O'Cinneide* (2005), p. 36; *Lüderitz* (2005), p. 89; AG *Trstenjak,* C-45/09 (*Rosenbladt*), para. 80 referring to C- 388/07 (*Age Concern*), Judgment of 5 March 2009, ECR 2009 I-1569, para. 43, 44.

832 see to this aspect AG *Trstenjak,* in: C-45/09 (*Rosenbladt*), para. 83.

833 see to this aspect *Lüderitz* (2005), p. 88; see for a general overview and discussion of potential legitimate aims chap. 12.3.

834 see to the question whether the prohibition against age discrimination should be applied less rigorously than the prohibition against sex discrimination AG *Jacobs*, Opinion delivered on 27 October 2005 in: C-227/04 P (*Lindorfer*), Judgement of 11 September 2007, Maria-Luise Lindorfer v Council of the European Union, ECR 2007 I-06767, para. 83-91 and AG *Sharpston*, Opinion delivered on 30 November 2006, in: C-227/04 P (*Lindorfer*), para. 51ff.; critical also whether the prohibition against age discrimination merely is a 'second class' prohibition: *Schmidt/Senne* (2002), p. 89.

to putting into effect in the Member States the principle of equal treatment'.[835] All the different forms of discrimination 'cannot be ranked: are equally intolerable'.[836] Nevertheless, the different grounds of discrimination may have similar features and thus may be combated in similar ways.[837] The experience that has been built up for example through the pioneering work on the grounds of discrimination – gender discrimination – may be used to benefit the protection of other forms of discrimination.[838] On the other hand, the unique feature of the diverse forms of discrimination should be accounted for.[839] This is inter alia done in the case of age discrimination by establishing the special justification provision in Art. 6 No. 1. Thus, even if age discrimination features unique characteristics in contrast to other discrimination grounds protected in Dir. 2000/78/EC, this does not constitute a sufficient basis to argue for a hierarchy of discrimination grounds. In view of effectively combating age discrimination, Art. 6 No. 1 Dir. 2000/78/EC has to be interpreted strictly and any difference in treatment on the grounds of age may only, in very exceptional circumstances, be justified.[840]

10.3.4 Positive action according to Art. 7 No. 1 Dir. 2000/78/EC

Aiming at ensuring full equality in practice, Art. 7 No. 1 in conjunction with Art. 1 Dir. 2000/78/EC allows member states, in light of the principle of equal treatment, to maintain or adopt specific measures to prevent or compensate for disadvantages that are related for example to the ground of age. Also, Art. 7 No. 1 in general constitutes a justification provision.[841]

---

835 Art. 1 Dir. 2000/78/EC.

836 Council decision of 27.11.2000 establishing a Community action programme to combat discrimination, OJ L 2000, 303/23, recital 5.

837 ibid., recital 7.

838 ibid.

839 ibid.; similar *Hahn* (2006), p. 95 f.

840 see to this aspect COM(1999), 565 final, Proposal for a Council Directive (2000/C 177 E/07) establishing a general framework for equal treatment in employment and occupation, OJ C 177 E/42, p. 12; *Lüderitz* (2005), p. 48, 90.

841 also viewing Art. 7 No. 1 as a justification provision: *Temming* (2008), p. 508; *Groß* (2010), p. 40, 54.

However, some argue that Art. 7 No. 1 merely constitutes an exception to the Directive's scope and not a justification provision.[842] Others seem not to make a clear distinction and rather use the notions of exception and justification as synonyms.[843] Moreover, it has been argued that positive measures in relation to chronological age may basically also already be justified via Art. 6 No. 1 s. 2 (a), as they may be subsumed under the justifiable difference in treatment when creating special conditions in order to promote the protection of employees in a specific age group. The reason for this is that any promotion or preferential treatment of one age group inevitably leads to discrimination of another age group, which is then exempted from the benefits.[844] Consequently, one might question the relevance of Art. 7 No. 1 in justifying matters of age discrimination.[845]

As stressed in the preparatory work to the Directive, such positive actions in the sense of Art. 7 No. 1 may include, inter alia, measures that are aimed at promoting the professional integration of young people, or the flexible transition from employment to retirement, as laid down by agreements concluded by the social partners.[846] However, it has to be kept in mind that the provision, in principle, is solely directed at the member states, so that positive measures laid down in collective agreements are only covered by Art. 7 No. 1 as long as the national law explicitly allows the social partners to do so.[847]

Art. 7 No. 1 is based on ex Art. 141 No. 4 EC (now: Art. 157 No. 4 TFEU) and Art. 2 No. 2 Dir. 76/297/EEC, according to which positive measures are allowed to combat disadvantages based on gender.[848] The introduction of such positive measures is based on the consideration that the mere formal equality approach to gender equality has been proven insufficient, as it does not lead to substantive gender equality.[849] In any case, as positive measures also constitute a derogation from the principle of equality, they should be interpreted strictly in light of the case law on sex discrimination.[850]

---

842 see e.g. *Schmidt/Senne* (2002), p. 83ff.

843 see e.g. *Boecken*, Winfried (2005), Die Altersgrenze von 68 Jahren für Vertragsärzte aus EG-rechtlicher Sicht, NZS 2005, pp. 393-400, p. 395 f.

844 see to this aspect *Rothermund/Temming* (2010), p. 78; similar also *Schlachter* (2014), p. 38 f.

845 see to the relation between Art. 6 No. 1 and Art. 7 Dir. 2000/78/EC *Schlachter* (2014), p. 39, who argues that the first provision is *lex specialis* to the latter in cases of promotional measures related to the employee's age in the sense of Art. 6 No. 1 s. 2 (a).

846 COM (1999) 565 final, p. 11.

847 *Schlachter* (2003) p. 364 f. and similar also recently *Schlachter* (2014), p. 36 f.; see also *Lüderitz* (2005), p. 123 f.

848 *Lüderitz* (2005), p. 123; see also for further details: *Polloczek* (2008), p. 100; *Rothermund/Temming* (2010), p. 78; *Schlachter* (2014), p. 36.

849 COM (1999) 565 final, p. 12; *Hahn* (2006), p. 134.

850 OM (1999) 565 final, p. 11; see in particular to the case law on gender quota rules and the difficulties to apply this argumentation to positive measures in favor of older employees *Hahn* (2006), p. 135, 138.

In general, the measures falling within the scope of Art. 7 No. 1 and pursuing a certain legitimate objective also have to fulfil the requirements of the proportionality test.[851]

10.3.5 Proportionality test: General considerations

In essence, the examined exception and justification provisions have in common that they all entail a proportionality analysis.[852] All provisions (either explicit or implicit) postulate that a differential treatment on the grounds of age needs to fulfil the requirements of the proportionality principle to be justified.[853] Most explicitly, Art. 4 No. 1 and Art. 6 No. 1 Dir. 2000/78/EC refer to the requirement of proportionality. In addition, to demonstrate that the unequal treatment in question is 'objectively and reasonably justified' by a legitimate aim, Art. 6 No. 1 s. 1 Dir. 2000/78/EC generally requires that the means of achieving the aim pursued have to be appropriate and necessary.

The wording of the proportionality requirements in Art. 6 No. 1 has been met with criticism.[854] As rightly stressed in the literature, the formulation 'objectively and reasonably justified' does not stipulate any further requirements and may be regarded as a *Worthülse*, so that it has no further meaning when it comes to the proportionality test.[855] Moreover, the criticisms are predominantly based on the diverging translations in the respective languages of the member states. This has been an issue of debate particularly in Germany. The term 'objectively and reasonably justified' for example has been translated in the German version to *objektiv und*

---

851 *Temming* (2008), p. 509; *Groß* (2010), p. 56, 57; see in detail to the proportionality requirement in Art. 7 No. 1 Dir. 2000/78/EC also *Lüderitz* (2005), p. 124 such as *Schlachter* (2014), p. 37 f.

852 see to the proportionality requirement also as regards Art. 2 No. 5, Art. 4 No. 1, Art. 6 No. 1 and Art. 7 No. 1 Dir. 2000/78/EC chap. 10.3.1 to 10.3.4 above; see also in detail *Krois*, Christopher, (2011), Altersgrenzen für Universitätsprofessoren, EuZA 2011, 351-361, p. 356.

853 similar *Groß* (2010), p. 54.

854 *Temming* (2008), p. 461; see also *Wank*, Rolf (2012), Altersgrenzen in Tarifverträgen nach der EuGH-Rechtsprechung, in: Arbeitsgerichtsbarkeit und Rechtsprechung, Festschrift für Klaus Bepler zu, 65. Geburtstag, Creutzfeldt, Malte/Hanau, Peter/Thüsing, Gregor/Wißmann, Hellmut (eds.), pp. 585-603, p. 595.

855 *Groß* (2010), p. 54; critcal also already *Schmidt*/*Senne* (2002), p. 85 fn. 55, who consider this formulation as being a '*Redaktionsversehen*' – an editing mistake.

angemessen. The terminological imprecisions become apparent if one further examines the German translation of 'appropriate and necessary' to *angemessen und erforderlich*. *Temming* therefore characterises the proportionality requirements in the German translation as *sinngemäße Pleonasmen*.[856] As clarified by AG *Trstenjak* in *Rosenbladt,* in contrast to the German wording that might indicate that unequal treatment itself has to be objective, the other language versions may not be interpreted to the effect that the objectivity of the difference in treatment constitutes a separate criterion.[857] Given the terminological uncertainties that arose with the German translation of Art. 6 No. 1, which is strongly related to the fact that both the notions of suitable and appropriate may be translated to *geeignet*, this would correspond to the second step in the proportionality assessment as laid down in this thesis.[858] Furthermore, both may also be translated to *angemessen*, which then corresponds to the proportionality stricto sensu evaluation. To avoid any misunderstanding, the notions' appropriateness or suitability are used in the thesis for the second step and proportionality stricto sensu will be reserved for the third step.[859]

Given the manifestation of the prohibition against age discrimination in EU primary law, the necessity of applying the principle of proportionality in justifying age discrimination becomes even more apparent and imperative. This is due to the fact that Art. 52 No. 1 CFREU explicitly demands that any limitation on the exercise of the rights recognised by the CFREU – which includes the right not be discriminated against, as manifested in Art. 21 No. 1 CFREU – is subject to the principle of proportionality. Accordingly, as clearly stipulated in Art. 52 No. 1 s. 2 CFREU, such limitations 'may be made only if they are necessary and genuinely meet objectives of general interest recognised by the Union or the need to protect the rights and freedoms of others'.

---

856 *Temming* (2008), p. 378 fn. 1600, p. 46 f.; see also *Husmann*, Manfred (2005), Die EG-Gleichbehandlungs-Richtlinien 2000/2002 und ihre Umsetzung in das deutsche, englische und französische Recht, Zeitschrift für Europäisches Sozial- und Arbeitsrecht (ZESAR) 2005, pp. 167-175, p. 170 f.; see also in detail as regards the diverging language versions *Wachter*, Gustav (2010), 'Sprachverwirrung' bei der Altersdiskriminierung, ZESAR 02/2010, pp. 49-54, in particular p. 52ff.; similar also *Bertelsmann* (2007), AGG, § 10 AGG, para. 48.

857 see AG *Trstenjak* in: C-45/09 (*Rosenbladt*), para. 152.

858 see chap. 12.2.

859 see ibid.

In a number of judgements, the CJEU has clarified and substantiated what is to be understood in particular by the proportionality requirements manifested Art. 6 No. 1 Dir. 2000/78/EC being the most central justification provision for age-discrimination cases. When justifying age discrimination, the proportionality analysis presupposes first of all the identification of a legitimate aim that underlies the measure in question, as explicitly stipulated by Art. 6 No. 1 Dir. 2000/78/EC. Even though the CJEU has already dealt with the legitimate-aim requirement of Art. 6 No. 1 in a number of judgements, an exact delineation or definition of what constitutes a legitimate aim is still lacking.[860] The aims that are considered legitimate in the sense of Art. 6 No. 1 basically have in common that they are social-policy objectives such as those related to employment policy, the situation in the labour market or vocational training.[861] Moreover, these legitimate aims should principally be of a public interest nature.[862] They need to be distinguished from purely individual reasons that are specific for the employer's situation, such as cost reductions or improving competitiveness.[863] However, it cannot be ruled out (as added by the CJEU) that a national provision may recognise, in the pursuit of those legitimate aims, a certain degree of flexibility for employers.[864] Subsequently, the CJEU seems to have *peu à peu* interpreted the requirement of having a social-policy objective less restrictively, as some of the aims referred to in Art. 6 No. 1 s. 2 (c) on their part may be related to the interests of the companies.[865] One of the questions that arises as regards social-policy objectives is whether the social partners may also refer to these social-policy objectives.[866] This may or example be relevant as regards mandatory retirement provisions laid down in a collective agreement and the question as to whether the age limit is based on a legitimate aim. This is for example questionable in cases of mandatory retirement for pilots that are typically manifested in collective agreements.[867]

---

860 see to this aspect *Schlachter* (2014), p. 32, who refers to the general overview given at *Wank* (2012), p. 593.
861 C-388/07 (*Age Concern*), para. 46.
862 ibid.
863 ibid; see also Joined Cases C-159/10 and C-160/10 (*Fuchs* and *Köhler*), para. 52.
864 C-388/07 (*Age Concern*), para. 46.
865 see to this aspect *Schlachter* (2014), p. 32.
866 ibid., p. 32 f.
867 This is assessed in chap. 15.

In case the provision in question does not expressly refer to a pursued objective or lacks precision in this regard, other elements derived from the general context of the measure concerned have to be taken into account to identify the provision's underlying aim.[868] It may basically be reliant upon several aims at the same time and, as stressed by the CJEU, the coexistence of several aims does not preclude the existence of a legitimate aim in the sense of Art. 6 No. 1.[869] The aims that are referred to may be linked to each other or classed in order of importance.[870] As further stressed by the CJEU, it is ultimately the task of the national court, having the sole jurisdiction to determine the facts of the dispute in question and to interpret the applicable national law, to determine whether and to what extent the provision in question may be justified by 'legitimate' aims in the sense of Art. 6 No. 1 Dir. 2000/78/EC.[871]

In choosing the means that are capable of achieving the social-policy objectives in question, the member states – and, as necessary, also the social partners at national level – in principle enjoy a broad discretion, according to the CJEU.[872] However, this broad discretion cannot, as

868 C-411/05 (*Palacios de la Villa)*, Judgement of 16 October 2007, ECR 2007 I-8531, para. 54ff., 57; C-388/07 (*Age Concern*), para. 43ff., 45; C-341/08 (*Petersen*), Judgement of the Court of 12 January 2010, ECR 2010, I-00047, para. 40; C-45/09 (*Rosenbladt*), para. 58; Joined Cases C-159/10 and C-160/10 (*Fuchs* and *Köhler*), para. 39; C-141/11 (*Hörnfeldt*), Judgement of 5 July 2012, ECR 2012 -00000, para. 24; C-286/12 (*Commission/Hungary*), Judgement of 6 November 2012, ECR 2012 -00000, para. 58.

869 C-388/07 (*Age Concern*), para. 45.

870 Joined Cases C-250/09 and C-268/09 (*Georgiev*), Judgement of 18 November 2010, ECR 2010 I-11869, para. 45, 46 and 68; C-341/08 (*Petersen*), para. 41 and 65; Joined cases C-159/10 and C-160/10 (*Fuchs* and *Köhler*), para. 46.

871 C-388/07 (*Age Concern*), para. 47; see for an overview of the CJEU's case-law in this regard: *Bagger*, Tuk (2013), Alder som diskriminationsgrund, in: Liber Amicarum et Amicorum in Honour of Ruth Nielsen, Festskrift, (2013), Fejø, Jens/ Neergaard, Ulla/Tvarnø, Christina D./Skovgaard Ølykke, Grith (eds.), pp. 61-79, pp. 70ff.

872 This has been stressed by the CJEU inter alia in: C -144/04 (*Mangold*), para. 63; C-411/05 (*Palacios de la Villa)*, para. 68; C-388/07 (*Age Concern*), para. 51; C-88/08 (*Hütter*), Judgement of 18 June 2009, ECR 2009 I-5325, para. 45; C-45/09 (*Rosenbladt*), para; 41, 69; C-141/11 (*Hörnfeldt*), para. 32; C-152/11 (*Odar*), Judgement of 6 December 2012ECR 2012 -00000, para. 47 and most recently in C-416/13 (*Vital Pérez*), Judgement of 13 November 2014, para. 67.

emphasised by the court in *Age Concern*, have the 'effect of frustrating the implementation of the principle of non-discrimination on grounds of age'.[873]

Part of the proportionality assessment is that the measure – for example a mandatory retirement provision – has to be suitable (respectively appropriate) to achieve the identified legitimate aim. This means it has to be rationally linked to the achievement of the previously identified legitimate aims.[874] It has been stressed by the court that mere generalisations regarding the capacity of a certain measure to contribute to social-policy objectives are not enough to demonstrate that the aim of that measure is capable of justifying a derogation from that principle of non-discrimination on the grounds of age as they do not 'constitute evidence on the basis of which it could reasonably be considered that the means chosen are suitable for achieving that aim'.[875] The court emphasised that general statements are not sufficient to substantiate whether the measure is appropriate in respect of it being suitable to achieve the legitimate aim.[876] As repeatedly stressed by the court, it has to be kept in mind that legislation is appropriate for ensuring attainment of the legitimate pursued aim only, if it genuinely reflects a concern to achieve it in a consistent and systematic manner.[877]

As regards the requirement of necessity, one might read the court's approach insofar that it encompasses that the age distinction is suitably tailored and does not disproportionally impact the disadvantaged age group.[878] In *Commission/Hungary,* the court made it clear, under reference to *Rosenbladt,* what was meant by this requirement:

> In order to examine whether the provisions at issue go beyond what is necessary for achieving that objective and unduly prejudice the interests of the persons concerned, those provisions must be viewed against their legislative

---

873 C-388/07 (*Age Concern*), para. 51.

874 see to the dictinction between appropriatness and necessity: *O'Cinneide/Tobler* (2012), p. 47 referring to C-499/08 (*Andersen*), Judgement 12 October 2010, ECR 2010, I-09343 and C-447/09 (*Prigge*).

875 C-388/07 (*Age Concern*), para. 51, referring by way of analogy to C-167/97 (*Seymour-Smith* and *Perez)* [1999] ECR I-623, para. 75 and 76.

876 ibid.

877 C-341/08 (*Petersen*), para. 53 referring to C-169/07 (*Hartlauer*), para. 55; see in this regard also C-88/08 (*Hütter*), para. 46 f; Joined cases C-159/10 and C-160/10 (*Fuchs* and *Köhler*), para. 85; C-476/11 (*Kristensen*), para. 67.

878 see *O'Cinneide/Tobler* (2012), p. 47 referring to C-499/08 (*Andersen)* and C-447/09 (*Prigge*).

> background and account must be taken both of the hardship they may cause to the persons concerned and of the benefits derived from them by society in general and the individuals who make up society [...].[879]

On closer examination, the necessity requirement entails (in addition to the suitability requirement) two further steps that need to be passed: first, a necessity assessment and second, a proportionality examination in the narrow sense (proportionality *stricto sensu*).[880] Such a rather strict approach inevitably results from the fact that the prohibition against age discrimination after *Mangold* and the coming into force of the Lisbon Treaty has fundamental right status or, as *Temming* put it, '*Grundrechtsqualität*'.[881] First, therefore, an assessment is required regarding whether the legitimate aim can be achieved by alternative means that are less restrictive and less harmful than the measure in question, but equally effective in terms of achieving the legitimate aim (necessity).[882] It has to be kept in mind that any strict application of the proportionality test and, in consequence, a strict assessment of the measure's necessity inevitably involves an intertwined *de lege ferenda* perspective when searching for alternative means.

Ultimately, in the final stage of the proportionality test – the proportionality stricto sensu evaluation – it has to be examined whether the effects of the chosen measure are disproportionate or excessive in relation to the interests affected. Here, the true weighing and balancing takes place, where, metaphorically speaking, *Justitia* takes action. The competing interests have to be balanced against each other. On the one scale is for example the employee's interest not to be discriminated against on the grounds of age due to compulsory retirement, and located on the other scale is the achievement of the legitimate aims in question such as employment policy or labour-market objectives or security aspects that underlie the mandatory retirement provision.[883]

---

879 C-286/12 (*Commission/Hungary*), para. 66 referring to C-45/09 (*Rosenbladt)*, para. 73.

880 arguing for such a three-step analysis, see also *Temming* (2008), p. 473 f. and *Groß* (2010), p. 57; for a similar stance, see also *Kilpatrick*, Claire (2011), The Court of Justice and labour law in 2010: A new EU discrimination law architecture, Industrial Law Journal, Vol. 40 No. 3, 2011, pp. 280-301, p. 290, 295.

881 *Temming* (2008), p. 473; see the required standard of proof in justifying direct age discrimination cases in detail in chap. 12.2.

882 similarly, see *Lüderitz* (2005), p. 89 and *Groß* (2010), p. 57.

883 similar *Lüderitz* (2005), p. 48, 90.

This means that an extensive reasoning is required to demonstrate whether the chosen measure is suitable, necessary and finally, proportional stricto sensu. Merely to conclude that an aim is legitimate is thus not sufficient to justify the age discrimination at issue.[884] Or, as the CJEU clarified in *Fuchs* and *Köhler*, any arguments that are referred to in order to support the use of age distinctions have to be based upon 'evidence of probative value'.[885] Whether this is the case is for the national courts to determine.[886]

10.3.6 Intermediate conclusion

In sum, the examined justification grounds do have, in principle, different justification requirements that need to be fulfilled. However, common to all of them is that it is either explicit, as for example in Art. 6 No. 1, or implicit, as for example in Art. 2 No. 5 or Art. 7 No. 1 Dir. 2000/78/EC, that the measure in question needs to be proportional. In any case, a strict application of the proportionality test is necessary. As regards the relationship of the different justification provisions to each other, it has to be noted that Art. 6 No. 1 is solely designed to justify discrimination on the grounds of age, while, by contrast, the other assessed justification provisions are generally applicable to all grounds, as prohibited by Art. 2 No. 1 Dir. 2000/78/EC. However, Art. 6 No. 1 is not *lex specialis* to the other justification provisions; rather, they are, in juxtaposition, autonomously applicable.[887]

Given the manifestation of the principle of non-discrimination on grounds in EU primary law, the justification requirements – in particular of Art. 6 No. 1 – have to be interpreted narrowly or as *O'Cinneide* and *Tobler* put it in their analysis of the CJEU's case law on age discrimination:

---

884 see to this aspect also *Schlachter* (2014), p. 33.

885 Joined Cases C-159/10 and C-160/10 (*Fuchs* and *Köhler*), para. 76ff., 82-83, operative part 1-2; see to this aspect also *O'Cinneide/Tobler* (2012), p. 44; see also in particular recital 15 Dir. 2000/78/EC.

886 Joined Cases C-159/10 and C-160/10 (*Fuchs* and *Köhler*), para. 82.

887 similar as regards Art. 4 No. 1, Art. 6 No. 1 and Art. 7 No. 1 Dir. 2000/78/EC conclusions by *Groß* (2010), p. 54.

The Court has stated that Article 6(1) constitutes a very specific derogation from the general principle of equal treatment. As such, this exception is to be read narrowly, in line with the general interpretative approach that the Court has applied in interpreting the provisions of the 2000 Directives. Furthermore, as the Court made clear in *Fuchs*, the right to work was protected by Article 15(1) of the EU Charter, and the provisions of Article 6(1) had to be read subject to this fundamental entitlement. As a result, the objective justification test set out in Article 6(1) has to be applied in a rigorous and demanding manner. Age distinctions which are not rationally linked to achieving a legitimate aim, or which are clearly incoherent, unreasonable, or excessive, will not satisfy the requirements of the 'appropriate and necessary' leg of the test.[888]

11 Prohibition against age discrimination in Norwegian and German law

11.1 Introduction

As the selected mandatory retirement provisions of Norwegian and German law are examined in light of Dir. 2000/78/EC and as regards their conformity with the justification requirements manifested therein, for a comprehensive analysis, it is also indispensable that an overview is provided of the implementation of Dir. 2000/78/EC into Norwegian and German law. This is carried out in the following chapter. However, it is not the focus of this thesis to examine the Norwegian and German anti-discrimination legislation in detail.

11.2 Implementation of Dir. 2000/78/EC into Norwegian law

The legal protection against discrimination in Norway is regulated in a number of different acts, whereof chap. 13 of the WEA basically transforms Dir. 2000/78/EC.[889]

---

888 *O'Cinneide/Tobler* (2012), p. 43 referring in this regard to the respective CJEU case law; see to the necessity for a strict standard of proof as regards the justification of direct age discrimination chap. 10.3.5.

889 see already chap. 2.4 above.

Originally, Directive 2000/78/EC was implemented into the WEA with effect from 1 May 2004 by introducing a new chapter XA on equal treatment in employment (*Likebehandling i arbeidslivet*).[890] Following further law reforms in 2005, chapter 13, in its current version, has been established.[891] Recently, the anti-discrimination legislation in Norway, which is spread across several laws, has been reformed and considerably harmonised,[892] even though these amendments had no considerable impact on chap. 13 WEA and the prohibition against age discrimination.

Implementing the Directive was a starting point and not a matter of legal obligation for the non-EU member Norway.[893] In this context, it has to be kept in mind that Dir. 2000/78/EC was based on Art. 13 Treaty establishing the European Community (TEC – now Art. 19 TFEU). As Art. 13 TEC came into force after the adoption of the EEA Agreement, the EEA Joint Committee had to decide about the Directive's implementation into the Agreement. A consensus could not be achieved in this regard and Dir. 2000/78/EC was thus not implemented.[894]

Via the EEA Agreement, Norway is legally bound to the principle of the equal treatment of women and men in employment in its Articles 69 and 70. The implementation of this principle is further specified in Annex XVIII to the EEA Agreement. In this Annex, reference is explicitly made to the EU gender directives that are thereby made part of the Agreement. In contrast to the gender equality directives that have thus been incorporated, the Agreement remains silent in terms of protection against age discrimination.[895]

Thus, in contrast to the gender Directives, Dir. 2000/78/EC is not part of the EEA Agreement. From a legal perspective, the EFTA member states are therefore not bound to having to implement the Directive. Even if Norway was thus not legally obliged to implement the Directive, it chose nevertheless to transform the Directive into national law based on an expediency assessment (*hensiktsmessighetsvurdering)*.[896]

---

890 see to the implementation of Dir. 2000/78/EC in general: *Strand*, Vibeke Blaker (2007), Vern mot direkte og indirekte diskriminering etter norsk rett – et ensartet vern?, Lov og Rett 2007, pp. 131-153, in particular p. 134 f. and as regards the protection against age discrimination in particular *Evju* (2006), p. 150 f.

891 see for an overview *Evju* (2006), p. 151.

892 see already chap. 2.4 above for further references.

893 see already *Hack* (2010 a), p. 348 f.; *Hack* (2012 a), pp. 358 f.

894 see in detail with further references *Hack* (2012 a), pp. 358 f.

895 ibid.

896 see Ot.prp. nr. 104 (2002-2003), *Om lov om endringer i lov 4. februar 1977 nr. 4 om arbeidervern og arbeidsmiljø mv. (likebehandling i arbeidslivet) m.m.*, chap. 3.2, p. 14: '*Fra norsk side har man, basert på en hensiktsmessighetsvurdering,*

Given that Norway is not obliged by the EEA Agreement to implement Dir. 2000/78/EC, Norwegian *EØS -lov* and its § 2 on the precedence of EEA law over Norwegian law is not applicable.[897] Likewise, the so-called *presumsjonsprinsipp*, which implies that Norwegian law is presumed to be in conformity with international law – and which generally has a strong impact on Norwegian law as a principle of interpretation – is per se not applicable.[898]

After having implemented the Directive, the key question that came up in Norway concerned to what extent chap. 13 WEA should be interpreted in view of Dir. 2000/78/EC and the relevant case law of the CJEU.[899] In the preparatory act to the WEA's equal treatment chapter, it has been pointed out that the objective should be that Norway should have protection against discrimination that should at least provide the same level of protection as guaranteed in the EU.[900] By contrast, the so-called Discrimination Act Committee, appointed to evaluate the harmonisation of the different discrimination acts, argued that Norway could act in a more unrestricted manner as regards Dir. 2000/78/EC and, in particular, as regards the prohibition against age discrimination.[901] The relationship between national law and the Directive's requirements has finally also been subject to several judgements of the Norwegian *Høyesterett*.[902] In its landmark decision in its first case on age discrimination and mandatory retirement,

---

gått inn for at hele ikke-diskrimineringspakken bør innlemmes i EØS-avtale.'; see also St.prp. nr. 11 (2003–2004), *Om samtykke til godkjenning av ei avgjerd i EØS-komiteen om innlemming i EØS-avtala av fellesskapshandlingsprogrammet om motkjemping av diskriminering (2001–2006),* p. 2 and Ot.prp. nr. 54 (2008-2009), *Om lov om endringer i arbeidsmiljøloven (likestilling av arbeidstiden for skift- og turnusarbeidere mv.)*, chap. 8.1, p. 52.

897 *Lov om gjennomføring i norsk rett av hoveddelen i avtale om Det europeiske økonomiske samarbeidsområde (EØS) m.v.* 27. november 1992 nr. 109; see in detail with further references *Hack* (2012 a), pp. 359.

898 see in general to the *presumsjonsprinsipp* among others: *Helgesen*, Jan E. (1982), Teorier om "folkerettens stilling i norsk rett", p. 30 f.; Rt. 2000 s. 1811 (*Finanger* I).

899 see in detail analyis in *Hack* (2012 a), pp. 357ff.

900 NOU 2003: 2, *Skjerpet vern mot diskriminering i arbeidslivet*, p. 14; requiring the same standard of protection also Innst. O. nr. 52 (2003-2004), *Innstilling fra kommunalkomiteen om lov om endringer i lov 4. februar 1977 nr. 4 om arbeidervern og arbeidsmiljø mv. (likebehandling i arbeidslivet) m.m.*, p. 2.

901 NOU 2009: 14, *Et helheltlig diskrimineringsvern*, chap. 7.7, p. 97, see also p. 198; critical *Hack* (2010 a), p. 348.

902 see Rt. 2010 s. 202 (*Kystlink*); Rt. 2011 s. 609 (*SAS*); Rt. 2011 s. 964 (*Gjensidige*); Rt. 2012 s. 219 (*CHC*); see also kjennelse Rt. 2010 s. 944 (*CHC*); see for a critical analysis *Hack* (2010 c), pp. 2-3; *Hack*, (2012 a), pp. 357-367, in particular p. 360ff.

the *Kystlink* case, the Norwegian *Høyesterett* clarified this relationship by stating that the national courts have to consider, as a starting point, the question as to whether the Directive should be invoked as the basis for applying and interpreting the national provisions in question, independently and based on 'the same sources of law that would apply if the question had been submitted to the ECJ'.[903]

In the aftermath of *Kystlink*, the *Høyesterett* has consistently referred to this formula in its cases on age discrimination and mandatory retirement.[904] It is thus beyond doubt that – when interpreting the prohibition against age discrimination in Norwegian law as manifested in chap. 13 WEA and the relevant justification provisions – both EU primary law and Dir. 2000/78/EC as secondary law, as well as the case law of the CJEU in this regard have to be considered.

11.3 Prohibition against age discrimination and central justification provisions in Norwegian law

11.3.1 The Working Environment Act

The protection against age discrimination is basically manifested in chap. 13 WEA. It prohibits, in its § 13-1 (1), both indirect and direct discrimination on the grounds of age.

Moreover, § 13-1 (2) inter alia prohibits harassment and instructions to discriminate on the grounds of age. Even though none of the discrimination acts contains an explicit provision that addresses issues of multiple discrimination, it is also considered to be prohibited according to Norwegian anti-discrimination legislation.[905] The argument has been made that protection against multiple discrimination follows from the fact that discrimination based on each ground of discrimination is prohibited.[906]

---

903 translation by author of Rt. 2010 s. 202 (*Kystlink*), para. 56; see to this case *Hack* (2010 c), pp. 2-3; *Hack* (2012 a), pp. 360-362.

904 Rt-2011-609 (*SAS*), para. 72; Rt. 2011 s. 964 (*Gjensidige*), para. 44; Rt. 2012 s. 219 (*CHC*), para. 46; see also to this aspect also kjennelse Rt-2010-944 (*CHC*), para. 9; see for a critical analysis of the *Kystlink* case; *Hack* (2010 c), pp. 2-3; *Hack* (2012 a), pp. 360-362 and for an analysis of further case law p. 362ff.

905 see e.g. Meld. St. (Melding til Stortinget) (2012–2013), *En helhetlig integreringspolitikk, Mangfold og fellesskap*, chap. 9.1.1, p. 111.

906 ibid.

As stated in § 13-2 (1), the chapter applies to all areas of employment including, according to § 13-2 (1) (d), termination of employment. The central provision for justifying discrimination is § 13-3. In its first paragraph it states that unequal treatment is not regarded as discrimination according to the WEA, provided that it first has a legitimate aim, second, is not an unproportional intervention as regards the person who is subject to the unequal treatment and third, that it is necessary for the exercise of the work or profession in question. As stressed in the preparatory work, this provision is considered to implement Art. 4 No. 1 Dir. 2000/78/EC. [907]

The second paragraph of § 13-3 is designed for age discrimination cases only. According to this paragraph, differential treatment that is necessary to achieve a legitimate aim and that is not unproportionally intervening as regards the person that is treated differently is not considered a violation of the prohibition against age discrimination.

As § 13-3 (2), moreover, also refers to indirect discrimination, it is assumed that both indirect and direct age discrimination are encompassed. As emphasised in § 13-3 (3), the Ministry may further concretise in a regulation the scope of the exceptions to the prohibition against age discrimination in § 13-3 (2). So far, such concretisation has not been enacted.

Norway adopted a so-called open approach by introducing a general objective justification test in chap. 13 WEA, without further specifying particular exceptions or circumstances as to when age discrimination is regarded as being justified.[908] This is in contrast to Art. 6 No. 1 s. 2 Dir. 2000/78/EC that at least gives a list of examples of legitimate aims. The Norwegian legislator consciously abstained from giving any examples to avoid any confusion and thus chose an open and indefinite formulation.[909] However, § 13-3 (2) is, according to the preparatory work, considered to be in line with Art. 6 Dir. 2000/78/EC.

---

907 Ot. prp. nr. 104 (2002-2003), *Om lov om endringer i lov 4. februar 1977 nr. 4 om arbeidervern og arbeidsmiljø mv. (likebehandling i arbeidslivet) m.m.*, chap. 8.4.4.2, p. 40.

908 see in general to the distinction between open and closed approaches *O'Cinneide*, Colm (2008), Age Discrimination, in: Bamforth, et al. (2008), Discrimination law: Theory and context, p. 1127, 1128.

909 Ot.prp. nr. 104 (2002-2003), chap. 8.4.5.3, p. 41 f.

Besides § 13-1 (1) WEA, the prohibition against age discrimination is also laid down in § 10-1 (1) *skiparbeidsloven*.[910] Protection against unobjective dismissal is regulated in its § 5-6, which basically corresponds to § 15-7 WEA. Dismissals based on age are further regulated in § 5-12. As in the case of § 15-13 a s. 1 WEA, the employment relationship may, according to § 5-12 (1) s. 1, be terminated when the employee has reached the age of 70. Lower age limits may be laid down, provided they are in conformity with the justification requirements stipulated in § 10- 3 (2).

With the enactment of the *skipsarbeidsloven*, the previously applicable *Sjømannsloven* has been replaced and abolished. The dismissal protection formerly regulated in § 19 of the Seafarers Act is now continued and largely harmonised with the WEA in chap. *5 skipsarbeidsloven*. As a result of the amendments, the previously applicable age limit for dismissal protection – that was central to the *Kystlink* case before – has been raised from 62 to 70 years of age. The general objective that more employees should extend their working lives has made it necessary to consider whether the 62-*årsgrense* should be raised.[911] As stressed in the preparatory acts, a raise in the age limit would provide access to personnel in an industry that is struggling with challenges related to the recruitment of workers.[912] Employment protection for seafarers should be guaranteed until the age of 70 in the same manner as in other sectors and exceptions might only be possible as long as they are objectively justified and are not a disproportionate intervention.[913] It has further been strongly emphasised that it is in the public interest that employment conditions should be favourable so that the population can stay in employment for as long as possible.[914]

Furthermore, the justification requirements of § 13-3 (2) do play a key role as regards termination of employment that is based on the employee's age. The employee's protection against unjustified dismissal (dismissals without a just cause (*saklig grunn*)) is basically manifested in § 15-7 WEA. An employee may not be dismissed as long as the dismissal is not objectively justified based on aspects related to the undertaking, the employer or the employee.[915]

Dismissals that are based on downsizing or rationalisation measures in the company (*driftsinnskrenkning eller rasjonaliseringstiltak*) are considered not to be justified (without a just cause) if the employer can alternatively offer the employee other suitable work in the company.[916]

---

910 *Lov 21. juni 2013 nr. 102 om stillingsvern mv. for arbeidstakere på skip (skipsarbeidsloven).*

911 Prop. 115 L (2012–2013), *Lov om stillingsvern mv. for arbeidstakere på skip (skipsarbeidsloven)*, chap. 1.3, p. 8.

912 ibid., chap. 1.3, p. 8.

913 ibid., p. 139; see in this regard also NOU 2012: 18, *Rett om bord, Ny skipsarbeidslov*, p. 37 f., p. 69 f. and in detail the Committee's analysis in chap. 12.3.7, p. 161ff.

914 Prop. 115 L (2012–2013), p. 140; NOU 2012: 18, p. 165.

915 § 15-7 (1) WEA.

916 § 15-7 (2) s. 1 WEA, see to this requirement in general: *Fanebust*, Arne (2013), Innføring i arbeidsrett, 3. edt., p. 253ff. and for a discussion of the requirement of just cause when it comes to modifications of the employment contract: *Hotvedt*, Marianne, Jenum/*Ulseth*, Terese Smith, Arbeidsavtalen og styringsrett: Harmoni i en domsoktett, Arbeidsrett, 2013, pp. 112-138, p. 119 f .

When determining whether the dismissal is based on a just cause related to *driftsinnskrenkning eller rasjonaliseringstiltak*, the company's interests have to be balanced against the detriments that the employee might suffer as a consequence of the dismissal.[917]

According to § 15-13 a (1) s. 1 WEA, the employment relationship may be terminated when the employee reaches 70 years of age.[918] It is further clarified in § 15-13 a (1) s. 2 in conjunction with § 13-3 (2) that lower age limits than the 70-year age limit may be laid down for example in a plant agreement or a collective agreement, provided that the age limit is objectively justified and not unproportionally intervening.

The provision's predecessor, § 15-7 (4) WEA, further stated that a dismissal before the age of 70 is not considered to be objective if the sole reason for dismissal is that the employee has achieved the general pension age of 67. Also, § 15-13 a (1) s. 1 WEA is basically based on this principle. Originally, the reason for introducing the 70-year age limit was that the general pension was lowered from 70 years of age to 67 in 1972 and the legislator wanted to clarify that the limit for dismissals on the grounds of age should remain at 70 years.[919] The primary objective of the 70-year age limit was to ensure the employee's right to remain in his position so that those employees who were able to and wanted to, could continue working even beyond the pension age.[920] In general, this led to enhanced dismissal protection for older employees. However, even if the provision – in contrast to the current § 15-13 a (1) s. 2 – did not explicitly refer to the possibility of laying down lower age limits, the preparatory work clarified that the provision did not prevent dismissals based on the pension age being reached that were manifested for example in a works council agreement or the individual employment contract.[921]

In contrast to the provision's predecessor § 15-7 (4) WEA, dismissals on the grounds of age are, with § 15-13 a, now regulated in a separate provision. Both as regards the previous applicable § 15-7 (4) and the current § 15-13 a subject to debate has been whether the 70-year age limit per se and whether lower age limits in particular are in conformity with the prohibition against age discrimination.[922]

---

917 § 15-7 (2) s. 2 WEA.

918 see already chap. 3.2 above, in particular as regards recent legal amendments.

919 see Ot.prp. nr. 17 (1972-1973), *Om lov om endringer i lov av 7. desember 1956 nr. 2 om arbeidervern*, p. 4; see to the pension age regulations in Norway already chap. 1.4.1.

920 NOU 1972: 21, *Oppsigelse ved nådd pensjonsalder etter lov om folketrygd, Om revisjon av reglene i Arbeidervernloven om vern mot usaklig oppsigelse*, p. 14.

921 Ot.prp. nr. 17 (1972-1973), pp. 4-6.

922 see among others *Evju* (2006), p. 156ff, in particular p. 158; *Evju*, Stein (2009), Proposisjon om "70-årsregelen" i arbeidsmiljølovens § 15-7, Nytt i privatretten, p. 4; *Hack* (2012 a), p. 364 f.; see for a critical discussion as to whether lower age limits are in conformity with the prohibition against age discrimination: *Roseth*, Kai O./*Kvalvik*, Christel, Aldersgrenser og aldersdiskriminering – er det lenger rom for å fastsette eller avtale særskilte aldersgrenser i norsk arbeidsliv?, Arbeid-

Common to the justification requirements in § 13-3 (1) and § 13-3 (2), such as § 15-13 a (1) s. 2 in conjunction with § 13-3 (2) WEA, is – in line with the Directive's requirements – that a proportionality test has to be fulfilled. This means following a strict understanding – as argued in this thesis – that three steps have to be fulfilled; that is, the measure needs to be suitable, necessary and finally proportional stricto sensu.[923] Even if such a proportionality test in particular, in its strict application, is a rather new concept in Norwegian law, it has to be acknowledged that applying balancing principles is an inherent part of Norwegian dismissal legislation and the respective case law. An example in this regard constitutes the just cause requirement (*saklig grunn*) in dismissals – where a balancing of the employer's and employee's interests takes place.[924] Proportionality – even though rather implicitly – has been an essential element in the overall evaluation of dismissals.[925] Traditionally, aspects of proportionality have come into play when evaluating dismissals of older employees. Weight has inter alia been put on seniority considerations.

---

srett 2012, pp. 142-165, p. 158ff., in particular p. 165; see moreover the recent legal proposal of the Ministry of Labour and Social Affairs to increase the 70-year age limit in § 15-13 a WEA up to the age of 72 and explicitly allow for laying down lower age limits in e.g. plant agreements that are set at the age of 70, see Prop. 48 L (2014–2015) *Endringer i arbeidsmiljøloven og allmenngjøringsloven (arbeidstid, aldersgrenser, straff mv.)*, p, 49, 86 and as regards lower age limits p. 55.

923 see to the requirement of three steps chap. 10.3.5; arguing generally for a three-step analysis in the Norwegian literature among others: *Lilli*, Marco (1999), Forholdsmessighetsprinsippet i EU-retten og dets betydning i norsk rett, *Lov og Rett,* 1999, pp. 515-536, p. 519; *Mathisen*, Gjermund (2007), Om proporsjonalitet som skranke for tiltak som gjør inngrep i EØS-avtalens fire friheter, Jussens Venner Vol. 42, 2007, pp. 80-92, in particular p. 82; see also *Hack*, Melanie R. (2010 c), Etter lek med ild, nå lek med vann: Aldersgrense, pensjonsalder, sjømenn Høyesterettsdom 18. februar 2010 (HR-2010-00303-A)' Nytt i privatretten. (2), 2010, pp. 2-3.

924 see the extensive analysis by *Evju*, Stein (2013), Saklighet og saklighetsprøvelse, en rettsgenetisk studie, Arbeidsrett Vol. 10 Nr. I, 2013, pp. 82-111, in particular as regards the requirement of having a just cause (*saklig grunn*), chap. 8, in particular p. 107 f.; see also in general to the just cause requirement: *Fanebust* (2013), p. 252 f.; and to a balancing of both employee's and employer's interests already: *Andersen*, Kristen (1967), Fra arbeidslivets rett, p. 288; see also *Lassmann*, Andreas (2007), Kündigung und Kündigungsschutz im norwegischen Arbeitsrecht, p. 221ff.

925 see the extensive analysis by *Evju*, Stein (2013), p. 107ff; see to this aspect also *Lassmann* (2007), p. 221 f.

The importance of proportionality has for example already implicitly been stressed in the preparatory work to the *arbeidervernlov* of 1956 – the predecessor to the WEA of 1977– according to which, tolerance should be practised against older employees in the objectivity assessment.[926] In addition, the preparatory work to the WEA may be interpreted in this regard. There, it has been stressed that in the evaluation of objective reasons in general, regardless of the employee's age, attention has to be paid as to whether the dismissal leads to consequences that are unproportional for the employee.[927]

Besides the justification provisions, affirmative active measures (*positiv særbehandling*) that contribute to the promotion of equal treatment, e.g. aiming at the protection or enhancing of the position of older or younger employees, are, according to § 13-6, not regarded as being a violation of the provisions of chap. 13 WEA.[928] This provision is to be understood as an exception rule that has to be interpreted narrowly. [929]

11.3.2 Prohibition against age discrimination on the constitutional level

Since 2014, both the principles of non-discrimination on the grounds of age and the principle of proportionality, became entrenched in the Norwegian Constitution. The principles of equality and non-discrimination have been explicitly manifested in the Norwegian Constitution in § 98 of the *Grunnloven* (Grl) that now explicitly states, '*Alle er like for loven. Intet menneske må utsettes for usaklig eller uforholdsmessig forskjellsbehandling'*.[930]

---

926 Ot. prp. nr. 8 (1956), *Om lov om arbeidervern,* p. 53: '*Det ville være urimelig ikke å vise like stor tolerance overfor de eldre*'; see to the aspect of old age and seniortity in dismissals already *Evju*, Stein (1979), Om kontraktsvern, arbeidstilsyn og straff, in: Evju, Stein/Jakhelln, Henning, (eds.) Arbeidsrettslige emner, 1979, pp. 215-376, p. 252 with reference in fn. 77 to Rt. 1972. 1330, 45; see to this aspect also *Lassmann* (2007), p. 221.

927 see Ot.prp. nr.41 (1975-76), *Om arbeidstid, oppsigelsesvern, arbeidstilsyn m.v. i lov om arbeidervern og arbeidsmiljø*; see in detail *Lassmann* (2007), p. 221 and for further examples of proportionality considerations p. 224.

928 see generally Ot.prp. nr. 49 (2004–2005), p. 328.

929 ibid.

930 'All are equal before the law. No human being shall be exposed to non-objective or unproportional unequal treatment'. (translation by author); amended with *grunnlovsvedtak 6 mai 2014 kunngjort ved res. 9 mai 2014 nr. 613, opphevet ved grunnlovsvedtak 13 mai 2014 kunngjort ved res. 14 mai 2014 nr. 628, tilføyd igjen ved grunnlovsvedtak 13 mai 2014 kunngjort ved res. 14 mai 2014 nr. 628, endret ved vedtak 27 mai 2014 kunngjort ved res. 20 juni 2014 nr. 778.*

In 2009, the so-called Discrimination Act Committee had already evaluated whether the principles of equality and non-discrimination should be implemented in the Norwegian Constitution. In its final proposal, the Committee explicitly recommended including age in the list of protected grounds.[931] By contrast, the Norwegian legislator finally deliberately refrained from listing several grounds of discrimination. In doing so, such an open approach should guarantee comprehensive protection against discrimination.[932] The principle of non-discrimination in § 98 (2) Grl has consequently to be interpreted as also including protection against discrimination on the grounds of age. The ban on non-discrimination encompasses both *usaklig* (unobjective) and *uforholdsmessig* (unproportional) discrimination. By referring to both criteria, the Norwegian legislator seems to perpetuate the requirement of having an objective reason or just cause by supplementing it with the proportionality criterion as inter alia known from discrimination legislation. One might argue that the referral to unobjectiveness is superfluous, as objectivity already implicitly is to be found in any proportionality analysis. However, by referring to both criteria, any discrimination explicitly needs to pass both tests, so that such a double standard might even lead to a strengthening of the protection against discrimination in the end.

As regards discrimination in the employment context, one might further consider examining the right to work as manifested in § 110 (1) of the Norwegian Constitution.[933] According to this provision, it is the state authority's responsibility to create conditions that enable every person that is capable of working to earn a living through his work. The provision generally entails an obligation for the government to conduct an active employment policy in order to avoid unemployment. However, it is only a program statement. Thus, it does not entail a legal right to work for the individual that could be enforced by filing a suit against the state.[934]

In sum, the prohibition against age discrimination is not only part of the Norwegian anti-discrimination legislation, but is also an explicit constitutional principle.

931 NOU 2009: 14, chap. 25, pp. 305-322, see in particular chap. 25.2 and also chap. 25.6, chap. 27.1.

932 see to this aspect: *Grunnlovsforslag 30 (2011-2012), Dok.nr.12:30 (2011-2012), Grunnlovsforslag fra Per-Kristian Foss, Martin Kolberg, Marit Nybakk, Jette F. Christensen, Anders Anundsen, Hallgeir H Langeland, Per Olaf Lundteigen, Geir Jørgen Bekkevold og Trine Skei Grande om grunnlovfesting av sivile og politiske menneskerettigheter*, p. 6.

933 NOU 2009: 14, chap. 25, 25.2.

934 NOU 2009:14, chap. 25.4.2.3 referring to Andenæs, Johs./Fliflet, Arne (2006), Statsforfatningen i Norge, p. 475.

11.4 Implementation of Dir. 2000/78/EC into German law

In Germany, the implementation of the Equal Treatment Directives[935] into German law took place in 2006 with the General Act on Equal Treatment (*Allgemeines Gleichbehandlungsgesetz* – AGG).[936] Also in Germany, the implementation of Dir. 2000/78/EC and the prohibition against age discrimination have been subject to vigorous debate both in case law and in the literature.[937]

---

935 Council Dir. 2000/43/EC of 29 June 2000 implementing the principle of equal treatment between persons irrespective of racial or ethnic origin; Council Dir. 2000/78/EC of 27 November 2000 establishing a general framework for equal treatment in employment and occupation; Dir. 2002/73/EC of the European Parliament and of the Council amending Council Dir. 76/207/EEC on the implementation of the principle of equal treatment for men and women as regards access to employment, vocational training and promotion, and working conditions; Council Dir. 2004/113/EC of 13 December 2004 implementing the principle of equal treatment between men and women in the access to and supply of goods and services.

936 The AGG entered into force on 18.08.2006. It is based on Art. 1 of the *Gesetz zur Umsetzung europäischer Antidiskriminierungsrichtlinien* of 14.08.2008, see BGBl. I, p. 1897; Further laws have been amended to comply with the Directives requirements, as indicated in Art. 16 of Dir. 2000/78/EC. Subject to amendments were e.g. the *Betriebsverfassungsgesetz* (BetrVG) – *Works Constitution Act* and the ArbGG. Moreover, the Act on equal treatment of soldiers (*Gesetz über die Gleichbehandlung der Soldatinnen und Soldaten* – SoldGG) had been established. See to these amendments and enactments: *Däubler* (2008), para. 2 and to the drafting process of the AGG: para. 8ff.; see for an overview of the drafting process and the discussions around the enactment of the AGG: *Over* (2009), pp. 85ff.

937 An extensive number of dissertations have analysed the implementation of the directive into German law and the prohibition against age discrimination, see among others and for further details and references: *Lüderitz*, Martin (2005) Altersdiskriminierung durch Altersgrenzen; *Hahn* (2006); *Senne* (2006); *Sprenger*, Markus (2006), Das arbeitsrechtliche Verbot der Altersdiskriminierung nach der Richtlinie 2000/78/EG; *Polloczek* (2008); *Temming* (2008); *Groß* (2010); *von Hoff*, (2009); *Over*, Henrik (2009) Das Verbot der Altersdiskriminierung im Arbeitsrecht nach dem Allgemeinen Gleichbehandlungsgesetz; *Müller*, Thomas (2011), Alter und Recht, Das menschliche Alter und seine Bedeutung für das Recht unter besonderer Berücksichtigung des europäischen und nationalen Antidiskriminierungsrecht; *Richter*, Claudia (2011), Benachteiligung wegen des Alters im Erwerbsleben, Eine Analyse der gesetzlichen Regelungen - unter besonderer Berücksichtigung des AGG und des KSchG - und ihre Handhabung in der betrieblichen Praxis and most recently: *Rehm*, Johannes

Germany belonged to the group of EU member states that were running late in implementing the Directive. In 2007, the European Commission opened infringement proceedings against Germany as regards the Directive's implementation into national law. In 2009, it finally sent formal requests to Germany to comply fully with Dir. 2000/78/EC. There, it was inter alia pointed out by the Commission that the protection against discriminatory dismissals was not covered by the German anti-discrimination law.[938] Ultimately, the Commission concluded in 2010 that, in view of recent changes, Germany had finally properly implemented Dir. 2000/78/EC.[939] In this context, it has to be kept in mind that Germany had not yet implemented Dir. 2000/78/EC at the time of the famous CJEU *Mangold* judgement. The problem that arose in *Mangold* concerned the fact that the court, in line with its established case law, could not directly apply the Directive's provisions in this case between private parties.[940] As a consequence, it could not rely on the Directive's prohibition against age discrimination.[941] The CJEU – by following AG *Tizzano's* suggestion – solved this problematic by referring to the prohibition against age discrimination as a general principle of EU primary law, that then could be relied upon directly by the private parties in the case.[942] One dimension of the *Mangold* case that was highly debated therefore concerned the Directive's horizontal applicability.[943] One argument that was brought forward in the discussion was that the CJEU, by referring to the general and, at that time, unwritten principle on age discrimination in EU primary law and by declaring that it is the national court's responsibility to set aside the national provision that regulated fixed-term contracts for older employees as being in conflict with this principle, acted ultra vires; that is, beyond its legal competences.[944] Therefore,

---

(2013), Ungleichbehandlungen aufgrund des Alters im Kündigungsrecht, Eine Untersuchung anhand deutscher und europarechtlicher Diskriminierungsverbote; *Kasprzyk*, Izabela (2014), Altersdiskriminierung im deutschen Arbeitsrecht.

938 http://europa.eu/rapid/press-release_IP-09-1620_en.htm (last accessed 17.12.2014).

939 http://europa.eu/rapid/press-release_IP-10-1429_en.htm (last accessed 17.12.2014).

940 *Schmidt*, Marlene (2005), The principle of non-discrimination in respect of age: Dimensions of the ECJ's Mangold judgment, German Law Journal, Vol. 07 No. 05, 2005, pp. 505-524, p. 520; the CJEU has consistently denied any direct applicability of Directives in cases between private parties see among others: C-152/84 (*Marshall*), Judgement of the Court of 26 February 1986, ECR 1984, 00723, para. 48; C-91/92 (*Faccini Dori*), Judgement of the Court of 14 July 1994, ECR 1994, I-03325, paras. 20-22; Joined cases C-397/01 to C-403/01 (*Pfeiffer* and others), Judgement of the Court of 5 October 2004, ECR 2004, I-08835, para. 108 f.

941 *Schmidt* (2005), p. 520.

942 see to a discussion of the several dimensions of the *Mangold* judgement among others: *Schmidt* (2005), p. 518ff. such as for an extensive analysis of the *Mangold* judgement: *Temming* (2008), p. 375ff.; see also chap. 10.1. above.

943 see to this problematic among others *Schmidt* (2005), p. 520 f.; *Temming* (2008), p. 375ff. and *Over* (2009), p. 100ff.; the issue of horiozontal applicability has also be explicitly pointed out by AG Bot in *Kücükdevei*, as a question that needs to be adressed by the Court, see Opinion of AG *Bot*, delivered on 7 July 2009, C-555/07 (*Kücükdeveci*), ECR 2010, I-00365, para. 90; see also Opinion of AG *Sharpston* in C--427/06 (*Bartsch*) delivered on 22 May 2008, ECR 2008, I-07245, para. 47 f.

some described *Mangold* as an *ausbrechender Rechtsakt*.[945] In the aftermath of the CJEU's decision, the German BVerfG finally clarified in its *Mangold* decision, also called the *Honeywell* decision, that *Mangold* was not an ultra vires act.[946] It has to be further kept in mind, as clarified by the CJEU in *Bartsch*, that there has to be a clear link between national law and Community law for the prohibition of non-discrimination on the grounds of age to be applicable. The CJEU stated that, 'the application, which the courts of Member States must ensure, of the prohibition under Community law of discrimination on the ground of age is not mandatory where the allegedly discriminatory treatment contains no link with Community law. No such link arises either from Article 13 EC, or, in circumstances such as those at issue in the main proceedings, from Directive 2000/78 before the time-limit allowed to the Member State concerned for its transposition has expired'.[947]

---

944 see C-144/04 (*Mangold*), para. 75 and 78.

945 see for an overview of the discussion: *Pötters*, Stephan/*Traut*, Johannes (2010), Eskalation oder Burgfrieden: Mangold vor dem BVerfG, ZESAR 2010, pp. 267-276, p. 272; see moreover in particular the critical analysis by *Gerken* Lüder/*Rieble*, Volker/*Roth*, Günter H./*Stein*, Torsten/*Streinz*, Rudolf (2009), 'Mangold' als ausbrechender Rechtsakt, p. 17ff.; see also *Bauer*, Jobst-Hubertus/*Arnold*, Christian (2006), Auf Junk folgt Mangold - Europarecht verdrängt deutsches Arbeitsrecht, NJW 2006, pp. 6-12, p. 8; *Frenz*, Walter (2010), Unmittelbare Arbeitnehmerrechte aus Richtlinien mit Anwendungsstopp durch das BVerfG? Die Verfassungsbeschwerde Honeywell, RdA 2010, pp. 229-234, p. 229; *Gerhardt*, Michael (2010), Europa als Rechtsgemeinschaft: Der Beitrag des Bundesverfassungsgerichts, Zeitschrift für Rechstpolitik (ZRP) 2010, pp. 161-165, p. 163; *Preis*, Ulrich/*Temming*, Felipe (2010 a), Der EuGH, das BVerfG und der Gesetzgeber – Lehren aus Mangold II, NZA 2010, 185-198, p. 193; critical also *Riesenhuber*, Karl (2007), Case ECJ – Mangold, European Review of Contract Law (ERCL), Band 3, Heft 1, 2007, pp. 62–71, p. 71.

946 BVerfG, Beschluss vom 06. Juli 2010 – 2 BvR 2661/06 –, BVerfGE 126, pp. 286-331; see to an overview of the *Honeywell*-decision and its critics: *Bauckhage-Hoffer*, Florian/*Umnuß*, Karsten (2011), Die 'Mangold'-Entscheidung des EuGH und das deutsche Arbeitsrecht - der vorerst letzte Akt, Europäisches Wirtschafts- und Steuerrecht (EWS), 2011, pp. 38-44, p. 40ff.; agreeing with the BVerfG inter alia: *Fuchs*, Maximilian (2011), Mangold – Kein ausbrechender Rechtsakt, ZESAR, 2011, pp. 3-9, see in particular p. 7ff.; see also *Temming*, Felipe (2012), Labour and the role of law, Kölner Schrift zum Wirtschaftsrecht (KSzWR) 2012, pp. 122-128, p. 127. *Temming* already denied in 2008 that *Mangold* constituted an ultra vires act; see his conclusion at *Temming* (2008), p. 404.

947 C-427/06 (*Bartsch*), Judgement of 23 September 2008, ECR 2008, I-07245, para. 25 and operative part; see also the detailed analysis of AG *Sharpston* in *Bartsch* C-427/06; see also analysis at *Bauer*, Jobst-Hubertus/*Arnold*, Christian (2008), Verbot der Altersdiskriminierung, Die Bartsch-Entscheidung des EuGH und ihre Folgen, NJW 2008, pp. 3377-3383; *Gerken* et. al. (2009), p. 13ff.

The AGG is inter alia, according to § 2 (1) No. 2 AGG, applicable as regards employment and working conditions, which includes 'reasons for dismissal, in particular in contracts between individuals, collective bargaining agreements and measures to implement and terminate an employment relationship'.[948]

The AGG's scope is further specified in § 2 (1). While the numbers 1 to 4 are only related to the employment sphere, Nos. 5 to 8 deal with circumstances beyond the scope of employment.[949] When it comes to dismissals, as stressed in § 2 (4), 'Only the provisions governing the protection against unlawful dismissal in general and specific cases shall apply to dismissals'. Given the AGG's general applicability to termination of employment according to § 2 (1) No. 2 AGG, it is no wonder that § 2 (4) is reason for further controversial debate, in particular in terms of its conformity with Dir. 2000/78/EC.[950] According to the dominating view in the literature and according to the BAG, the AGG also has to be applied in cases under the KSchG.[951] The prohibition against age discrimination laid down in the AGG has thus also to be considered in matters primarily examined under the Protection against Unfair Dismissal Act (*Kündigungsschutzgesetz* – KSchG).[952] This problematic becomes particularly apparent in cases of a *betriebsbedingte Kündigung* – dismissal due to operational reasons. In such cases, an employee's age and his seniority inter alia have to be con-

948 see § 2 (1) Nr. 2 AGG (English version: http://www.antidiskriminierungsstelle.de/SharedDocs/Downloads/EN/publikationen/agg_in_englischer_Sprache.pdf?__blob=publicationFile (accessed: 17.12.2014)).

949 see to the material scope e.g.: *von Steinau-Steinrück*, Robert/*Schneider*, Volker (2010), in: AnwaltKommentar Arbeitsrecht, § 2 AGG, para. 2.

950 see among others for an overview: *Bauckhage-Hoffer*/*Umnuß* (2011), p. 43 f.; see extensive analysis at *Polloczek* (2008), p. 213ff.; *Over* (2009), pp. 133ff.

951 see e.g. in general *Steinau-Steinrück*/*Schneider* (2010), § 2 AGG, para. 23; arguing generally for an interpretation of § 2 (4) AGG in conformity with EU law (*europarechtskonforme Auslegung*) inter alia *Over* (2009), p. 139, who nevertheless points to the limitations of such an understanding, see p. 140ff.; see for an overview of the discussion in literature: BAG, Urteil vom 06. November 2008 – 2 AZR 523/07 –, BAGE 128, pp. 238-255, paras. 30-33.

952 see in this regard BAG, Urteil vom 06. November 2008 – 2 AZR 523/07 –, BAGE 128, pp. 238-255, where the BAG in para. 28 clarified: '*Die Diskriminierungsverbote des AGG (§§ 1 - 10 AGG) sind im Rahmen der Prüfung der Sozialwidrigkeit von Kündigungen zu beachten. Eine Kündigung kann sozialwidrig sein, wenn sie gegen Diskriminierungsverbote verstößt. Die Regelung des § 2 Abs. 4 AGG steht dem nicht entgegen. Das ergibt die Auslegung.*'

sidered as manifested in § 1 (3) s. 1 of the (KSchG during a social selection (a so-called *Sozialauswahl*) that has to be undertaken to determine which position shall become redundant.[953] Following an interpretation of § 2 (4) AGG in conformity with EU law, these criteria in dismissal legislation also need to be critically examined in terms of their compatibility with the prohibition against age discrimination.[954]

11.5 Prohibition against age discrimination and central justification provisions in German law

11.5.1 General Act on Equal Treatment

As already emphasised in the beginning of the Act, its purpose is to prevent or to stop discrimination inter alia on the grounds of age.[955] In line with the Directive's requirements, both direct and indirect age discrimination such as harassment and instructions related to age are prohibited.[956]

Direct age discrimination is prohibited under § 3 (1) s. 1 in conjunction with § 1 AGG. Indirect age discrimination is prohibited according to § 3 (2) in conjunction with § 1 AGG. Age-related harassment is deemed to be discrimination according to § 3 (3) in conjunction with § 1 AGG. Instructions to discriminate on the grounds of age are prohibited by § 3 (5) in conjunction with § 1 AGG. According to § 7 (1) s. 2, age discrimination is also prohibited in cases where the person committing the act of discrimination only assumes the existence of any of the grounds referred to in § 1 including age.

Moreover, the AGG explicitly addresses the issue of unequal treatment related to several grounds of discrimination (multiple discrimination).[957] According to its § 4, unequal treatment based on several grounds prohibited by § 1 AGG may only be justified under §§ 8 to 10 and § 20, provided that the justification extends to all the grounds that are affected by the unequal treatment.

---

953 see in detail among others: *Rothermund/Temming* (2010), p. 54ff.' who inter alia critize the use of the criterion 'age' in a *Sozialauswahl*, see p. 56 f.

954 see for a thorough critical analysis in this regard *Temming* (2008), pp. 156ff., in particular pp. 170ff. and 537ff., who inter alia argues that the use of criterion age in the social selection process is a violation of the prohibition against age discrimination that cannot be justified, see p. 546, p. 551; see also *Temming/Rothermund* (2010), pp. 99ff. who advocate a strict proportionality analysis and questions in particular the proportionality of the age criterion, see p. 100.

955 § 1 AGG.

956 see in general to the prohibition against age discrimination: §§ 1, 7, 19, 24 AGG.

957 see generally to the various forms of multiple discrimination already chap. 10.2.2.3 above.

The key justification provisions when it comes to direct discrimination on the grounds of age are § 8 on occupational requirements and the specific justification clause for age discrimination in § 10. Moreover, positive action measures are permissible according to § 5. As regards unequal treatment on the grounds of age, § 10 contains a sweeping clause (*Generalklausel*) that is further concretised in a list of particular justification options.[958] Besides this, in cases of indirect age discrimination, the justification requirements are intrinsic to the definition of indirect discrimination (*tatbestandsimmanent*) in § 3 (2).[959] Direct age-discrimination is thus only justifiable according to §§ 8, 10 and § 5.[960]

The relationship between § 8 and § 10 is not clear and is subject to debate. Some have raised the question as to whether or not it is a competitive relationship (*Konkurrenzverhältnis*).[961] Others have argued that only when the requirements of § 10 are not fulfilled, might one fall back on a justification according to § 8.[962] Others have advocated that both provisions are parallely applicable.[963]

According to § 8 – which basically transforms Art. 4 No. 1 Dir. 2000/78/EC – a difference in treatment inter alia on the grounds of age shall be permissible for reasons of GORs that are related to the nature or context of the particular occupational activity.[964] According to § 10 s. 1, which implements Art. 6 No. 1 Dir. 2000/78/EC, unequal treatment on the grounds of age shall, notwithstanding § 8, not constitute discrimination, provided that it is objectively and reasonably justified by a legitimate aim.[965] As explicitly stated in § 10 s. 2, the means of achieving the aim in question have to be appropriate and necessary. As regards unequal treatment on the grounds of age, § 10 contains a sweeping clause (*General-*

---

958 see *Falke*, Josef (2007), in: AGG, Rust, Ursula/Falke, Josef (eds.) (2007), § 8 AGG, para. 32.

959 see to this aspect e.g. *Steinau-Steinrück*, Robert von/*Schneider*, Volker/*Wagner*, Tobias (2005), Der Entwurf eines Antidiskriminierungsgesetzes: Ein Beitrag zur Kultur der Antidiskriminierung? NZA 2005, pp. 28-32, p. 28 f.; *Trasch*, Timo (2008), Der Prüfungsmaßstab des § 10 Satz 1 AGG bei der Rechfertigung der unmittelbaren Diskriminierung wegen des Alters, p. 33.

960 see to the relation of § 3 (2) to §§ 8, 10 and § 5: *Trasch* (2008), p. 33 f.

961 see to this question e.g. *Trasch* (2008), p. 14, 33 f.

962 see *Falke* (2007), § 8 AGG, para. 32.

963 *Brors* Christiane (2008), in: Allgemeines Gleichbehandlungsgesetz. Däubler, Wolfgang/Bertzbach, Martin (eds.), § 8, para. 2.

964 see *Brors*, (2008), § 8, para. 1; *Falke* (2007), § 8 AGG, para. 1

965 § 10 (1) s. 1 AGG; see for an extensive and critical analysis of the justification requirements in § 10 s. 1 AGG: *Trasch* (2008).

klausel) that is concretised in a list of examples for further particular justification options in § 10 s. 3.[966] Additionally, the German legislator chose an open approach by abstaining from a closed list of justification examples.[967]

Of the listed examples in § 10 s. 3, it is worth mentioning in particular No. 5, referring to 'agreements providing for the termination of the employment relationship without dismissal at a point in time when the employee may apply for payment of an old-age pension'. It further states that § 41 SGB VI, which regulates for pension entitlements not impacting the employee's dismissal protection, shall remain unaffected.

In order to maintain the older employee's dismissal protection, § 41 Social Code Book VI ensures, as clarified in its s. 1, that the entitlement to an old-age pension is not regarded as a reason that may cause the termination of the employment relationship according to the KSchG.

By adding Nr. 5, which has no corresponding provision in Art. 6 No. 1 Dir. 2000/78/EC, the German legislator aimed at clarifying that age could still be taken into account in the termination of employment relationships.[968] The original aim of § 10 AGG to contribute in respect of enhancing the protection especially of older employees against age discrimination, has thus not rigidly been adhered to. Quite the contrary, § 10 s. 3 No. 5 seems to be in contradiction to that.[969] Not surprisingly, given these discrepancies, § 10 s. 3 No. 5 has become one of the most controversial examples in the discussion in the legal literature concerning the confor-

---

966 Bt-Drs. 16/1780, *Entwurf eines Gesetzes zur Umsetzung europäischer Richtlinien zur Verwirklichung des Grundsatzes der Gleichbehandlung*, p. 36; similar also *Löwisch*, Manfred (2006), Kollektivverträge und Allgemeines Gleichbehandlungsgesetz, Der Betrieb (DB) 2006, pp. 1729-1732, p. 1730; *Falke* (2007), § 8 AGG, para. 32; *Brors* (2008), § 10, para. 18.

967 see in general the wording in § 10 s. 1 and s. 3 and in particular the use of '*insbesondere* ' in § 10 s. 3 AGG; arguing that § 10 AGG rather should be interpreted as listing concretised exceptions: *Bertelsmann* (2007), § 10 AGG, para. 41ff., in particular para. 45.

968 Bt-Drs. 16/1780, p. 36; see to the legislative history of § 10 s. 3 No. 5 AGG: *von Roetteken*, Torsten (2014), AGG, 36. update 07/14, § 10, para. 2 and para. 8 referring to Bt-Drs. 15/5717, p. 9, 36 and Bt-Drs. 16/1780, p. 9, 36.

969 see to this discrepancy also *von Roetteken* (2014), § 10, para. 2.

mity of § 10 s. 3 with Dir. 2000/78/EC and the prohibition against age discrimination.[970] Some for example argue that the national legislator failed to refer to a reason as to why any such age limit should be justified.[971] Others generally put into question the German legislator's legal competence to lay down retirement ages, as they are not explicitly listed in the Directive's Art. 6 No. 1.[972]

In any case, mandatory retirement age limits falling under the scope of § 10 s. 3 No. 5 have to be justified in light of EU law and the respective case law of the CJEU.[973] Most importantly, they have to pass the proportionality test. In particular, in the case of general age limits laid down e.g. in works council agreements or collective agreements, this hurdle may hardly be overcome if one follows a strict understanding of the proportionality test.[974]

The principle of equality is not an unknown concept in the German employment-law context, where the so-called *arbeitsrechtlicher Gleichbehandlungsgrundsatz* (principle of equality in employment law) has traditionally been referred to in cases dealing with issues of unequal treatment.

The *arbeitsrechtlicher Gleichbehandlungsgrundsatz* is part of employment customary law, being established long before the coming into force of the AGG.[975] The AGG did not replace this principle, which is still applicable.[976] It basically says that it is prohibited for employers to exempt

---

970 see generally for an overview of the arguments brought forward in literature: *Brors* (2008), § 10, para. 85; *Belling*, Detlev W. (2011), in: Erman BGB, Kommentar, Westermann, Harm P. (edt.), 13.edt., § 10 AGG, para. 13 e.g advocates the provision's conformity with EU law.

971 see for an overview of the discussion: *Brors* (2008), § 10, para. 85; critical in this regard also *von Roetteken* (2014), § 10, paras. 2ff.

972 see for an overview references given at *Brors* (2008), § 10, para. 85.

973 see references given at *Brors* (2008), § 10, para. 85.

974 critical also among others *Temming* (2008), p. 604 f, who denies a justification according to § 10 s. 3 No. 5 AGG of general mandatory retirement ages in collective agreements, see also fn. 2456 for an extensive list of further critical voices in literature as regards general mandatory age limits and their conformity with EU law.

975 see for an overview as to the principle's development and its dogmatic derivation: *Senne* (2006), p. 233 f.

976 That the application of other prohibitions of discrimination or laws on equal treatment shall remain unaffected by the AGG has been explicitly stressed in its § 2 (3) s. 1 AGG; see to this principle in detail: *Senne* (2006), p. 232ff. such as *Kasprzyk* (2014), chap. C. I.

certain employees or groups of employees from general positive measures and thus treat these individuals in a worse manner (based on arbitrary and unobjective reasons) than other employees are treated, who are comparable to these employees' respective group of employees.[977]

Protection against age-based differentiations is, moreover, generally provided via § 75 (1) BetrVG. According to this provision, employers and the works council are obliged to oversee that the employees are treated in line with the principles of *Recht und Billigkeit* and, in particular, that discrimination based inter alia on the grounds of age does not take place.[978]

11.5.2 Prohibition against age discrimination on the constitutional level

On the constitutional level, Germany has – besides the general principle of equality before the law in Art. 3 (1) *Grundgesetz* (GG) – a special equality provision (*besonderer Gleichheitssatz*) manifested in Art. 3 (3) GG of its Constitution. This equality provision concretises the general equality principle of Art. 3 (1) in its scope, so that from a systematic point of view, the relationship of Art. 3 (3) to Art. 3 (1) GG is that of *lex specialis* to *lex generalis*.[979]

In its s. 1 Art. 3 (3) GG, it prohibits any disfavourable or favourable treatment related to 'sex, parentage, race, language, homeland and origin, faith, or religious or political opinions'.

It further prohibits any disfavourable treatment on the grounds of disability in its s. 2. Gender equality is guaranteed in Art. 3 (2) GG.

---

977 see BAG, Urteil vom 26. Oktober 1994 – 10 AZR 109/93 –, juris, para. 21 and definition given at *Senne* (2006), p. 233.

978 see to the principles of '*Recht und Billigkeit*' and the prohibition against age discrimination in 75 (1) BetrVG among others: *Berg*, Peter (2014), in: BetrVG, Däubler, Wolfgang/Kittner, Michael/Klebe, Thomas/Wedde, Peter (eds.), 14.edt. 2014, § 75, para. 7 and para. 55ff. One of the works council's tasks is moreover to promote employment of older workers in the company, see § 80 (1) No. 6 BetrVG.

979 see in detail *Temming* (2008), p. 101 f.

The list of discrimination grounds in Art. 3 (3) s. 1 GG is exhaustive.[980] Age is not included.[981] Germany has therefore no explicit protection against age discrimination manifested in its Constitution.[982] In an analysis as to whether the protection of employees against age discrimination is constitutionally provided for, one may thus solely refer to the general principle of equality in Art. 3 (1) GG.[983] It has been argued that the BVerfG, despite the shortcomings in Art. 3 (3) GG, already has, with Art. 3 (1) GG, a legal instrument with which to critically assess age-based differentiations in the employment context based on a strict proportionality analysis.[984]

Compared to the AGG, one may thus ascertain that the protection against age discrimination provided for in the AGG is wider than the one in the Constitution is. If one argues that the prohibition against age discrimination being a fundamental right of the CFREU should be taken seriously, and thus any exception to it should be allowed for only by following a strict standard of scrutiny, there would ultimately be a discrepancy between the national and European provided protection of this basic right.[985]

---

980 see to this aspect in detail *Senne* (2006), p. 208ff. and *Temming* (2008), p. 108.

981 In 1994 Art. 3 (3) GG was amended as to include also the discrimination ground disability. There have also been discussions as to whether Art. 3 (3) GG may be interpreted as also encompassing age, see to the discussion in detail *Polloczek* (2008), p. 110ff. who denies that age may be subsumed under Art. 3 (3) s.1 GG; denying also *Senne* (2006), p. 212.

982 see in this regard also *Temming* (2008), p. 108 and 114 referring e.g. to § 6 (2) of the Finnish Constitution, see also conclusion at p. 116.

983 *Senne* (2006), p. 211; *Temming* (2008), p. 108ff.; similar also *Polloczek* (2008), p. 111ff.

984 see in detail analysis at *Temming* (2008), p. 108ff. and conclusion at p. 116 and p. 416; similar also already *Senne* (2006), p. 214 f.

985 similar in view of the *Mangold* judgement and the establishment of a general principle of non-discrimination on grounds of age in EU law versus the German constitutional protection: *Temming* (2008), p. 416; see to the necessity for a strict standard of proof chap. 12.2.

The judgements of the BVerfG for example concerning age limits for statutory health insurance for physicians and pilots can be seen as an indicator that the constitutional court does not want to revise its case law on Art. 3 (1), but rather seems to leave it to the CJEU to further clarify matters of age discrimination.[986] Given that the CJEU in turn leaves it to the national courts to concretise whether or not the respective age discrimination is justifiable in view of the de facto national situation, *Temming* rightly fears that the prohibition against age discrimination in this back-and-forth process might finally be *weichgespült*, meaning that it might lose its strength and be weakened.[987]

To dissolve a potentially emerging conflict of a diverging standard of protection provided, on the one hand, on a national constitutional level, and on EU level on the other hand, it has been suggested that Art. 3 (3) s. 1 should be reformed *de lege ferenda* to also encompass age as a protected ground.[988]

It has to be further noted that age-discrimination cases in the employment context, in particular those concerned with mandatory retirement, typically feature a reference to the freedom of profession (*Berufsfreiheit*) manifested in Art. 12 (1) GG.[989] It guarantees that 'All Germans have the right to freely choose their occupation, their place of work, and their place of study or training'. The freedom of profession in Art. 12 (1) GG has, in the field of unequal treatment on the grounds of age, in particular as

986 *Temming* (2008), p. 416 referring to BVerfG, Nichtannahmebeschluss vom 26. Januar 2007 – 2 BvR 2408/06 –, juris (*Verkehrspilotenaltersgrenze*) and BVerfG, Nichtannahmebeschluss vom 07. August 2007 – 1 BvR 1941/07 –, juris (*Altersgrenze für Vertragszahnärzte*).

987 ibid., p. 417.

988 see in this regard ibid., p. 418; see to the option of including age in Art. 3 (3) GG also already *Lüderitz* (2005), p. 243, who however rightly stresses that Dir. 2000/78/EC does not require any amendments on constitutional level.

989 see to this aspect *Temming* (2008), p. 116 and p. 417 f.; *Polloczek* (2008), p. 113 f.

regards the constitutional legitimacy of age limits, played a pivotal role.[990] According to the BVerfG, the freedom of profession also encompasses the employee's free decision to terminate their profession.[991]

When it comes to the limitations of the freedom to choose one's profession in the meaning of Art. 12 (1) GG (*durch Gesetz oder aufgrund eines Gesetzes)*, subjective and objective requirements need to be distinguished between in terms of access to the profession in question, the so-called *Berufszugangsvoraussetzungen.*[992] While subjective requirements are related to factors that depend on the person, objective requirements are based on general criteria, independent from the individual's personal qualifications.[993] Maximum age limits for entering a profession (*Höchstaltersgrenzen*) are, according to the BVerfG, considered subjective requirements.[994] The fact that the individual does not have an impact on his age is thereby, according to the BVerfG, irrelevant.[995] Such subjective requirements for entering a profession are in conformity with the Constitution, provided they serve the protection of important public goods (*wichtige Gemeinschaftsgüter*), which are to give precedence over the individual's freedom, and provided that the principle of proportionality is fulfilled.[996]

---

990 see as regards the case-law of the BVerfG e.g.: BVerfG, Beschluss vom 30. April 1952 – 1 BvR 14/52, 1 BvR 25/52, 1 BvR 167/52 –, BVerfGE 1, 264-281 (*Bezirksschornsteinfeger)*; BVerfG, Beschluss vom 16. Juni 1959 – 1 BvR 71/57 –, BVerfGE 9, 338-354 (*Altersgrenze für Hebammen*); BVerfG, Beschluss vom 04. Mai 1983 – 1 BvL 46/80, 1 BvL 47/80 –, BVerfGE 64, 72-86 (*Prüfingenieur*); BVerfG, Beschluss vom 10. April 1984 – 2 BvL 19/82 –, BVerfGE 67, 1-25 (*Emeritierungsalter*); BVerfG, Nichtannahmebeschluss vom 07. August 2007 – 1 BvR 1941/07 –, juris (*Altersgrenze für Vertragszahnärzte*); see to the role of Art. 12 (1) GG and for further references inter alia as regards case law of the BAG: *Polloczek* (2008), p. 30, 113, fn. 83.

991 BVerfG, Entscheidung vom 11. Juni 1958 – 1 BvR 596/56 –, BVerfGE 7, 377-444 (*Apotheken-Urteil*); see also: BVerfG, Beschluss vom 16. Juni 1959 – 1 BvR 71/57 –, BVerfGE 9, 338-354, (*Altersgrenze für Hebammen*), see para. 22; to this aspect *Polloczek* (2008), p. 113.

992 see as regards the distinction between *subjektive* and *objektive Berufszugangsvoraussetzungen:* BVerfG, Entscheidung vom 11. Juni 1958 – 1 BvR 596/56 –, BVerfGE 7, 377-444 (*Apotheken-Urteil*), para. 77 f.; see to this distinction also *Senne* (2006), p. 228 f.; *Polloczek* (2008), p. 113 f.

993 ibid.

994 ibid.

995 see BVerfGE 9, 338-354, (*Altersgrenze für Hebammen*) at p. 345, para. 23; see also *Polloczek* (2008), p. 113 f.

996 see BVerfG, Entscheidung vom 17. Juli 1961 – 1 BvL 44/55 –, BVerfGE 13, 97 (*Befähigungsnachweis für Handwerker*), para. 22 f.; BVerfG, Beschluss vom 12. März 1985 – 1 BvL 25/83, 1 BvL 45/83, 1 BvL 52/83 –, BVerfGE 69, 209-220, BStBl II 1985, 471, p. 218, para. 22 f.; see to these cases *Polloczek* (2008), p. 113 f.

As emphasised by the BVerfG, the principle of proportionality does not oblige the legislator – when determining age limits – to assess the capability of the employee on a case-by-case basis; quite the contrary, generalised assumptions in this regard are sufficient.[997] The BVerfG had to deal with age limits in a number of judgements. Subject to its evaluation were e.g. age limits for midwives, district chimneysweepers, inspection engineers for construction analysis (*Prüfingenieure für Baustatik*), notaries and statutory health-insurance dentists.[998] Common to all cases is that any interference (*Eingriff*) in the employee's freedom of profession could be justified by reffering to 'important public goods'.[999]

11.6 Intermediate conclusion

Both in Norway and in Germany, Dir. 2000/78/EC has been implemented into national law. The prohibition against age discrimination is manifested in both countries on a national level in the WEA, and respectively, in the AGG, and age discrimination may only be justified under certain justification criteria that principally correspond to the Directive's justification provisions. To meet these justification criteria, any measure needs to pass a proportionality analysis that entails, according to a strict understanding, a three-step test.[1000]

---

997 see BVerfGE 9, 338-354, (*Altersgrenze für Hebammen*), para. 27 f.; such as similar BVerfG, Kammerbeschluss vom 29. Oktober 1992 – 1 BvR 1581/91 –, (Nichtannahmebeschluß: Verfassungsmäßigkeit der *Höchstaltersgrenze von 70 Jahren für die Ausübung des Notarberufs*), para. 12; see to these cases *Polloczek* (2008), p. 113 f.

998 BVerfG, Beschluss vom 16. Juni 1959 – 1 BvR 71/57 –, BVerfGE 9, 338-354, (*Altersgrenze für Hebammen*); BVerfG, Beschluss vom 04. Mai 1983 – 1 BvL 46/80, 1 BvL 47/80 –, BVerfGE 64, 72-86 (*Prüfingenieur*); BVerfG, Beschluss vom 30. April 1952 – 1 BvR 14/52, 1 BvR 25/52, 1 BvR 167/52 –, BVerfGE 1, 264-281 (*Bezirksschornsteinfeger*); BVerfG, Kammerbeschluss vom 29. Oktober 1992 – 1 BvR 1581/91 –, (Nichtannahmebeschluß: Verfassungsmäßigkeit der *Höchstaltersgrenze von 70 Jahren für die Ausübung des Notarberufs*); BVerfG, Nichtannahmebeschluss vom 07. August 2007 – 1 BvR 1941/07 –, juris (*Altersgrenze für Vertragszahnärzte*).

999 see to this aspect *Polloczek* (2008), p. 114.

1000 Even if the order in which the three elements are mentioned and the terminology might differ this does not lead to changes with regard to the proportionality test's substance; similar *Fredriksen Haukeland*, Halvard (2007), Domstolenes

For the understanding of both Norwegian and German law on age discrimination, a thorough analysis of the underlying Dir. 2000/78/EC and its interpretation through the CJEU is pivotal. Examining the Directive and the relevant case law is a *sine qua non* for any comprehensive analysis of the law on age discrimination on the national level. The question as to whether selected examples on mandatory retirement in Norway and Germany are in conformity with Dir. 2000/78/EC is therefore analysed in detail in the following chapters.

---

prøving av EØS-avtalens proporsjonalitetsgrunnsetning – En kommentar til Høyesteretts dom i spilleautomatsaken, Jussens Venner 2007 Nr. 5, pp. 295-305, p. 297.

Part III

12 Justifying direct age discrimination in the case of mandatory retirement: General considerations

12.1 Applicability of Dir. 2000/78/EC to provisions on mandatory retirement

As a necessary step prior to any justification analysis in light of Dir. 2000/78/EC, it has first to be examined whether provisions on mandatory retirement actually do fall within the Directive's scope. This question has been addressed by the CJEU in the *Palacios* case, where the court made it clear that recital 14 of Dir. 2000/78/EC, which states that the Directive 'shall be without prejudice to national provisions laying down retirement ages', does not constitute a hindrance to the Directive's applicability to mandatory retirement provisions.[1001] Later on in its further case law on retirement ages, the CJEU applied a similar approach as in *Palacios* and held that the controversial age limits were to fall within the Directive's scope.[1002]

The controversial provision in *Palacios* permitted the automatic termination of an employment relationship once the employee had reached the age of 65.[1003] In doing so, it affected the duration of the employment relationship between employer and employee 'and, more generally, the engagement of the worker concerned in an occupation, by preventing his future participation in

---

1001 C-411/05 (*Palacios de la Villa*), para. 44; see in detail to the *Palacios* judgement and national retirement ages analysis at *O'Cinneide*, Colm/*Tobler*, Christina (2012), The evolution and impact of the case-law of the Court of Justice of the European Union on Directives 2000/43/EC and 2000/78/EC, p. 26 f.

1002 C-388/07 (*Age Concern*); C-341/08 (*Petersen)*; C-45/09 (*Rosenbladt)*; Joined Cases C-250/09 and C-268/09 (*Georgiev*), Judgement of 18 November 2010, ECR 2010, I-11869; Joined Cases C-159/10 and C-160/10 (*Fuchs and Köhler*); C-447/09 (*Prigge*); C-286/12 (*Commission/Hungary*); see for an overview in this regard *O'Cinneide/Tobler* (2012), p. 27 f.

1003 C-411/05 (*Palacios de la Villa*), para. 45.

the labour force'.[1004] According to the court's conclusion, the provision felt within the Directive's scope, as it established rules that were related to 'employment and working conditions, including dismissals and pay' within the meaning of Art. 3 (1) (c) Dir. 2000/78/EC.[1005]

As concretised in Art. 3 No. 1 (c), the Directive is, moreover, applicable to all persons as regards the public as well as private sectors, including public bodies, in relation to employment and working conditions, including dismissals. Mandatory retirement age limits constitute, in general, a condition that regulates the employment relationship, as they automatically terminate the employment relationship in cases where the employee has reached a certain chronological age. Such age limits are basically thus to be subsumed under Art. 3 No. 1 (c). Moreover, as already ascertained, provisions on mandatory retirement constitute direct age discrimination.[1006] The key question, therefore, is whether this direct age discrimination may be justified according to Dir. 2000/78/EC or not.

12.2 Standard of scrutiny

The central question when it comes to justifying age discrimination in cases of mandatory retirement concerns the standard of scrutiny that should be applied. When examining the CJEU's case law, the answer to this question is not easy to find. As rightly stressed by *Preis,* the Court's approach in its case law on age discrimination rather seems to resemble *Schlangenlinien.*[1007] In general, two approaches by the CJEU in applying the justification test in cases concerning age discrimination may be identified. In some cases, the Court applies a rather soft standard of proof, while in others, a rather stricter standard of proof has been applied. Examples of a soft standard of proof are *Palacios*, *Rosenbladt* and *Hörnfeldt*,[1008] while

1004 ibid., para 45.

1005 ibid., para. 46; AG *Mazák* suggested that the Court should rather adopt a 'restrained approach' when determining the Directive's scope and argued on the contrary that provisions providing for the setting of a compulsory retirement age do not fall within the Directive's scope, see analysis in C-411/05 (*Palacios de la Villa*) AG *Mazák* opinion, delivered on 15 February 2007, ECR 2007, I-08531, para. 52 ff., in particular, para. 67; see for an overview of the arguments brought forward by AG *Mazák*: *O'Cinneide/Tobler* (2012), p. 27.

1006 see chap. 10.2.3.

1007 *Preis*, Ulrich/*Temming*, Felipe (2010 b), Schlangenlinien in der Rechtsprechung des EuGH zur Altersdiskriminierung, NZA 2010, pp. 1323-1328.

1008 C-411/05 (*Palacios de la Villa*); C-45/09 (*Rosenbladt*); C-141/11 (*Hörnfeldt*).

for example *Mangold*, *Kücükdeveci*, *Hütter*, *Petersen*, *Andersen*, *Hennings* and *Prigge*,[1009] on the contrary, illustrate a rather rigorous justification analysis.[1010] In line with *Schlachter*, one may further distinguish (as regards the Court's approach) between a 'control standard' that has been applied as regards general mandatory retirement age limits, such as for example in *Rosenbladt*, versus a more rigorous standard that has been applied in cases that were concerned with special age limits; that is, mandatory retirement designed for specific professions such as for example statutory health-insurance dentists in *Petersen*, university professors in *Georgiev* or pilots in *Prigge*.[1011] The Court's approach is rather astonishing. In fact, it would have been more logical when it comes to mandatory retirement ages to apply the standard of proof exactly the other way around: rigorous as regards general mandatory retirement ages and rather loose in terms of specific mandatory retirement ages. The reason for this is that when it comes to such specific, professional mandatory retirement age limits such as for pilots or physicians, it is basically easier to refer to public interests such as security or health aspects that might counterbalance the employee's interests in a proportionality assessment. For general age limits, such general societal interests are harder to find.[1012]

1009 C-144/04 (*Mangold*); C-555/07 (*Kücükdeveci*); C-88/08 (*Hütter*); C-341/08 (*Petersen*); C-499/08 (*Andersen*); C-297/10 (*Hennings*); C-447/09 (*Prigge*).

1010 similar *Brors*, Christiane (2012), Wann ist eine Altersdiskriminierung nach der Rechtsprechung des EuGH gerechtfertigt? RdA 2012, pp. 346-353, in particular p. 350 f., 353; similar also *Wank* (2012), p. 595; indentifying a looser standard of review in retirement cases versus a tighter standard of proof in other age discrimination cases also *Kilpatrick* (2011), pp. 288ff, in particular p. 293, 296 f.; analysing the '*Prüfungsintensität*' of the principle of proportionality as applied by the CJEU in cases on age discrimination also *Rothermund/Temming* (2010), p. 82ff. who finally advocate a strict application of the proportionality test see e.g. p. 100 such as p. 117 at Nr. 9; see as regards different control standards also already *Preis/Temming* (2010 b), p. 1327 f.

1011 see Joined cases C-250/09 and C-268/09 (*Georgiev*); *Schlachter*, Monika (2011), Mandatory retirement and age discrimination under EU law, International Journal of Comparative Labour Law and Industrial Relations Vol. 27 Issue 3, pp. 287-299, p. 290; see to this aspect also *Numhauser-Henning*, Ann (2013), Age Discrimination and compulsory retirement, in: Introduction to the Norma Elder Law Research Environment, Numhauser-Henning, Ann (ed.), p. 48; see in general to the distinction between general and special mandatory retirement age limits chap. 3.2 above.

1012 see for a critical review of the justification patterns applied in cases of mandatory retirement chap. 12.3.

Despite the different standards that have been applied by the CJEU, common to all of the cases is that the Court, since *Kücükdeveci*, has invoked the prohibition against age discrimination as a general principle of EU law that is explicitly manifested in the CFREU.[1013] This manifestation in EU primary law shall be the initial point in this thesis for the application of a strict justification analysis.

It is therefore argued in this thesis that following a strict standard of proof that is rooted in the general principle of the prohibition on age discrimination includes three steps that have to be assessed. The key steps, which are examined – after having first identified the legitimate aim of the provision in question –, are the following:

Suitability or appropriateness
Necessity
Proportionality stricto sensu.[1014]

Only if these conditions of the proportionality principle are fulfilled in a cumulative fashion, can the measure in question be considered as proportional and thus not a violation of the principle of non-discrimination on the grounds of age. According to the view held in this thesis, only the application of a strict standard of proof is rigorous enough when the aim is to take the prohibition against age discrimination seriously.

12.3 Typically used justification patterns

12.3.1 Introduction

The justification patterns that are typically referred to in any discussion of mandatory retirement may be distinguished as belonging to three main categories: first, arguments that are related to the employee in persona, second, arguments that are related to the employer and finally, aspects that are primarily related to third-party interests beyond the employee–

1013 see chap. 10 above.

1014 similarly arguing for a rather strict standard of proof in his analysis of German employment law in view of the prohibition against age discrimination in EU primary law: *Temming* (2008), p. 517; subsequently interpreting the CJEU case law in favour for a three-steps-analysis also *Rothermund/Temming* (2010), p. 82; arguing for a three-step analysis also *Wank* (2012), p. 595.

employer relationship.[1015] These justification patterns are also to be found in the selected examples on mandatory retirement as analysed in chap. 13 to 15. However, before any further thorough justification analysis of the selected examples on mandatory retirement takes place, it is necessary to shed a critical light on these arguments from a general perspective.

12.3.2 Justification patterns related to the employee

12.3.2.1 Decline of capabilities and maintaining dignity

Justification patterns that are strongly related to the employee in question are primarily those that refer to the employee's capabilities. One of the central arguments that has been brought forward in justifying mandatory retirement is that older employees, after having reached a certain age, are regarded as inefficient employees on the grounds of deterioration both in their mental and physical capabilities.[1016] A prominent example where this argument has been discussed before the CJEU the joint case, the *Fuchs* and *Köhler* case, that was based on a German reference for a preliminary ruling, where the so-called irrefutable presumption of 'disability for service' (*unwiderlegliche Vermutung der Dienstunfähigkeit*) played a considerable role.[1017] This argument has inter alia been central in the debate about the legitimacy of mandatory retirement for university professors, as further assessed in detail in chap. 14.4.3.1.2.

However, as the review of geronotological findings in chap. 6.3.5 has clearly demonstrated, the argument that ageing has to be equalised with a mere process of decline in mental and physical capabilities has been unmasked as a myth. In general, it has thus to be ascertained that the

---

1015 see for a critical overview of often referred reasons for mandatory retirement also *Temming* (2008), pp. 311ff., p. 334 and in detail at pp. 462ff. *Temming* distinguishes between four categories of explanatory models: first economic-rational models, second (macro-)economic (*volkswirtschaftliche*) aspects, third intertemporal decisions of the employee and finally cultural and psychological based arguments, see introduction at p. 312. and in particular as regards Art. 6 No. 1 Dir. 2000/78/EC also *Groß* (2010), p. 104ff.

1016 see to this aspect already the review of ageing theories chap. 6.3.5 above; *Chen* (1987), p. 170 with critical evaluation of the commonly used justification arguments on p. 170ff.; critical also *von Hoff* (2009), p. 279ff.

1017 Joined Cases C-159/10 and C-160/10 (*Fuchs* and *Köhler*).

employee's de facto capability and capacity should be the decisive factor, not his alleged incapacity based on his chronological age. Nevertheless, there are certain occupational groups where physical and mental fitness might nevertheless be essential for the job. This might particularly be the case in security-relevant professions, such as pilots, and for those in the fire service or in the police force. The question as to whether capability arguments may serve as legitimate aims in justifying mandatory retirement for pilots is further assessed in chap. 15.3.3.1.

A further central employee-related argument claims that mandatory retirement serves to spare the employee from any humiliating situation that might occur in a dismissal based on an alleged decline of capabilities.[1018] It has been argued that the employee should get a dignified transition to retirement rather than being exposed to a degrading and incriminatory situation in the case of an individual assessment of his mental and physical capabilities.[1019] Retiring via fixed age limits is a process that takes place free from value judgements and without consideration of the individual employee, according to the argumentation.[1020] It affects every employee in equal measure and guarantees planning reliability for the prospective retiree, according to this argumentation.[1021] According to this view, flexible solutions that lead (in the worst case for the employee) to the appraisal of his disability for service and consequently, to retirement, are equitable with a stigma.[1022]

As regards the capacities of the employee, it has to be noted, as made clear in recital 17 of Dir. 2000/78/EC, that the Directive in general does not require employers to recruit, promote, train or maintain in employment an employee who in fact is not competent, capable and available to perform the essential functions of the post in question or to undergo relevant professional training.

1018 see to such argumentation in the Norwegian context Ot.prp. nr. 54 (2008-2009), *Om lov om endringer i arbeidsmiljøloven (likestilling av arbeidstiden for skift- og turnusarbeidere mv)*, p. 66. This line argumenation played e.g. a role in the case law of the German BAG. However, the BAG does in its recent case law no longer refer to such argumentation, see for an overview of the German caselaw in this regard: *Temming* (2008), p. 334.

1019 see e.g. argumentation by *Gärditz,* Ferdinand K. (2010), Zur Vereinbarkeit beamtenrechtlicher Altersgrenzen mit der EG-Gleichbehandlungsrichtlinie 2000/78/EG, Zeitschrift für das Privatrecht der Europäischen Union (GPR) 2010, pp. 17-19, p. 18, 19.

1020 ibid.

1021 see to a critical evaluation of such arguments already *Chen* (1987), p. 170ff.

1022 *Gärditz* (2010), p. 19.

However, referring to human dignity to justify the maintenance of mandatory retirement may be characterised as being paternalistic or rather, as *Fredman* put it,

> ... it is also an affront to human dignity of the individual to assume that he or she automatically shares the characteristics of everyone else in his or her age group. Personal appraisal is now a part of working life of most individuals of whatever age: it is only degrading if actual diminishing of capability due to age is considered stigmatic. Far better to respect each individual regardless of her capability, but also to avoid attaching stereotypical views of capability to certain age groups.[1023]

It is beyond doubt that some form of determining an exit from working life is necessary. A process is needed where both the employer and employee can be actively involved. Instead of using compulsory absolute age limits, performance management of staff could be carried out consistently and objectively for all employees, irrespective of chronological age.[1024] Using capability procedures rather than rigid statutory procedures such as compulsory retirement should be the preferred route. Whatever the *de lege ferenda* solutions might look like in view of gerontological findings, existing mandatory retirement provisions based on blanket assumptions about older employees' incapacity when having passed a certain chronological age can no longer be maintained unless the reverse is scientifically and factually demonstrated.[1025]

In addition to the argument of having some kind of predictability for both employer and employee by operating with mandatory retirement, one might argue that the employer's margin of discretion in the termination decision could also be reduced. Treating all employees the same with regard to the termination of employment could thus, according to this view, reduce potential unequal treatment. However, such argumentation does not take into consideration that treating all employees equally does not automatically imply that such treatment is just. It simply neglects the fact that ageing is an individual process.

1023 *Fredman* (2003), p. 45; similar also *Temming* (2008), p. 328 f., 334.

1024 This has been stressed e.g. by the UK Government in their analysis on the default retirement age: *BIS* (Department for Business Innovation and Skills) (2011), Phasing out the default retirement age - Government Response to Consultation, January 2011, p. 7; see for further *de lege ferenda* considerations chap. 16.

1025 in this regard also already *Chen* (1987), p. 171.

Moreover, mandatory retirement has been regarded as something that works to the benefit (*et gode*) of the older employee.[1026] In particular, in professions that are physically strenuous, getting the opportunity to exit working life and retire might in fact be something positive for the employee. However, this line of argumentation is also paternalistic, as the forced exit from employment under the cloak of protecting the employee's health simply defies the interests of those employees who still want to and are able to work. Being forced to retire can lead to social exclusion and deprivation for those who are willing to and able to work longer in terms of their right to work.

Moreover, an inherent part of employee-related arguments that is often referred to is the cost reason. One might for example argue against individual and flexible approaches, that systems with strict retirement ages are more cost-efficient than systems where, instead of using mandatory retirement, a capability analysis of each individual employee is carried out.[1027] Furthermore, the argument might be made that older employees are too cost-intensive in relation to their productivity in contrast to younger workers. In general, it cannot be neglected that the wages of older employees and alleged overpayment may also contribute to their vulnerable situation.[1028] Some argue therefore that for example in collective redundancies, cost factors may justify the favoured dismissal of higher paid employees during redundancy programmes, even though it cannot be ignored that this would be likely to have a negative impact on older employees.[1029]

In this context, the so-called *Lazear* model is worth mentioning. It revealed that younger employees are traditionally paid less than their relative productivity in efficient long-term incentive contracts whereas their older colleagues are paid comparatively more than their relative productivity in efficient long-term incentive contracts.[1030]

1026 see to such argumentation e.g. NOU 2004:5, *Arbeidslivslovutvalget, et arbeidsliv for trygghet, inkludering og vekst,* p. 312 and Ot.prp. 54 (2008-2009), *Om lov om endringer i arbeidsmiljøloven (likestilling av arbeidstiden for skift- og turnusarbeidere mv),* p. 63.

1027 arguing in this regard e.g. *Lüderitz* (2005), p. 54, 55; critical to such argumentation *Temming* (2008), p. 314 f.

1028 see to this aspect in detail *Meenan* (2007 a), p. 286 f.; see to the relation of the amount of pay and age also *Issacharoff*, Samuel/ *Harris Worth*, Erica (1997), Is age discrimination really age discrimination?: The ADEA's unnatural solution, in: New York University Law Review, 1997, 787 f., who analyse this relation inter alia under the term 'The Life-Cycle Model' or 'career-wage-model'.

1029 *O'Cinneide* (2005), p. 26.

1030 see in detail *Meenan* (2007 a), p. 286 f.

It has been suggested that the seniority elements of pay should be critically reviewed in order to bring pay closer to productivity, which then could be an incentive for employers to both hire and keep older employees.[1031] Moreover, it has been argued that the focus should perhaps be shifted to the entire worklife of a long-term employee, as this might reveal 'that wages and marginal productivity are separated not only at the late stages of employment, but throughout a typical employee's career'.[1032]

From the perspective of society as such, one might raise the question of whether an even much greater cost burden arises as a result of the still prevailing early retirement schemes and the pressure on the social security systems.[1033] Furthermore, the implicitly referred to correlation between ageing and a decline in productivity is highly questionable if this is not accompanied by an individualised assessment of the de facto capabilities of the employee in question.[1034] The aspect that older employees might compensate for potential age-related deficits via their know-how and professional experience needs to be considered and might counterbalance cost arguments. In any cost-efficiency evaluation, it should therefore be kept in mind that older employees constitute a valuable resource, which, particularly in view of the increasing skills shortage, should not be disregarded.[1035]

1031 ibid.

1032 *Issacharoff/Harris* (1997), pp. 787ff.

1033 see to this aspect e.g. analysis by *Econ Pöyry* (2010), Sammfunnsøkonomisk gevinst ved økt pensjoneringsalder, utarbeidet for Senter for seniorpolitikk, Notat 2010-020.

1034 see to this aspect in detail *Mégret* (2011), p. 63; critical to equalizing chronological age with productivity also *Temming* (2008), p. 313 f.; see for a thorough analysis of the correlatian between age and productivity in the case of pilots chap. 15.3.3.1.1.

1035 ibid.

12.3.2.2 Sufficient financial stability due to pension eligibility

Proponents of maintaining mandatory retirement age limits also regularly refer to the fact that the employee subject to the age limit will be in a financially stable situation due to his eligibility for pension entitlements.[1036] The argument is thus made that the older employee is no longer dependant on his job income, so that it is legitimate when balancing the involved interests to end his employment.[1037] This argumentation has been central in cases of (mass) redundancies where the interests of older employees had to be weighed against younger employees' interests with worse financial safeguards.[1038]

In addition, the CJEU has consistently referred to the aspect of pension eligibility. The amount of the employee's pension was not decisive.[1039] The right to claim a pension is per se considered sufficient. The Court goes even further – as argued in the *Rosenbladt* case – by stating that the employee subject to the age limit might apply for a new job.[1040]

In redundancies, where a selection has to be made, considerations of financial stability might generally play a role. However, such arguments should only be one of several factors that are to be considered and not the decisive element in maintaining compulsory retirement. The reason for this is that younger employees may also, in principle, have sufficient financial stability. The argument of financial stability merely derived from pension entitlements is thus one that is highly questionable, especially if it is applied as the sole criterion and is only related to the employee's

---

1036 The entitlement to financial compensation by means of a replacement income in form of a retirement pension at the end of working life has also repeatedly been stressed by the CJEU, see e.g. C-141/11 (*Hörnfeldt*), para. 42 referring to that aspect and by way of analogy to C-45/09 (*Rosenbladt*), para. 48.

1037 critical to this argumentation *Temming* (2008), p. 327 f.; *Temming* even calls this argument as the '*Gretchenfrage*' (p. 179 as regards social selection procedure in § 1 KSchG) or the '*Dreh- und Angelpunkt in der Debatte um die Wirksamkeit allgemeiner Altersgrenzen*', see p. 310, see also p. 311.

1038 One example in this regard constitutes the Norwegian SAS case Rt. 2011 s. 609 (*SAS*), where the aspect of financial stability due to pension eligibility was discussed (see para. 90, in particular para. 95ff.) and where the Høyestrett conluded that given the employees' eligibility to pension entitlements the dismissal of those employees did not constitute unjustified age discrimination (para. 104 f.).

1039 see e.g. argumentation given by the CJEU in C-45/09 (*Rosenbladt*), para. 47 f.; see also C-141/11 (*Hörnfeldt*), para. 42ff., in particular para. 45 and 47.

1040 see ibid, para.74 and 75.

age.[1041] Furthermore, the respective pension amount might be so low that the employee is simply forced to continue working to afford a living.[1042] In such cases, the pension entitlement per se is thus a poor indicator for financial stability. Moreover, the argument of pension entitlements runs counter to the explicitly declared objectives of recent pension reforms to motivate employees to extend their working careers as long as possible. As for example the Norwegian pension reform with its aim of encouraging older employees to extend their working life clearly illustrates – it is essential for employees and prospective retirees to be allowed the possibility of being able to gain further pension points to achieve a sufficient pension amount.[1043] Despite the entitlement to a pension and the respective pension amount, it has to be noted that being able to work and to earn a living in an occupation freely entered into has an intrinsic value, as being retired cannot be compared to being in an occupation.[1044]

1041 similarly critical to the use of the criterion '*Rentennähe*' in dismissals according to § 1 KSchG *Temming* (2008) pp. 177ff, in particular at p. 181 f., who stresses as regards mandatory retirement however that older employees eligible for pension even if it should be a low pension often do no longer have caring responsibilities for a family, see p. 328; critical in the German context also already *Schröder* (1984), p. 110 f.

1042 This was e.g. the case in C-45/09 (*Rosenbladt)*. Also in C-141/11 (*Hörnfeldt*) the claimant received a rather low pension compared to Swedish standards, see to this aspect e.g. *Numhauser-Henning* (2013), p. 46 fn. 20; critical to the *Hörnfeldt* judgement also *Wachter*, Gustav (2013), Altersdiskriminierung, Diskriminierung/Höhe der Altersrente, Zeitschrift für europäisches Sozial- und Arbeitsrecht (ZESAR) 03/13, pp. 125-133, p. 131ff.

1043 see already chap. 1.4.1.

1044 This has been e.g. rightly stressed by the claimant in the *Kystlink*-case Rt. 2010 s. 202 (*Kystlink*), para. 58; stressing this aspect also among others: *Blanpain*, Roger (2011), Discrimination on the basis of age, The EU: Only a beginning, in: labour law between change and tradition, Blanpain, Roger/Hendrickx, Frank (eds.), pp. 1-9, p. 9.; see also already *Schröder* (1984), p. 114, who stressed: '*Wer den Zweck beruflicher Tätigkeit auf die materielle Existenzsicherung reduziert, verkennt nicht nur deren tatsächliche Bedeutungsvielfalt, sondern geht auch an den Wünschen der betroffenen Arbeitnehmer vorbei.*'

12.3.3 Justification patterns related to the employer

On behalf of the employer, be it a private- or public-sector employer, the typically referred to arguments for the justification of mandatory retirement concern the employer's interest in maintaining a balanced age structure among its employees, to guarantee planning reliability as regard succession planning and the aspect that older employees need to exit the workforce to free up posts and career opportunities for their younger colleagues.[1045] Part of this line of argumentation concerns fair job allocation among the generations. Strongly related to this is again the argument that older employees who withdraw from the workforce due to mandatory retirement in general are eligible to achieve a pension and thus are not financially dependent on their job income, while by contrast, younger employees may need to take care of a family.

In this context, a further argument that is steadily referred to is the so-called fair innings argument.[1046] According to this reasoning, discrimination against older employees has often been defended by employers on the grounds that older workers have had a 'fair innings' and that they should therefore give way to younger workers.[1047] The early retirement policy, which dominated the last decades in most of the countries in the EC, based its justification inter alia on this argument and it still remains in the current debates around mandatory retirement.[1048] One recent example of such an argumentation can again be seen in the *Hörnfeldt* case, where the CJEU stated, 'It may also be accepted that, depending on the situation in the relevant labour market or in the undertaking involved, where the number of employees affected is limited, that rule makes it easier for young people to enter and/or remain in the labour market'.[1049]

1045 critical *Fredman* (2003), p. 47 f.; see also *Temming*, pp. 327ff., in particular p. 330; critical to such argumentation also *Mégret* (2011), pp. 37-66, p. 61.

1046 see for a critical analysis *Fredman* (2003), p. 47 f.; see for the discussion of the 'fair innings'argument in the context of health care e.g. *Rivlin*, Michael M. (2000), Why the fair innings argument is not persuasive, BMC Medical Ethics 2000, 1:1.

1047 *Fredman* (2003), p. 47.

1048 ibid., p. 47.

1049 C-141/11 (*Hörnfeldt)*, para. 34.

However, the 'fair innings' argumentation can be unmarked as a 'lump of labour fallacy'.[1050] The lump of labour theory is based on the view that the economy has a fixed number of jobs available and that the employment of one group – such as older employees – leads to the unemployment of another group – in this case, younger employees. The argument for the lump of labour theory has been inter alia used to advocate a complete withdrawal from work.[1051] The main counterargument against the 'fair innings' reasoning is that it disregards the essential fact that jobs de facto can contribute to the creation of further jobs.[1052] The number of available jobs is simply not of a predictable limited size, as the labour market is dynamic, not static.[1053] Or, in other words, the labour market is 'determined by the scale of demands for jobs, not the supply of jobs'.[1054] Not surprisingly, among economists, the lump of labour theory has been widely acknowledged as being a fallacy. One of the theory's fundamental flaws is that it is fixated on the short term and neglects long-run labour-market adjustments.[1055] In the short-term perspective or in isolated circumstances, it may be the case that jobs are created and filled by new cohorts of employees as a result of the exit of for example older workers from the work sphere.[1056] However, given a long-term perspective, one cannot ignore the fact that higher employment results in economic growth, which in turn increases the demand for labour.[1057] Rather, it has to be recognised, as for example stressed by the UN Madrid Plan, that the continued employment of older workers need not lead to a reduction of labour-market opportunities for younger persons and may, quite the con-

---

1050 *Fredman* (2003), p. 47; see also *Macnicol* (2006), p. 96ff.; *Temming* (2008), p. 321 with further references.

1051 critical *Knapp*, Kenneth A. (2007), The fallacy of the lump of labor: Adding to the costs of ageism, International longevity center – USA (ILC) Issue Brief, December 2007.

1052 *Fredman* (2003), p. 47; similar with further references *Rothermund/Temming* (2010), p. 17.

1053 *Rothermund/Temming* (2010), p. 17.

1054 *Fredman* (2003), p. 47.

1055 *Knapp* (2007), p. 1.

1056 ibid., p. 1.

1057 ibid., p. 1.

trary, provide an ongoing and valuable contribution to the improvement of the respective national performance and output that benefits all members of society.[1058]

In this regard, it is interesting to look at the United Kingdom (UK). The UK government decided that the existing default retirement age (DRA) – which was highly debated before the CJEU in the *Age Concern* case C-388/07[1059] – should be phased out. With effect from 1 October 2011, the DRA in the UK has been abolished. In its Regulatory Impact Assessment of the DRA, the UK government stated:

'The Government does not believe that the abolition of the DRA will have a negative impact on opportunities for younger workers. As set out in the impact assessment, the effect on economic activity and labour supply of removing the DRA is likely to increase economic activity in the economy as a whole. Furthermore, it is not often the case that younger and older workers are direct substitutes. Where there are genuine succession planning considerations (perhaps involving particular training requirements) employers could consider retaining a retirement age if it can be objectively justified. [...] Furthermore, although there is a persistent assumption that older people in work "block" younger people from finding work, evidence suggests this is incorrect. The number of jobs in the economy is not fixed, but depends on Government and private spending (when spending increases the number of jobs increases). Evidence suggests the employment rate of older people has little effect on the employment of younger people, and if anything a higher employment rate of older people tends to slightly increase the employment rate of younger people. Gruber et al. (2009)5 considered a variety of evidence from 12 countries and follows a number of analytical estimated techniques, coming to the conclusion that "the overwhelming weight of the evidence, as well as the evidence from each of the several different methods of estimation, is contrary to the fixed job theory. We find no evidence that increasing the employment of older persons will reduce the employment opportunities of youth" (Gruber et al., 2009). The same paper found that attempts in Denmark to raise youth employment by encouraging older employees to retire had the opposite effect – youth employment fell and unemployment rose'.[1060]

Moreover, the number of posts that become available using age limits has to be considered; that is, how much turnover de facto is created by using mandatory retirement.

The Norwegian *Gjensidige* case demonstrates this vitally, where, it has been stressed in the first instance of the case, a closer look at the number of employees revealed that the use of compulsory retirement led to merely freeing up 9 posts per year of a total of 2000 employees at Gjensidige.[1061]

1058 *Madrid Plan* (2002), para. 26.

1059 C-388/07 (*Age Concern*).

1060 *BIS* (2011), p. 7, 8 referring to Gruber, J./, Milligan K./Wise, D. (2009), Social security programs and retirement around the world: The relationship to youth employment, Introduction and summary, National Bureau of Economic Research Working Paper No. 14647, January 2009.

1061 see TOSLO-2009-143503, Judgement of Oslo tingrett of 16. April 2010.

Examples of mandatory retirement provisions where arguments of intergenerational equity play a role are typically to be found in the higher education sector and in the health sector, as the CJEU case *Georgiev* on mandatory retirement for university professors and the *Petersen* case on compulsory retirement for statutory health-insurance dentists illustrate. Moreover, they have been brought forward in the discussion of mandatory retirement for pilots as e.g. illustrated by the CJEU case *Prigge*. Such argumentation is further elaborated on in chapters 13 to 15 as regards selected mandatory retirement age limits for physicians, university professors and pilots.

To conclude, it is, beyond doubt, important to create job opportunities for the young; however, as stated already by *Chen* in 1987:

> … the policy of making room for the young at the expense of active older bread earners – in complete disregard of actual capacity and fitness – is nothing more than 'the shifting of the problem of insufficient jobs from one age group to another'. Blatant waste of enormously useful talents and skills, seasoned by years of practical experience, is scarcely the way to argument the common interest.[1062]

12.3.4 Justification patterns related to third parties

In justification patterns that are related to third parties, the argument that older employees constitute a safety hazard as a result of their supposed capability decline is often referred to.[1063] Such arguments are also typically brought forward in the discussion of mandatory retirement for professions such as pilots, police officers, firefighters and also with regard to physicians. Classic examples are the potential threat to life and limb of passengers or the flight crew, or an error in medical treatment caused by physicians with decreased capabilities due to their age. Both of these arguments play a pivotal role in justification analysis, according to Art. 2 No. 5, such as Art. 4 No. 1 Dir. 2000/78/EC.[1064] Even if the aim of protecting the health and life of other persons by all means might be considered legitimate, nevertheless, the key question has to be addressed in a justification

---

1062 *Chen* (1987), p. 171.

1063 see for a discussion of '*Altersgrenzen aus Sicherheitsgründen oder zum Schutz Dritter*' in view of the AGG *von Hoff* (2009), p. 283ff.

1064 see already above chap. 10.3.1 and 10.3.2, such as for selected examples chap. 13 and 15.

analysis as to whether alternative measures to the absolute age limit are available that might likewise ensure the safety and health of third parties. This entails assessing whether health tests at regular intervals and so-called functioning tests might replace and finally supersede the age limit in question.[1065] If regularly and frequently conducted, such tests might, in the end, also lead to an increase in security during the entire working life, as already with existing age limits as a result of the individual ageing process, a performance decline and thus a security and health risk might occur long before the age limit is reached. These examples are going to be explored in detail as regards their conformity with Dir. 2000/78/EC justification requirements in chap. 13 to chap. 15.

13 *Mandatory retirement in medical professions: The example of physicians*

13.1 Introduction

Examining mandatory retirement provisions for physicians and their justification is very interesting, as physicians encompassed by such age limits are in a unique position as they work with the life and health of others, which in turn has a strong impact on the justification analysis and the interests that are involved. Moreover, employees and self-employed persons working in this occupational field are in an exceptional position, as they are often exposed to high levels of physical and mental stress due to shift work and the heavy responsibility that has to be held in this job. These aspects principally might also impact the worker's ability to work when getting older. To determine exactly how ageing affects a physician's performance is complicated. As stressed by *Collier,* it is not an easy task, 'to decide at what point older doctors should be encouraged to hang up

1065 see analysis as regards e.g. pilots in chap. 15.3.3.2.1; see in general for an overview of the different ways to conduct individual capabilities assessments NOU 2000: 27 *Sykefravær og uførepensjonering*, chap. 10.3 '*Nærmere om funksjonsvurdering*', in particular chap. 10.3.1 '*Ulike måter å foreta funksjonsvurderinger*'; see also to the question as to whether capability assessments are justifiable the analysis by *von Hoff* (2009), pp. 306ff.

their stethoscopes rather than be encouraged to improve their skills. Refusing to employ capable doctors because they have a lot of candles on their birthday cakes reeks of ageism'.[1066]

On the contrary, one cannot deny the fact that allowing older physicians to continue working long after their skills have decreased might endanger the public.[1067] However, most experts generally agree that even in old age, physicians make valuable contributions to health care and are a valuable resource both for society as such and the individual patient, who might benefit from the older physician's experience and know-how.[1068] In particular, in the case of general practitioners, the mutual trust built up between the patient and physician over the years may come into play. In Norway as well as in Germany, mandatory retirement for physicians has been highly debated, with the CJEU *Petersen* case as the most prominent example.[1069] Based on these considerations, it is very fruitful from a normative perspective to analyse more closely mandatory retirement for physicians as a further selected example. As pointed out by *Janbu* as regards the Norwegian legislation, the examination of the existing age limit's legitimacy is not a 'static' assessment, the ongoing demographic change and the politically expressed will to encourage older workers to extend their working life somewhat actualises the problem, whether such age limits are justifiable or not.[1070]

Even if a number of professions fall under the term 'healthcare personnel' or medical professions, this chapter predominantly sheds light on the specific age limits for general physicians; that is, those physicians that are responsible for providing the necessary primary healthcare service (*allmennlegetjeneste/Allgemeinmedizin*).[1071] Physicians are specialised in a variety of medical disciplines, which might differ considerably from each other when it comes to job profile and job-related tasks and requirements.[1072] The occupational profile of a dermatologist differs for example

---

1066 *Collier*, Roger (2008), Diagnosing the aging physician, Canadian Medical Association Journal (CMAJ), April 22, 2008, pp. 1121-1123, p. 1121.

1067 ibid.

1068 similar ibid.

1069 see C-341/08 (*Petersen*); see for references to the Norwegian debate chap. 13.2.6 and as regards Germany chap. 13.5.1.

1070 *Janbu*, Torunn (2011), Eldre leger og lisens, Tidsskrift for den norske legeforening (Tidsskr Nor Legeforen) nr. 2, 2011, 131, p. 111.

1071 see e.g. § 1 *Forskrift om fastlegeordning i kommunene* FOR-2012-08-29-842.

1072 similar *Boecken*, (2005), p. 396.

considerably from that of a heart surgeon. In view of these significant differences, which also have an impact on the justification patterns that have to be considered when analysing mandatory retirement, physicians working in the field of primary health care (general physicians) constitute the chosen example for the following analysis. Given the underlying complex and different regulatory frameworks on the national level, the compatibility assessment is therefore going to be conducted for Norway and Germany separately.

13.2 De lege lata situation in Norway

13.2.1 Introduction

In general, in Norway, one has to distinguish between healthcare personnel, working in the private sector and employees who are working in the public sector, such as e.g. in communal hospitals.[1073] The central act in Norway regulating employment aspects of personnel working in the healthcare sector is the so-called Health Personnel Act (hlspl.).[1074]

The so-called *fastlege* plays a key role in the Norwegian system – a general practitioner (GP) who is responsible for primary care and who participates via an agreement with the municipality in the so-called *fastlegeordning* (GP scheme).[1075] Approximately 99% of the Norwegian population is registered for the regular GP scheme.[1076] The GP scheme is a list system, which has at its main objective, strengthening the relationship between the physician and the patients.[1077] It was implemented in 2001 as

1073 In general it has to be noted that in Norway as with the other healthcare systems in Scandinavian countries, these systems often are characterized as being run according to a decentralized modell due to which funding is raised by taxation and where the main players are public, see *Johnsen*, Jan R. (2006), Health systems in transition, Norway, European Observatory on Health Systems and Policies, p. 21 referring to Rice, N./Smith, P. (2002), Strategic resource allocation and funding decisions, in: Mossialos, E. et al. (eds), Funding health care: Options for Europe.

1074 Lov 7. juli 1999 nr. 64 *om helsepersonell m.v.* (*helsepersonelloven eller hlspl*) (Health Personnel Act – hlspl).

1075 see *Forskrift om fastlegeordning i kommunene*; see also *Befring*, Anne K./*Grytten*, Nils J./*Ohnstad*, Bente (2002), Jus for leger, pp. 66, 446ff., 454 f.

1076 *Johnsen* (2006), p. 19.

1077 ibid., p. 19.

part of a major health reform in Norway, which moreover aimed at improving the quality of the medical services on the local level and improving the continuity of care.[1078]

One of the GP scheme's basic principles constitutes the patients' freedom and right to choose whether or not to participate in it.[1079] If they participate and enrol in the system, they may select their physician from a pool of GPs within the national health plan and sign onto the list of the GP of their choice.[1080]

The GP scheme's core element constitutes an agreement between the GP, who is self-employed in his private practice, and the municipality, the so-called *fastlegeavtalen*.[1081]

13.2.2 Authorisations and licences

To be entitled to practise medicine in Norway, it is necessary to have an authorisation (§ 48 hlspl.)[1082] or licence (§ 49 hlspl.). This applies regardless of whether one works as a GP or not. Authorisations represent full and permanent approval, while licences impose one or more limitations with respect for example to duration, independent or supervised practise. The authorisation's main objective is to ensure that the physicians possess the necessary relevant qualifications, which in turn is an indispensable requirement to guarantee the patients' safety and quality within the health

1078 see § 1 *Forskrift om fastlegeordning i kommunene.*

1079 § 2-1 c (1) Lov 2. juli 1999 nr. 63 *om pasient- og brukerrettigheter (pasient- og brukerrettighetsloven*). As participation in the GP-scheme is voluntary, patients are free to find a doctor outside the GP-system, even though that might require the patient to pay a higher patient's payment premium.

1080 Despite this the patient has twice a year the right to choose another physician as his GP and moreover the right to obtain a second opinion from another GP, see § 2-1 c (2) *pasient- og brukerrettighetsloven.*

1081 §§ 2 (b), 30ff. *Forskrift om fastlegeordning i kommunene.* Per-capita grants from the municipality, such as the rates for own contribution by the patients and reimbursement from the insurance for the work performed form the income of GPs, see *Johnsen* (2006), p. 19; 93.5 percent of primary care physicians are in private practice, while the remaining 6.5 percent are employed in the municipality, see https://www.regjeringen.no/nb/tema/helse-og-omsorg/helse--og-omsorg stjenester-i-kommunene/fastlegeordningen/id115301/ (last accessed: 17.12.2014)

1082 Physicians are explicitly listed in § 48 (1) (n) hlspl.

service.[1083] According to § 48 (2) hlspl., authorisation may be granted to any physician under the following cumulative conditions: first, that the physician in question has passed an examination in the relevant subject at a Norwegian university or college or through occupational training at a secondary level (§ 48 (2) (a) hlspl.), second, that the physician has completed practical training in conformity with regulations laid down by the Ministry of Health and Care Services (§ 48 (2) (b) hlspl.), third, that the physician is under 75 years of age (§ 48 (2) (c) hlspl.) and finally, that he is not considered to be unfit (*uegnet*) for the profession (§ 48 (2) (d) hlspl.). In case the applicant does not meet the necessary requirements for getting the authorisation, a licence may be issued instead, which may contain limitations on the holder's rights.[1084] The licence could for example be restricted in relation to tasks, responsibilities, a special field of medicine, that the work shall be subject to supervision or that it may only be granted following a concrete and individual assessment of whether the licencee is de facto capable of practising his profession in a responsible manner.[1085]

13.2.3 The student licence, turnus licence and licence for medical practitioners above the age of 75

One has, in general, to distinguish between the student licence, the *turnus* licence and the licence for medical practitioners above the age of 75. The student licence permits the student to practise medicine in a subordinate capacity, which entails permission to prescribe medication to a limited extent in relation to the work in such a capacity.[1086] A *turnus* or 'practical service' licence is required for practising as a medical practitioner in a subordinate capacity at a hospital, such as e.g. work in a casualty unit, dur-

1083 §§ 1, 48 (2) hlspl.; see Ot.prp. nr. 1 (1979-80), *Om lov om leger og om lov om tannleger*, chap. 5.3.9, p. 49; Innst. O. nr. 55. (1979-80), *Innstilling fra sosialkomitéen om lov om leger og om lov om tannleger*, p. 4.

1084 see § 49 (1), (3) hlspl.; see in detail *forskrift om lisens til helsepersonell*, FOR 2000-12-21-1379.

1085 § 49 (3) hlspl.; see e.g. limitations manifested in § 8 *forskrift om lisens til helsepersonell* as regards licences for health personell above the age of 75.

1086 § 4 *forskrift om lisens til helsepersonell.*

ing a state-organised *turnus*.[1087] Work during *turnus* encompasses work in a hospital and periods in the primary district healthcare service.[1088] In contrast to a student licence, it provides for more extensive areas of responsibility. The successful completion of *turnus* is, since legal amendments in 2012, no longer an indispensable requirement to get an authorisation, but constitutes a compulsory part of the physician's professional specialisation.[1089] Finally, a special licence exists for physicians having reached the age of 75.[1090] This is due to the fact that, according to § 54 (1) s. 1 hlspl., authorisation, a licence or the certificate of completion of specialist training expires when the holder turns 75 years of age.

13.2.4 Expiration of authorisation at the age of 75: The age limit in § 54 (1) s. 1 hlspl.

The age limit in § 54 (1) s. 1 hlspl. as such may be characterised as a mandatory retirement provision. However, under certain conditions, stated in § 54 (2) in conjunction with §§ 49, 51 hlspl., a physician will have the possibility of extending his working life beyond the age limit by applying for a licence. Provided that the age limit is supplemented by the option to apply for a licence, it may rather be characterised as a soft age limit, opening up for flexible opportunities for extending working life. Nevertheless, one cannot ignore the fact that the licence in reality often imposes restrictions on the physician in the exercise of his profession compared to the previous applicable authorisation. Moreover, one has to consider that if the licence or authorisation finally expires, the employee is not allowed to

1087 see e.g. § 9 *Forskrift om spesialistgodkjenning av helsepersonell og turnusstillinger for leger*, FOR-2000-12-21-1384; § 3 (1) b) *Forskrift om veiledet tjeneste for å få adgang til å praktisere som allmennlege med rett til trygderefusjon*, FOR-2005-12-19-1653; § 1a-1 *forskrift om lisens til helsepersonell.*

1088 see in detail information given at: http://legeforeningen.no/Student/Norsk-medisinstudentforening/Turnus/Temaer-A-A1/Turnus-FAQ/ (last accessed: 17.12.2014)

1089 see in detail *Helsedirektoratet* (2012), Ny turnusordning for leger, Informasjon og veiledningsmateriell, 1. edt., p. 4.

1090 §§ 48 (2) (c), 49 hlspl.; §§ 6ff. *forskrift om lisens til helsepersonell.*

work any longer as a physician, as these requirements are compulsory.[1091] In this respect, the age limit is absolute and may even be characterised as an occupational ban.[1092]

13.2.5 The age limit for practising as a general practitioner in the fastlege system

The age limit for practising as a GP in the *fastlege* system is even lower than the age limit for withdrawal of authorisation. This is due to the fact that according to a framework agreement between the *Legeforeningen* (Norwegian Medial Association – NMA)[1093] and the *Kommunens Sentralforbund* (The Norwegian Association of Local and Regional Authorities – KS),[1094] the individual contract between the municipality and the GP terminates without further notice automatically when the age of 70 is reached.[1095] Therefore, the contract expires solely based on the physician reaching the age limit of 70. It has to be kept in mind that the physician is not protected against unilateral termination of the contract and the automatic expiry of the contract after having reached the age of 70. However, the agreement between the KS and NMA opens up for a prolongation. The municipality and the physician may enter into a temporary employment contract concerning practising as a GP above the age of 70, but this does

1091 see § 54 (1) hlspl.

1092 *Pande*, Helene/*Holmsen*, Eva (2006), Palliativ medisin – en oppgave for pensjonerte leger?, Tidsskrift for den norske lægeforening (Tidsskr Nor Lægeforen) nr. 24, 2006, 126, pp. 3283–3284, p. 3284.

1093 http://www.legeforeningen.no/id/81039 (last accessed 17.12.2014).

1094 http://www.ks.no (last accessed 17.12.2014).

1095 see part VI para 16, s. 3 of Framework agreement between NMA and KS: *'Den individuelle avtalen opphører uten oppsigelse når legen fyller 70 år.'*, available at: http://legeforeningen.no/Emner/Andre-emner/Avtaler/Avtalearkiv/Naringsdrivende/Fastleger-KS/Rammeavtalen-mellom-KS-og-Den-norske-legeforening-om-allmennpraksis-i-fastlegeordningen-i-kommunene/ (last accessed 17.12.2014); In addition the *fastlege* has to sign an individual agreement *'om allmennpraksis i fastlegeordning'* with the municipality. Due to this agreement the fastlege is obliged to follow the rights and duties laid down in the framework agreement.

not apply after the doctor has reached 75 years of age.[1096] With the withdrawal of the authorisation at the age of 75, the individual agreement also expires with immediate effect.[1097] Whether the contract between the age of 70 and 75 may be extended depends in the end on the municipalities' evaluation.[1098] If the agreement is not prolonged, the physician in question is no longer entitled to work as a *fastlege*. Nevertheless, he might apply for a licence and could then work as a physician outside the *fastlege* system.

It has to be noted that GPs often face difficulties when applying for a prolongation of the agreement. Reasons for not extending the agreement are often the fear of age-based decline in the GP's performance, which would put the health of the patients at risk and which might lead to an irresponsible increase in the municipality's responsibility.[1099] Moreover, one might refer to further aspects such as the good recruitment of younger GPs, meaning that there would be no need to have the older physicians further employed.

As laid down in §§ 54 (2), 49 (4) hlspl. in conjunction with §§ 6-9 *Forskrift om lisens til helsepersonell,* exemptions from the general rule that the authorisation or license expires at the age of 75 years can be made. The physician may still use his professional title (§ 54 (1) s. 2)[1100] and apply for a licence to engage in limited medical practise (§ 54 (2)), such as for example the limited right to issue prescriptions of drugs or a limitation to a particular professional position.[1101] Working as a health professional

1096 see part VI para. 16, s. 4 Framework agreement between NMA and KS: 'Kommunen og legen kan inngå en tidsbegrenset avtale om fastlegevirksomhet ut over fylte 70 år, likevel ikke etter at legen er fylt 75 år.'

1097 see § 54 (1) s. 1 hlspl. i.c.w. part VI para. 16, s. 5 Framework agreement between NMA and KS.

1098 *Herlofsen*, Erik R. (2008), Diskriminerende aldersgrenser for leger, "Autorisasjonen er inndratt", Vi Over 60, Nov. 2008, pp. 68-69, p. 68 with further details; the fact that the municipality 'may ' extent the contract but is not obliged to to so, has also been referred to by the defendant in case LE-2009-47936, Judgement of 24. June 2009, *Eidsivating lagmannsrett, kjennelse*. The case inter alia concerned the prolongation to work as a fastlege beyond the age of 70.

1099 see to this aspect among others: *Tangen*, Erik (2011), Diagnose: For gammel, in: nyhet BÆRUM, 12. Februar 2011, p. 12.

1100 see commentary (available via www.lovdata.no) to § 6 *Forskrift om lisens til helsepersonell*.

1101 see §§ 54 (2), 49 (3) hlspl.

beyond the age of 75 years entails for example being able to take assignments as an expert witness (*sakkyndig*) or engage in teaching.[1102] It is primarily clinical, patient-oriented activities that the health personnel will be cut off from.[1103] However, according to § 54 (2) hlspl., regulations on the licensing of health professionals over 75 years may be given so that they can also provide health care beyond the age of 75. This has been predominantly regulated in chap. 2 (§§ 6-9) of *Forskrift om lisens til helsepersonell.*[1104] As laid down in its § 6 (1), health personnel over the age of 75 may apply for a licence to continue to practise their professions.[1105] Such a licence shall be granted for a specified period, which shall not exceed two years at a time while the applicant is less than 80 years of age.[1106] Its duration shall not exceed one year in cases where the applicant is 80 years of age or older.[1107] A physician may thus get a successive licence for the respective period several times. Some even hold a licence above the age of 90.[1108] The central rationale for the shorter duration of licences is to increase the number of control assessments to ensure that the licensee is still fit to practise the profession.[1109] The content of the application for the licence is further substantiated in § 7. As stated in § 7 (1) (a), (b), information shall be given about the 'nature and extent' of the business where the

1102 see commentary § 6 *Forskrift om lisens til helsepersonell.*

1103 see ibid.

1104 see §§ 6-9 *Forskrift om lisens til helsepersonell.*

1105 see in general the cross-sectional study carried out in 1993 among Norwegian physicians regarding inter alia their licences and professional activity. Due to the survey 76% of the respondents between the age of 75 and 79 still had a licence, while the numbers of licencee holders dropped down to 64% for the age group 80-84 and 41% for those aged 85 to 89. The study did not specify the respective nature and extent of the licence, see in detail: *Gogstad* Anders/ *Aasland* Olaf G. (1998), Hvordan har de pensjonerte legene det? Tidsskr Nor Lægeforen 1998, 118, pp. 1378–82, p. 1379, 1381.

1106 § 6 (2) *Forskrift om lisens til helsepersonell.*

1107 § 6 (2) *Forskrift om lisens til helsepersonell.*

1108 *Aasland*, Olaf G./*Bringedal*, Berit/*Ronge*, Kari (2010), Aldersgrense for legers autorisasjon og lisens, Tidskr Nor Legeforen nr. 19 2010, 130, pp. 1917-20, p. 1919, Tabell 1.

1109 see commentary to § 6 *Forskrift om lisens til helsepersonell*: 'Tidsbegrensningen må ses i sammenheng med forskriftsutkastet § 9, om endringer i lisensperioden. Den sentrale begrunnelsen for kortere varighet av lisenser enn tidligere, er å øke antall kontrollpunkter for å sikre at lisensinnehaveren fortsatt er skikket til å utøve yrket.'

licence is needed.[1110] This means that information should be given about what type of business will be operated, for example, if the licence is needed for the business of being a medical advisor or for conducting patient-oriented activities. Information shall also be provided about the approximate extent of the business operations.[1111] Finally, according to § 7 (2), every application should be accompanied by a medical certificate, which is more than the normally required health certificate. The medical certificate shall be issued by the applicant's GP or any other physician who possesses an authorisation. In addition to assessing the health of the applicant, the issuing physician also has to consider whether the applicant is physically and mentally able to handle the concrete activities that the applicant has applied for.[1112] The issuing physician has (in other words) to be familiar with the type of business that the applicant intends to practise and with the business that the licence is being applied for, before the medical certificate can be issued.[1113] When awarding the licence, the applicant's suitability shall be analysed in relation to the nature and extent of the applicant's intended work. It is particularly stressed that great emphasis should be placed on how the applicant has kept abreast of the latest

1110 Moreover the application should contain the following information: the type of work performed by the applicant, particularly during the last five years, see § 7 (1) (b) *Forskrift om lisens til helsepersonell*; if an (unrestricted) authorisation to prescribe (*forskrivingsrett*) is desired and the period of time for which the licence should be valid, see § 7 (1) (d) *Forskrift om lisens til helsepersonell.*

1111 commentary to § 7 *Forskrift om lisens til helsepersonell*: 'Omfang kan være et fast antall dager eller timer pr. uke, eller det kan være av mer tilfeldig karakter, avhengig av oppgavetilflyt og/eller ønske om kun periodevis virksomhet'; It was originally specified that the activities of the physicians with a licence should not be less than equivalent to a 20% position, but this met resistance in the Social Committee. The Parliament majority rather voted in 2004 for a proposal that the county physician could grant license after a specific and discretionary assessment without absolute requirements concerning nature of the business and that it's scope has to exceed a certain percentage of the position; see to this aspect Innst. S. nr. 76 (2002–2003) Innstilling fra sosialkomiteen om forslag om en endring i FOR 2000-12-21-1379; *Forskrift om endring i forskrift om lisens for helsepersonell*, FOR-2004–08–30-1224; see to this aspect *Aasland* et al. (2010), p. 1917.

1112 § 7 (2) s. 2 *Forskrift om lisens til helsepersonell*: 'Legeattesten skal bekrefte at lisenssøker er psykisk og fysisk i stand til å ivareta slik virksomhet som det søkes om lisens for'.

1113 commentary to § 7 *Forskrift om lisens til helsepersonell.*

developments within his or her field, and how the applicant plans to maintain his or her competence.[1114] The licence may be awarded with a full, limited or without any prescribing right.[1115]

The licence to engage in organised patient-related activities of a certain scope may be provided with full prescribing rights (§ 8 (2) s. 1).[1116] A licence to engage in patient-related activities not covered by § 8 (2) s. 1 may be provided with limited prescribing rights.[1117] A licence without a right to prescribing is awarded in cases where the applicant solely intends to engage in patient-oriented business that only includes family, friends and other relatives, and where the licence should not be used for patient-related activities.[1118]

No specific requirements exist for determining whether one or the other type of licence shall be issued.[1119] It is up to the issuing authority's discretion to assess whether and to what extent the licence should be granted.[1120] In exercising this discretionary margin, the issuing authority shall in particular take into consideration the nature and extent of past activities, what activities the applicant intends to exercise, how the applicant has kept and will keep up to date and other factors that may affect licence issuance.[1121] In the event that a change should occur in the state of physical or mental health of a licensee, in a manner that might have an adverse effect on the licensee's ability to carry on their profession, the licensee shall immediately notify the Norwegian Directorate for Health and Social Affairs.[1122] Licensees may voluntarily renounce their licence to practise.[1123] Besides this, it is incumbent on any health professional who becomes aware of such a change in the state of health of a licensee or of any matter that may be of relevance for the licensee's ability to carry on their profession prop-

1114 § 8 (1) *Forskrift om lisens til helsepersonell.*

1115 § 8 (2) *Forskrift om lisens til helsepersonell*; commentary to § 8 *Forskrift om lisens til helsepersonell.*

1116 commentary to § 8: '*Kun leger med lisens med full forskrivningsrett kan forskrive medisiner på blåresept.*' This is decisive as it may preclude the physician from working in areas where these prescriptions typically are needed.

1117 § 8 (2) s. 2 *Forskrift om lisens til helsepersonell.*

1118 § 8 (2) s. 3 *Forskrift om lisens til helsepersonell.*

1119 similar *Gislerud*, G./*Claussen*, B./*Bruusgaard*, D. (2000), Lisens for leger, Tidsskr Nor Lægeforen 2000, 120, pp. 2446-2447.

1120 commentary to § 8 Forskrift om lisens til helsepersonell; critical to this discretion *Gislerud* et al. (2000), pp. 2446-2447; see also *Mellbye*, Fredrik (1996), Aldersgrense for licentia practicandi, Tidsskr Nor Lægeforen 1996, 116, p. 1137.

1121 commentary to § 8 *Forskrift om lisens til helsepersonell.*

1122 § 9 (1) *Forskrift om lisens til helsepersonell.*

1123 § 9 (2) *Forskrift om lisens til helsepersonell* i.c.w. § 61 hlspl.

erly, to notify the Board on Health Supervision or the Norwegian Directorate for Health and Social Affairs. Thus, this provision imposes an obligation to act (*aktivitetsplikt*) on the licensee or any other persons who might have noticed that the licensee's health condition has changed, thus making him unfit to possess a licence as a healthcare professional.[1124] Not all changes have to be notified, only those that 'may have an affect on the licencee's suitability'.[1125] The same obligation is imposed on the physician who has been issued with the medical certificate, as stipulated in § 7 (2). He has to give such notification without being restricted by the duty of confidentiality.[1126] This is in line with § 17 hlspl., which imposes an obligation on health professionals to report any circumstances that may endanger patients' safety. However, as the phrase 'may have' in § 9 (1) implies, the final assessment of whether a change in health condition justifies the revocation of the licence ultimately rests with the Board of Health Supervision.[1127]

1124 commentary to § 9 *Forskrift om lisens til helsepersonell.*

1125 see § 9 (1) *Forskrift om lisens til helsepersonell.*

1126 § 9 (3) *Forskrift om lisens til helsepersonell* i.c.w. § 23 hlspl.

1127 commentary to § 9 *Forskrift om lisens til helsepersonell.*

13.2.6 Critics to the age limit in § 54 (1) s. 1 hlspl.

The 75-year age limit for the withdrawal of authorisation is at present highly debated.[1128] In 2008, the NMA made a proposal that the age limit should be raised; however, the Ministry did not propose any amendments.[1129] In 2010, the research centre of the NMA evaluated, with the help of questionnaires, the attitude of physicians towards the controversial 75-year age limit.[1130]

In a further questionnaire sent out in April 2008, physicians were asked about their view on the withdrawal of the authorisation.[1131] Fifty-six per cent of the respondents disagreed with the withdrawal of authorisation at the age of 75, and stated, for example, that the criterion for the authori-

---

1128 see to the debate among others: critical *Mellbye* (1996), p. 1137; *Pande/Holmsen* (2006), pp. 3283ff.; *Herlofsen* (2008), p. 68 f.; *Pahle*, Egill/*Hansen*, Jan A. (2008), Diskriminerende aldersgrense for leger, Tidsskr Nor Legeforen nr. 13-14, 128, p. 1546; *Pande*, Helene/*Noreik*, Kjell (2008), Eldre legers syn på tap av autorisasjon ved 75 år, Tidsskr Nor Legeforen nr. 24, 2008, 128, p. 2843; *Hagen*, Steinar (2009), Samfunnets hån mot eldre leger, Tidsskr Nor Legeforen nr. 4, 2009, 129, pp. 311-312, p. 311 f.; *Steinsvoll*, Steinar, P. (2009), Diskriminering av eldre leger, Tidsskr Nor Legeforen nr. 7, 2009, 129, p. 650; *Aasland* et al. (2010), p. 1918 f., 1920; *Ekroll*, Torbjørn (2011), Når de yngste fåe bestemme, Tidsskr Nor Legeforen nr. 9, 2009, 129, pp. 892-893, p. 892 f.; *Hustad-Johansen*, Finn E. (2009), Tanker omkring 70-årseregelen for fastlegehjemmel, Tidsskr Nor Legeforen nr. 9, 2009; 129, p. 892; *Hunstad*, Nils (2009), Opphør av autorisajon ved fylte 75 år, Tidsskr Nor Legeforen nr. 9, 2009, 129, p. 892; *Janbu* (2011), p. 111; arguing e.g. for maintaining the existing licence system *Svabø*, Harry M. (1996), Eldre legers kår, Tidsskr Nor Lægeforen 1996,116, p. 1064; similar also *Bruusgaard*, Dag (2010), Forsvarlighet og autorisasjon, Tidsskr Nor Legeforen nr. 19 2010, 130, p. 1906 such as also *Haugum*, P. (2008), Eldre leger diskrimineres ikke, Tidsskr Nor Legeforen nr. 13-14, 2008; 128, pp. 1545-1546; The age limit of 75 years in § 54 (1) s. 1 hlspl., as well as the awarding of licences (§ 49 hlspl.) to physicians above the age of 75 has also been subject-matter of several decisions by Norwegian Appeal Board for Health Personnel (*Statens Helsepersonellnemnd-HPN)*, see e.g. only in the past decade: vedtak 2010-05-26, HPN 2010-62; vedtak 2008-10-21, HPN-2008-97; vedtak 2007-11-21. HPN-2007-9; vedtak 2007-11-20. HPN-2007-132; vedtak 2006-12-18, HPN-2006-181; vedtak 2005-01-20. HPN-2004-137; vedtak: 2003-11-25. HPN-2003-126; even though rather implict it was also subject to the case LE-2009-47936 of the Eidsivating lagmannsrett.

1129 see to this aspect *Janbu* (2011), p. 111.

1130 see for the details of the chosen material and method *Aasland* et al. (2010), pp. 1917-1920; see also *Pande/Noreik* (2008), p. 2843.

1131 ibid.

sation should be related to physical or mental health rather than age and that a professional body like the GP scheme or the *fylkeslege* (Chief County Medical Officer) should function as a kind of control body.[1132] Some stated, moreover, that the existing regulation is contrary to the official senior policy, which claims that there should be an extension of working life.[1133]

Both physicians under the age of 75 (non-retired) and above the age limit (retired) were involved.[1134] The participants were asked about their opinion concerning the requirement that those over 75 years have to renew their licence.[1135] While 80% of the non-pensioners replied that they agreed with the existing age limit and the requirement to renew the licence, only 34% of the respondents who were retired physicians agreed.[1136] Not surprisingly, the attitude of the respondents changed the closer they got to the 75-year age limit. After the age of 55, the proportion of those respondents who claimed that the decision of prolongation should be left to the physicians alone increased remarkably.[1137] After the age of 75, the majority of the respondents was in favour either of a lifelong licence – regardless of the age or health of the physician in question – or that the physician should self-determine if he wanted to renew the licence or not.[1138] Of those respondents who in principle endorsed an age limit, 9.7% of the non-retired and 15.4% of the retired respondents recommended an alternative age limit.[1139] In addition, in this regard, a clear trend was observable

1132 ibid.

1133 ibid.

1134 The term retired/non-retired is used to distinguish between the respondents under and above the age limit of 75, who were asked in two separate questionnaires about the same question.

1135 *Aasland* et al. (2010), p. 1918.

1136 ibid., p. 1918, Figure 1.

1137 ibid., p. 1918.

1138 ibid., p. 1918; similar already study concerning the professional activity and retirement patterns among Norwegian physicians, where according to a questionaire retired physicians considered the 75 years-age limit as too low, see *Hensrud,* Anne/*Kristiansen*, Ivar S. (1994), Yrkesaktivet og pensjonering blant norske leger over 55 år, Tidsskr Nor Laegeforen, 1994;114(26), pp. 3093-3096, p. 3096.

1139 ibid., p. 1918, Figure 1.

where the older the respondents were, the higher the proposed alternative age limit was.[1140] Moreover, the questionnaire revealed that a quarter of the respondents above the age of 75 held a licence.[1141]

Of those physicians who replied that they did not apply for a renewal of their licence, the majority indicated that they feared they would not meet the requirement stipulated in § 8 (2) *Forskrift om lisens til helsepersonell* in which organised patient-oriented activities have to be of a certain scope.[1142] However, these concerns might be unsubstantiated, as the SAFH states that in the years 2005–2008, 96% of the physicians (above the age of 74) who applied for a renewal of their licences, ultimately got the approval.[1143]

In a further Norwegian study among working physicians inter alia the impact of adverse events that had caused patient injury and for which the physician felt responsible, such as differences with respect to age, were investigated.[1144] The study revealed a peak at the age of 52.1, when the partial effect of age – on the logit of the probability – of having experienced serious patient injury was estimated.[1145] Similarly, in an American survey, the extent to which it was possible to identify physicians with increased risk of malpractice, based on data from 8000 physicians, revealed a certain positive correlation between age and risk, but this risk similarly levelled off at 50 years of age.[1146] As no scientific data seem to be available to strengthen the need to set the age limit at 75, the limit being set at that specific age seems rather arbitrary.[1147] Critics of the withdrawal of the authorisation at the age of 75 point out that it is humiliating

---

1140 The majority of the retired physicians (those above 75) for example proposed an alternative age limit of 80. But also of the non-retired nearly 50% proposed 80 as the alternative age limit, see ibid., p. 1918, Figure 1.

1141 *Aasland* et al. (2010), p. 1918.

1142 ibid., p. 1918; see to the critics also *Pahle/Hansen* (2008), p. 1546.

1143 *Aasland* et al. (2010), p. 1918. But these data entail no information about the character of the licence (e.g. whether it entails a full or rather a limited prescribing right) and the duration of the licence.

1144 *Aasland*, Olaf G *Førde*, R. (2005), Impact of feeling responsible for adverse events on doctors' personal and professional lives: the importance of being open to criticism from colleagues, Quality and Safety in Health Care (Qual Saf Health Care) 2005: 14, pp. 13–17, p. 14.

1145 *Aasland/Førde* (2005), p. 14, figure 1. However it has to be noted that the analysis was based on self-reporting by the physicians, see *Aasland* et al. (2010), p. 1918 f.

1146 *Aasland* et al. (2010), p. 1918 f. referring to Rolph J. E./Adams J. L./Kimberly A. (2007), Identifying mal- practice-prone physicians, Journal of Empirical Legal Studies 2007, 4, pp. 125–53.

1147 *Herlofsen* (2008), p. 68; *Pahle/Hansen* (2008), p. 1546.

after a long working life to be deprived of one's authorisation solely because of age.[1148] The older physicians tend to represent lifelong experience and knowledge, they have often developed mutually trusting relationships with their patients in their decades of practising, which a younger physician can hardly replace, and finally, they could contribute towards unburdening the healthcare system.[1149] In light of increased life expectancy and the current and further expected shortage of physicians in Norway, the maintenance of the 75-year age limit for the authorisation thus seems questionable, according to its critics.[1150] Others even call the withdrawal of authorisation a *Kollektiv 'straff'*[1151] as the age limit is based on the misperception that many physicians are not able to realise when the time is ripe to withdraw.[1152] Patients might also function as a kind of corrective, as they would change their physician in cases of a suspected decline of mental and physical abilities in their present physician.[1153] In the interests of those few who apparently do not understand their own good, the others are 'punished' according to this argumentation, including those healthy, skilled and experienced physicians who are desperately needed in the Norwegian health system and who would prefer to make their own decision regarding when to retire.[1154] In line with this, critics even call the withdrawal of authorisation at the age of 75 'scornful' and a 'restriction of liberty'.[1155] By contrast, those who claim for the maintenance of the existing regulation argue that physicians may not be able to realise themselves when it is time to retire and that it therefore should be up to the legislator to determine the point of withdrawal.[1156] Due to this argumentation, the regulations are rather designed so that those who are fit

1148 *Steinsvoll*, (2009), p. 650.

1149 *Bruusgaard* (2010), p. 1906; *Pahle/Hansen* (2008), p. 1546; *Steinsvoll* (2009), p. 650; similar *Hagen* (2009), p. 311.

1150 *Steinsvoll* (2009), p. 650; to the aspect that older physicians may be a needed resource also *Torp*, Kå Hå (1996), Må en lege alltid være lege? Tidsskr Nor Lægeforen, 1996 nr. 9, p. 1120, *Pahle/Hansen* (2008), p. 1546; *Hagen* (2009), p. 311 and Innst. O. nr. 55 (1979-80), *Innstilling fra sosialkomitéen om lov om leger og om lov om tannleger*, p. 4.

1151 *Herlofsen* (2008), p. 69.

1152 ibid.

1153 *Hunstad* (2009), p. 892.

1154 *Herlofsen* (2008), p. 69; similar *Hagen* (2009), p. 311.

1155 *Hagen* (2009), p. 311.

1156 *Haugum* (2008), p. 1546.

and suitable for the continued exercise of the medical profession should have the opportunity to do so.[1157] However, others argue that the fact that one can obtain a licence with various limitations cannot countervail the discrimination.[1158] According to this view, this in inter alia based on the fact that no scientific evidence exists for the steadily mentioned lack of ability of older physicians to be aware of the impact of ageing and to assess when they should retire.[1159] Some argue that any impaired ability to practise medicine as a physician would at least be caught by the Norwegian Board of Health Supervision.[1160] A counterargument here would be that the risk of malpractice could then be too high.

With regard to the possibility of being able to apply for a licence, in particular, the legitimacy of the exercise of discretionary power by the issuing authority may be criticised. The decision to award a licence or not depends largely on whether the assessment of mental and physical fitness can be regarded as entirely objective. This raises the question of the decision's verifiability. The decision of the issuing authority is based on discretion, which in the end may lead to diverging results depending on who has assessed the older physician.[1161] Moreover, the limitation of the right to issue prescriptions in § 8 (2) *Forskrift om lisens til helsepersonell* supplementing § 54 (1) s. 1 hlspl. has been criticised. This is due to the fact that it de facto implies that older physicians cannot stand in, when required, for their younger colleagues with full prescription rights.[1162] Consequently, the criticism regarding issuing a licence without, at the same time, giving the physician the right to issue prescriptions fully is like 'providing a hunting licence for hunters without a licence to use guns'.[1163]

Moreover, one of the counterarguments to the introduction of these rules concerned the provision's inconsistency. In contrast to physicians above the age of 75, physicians under the age limit have full rights, with-

---

1157 ibid.
1158 *Pahle/Hansen* (2008), p. 1546.
1159 ibid.
1160 *Mellbye* (1996), p. 1137.
1161 critical also *Gislerud* et al. (2000), p. 2447; *Mellbye* (1996), p. 1137.
1162 *Pahle/Hansen* (2008), p. 1546.
1163 translation by author of ibid., p. 1546; see also *Pande/Noreik* (2008), p. 2843.

out being required in any way to prove their patient-related activities and without being subject to capability assessments during the course of their working career.[1164]

13.3 Compatibility of the 75-year age limit in § 54 (1) s. 1 hlspl. with Dir. 2000/78/EC

13.3.1 Scope of Dir. 2000/78/EC

GPs affiliated to the *fastlege* system fall under the group of self-employed working in the public sector and providing services in the public health sector. Beside this, physicians may also work outside the *fastlege* system, in particular, in cases where they have passed the 70-year age limit as manifested in the Framework agreement between the NMA and KS and did not get a prolongation of their contract.[1165] Even if, as a rule, GPs in Norway are self-employed, this is, according to the wording of Art. 3 No. 1 (a), encompassed by the Directive. Moreover, the 'age limits' - that is, both the withdrawal of the authorisation and the limitation of the licensing[1166] - constitute a 'condition for access to employment' in the sense of Art. 3 No. 1 (a). Access to employment incorporates not only the first instance of access to employment, but also the continuation of employment.[1167]

However, it has to be kept in mind that physicians working as a *fastlege* and being self-employed are not covered by the Norwegian WEA and its chap. 13, which basically transforms Dir. 2000/78/EC. The special regulation in § 13-2 (2) WEA concerning the Act's applicability to self-employed persons merely regulates that the provisions of chap. 13 shall correspondingly apply to the employer's choice and treatment of self-

1164 see § 8 *Forskrift om lisens til helsepersonell*; to the crictics see *Janbu* (2011), p. 111.

1165 Del VI, para. 16, s. 3 *rammeavtale mellom KS og den norske legeforening*.

1166 As as manifested in § 54 (1) s. 1 hlpsl. and the regulations concerning the licence are manifested in § 54 (2) in conjunction with §§ 49 (4), 51 hlpsl., §§ 6-9 *Forskrift om lisens til helsepersonell.*

1167 see to this aspect in the German context *Boecken* (2005), p. 394; *Schüffner*, Marc/*Schnall*, Laura (2009), Hypertrophie des ärztlichen Sozialrechts, Verfassungs- und europarechtliche Regelungen des (zahn-)ärztlichen Berufsrechts anhand ausgewählter Beispiele, p. 76.

employed persons. As referred to in the preparatory acts, the provision only focuses on the employment contract and on the employer's choice, and not on the applicability of the chapter's provisions as such to self-employed persons.[1168] This is a decisive difference to the Directive's scope, which also applies in all matters to self-employed persons.[1169]

With § 13-2 (2) WEA, what was established during the process of implementing Dir. 2000/78/EC into Norwegian law by § 54 A No. 3 of the WEA of 1977 is continued, and it came into force by the amending act *endringslov* Nr. 15/2004.[1170] § 54 A replaced, in turn, the former applicable § 55 A, where self-employed persons were not encompassed.[1171] The protection against discrimination has thus, with § 13-2 (2) WEA, compared to its antecessor in § 55 A WEA, a wider scope of applicability. There were, however, even before the amendments, several examples to be found according to which the WEA had also been made applicable for the group of self-employed persons through further regulations.[1172] Finally, in the preparatory act for § 54 A WEA, the legislator could not find a good reason to explicitly exclude the self-employed from protection against discrimination.[1173]

Even if the Norwegian legislator seems to have been aware of the Directive's wider scope encompassing employment and occupation – and not merely the employment relationship per se – from the Norwegian legislative perspective, nothing more has so far been done as regards the situation of the self-employed. Here again, it has to be kept in mind that Norway was not legally bound to implement Dir. 2000/78/EC.[1174] Nevertheless, one might at least argue that the Norwegian legislator has not explicitly excluded self-employed persons from the scope of applicability of chap. 13 WEA. Given the 'lack' of transformation of the Directive in terms of its applicability to self-employed persons, the compatibility analysis of the Norwegian provisions with Dir. 2000/78/EC lacks a certain corresponding implementation into Norwegian law, so that the analysis is of a rather 'hypothetical' nature. Despite these uncertainties, the chosen

---

1168 see commentary in Ot.prp. nr. 49 (2004-2005), *Arbeidsmiljø, arbeidstid og stillingsvern mv. (arbeidsmiljøloven)*, p. 326; Ot.prp. nr. 104 (2002–2003), chap. 8.1.3, p. 24.

1169 Art. 3 No. 1 (a) Dir. 2000/78/EC.

1170 see Ot.prp. nr. 49 (2004-2005), p. 326; see in general already chap. 11.3.1. above.

1171 see Ot.prp. nr. 104 (2002–2003), chap. 8.1.1, p. 23.

1172 see commentary to § 13-2 (2) WEA by Universitetsforlaget lovkommentar (available via lovdata).

1173 Ot.prp. nr. 104 (2002–2003), chap. 8.1.5.3, p. 25; see commentary to § 13-2 (2) WEA by Universitetsforlaget lovkommentar.

1174 see chap. 11.2.

common parameter for the compatibility assessment in any case constitutes Dir. 2000/78/EC, which the selected provisions on the national level shall be measured against.

The fact that due to Art. 3 No. 3, the Directive is not applicable to payments of any kind made by state schemes or similar schemes, including state social security or social protection schemes, does not constitute a hindrance of the Directive's applicability with regard to the admission of physicians as a *fastlege,* as the admission and the age limit do not constitute a payment in the sense of Art. 3 No. 3, but rather a limitation to the exercise of the profession.[1175]

To conclude, physicians in Norway, who are subject to the 'age limit' in § 54 (1) s. 1 hlspl., are thus encompassed by the personal and material scope of Dir. 2000/78/EC, so that the Directive is applicable with regard to the withdrawal of the authorisation and the licensing requirements.

13.3.2 Direct age discrimination

Both the regulations in § 54 (1) s.1 hlspl. as well as in §§ 54 (2), 49 hlspl. in conjunction with §§ 6-9 *Forskrift om lisens til helsepersonell* are directly tied to the criterion of age; namely, to the age of 70 and 75, respectively. This constitutes less favourable treatment compared to that of younger physicians, so that direct age discrimination in the sense of Art. 2 No. 2 (a) in conjunction with Art. 2 No. 1 Dir. 2000/78/EC is in play.

13.3.3 Justification of direct age discrimination

The key issue then is whether the direct age discrimination is capable of being justified based on Art. 2 No. 5, Art. 6 No. 1, Art. 4 No. 1 and Art. 7.[1176] However, before going into the justification analysis, it is necessary to identify a legitimate aim underlying § 54 (1) s. 1 hlspl.

1175 similar *Schüffner/Schnall* (2009), p. 76.

1176 see in detail to the different justification grounds of Dir. 2000/78/EC and their relation to each other chap. 10.3.

13.3.3.1 Legitimate aim

In the assessment of mandatory retirement for physicians, in general, three objectives might be of relevance as legitimate aims:[1177] first is the protection of the health of patients, who are covered by the health-insurance scheme that the physician in question is a member of. The key argument referred to here is typically that the performance of the physicians declines after a certain age and that the physician's age, in consequence, is considered a risk factor.

Second is the aim of generational equity; that is, the fair distribution of employment opportunities among the generations. Via the mandatory retirement provision, posts for younger physicians might be freed up and they then might be enabled to enter the labour market and get the opportunity to start their own 'business' and afford a living, so the argument goes. Finally, the third objective that might come into play concerns the financial balance of the national health system.[1178] This aim is generally based on the argumentation that a rising number of physicians might lead to an excessive increase in the supply of healthcare, which in turn might result in an excessive level of expenditure to be borne by the state.[1179] The central argument here is that the departure of the oldest of those physicians would make it possible to reduce that expenditure and, in doing so, might avert a risk of serious harm to the balance of the social security system.[1180]

13.3.3.1.1 Securing the patients' health and the public health

As regards the question as to whether the first aim of securing the patients' health and the public health underlies § 54 (1) s. 1 hlspl., it is fruitful to look at § 1 hlspl. It explicitly states that the law's purpose is to promote safety for patients and quality of healthcare services as well as trust in health care and the healthcare services. The provision had been included

---

1177 see to the aspect that several legitimate aims may be referred to already chap. 10.3.5 above.

1178 similar objectives referred to by the referring German court in C-341/08 (*Petersen*), para. 38, which the CJEU then discussed, see para. 44ff., 65ff.

1179 see similar arguments brought forward by the defendant in LE-2009-47936; similar also C-341/08 (*Petersen*), para. 52.

1180 see similar ibid., para. 52.

to illustrate the rationale for regulating health professionals' practice.[1181] The importance of also considering the objectives set out in § 1 in the interpretation of further provisions of the hlspl. – like § 54 (1) s. 1 hlspl. – has also been stressed in the preparatory acts to § 1 hlspl., as the overarching objectives are reflected in § 1 as guidance for the legal interpretation of the provisions.[1182] It has inter alia been stressed that the key objectives set out in § 1 hlspl. also imply that it should be guaranteed that the respective person possesses the necessary professional prerequisites to exercise their profession in a responsible manner, and that thus the control aspect as regards the professional's qualifications will be more obvious.[1183] In addition, it has to be kept in mind that one of the cumulative requirements in granting an authorisation is that the physician in question may be regarded as fit (*ikke uegnet*) for the profession, as stipulated in § 48 (2) (d) hlspl. Moreover, the concern for the patients' safety is explicitly stressed in § 48 (4) hlspl., regulating the requirements for authorisations that do not fall under § 48 (2) hlspl. but may be issued upon request and in cases where certain conditions are fulfilled.

The aim of promoting the patients' safety and quality of the healthcare service also becomes apparent when examining the respective preparatory acts regarding the age limit. First, it has to be noted that before the age limit in § 54 (1) s. 1 hspl. came into force, it was not possible to revoke a physician's authorisation or licence with the argument that he was incapable or not fit (*uskikket)* to exercise the profession of a physician based on old age.[1184] The right to practise as a physician, quite the contrary, was normally awarded for one's lifetime.[1185]

However, there were e.g. possibilities to revoke the right of the physician to prescribe anaesthetics.[1186]

1181 Ot. prp. nr. 13 (1998-1999), chap. 26 *Merknader til de enkelte bestemmelser, til* § 1.

1182 NOU 1993: 33, *Helsepersonells rettigheter og plikter*, chap. 21, to § 1, see also chap. 12.3.

1183 ibid.

1184 see for a historical overview over previous applicable regulations *Haave*, Per (2007), Da legene skulle autoriseres, Tidsskr Nor Lægeforen nr. 24 2007, 127, pp. 3267-3271, p. 3267ff.

1185 NOU 1976: 1, *Legers og tannlegers rettigheter og plikter*, chap. 5.3.9, p. 36; Innst. O. nr. 55 (1979-80), p. 2; Ot. prp. nr. 1 (1979-80), chap. 5.3.9, p. 48.

1186 NOU 1976: 1, chap. 5.3.9, p. 36; Ot. prp. nr. 1 (1979-80), chap. 5.3.9., p. 48.

The authorisation by the state was originally introduced in 1927 with the first *legelov* and this removed the automatic right to practise for students of medicine.[1187] The purpose of its introduction was to maintain the population's confidence in practising physicians by excluding those physicians who were regarded as 'unfit' to do their job.[1188] In 1980, the 75-year age limit was introduced and the provision was continued in the Health Personnel Act of 1999.[1189] The age limit may be regarded as an instrument to control the physicians, while at the same time guaranteeing the best possible treatment for the patients.[1190] The *legelov* of 1927 for the first time required medical students to gain authorisation by the state before they were allowed to practise medicine and use the title of 'medical doctor'.[1191] The main aim of the introduction of the state authorisation was to protect the medical profession against 'unfit' members; that is, those physicians who did not fulfil the ideals of their professional ethic.[1192] Thus, 'it was not a question of monopolising medical work or preventing other groups from working within the healthcare services'.[1193] To put this into context, it has to be noted that the labour market for physicians at the beginning of the 20th century had gone through a transition from a bureaucratic to a free labour market.[1194] Most of the physicians were no longer engaged by the state, but rather had to practise in a private market.[1195] This change resulted in the fear that this might undermine the physicians' authority and status for those who were no longer per se employed by the state and thus

1187 *Aasland* et al. (2010), p. 1917 referring to Lov av 29. april 1927 *om lægers rettigheter og plikter*.

1188 *Haave* (2007), pp. 3267-3271; *Aasland* et al. (2010), p. 1919.

1189 see overview given by *Aasland* et al. (2010), p. 1919.

1190 *Aasland* et al. (2010), p. 1917.

1191 Previously the passed state exam (*embetseksamen*) together with the medical oath and a completed traineeship period (*praktikanttjeneste*) lead automatically to the right to practice medicine. See for an historical overview over the debates about the enactment of the *legelov* and the new requirement of authorisation: *Haave* (2007), pp. 3267-3271.

1192 ibid., p. 3269 f.

1193 translation by author of ibid., p. 3267.

1194 ibid., p. 3269 f., who points – under reference in fn. 27 to Larsen, Ø. (1986), Leger i Norge, in: Larsen Ø./Berg, O./Hodne, F., Legene og sammfunnet, Oslo: Seksjon for medisinisk historie, Universitetet i Oslo/Den norske lægeforening, 1986 – to the fact that privat practising physicians constituted in 1910 about 60% of the countries physicians as opposed to 7,5% in 1832.

1195 ibid., p. 3269 f.

'controlled'.[1196] To restore the state control that was thought to have been lost, the authorisation by the state was considered a necessary solution for safeguarding the public's confidence in the physicians and their work.[1197] Interestingly enough, in the years between 1927 and 1980, an interesting change in perspective took place, to the extent that in 1927, the main purpose referred to by the act was to protect the physicians against other non-professionals and therewith to avoid a weakening in the population's confidence in the medical profession. In 1980, the aim was to protect the patients against 'unfit' physicians.[1198] The Ministry for Social Affairs and Health's[1199] (now the Ministry of Health and Care Services) original rationale for the implementation of the age limit was that experience had demonstrated that particular control over the older cohorts of physicians seemed necessary in order to avoid the risks of serious malpractice both for the patients as well as for the physician himself.[1200] The question of whether older physicians should be allowed to continue working even in old age came up and was discussed in the preparatory acts underlying the age limit in § 54 s. 1 hlspl.[1201] Two options were debated in the preparatory acts: the first option was to revoke an authorisation based on the physician's age (*høy alder*), meaning that old age would be an additional explicit reason to withdraw an authorisation.[1202] The second option was to introduce an absolute age limit for authorisation that could be combined with the opportunity to get a temporary licence afterwards.[1203] The risk for the patients' health caused by an older physician's declining capabilities was thereby the key reason that was discussed regarding the introduction of these options.[1204] The argument was made that physicians are in a

---

1196 ibid., p. 3268ff.
1197 ibid., p. 3269 f.
1198 see to this aspect *Aasland* et al. (2010), p. 1919.
1199 Sosial- og helsedepartementet.
1200 see to this aspect *Aasland* et al. (2010), p. 1917.
1201 see to the NOUs mandat NOU 1976: 1, chap. 5.3.9 referring to chap. 1 b, 2.1.
1202 see Ot.prp. nr. 1 (1979-80), chap. 5.3.9, p. 49 referring to the former applicable § 16 *legelov*, p. 50; NOU 1976:1, chap.5.3.9., p. 36.
1203 see Ot.prp. nr. 1 (1979-80), chap. 5.3.9, p. 49, 50; NOU 1976:1, chap. 5.3.9., p. 36.
1204 NOU 1976:1, chap. 5.3.9, p. 36; Ot.prp. nr. 1 (1979-80), chap. 5.3.9, p. 48.

unique position as they work with the life and the health of others, which might put their patients at risk in cases where they are not competent.[1205] It has also been stressed that it might normally be difficult for patients to evaluate the physician's work and qualifications.[1206] It has been brought forward that one may not rely on the physician's ability to self-criticise and his or her ability to determine whether his or her own expertise will last into old age.[1207] The authorisation has therefore been regarded as a guarantee for the public that the physicians are qualified.[1208]

Interestingly enough, in the preparatory work, it was acknowledged that how long the individual might finally be able to exercise his profession largely varies from individual to individual. [1209] Thus, it was argued that a more individual assessment would better correspond to the real situation at hand.[1210] Relevant aspects might be, in general, the physician's mental and physical health and his professional interest and willingness to keep 'up to date'.[1211] However, as stressed by the NOU Committee, in old age (*høy alder*) both health and interest might decrease.[1212] Even if most of the physicians probably would choose to reduce their professional activity in awareness of a decline due to age, and even if patients were to choose other physicians instead in cases where the patients feared that there were age-related risks, it has been pointed out that the risk that serious symptoms would been overlooked and that an inappropriate treatment would be prescribed might nevertheless evolve.[1213]

In view of the then-in-force pensionable age and dismissal protection legislation that had been limited to the age of 70, introducing an absolute age limit for authorisation that could correspondingly be set at 70 with a maximum cohesive licence period of 5 years was discussed.[1214] The Ministry endorsed as appropriate, in cases of an age limit combined with access to get a licence, an age limit of 75, as most of the physicians would be capable of exercising their profession above

---

1205 Ot.prp. nr. 1 (1979-80), chap. 5.3.9., p. 49; see also Innst. O. nr. 55 (1979-80), p. 4.
1206 ibid.
1207 Ot.prp. nr. 1 (1979-80), chap. 5.3.9., p. 49.
1208 Ot.prp. nr. 1 chap. 5.3.9., p. 49; Innst. O. nr. 55 (1979-80), p. 4.
1209 Ot.prp. nr. 1 (1979-80), chap. 5.3.9., p. 50.
1210 ibid.
1211 ibid., p. 49, see arguments brought forward in the consultative bodies (*høringsinstansene*), p. 49.
1212 NOU 1976: 1, chap. 5.3.9, p. 36.
1213 Ot.prp. nr. 1(1979-80), chap. 5.3.9., p. 49.
1214 NOU 1976: 1, chap. 5.3.9, p. 36.

the age of 70.[1215] The NOU Committee had pointed to the advantage for the public authorities of operating with an age limit and the temporary granting of licences when handling cases where older physicians might be a risk for their patients, as it would simply be easier to deny a request for the renewal of a licence than to revoke an authorisation.[1216] By contrast, it would be difficult to prove that a physician would be unfit to exercise the medical profession because of old age (*uskikket til å utøve legeyrket på grunn av høy alder).* Moreover, the Committee felt that the authorisation's withdrawal based on unfitness (*usikkhet*) might be a stigma that older physicians should be spared of, as it might have a defamatory effect and, inevitably, a certain penalising effect.[1217]

One of the counterarguments brought forward against the expiration of the authorisation combined with the opportunity to grant a licence has been that many physicians might perceive it as unfair that they need apply for a new licence when they have continued to exercise their profession as well as they always have done.[1218] It has been feared that some physicians – who otherwise might be a valuable supplement to the healthcare service – might therefore refrain from applying for a renewal of their licence, which in turn might lead to an increased shortage of physicians.[1219]

After having considered the pros and cons of the option to introduce an automatic expiration of authorisation, the Committee and the Ministry finally concluded that such a provision should not be enacted.[1220] In lieu thereof, a system incorporating a reason for the withdrawal of authorisation including *høy alder* was favoured.[1221] Referring to 'old age' rather than potential mental and physical deficits could be an easier and gentler route towards retirement, so the argument goes.[1222] A general control in the older age groups regarding the physician's fitness has been mentioned as a possible alternative.[1223] However, the majority in Innst. O. Nr. 55 (1979–80) finally argued that in light of the high demands on achieving an authorisation to practise as a physician in Norway, the requirements to

1215 Ot.prp. nr. 1 (1979-80), chap. 5.3.9., p. 49.

1216 see also the arguments brought forward in the *høringsinstansene*, Ot.prp. nr. 1 (1979-80), chap. 5.3.9., p. 49.

1217 NOU 1976: 1, chap. 5.3.9, p. 36.

1218 NOU 1976: 1, chap. 5.3.9, p. 36.

1219 NOU 1976: 1, chap. 5.3.9, p. 37; see in this regard also the argumentation in Innst. O. nr. 55 (1979-80), p. 4; see also the argumentation of the minority in Innst. O. nr. 55 (1979-80), p. 4; Ot.prp. nr. 1 (1979-80), chap. 5.3.9., p. 50.

1220 NOU 19761, chap. 5.3.9, p. 37; Ot.prp. nr. 1 (1979-80), chap. 5.3.9., p. 48.

1221 see NOU 1976:1, p. 31ff.; Ot.prp. nr. 1 (1979-80), chap. 5.3.9., p. 50.

1222 Ot. prp. nr. 1 (1979-80), chap. 5.3.9., p. 50.

1223 see NOU 1976:1, p. 31ff.; Ot.prp. nr. 1 (1979-80), chap. 5.3.9., p. 50.

keep such an authorisation should be similarly strict.[1224] The majority's key argument ultimately was that considering the patient's life should be prioritised (*hensynet til pasientenes liv som må komme i første rekke*[1225]). Consequently, the argument was made that there should be an age limit for physicians as for other professions related to important duties in society (*sammfunnsfunskjoner*). Given the interindividual different capabilities and interests with increasing age, the aim was not to introduce an age limit to hinder capable and interested older physicians in performing a profession they are eligible for, but rather to give the public authorities a real and simplified opportunity to intervene quickly if there was any irresponsible medical practice.[1226] This consideration must, according to the majority's opinion, outweigh the individual's desire to retain a lifelong authorisation.[1227]

In opposition to this, the minority did not opt for the age limit combined with a licence, with the key argument being that other liberal professions did not operate with such age limits and that the existing regulations already encompassed the possibility of being able to withdraw an authorisation/licence in case the physician were to practise in a non-acceptable manner.[1228]

As most of the cases where an age-related decline of capabilities led to negative consequences were experienced after the age of 75, the age limit was finally proposed to be set at the age of 75 in combination with access to temporary licences.[1229] The majority's proposal was adopted by the parliament in the end. The age limit was finally incorporated into the Health Personnel Act of 1999.[1230]

As referred to by *Aasland* et al. in their article concerning the age limit in § 54 hlspl., the Norwegian Ministry of Health and Care Services has been asked to give an analysis of the age limit and the potential need to review it in light of new arguments such as the fact that the population is living longer and is in better health and in view of the expressed wish of the public authorities to extend working life.[1231] The Ministry, in its response of 23 April 2009, repudiated the necessity of reviewing the existing age limit, stressing that the provision serves to maintain the patients' security, the quality of health care and the overall trust in the healthcare services.[1232] Even though

1224 Innst. O. nr. 55 (1979-80), p. 4.
1225 ibid.
1226 ibid.
1227 ibid.
1228 ibid.
1229 ibid.
1230 see *Lov av 2. Juli 1999 nr. 64 om helsepersonell mv.*; see to this aspect *Aasland* et al. (2010), p. 1917.
1231 *Aasland* et al. (2010), p. 1919.
1232 ibid., p. 1919.

this is not a legal source in the strict sense, this might nevertheless at least be a further indication that the safety of the patients and the quality of the health care (such as the overall confidence in the healthcare services) represent the key objectives behind the provision's age limit.

The potential age-based capability decline of the physician also plays a considerable role in the evaluation as to whether the *fastlege* agreement will be prolonged beyond the age of 70 or not. If the prolongation of the agreement were to be denied due to such reasons, the refusal would lead to a paradoxical situation: the physician in question is at that point no longer allowed to practise as a GP in the *fastlege* system, but is nevertheless in the possession of his authorisation, due to which he is allowed to practise as a physician until having reached the age of 75. Moreover, additionally, he has, in principle, the opportunity to apply for a licence after having reached the age of 75. If the key argument for not extending the *fastlege* contract were to be the age-based decline of the respective physician's capabilities, this argumentation would then be inconsistent, as the exercise of his profession as a physician until the age of 75 – and above the age of 75 under the licence – also might imply a risk for the patients' health. If one continues this argumentation in favour of maintaining the age limit for GPs at the age of 70, this would finally imply that patients under the GP scheme would be more 'protected' than those patients of physicians practising above the age of 70 and who were outside the GP system, as these physicians are allowed to work at least until the withdrawal of authorisation at the age of 75.[1233] A similar incongruency was criticised by the CJEU in the *Petersen* case.[1234] In *Petersen,* the situation in Germany was as follows: dentists practising outside the statutory health-insurance scheme could practise their profession at any age and where not encompassed by the 68-year age limit otherwise applicable for Statutory Health Insurance (SHI) dentists. One of the legislation's central aims referred to under the proceedings for the 68-year age limit was the protection of patients' health against a decline in the performance of dentists older than 68 years of age.[1235] However, patients could be treated by privately practising dentists older than 68 years of age and were consequently not protected against the presumed performance decline. According to the CJEU's analysis, the exception for private practising dentists therefore

1233 critical also: *Hustad-Johansen* (2009), p. 892; *Tangen*, Erik (2011), Diagnose: For gammel, nyhet Bærum, 12. February 2011, p. 12.

1234 C-341/08 (*Petersen*).

1235 ibid., para. 88.

runs 'counter to the objective pursued',[1236] inter alia as it potentially applied to all dentists and appeared to concern 'a not inconsiderable number of patients'.[1237] In light of one of the objectives pursued by the age limit, namely the protection of the health of patients, due to the CJEU, the measure lacked consistency, as dentists outside the system were exempted from it.[1238] The Court therefore concluded, 'In that case the age limit imposed on panel dentists is not necessary for the protection of health within the meaning of Article 2(5) of the Directive'.[1239]

In sum, securing the patient's health and the public health was a key underlying aim of the age limit in § 54 (1) s. 1 hlspl. This may also be considered legitimate if it is not applied in an inconsistent manner.[1240]

13.3.3.1.2 Financial stability of the national health system

Related to the aim of securing the quality of health care is, moreover, the aim of the financial stability of the national health system.[1241] However, as regards this objective, neither in law, the provision's context,[1242] preparatory acts nor in any other relevant sources of law is any evidence to be found that such an aim underlies the age limit in § 54 (1) s. 1 hlspl.

13.3.3.1.3 Fair distribution of employment opportunities among generations

While the fair distribution of employment opportunities for physicians among the generations was discussed as a legitimate aim in CJEU *Petersen* and played a role in the debate concerning German provision § 95 (7) s. 3 of the Fifth Book of the Social Code (*Sozialgesetzbuch* (SGB) V) in its former applicable version, as regards Norway, the situation is

---

1236 ibid., para. 61.
1237 ibid., para. 61.
1238 ibid., para. 62.
1239 ibid., para. 62.
1240 Recognizing this aim as legitimate also ibid., para. 52.
1241 C-341/08 (*Petersen*), para. 44.
1242 The possibility to merely identify a legitimate aim out of the provison's context has been explicitly recognized by the CJEU, see chap. 10.3.5.

considerably different.[1243] Quite the contrary, in the past decades, a feared shortage of physicians coined discussions in Norway.[1244] This is also corroborated by examining the preparatory acts to § 54 (1) s.1 hlspl., where the risk of a shortage of physicians caused by the introduction of an age limit has been explicitly referred to on several occasions.

However, as regards the age limit in the Framework agreement between the KS and NMA, considerations such as creating job opportunities for younger physicians might have played a role. However, this provision is not assessed in detail in this thesis in terms of its compatibility with Dir. 2000/78/EC.

13.3.3.1.4 Intermediate conclusion

To sum up, the key aim underlying § 54 (1) s. 1 hlspl. is that of securing the patients' health and the public healthas well as the quality of the healthcare system as such. After having identified this, the next step is to determine which justification provision of Dir. 2000/78/EC is most appropriate for the purpose of examining the justification of the age-discriminatory age limit in § 54 (1) s. 1 hlspl.[1245] It has to be kept in mind that the aims that may be regarded as legitimate within the meaning of Art. 6 No. 1 Dir. 2000/78/EC, as explicitly stated by the CJEU in *Age Concern*, have to be social-policy objectives, such as those related to employment policy, the labour market or vocational training.[1246] In line with the argumentation of Advocate General *Bot* in the CJEU in the *Petersen* case, the aim of protecting the public health in general, and the health of the patients in particular may hardly be subsumed under these social-policy objectives.[1247]

1243 see to the German legal situation that was subject to C-341/08 (*Petersen*), para. 11ff.

1244 see to the problem of shortage of physicians e.g. Ot.prp. nr. 4 (1998-99), *Om lov om endringer i folketrygdloven og i enkelte andre lover*, chap. 17.2; see to the discussion e.g. *Vigen*, Terje (1999), Legemangelmysteriet - kan det løses?, Tidsskr Nor Lægeforen 1999, 119, p. 487.

1245 similar AG *Bot*, in C-341/08 (*Petersen*), Opinion delivered on 3 September 2009, ECR 2010, I-00047, para. 54.

1246 see AG *Bot*, in C-341/08 (*Petersen*), para. 55 referring to C-388/07 (*Age Concern)*, para. 46, such as C-88/08 (*Hütter*), para. 41 and case law cited therein.

1247 AG *Bot*, in C-341/08 (*Petersen*), para. 55.

Consequently, when it comes to the aim of protecting the public health, this aim has to be examined in light of Art. 2 No. 5 Dir. 2000/78/EC, which explicitly refers to the protection of public health.[1248]

13.3.3.2 Exception according to Art. 2 No. 5 Dir. 2000/78/EC

This provision refers to the protection of health as a reason that is capable of justifying a difference in treatment on the grounds of age.[1249] In conformity with that provision, the Directive, without prejudice, concerns measures manifested in national law that, in a democratic society, are necessary inter alia for the protection of health.[1250] Hence, it is necessary to determine whether § 54 s. 1 hlspl. constitutes a measure that may be considered as being necessary for the protection of health as manifested in Art. 2 No. 5.[1251]

It has to be noted that Art. 2 No. 5 solely aims at protecting the health of third parties and not the health of the employee as such.[1252] This is also bolstered by recital 18, which primarily refers to preserving the operational capacity of e.g. the emergency services and not to the protection of the employee's health.[1253]

As stressed by the CJEU in *Petersen*, when it comes to measures in the area of health, it has to be recalled that member states retain the power to organise their social security systems and to adopt, in particular, provisions intending to govern the organisation and delivery of health services and medical care.[1254] In principle, the member states have to exercise that power in compliance with Community law, but as stated in *Petersen,*

1248 ibid.

1249 see in this regard C-341/08 (*Petersen*), Judgement, para. 49; see to the provision in general already chap. 10.3.1 above.

1250 C-341/08 (*Petersen*), judgement, para. 49.

1251 similar AG Bots, in C-341/08 (*Petersen*), para. 56 as regards the controversial German provision § 95 (7) SGB V (old version).

1252 *Lüderitz* (2005), p. 55.

1253 ibid., p. 55.

1254 C-341/08 (*Petersen*), Judgement, para. 51 referring to Art. 152 (5) EC Treaty, C-169/07 (*Hartlauer*), Judgement of 10 March 2009, ECR 2009, I-01721, para. 29, 30 and Joined Cases C-171/07 and C-172/07 (*Apothekerkammer des Saarlandes and Others*), Judgement of 19 May 2009, ECR I-04171, para. 18, 19.

> ... when assessing whether that obligation has been complied with, account must be taken of the fact that a Member State may determine the level of protection which it wishes to afford to public health and the way in which that level is to be achieved. Since the level of protection may vary from one Member State to the other, Member States must be allowed discretion.[1255]

Or, as pointed out by Advocate General *Bot*, this discretion provided for the member states results from the fact that the health and life of human beings rank foremost among the assets and interests that are protected by the EC Treaty.[1256] In general, it thus falls under the discretionary power of the member state to lay down a provision setting an age limit for the authorisation to practise as a physician with the view to having a high level of protection for public health and in order to protect the health of the patients.[1257] Even if Norway is not an EU member, in line with the case law of the Norwegian *Høyesterett*, this aspect also has to be considered when examining the age limit in § 54 s. 1 hlspl. in terms of its conformity with Dir. 2000/78/EC.[1258]

13.3.3.2.1 Necessity and appropriateness

Central to the necessity analysis is to assess whether less restrictive means than the age limit in § 54 (1) s. 1 hlspl are available to achieve the legitimate aim of securing the public health and the health of the patients. Moreover, it has to be remembered, as stressed in *Petersen*, that legislation is considered appropriate for ensuring the attainment of the legitimate aim being pursued 'only if it genuinely reflects a concern to attain it in a consistent and systematic manner'.[1259]

The necessity analysis in essence means examining whether alternatives to an absolute age limit are available. The answer depends on whether the age limit in § 54 (1) s. 1 hlspl. opens up for flexibility or whether it is absolute and fixed and thus constitutes an insuperable limit for any further exercise of this profession. Looking solely at § 54 (1) s. 1 hlspl., the age

---

1255 ibid.; see also AG Bot in C-341/08 (*Petersen*), para. 57.

1256 AG Bot, in C-341/08 (*Petersen*), para. 57.

1257 similar ibid., para. 58 w.f.r.; Judgement C-341/08 (*Petersen*), para. 52.

1258 see as regards Norway's relation to Dir. 2000/78/EC and the respective case law chap. 11.2 above.

1259 C-341/08 (*Petersen*), Judgement, para. 52, 53 referring to C-169/07 (*Hartlauer)*, para. 55.

limit is absolute. Such a compulsory termination of the exercise of the profession cannot be regarded as necessary, as, in general, an individual assessment of the physician's mental and physical capabilities might likewise contribute to ensuring the aim of protecting the patients' health and the public health.[1260] Such a measure would be equally effective, but without violating the physician's right not to be discriminated against on the grounds of age and without affecting his right to work. If applied strictly, the age limit makes any further exercise of the profession as a physician unfeasible. Given the fact that probably a manageable number of physicians that are interested in extending their working career beyond the age limit would apply for such an individual assessment, such a measure may, moreover, not be regarded as disproportional.[1261] In this regard, an analogy may be drawn to the situation of pilots, who similarly work in a unique position, as they might be confronted with situations of potential hazard in terms of the life and health of their passengers.[1262] In addition, pilots need to pass regular tests regarding their individual mental and physical capabilities. In light of these considerations, an absolute age limit such as § 54 (1) s. 1 hlspl. does not per se constitute a necessary measure with which to achieve the legitimate aim of securing the public and patients' health, as other means such as individual health tests, as provided for in § 49 hlspl. in conjunction with § 8 (1) *Forskrift om lisens til helsepersonell*, would also be available to pursue the legitimate aim.[1263] The provision § 54 (1) s. 1 hlspl. alone therefore does not pass the proportionality test, as all its criteria have to be fulfilled in a cumulative manner.

The same applies in general as regards the age limit of 70 years as laid down in the agreement between the KS and NMA provided that the prolongation of the physician's contract is denied on the generalised assumption of the physician's age-based decline in capabilities.[1264]

1260 see for a discussion of individual assessments and control as an alternative to the age limit for authorisation *Aasland* et al. (2010), p. 1919 f., similar argumentation in view of the German context *Schüffner/Schnall* (2009), p. 65, 66, who also argue that such individual assessment would not contradict financial aspects as the respective physicians could bear the costs of the testing.

1261 similar argumentation in view of the German context *Schüffner/Schnall* (2009), p. 65, 66.

1262 see in detail analysis in chap. 15; see to this aspect also in view of the German context *Boecken* (2005), p. 396; *Schüffner/Schnall* (2009), p. 65, 66.

1263 ibid.

1264 see chap. 13.2.5. This provision is however not assessed in detail in this thesis.

However, it has to be kept in mind that the age limit in § 54 (1) s. 1 hlspl. is supplemented by the option to get a licence according to §§ 54 (2), 49 hlspl. in conjunction with §§ 6-9 *Forskrift om lisens til helsepersonell.* Therefore, the age limit actually constitutes a softer or more flexible age limit, as it offers the opportunity to get a licence for a limited period above the age of 75, provided that the (individual) physician both possesses the physical and mental capabilities and that he is up to date concerning the state of the art in his field. Not only is the assessment of the physician's health important, but also the monitoring of his level of knowledge. This requirement is made explicitly clear in § 8 (1) *Forskrift om lisens til helsepersonell.* With the individual assessment of the individual physician, as stipulated in § 8 (1) *Forskrift om lisens til helsepersonell*, a less restrictive measure is available. Therefore, this regulation is, in principle, less harmful to the physician's right to exercise his profession than an absolute age limit would be, but nevertheless, it is equally effective at achieving the aim of securing the patient's (and the physician's) health and life.

Thus, § 54 (1) s. 1 hlspl., together with §§ 54 (2), 49 hlspl., §§ 6-9 *Forskrift om lisens til helsepersonell,* constitutes a necessary measure in the sense of Art. 2 No. 5 Dir. 2000/78/EC to protect the health of the patients and the public in general. Moreover, this is an appropriate measure with which to achieve this aim.

However, the measure's necessity strongly depends on whether the opportunity to apply for a licence really is provided for the physicians. As widely criticised, it has to be noted in this context that the issuing of the licence strongly depends on the discretion of the responsible physician who is conducting the health test. Thus, the process of awarding the licence may be criticised for lacking objective criteria. Moreover, it has to be considered if the licence system really enables the physician to be integrated into the system. It is therefore crucial to consider the real conditions under which the physician is going to be allowed to work above the age of 75. Economic considerations also come into play here, as it has to be assessed whether for example a physician who has previously worked as a *fastlege* and now might be allowed to work outside the *fastlege* system, might be confronted with a financial loss in his income, as he is no longer paid under the GP regulations. Thus, the physician might be economically dependent on practising under the *fastlege* system.

13.3.3.2.2 Proportionality stricto sensu

The age limit in § 54 (1) s. 1 hlspl in conjunction with §§ 54 (2), 49 hlspl., §§ 6-9 *Forskrift om lisens til helsepersonell* might be proportional, provided that the proportionality stricto sensu requirement is fulfilled.[1265] Predominantly, the interests that have to be weighed against each other are the interests of the patients versus the interests of the physician. Generally speaking, it is a balancing act between the protection of the patient's health and the public health, the patient's confidence in the physician and the health system versus the physician's professional and personal self-fulfilment related to the exercise of his right to work. On the one hand, it has to be considered that the deprivation of the authorisation based on the age limit might have a considerable impact on the physician's purpose in life, as exercising one's profession plays an important role in terms of the individual's persona and in achieving a fulfilling life.[1266] On the other hand, there is the risk of potential harm to the life and limb of the patients caused by physicians who no longer possess the needed mental and physical capabilities. Life and health are sensible assets that far outweigh the physician's interest in his professional and personal self-fulfilment. This is even truer when physicians are working for example as surgeons, where the requirements regarding the physician's fitness might be even higher. In the end, the withdrawal of the authorisation and the need to undergo health tests and assessments to determine whether the physician is up to date in his professional field to enable him to obtain a further licence above the age of 75 is a less harmful measure for the physician than the potential hazard to the patient caused by medical malpractice. The age limit, in combination with the requirements for granting the licence, is a hedging instrument to secure the aim is maintained in terms of guaranteeing the patients' health and public health and quality of health care in general. If the physician fulfils the necessary requirements to obtain the licence, and provided that the granting of the licence is not arbitrarily and generally applied, he might exercise his right to work even beyond the age of 75, so that his interests are also considered. As regards setting the age limit at 75, this seems, in this regard, not to be unproportional. However, one might

1265 A proportionality stricto sensu analysis has also to take place as regard Art. 2 No. 5 Dir. 2000/78/EC, see chap. 10.3.1.

1266 similar argumentation by *Schüffner/Schnall* (2009), p. 67 as regards the German context.

consider from a *de lege ferenda* perspective to give the physician also the opportunity - provided that the licence criteria are met - to continue working in the fastlege system even beyond the age of 75.[1267]

In light of this balancing of interests, the age limit in § 54 (1) s. 1 hlspl.in conjunction with §§ 54 (2), 49 hlspl., §§ 6-9 *Forskrift om lisens til helsepersonell* has to be regarded as *proportional stricto sensu*, as it allows for both interests to a sufficient extent.

13.3.3.3 Justification according to Art. 4 No. 1 Dir. 2000/78/EC

As explicitly expressed by Art. 4 No. 1 in conjunction with Art. 1 Dir. 2000/78/EC, member states may provide that a difference in treatment which is based on a characteristic related to age shall not constitute age discrimination where, based on the nature of the particular occupational position in question, such a characteristic constitutes a GOR,[1268] provided that the objective is legitimate and the requirement is proportionate. As pointed out by *Sodan*, this 'characteristic' may be compared to the special indispensable requirement in Art. 2 No. 2 Dir. 76/207/EEC, where the CJEU in the *Sirdar* case confirmed its previous judgements 'that sex may be a determining factor for posts such as those of prison warders and head prison warders [...] or for certain activities such as policing activities where there are serious internal disturbances'.[1269]

Similarly, as in *Sirdar*, age might, in principle, be a determining factor in justifying age limits for certain professions, where the physical capacity constitutes an essential precondition for the exercise of the profession and where an increased public interest and the interest of the physician himself might exist to differentiate on the grounds of age, on the grounds of safety or rather the protection against hazards of health and life caused by age-

---

1267 see to this aspect de lege ferenda chap.16.3.2.

1268 *O'Cinneide* (2005), p. 34; see also chap. 10.3.5 above.

1269 *Sodan* (2009), p. 67 reffering to C-273/97 (*Sirdar*), Judgement of of 26 October 1999, ECR 1999, I-07403, para. 24; *Sodan* refers to Council Directive 76/207/EEC of 9 February 1976 on the implementation of the principle of equal treatment for men and women as regards access to employment, vocational training and promotion, and working conditions OJ L 039.

related performance decline.[1270] Nevertheless, the problem remains in determining at what exact age the factor of 'age' might constitute a GOR.[1271]

Looking at the wording of the hlspl., the age of 75 seems at first glance to constitute a GOR or, in the US terminology, a BFOQ.[1272] The criterion of being under the age of 75 is laid down twice as one of the indispensable cumulative requirements for awarding a licence in § 48 (2) (c) hlpsl. and as a mandatory criterion leading to the authorisation's expiration in § 54 (1) hlpsl.[1273] Nevertheless, this characteristic only constitutes a GOR according to the explicit wording in Art. 4 No. 1 Dir. 2000/78/EC provided that its underlying objective is legitimate and that the age requirement is proportionate.[1274] However, before going into the proportionality analysis, it is first necessary to assess whether age might constitute a suitable GOR at all. This entails evaluating the use of age as a proxy for a quality or characteristic that constitutes a GOR for the profession of a physician. As the age limit in § 54 (1) hlpsl. is applicable for GPs as well as specialists, the determination of a general applicable age limit is rather questionable, especially in view of the variety of different medical disciplines and the different specific job-related requirements related to them.[1275] As highlighted in several studies, reaching a certain age does not necessarily mean that the physician in question automatically lacks the required level of mental and physical fitness. Age is thus an inadequate proxy and not sufficiently precise enough an indicator for any of the requirements needed to practise as a physician,[1276] so that it hardly qualifies as a 'substitute for a "real" GOR'.[1277]

1270 similar *Schüffner/Schnall* (2009), p. 78 f.; *Sodan* (2009), p. 67. Both authors however conclude that for the German context, the age limit in § 95 (7) s. 3 SGB V (old version) cannot be justified under Art. 4 No. 1 Dir. 2000/78/EC.

1271 see to this problematic in general *O'Cinneide (*2005), p. 34.

1272 see chap. 10.3.2. above.

1273 § 48 (2) (c) hlpsl. stipulates that one of the cumulative requirements for the right to be granted an authorisation constitutes that the applicant is under 75 years of age.

1274 see in detail 10.3.2. above.

1275 similar for the German context *Sodan* (2009), p. 67.

1276 similar *Aasland* et al. (2010), p. 1918 f. and *Pahle/Hansen* (2008), p. 1075.

1277 *O'Cinneide* (2005), p. 34 f.

As pointed out by *O'Cinneide*, the use of age limits, even for reasons of protecting public safety, cannot be justified where the individual assessment of the employee's capabilities is possible.[1278] That is to say, where alternative measures are available to achieve the aims being pursued (the necessity test). This is in line with recital 23 of Dir. 2000/78/EC, stressing that a justification according to Art. 4 No. 1 Dir. 2000/78/EC may only take place 'In very limited circumstances'.[1279] The licence system in Norway, which requires health tests both before and after the 75-year age limit, clearly demonstrates that the individual assessment of physicians is practicable. This is even truer in light of the fact that a physician might practise beyond the 75-year age limit, provided that he fulfils the criteria for getting a licence. As for the licence, the intellectual and physical capabilities of the individual physician in question should similarly be decisive for awarding the authorisation. As the justification analysis as regards Art. 2 No. 5 Nr. 1 2000/78/EC has already demonstrated, the age limit in § 54 (1) s. 1 hlspl. is, as such, not necessary, as alternative measures are available, as the licence system with its health assessments illustrates.

In sum, being of a certain age to be able practise medicine either as a *fastlege* or as a physician outside the *fastlege* system is not a necessary GOR and thus is not proportionate in the sense of Art. 4 No. 1 Dir. 2000/78/EC. Thus, the age discrimination cannot be justified according to Art. 4 No. 1 Dir. 2000/78/EC.

13.3.3.4 Justification according to Art. 7 No. 1 Dir. 2000/78/EC

As stated in Art. 7 No. 1 in conjunction with Art. 1 Dir. 2000/78/EC, in light of ensuring de facto full equality in practice does not contradict the principle of equal treatment in terms of maintaining or adopting specific measures in working life to prevent or compensate for disadvantages on the grounds of age. However, maintaining the age limit in § 54 (1) s. 1 hlpsl. does not constitute such a measure; that is, a positive discrimination in the sense of Art. 7 No. 1 Dir. 2000/78/EC. Thus, § 54 (1) s. 1 hlpsl. may not be justified due to Art. 7 No. 1 Dir. 2000/78/EC.

1278 ibid., p. 35.
1279 recital 23 Dir. 2000/78/EC.

13.3.4 Intermediate conclusion

To conclude, § 54 (1) s. 1 hlpsl. in conjunction with §§ 54 (2), 49 hlspl. and §§ 6-9 *Forskrift om lisens til helsepersonell* passes the proportionality test, and the age discrimination can thus be justified according to Art. 2 No. 5 Dir. 2000/78/EC, while regulation § 54 (1) s. 1 hlspl. does not pass the necessity hurdle and thus cannot be justified under Art. 2 No. 5 Dir. 2000/78/EC.

13.4 Further examples of mandatory retirement in the Norwegian health sector

Besides physicians, other health personnel listed in § 48 (1) hlspl. are also encompassed by the authorisation requirement and consequently, by the 75-year age limit for the withdrawal in § 54 (1) s. 1 hlspl. Examples are physiotherapists (§ 48 (1) (h) hlspl.), auxiliary nurses (§ 48 (1) (j) hlspl.), psychologists (§ 48 (1) (t) hlspl.), general nurses (*sykepleier*) (§ 48 (1) (v) hlspl.), and dentists (§ 48 (1) (x) hlspl.), as well as certain types of pharmacists (§ 48 (1) (ø) hlspl.) and (§ 48 (1) (å) hlspl.)).

It has to be noted that besides the hlpsl., a number of other acts are applicable for the different medical professions, in particular, when it comes to regulating retirement and pension issues. One example constitutes the *Lov om pensjonsordning for apotekervirksomhet.*[1280] It regulates all aspects concerning the pensions of pharmacists and those employees who are permanently employed at a pharmacy, provided that they have an average working time of at least 15 hours per week, or are employed at a pharmacy operating around-the-clock (fast vaktapotek) with a tariff salary that is at least equal to the tariff salary for 15 hours a week on a *dagtjeneste* (day shift).[1281] Its central provision constitutes § 6, manifesting a right to retire after having reached the age limit of 70 years of age while at the same time stipulating an obligation to retire when this age limit is reached. The question arises as to whether the age limit in § 6 *Lov om pensjon for apotekervirksomhet* is in conformity with hlspl., as according to its § 3 (1) No. 2, (3) in conjunction with § 48 (1) (ø) and (å), pharmacists are also encompassed by the hlspl. Thus, the key question is whether there is conformity between § 6 *Lov om pensjon for apotekervirksomhet* and § 54 (1) hlspl. While § 6 *Lov om pensjon for apotekervirksomhet* determines the age limit at the age of 70, the authorisation expires, by contrast, due to § 54 (1) hlspl. – which is, according to § 48 (1) (ø) and (å) in conjunction with § 3 (1) No. 2, (3) hlspl., also applicable for pharmacists– at the age of 75. This means that even if the pharmacist in question possesses the authorisation until the age of 75, he is nevertheless, according to § 6 *Lov om pensjon for apotekervirksomhet*, obliged to retire at the age of 70. Thus, there is a discrepancy between both regulations, which in turn raises the question as to which of the two regulations has precedence in a case involving conflict. In contrast to medical

---

1280 *Lov 26. juni 1953 nr. 11 om pensjonsordning for apotekvirksomhet mv.*

1281 see for further details § 1 *Lov om pensjon for apotekervirksomhet.*

practitioners, pharmacists do not have the possibility of prolonging their working career beyond the age limit, as their age limit is absolute and does not open up for any prolongation. They are obliged to retire at the age of 70, which stands in sharp contrast to the fact that they legally possess the authorisation to work as pharmacists until the age of 75. Thus, the question arises as to whether less harmful measures than an absolute age limit would be available here. Similarly, as in the case of GPs, medical health-assessment tests and the assessment that their work is state of the art could constitute an alternative measure, which makes it rather questionable as to whether this age limit would pass a strict proportionality analysis. [1282]

13.5 De lege lata situation in Germany

13.5.1 Introduction

Aspects concerning the authorisation to work as a physician under the German statutory health-insurance (SHI) system, such as requirements for its expiration, are regulated in the SGB V. The core provision in this regard is § 95 SGB V. For reasons of comparability, the situation of GPs working as a *Vertragsarzt* (SHI physicians) shall be elaborated on in this chapter, as they show the closest similarity to the Norwegian *fastlege*. In general, any fully qualified physician in Germany can set up his practice wherever he wants. This allows for treating self-paying patients and those with private health insurance. However, in order to be eligible for reim-

1282 As only selected examples of age limits are analysed regarding their conformity with the prohibition of age discrimination in Dir. 2000/78/EC, this thesis does not evaluate further age limits in detail. A deeper analysis of the age limits for pharamacists, nurses or other health care personnel is not provided for in this examination; see for a critical analysis e.g. *Herlofsen*, Erik R. (2013), Særaldersgrenser på gyngende juridisk grunn? published at: www.seniorpolitikken.no (last accessed); see moreover: *Hyggen*, Christer (2008), Slitne kvinner og farlige menn – Om grunnlaget for særaldersgrenser i Norge, Fafo-rapport 2008:16, p. 6ff; see in detail to the retirement decisions of employees at municipal and private hospitals *Enehaug*, Heidi/*Hilsen*, Anne I./*Steinum*, Trude (2008), Særaldersgrenser og virksomhetens handlingsrom, p. 19; The entitlement to pension is regulated in §§ 7-11 *Lov 22. juni 1962 nr. 12 om pensjonsordning for sykepleiere (sykepleierpensjonsloven).*

bursement from the SHI, the physician has to become an SHI physician.[1283] About 90% of the German population is covered by SHI (*gesetzliche Krankenkasse*).[1284]

Membership in the public insurance scheme is, in principle, mandatory. Employees and their dependents are enrolled in the SHI scheme. The scheme is financed by the contributions of its members that are paid as payroll taxes by the employer and employees. For individuals who are unemployed, the SHI contributions are paid by the employment agency. Self-employed persons are not covered by the SHI and they may buy private insurance. Employees with an income above a certain threshold and the self-employed have the possibility of opting out of the statutory system and insuring themselves privately. Those who choose not to opt out are 'voluntarily insured'. The only income that is subject to insurance contributions is income derived from employment.[1285]

The work of a *Vertragsarzt* working as a GP is thus essential in covering the basic primary health care for the German population, a situation that is basically comparable to that of the *fastlege* system in Norway. They practise their profession as self-employed persons.[1286] Working as an SHI physician basically requires the physician's approbation and medical specialist's training (*Facharztausbildung*). If these requirements are met, a committee decides on the physician's request to be admitted to the so-called *vertragsärztliche Versorgung* (care by SHI physicians).[1287] If admitted, the physician will become a member of the *Kassenärztliche Vereinigung* (Association of Statutory Health Insurance Physicians).[1288] The physician will then be both eligible and obliged to take part in the statutory healthcare system.[1289]

1283 see for an overview: *Obermann*, Konrad/*Müller*, Peter/*Müller*, Hans-Heiko/*Schmidt*, Burkhard/*Glazinski*, Bernd (2013), Understanding the German health care system, p. 86, in particular p. 87.

1284 see for an overview: http://www.vdek.com/gesetzliche_krankenversicherung.html (last accessed at 17.12.2014); see to this aspect also C-341/08 (*Petersen*), para. 33; *Boecken* (2005), p. 394.

1285 see for an overview: *Obermann* et. al (2013), p. 20, p. 140.

1286 *Boecken* (2005), p. 394; see in detail to the legal framework conditions for *Vertragsärzte* as self-employed persons *Wenner*, Ulrich (2009), Neue Rollenanforderungen an den Vertragsarzt, Freiberuflicher Unternehmer, Funktionsträger im Gesundheitskonzern, Restverwalter oder Vollzugsakteur staatlicher Gesundheitspolitik?, GesundheitsRecht (GesR) 2009, pp. 505-518, p. 505 f.

1287 see elaborately *Becker* Ulrich (1999), Zur verfassungsrechtlichen Stellung der Vertragsärzte am Beispiel der zulassungsbezogenen Altersgrenzen, NZS 1999, pp. 521-530.

1288 see in detail ibid., p. 522.

1289 see in detail ibid., p. 522.

According to § 32 (1) s. 1 of the *Zulassungsverordnung für Vertragsärzte* (Ärzte-ZV), the *Vertragsarzt* has to exercise his profession in person and in *freier Praxis*. *Vertragsärzte* fall, in principle, under the category of *freie Berufe* (free professions). This is explicitly manifested in § 1 (2) *Bundesärzteordnung*, stating, '*Der ärztliche Beruf ist kein Gewerbe; er ist seiner Natur nach ein freier Beruf*'.[1290]

Until 2008, § 95 (7) SGB V encompassed in its s. 3 a mandatory retirement age limit according to which the physician's admission was terminated when he turned 68 years of age.[1291] The legislator's original rationale behind this age limit, when introducing it in 1992, was to curtail a surplus of medical practitioners and to ensure the financial stability of the statutory health-insurance scheme.[1292] Additionally, the BVerfG also justified the age limit's maintenance by referring to the high requirements – to the mental and physical capabilities that are part of practising as a SHI physician – which older physicians, due to their age, no longer might be able to cope with.[1293] The age limit would thus contribute to avoiding

1290 see in detail *Wenner* (2009), p. 505 f.

1291 see to the provision and its exemption regulations: C-341/08 (*Petersen*), paras. 11-17.

1292 see Bt-Drs. 12/3608, Entwurf eines Gesetzes zur Sicherung und Strukturverbesserung der gesetzlichen Krankenversicherung (Gesundheits-Strukturgesetz), p. 93, see to this aspect also *Becker* (1999), pp. 521-530, in particular p. 522; see also *Groß* (2010), p. 124ff.

1293 BVerfG, Kammerbeschluss vom 31. März 1998 – 1 BvR 2167/93, 1 BvR 2198/93 –, juris., para. 30.

potential hazards for the patients and the public.[1294] As rightly pointed out by the German legal literature,[1295] as well as by the CJEU in *Petersen,*[1296] this argumentation was untenable. This was because physicians working solely for patients with private health insurance were not encompassed by the age limit, even though these physicians might also have created risks for the patients. Additionally, in the previous regulation, several exemptions to the age limit existed for SHI physicians, e.g. in areas where there was a shortage of physicians, the SHI physician could even work beyond the age limit.[1297] Despite these inconsistencies, the German BVerfG has endorsed this provision.[1298] In its settled case law, the Federal Social Court (*Bundessozialgericht*) also held the view that the age limit was justi-

---

1294 ibid.; critical inter alia *Groß* (2010), p. 124ff.

1295 see among others: *Becker* (1999), pp. 521-530; *Senne* (2006), p. 302ff.; *Kazemi*, Robert/*Leopold* Anders (2007), Ist die Altersgrenze von 68 Jahren in § 95 SGB V noch verfassungsgemäß?, Arzt Zahnarzt Recht (AZR) 2007, pp. 118-122; *Rixen*, Stephan (2007), Rettung für den altersdiskriminierten Vertragsarzt durch den EuGH, ZESAR 2007, 345-535; *Jaeger*, Berit (2008), 68-Jahres-Altersgrenze für Vertragsärzte mit deutschem und europäischem Recht vereinbar, Medizinrecht (MedR), 2008, pp. 456-458; *Haak*, Sabine (2009), Das Ende der Zwangspensionierung, Gesetzliche Altersregelung für Ärzte, Hartmannbund (HM) Magazin, 2009, Nr. 1, 10; *Meixner*, Rüdiger (2009), Betroffene gehen rechtlich gegen Altersdiskriminierung vor, Trotz Ende der 68er-Altersgrenze, Niedergelassene Arzt 2009, Nr. 3, 31; *Riedel*, Daniel (2009), Das Teilhabegrundrecht auf Zulassung zur vertragsärztlichen Versorgung, NZS 2009, pp. 260-264; *Beschorner*, Jürgen (2010), Zulässigkeit von Altersgrenzen für Vertragszahnärzte nach der Richtlinie 2000/78/EG, Zeitschrift für ausländisches und internationales Arbeits- und Sozialrecht (ZIAS) 3/2010, pp. 252-265; *Groß* (2010), p. 124ff.

1296 see C-341/08 (*Petersen*), para. 16.

1297 *Gesetz zur Veränderung des Vertragsarztrechts und anderer Gesetze* (*Vertragsarztrechtsänderungsgesetz*) of 22.12.2006 (enacted on 01.01.2007, BGBl. 2006, I, S. 3439) introduced exemption in § 95 (7) s. 8 and s. 9 SGB V (old version); see *Schüffner*/*Schnall* (2009), p. 63.

1298 BVerfG, Kammerbeschluss vom 20. Dezember 1996 – 1 BvL 10/96 –, juris; BVerfG, Kammerbeschluss vom 31. März 1998 – 1 BvR 2167/93, 1 BvR 2198/93 –, juris; BVerfG, Beschluss vom 20. März 2001 – 1 BvR 491/96 –, BVerfGE 103, 172-195; BVerfG, Nichtannahmebeschluss vom 04. Oktober 2001 – 1 BvR 1435/01 –, juris; BVerfG, Nichtannahmebeschluss vom 04. Oktober 2001 – 1 BvR 1418/01 –, juris; BVerfG, Nichtannahmebeschluss vom 07. August 2007 – 1 BvR 1941/07 –, juris; BVerfG, Nichtannahmebeschluss vom 30. Juni 2008 – 1 BvR 1159/08 –, juris; see to the critics e.g. *Senne* (2006), p. 304; *Schüffner*/*Schall* (2009), p. 64ff; *Sodan* (2009), p. 47ff.

fiable and in conformity with both constitutional law and the prohibition against age discrimination in EU law.[1299] It inter alia argued that the age limit was justified to protect younger physicians' entry into the SHI system.[1300] However, in view of the prohibition against age discrimination in EU law, several authors doubted the provision's conformity with EU law.[1301] However, even the CJEU judgement in *Petersen* did not explicitly declare the provision as being against the prohibition of age discrimination. The Court rather stated that a member state might regard it as necessary to impose such an age limit that aims at facilitating the access to employment by younger physicians, provided that it is consistently applied.[1302] Central to the CJEU thus was the provision's coherence.[1303] According to the CJEU, it was up to the German courts to review the provision in light of these aspects.[1304]

The maximum age limit for SHI physicians – including dentists and psychotherapists – has been abolished since 2009.[1305] According to the *de lege lata* status quo, physicians are now allowed to work beyond the age of 68, without being restricted by an age limit. The abolishment was based on the consideration that the experiences of private patients regarding

---

1299 see BSG, Urteil vom 09. April 2008 – B 6 KA 44/07 R –, juris; BSG, Urteil vom 06. Februar 2008 – B 6 KA 41/06 R –, BSGE 100, 43-51; BSG Urteil vom 24.11.1993 BSGE 73, 222; BSG, Beschluss vom 18. August 2010 – B 6 KA 18/10 B –, SozR 4-2500 § 95 Nr. 17; see to the critics among others: *Boecken*, Winfried (2008), Höchstaltersgrenze für Vertragsärzte, ArztRecht (ArztR) 2008, pp. 299-302, p. 301.

1300 see BSG, Urteil vom 25. November 1998 – B 6 KA 4/98 R –, SozR 3-2500 § 95 Nr. 18, BSGE 83, 135-145, para. 31; Bundessozialgericht (BSG), Beschluss vom 18. August 2010 – B 6 KA 18/10 B –, SozR 4-2500 § 95 Nr. 17, para. 9.

1301 see in detail: *Boecken* (2005), pp. 393-400, in particular p. 396ff.; *Eichenhofer*, Eberhard (2007), Gesetzliche Altersgrenze im Vertrags(zahn)arztrecht: Kann nach dem AGG alles beim Alten bleiben? Die Sozialgerichtsbarkeit (SGb) 2007, pp. 580-585, p. 585; *Sodan* (2009), pp. 65ff, in particular p. 69; *Schüffner/ Schnall* (2009), p. 75ff., in particular p. 84.

1302 C-341/08 (*Petersen*), paras. 16, 73-75.

1303 ibid., paras. 16, 73-75; see to the aspect of consistency also chap. 10.3.5. above.

1304 C-341/08 (*Petersen*), para. 74.

1305 *Gesetz zur Weiterentwicklung der Organisationsstrukturen in der gesetzlichen Krankenversicherung* (GKV-OrgWG) of 15. 12. 2008, BGBl. I, p. 2426.

physicians practising above the age of 68 outside the panel system justified setting aside the age limit.[1306] Moreover, the abolishment would lead to enhanced succession planning and increased leeway in the organisation of the physician's succession, so the argumentation goes.[1307] Moreover, problems as regards the supply of medical services could be avoided.[1308]

Remarkably, the introduction of the AGG had no influence on the age limit in § 95 (7) s. 3 SGB V; it neither lead to an abolishment nor to a modification of the already existing provision.[1309] It was rather the increased demand for medical services that led to rethinking as regards the age limit's necessity.

13.5.2 Authorisation

In general, the entitlement to practise medicine depends on whether the authorisation requirements laid down in § 95 SGB V are fulfilled. Decisive in this regard is the interplay of § 95 SGB V and the detailed regulations in the *Ärzte-Zulassungsverordnung*.[1310] Formally, a written request, such as evidence on the registration in the index of physicians, is necessary.[1311] Besides this, the substantive subjective requirements that have to be fulfilled by the physician are their approbation as a physician, such as evidence of speciality training (*Facharztausbildung*), and finally, evidence regarding the physician's personal fitness (*Eignung*).[1312]

1306 Bt-Drs. 16/10609, *Beschlussempfehlung und Bericht, des Ausschusses für Gesundheit (14. Ausschuss), zu dem Gesetzentwurf der Bundesregierung – Drucksachen 16/9559, 16/10070 – Entwurf eines Gesetzes zur Weiterentwicklung der Organisationsstrukturen in der gesetzlichen Krankenversicherung* (GKV-OrgWG), p. 55; see to this aspect also *Joussen*, Jacob (2012), § 95 Teilnahme and der vertragsärztlichen Versorgung, in: Becker, Ulrich/Kingreen, Thorsten, SGB V, Gesetzliche Krankenversicherung, 3. edt. 2012, § 95, para. 28.

1307 ibid.

1308 ibid.

1309 see to this aspect AG *Bot* in C-341/08 (*Petersen*), para. 15.

1310 *Joussen*, § 95, para. 2.

1311 see § 95 (2) SGB V; ibid., para. 3.

1312 *Neumann*, A. (2011), in: Beck'scher Online-Kommentar Sozialrecht, BeckOK SGB V, Rolfs, Christian/Giesen, Richard/ Kreikebohm, Ralf/Udsching, Peter (eds.), § 95, edt. 30, Stand: 01.03.2011, para. 4; *Joussen* (2012), § 95, para. 5 with further details.

The authorisation to practise as a panel physician may, under certain conditions, be of a temporary nature.[1313] In doing so, the appearance and manifestation of so-called *Überversorgung* – that is, situations where more physicians than are actually needed are practising – shall be reduced.[1314] In cases where a temporary limited authorisation has been issued, the authorisation automatically ends with the end of the terminability.[1315]

13.5.3 Withdrawal and expiration of authorisation

The authorisation's termination might first be caused by its withdrawal.[1316] The conditions for withdrawal of the authorisation are laid down in § 95 (6) s. 1 SGB V. Three exclusive listed reasons lead to withdrawal: first, the authorisation may be withdrawn if its conditions no longer exist, second, the physician does not start working as a panel doctor or no longer works as a panel physician and finally, if the physician grossly violated his obligations as a panel physician. In cases where these reasons are given, the withdrawal is compulsory.[1317] When assessing if the conditions for withdrawal are at hand, the principle of proportionality has to be considered. Any withdrawal may always be the *ultima ratio* option.[1318] A readmission is, in principle, possible.[1319]

In addition to these options for withdrawal, the law lays down in § 95 (7) SGB V the expiration of the authorisation by an act of law. According to § 95 (7) s. 1 and s. 2 SGB V, the authorisation compulsorily expires in cases where the panel physician dies, where he provides a waiver for the declaration or when he moves away from the panel district.[1320]

1313 *Joussen* (2012), § 95, para. 26; see § 98 (2) Nr. 12 SGB V as well as § 19 (4) *Zulassungsverordnung für Vertragsärzte* (Ärzte-ZV).

1314 *Joussen* (2012), § 95, para. 26.

1315 ibid., para. 26 with further details.

1316 ibid., para. 21.

1317 ibid. with further details.

1318 ibid., para. 23

1319 see in detail to the requirements for readmission: *Hesral*, Harald (2013), chap. 3, B. Anspruch auf Wiederzulassung zur vertragsärztlichen Versorgung, in: Disziplinarrecht für Ärzte und Zahnärzte, Ehlers, Alexander (edt.) 2. edt. 2013, para. 626ff.

1320 see *Joussen* (2012), § 95, para. 25; *Neumann* (2011), § 95, para. 58.

13.5.4 Obligation to undertake advanced training

To safeguard the quality of the health care provided by the SHI physicians, § 95 d SGB V stipulates the obligation to undertake continuous advanced training.[1321] In doing so, the requirements of § 72 (2) SGB V, according to which the health care provided by physicians has to reflect the recent status quo of medical science, shall be accounted for.[1322] The obligation aims at maintaining the physician's expertise to enable the physician to get the authorisation through e.g. the modification and further development of his professional knowledge.[1323] The advanced training, as stressed in § 95 d (1) s. 2 SGB V, has therefore to correlate with the state of the art in medical science and research.[1324] The legal determination of this obligation implies that it is a core obligation of the physician that results from the authorisation.[1325] To achieve this up-to-date knowledge, all authorised physicians are obliged to complete such advanced training.[1326] The basic details of this advanced training are manifested in § 95 d SGB V. It is important to note that the physician has to prove that he has completed the training.[1327] In case he disregards the obligation, the provision also allows for sanctions.[1328] In line with § 95 d (3) SGB V, every physician participating in the panel system has to complete the training to a sufficient extent within every fifth year. If not, the withdrawal of the authorisation may be requested.[1329]

1321 see in detail *Joussen* (2012), § 95 d, in: BeckerKingreen, SGB V, para. 2 referring to § 137 Abs. 3 S. 1 No. 1 SGB V i.c.w. *G-BA-Regelung zur Fortbildung der Fachärzte im Krankenhaus* and Hübner, M./Loof, Ariane (2010), Fortbildungspflicht der Fachärzte im Krankenhaus und damit verbundene berufs- und arbeitsrechtliche Implikationen, MedR 2010, p. 547.

1322 *Joussen* (2012), § 95 d, para. 1.

1323 ibid., para. 1, 2.

1324 ibid.

1325 § 95 d SGB V.

1326 *Joussen* (2012), § 95 d, para. 1-2.

1327 § 95 d (2) SGB V.

1328 *Joussen* (2012), § 95 d, para. 1, 4.

1329 see in detail *Neumann* (2011), § 95 d, para. 22, 23.

13.6 Compatibility of § 95 (7) SGB V with Dir. 2000/78/EC

The authorisation provision in § 95 (7) SGB V regulates 'conditions for access to employment, to self-employment or to occupation' such as 'employment and working conditions', as laid down in Art. 3 No.1 (a), (c) Dir. 2000/78/EC. The provision thus falls within the Directive's scope.

Even though on a national level part. 2 (§§ 6–18) of the AGG is titled *Protection of employees against discrimination,* these provisions shall also apply *mutas mutandis* according to § 6 (3) AGG to self-employed persons such as SHI physicians, insofar as the conditions for access to gainful employment and promotion are concerned.[1330]

However, in contrast to the situation in *Petersen*, the provision no longer entails an age limit or any other regulation that has a direct or indirect age-discriminatory effect in the meaning of Art. 2 No. 2 (a), (b) of Dir. 2000/78/EC. In the absence of direct age discrimination, ergo, no further justification analysis is required.

Even if no compatibility test according to Dir. 2000/78/EC has to be conducted, it is nevertheless fruitful for the comparison with the Norwegian situation to assess the *de lege lata* status quo critically.

13.7 Critical analysis of the de lege lata status quo in Germany

As regards Germany, it has to be noted that in the current situation there is no particular control mechanism concerning the physician's health that applies after the physician has reached a certain age, neither for panel physicians nor for private practising physicians. Consequently, both sorts of patients are now confronted with the risk of potentially under-performing dentists. By stipulating continuous advanced training of the physicians, the current regulation serves the protection of the patients' and the public health only to a minor degree. Rather, it still entails a potential hazard for the life and health of the patients. Even if the ageing process is intra- and interindividually different, it is a process that is unavoidable in the end. The idea of being for example examined by a dentist who is no longer able to hold the dental drill due to senility or who might no longer focus on the carious spot due to age-based debility of sight is more than

1330 see *Sodan* (2009), p. 63 f.; *Schüffner/Schnall* (2009), p. 74.

unpleasant. This raises the question as to why the German legislator, when abolishing the age limit, did not choose a solution with a kind of monitoring and control function instead. If individual health tests were to be compulsorily performed, the risks for the patients' health could at least be minimised. The continuous granting of the authorisation could be made dependent on the positive graduation of such tests by the physician. The inconsistency that has been inter alia criticised in *Petersen* as regards the previous legislation could have been avoided as long as all physicians had been required to pass these tests. Such a solution would take better account of the aim of protecting the health of the patients than all previous and current regulations.

13.8 Final discussion, comparison and conclusion

The primary aim underlying the mandatory age limit for physicians in Norway has been to secure the patients' and the public health and to guarantee the quality of the healthcare system as such. In contrast to this, the primary aim of introducing the previous valid 68-year age limit in § 95 (7) s. 3 SGB V in Germany was to guarantee the financial stability of the German social security system, while the protection of the patients' health was not the legislator's intention when introducing the age limit. However, when reviewing the age limit, the BVerfG used this argument to justify the age limit's maintenance. Nevertheless, as the *Petersen* case demonstrated, the German regulation was inconsistent, as SHI physicians were forced to retire at the age of 68, while physicians working in the private sector were allowed to work without limitation. In light of the argument concerning protecting the health of the patients, this inconsistency could no longer be maintained, as the CJEU stated in *Petersen*. The decisive difference as regards the German regulations in comparison to the Norwegian situation is that according neither to the previous nor to the current legal situation in Germany is any individual health assessment required after a certain age has been reached to keep the authorisation in old age. Previously, the argument concerning the physician's mental and physical decline was rather based on the generalised assumption that such a decline would take place after the age of 68. By contrast, the individual assessment of the physician's capabilities plays a central role in the Norwegian system of licensing. By combining the granting of the licence with a control measure relating to the physician's capabilities, this solution offers the opportunity to be able to protect the health of the patients while at the same time considering the physician's interests in extending his working career beyond the age of 75, provided that the licence requirements are fulfilled. However, it has to be acknowledged that the granting of the licence, as criticised in the literature, may lead to a limitation of the physician's right to work (e.g. in restricting the right to issue prescriptions) that may not be justified in terms of the physicians' alleged decline in capabilities and may actually be the result of the issuing authority's discretionary power rather than of an objective analysis of the physician's capabilities. In view of the prohibition against age discrimination, it is therefore necessary that the licence system is applied thoroughly and that the right of the physician not to be discriminated against on the grounds of age, such as his right to work, are respected. Any restriction in this regard has therefore to be *ultima ratio* in light of the proportionality principle. Or, as pointed out by *Svabø, 'Får vi kontrollinstansene til å håndheve reglene med klokskap og medmenneskelig forstand, burde vi kunne leve med det'.*[1331]

The total abolishment of the age limit in the German context enabled older physicians to extend their working career without restrictions and thus to exercise their right to work, but this legal amendment might have been enacted at the expense of the quality of the German healthcare system and patient safety, as no such control mechanisms that are present in the Norwegian case are available in the German scenario. The existing obligation of advanced training in Germany is, compared to the licence requirements in Norway, a rather insufficient way to guarantee the patients' health. As in the Norwegian regulations, the controls should be used more frequently with increasing age, plus the necessity of having to pass regular health tests should be required in the case of Germany.

If the licence requirements such as those in Norway are ensured, thus enabling the older physician to continue working, this might eventually prove to be a win–win situation for both the physician and his patients, all of whom could benefit from the physician's experience or, as pointed out by *Pande* and *Holmsen, 'Vi vil her peke på at den gamle huslegen holdes*

1331 'If the supervisory authorities do enforce the regulations with both wisdom and humane intelligence, then we should be able to live with that.', translation by author of *Svabø* (1996), p. 1064.

frem som et savnet motstykke til dagens travle leger. Han (eller hun) var nettopp en som gikk hjem til pasienten, en som hadde erfaring og god tid, og alderen ble ikke sett på som noe negativt'.[1332]

14 Mandatory retirement in higher education: The example of public university professors

14.1 Introduction

Alongside mandatory retirement for pilots and physicians, rules on compulsory retirement for employees in higher education such as university professors belong to the 'classic' and highly debated examples when discussing the legitimacy of mandatory retirement. The profession of a university professor constitutes a further unique example, as it has an entirely different job profile than that of employees working in security-relevant professions, such as pilots (see chap. 15) or in the health sector, such as physicians (see chap. 13). Unlike pilots or physicians, aspects such risks to life and limb of other human beings do not play a central role in the balancing of the involved interests. The most referred to considerations are succession planning, general age-related capability decline and budgetary savings. Factors that lead, in turn, to different justification patterns; patterns that have to be analysed and applied when discussing the age limit's conformity with the prohibition against age discrimination, as concretised in the Directive. Both in Norway and in Germany, compulsory retirement for professors has been subject to vigorous debate.[1333] As in other sectors,

---

1332 'We would like to note in this regard the old family doctor being referred to as the deficient counterpart to today's busy physicians. He (or she) was the one who went to the patient's home, who had a wealth of experience and who had enough time, and precisely because of this, his or her age was not considered as something negative.' translation by author of *Pande*, Helene/*Holmsen*, Eva (2006), Palliativ medisin – en oppgave for pensjonerte leger?, Tidsskrift for Den norske legeforening. Nr. 24, 2006, 126, pp. 3283–3284, p. 3284; see similar *Collier* (2008), p. 1123; *Steinsvoll* (2009), p. 650.

1333 see for the Norwegian context e.g.: Likestillings- og diskrimineringsnemnda (LDN) case 36/2009, uttalelse 14. December 2009; LDN case 24/2011, uttalelse 22. November 2011; *Landsverk*, Johanne (2010), Ingen propp i systemet, Forskerforum 1 2010, pp. 13-17; *Materstvedt*, Lars. J. (2010), En "prop" snakker ut- om aldersgrenser for professorer, universitetsavisa.no, 18.02.2010; *Holgersen*, Gudrun (2013), Aldersdiskriminering, in: Undring og erkjennelse,

demographic change also affects the university sphere. In addition, some even fear a 'brain drain' of leading scientists to US universities where compulsory retirement of university professors principally is unknown.[1334]

In the US, the situation has not always been as positive for older academics as it is at present. Even though the ADEA of 1967 and its second amendment passed in 1986 explicitly prohibited mandatory retirement, colleges and universities were granted an exemption valid until further amendments in 1994. The amendments in 1994 ultimately led to the abolishment of mandatory retirement at universities and colleges in the US. Before that, academics were forced to retire at the age of 65 unless they were invited to continue working, an exemption that has typically been granted to the more eminent researchers. The referred to reason for this exceptional position of professors until 1994 was the steady inflow of young faculty and the promotion of hiring women and minorities. Abolishing mandatory retirement for academic staff in the US has changed the participation of senior employees fundamentally, as the percentage of those above the age of 70 increased from 10% to 40%. The percentage of tenured professors e.g. at Harvard University Faculty of Arts and Sciences that were 70 years and older increased e.g. from 0% in 1992 to 9.1% in 2006.[1335]

In addition, the CJEU already had to deal with such age limits. The combined cases in *Georgiev* concerned two central questions: first, the compatibility with Dir. 2000/78/EC of fixed-term employment contracts for professors who have reached the mandatory retirement age and second, if the mandatory age limit as such could be justified under the Directive.[1336] Besides *Georgiev,* it is worth looking at the combined cases of *Fuchs* and *Köhler*, dealing similarly with mandatory retirement and the option for prolongation for permanent civil servants in the judiciary, in this case,

---

Festskrift til Jan Fridthof Bernt 70 år, Søvig, Karl H/Schütz, Sigrid Eskeleand/ Rasmussen, Ørnulf (eds), pp. 207-219, p. 216, 217; see as regards Germany e.g. already BVerfG, Beschluss vom 10. April 1984 – 2 BvL 19/82 –, BVerfGE 67, 1-25 (*Emeritierungsalter*); see recently e.g. as regards mandatory retirement for teachers in Hessen: Hessischer Verwaltungsgerichtshof (VGH), Judgement of 30.10.2013, 1 B 1638/13; see for the discussion in literature e.g. already *von Lübtow*, Ulrich (1967), Die Rechtsstellung des entpflichteten Professors; and recently *Poguntke*, David (2011), Das Hinausschieben der Altersgrenze auf Initiative des Beamten, Die Öffentliche Verwaltung (DÖV) 2011, pp. 561-568.

1334 *Mohr*, Joachim (2007), Die Vertreibung der Weisen, Der Spiegel. *Kämmerer*, Jörg A. (2008), Deutsches Beamtenrecht und Verbot der Altersdiskriminierung, Zeitschrift für Beamtenrecht (ZBR) 10/2008, pp. 325-339, p. 326; similar for the Norwegian context *Brock-Utne*, Birgit (2010), „Det er arbeidet som gir mitt liv innhold“, Morgenbladet 30. April 2010.

1335 see in detail *Stroebe*, Wolfgang (2010), The graying of academia, American Psychologist 2010, Vol. 65 No. 7, pp. 660-673, p. 660; see for a discussion in the US context among others *Posner*, Richard. A (1995), Aging and old age, pp. 351ff., in particular p. 354ff.

1336 Joined cases C-250/09 and C-268/09 (*Georgiev*).

prosecutors.[1337] In Norway as well as in Germany, it may generally be ascertained that university employees are predominantly working in the public sector and that the mandatory retirement age is, in both cases, manifested by law. In the following analysis, the focus rests on university professors working at public universities.[1338]

14.2 De lege lata situation in Norway

14.2.1 Mandatory retirement age limit

The majority of professors working in Norway is employed at public universities, which is ultimately due to the fact that only a small number of private higher education institutions exist in Norway.[1339] The central act for this analysis constitutes the *aldersgrenselov*.[1340] It contains in its § 2 (1), a 70-year mandatory age limit that is applicable for public university professors, being employees of the state (*tjenestemenn*).[1341]

1337 Joined cases C-159/10 and C-160/10 (*Fuchs* and *Köhler*), para. 32.

1338 The legal analysis is restricted to university professors alone, meaning those employees who are in the possession of the title 'university professor' and are employed at a public university in Norway respective Germany. It has to be noted however that besides university professors also other scientific staff working at public universities are encompassed as civil servants by the respective applicable age limits in Norway and Germany. This group of employees is not going to be analysed in detail.

1339 An example for a private university constitutes the *Handelshøyskolen BI,* based in Oslo, Bergen, Trondheim, Stavanger, Kristiansand and Drammen.

1340 Lov 21. desember 1956 nr. 1 *om aldersgrenser for offentlige tjenestemenn m.fl. (aldersgrenselov)*; see for an overview of further generally applicable regulations: *Hack*, Melanie R. (2012 b), Should I stay or should I go? Altersgrenzenregelungen für Professoren in Norwegen' in: Altersdiskriminierung, Jahrbuch 2012. Wachter, Gustav (ed.), pp. 193-214, p. 202ff.

1341 According to the definition goven in § 1 No. 2 s. 2 of the Lov 4. april 1983 nr. 3 *om statens tjenestemenn m.m.* (tjenestemannsloven –tjml) '*tjenestemenn'* are those employees of the public service who do not fall under the category "embetsmann". The latter category encompasses according to § 1 No. 2 s. 1 tjml those senior civil servants who are appointed by the Royal Decree. Previously also university professors have been *embetsmenn* from 1813 until law amendments in 1989, see extensive analysis given at: *Jakhelln*, Henning (1989), Embetsmenn eller tjenestemenn, in: Institutt for offentlig retts skriftserie nr. 2/1989, chap. 2. For easier terminological reference *'tjenestemenn'* are in the following referred to as civil servants.

The age limit came into force in 1917 with the *lov om aldersgrenser for offentlige tjenestemenn (aldersgrenselov)*.[1342] It laid down that civil servants paying into the Norwegian Public Service Pension Fund (*statens pensjonskasse*, SPK) were subject to an age limit of 70 years of age.[1343] This age limit was originally solely applicable for men. For women, by contrast, the age limit was set at 65 years. Already at the time of enactment, this gender-based difference was subject to debate. It took until 1956 to abolish in order to equalise the age limits. It was stressed in the discussion that the difference between men and women could not be justified, as there was no empirical evidence for an earlier female ageing process. Therefore, no legitimate medical reason could be found for a lower age limit for women.[1344]

From the perspective of the university professor, a multitude of options seems to be available for the transition from work to retirement.[1345] At most of the possible stages for entry into retirement, it is up to the university professor to decide whether he wants to continue working or wants to retire. This available flexibility and freedom of choice when determining the exit from active employment is reflected in §§ 19-1 (1), 20-1 *folketrygdlov* (ftrl), due to which the objective of the old-age pension should be to guarantee those who are eligible for a pension a secure income in retirement and to facilitate a flexible, smooth and gradual transition from working life to retirement.[1346] The professor may e.g. under certain conditions already retire at the age of 62, 65 or 67.[1347] Beyond terminating the employment relationship at an earlier stage in line with pension regulations, the university professor has the opportunity to continue working until the general age limit of 70 years in § 2 *aldersgrenselov*. Until then, he may not be dismissed on the sole fact that he has reached a certain age. It has to be noted that employees of the state are not encompassed by the dismissal protection of the WEA, but by the dismissal protection laid down in the *tjenestemannslov* (tjml).[1348] However, as profes-

1342 see for an overview: *Hack* (2012 b), p. 202ff.

1343 see in detail *Hippe* et al. (2012), p. 23 f.

1344 ibid.

1345 *Hack* (2012 b), p. 202ff.

1346 see for further details as regards the different applicable pension regulations *Hack* (2012 b), p. 206 f.

1347 This is mainly regulated in § 21 (1)- (4) of the Lov 28. juli 1949 nr. 26 *om Statens pensjonskasse* (*stpkl*), which also encompasses university professors, see for further details: ibid.

1348 see § 1 No. 2 s. 2 tjml, § 1-2 (3) WEA. An exception to this by a further regulation issued by the King has so far not been made; see also Ot.prp. nr. 54 (2008-2009), chap. 13, p. 86; LDN– uttalelse sak 24/2011, 22.11.2011, p. 6.

sors are obliged to terminate their employment by the next month following them reaching the age of 70, dismissal protection generally provided for by the tjml is likewise not available beyond that age limit.[1349]

For those encompassed by dismissal protection in the tjml, the central provision is § 10 tjml. It states that provided that the employee has been employed on a permanent basis and has been employed for at least two consecutive years as a *tjenestemenn* in the sense of § 1 No. 2 (2), a dismissal may only take place in four cases: first, in cases where the position is going to be removed or the work ceases to exist (§ 10 No. 1 tjml), second, in cases where the employee is steadily not capable of continuing to work (§ 10 No. 2 (a) tjml), thirdly, if he no longer possesses the qualifications that are necessary for the post in question (§ 10 No. 2 (b) Alt. 1 tjml) or finally, if he permanently turns out to be unsuitable for the position due to other grounds (§ 10 No. 2 (b) Alt. 2 tjml).[1350]

In any case, the flexibility and the professor's freedom of choice in determining the point of exit form his working life meet boundaries as soon as the respective employee reaches the general age limit of 70 in § 2 (1) s. 1 *aldersgrenselov*. Only under certain conditions is a prolongation of the employment relationship up to the age of 75 via fixed-term employment contracts possible, as further laid down in § 3 *aldersgrenselov*. Being an absolute age limit, the age of 75 constitutes the ultimate benchmark for the professor's freedom of choice in making use of his right to work.[1351]

Professors who are primarily concerned with physical education, teaching and research in activity disciplines (*aktivitetsfag*) and practical subjects at the Norwegian School of Sports and Science, such as for example in the security training centre (*sikkerhetsopplæringssenter*), are subject to a lower mandatory retirement at age 65.[1352]

Exceptions to this are professors at private universities, which are not encompassed by the special dismissal provisions in the *tjml*, but underly the general rules on dismissal in the WEA.

1349 § 2 (4) *aldersgrenselov*. Encompassed by this age limit are inter alia judges and federal prosecutors. In principle not encompassed are professors, employed at private universities, such as at the *Det teologiske Menighetsfakultet*, the *Handelshøyskole BI*, or at some religious universities such as the *Misjonshøyskole* in Stavanger. Professor positions at the BI are related to the SPK. However, it should be borne in mind that the *pensjonskasseloven* not obligatory prescribes a certain age limit. Despite this, one may assume that also these universities operate with an age limit of 70 years of age.

1350 The requirements for dismissal in the first year of civil service are regulated in § 9 tjml. See to previous applicable rules on dismissal of professors as *'embetsmenn'*: *Jakhelln* (1989), chap. 2.5, 2.6.

1351 see § 3 (1) s. 3 *aldersgrenselov*.

1352 see *Fornyings- og administrasjonsdepartementet* (2009), Aldersgrensene i staten og aldersgrensene for øvrige medlemmer i statens pensjonskasse, p. 24; Innst. S. nr. 77 (1995-1996), *Innstilling fra familie-, kultur- og administrasjons-*

14.2.2 Exceptions to the age limit: Extensions per fixed-term employment contracts

According to § 3 *aldersgrenselov*, the employment relationship of university professors after having reached the 70-year age limit may be prolonged per fixed-term employment contracts up to the age of 75.[1353] The central precondition for the prolongation is that the civil servant in question still fulfils the requirements that are necessary for the position in question.[1354] As indicated by the provision's wording, the employer (*tilsettingsmyndighet*) 'may' decide that the employee cannot continue in employment (*fortsette i tjeneste*).[1355] Consequently, he has no right to prolongation.[1356] The decision rests with the university or the department at the respective responsible faculty. The King may determine further rules on how this discretionary power may be exercised.[1357] The circumstances of the respective agency, the demographic development and the respective employment/labour-market (*sysselsettingen*) situation shall be taken into account when deciding upon the prolongation.[1358]

By principally offering the opportunity for fixed-term employment, § 2 combined with § 3 *aldersgrenselov* seems at first glance to provide a rather more flexible solution than the mandatory retirement regulation in § 2 alone does. However, it has to be borne in mind that the employment in cases of first time prolongation are only allowed for a period of one to two years. After that, fixed-term contracts may only be granted for a period of one year. In total, the prolongation shall not exceed the maximum of five years.[1359] Taking a closer look at the wording of § 3 *aldersgrenselov*, a number of questions arise, such as the question regarding what kind of 'requirements' have to be fulfilled by the professor, as stipu-

---

komiteen om aldersgrenser for offentlige tjenestemenn m.fl.; This age limit is not going to be subject to a closer proportionality analysis as only the general mandatory retirement age limit for university professors in Norway and Germany is going to be examined as a selected example.

1353 § 3 i.c.w. § 2 *aldersgrenselov*.

1354 § 3 (1) s. 2 *aldersgrenselov*.

1355 § 3 (1) s. 1 *aldersgrenselov*.

1356 LDN – uttalelse case 24/2011, 22.11.2011, p. 6, 7; LDN case 36/2009, uttalelse 14. December 2009, p. 5.

1357 § 3 (2) s.1, see also s. 3 *aldersgrenselov*.

1358 § 3 (2) s. 2 *aldersgrenselov*.

1359 § 3 (1) s. 3 *aldersgrenselov*.

lated in § 3 (1) *aldersgrenselov*, for him to be allowed to continue working.[1360] What are the exact requirements for the position of a university professor? In the case of doubtful evidence in this regard, how such evidence should be provided is not further clarified.[1361] In the case of professors, it might not so much be the physical, but rather the mental capacities that are decisive for a capability assessment. To determine a professor's intellectual capacity objectively might be a difficult task.[1362] How this may finally be determined in terms of whether the individual professor still fulfils the requirements of the position as stipulated by § 3 *aldersgrenselov* therefore seems to be more than questionable. Moreover, it has to be kept in mind that the final decision about extending the contract ultimately comes down to the employer's discretion, being the final decision-maker in this regard.[1363] In addition to these uncertainties, the meaning of the formulation *fortsette i tjeneste* in § 3 (1) s. 1 *aldersgrenselov* is rather ambiguous.[1364] It leaves several questions unanswered such as what does the prolongation in fact look like; that is, to what extent may the employment relationship be modified in terms of job profile and remuneration? Will the job under the fixed-term contract, apart from the limitation concerning time, correspond in its entirety to the previous work?[1365] To find the answers to these questions is rather difficult, as scientific, reliable and empirically substantiated data concerning the use of § 3 *aldersgrenselov* at Norwegian universities are inexistent. As the question of prolongation according to § 3 *aldersgrenselov* has not yet been subject to court decisions, looking at cases before the Norwegian Equality Tribunal (*Likestillings- og diskrimineringsnemnda* (LDN)) and the Equality and Discrimination Ombudsperson (*Likestillings- og diskrimineringsombudet* (LDO)) may therefore shed light on how to interpret § 3 *aldersgrenselov*.[1366] In case 36/2009,[1367] the key question was whether the rejection of a request

1360 *Hack* (2012 b), p. 205.
1361 ibid.
1362 ibid.
1363 ibid.; see to the aspect of discretion also LDN case 36/2009, uttalelse 14. December 2009.
1364 *Hack* (2012 b), p. 205.
1365 ibid., p. 206.
1366 see cases LDN case 36/2009, uttalelse 14. December 2009; LDN case 24/2011, uttalelse 22. November 2011; see to this cases also *Holgersen* (2013), p. 216, 217; see in general to the Norwegian ombud-system *Hack* (2010 a), p. 350 f.
1367 LDN case 36/2009, uttalelse 14. December 2009.

to continue working as a professor beyond the age of 70 violated the prohibition against age discrimination as manifested in chap. 13 WEA. The faculty rejected the request for prolongation, as they wanted to maintain the established principle (*fast prinsipp*) that the mandatory retirement age is set at 70 years of age. After that, the professor might be engaged as a researcher in a so-called *forskerstilling*. He may then use the title of professor emeritus, so their argument went. The plaintiff criticised the categorical rejection of the request and claimed that each request should be treated individually. Moreover, he referred to Ot. prp. nr. 60 (1956), where it is stated that not only the interests of the civil service as such, but also other interests of society and the interests of the civil servant should be accounted for in the decision about prolongation.[1368] The defendant challenged this. The faculty admitted that calling the age limit a 'principle' was rather unfortunate, but stressed that the rejection was based on an individual evaluation after weighing up the employee's interests versus the university's interests – particularly economic reasons. In its analysis, the LDN interestingly enough referred to the fact that the question as to whether a general age limit of 70 years was in conformity with the prohibition against age discrimination had already been evaluated several times by the legislator, who concluded that there was no violation of the prohibition if an employee was forced to retire at the age of 70 and that a further analysis of other factors than the employee's age did not appear to be necessary.[1369] According to the LDN, it is up to the parliament and not the LDN to decide whether this position should be changed. Moreover, the LDN stressed that the wording of § 3 (1) *aldersgrenselov* (*kan treffe bestemmelse*) explicitly leaves it to the employer's discretion as to whether the professor may continue or not. In light of these considerations, the LDN finally concluded that the rejection of the request for prolongation was not against the prohibition of age discrimination.[1370]

1368 ibid., referring in this regard to Ot.prp. nr. 60 (1956) *Om lov om aldersgrenser for offentlige tjenestemenn m. fl.*, see to such arguments in particular p. 52 f.

1369 ibid.; It has to be noted that the legislator's evaluation the LDN is referring to the former 70-years-age limit in § 15-7 (4) WEA (now: § 15-13 a (1) WEA), which has to be distinguished from the age limit in § 2 *aldersgrenselov*. While the former concerns the loss of dismissal protection after achieving the age of 70, the latter constitutes a 'real' age limit as the employee is obliged to terminate the employment relationship. Thus, both regulations are only to some extend comparable.

1370 ibid., agreeing also *Holgersen* (2013), p. 216, 217.

The LDN case 24/2011[1371] concerned a professor who, after having reached 70 years of age, continued to work in the position as a professor for one more year and who, after that period, received an offer to continue working under pensioner's terms (*pensjonistvilkår i staten*). The professor felt discriminated against on the grounds of age based on this job offer. The plaintiff argued that the job offer implied the same amount of teaching obligations had to be fulfilled as when he was engaged as a full-time professor in previous years. He stressed that he sufficiently met the required qualifications for the position, which he tried to substantiate by the fact the he continued working after having reached the age limit. Moreover, he claimed that the 70-year age limit for civil servants as such was age discrimination. In its analysis, the LDN stated again that the employer possesses a discretionary power when evaluating if the professor may continue to work, according to § 3 *aldersgrenselov*, which also implies that the employer may offer reduced teaching duties under *pensjonistvilkår*. According to the LDN, the job offer did not therefore constitute age discrimination. Regarding the 70-year age limit, it referred again to the legislator's evaluations of the 70-year age limit in the WEA and stated that it was not up to the LDN, but rather up to the parliament to determine whether such an age limit was contradictory to the prohibition against age discrimination.

Similarly, in case 09/1839[1372] before the LDO, the plaintiff got a job offer to continue working beyond the age limit, which, according to his argumentation, de facto constituted a prolongation of his previous post as a professor. However, the LDO referred to the fact that his previous post and the conditions of the job offer could not be equated, as the latter did not include research projects, which were part of a full-time position as a professor. In consequence, the job offer did not violate the prohibition against age discrimination. Interestingly enough, the LDO pointed out that the question as to whether the hourly rate for pensioners is in conformity with the prohibition of discrimination on the grounds of age might be evaluated on a general basis. According to the LDO, the situation where the retired professor continues to work at the same place after having reached the age of 70 and has fully accrued pension rights raises particular questions, which the ombudsperson is going to address further in its policy work.

In case 10/142,[1373] the LDO decided that age was not the decisive factor for not being invited for a job interview for the position of a professor. The ombudsperson specified that the prohibition against age discrimination is not absolute and that the employer may, to a certain extent, treat the employees differently on the grounds of age as long as it is necessary to achieve a legitimate aim

1371 LDN case 24/2011, uttalelse 22. November 2011.

1372 LDO case 09/1839, uttalelse 11. February 2011, anonymized version sended on request to the author.

1373 LDO case 10/142, uttalelse 11 April 2011.

and does not disproportionately interfere with the employee's rights as expressed in § 13-3 (2) WEA. The LDO particularly stressed that a reasonable age structure may constitute an objective reason to discriminate on the grounds of age.[1374]

Common for these cases is a relatively short analysis of whether age discrimination has taken place and if it may be justified. A strict standard of justification is not applied. Instead, it has rather cursorily been ascertained that the prohibition against age discrimination has not been violated. Moreover, it seems to be left to the legislator to change the legal situation *de lege ferenda*. In doing so *de lege lata*, a rather restrictive application of § 3 *aldersgrenselov* is applied. At least this provision has been used by universities when allowing professors who have reached the age of 70 before the end of term (*semesterslutt*) to continue to work until the end of the semester.[1375] In sum, the use of prolongation up to the maximum age of 75 years seems to be the rare exception.[1376]

The author does not have any scientific, empirically reliable information as to whether, how often and to what extent prolongation according to § 3 *aldersgrenselov* is applied. On enquiry via email in February 2012, the human resource departments of several Norwegian universities replied. At the University of Trondheim, at least two professors made use of § 3, and one of them may even be employed until the age of 74; at the University of Tromsø, only in minor cases was a prolongation of 1–2 years used, while no information was available concerning an extension up to 75 years of age. The personnel policy plan (*personalpolitiske handlingsplan*) of the University of Stavanger stipulates that one should make use of the option to extend working life according to § 3 when evaluating if the university has a demand for further employing the respective professors. Until February 2012, the provision was made use of in only one case. According to the feedback from the University of Oslo (UiO) as regards the period 2006 to February 2012, prolongation up to the maximum of 75 years has not yet been granted; rather, professors had been engaged in minor roles as censors in exams or in similar engagements.

This contrasts with the expressed appeal made in the governmental human resources handbook (*Statens Personalhandbok* (SPH)) that public employers should facilitate older employees to stay in active employment.[1377] Moreover, the prevailing application of § 3 *aldersgrenselov* contrasts with the provision's wording itself, which in principle leaves room for an

1374 ibid.; This argument has also been brought forward by NOU 2003: 2, chap. 12, p. 66.

1375 *Hack* (2012 b), p. 206.

1376 ibid.; see also *Toft*, Martin (2010), Snart 70 – nektar å pensjonera seg, UNIFORM 04, 11.03.2010.

1377 see e.g. chap. 5.2.2 (1) of the SPH where it is explicitly laid down that: '*Statlige arbeidsgivere oppfordres til å legge til rette for at eldre arbeidstakere kan fortsette i tjenesten.*'; see to this aspect also *Toft* (2010).

extensive use of the option to prolong the professor's employment, as it is up to the employer's discretion to decide whether to make use of § 3 *aldersgrenselov*.

14.2.3 Further employment under pensjonistvilkår/pensioner's terms and affiliation to the university as professor emeritus

In case the public-sector university professor should retire, he nevertheless has the opportunity to be further engaged as an old-age pensioner (*alderspensjonist*).[1378] The conditions for further employment under pensioner's terms are laid down in the SPH and in further guidelines at the level of the respective university.[1379]

Examining the regulations of the UiO may provide an example of how a further professional affiliation between the retired university professor and his institution may look.[1380] The main aim of these regulations is to facilitate work for pensioners who still wish to contribute to the UiO research activities, either through research or through supporting functions that are related to research or teaching.[1381] Usually, these university professors will be affiliated to the university under the status of professor emeritus.[1382] This is in line with the regulation's aim of maintaining the pensioner's status as a professor, even beyond active employment. The professorial status shall remain unaffected. Under the regulations, the professor emeritus shall be offered an extended affiliation to the university without being employed, as long as the professor emeritus' activity is 'of value for the UiO'.[1383] It is up to the head of the respective unit in every single case to decide whether such an offer should be made. Consequently,

---

1378 see for further details SPH, chap. 10.12.1.

1379 see *Hack* (2012 b), p. 203 for further details.

1380 see e.g. *Reglementshåndbok for Universitetet i Oslo* (version of 2008), chap. 7.16, enacted 1. February 2008.

1381 Reglementshåndbok for Universitetet i Oslo, chap. 7.16.

1382 Even if the regulations do not explicitly name it, they regulate the status as professor emeritus. The right to get the status as 'emeritus' itself is not explicitly laid down by law or regulation. It has rather the character of a customary right. However, it is to some extend related to the right to use the professional title 'professor' even after retirement as manifested in § 6-7 (3) Lov 1. april 2005 *om universiteter og høyskoler (universitets- og høyskoleloven– univl.)*.

1383 Reglementshåndbok for Universitetet i Oslo, chap. 7.16.

the retired professor in question has no right to claim continued affiliation to the university.[1384] It has to be kept in mind that these regulations only apply to retirees who are not in paid employment with the UiO, as those in paid employment – even for temporary assignments – would be defined as employees and thus fall out of the regulation's scope.[1385] Examples for the engagement of retired university professors without financial compensation may be participating in research projects, continuing and completing existing research projects or mentoring and supporting younger scientists.[1386] The continued affiliation to the university has to be laid down in an agreement between the retired professor and the responsible director.[1387] As the professor's formal contractual employment relationship with the university is terminated, no expectations concerning the duty to work or the delivery of concrete results may be demanded.[1388] What the affiliation de facto may include is subject to an individual assessment in each individual case and is decided by the management of the relevant unit. Examples of what may be offered to the university professors are allocation and access to a virtual workstation, access to the library, a physical place to work, scientific facilities and infrastructure or technical support. Such agreements should not normally be made for more than one year at a time. [1389]

14.3 De lege lata situation in Germany

14.3.1 Mandatory retirement age limit

In Germany, professors working at public universities are generally civil servants. In addition, these professors are confronted with a mandatory retirement age limit. The German legal situation is rather complex, as both

1384 ibid., in particular para. 2.
1385 ibid., para. 1.
1386 ibid., para. 2.
1387 ibid., para. 3.
1388 ibid., para. 3.
1389 ibid., para. 3; One aspect that has to be considered is whether the entity has the necessary financial ressources, see para. 4.

regulations on federal and state (*Länder*) level apply. Further matters concerning the employment relationship of civil servants are also regulated in collective agreements.[1390]

As regards legal relations of persons employed by the federation (*Bund*) and by federal corporations under public law, the federation shall have exclusive legislative power (*ausschließliche Gesetzgebungskompetenz*).[1391] This finds its legal expression in the law for federal civil servants, the *Bundesbeamtengesetz* (BBG), in particular § 147 (3) BBG. However, as regards statutory rights and duties of civil servants on the state level, such as in the case of university professors, the legislative competence rests, in principle, on the states, with the so-called concurrent legislative power (*konkurrierende Gesetzgebung*), so long as and to the extent that the federation has not exercised its legislative power by enacting a law.[1392]

Since 2008, the *Beamtenstatusgesetz* (BeamtSTG) has laid down rules in its §§ 21ff. for the termination of the civil servant employment relationship. In § 21 No. 4 in conjunction with § 25 BeamtSTG, it is generally manifested that tenured civil servants (*Beamte auf Lebenszeit*) have to retire when having reached the age limit.[1393] As in BeamtSTG, no explicit age for compulsory retirement is laid down; it is up to the 16 states and the federation to determine the respective mandatory retirement ages.[1394] For civil servants on the federal level, the general age limit of 67 is laid down in § 51 BBG.[1395] For federal civil servants born after 1947, the age limit

1390 see as regards mandatory retirement provisions in general § 33 (1) (a) *Tarifvertrag für den öffentlichen Dienst* (TVöD), § 33 (1) (a) *Tarifvertrag für den öffentlichen Dienst der Länder* (TV-L); see for an overview of the different applicable regulations on federal, state level and in the relevant collective agreements: *Summer*, Rudolf (2009), Die Altersgrenze für den Wechsel aus dem aktiven Beamtenverhältnis in den Ruhestand und die individuellen Abweichungen, Die Personalvertretung (PersV) 5 2009, pp. 164-168, p. 164 f; see moreover *Wulfers*, Christian/*Hecht*, Diana (2007), Altersdiskriminierung durch Tarifbestimmungen – Eine Analyse des TvöD und TV-L, Zeitschrift für Tarifrecht (ZTR) 2007, pp. 475-483, in particular chap. 3.2.3 as regards the age limit in § 33 (1) (a) TVöD/TV-L and its conformity with Dir. 2000/78/EC.

1391 see Art. 73 No. 8 GG.

1392 see Art. 74 (1) No. 27, Art. 72 (1) GG.

1393 see moreover § 23 (1) s. 1 BeamSTG.

1394 see Bt-Dr. 16/4027, *Entwurf eines Gesetzes zur Regelung des Statusrechts der Beamtinnen und Beamten in den Ländern (Beamtenstatusgesetz* – BeamtStG), S. 28; see also joined cases C-159/10 and C-160/10 (*Fuchs* and *Köhler*), para. 11; Previously, that is to say before the major so-called *Föderalismusreform* (federalism reform), there was one general mandatory retirement age limit for civil servants laid down on federal level, which the *Länder* implemented in their respective in legislation.

1395 see § 51 (1) BBG.

increases stepwise until the age of 67.[1396] In most of the states, the mandatory age limit is set at the age of 65, with a gradual increase up to the age of 67 in line with the pension reform amendments.[1397] In principle, professors have the opportunity to apply for a prolongation of the employment relationship via fixed-term contracts up to a further maximum age limit.

14.3.2 Exceptions to the age limit: Extensions per fixed-term employment contracts

Both on the federal level and in all *Länder*, the option to postpone the exit from active employment and thus the retirement start date is generally provided for civil servants in German law.[1398]

Besides these regulations in public law, professors might also be further employed via an employment contract under private law conditions after their retirement.[1399] This might be e.g. of interest in cases where the chair (*Lehrstuhl*) is still vacant and needs to be reoccupied until the successor of the chair has been employed.[1400]

1396 see § 51 (2) BBG.

1397 see to the pension reform in general chap. 1.4.2.

1398 see on federal level: § 53 (1) BBG; see on *Länder* level e.g.: Art. 63 Bayerisches Beamtengesetz (BayBG) in Bayern; § 38 (2) Landesbeamtengesetz (LBG) in Berlin; § 45 (3) LBG in Brandenburg; § 35 (4) Bremisches Beamtengesetz (BremBG) in Bremen; § 35 (4) Hamburgisches Beamtengesetz (HmbBG); § 34 (1) Hessisches Beamtengesetz (HBG) in Hessen; § 35 (3) Beamtengesetz für das Land Mecklenburg-Vorpommern (LBG M-V); § 38 LBG in Rheinland-Pfalz; § 43 (3) Saarländisches Beamtengesetz (SBG) in Saarland; § 47 Sächsisches Beamtengesetz (SächsBG) in Sachsen; § 39 (2) Beamtengesetz des Landes Sachsen-Anhalt (LBG LSA) in Sachsen-Anhalt; § 35 (4) LBG Schleswig-Holstein in Schleswig Holstein and § 43 (6) Thüringer Beamtengesetz (ThürBG) in Thüringen.

1399 see in detail *Mohr*, Jochen (2009), Die Rechtsstellung pensionierter und emeritierter Hochschullehrer bei vertraglicher Verpflichtung zur Vertretung ihres Lehrstuhls in Lehre, Forschung und Prüfung bis zur Wiederbesetzung, NZA 2009, pp. 1-6, p. 3ff.

1400 see in detail ibid. pp. 1-6.

Interestingly enough, § 25 BeamtSTG neither stipulates nor prohibits such provisions on the *Länder* level.[1401] In theory, an age limit may therefore e.g. be set at 75 or 80 or may even be abolished.[1402] All regulations on the *Länder* level have in common that they operate with mandatory age limits. These age limits are not exclusively applicable for university professors, but rather generally encompass civil servants as such. However, some *Länder* explicitly allow university professors to remain in employment, even after having reached the age limit, until the university term (the semester/trimester) during which they have reached the age limit ends.[1403] In ten *Länder,* the age limit is laid down at the age of 67.[1404] With the exception of *Baden-Würrtemberg* and *Hamburg*, all these *Länder* open up for a postponement of retirement up to a maximum of three years, that is, up to the age of 70, while it is only 68 in the case of *Baden-Würrtemberg.*[1405] Only *Hamburg* explicitly refuses university professors the opportunity to postpone the retirement start.[1406] On the contrary, six *Länder* still have a lower age limit set at the age of 65.[1407] They provide for a postponement of the retirement start up to the age of 68.[1408] In general, the reason for postponing may be so-called *dienstliche Gründe* (official reasons) on behalf of the employer or following a request from the employee, provided that the so-called *dienstliche Interessen* (official interests of the service) do not conflict with the employee's request to prolongate his

1401 *Poguntke* (2011), p. 561.

1402 see to this aspect also *von Roetteken,* Thorsten/*Rothländer*, Christian/*Burkholz*, Bernhard/*Kohde*, Jens (2013), in: von Roetteken, Thorsten/Rothländer, Christian (eds.), BeamtStG Kommentar zum Beamtenstatusgesetz, § 25 Ruhestand wegen Erreichens der Altersgrenze, IV. Ergänzung durch Landesrecht, 16. Update 12/13, para. 27, 29ff.; critical *Summer* (2009), p. 164, 166.

1403 see § 35 (1) BremBG; § 35 (1) HmbBG; § 33 (2) No. 2 HBG; § 35 (1) LBG Schleswig-Holstein; § 39 (1) LBG LSA; see to this aspect also C-159/10 and C-160/10 (*Fuchs* and *Köhler*), para. 91.

1404 see § 36 (1) LBG Baden-Württemberg; § 35 (1) BremBG; § 35 (1) HmbBG; § 33 (1), (2) No. 2 HBG; § 35 (1) LBG M-V; § 35 (2) Niedersächsisches Beamtengesetz (NBG), § 35 (2); § 31 (1) Beamtengesetz für das Land Nordrhein-Westfalen (LBG NRW); § 46 (1) SächsBG; § 35 (1) LBG Schleswig-Holstein; § 43 (1) ThürBG.

1405 see § 39 LBG Baden-Württemberg.

1406 § 123 i.c.w. § 35 (4) No. 5, (5) HmbG; see moreover *Poguntke* (2011), p. 565.

1407 see Art. 62 s. 1 BayBG; § 38 (1) s. 1 LBG Berlin; § 65 (1), (2) LBG Brandenburg; § 54 (1) LBG Rheinland-Pfalz; § 43 (1) SBG; § 39 (1) LBG LSA.

1408 Art. 63 (1), (2) BayBG; § 38 (2) LBG Berlin; § 65 (3) LBG Brandenburg; § 55 (1) LBG Rheinland-Pfalz; § 43 (3) SBG; § 39 (2) LBG LSA.

employment contract. In any case, the existence of *dienstliche Gründe* or *dienstliche Interessen* is an indispensable requirement for postponing the retirement start in all the respective *Länder* provisions.[1409] As a vague legal concept (*unbestimmter Rechtsbegriff*), the interests of the service refers to the interests involved in the proper and smooth accomplishment of tasks.[1410] It depends to a considerable extent on the previous organisational and personnel decisions of the employer, and is determined by the order of the respective department and the available related human resources and organisational alternatives.[1411] Only *Berlin* explicitly clarifies in § 38 (2) s. 2 LBG that organisational, staff-related aspects as well as fiscal interests are in the interests of the service.

In the German literature, it has been discussed whether postponing the age limit constitutes a subjective right of the employee.[1412] Moreover, common to all the provisions concerning the postponement of the age limit is the controversy around whether it should solely serve the public or also the subjective interests of the respective civil servant.[1413] The argument that subjective interests should also be accounted for at least finds support when examining the respective *travaux preparatoires* on the *Länder* level. There, it has been stressed several times that the mandatory retirement age should be flexibilised by making use of the prolongation option to enhance the employee's possibilities to plan their transition from work to retirement individually.[1414] In the interests of the civil servant, the decision about his request should at least be exercised *ermessensfehlerfrei*; that is, without any mistakes in the discretionary decision.[1415]

In short, the requirements for postponing the age limit based on the employee's request are first, the request for prolongation itself, second, that the employee has not yet exceeded the respective maximum age limit for entry into retirement and finally, that no *dienstliche* reasons or interests may be identified that conflict with the postponement.[1416] Since the legal

---

1409 Sometimes no distinction is made between '*dienstliche Gründe*' and '*dienstliche Interessen*', such as in NRW where § 32 LBG NRW just speaks of '*dienstliche Gründe*'. In Thüringen the formulation '*dringende dienstliche Belange*' is used in § 43 (3) ThürBG, while in Bayern Art. Art. 62 s. 1 BayBG uses the expression '*zwingende dienstliche Rücksichten*'.

1410 *Poguntke* (2011), p. 563; critical to the term '*dienstliches Interesse*': *Summer* (2009), p. 167.

1411 *Poguntke* (2011), p. 563.

1412 see in detail e.g. *Schäfer*, Hauke (2009), Hat der Beamte ein subjektives Recht auf Dienstzeitverlängerung?, ZBR 2009, pp. 301-305, 303 f. with particular focus on the situation of university professors: p. 301, 304.

1413 see in detail to the discussion *Poguntke* (2011), p. 562 fn. 15.

1414 ibid.

1415 ibid.

1416 ibid.

amendments in 2008, a paradigm shift has taken place as regards the requirement of *dienstliches Interesse*. Before the amendments, the *Dienstunfähigkeit* (disability for service) of the civil servant in question who had reached the age limit was irrefutably assumed. By contrast, *de lege lata* the existence of the *dienstliches Interesse* has to be ascertained explicitly.[1417] A mere fictitious *dienstliches Interesse* is no longer sufficient. Examples may be maintaining continuity in the exercise of the professional tasks, difficulties in filling jobs that are available or an interest in a certain age structure.[1418] An example for conflicting *dienstliche Gründe* could be if the employee in question remains in his post beyond the mandatory retirement threshold when the fulfilment of his job-related tasks is negatively affected.[1419] It is questionable as to whether the *dienstliche Gründe* are solely those related to the employer or if they may also be based on the civil servant as such, e.g. insufficient capabilities and a lack of willingness to perform tasks or absences from work.[1420] In any case, the decision as to the professor's request for prolongation being granted or not depends on the responsible public authority's discretion. The fact that the provisions for prolongation solely refer to *dienstliche Interessen* without explicitly mentioning reasons that rest in the employee's person and that may conflict with the prolongation request, militates at least for a restrictive application in favour of the employee. Otherwise, the legislator's emphasis on enhancing the employees' flexibility by giving them opportunities for the prolongation of their working career would be foiled.[1421]

14.3.3 Emeritus regulations

Emeritus regulations are, in principle, subject to the law of the *Länder*; however, the *Hochschulrahmengesetz* (HRG – Framework Act for Higher Education) of 1976 abolished the legal institution of *Emeritierung* with

1417 in detail ibid., p. 563, fn. 26-29.
1418 ibid.
1419 ibid.
1420 ibid.
1421 ibid., p. 565 who advocates that solely employer's interests should be accounted for in the decision on prolongation; stressing the individual interests of the employee in the discretionary decision also *Schäfer* (2009), p. 305.

effect *pro futuro* for those professors appointed after a certain point in time.[1422] Professors appointed prior to that date are still therefore encompassed by the emeritus regulations. In general, the mandatory retirement age has replaced the emeritus provisions. According to § 36 (2) HRG, retired professors are still entitled to give lectures and be part of examination procedures, which may, in principle, be compared to the previous applicable emeritus entitlements.[1423]

Whether the professor may even hold his title in retirement is subject to the various regulations on the *Länder* level.[1424] Given the uncertainties due to the different and fragmented regulations, and in view of the habitualness in international academia, some argue for maintaining the nomenclature of 'emeritus'.[1425] Some use the denomination a.D. (*außer Dienst*), while others use i.R. (*im Ruhestand*). Both terms have met with criticism for being terminologically improper, as a retired professor is not really off duty (*außer Dienst*) but may actually still be professionally active, see e.g. § 36 (2) HRG.[1426]

14.4 Compatibility analysis

Given the multitude of regulations on the *Länder* level in Germany, for reasons of comparability, the provisions concerning mandatory retirement for professors in the *Land Hessen*, as manifested in §§ 33 (1), (2) No. 2, 34 (1) HBG, shall be the selected example for the compatibility analysis. The main reason for this is that these provisions at least in part have already been subject to the CJEU case of *Fuchs* and *Köhler* regarding civil servants.

The subject of the *Fuchs* and *Köhler* case was the age limit for civil servants that, previous to legal amendments in March 2014, was laid down in § 50 HBG.[1427] The age limit has basically been maintained in the current § 33 HBG, in force since 1 March 2014.

1422 *Hartmer*, Michael (2009), Prof. em. oder Prof. a.D.? Zur Titelführung von pensionierten und emeritierten Hochschullehrern, Forschung & Lehre, 10. Oktober 2009; *Mohr* (2009), p. 2 f.; see §§ 72, 76 *Hochschulrahmengesetz* (HRG).

1423 arguing in this regard *Hartmer* (2009); see also e.g. Art. 13 *Bayerisches Hochschulpersonalgesetz* - BayHSchPG: *'Professoren und Professorinnen stehen auch nach dem Eintritt in den Ruhestand die mit der Lehrbefugnis verbundenen Rechte zur Abhaltung von Lehrveranstaltungen und zur Beteiligung an Prüfungsverfahren zu.'*

1424 see e.g. Art. 12 (1) BayHSchPG, § 61 (4) s. 3, (9) *Hessisches Hochschulgesetz*.

1425 see e.g. *Hartmer* (2009).

1426 see to the critic ibid.

1427 see for an overview joined cases C-159/10 and C-160/10 (*Fuchs* and *Köhler*), para. 9ff.

Moreover, they operate in line with the majority of the *Länder* with a mandatory age limit set at the age of 67, so that this example also has a kind of representative function. The legal situations in Norway and Germany are, in terms of their compatibility with Dir. 2000/78/EC, examined together, as they both feature similar regulations to end the employment of university professors having achieved mandatory retirement through §§ 2 (1) s. 1, 3 (1) *aldersgrenselov* and §§ 33 (1), (2) No. 2, 34 (1) HBG. When interpreting the Directive's provisions in the compatibility analysis, besides *Fuchs* and *Köhler*, the CJEU *Georgiev* case concerning mandatory retirement for university professors has the closest similarity to the situation in Norway and in Germany. Comparable to the situation in the *Georgiev* case, also in the Norwegian and German context, two central questions concerning the compatibility with the prohibition against age discrimination have to be adressed:[1428] first, the compatibility as regards the mandatory retirement age in § 2 (1) s. 1 *aldersgrenselov* and §§ 33 (1), (2) No. 2 HBG and second, the option to extend the employment contract beyond the age limit of 70 and 67 via fixed-term contracts at most to the absolute age limit of 75, respectively, as stipulated in § 3 (1) s. 3 *aldersgrenselov* and § 34 (1) HBG.

14.4.1 The scope of Dir. 2000/78/EC

Both §§ 2 (1) s. 1, 3 (1) *aldersgrenselov* and §§ 33 (1), (2) No. 2, 34 (1) HBG concern employment and working conditions in terms of Art. 3 No. 1 (c) Dir. 2000/78/EC, as they have a direct impact on the duration and the modalities of the employment relationship, as well as, more generally, on the exercise of the professional activity of university professors, in that they limit their future participation in the labour force beyond the age of 70 and 67, respectively, and preclude entirely such participation beyond the age of 75 and 70, respectively.[1429] Thus, the selected Norwegian and

---

1428 see the questions referred for a preliminary ruling in C-250/09 and C-268/09 (*Georgiev*), para. 23; see also opinion AG *Bot* in joined cases C-250/09 and C-268/09 (*Georgiev*), para. 21, 23, 25; *Hack* (2012 b), p. 208.

1429 similar opinion AG *Bot* delivered on 02.09.2010, in joined cases C-250/09 and C-268/09 (*Georgiev*), para. 23 referring to C-411/05 (*Palacios*), para. 45, 46 and C-388/07 (*Age Concern*), para. 27, 28; see finally C-268/09 (*Georgiev*), para. 29, 30; see in general to the Directive's scope chap. 10.2.1.

German provisions affect employment and working conditions such as dismissals in the public sector in the sense of Art. 3 No. 1 (c) and hence come within the scope of Dir. 2000/78/EC.

14.4.2 Direct age discrimination

Professors affected by §§ 2 (1) s. 1, 3 (1) *aldersgrenselov* and §§ 33 (1), (2) No. 2, 34 (1) HBG, solely experience less favourable treatment – compulsory retirement due to age – than other persons in a comparable situation practising the same profession on the sole ground that they have reached the age limit of 70 and 67, respectively, as stipulated in § 2 *aldersgrenselov* and § 33 (1), (2) No. 2 HBG.[1430]

Also with regard to the application of fixed-term contracts – regulated in §§ 2 (1) s. 1, 3 (1) *aldersgrenselov* and §§ 33 (1), (2) No. 2, 34 (1) HBG – after having reached the age limit of 70 and 67, respectively, the following can be ascertained: by stipulating that, beyond the respective age limit, the employment relationship may be extended solely via fixed-term contracts for a maximum total of five years in the case of Norway and three years as regards Germany, both provisions treat university professors who have reached the age of 70 and 67, respectively, as well as those who have reached the age of 75 and 70, respectively, less favourably than other university professors who are working in the same profession and are younger than the age limit.[1431] In contrast to other professors who are under this age limit and who, in principle, benefit from a contract of indefinite duration, professors who are above the age limit are forced to accept a fixed-term contract if they wish to extend working life beyond the age limit.[1432] Consequently, these professors are deprived of the option to continue with the exercise of their profession via unlimited employment con-

---

1430 C-250/09 and C-268/09 (*Georgiev*), para. 32 referring to C-411/05 (*Palacios*), para. 51.

1431 similar opinion AG *Bot* in C-250/09 and C-268/09 (*Georgiev*), para. 25 and judgement C-250/09 and C-268/09 (*Georgiev*), para. 32, 33.

1432 similar opinion AG *Bot* in C-250/09 and C-268/09 (*Georgiev*), para. 25.

tracts.[1433] Furthermore, professors who reach the age of 75 and 70, respectively, are also deprived of the possibility of working under a fixed-term contract, as this age limit constitutes an absolute age limit.

In addition, a comparison with employees who are affected by a general age limit that is lower than that of professors does not alter that conclusion. As pointed out by AG *Bot* in *Georgiev*, the mere fact that a lower mandatory retirement age limit might exist for other employees does not lead to the conclusion that, from the perspective of those affected by the lower age limit, university professors might appear to be 'in an advantageous position in comparison with other employees'.[1434] Such a conclusion excludes the possibility that these professors may be subject to a difference in treatment on the grounds of age, contrary to the Directive.[1435] The chosen comparators solely have to be university professors, who have not yet reached the mandatory retirement age in respect of the absolute age limit for the fixed-term contract.[1436]

Arguments that such legislation is not unfavourable to the professors concerned because it makes it possible for them, where appropriate, to work for another couple of years – in the case of Norway, at most up to the age of 75 – after reaching the age at which they may be made to take retirement with a pension, are not capable of undermining this finding.[1437] The reason for this is that such a situation does not prevent professors from working under more precarious working conditions than younger professors under the age limit do, as they no longer have employment of an indefinite duration.[1438] Consequently, both §§ 2 (1) s. 1, 3 (1) *aldersgrenselov* and §§ 33 (1), (2) No. 2, 34 (1) HBG lead to a difference in treatment, which is based directly on the grounds of age in terms of Art. 2 No. 1, No. 2 (a) in conjunction with Art. 1 Dir. 2000/78/EC.[1439]

1433 similar joined cases C-250/09 and C-268/09 (*Georgiev*), para. 33; similar opinion AG *Bot* in C-250/09 and C-268/09 (*Georgiev*), para. 25.

1434 Opinion AG *Bot*, C-250/09 and C-268/09 (*Georgiev*), para 25.

1435 ibid.

1436 ibid.

1437 similar CJEU in joined cases C-250/09 and C-268/09 (*Georgiev*), para. 34.

1438 ibid.

1439 similar joined cases C-250/09 and C-268/09 (*Georgiev*), para. 32, 33 referring to C-411/05 (*Palacios*), para. 51; see also Opinion of AG *Bot*, C-250/09 and C-268/09 (*Georgiev*), para. 25.

14.4.3 Justification of direct age discrimination

A justification of the ascertained direct age discrimination might be possible based on Art. 6 No. 1, Art. 4 No. 1 and Art. 7 Dir. 2000/78/EC.[1440] The most central justification provision as regards mandatory retirement for university professors constitutes Art. 6 No. 1 Dir. 2000/787EC.[1441] Before going into the justification analysis, it is necessary to identify a legitimate aim underlying §§ 2 (1) s. 1, 3 (1) *aldersgrenselov* and §§ 33 (1), (2) No. 2, 34 (1) HBG.

14.4.3.1 Legitimate aim

In the assessment of mandatory retirement for professors, in general, three objectives might be of relevance as legitimate aims: first, by enabling pathways and career opportunities and promotion for younger scientific staff, a favourable and balanced age structure might be established and maintained at the universities.[1442] Related to this is often the aspect of planning staff departures and enjoying planning certainty as regards the retirement of professors.[1443] Second, the aim is often referred to that by making use of mandatory retirement, individual legal disputes with older professors over their continued fitness for service could be prevented.[1444] Finally, cost factors such as high wages for employees who are close to retirement age and, more generally, the scarcity of financial resources are brought forward.[1445] The potential legitimate aim that might come into

---

1440 see in general to these justification provisions chap. 10.3.

1441 see in this regard joined cases C-250/09 and C-268/09 (*Georgiev*), para. 35ff. and joined cases C-159/10 and C-160/10 (*Fuchs* and *Köhler)*, para. 35ff.

1442 joined cases C-159/10 and C-160/10 (*Fuchs* and *Köhler)*, para 28, 32; previous instance: VG Frankfurt, Beschluss vom 29. März 2010 – 9 K 3854/09.F –, juris.

1443 joined cases C-159/10 and C-160/10 (*Fuchs* and *Köhler)*, para. 28, 32.

1444 similar: ibid.; see to this aspect e.g. *Summer*, Rudolf (2007), Die Altersgrenze für den Eintritt in den Ruhestand – Probleme durch Europarecht, ZBR 11/2007, pp. 368-371, p. 371.

1445 *Hack* (2012 b) reffering to *Oksholen*, Tore (2010), Hvor gammel får en professor bli?, in: Universitetsavisa 18.01.2010 and to the critics by *Brock-Utne* (2010); *Manfredi*, Simonetta/*Vickers*, Lucy (2009), Retirement and Age Discrimination: Managing Retirement in Higher Education, Industrial Law Journal Vol. 38, No. 4, 2009, pp. 343-364, p. 353ff.; *von Lübtow*, Ulrich (1967), Die Rechtsstellung des entpflichteten Professors, p. 19, 20.

play here relates to the achievement of budgetary savings and labour cost savings through avoiding the recruitment of new staff and so reducing the expenditure on personnel.[1446]

In general, it has to be noted that as regards the lack of precision in the legislation concerning the pursued aim – neither the *aldersgrenselov* nor the HBG expressly state any pursued aim. In such cases, the CJEU stressed again in *Fuchs* and *Köhler* that it is important to examine other elements derived from the general context of the measure at issue to identify the underlying aim.[1447] According to the CJEU, despite changes in circumstances, the law in question may thereby be maintained for other reasons, without preventing the aim from being legitimate.[1448] In *Fuchs* and *Köhler* e.g. the change concerned two aspects: first, the perception of fitness to work beyond the age limit – the CJEU referred to the fact that the previous applicable § 50 HBG (now § 33 HBG) was originally based 'on the irrebuttable presumption that a person is unfit to work beyond the age of 65' and, according to the representatives of the *Land Hessen* and the German government in the hearing, this should no longer be viewed as underpinning the retirement age; instead, the legislature had now accepted that people may be fit to work beyond that age.[1449] Second, the change concerned the aspect that the age limit in question was introduced during a period of full employment and then maintained during a period of unemployment.[1450]

Furthermore, the Court stressed that the means used to achieve a legitimate aim of public interest may be altered on the national, regional or sectoral level to adapt them to changing circumstances in the employment situation of the respective member state.[1451]

---

similar concerns brought forward by British academics *Manfredi/Vickers* (2009), p. 358.

1446 joined cases C-159/10 and C-160/10 (*Fuchs* and *Köhler),* para. 28, 32.

1447 ibid., para. 39 referring to C-411/05 (*Palacios*), para. 56, 57; C-341/08 (*Petersen*), para. 40; C-45/09 (*Rosenbladt*), para. 58.

1448 ibid., paras. 41-43.

1449 ibid., para. 40.

1450 ibid., para. 43.

1451 ibid., para. 54, 55 referring to C-411/05 (*Palacios*), para. 70; The fact that the mandatory retirement age was determined on *Länder* level, did consequently not prevent that the § 50 HBG was pursuing a legitimate aim, see para. 55.

The coexistence of a number of aims does not preclude the existence of a legitimate aim within the meaning of Art. 6 No.1 Dir. 2000/78/EC.[1452] They may be linked to another aim or classed in order of importance.[1453] Moreover, the CJEU clarified in *Fuchs* and *Köhler* again that aims that may be regarded as 'legitimate' in the sense of Art. 6 No. 1 have to be of a public interest nature.[1454] Such aims have to be distinguished from purely individual reasons that are particular to the employer's situation.[1455] Examples of purely employer-related interests are cost reductions or the improvement of competitiveness.[1456] Nevertheless, as pointed out in *Age Concern*, it may not be ruled out 'that a national rule may recognise, in the pursuit of those legitimate aims, a certain degree of flexibility for employers'.[1457] According to the CJEU, all the aims referred to in the proceedings in *Fuchs* and *Köhler* – which were similar to the three aims referred to above, with reservations as regards the aim of budgetary savings – may be regarded as aims of public interest.[1458] In contrast to the CJEU's line of argumentation, concerns were brought forward by the VG *Frankfurt* as to whether measures such as the age limit in the previous applicable § 50 (1) HGB really were in the public interest, instead of solely meeting the employer's interests.[1459] It doubted, in particular, whether the measures adopted by *Land Hessen* in respect of some of the civil servants were covering a too limited group of employees to constitute a measure pursuing an aim in the public interest.[1460]

1452 ibid., para. 37, para. 44, 45 referring to C-45/09 (*Rosenbladt*), para. 43, 45; see in general already chap. 10.3.5.

1453 ibid., para 46 w.r.t joined cases C-250/09 and C-268/09 (*Georgiev*), para. 45, 46, 68; C-341/08 (*Petersen*), para. 41, 65.

1454 ibid. para. 52.

1455 ibid., para. 52.

1456 ibid., para. 52.

1457 ibid. para. 52 referring to C-388/07 (*Age Concern*), para. 46.

1458 ibid. para 53, see also para 47, 50; see with regard to the question of whether the aim of budgetary savings falls under the category social policy objectives, para. 69ff., in particular para. 74.

1459 ibid., para. 51.

1460 ibid., para. 51.

14.4.3.1.1 Intergenerational equity argument: Balanced age structure

By referring to intergenerational equity, it is often brought forward that the use of mandatory retirement remedies an age 'imbalance' in the academic workforce. Age limits might thus function as an instrument to guarantee a 'turnover' of scientific staff and to facilitate long-term and predictable workforce planning at the universities.[1461] It has been argued that extending the working life of university professors beyond the mandatory retirement age limit, by either postponing the retirement start via increasing the age limit or by entirely abolishing it, might threaten this generational 'balance'.[1462] Some even argue that the older employees' wish to extend their working life might be realised at the expense of career opportunities for younger colleagues.[1463] Whether generational equity might function as a legitimate aim was also subject to the proceedings in *Georgiev*, where the CJEU recognised once more, 'that encouragement of recruitment undoubtedly constitutes a legitimate aim of Member States' social or employment policy [....], in particular when the promotion of access of young people to a profession is involved'.[1464]

In light of its previous jurisdiction, the encouragement of recruitment by means of offering posts as professors in higher education to younger people may, according to the Court, constitute a legitimate aim.[1465] Moreover, the CJEU stressed that the mix of different generations of teaching

1461 see to this aspect *Hack* (2012 b), p. 210; see in general to this justification pattern already chap. 12.3.3.

1462 similar e.g. LDO case 10/142, uttalelse 11.04.2011; similar also BVerfG, Beschluss vom 10. April 1984 – 2 BvL 19/82 –, BVerfGE 67, 1-25(*Emeritierungsalter*), para. 43, 44; similar concerns have also been brought forward by British academics, see to this aspect *Manfredi*/*Vickers* (2009), p. 358.

1463 see e.g. *Summer* (2007), p. 369 f.

1464 joined cases C-250/09 and C-268/09 (*Georgiev*), para. 45 referring to C-411/05 (*Palacios*), para. 65, C-341/08 (*Petersen*), para. 68; see also joined cases C-159/10 and C-160/10 (*Fuchs* and *Köhler*), para. 58.

1465 joined cases C-250/09 and C-268/09 (*Georgiev*), para. 45; This has been also stressed as regards the recruitment of prosecutors in joined cases C-159/10 and C-160/10 (*Fuchs* and *Köhler*), para. 49.

staff and researchers may promote an exchange of experiences as well as innovation, which might contribute to the development of quality teaching and research at universities.[1466]

Furthermore, as stressed by AG *Bot* in his analysis in *Georgiev*, it has to be kept in mind that the number of vacant posts within academia is limited, and that careers within that sector may be relatively long, so that it is, according to *Bot*, reasonable to take the view that a maximum age limit will facilitate younger people in entering the profession.[1467]

It has to be noted that the CJEU was in doubt as to whether the aims put forward by the German and Slovak governments and the Commission in *Georgiev* de facto corresponded to those of the Bulgarian legislature in view of the case file.[1468] Mr. Georgiev criticised how the university and the Bulgarian government merely made assertions that did not correspond to the reality of the labour market.[1469] He pointed out that the mean age of university professors was 58 and that there were no more than 1000 of them, which was ascribed to the absence of interest by younger people in an academic career as a university professor.[1470] Consequently, the claimant argued that the legislation at issue did not serve to encourage the recruitment of young academics.[1471] In light of prevailing uncertainties, the CJEU finally stated that it was up to the national court to examine the facts and to determine whether the aims alleged by the university and the Bulgarian government in reality were in accordance with the facts.[1472] As in its previous case law, the CJEU's analysis is not tantamount to a 'blanco-cheque' for the practising of the mandatory retirement age limit; rather, the Court played the ball back to the national court to analyse whether the criteria of the proportionality principle were fulfilled.[1473]

After having said this, it is essential to assess whether this aim may also be considered as a legitimate aim in the Norwegian and German contexts. As regards §§ 2 (1) s. 1, 3 (1) *aldersgrenselov*, examining the discussions prior to the coming into force of the 70-year age limit for civil servants might be fruitful. In the discussions, the argument of creating better job

1466 joined cases C-250/09 and C-268/09 (*Georgiev*), para. 46 referring to AG *Bot* in joined cases C-250/09 and C-268/09 (*Georgiev*), para. 34; see to this aspect as regards prosecutors also joined cases C-159/10 and C-160/10 (*Fuchs* and *Köhler*), para. 49.

1467 Opinion AG Bot, in joined cases C-250/09 and C-268/09 (*Georgiev*), para. 34.

1468 joined cases C-250/09 and C-268/09 (*Georgiev*), para. 47, see to the referred aims para. 41ff.

1469 ibid.

1470 ibid.

1471 ibid.

1472 ibid., para. 48, *Hack*, Melanie R. (2011), Gamle professorer, bedriftsfastsatte aldersgrenser og eldrebølgen, Nytt i privatretten: nyhetsbrev for informasjon på det privatret 2011 (2), pp. 5- 6, p. 6.

1473 *Hack* (2011), p. 6.

opportunities for younger employees was also brought forward.[1474] Moreover, it is worth looking more closely in this regard at § 3 (2) s. 1 *aldersgrenselov*, which explicitly stresses that employment aspects have to be considered when deciding upon the prolongation of the contract. This may in turn be interpreted also to the extent that factors such as increasing the employment of younger employees may play a role.

Among the identified aims, the aim of creating a balanced age structure and thus a balance between the generations constituted, according to the German government and the *Land Hessen*, the principal aim of the previous applicable § 50 HBG.[1475] The *Land Hessen* and the German government argued in the proceedings in *Fuchs* and *Köhler* that the presence of different ages within the employee network would also guarantee the transfer of experience from older staff and the transfer of recently acquired knowledge from younger staff to their respective younger or older colleagues, which in turn would contribute to the provision of a high-quality public justice service.[1476] This aim not only encompasses the civil servants covered by the formerly applicable § 50 (1) HBG as subject to *Fuchs* and *Köhler*, but is also of relevance as regards professors being now subject to §§ 33 (1), (2) No. 2, 34 (1) HBG. Due to the case law of the German Federal Constitutional Court, age limits for professors were justified with regard to Art. 12 GG, as they served the promotion of younger academics,

1474 NOU 1998: 19, *Fleksibel pensjonering*, chap. 5.10, p. 183; *Hyggen* (2008), p. 20.

1475 see to this aspect joined cases C-159/10 and C-160/10 (*Fuchs* and *Köhler*), para. 25, 47; see also *Rombach,* Annett (2010), 'Age Concern Germany': Zur gemeinschaftsrechtlichen (Un-)Zulässigkeit von Altershöchstgrenzen im öffentlichen Dienst, Neue Zeitschrift für Verwaltungsrecht (NVwZ) 2010, pp. 102-104, p. 104, fn. 24, who refers to the legislative history of § 50 (1) HBG given by the government in Hessen in 1962 according to which the provision aimed at avoiding a disadvantageous age structure of the civil servants, see reference to Lt-Dr. IV/940, p. 263; see also Hessischer Verwaltungsgerichtshof (VGH) (judgement) of 28.09.2009, 1 B 2487/09, para. 10; VG Frankfurt, Beschluss vom 29. März 2010 – 9 K 3854/09.F –, juris, para. 276; see recently as regards mandatory retirement for teachers in Hessen: Hessischer VGH, Beschluss vom 28. Oktober 2013 – 1 B 1638/13 –, juris, para. 5; see in general for an overview of legislative history of age limits for civil servants in Germany and the respective underlying aims *Sembdner*, Friedrich (2007), Zur Verlängerung der aktiven Dienstzeit des Beamten bis zur Vollendung des 67. Lebensjahres, Die Personalvertretung 6/7 2007, pp. 312-316, p. 313.

1476 joined cases C-159/10 and C-160/10 (*Fuchs* and *Köhler*), para. 48.

so the argumentation goes.[1477] In addition, exponents in the German legal literature followed this approach.[1478] In particular, in the case of the lifetime appointment of professorships, only the use of a fixed age limit releases a new post, so the argument goes.[1479] What comes into play here is that the redundancy instrument, due to business operations (*betriebsbedingte Kündigung*), is not applicable when it comes to civil servants.[1480]

However, taking a closer look at the argument for achieving a balanced age structure and serving generational equity reveals a number of shortcomings. First, it is questionable as to at what point a 'balanced' age structure would be achieved and how its existence would be proven.[1481] Should one introduce positive measures such as quota rules to guarantee the representation of certain age groups? Should the representation of the age groups be statistically proven? The chronological age would then again function as the decisive proxy, which is, as shown in chap. 6, more than questionable. A balanced and, for the university, enriching mix of employees with different backgrounds does not result from a different mix of ages alone. Rather, a multitude of factors should constitute the basis for choosing the employees, among these, first should be the academic profile. Second, several counterarguments may be raised concerning the level of the next step; namely, the suitability of the age limit: one of the arguments rightly raised by critics is that the age limit often does not have an impact on whether the vacant chair in question is refilled or omitted entirely.[1482]

1477 BVerfG, judgement of 10.4.1984 - 2 BVL 19/82 – BverfGE 67, 1-25, juris, para. 43; the argument of creating posts for younger civil servants was already brought forward by Reichsgericht (RG), 3. Zivilsenat, Urteil vom 14.03.1922, Akz. III 689/21104, RGZ 58 (63), juris.; critical already *von Lübtow* (1967), p. 19 f.

1478 see e.g. *Lüderitz* (2005), p. 102; 159; see also already *Linsenmaier* (2003), p. 31.

1479 *Lüderitz* (2005), p. 100ff., 159; see also already *Linsenmaier* (2003), p. 31.

1480 *Senne* (2006), p. 300 f.; see for an overview of German law chap. 11.5.

1481 see in general to the shortcomings of the balanced-age-structure-argument: *Martin*, Brian (1984), Age discrimination in academia, ANU reporter Vol. 15, No. 11, 27 July 1984, p. 2.

1482 *Bjørgen*, Ivar A. (2010), Aldersgrenser som diskriminering, adressa.no 18.2.2010; *Materstvedt* (2010), En "propp" snakker ut- om aldersgrenser for professorer, universitetsavisa.no, 18.02.2010; *Landsverk* (2010), p. 14; critical also *Senne* (2006), p. 300ff.

Consequently, practising the age limit is no guarantee for the move up the job ladder of younger generations of scientists.[1483] Critics therefore mainly point out that it was irrelevant for the practising of the age limit as to whether the vacant post was filled with a younger employee or was omitted entirely.[1484] It may therefore be argued that the age limit is not suitable for bringing younger scientists into work, as the allocation of jobs between generations constitutes a fallacy due to the fact that the amount of available work is not static.[1485] As pointed out by *Krois*, one might in fact generally argue that the continued employment of older employees could contribute to generating additional job opportunities for younger employees.[1486] Nevertheless, one might also argue that in regulated labour markets such as the higher education sector, the idea of fair job allocation between generations might apply, as the number of professorships or lecturing positions is often constant.[1487]

The generational equity argument might also be put forward in terms of the opportunity to conclude fixed-term contracts up to a further age limit – as in § 3 (1) *aldersgrenselov* and § 34 (1) HBG – as it similarly might allow for a generationally equitable distribution of employment opportunities and might enable universities to realise generation change in a flexible manner.[1488] However, such regulations still need to pass the necessity hurdle and may only do so as long as more positions are not offered than are de facto demanded; that is, as long as full employment does not exist.[1489]

1483 *Hack* (2012 b), p. 209; similar arguments brought forward by *Landsverk* (2010), p. 14, 15.

1484 *Senne* (2006), p. 302; similar *Landsverk* (2010), p. 14, 15.

1485 *Temming* (2008), p. 321 f.; *Krois*, Christopher, (2011), Christopher, Altersgrenzen für Universitätsprofessoren, EuZA 2011, 351-361, p. 359; see in detail to the lump of labour fallacy chap. 12.3.3.

1486 *Krois* (2011), p. 359.

1487 in this regard ibid., p. 360 referring to AG *Bot*, Joined cases C-250/09 and C-268/09 (*Georgiev*), para. 40.

1488 similar ibid., p. 359 f.

1489 ibid., referring to C-341/08 (*Petersen*), para. 71. In his analysis of the *Georgiev* judgement *Krois* forecasts for the situation in Germany, that provided fewer jobs are available in academia than demanded and provided that no incoherent exceptions are made as regards other teaching positions at the universities, mandatory retirement for professors in Germany might be justified in view of a inter-generational equity, see conclusion p. 361.

Regardless of whether one recognises the aim of generational equity or not, it has generally to be doubted – in contrast to the CJEU who acknowledged this aim as being a social-policy objective – whether a balanced age structure of any kind may constitute a legitimate aim of public interest, as stipulated in Art. 6 No. 1 Dir. 2000/78/EC. In principle, aims related to human resource planning are objectives linked to the employer's private autonomy and they do not belong to the category of social-policy objectives that are of general interest.[1490] Besides this, these aims may lack objectivity, as no explicit criteria are given on what the personnel structure should actually look like.[1491] Personnel planning should be objectively reproducible.[1492] These considerations have also been brought forward by the VG Frankfurt am Main (a.M.) – the referring court in *Fuchs* and *Köhler* – as regards the previous applicable § 50 HBG, which, moreover, criticised the lack of correlation between civil servants leaving the workforce due to mandatory retirement and younger persons entering the profession in question.[1493] The aim of achieving and maintaining a certain age structure may therefore, at the most, be regarded as a social-policy objective, provided that the envisaged age structure is examined in light of the specific employment and labour-market situation at issue and provided that it is, in the respective case, clarified regarding why such an age structure constitutes a social-policy objective in the public interest.[1494] In this regard, the difficulty remains that the aim of achieving a balanced age structure always depends on the respective employer's aims, which are hardly objective.[1495]

Even if the university sector is characterised by a strongly regulated labour market, vacancies that become available for younger employees in cases where a university professor retires are not necessarily filled and

1490 see in detail VG Frankfurt a.M., Beschluss vom 29. März 2010 – 9 K 3854/09.F – juris, para. 266, 270; C-159/10 and joined cases C-160/10 (*Fuchs* and *Köhler*), para. 25.

1491 ibid.; see to the critics also *Rombach* (2010), in particular fn. 28; such as *Martin* (1984), p. 2.

1492 in this regard also *Rombach* (2010), p. 104 in particular fn. 28.

1493 VG Frankfurt a.M., Beschluss vom 29. März 2010 – 9 K 3854/09.F – juris, para. 273ff; see in detail joined cases C-159/10 and C-160/10 (*Fuchs* and *Köhler*), para. 25.

1494 *Rombach* (2010), p. 104 in particular fn. 28 referring to VG Frankfurt a.M. 21.4.2008 - 9 E 3856/07, para. 87.

1495 ibid.

might, on the contrary, be removed.[1496] Thus, the claimed legitimacy of the compulsory retirement of university professors to promote young academics may turn out to be a fallacy and may not be referred to as a legitimate aim in the justification analysis.[1497] Therefore, the lump of labour fallacy casts doubt on the suitability of the mandatory retirement provisions.

14.4.3.1.2 Mental and physical decline of abilities due to the ageing process

Moreover, it has often been brought forward that practising a mandatory retirement age limit for university professors contributes to preventing possible disputes concerning the employee's fitness to work beyond a certain age.[1498] According to this argumentation, a generalised age limit functions as an instrument that facilitates employers in getting rid of older employees without the necessity of discussing the exit from working life with the individual employee and without considering the de facto existing capabilities of the respective employee.[1499]

In addition, as regards Norway, the aspect of capability decline with increasing age has been brought forward as the key aim in the preparatory acts underlying the age limit in § 2 (1) s. 1 *aldersgrenselov*. Prior to the coming into force of the *aldersgrenselov*, three separate pension committees dealt with pension schemes for civil servants and discussed age limits.[1500] The setting of age limits arose through the need in the public sector to get rid of allegedly unproductive employees and the desire to create better career opportunities for younger workers.[1501]

1496 *Brors* (2008), § 10, para. 92.

1497 similar ibid., § 10, para. 277ff.

1498 see in general to this argument already chap. 12.3.2.1 above; similar as regards civil servants in general in joined cases C-159/10 and C-160/10 (*Fuchs* and *Köhler*), para. 50; see also *Gärditz* (2010), p. 19.

1499 see e.g. *Gärditz* (2010), p. 18, 19 who inter alia argues that practising absolute mandatory retirement age limits instead of flexible approaches serves the protection of the employee's dignity (*Persönlichkeitsschutz*); see for a critical analysis of such argumentation chap. 12.3.2.1.

1500 see for an overview *Hack* (2012 b), pp. 196ff.

1501 *Hyggen* (2008), p. 20.

As early as 1896, the first so-called pension committee pointed out that it was common knowledge that besides the civil servants being enlisted on the pension list, employees were to be found who were still working, even if they de facto could be equated with retirees.[1502] The reason that was referred to in this case was that increasing age had already reduced their physical strength, that their capabilities were blunted and that their vitality decreased, so that these employees, in a way, were in reality retired, while at the same time claiming their further salary income.[1503] According to the committee, the persistence of the elderly in posts that required the full vigour of their owners constituted an illegitimate form of 'self-retirement'.[1504] As stressed by the committee, the decisive argument for introducing age limits was therefore the improved career opportunities for young professionals.[1505] Remarkably, in contrast to that argumentation, the second pension committee in 1904 voted for a more flexible approach in regulating the 'exit age' from the labour market or rather, the transition to retirement.[1506] The main reason for this committee opting for flexible solutions was that the ageing process of the civil servants did not proceed in a linear fashion, but rather was different from person to person, which in turn has an impact on the age-related work capability of the employee in question.[1507] From this, it follows, due to the committee's argumentation, that it is nearly impossible to determine an age limit that is uniformly applicable to all employees.[1508]

In 1906, the third pension committee finally recommended an age limit, which was to be set as high as possible without affecting the work of the respective employee as a result of the ongoing ageing process.[1509] A higher age limit would force the civil servants to terminate the employment relationship and a lower age limit would facilitate the administration in dismissing those employees who were no longer mentally or physically fit enough for service.[1510] These arguments were also put forward in the *travaux preparatoires* of the *aldersgrenselov* of 1917, which today mostly has the same wording as it did almost a century ago at the time of enactment.[1511] Ultimately, in 1917, a mandatory retirement age of 70 years – which is still applicable today – was entrenched in the *aldersgrenselov*. University professors were also encompassed by this age limit. As civil servants, they were no longer appointed for life – as was previously the case for *embetsmen*. In the following decades, the existing age limits in the public sector were consistently subject to evaluation. Particularly note-

---

1502 NOU 1998: 19, chap. 5.10, p. 182 f.; *Hack* (2012 b), p. 196.
1503 NOU 1998: 19, p. 182 f.
1504 ibid., p. 183.
1505 ibid., p. 183.
1506 ibid.; *Hack* (2012 b), p. 196.
1507 NOU 1998: 19, p. 183.
1508 ibid.
1509 ibid.
1510 ibid.
1511 Ot.prp. nr. 4 of 1917.

worthy is the so-called *aldersgrensekomitee* of 1954, which took a critical stance on the existence of fixed age limits in the face of individually different ageing processes.[1512]

Traditionally, provisions on mandatory retirement in German civil servant law (*Beamtenrecht*) are based upon the irrefutable presumption of the employee's disability for service (*unwiderlegliche Vermutung der Dienstunfähigkeit*) after having reached the mandatory age limit. This argumentation constituted the basis for introducing the age limits in the public sector by imputing *Dienstunfähigkeit* to the employee who had reached a certain age. The underlying key argument for the introduction of these age limits has been that the *Dienstunfähigkeit* does not have to be proven in the individual case, but may rather be similarly presumed for all civil servants following a generalised regulation based on the general experience that capabilities do decrease after a certain age.[1513]

Both in German case law and in the literature, this argumentation of a generalised assumption of *Dienstunfähigkeit* has been criticised as being in contradiction to the recent findings from gerontological research.[1514] As rightly stressed by *von Lübtow* as early as 1967, scientific findings do not support the view that it corresponds to the general experience in life that the physical and mental capabilities of a university professor decline after having reached mandatory retirement age.[1515] The exit from working life should not be determined by an absolute and fixed age limit – as is finally the case in Norway and Germany, even when a prolongation is granted

---

1512 see for further details NOU 1998: 19, chap. 5.10, pp. 183-185.

1513 see in this regard already RG of 14.03.1922 concerning the Prussian Altergrenzengesetz, RGZ 104, 62; BVerfG, Judgement of 16.06.1959 – 1 BvR 71/57 –, BVerfGE 9, 338 (*Altersgrenze für Hebammen*) - juris, para. 23ff., 26; BVerfG, Nichtannahmebeschluss vom 23. Mai 2008 – 2 BvR 1081/07 –, juris, para. 12; Hessischer Verwaltungsgerichtshof (VGH), Urteil vom 28. September 2009 – 1 B 2487/09 –, juris, para. 10; critical to this argument referring national Court in joined cases C-159/10 and C-160/10 (*Fuchs* and *Köhler*), para. 24; critical to the presumed decline of capabilities already BAG, Urteil vom 28. 9. 1961 - 2 AZR 428/60, NJW 1962, pp. 73-74, p. 74; see to the critics also already *von Lübtow* (1967), p. 17, 18.

1514 see among others: *Nussberger*, Angelika (2002), Altersgrenzen als Problem des Verfassungsrechts, Juristen-Zeitung (JZ), 2002, pp. 524-532, p. 532; such as already *Simitis*, Spiros (1994), Altersdiskriminierung - die verdrängte Benachteiligung, NJW 1994, pp. 1453-1454, critical also referring national Court in joined cases C-159/10 and C-160/10 (*Fuchs* and *Köhler*), para. 24.

1515 *von Lübtow* (1967), p. 18 f.

according to § 3 (1) *aldersgrenselov* and § 34 (1) HBG – the exit should rather comply with the individual's mental and physical capabilities.[1516] As already stressed in chap. 6.4, it is, in contrast to the argumentation underlying the age limits in Norway and Germany, essential to take into account the intra- and interindividual ageing process. This has also been particularly stressed by the research concerned with the relationship between scientifically proven productivity and age. Whereas early research typically demonstrated a decline in productivity after the ages of 40 to 45 years, this decline has been absent in more recent studies.[1517] Remarkably, a Norwegian study that particularly examined the common contentions that the collective ageing of tenured academics has negative impacts on the research performance of universities due to the negative effects of ageing itself and a lack of newcomers revitalising the research, also could not demonstrate any scientifically reliable differences in productivity.[1518] Age was, according to this study, a poor predictor of productivity in the research. [1519]

To conclude, individual capabilities rather than general assumptions should be accounted for.[1520] The university professor's past performance is a much better predictor of his scientific productivity than his age is.[1521] The decision on continuing employment should therefore be based at any stage on individual merit rather than age.[1522] This is even truer for the profession of a professor, where the exercise of the profession basically is also possible in old age and thus has to be distinguished fundamentally from security-relevant professions such as pilots, who have an entirely different job profile.[1523] In particular, arguments concerning the physical burden on university professors play a minor role compared to the situation of

---

1516 ibid.

1517 see in detail for an extensive overview of research regarding the association of scientific productivity and age *Stroebe* (2010), pp. 660-673; see also *Kyvik,* Svein/*Olsen*, Terje B. (2008), Does the aging of tenured academic staff affect the research performance of universities?, Scientometrics Vol. 76 No. 3 (2008), pp. 439-455, p. 440, 454.

1518 see in detail *Kyvik*/*Olsen* (2008), pp. 439-455.

1519 ibid., p. 447 f., p. 454.

1520 so already *von Lübtow* (1967), p. 18, 19; see also *Stroebe* (2010), p. 672.

1521 *Stroebe* (2010), p. 671.

1522 ibid., p. 672.

1523 *von Lübtow* (1967) p. 21; *Hack* (2012 b), p. 210; similar *Senne* (2006), p. 46ff., 300ff.; see also for the analysis of age limits for pilots chap. 15.

e.g. health personnel or pilots. Moreover, teaching and even more so, research activity, often reaches its peak in old age for professors, as the increased experience may lead to a fruitful synopsis of the professor's area of expertise.[1524] To force university professors to terminate their employment based on a mere chronological age would already make no sense from a purely scientific point of view. Rather, it would run counter to a university's interests in promoting outstanding research.[1525] The job of a university professor may thus rightly be characterised as an '*echter Beruf auf Lebenszeit*'[1526] – a real lifelong job – as the ability to teach and carry out research work does not automatically end at a certain age.[1527] Fixed age limits like those in §§ 2 (1) s. 1, 3 (1) *aldersgrenselov* and §§ 33 (1), (2) No. 2, 34 (1) HBG are thus hardly compatible with these findings.[1528] Furthermore, particularly from a Norwegian perspective, they run counter to the targeted aim of the pension reform to motivate older employees, which also includes university professors, to extend their working life and to stay as long as possible in active employment. Thus, neither with regard to the age limit in §§ 2 (1) s. 1, 3 (1) *aldersgrenselov* nor with regard to §§ 33 (1), (2) No. 2, 34 (1) HBG can the argument of declining capabilities with old age be maintained as a legitimate aim.

14.4.3.1.3 Saving costs

It is often stressed that senior academics are too cost-intensive as they typically have higher wages, which may not justify their scientific productivity, so this argumentation goes.[1529] This argument is therefore often related to the aspect of capability decline with increasing age that is referred to. The aspect of saving costs is neither explicitly referred to as a legitimate aim in the Norwegian legislative context as regards §§ 2 (1) s. 1, 3 (1) *aldersgrenselov*, nor as an aim explicitly pursued by §§ 33 (1), (2)

1524 *Thieme*, Werner (1956), Deutsches Hochschulrecht, p. 271; *von Lübtow* (1967), p. 21; *Hack* (2012 b), p. 210; similar *Landsverk* (2010), p. 18.

1525 in this regard *von Lübtow* (1967), p. 21. It is noteworthy that *von Lübtow* already in 1967 advocated a flexible system instead of compulsory retirement via an age limit; similar also *Stroebe* (2010), p. 672.

1526 *Thieme* (1956), p. 271; *von Lübtow* (1967), p. 21.

1527 *von Lübtow* (1967), p. 21.

1528 *Hack* (2012 b), p. 210.

1529 see to this aspect e.g. research findings by *Manfredi/Vickers* (2009), p. 358.

No. 2, 34 (1) HBG.[1530] It generally has to be ascertained that – as rightly stressed by the CJEU – EU law does not preclude the member states from also taking account of budgetary considerations as long as they, in particular, are in conformity with the general principle of the prohibition of age discrimination.[1531] Whether or not saving costs may be referred to as a legitimate aim is particularly of relevance when it comes to the application of Art. 6 No. 1 Dir. 2000/78/EC –, which is pivotal for the compatibility assessment of mandatory retirement for professors with Dir. 2000/78/EC. Even if budgetary considerations may specifically underpin a chosen social policy of a member state and have an impact on the nature or extent of the intended measures, such considerations cannot (as clarified in *Fuchs* and *Köhler*) in themselves constitute a legitimate aim within the meaning of Art. 6 No. 1 of Dir. 2000/78/EC.[1532] Individual motives, and also those of public employers such as in the case of public university professors, that are related to a particular situation of the respective employer, such as cost reductions and general budgetary considerations, do thus not in themselves constitute social-policy objectives.[1533] However, the employment relationships of civil servants feature certain characteristics that are different from those present in the relationships between workers and private employers. The cost efficiency of a public service, which is primarily tax-financed, is, in general, apparently of a public interest nature.[1534] However, using mandatory retirement as an instrument to control public spending is questionable in times of demographic change where it tends to be in the public interest to keep civil servants on rather than reducing personnel. Reducing public spending may be achieved by a multitude of measures, where cost reductions due to reduced professor posts as a result of mandatory retirement play a rather minor role. Moreover, it is, as pointed out, problematic to subsume this aim per se under the social-policy objectives.

1530 see to § 50 (1) HBG, C-159/10 and C-160/10 (*Fuchs* and *Köhler*), para. 70.

1531 joined cases C-159/10 and C-160/10 (*Fuchs* and *Köhler*), para. 65, 74; The CJEU generally stated that it is for the national to court to determine whether this aim belongs to those pursued by § 50 (1) HBG, para. 69ff., 71; Both the *Land Hessen* and the German Government had stated that the provision did not pursue that aim, see para. 70.

1532 joined cases C-159/10 and C-160/10 (*Fuchs* and *Köhler*), para. 74.

1533 see to the public interest nature of social policy objectives in the sense of Art. 6 No 1 Dir. 2000/78/EC C-388/07 (*Age Concern*), para. 46; see also *Rombach* (2010), p. 104.

1534 in this regard *Gärditz* (2010), p. 18.

In view of these aspects, the aim of saving costs by operating with mandatory retirement for university professors does not constitute a legitimate aim as required by Art. 6 No. 1 Dir. 2000/78/EC.

14.4.3.2 Justification according to Art. 6 No. 1 Dir. 2000/78/EC

14.4.3.2.1 Necessity and suitability

If one acknowledges the aim of a balanced age structure as a legitimate aim, then the age limits in §§ 2 (1) s. 1, 3 (1) *aldersgrenselov* and §§ 33 (1), (2) No. 2, 34 (1) HBG, respectively, have to be necessary and suitable in terms of achieving the identified legitimate aim.[1535] In essence, this first involves analysing whether alternative, less harmful measures are available to the Norwegian and German mandatory retirement provisions for professors. In general, the CJEU stated that as regards the determination of the measures that are capable of achieving the legitimate aim, the member states enjoy a broad discretion.[1536] It is remarkable that the CJEU explicitly stressed that this does not apply in an unrestricted manner as, 'the Member States may not frustrate the prohibition of discrimination on grounds of age set out in Directive 2000/78. That prohibition must be read in the light of the right to engage in work recognised in Article 15(1) of the Charter of Fundamental Rights of the European Union'.[1537]

The Court clearly follows therewith its jurisdiction in *Age Concern*[1538] and *Kücükdeveci.*[1539] What is noteworthy is the fact that the Court does not merely refer to the CFREU and that the prohibition against age discrimination has to be read in light of the Charter, but that it explicitly refers to the right to engage in work, as manifested in Art. 15 (1) CFREU. The Court emphasised, in particular, that this is true for older employees, as it stated:

1535 joined cases C-250/09 and C-268/09 (*Georgiev*), para. 68, see also the ruling in para 79; joined cases C-159/10 and C-160/10 (*Fuchs* and *Köhler*), para. 56.

1536 joined cases C-159/10 and C-160/10 (*Fuchs* and *Köhler*), para. 61 w.r.t. C-411/05 (*Palacios*), para. 68.

1537 ibid., para. 62.

1538 see C-388/07 (*Age Concern*), para. 51.

1539 see C-555/07 (*Kücükdeveci*), para. 21, 22.

> It follows that particular attention must be paid to the participation of older workers in the labour force and thus in economic, cultural and social life. Keeping older workers in the labour force promotes diversity in the workforce, which is an aim recognised in recital 25 in Directive 2000/78; moreover, it contributes to the realising of their potential and to the quality of life of the workers concerned, in accordance with the concerns of the European Union legislature set out in recitals 8, 9 and 11 in that directive.[1540]

When assessing the necessity of such age limits, it has often been argued (in line with the argumentation in *Georgiev*) that mandatory retirement provisions have to be regarded as a necessary instrument with which to terminate the employment relationship after the employee in question has achieved pensionable age.[1541] Employees are generally covered and protected by their pension eligibility, so this argumentation goes.[1542] Moreover, the employee may be prepared for his exit from working life, as he is often already aware of the mandatory retirement age in advance when entering the employment contract.[1543] However, in line with its ruling in *Age Concern*, the CJEU points out that mere generalisations that might indicate a measure's likeliness to contribute to employment policy, labour-market or vocational training objectives is not enough to demonstrate that the aim of the measure in question 'is capable of derogating from the principle of non-discrimination on grounds of age and do not constitute evidence on the basis of which it could reasonably be considered that the means chosen are likely to achieve that aim'.[1544]

The CJEU emphasised again that Art. 6 No. 1 Dir. 2000/78/EC 'imposes on Member States the burden of establishing to a high standard of proof the legitimacy of the aim relied on as a justification'.[1545]

If one applies these aspects to the mandatory retirement provisions for university professors in Norway and Germany, it is questionable as to whether the age limit is at all necessary for achieving the pursued aim. A less harmful but equally effective measure to achieve the aim of a balanced age structure might constitute options for flexible retirement, part-

---

1540 joined cases C-159/10 and C-160/10 (*Fuchs* and *Köhler*), para. 63.

1541 *Tempelmann*, Achim/*Stenslik*, Bastian-Peter (2011), Altersgrenzenregelungen im Arbeitsrecht, Deutsches Steuerrecht (DStR), 2011, pp. 577-581, p. 580.

1542 ibid.

1543 *Tempelmann/Stenslik* (2011), p. 580.

1544 joined cases C-159/10 and C-160/10 (*Fuchs* and *Köhler*), para. 77 referring to C-388/07 (*Age Concern*), para. 51.

1545 ibid., para. 78 referring to para. 67 in the same judgement.

time employment or job-sharing models that would offer a smooth transition to retirement by, at the same time, opening up for younger successive employees to enter academia. In doing so, the existing know-how, experience and networks of the senior employees could be passed on to the following generation of academic employees. With such a flexible solution, an appropriate balance of the interests of the professor in voluntarily deciding about ending or extending his working life, his interest in exercising his right to work and the interest of the university in succession planning and guaranteeing a balanced age structure among its employees could finally be achieved. This could be a solution that would benefit both the universities and the employee. In this regard, the option for prolongation as provided for in § 3 (1) *aldersgrenselov* as well as § 34 (1) HBG might constitute such an alternative, less harmful measure than the mandatory retirement age laid down in § 2 (1) s. 1 *aldersgrenselov* and § 33 (1) HBG. In principle, the extension of the employment contract via fixed-term employment constitutes a flexible measure that provides the professor with the opportunity to extend his working career even beyond the compulsory retirement age. Interestingly enough, the argument of increasing the age limit's flexibility to enhance the options for the respective civil servant to individually plan his work and retirement has also been stressed several times in the preparatory acts on the *Länder* level in Germany concerning the provisions for postponing the start of retirement.[1546] As stressed by *Poguntke,* arguing that postponing the employee's retirement start would deteriorate the access and promotion opportunities for younger colleagues may not substantiate a *dienstliches Interesse* as required e.g. in § 34 (1) HBG. Referring to this general argument would minimise the civil servant's freedom in determining his exit from working life and would thus run counter to the expressed aim of the legislators on the *Länder* level to achieve more flexibility for the employee.[1547] In contrast, moreover, an extension of the working career on an individual basis may

1546 *Poguntke* (2011), p. 562 referring in fn. 22 to Bürgerschaft HH, Drs. 19/3757, p. 7, 63 f.; Brem. Bürgerschaft, Drs. 177/882, p. 142; Nds. LT-Drs. 16/665, p. 115; Nds. Landtag, Plenarprot. 25.03.2009, p. 3921; LT-Drs. NRW 14/8176, p. 126; Landtag NRW, Plenarprot. 01.04.2009, p. 1395ff.; LT-Drs. SH 16/2306, p. 179.

1547 see in detail to the preparatory work on *Länder* level and the aspect of flexibility *Poguntke* (2011), p. 562 f., 564.

contribute more to an enriching mixture of employees of different ages, which in turn may positively affect the transfer of knowledge and expertise among the generations.[1548]

Despite these considerations, it has to be kept in mind that this alleged flexibility is restricted both in Norway as well as in Germany by the limitation of the opportunity for prolongation via a further absolute age limit, set at the age of 75 in Norway and 70 in the case of Hessen. This age limit is final in both cases and does not allow – besides professor emeritus regulations – for any further extension of the working career. Thus, the age limits in § 2 (1) s. 1 *aldersgrenselov* and § 33 (1) HBG are absolute age limits and thus do not constitute a less harmful measure. Therefore, a less harmful measure could be a flexible system for the transition from work to retirement instead of these absolute and fixed age limits, even if one were to conclude that there is no alternative to the compulsory retirement of professors to achieve the legitimate aim being pursued.[1549] The mandatory age limit nevertheless has to be proportional stricto sensu.

As stressed by the CJEU in *Fuchs* and *Köhler*, potentially diverging interests have to be considered; namely, the interests of those employees who wish to exit working life when having reached retirement age and are entitled to a pension versus the interests of those persons who instead wish to extend their working career.[1550] In addition, mandatory retirement clauses may 'in the interests of sharing work among the generations, promote the entry of young workers into the labour force'.[1551] Due to the CJEU, the national authorities may, when determining their social policy based on political, economic, social, demographic and/or budgetary considerations, choose to promote the extension of people's working life or vice versa to provide for early retirement.[1552] Finding the right balance between the different interests involved, while at the same time ensuring that the measures do not go beyond what is appropriate and necessary to achieve the legitimate aim being pursued is a task for the respective national authorities.[1553] Interestingly enough, in this regard, the CJEU stressed once again the role of the worker's entitlement to a pension at a reasonable level, alongside the general opportunity for him being able to apply for a new job.[1554] Here, the CJEU seems to repeat the strange line of argumentation in the *Rosenbladt* case: advocating

1548 ibid.; similar *Landsverk* (2010), p. 14, 15.
1549 arguing for a flexible system already *von Lübtow* (1967), p. 21.
1550 joined cases C-159/10 and C-160/10 (*Fuchs* and *Köhler*), para. 64.
1551 ibid.
1552 ibid., para. 65 referring to C-411/05 (*Palacios*), para. 68, 69.
1553 ibid., para 65. referring C-411/05 (*Palacios*), para. 69, 71 and C-45/09 (*Rosenbladt*), para. 44.
1554 joined cases C-159/10 and C-160/10 (*Fuchs* and *Köhler*), para. 66 referring to C-411/05 (*Palacios*), para. 73; C-45/09 (*Rosenbladt*), para. 73-76.

the legitimacy of a mandatory retirement provision, while at the same time arguing that the employee may continue to remain in working life as it is against the prohibition of age discrimination to exclude older workers from seeking a job.[1555]

When assessing the age limits' proportionality in its strict sense, the universities' interests in achieving a balanced age structure have to be weighed against the rights and interests of the individual professor in exercising his right to work without being discriminated against on the grounds of age and the interrelated possibility for self-realisation in the workplace. Also in this regard, it is difficult to understand why it should be in the interests of the universities and in the public interest to compulsory retire professors and, in doing so, to lose distinguished academics. This is even more questionable in view of the brain drain of top scientists that takes place from countries such as Germany or Norway to e.g. the USA, which does not have such age restrictions.

14.4.3.2.2 Intermediate result

An absolute age limit such as laid down both in § 2 (1) s. 1, 3 (1) *aldersgrenselov* and §§ 33 (1), (2) No. 2, 34 (1) HBG is not a necessary measure as an option for prolongation – without being restricted by a further age limit – would constitute a less harmful and alternative measure that would likewise be appropriate in terms of achieving the aim being pursued. Additionally, the options for prolongation provided for in § 3 *aldersgrenselov* and § 34 (1) HBG do not pass the proportionality stricto sensu requirements, as, due to the absolute age limit for prolongations, they highly limit the employee's interests in terms of continuing his working career.

To conclude, both the Norwegian as well as the German mandatory retirement regulations hardly pass the necessity hurdle, as alternatives to absolute and compulsory age limits are imaginable that would be equally effective in achieving the alleged aim being pursued. In addition, flexible

---

1555 see to the critics of this argumentation among others: *Kohte*, Wolfhard (2011), Altersdiskriminierung von Universitätsprofessoren ("Georgiev"), jurisPR-ArbR 2/2011, Anm. 7, Kohte.

solutions might be an option here.[1556] The age limits in §§ 2 (1) s. 1, 3 (1) *aldersgrenselov* and §§ 33 (1), (2) No. 2, 34 (1) HBG do not pass the proportionality test in Art. 6 No. 1 Dir. 2000/78/EC and are consequently not in conformity with the principle of non-discrimination on the grounds of age as concretised in the Directive. Taking age equality seriously in the context of the compulsory retirement of university professors leads to the conclusion that such age limits cannot be justified.

14.4.3.3 Justification according to Art. 4 No. 1 Dir. 2000/78/EC

Age does not constitute a GOR; that is, an adequate proxy for any of the requirements generally needed to exercise the profession of a professor.[1557] A justification according to Art. 4 No. 1 Dir. 2000/78/EC is therefore out of question when it comes to examining university professors' mandatory retirement compatibility with Dir. 2000/78/EC.

However, in cases of professors working in e.g. disciplines such as sports or security, age might be a GOR. However, also in this case, the question still remains as to whether these age limits pass the necessity test, as alternative measures such as regular health tests are available to ensure that the professor is mentally and physically fit.

1556 see in detail to *de lege ferenda* considerations chap. 16, 16.3.3.; arguing on the contrary for a justification of mandatory retirement for civil servants in Germany: *Baßlsperger*, Maximilian (2008), Altersdiskriminierung durch Beamtenrecht, Zeitschrift für Beamtenrecht 10/2008, pp. 339-350, p. 345 f., p. 350; see in general to Art. 4 No. 1 Dir. 2000/78/EC and the GOR-requirement, chap. 10.3.2.

1557 similar *Baßlsperger* concerning a justification according to § 8 AGG – the respective German provision to Art. 4 No. 1 Dir. 2000/78/EC, see in detail *Baßlsperger* (2008), p. 345; denying a justification according to Art. 4 No. 1 Dir. 2000/78/EC as regards mandatory retirement for civil servants also: *von Roetteken*, Torsten/*Rothländer*, Christian/*Burkholz*, Bernhard/*Kohde*, Jens (2013), Kommentar BeamStG, § 25 Ruhestand wegen Erreichens der Altersgrenze, VI. Unvereinbarkeit von Altersgrenzen mit der RL 2000/78/EG und Art. 21 Abs. 1 GRCh, para. 47ff.; arguing that age is a poor indicator for scientific productivity also *Stroebe* (2010), p. 671 f.; *Kyvik*/*Olsen* (2008), p. 447 f., 454.

14.4.3.4 Justification according to Art. 7 No. 1 Dir. 2000/78/EC

The age limits in §§ 2 (1) s. 1, 3 (1) *aldersgrenselov* and §§ 33 (1), (2) No. 2, 34 (1) HBG may constitute a positive action in the sense of Art. 7 No. 1 Dir. 2000/78/EC. Both provisions might constitute such a specific measure, as they might contribute to advancing the access of younger scientists to professor posts to counterbalance existing disadvantages on the grounds of age between younger and older scientists. However, this assumption is questionable. To force older employees to retire to make place for younger colleagues does not per se serve equality in the working sphere, as it rather, on the contrary, excludes the group of older workers from working life.[1558] Even if the wording in Art. 7 No. 1 were to be interpreted in a wide sense, it is more than questionable as to whether mandatory retirement for university professors might constitute a positive action. This is particularly questionable, as these age limits should constitute specific measures in favour of younger employees, which is not fulfilled due to two reasons: first, not every vacancy for a professorship that is available due to retirement is filled again and second, in the case of replacement, this has not necessarily to be carried out with a younger employee.[1559] In view of these aspects, it must be concluded that the age limits in §§ 2 (1) s. 1, 3 (1) *aldersgrenselov* and §§ 33 (1), (2) No. 2, 34 (1) HBG do not constitute a measure that is designed to balance or frustrate the detrimental treatment of younger employees in the sense of Art. 7 No. 1 Dir. 2000/78/EC.[1560]

14.5 Final discussion, comparison and conclusion

Both Norway and Germany have chosen a similar modus operandi to determine the exit of university professors from their working life: the manifestation of a mandatory retirement that is supplemented by the opportunity for further employment via fixed-term contracts that, in turn, are limited by an absolute age limit. However, one crucial difference

1558 *Senne* (2006), p. 302.

1559 critical also *Senne* (2006), p. 302; *Schlachter* (2003), p. 366; by contrast: arguing in general for creating posts for younger civil servants via mandatory retirement: *Summer* (2007), p. 370; *Baßlsperger* (2008), p. 346.

1560 see also *Hack* (2012 b), p. 209 as regards the situation in Norway.

remains – the applicable age limits for university professors in Germany are much lower than they are for their Norwegian counterparts. Some *Länder* even operate with a general age limit, which is five years below the general age limit in Norway, and is open to prolongation only up to the age of 68. Notably, in none of the 16 German federal states is the absolute mandatory retirement age higher than the age of 70. If one considers the possible option for prolongation until the absolute age limit of 75 in Norway, this constitutes a remarkable difference of seven to ten years, depending on the respective *Bundesland.* Common to both is that neither in the case of Norway nor in Germany can the existing age limits for university professors working at public universities be justified, as alternatives to an absolute age limit are imaginable. None of the evaluated age limits passes the necessity step of the proportionality analysis. Consequently, the key question is whether flexible approaches might be the solution instead of absolute age limits. *De lege lata* the age-discriminatory effect of the examined mandatory retirement provisions could at least be minimised if the university professor's options for prolongation would de facto be applied less restrictively.[1561] Otherwise, as rightly stressed by *Temming* in referring to the civil servant's right to work as enshrined in Art. 15 CFREU – as the CJEU did e.g. in *Fuchs* and *Köhler* – it 'is nothing but a mere lips [sic] service'.[1562] From the German perspective, the age limits seem to be even more difficult to justify, given the fact that the applicable age limits are considerably lower than in the case of Norway, where the age limits in §§ 33 (1), (2) No. 2, 34 (1) HBG are already hard to justify. Thus, even if contested, the Norwegian regulation, with its option for prolongation of the employment relationship up to the age of 75, might at least from a German point of view function to some degree as a best-practice model.[1563] Notwithstanding this potential role-model function, it is important to note that the age limit for professors is not without controversy in Norway. In the Norwegian discussion, which is more a case

1561 similar to this aspect from the German perspective *Poguntke* (2011), p. 568; similar from a British perspective also findings by *Manfredi/Vickers* (2009), p. 359.

1562 *Temming*, Felipe (2012), Compulsory retirement and the fixing of a maximum age for recruitment - lawful or unlawful age discrimination, p. 14, available at http://www.equineteurope.org/IMG/pdf/felipe_temming___presentation-2.pdf (last accessed: 17.12.2014); see C-159/10 and C-160/10 (*Fuchs* and *Köhler*), para. 62.

1563 *Hack* (2012 b), p. 212.

of legal politics than of legal doctrine, some argue for its abolishment, while others merely advocate for an increase in the age limit.[1564] Notably, no one discusses a lowering of the age limit.

To conclude, it is more than questionable as to whether both Norway and Germany are able to afford the loss of highly skilled employees, e.g. via the 'brain drain' to the US. This is even truer if one considers the labour shortage caused by the demographic change, which may lead to a race for talented employees irrespective of their age, where the decision to keep on and hire such employees should be based on academic grounds and not on age. The referring court in *Fuchs* and *Köhler* put this problematic in a nutshell in view of the situation of public employees by inter alia asking:

> In view of the gaps already to be seen in the labour market owing to demographic trends and of the impending need for skilled staff of all kinds [...], is it reasonable and necessary to force civil servants able and willing to continue working to retire from the civil service at a time when there will soon be a major demand for personnel which the labour market will hardly be able to meet?[1565]

By taking age equality and thus the prohibition against age discrimination seriously, one might overcome existing inflexibilities when it comes to the transition from employment to retirement in the academic working sphere and might rather promote and utilise the intellectual capacities and talents of academics of all ages. Due to population ageing, the university workplace is also confronted with developing strategies for embracing older workers, including older professors.[1566] *De lege ferenda* for example flexible work schedules such as job-sharing models may have to be discussed in view of a changing and ageing academic workforce.[1567] As stressed by

---

1564 The age limit has so far not been subject to court decisions in Norway, however see chap. 14.2.2 above as regards decisions by the *LDN* and *LDO*. Advocating a removal of the age limit e.g.: *Brock-Utne* (2010); *Bjørgen* (2010); to the discussion in general *Landsverk* (2010), pp. 13-17; *Oksholen* (2010); critical also *Toft*, Martin (2010), Snart 70 – nektar å pensjonera seg, UNIFORM 04, 11. März 2010, p. 4.

1565 see C-159/10 and C-160/10 (*Fuchs* and *Köhler*), para. 28.

1566 *Stein*, David/*Rocco*, Tonette S./*Goldenetz*, Kelly A. (2000), Age and the University workplace, Human Resource Development Quarterly, vol. 11, no. 1, pp. 61-80, p. 78.

1567 ibid.; see also *Martin* (1984), p. 2; see in detail *de lege ferenda* considerations chap. 16, in particular 16.3.3.

Stein et al., to build intergenerational work teams in academia constitutes an area of future research that will require creative ways of blending training opportunities, flexible employment patterns and policies that are supportive of the life needs of an ageing workforce.[1568] *De lege lata* universities, even though they are generally reflective and progressive institutions that should be on the leading edge, when it comes to responding to coming shifts in employment practices and patterns, they still seem to be 'bastions of old images'.[1569] By continuing to operate with mandatory retirement provisions, valuable resources of human capital might be wasted, which in the end might lead to lowered competitiveness of Norwegian and German universities compared to e.g. their US counterparts, where productive researchers are not prevented by age limits from continuing to make major scientific contributions.[1570]

15 Mandatory retirement in security-relevant professions: The example of pilots

15.1 Introduction

A further classic example for mandatory retirement are age limits for aviation employees, in particular, for pilots. As *Meenan* put it in a nutshell, 'While airline pilots are not the most everyday example, their position highlights the complex interplay of capability, mandatory retirement, public safety, national, and international regulation in a way that few other professions do'.[1571]

How controversial age limits are, in particular for pilots, may be illustrated by examining recent judgements on the national and European level. The cases *CHC* before the Norwegian *Høyesterett* and the CJEU case *Prigge*, which was based on a reference for a preliminary ruling by the German BAG, are very illustrative in this regard.[1572] Besides the controversy around mandatory retirement for pilots, the age of pilots played a further essential role in debates about the legitimacy of seniority lists in

---

1568 *Stein* et al. (2000), p. 78; see to *de lege ferenda* considerations chap. 16.3.3.
1569 *Stein* et al. (2000), p. 64.
1570 similar *Stroebe* (2010), p. 672.
1571 *Meenan* (2005), p. 21.
1572 Rt. 2012 s. 219 (*CHC*); C-447/09 (*Prigge*).

redundancies (*nedbemanning*). Aspects such as the proximity to the pension and the employee's financial coverage due to pension entitlements are the key arguments that have been referred to in the dismissal processes.[1573]

Remarkably, *CHC* was decided based upon reliance on a CJEU judgement; namely, the *Prigge* case. It is noteworthy that the *Høyesterett* set aside the proceedings in *CHC* as it was waiting for the decision in *Prigge.* The proceedings in *CHC* vitally demonstrate the increasing impact on EU law and, in particular, of Dir. 2000/78/EC and the related CJEU case law on Norwegian cases on age discrimination.[1574] Moreover, the *Prigge* and *CHC* cases demonstrate that the legal situation in Norway and Germany is very similar, which is due to the fact that the normative framework is based on the same international and European legal standards in both countries.[1575] Moreover, mandatory retirement for pilots is typically regulated in Norway as well as in Germany in collective agreements, with the regulations being subject to *Prigge* and *CHC* being the most prominent examples. These examples are chosen as they first illustrate a conglomerate of different applicable regulations: international regulations, EU law, national laws and finally, on the national level, collective agreements. Second, they are interesting in terms of them shedding light on the relationship between the prohibition against age discrimination and the right of

---

1573 The analysis is not going to evaluate in detail the compatibility of seniority criteria in dismissals with Dir. 2000/78/EC as the primary focus rests on mandatory retirement provisions; see for a critical analysis of the use of seniority in aviation employment relationships *Rieble*, Volker (2010), Seniorität in der Luftfahrt, Festschrift für Eduard Picker zum 70. Geburtstag, Lobinger, Thomas (ed.), pp. 1117-1130, who argues that such seniority-based rules are an unproportional limitation of the pilot's professional freedom, see. e.g. pp. 1122ff., 1130; see moreover as regards relevant cases: Høyesterett, Rt. 2011 s. 609 (SAS), according to which the prohibition against age discrimination was not violated and the dismissals could be justified, see analysis in para. 66ff., 105.; similar cases: *Svensk Arbetsdomstolen*, Dom nr. 37/11, Mål Nr. A 110/10, Judgement of 04. Mai 2011, concerning dismissal of cabin crew members based on seniority rules that was considered being against the prohibition of age discrimination according to the judgement; see also as to dismissals of pilots based on seniority lists and entitlement to pension, *Københavns Byret*, sag nr. BS 32C-1356/2010, Judgement of 4. April 2011, where the Court concluded that the dismissals were age discriminatory and could not be justified.

1574 see in detail *Hack* (2012 a), p. 366.

1575 see to this aspect Rt-2012-219 (*CHC*), para. 47, 48.

the social partners to determine mandatory provisions via collective bargaining.[1576] Finally, when it comes to mandatory retirement in security-relevant professions such as pilots, several interests are involved that make the compatibility analysis with Dir. 2000/78/EC particularly interesting as a chosen example: the life and limb of the passengers, the crew and the people living in the area that the pilot is flying over versus the pilot's interests in his individual and professional self-fulfilment. Besides the different applicable legal regulations, mandatory retirement for pilots also has a further interesting dimension: in cases where one state may have a different age limit for pilots than other states, this could lead to strange cross-border effects – that have not been covered by the Directive –, as pilots from countries with a higher mandatory retirement age would be restricted in their routes, having to avoid flying over any country with a lower age limit.[1577] Moreover, this might have a negative impact on the employer's ability to roster pilots for cross-border or international work and might make them more vulnerable in case of downsizings.[1578]

15.2 De lege lata legal framework

15.2.1 International legal framework

The relevant international legislation as regards private and professional airline pilots was originally developed by an international institution, the Joint Aviation Authorities (JAA), which both Norway and Germany were members of.[1579] When it came to the legal situation of pilots, a pivotal part of this legislation constituted the so-called Joint Aviation Requirements – Flight Crew Licensing 1 (the JAR-FCL 1) – that were adopted on 15 April

1576 see to the legal situation before the applicability of the prohibition against age discrimination in Germany e.g. *Mohr*, Jochen (2013), Unwirksamkeit tariflicher Altersgrenzen für das Cockpitpersonal von Fluggesellschaften, Sammlung Arbeitsrechtlicher Entscheidungen (SAE) 02/2013, pp. 36 -44, p. 37 f., 41 f.

1577 see to this aspect *Meenan* (2007 a), p. 303 f. referring to Martinair Holland NV v. Vereniging van Nedelandse Verkeervliegers NR. C03/077HR, Dutch Supreme Court, 8. October 2004; see also *O'Cinneide* (2005), p. 38, fn. 94.

1578 *Meenan* (2007 a), p. 303 f.

1579 see in general see for a historic overview of the JAA's role: http://www.jaa.nl/introduction/introduction.html (last accessed: 17.12.2014).

2003.[1580] The JAR-FCL 1, in particular, contained age restrictions that were applicable to holders of pilot licences above the age of 60.[1581] In 2009, the JAA system was disbanded and instead, the JAA Training Organisation was kept running. A further important change created the adoption of EC Regulation 1592/2002 (now Commission Regulation (EU) No. 6/2013 of 8 January 2013)[1582] that lead to the establishment of a European Aviation Safety Agency (EASA). Being an EU agency with regulatory and executive tasks in the field of civilian aviation safety, several of the functions of the JAA have since then been taken over by EASA, which both Norway and Germany are member states of.

On the international level *de lege lata* the international standards on personnel licensing for pilots are contained in Annex 1 – Personnel Licensing to the Convention on International Civil Aviation (the so-called Chicago Convention). The Council of the ICAO adopted an amendment to Annex 1 — Personnel Licensing on 10 March 2006 that increased the upper age limit by five years for commercial pilots operating two-pilot aircraft, subject to further conditions – the so-called Amendment 167 to Annex 1.[1583] In short, it regulates that the holders of pilot licences shall not be permitted by the contracting state to act as a pilot-in-command on an aircraft engaged in international flights if the pilot has already reached his 60th birthday or, in the case of operations with more than one pilot where the other pilots are younger than 60 years of age, the pilot should not be older than 65. Moreover, it has been recommended that contracting states, having issued pilot licences, should not permit the holders thereof to act as co-pilots of an aircraft engaged in international flights if the licence holders are older than 65 years of age.

As clarified in Amendment 167 to Annex 1, a so-called pilot-in-command who is between the ages of 60 to 64 may not, in line with Art. 33 of the Convention on International Civil Aviation, be prevented by reason of age from working as a pilot, provided that he is engaged in operations

---

1580 see for an overview AG Villalón in C-447/09 (*Prigge*), para. 3.

1581 ibid.

1582 Commission Regulation (EU) No. 6/2013 of 8 January 2013 amending Regulation (EC) No. 216/2008 of the European Parliament and of the Council on common rules in the field of civil aviation and establishing a European Aviation Safety Agency, and repealing Council Directive 91/670/EEC, Regulation (EC) No. 1592/2002 and Directive 2004/36/EC Text with EEA relevance, OJ L 4, 9.1.2013, p. 34–35.

1583 The new provisions became applicable on 23 November 2006.

with more than one pilot. In augmented crews consisting of two or more pilots, at least one pilot should be under the age of 60.[1584] However, in cases where the pilot is working in single-pilot commercial air transport operations, the upper age limit is set at the age of 60.[1585]

As further stressed, a state may nevertheless impose a lower maximum age limit than the one specified by ICAO in § 2.1.10.2 of the Amendment, but it may not prevent, under reference to age, an aircraft from another state operated by a pilot-in-command, who holds a licence issued or validated by that state and who is below the ICAO upper age limit, from operating in the airspace above the territory of the state with the lower age limit.[1586]

According to Amendment 167 to Annex I, a contracting state that has issued pilot licences shall not permit the holder of such a licence who is engaged in pilot-in-command flights consisting of just one pilot to fly any longer if the pilot in question has reached his 60th birthday. In cases of flight operations where at least two pilots are engaged, the age limit is set at 65, provided that the other pilot involved is younger than 60 years of age.[1587] As stated in Amendment 167 to Annex 1, Arts. 39, 40 of the Convention on International Civil Aviation are also of relevance to the age limit concerning pilots-in-command that are 65 years of age or older, as they also authorise international flights by flight crew who do not meet all of the international licensing standards, as long as an authorisation is given by each state in which the aircraft is operated.[1588] For pilots above the age of 60, a six-monthly medical assessment is necessary.[1589] Moreover, the ICAO specifies an annual medical assessment for pilots who are under the age of 60 and who are engaged in two-pilot operations.[1590]

1584 Amendment 167 to Annex 1 para. 1), available at http://www.icao.int/safety/aviation-medicine/Pages/medFAQ_en.aspx#age: (last accessed: 17.12.2014).
1585 ibid. para. 1).
1586 ibid. para. 1).
1587 ibid. para. 1), 3).
1588 Amendment 167 to Annex 1, para. 2).
1589 ibid. para. 4).
1590 see reference made by Amendment 167 to Annex 1, para. 4).

15.2.2 The legal framework on the EU level

On the EU level, the most relevant regulatory framework constitutes Commission Regulation (EU) No 1178/2011 that lays down technical requirements and administrative procedures related to civil aviation aircrew.[1591] As regards pilot licensing and medical certification, Art. 3 Regulation (EU) No 1178/2011 refers to its Annex I, where age restrictions for pilots above the age of 60 are manifested in 'FCL.065 Curtailment of privileges of licence holders aged 60 years or more in commercial air transport requirements for pilots'.[1592] These restrictions correspond to the international requirements in Annex I of the Chicago Convention. According to FCL.065, pilots aged 60 to 64 are only allowed to fly provided that they are first a member of a multi-pilot crew and second, that the 60+ pilot is the only pilot in the cockpit crew who is above the age of 60.[1593] Moreover, it is explicitly stated that pilots above the age of 65 shall no longer act as a pilot of an aircraft that is engaged in commercial air transport.[1594]

15.2.3 De lege lata situation in Norway and Germany

In both countries, the international regulations, such as EU regulations, have a strong impact on the respective regulations of public law. For this reason, both countries are examined together.

In Norway, public law regulates that pilots that do have a flight licence are allowed to fly in commercial flights until they have reached the age of 65, provided that further requirements are fulfilled.[1595] For pilots working after having reached the age of 60, the cockpit crew has to consist of at

---

1591 Commission Regulation (EU) No. 1178/2011 of 3 November 2011 laying down technical requirements and administrative procedures related to civil aviation aircrew pursuant to Regulation (EC) No. 216/2008 of the European Parliament and of the Council Text with EEA relevance, OJ L 311, 25.11.2011, pp. 1–193. This regulation has been amended by Commission Regulation (EU) No. 290/2012 of 30 March 2012 OJ L 100, 5.4.2012, pp. 1–56.

1592 see as regards requirements for cabin crew members Art. 11 Regulation (EU) No. 1178/2011

1593 Regulation (EU) No. 1178/2011, Annex I, FCL.065, (a), (1)-(2).

1594 ibid., (b).

1595 see overview to the existing regulations given at Rt. 2012 s. 219 (*CHC*), para. 48.

least two pilots, whereof the other pilot has to be younger than 60 years of age. The international regulations have been implemented into Norwegian law via *forskrift 20. November 2009 nr. 1407 om sertifisering av flygere og krav til flygetreningsorganisajoner for fly og helikopter,helicopter* – the so-called *JAR-FCL-forskriften.*[1596] To comply with the new regulations on the EU level that also have been integrated into the EEA Agreement and are thus now also applicable to the non-EU member Norway, the *JAR-FCL-forskrift* will be abolished by 8 April 2016[1597] and replaced by *Forskrift om sertifisering av besetningsmedlemmer som gjennomfører forordning 1178/2011*, which has been amended by EU Commission Regulation 290/2012[1598] (Regulation on Aircrew). The new regulations on the EU level (Regulations 1178/2011, 290/2012 and 216/2008) have therefore also been implemented in Norway.[1599] As a consequence of implementing the new regulations, several national provisions will be abolished.[1600] The areas that are not encompassed by the Regulation on Aircrew are still going to be regulated by national provisions.[1601] As stressed by the Norwegian *Luftfartstilsynet* (Civil Aviation Authority Norway), during the transitional period, the existing legal framework will be adjusted to the new regulations. During this transformation period, the old and the new regulations will both be applicable and, in case of conflicting regulations, the *forskrift om sertifisering av besetningsmedlemmer* will take precedence over the other still-existing national provisions.[1602]

1596 see ibid.

1597 see § 7 *Forskrift om sertifisering av besetningsmedlemmer* (FOR-2013-07-16-916).

1598 Commission Regulation (EU) No. 290/2012 of 30 March 2012 (OJ L 100, 5.4.2012, p. 1).

1599 Commission Regulation (EU) No. 1178/2011, such as Commission Regulation (EU) No. 290/2012 and Regulation (EC) No. 216/2008 are part of the EEA agreement via Annex XXIII Transport, Part. I, VI. Civil Aviation, p. 76, 66ne; see § 1 *Forskrift om sertifisering av besetningsmedlemmer.*

1600 this is e.g. the case for *Forskrift om gjennomføring av felleseuropeiske bestemmelser om medisinske krav for tjenestegjørende på luftfartøy*, BSL JAR-FCL 3 (Flight Crew Licencing) *endring* 5, FOR-2008-06-19-617, that already has been abolished since 19. July 2013, see § 7 *Forskrift om sertifisering av besetningsmedlemmer.*

1601 see for details and overview at luftfarttilsynet.no

1602 see in general luftfarttilsynet.no, see in detail for the temporary provisions as regards the implementation of Commission Regulation (EU) No. 1178/2011: § 8 *Forskrift om sertifisering av besetningsmedlemmer.*

Besides these complex provisions in public law, the social partners in the aviation sector have manifested certain mandatory retirement provisions in collective agreements. One example in this regard is the mandatory retirememt age limit that was subject to the proceedings in *CHC*.[1603]

Like in Norway, a complex set of public law rules is also applicable for pilots in Germany. When it comes to provisions on mandatory retirement for pilots, two provisions are pivotal: first, § 20 (2) No. 1 *Luftverkehrs-Zulassungs-Ordnung* (LuftVZO) and second, § 127 *Verordnung über Luftfahrtpersonal* (LuftPersV).[1604] The first provision, § 20 (2) No. 1 LuftVZO, basically transforms the international requirements set out in JAR-FCL 1. In line with the international regulations, pilots that are 60+ are therefore allowed to fly on international flights, provided that they are not older than 65 and that they are a member of a multi-person cockpit crew, where the other pilots have not yet reached the age of 60. This provision is also applicable to situations where merely two pilots are sitting in the cockpit. By contrast, § 127 LuftPersV is less restrictive, as it explicitly allows for pilots above the age of 60 and until they have reached the age of 65 to be engaged even in flights where just one pilot is in the cockpit. However, this is restricted to the German territory. Since 2012, this twofold regime with different regulations depending on whether the aircraft is operating solely above German ground or internationally, has been replaced by Regulation (EU) No. 1178/2011, which, in principle, adopts with its Art. 3 in conjunction with Annex I. (FCL.065), when compared to § 127 LuftPersV, a somewhat stricter internationally applicable age limit.[1605]

1603 see Rt. 2012 s. 219 (*CHC*), para. 4; see for an overview: http://tariffavtaler.nho.no/?sort=arbeidsgiver&type=overenskomster&catid=32 (last accessed: 17.12.2014).

1604 see for an overview to the applicable public regulations in Germany: *Temming*, Felipe (2012), Diskriminierende Beendigung der Arbeitsverträge von Piloten bei Vollendung des 60. Lebensjahres, EUZA Vol. 5 2012, pp. 205-224, p. 210 f.

1605 Regulation (EU) No. 1178/2011 has been implemented into German law via: *Gesetz zur Anpassung des Luftverkehrsrechts an die Verordnung (EU) Nr. 1178/2011 der Kommission vom 3. November 2011 zur Festlegung technischer Vorschriften und von Verwaltungsverfahren in Bezug auf das fliegende Personal in der Zivilluftfahrt gemäß der Verordnung (EG) Nr. 216/2008 des Europäischen Parlaments und des Rates vom 20. Februar 2008 vom 07. August 2013*, BGBl I 2013, 3123; see in general to the two systems *Temming* (2012), p. 210 f.

Both in Norway and in Germany, absolute mandatory retirement age limits set at the age of 60 were subject to highly debated court decisions. The highly disputed provision in the *Prigge* case was laid down in § 19 (1) of the so-called *Manteltarifvertrag Nr. 5 a* for the cockpit personnel of *Deutsche Lufthansa*. In its version of 14 January 2005, the *Manteltarifvertrag Nr. 5 a* stated in § 19 I, 'The employment relationship shall terminate, without notice of termination, at the end of the month on which the 60th birthday falls'.[1606]

In *Prigge*, the CJEU finally ruled that the mandatory retirement age for pilots of 60 years of age constituted age discrimination that could not be justified according to Dir. 2000/78/EC. The Court stressed, in particular, that it could not be regarded as necessary in achieving the legitimate aim of air safety given the fact that particularly on the international level, the respective provisions explicitly allowed for a further engagement of the pilot beyond the age of 60 in a multi-pilot crew setting and where the age limit was set at 65.[1607] By contrast, until *Prigge*, both the BAG and BVerfG had recognised in settled case law that the mandatory retirement age of 60 years of age for pilots laid down by collective agreements did not constitute unjustified age discrimination.[1608] However, according to the judgement of the BAG in the aftermath of *Prigge* and in line with the CJEU's ruling, the controversial age limit in § 19 (1) s. 1 *Manteltarifvertrags* Nr. 5 a violated the prohibition against age discrimination as manifested in § 7 (1) i.c.w. § 1 AGG. The mandatory retirement age limit has been declared legally void due to § 7 (2) AGG.[1609]

In its decision in *CHC* or the *Helicopter* case[1610] the *Høyesterett* held that a retirement age of 60 years imposed upon helicopter pilots by means of a collective agreement did violate the prohibition against age discrimination. The *Høyesterett* set aside the case as it was waiting for the CJEU's decision in *Prigge*.[1611] The *Prigge* case had thus a particular impact on

1606 see C-447/09 (*Prigge*), para. 18.

1607 C-447/09 (*Prigge*), para. 83.

1608 see e.g. BAG, Urteil vom 21. Juli 2004 – 7 AZR 589/03 –, juris; BVerfG, Nichtannahmebeschluss vom 26. Januar 2007 – 2 BvR 2408/06 –, juris; BVerfG, Nichtannahmebeschluss vom 25. November 2004 – 1 BvR 2459/04 –, juris; *Beitze* (2009), § 10, para. 100. p. 262 f.; see for an overview of the previous BAG jurisdiction *Mohr* (2013), p. 37 f., 41 f.

1609 BAG, Urteil vom 18. Januar 2012 – 7 AZR 112/08 –, BAGE 140, 248-260.

1610 Rt. 2012 s. 219 (*CHC*).

1611 Rt. 2010 s. 944; see in detail *Hack* (2012 a), 365 f.

both the understanding of German law and Norwegian law. *CHC* therefore illustrates par excellence the increasing impact of EU law on Norwegian law in the field of age discrimination.[1612]

The controversial provisions subject to *CHC* were laid down in § 11 of the collective agreement between *Nærlingslivets Hovedorganisajon (NHO) Luftfart* and *CHC Helikopter Service AS*, on the one hand, and *Norsk Flygerforbund/Helikopter Service AS Flygerforening* on the other hand. § 11. 1 laid down the pension age at 58 and, in § 11.2, employment beyond this pension age was regulated. It stated in § 11.2.1 s. 1, 'The pilot has the right to continue as a pilot above the age of 58 until he has achieved the age of 60, provided that the necessary certificates and qualifications are at hand'.[1613]

These provisions in the pension regulations had, according to the social partners, to be interpreted to the extent that the employment relationship had to be terminated after the pilot had reached the age of 60.[1614] In its analysis, the *Høyesterett* paid attention to, inter alia, the fact that the age limit could not be justified by referring to risks for air safety and, in particular, the health of third persons caused by a potential capability decline of the pilot above the age of 60.[1615] The *Høyestrett* finally held that to achieve the aim of air safety by establishing a mandatory retirement provision of 60 years of age in a collective agreement constitutes an unproportional intervention, when national and international legislation allowed pilots to continue working until the age of 65 years, provided that they fulfilled the necessary health requirements.[1616] The age limit could thus not be justified and was considered a violation of the prohibition against age discrimination.

15.2.4 Intermediate conclusion

Besides the regulations in international and national public law, the social partners have laid down mandatory retirement provisions for pilots in collective agreements. It is anticipated that the social partners, as a reaction to

1612 see ibid.
1613 translation by author.
1614 Rt. 2012 s. 219 (*CHC*), para. 45.
1615 ibid., para. 55.
1616 ibid., para. 56.

the judgements in *Prigge* and *CHC,* will raise their compulsory retirement age limits in accordance with the respective international and EU regulations. Two central stages that are demarcated by age limits for pilots may be distinguished: first, a period where a pilot can fly without particular age-related restrictions until the age limit of 60 years has been reached and second, the period between 60 and 65 years of age where the pilot is only allowed to fly provided that he is part of a multi-pilot crew and provided that the other pilots are younger than 60.

15.3 Compatibility analysis

In view of the close similarity between the mandatory retirement provisions for pilots manifested in collective agreements in Norway and Germany, the following analysis focuses on such provisions as a test case for the conformity of such age limits with Dir. 2000/78/EC. In this analysis, both countries are therefore examined together. Anticipating that *de lege lata* in the aftermath of the judgements in *CHC* and *Prigge*, the previously valid age limits of 60 years of age have been adjusted to the respective international and EU law standard, the following examination concentrates both on the question of the legitimacy of having the age of 60 as a mandatory age threshold – as was the case in *Prigge* and *CHC* – as well as on having the age of 65 as a compulsory retirement age limit for pilots.

15.3.1 Scope of Dir. 2000/78/EC

By stipulating that the pilot's employment relationship terminates (without the need for notice to terminate the employment contract) at the end of the month in which the pilot turns 60 – as was e.g. the case in *Prigge* and in *CHC* – such provisions concern the employment conditions of employees within the meaning of Art. 3 No. 1 (c) Dir. 2000/78/EC.[1617] This is also the case as regards provisions providing a termination of the employment contract at the age of 65. The Directive is therefore applicable to both the lower as well as the higher limit.[1618]

1617 C-447/09 (*Prigge*), para. 41.

1618 As regards the lower age limit see C-447/09 (*Prigge*), para. 41.

However, when it comes to the Directive's scope, the question arises as to whether collective agreements must also respect the principle of non-discrimination on the grounds of age as implemented by the Directive. As clarified by the CJEU, the fact that a national legislation authorises, for an objective reason, a collective agreement to lay down provisions on the automatic termination of employment contracts at a certain age, does not dispense with the requirement that the respective collective agreement also has to be in accordance with EU law, more particularly, with Dir. 2000/78/EC.[1619] In addition, the social partners are therefore bound, beyond doubt, by the prohibition against age discrimination.[1620] This has also been emphasised by the CJEU.[1621] However, in determining their measures to achieve the legitimate aims, the social partners do, in principle, enjoy a broad discretion.[1622] The right to collective bargaining as set out in Art. 28 CRFEU must, within the scope of EU law, therefore be performed in accordance with EU law.[1623] Thus, where the social partners adopt measures that fall within the Directive's scope, which gives specific expression in the area of employment and occupation to the principle of non-discrimination on the grounds of age, the social partners have to respect the Directive.[1624] Consequently, the principle of non-discrimination on the grounds of age as concretised by the Directive also has to be respected by the social partners.[1625] In any case, any limitation of a basic

1619 C-447/09 (*Prigge*), para. 46 referring to C-45/09 (*Rosenbladt*), para. 53.

1620 see Art. 13, 16 (b) and Art. 18 Dir. 2000/78/EC; see to this aspect *Forst* (2012), p. 227.

1621 joined cases C-297/10 and C-298/10 (*Hennigs* and *Mai*), Judgement of 8 September 2011, ECR 2011, I-07965, para. 68

1622 C-447/09 (*Prigge*), para. 48 f.; joined cases C-297/10 and C-298/10 (*Hennigs* and *Mai*), para. 65; see also C-45/09 (*Rosenbladt*) para. 49; C-411/05 (*Palacios*), para. 68.

1623 C-447/09 (*Prigge*), para. 47 referring to C-438/05 (International Transport Workers' Federation and Finnish Seamen's Union, '*Viking Line*') [2007] ECR I-10779, para. 44, and C-341/05 (*Laval* un Partneri) [2007] ECR I-11767, para. 91; see also joined cases C-297/10 and C-298/10 (*Hennigs* and *Mai*), para. 67 f.

1624 C-447/09 (*Prigge*), para. 48 referring to. C-127/92 (*Enderby*), ECR I-5535, para. 22; see also joined cases C-297/10 and C-298/10 (*Hennigs* and *Mai*), para. 67 f.

1625 C-447/09 (*Prigge*), para. 49; see also C-297/10 and C-298/10 (*Hennigs* and *Mai*), para. 63, 68; see also C-45/09 (*Rosenbladt*), para. 52; The *Høyesterett* did not go any further into this, see para. 65; see in detail to the question how much leeway should be granted to the social partners in determing mandatory retirement chap. 15.3.3.5.

Charter right, be it the individual employee's right to be protected against age discrimination or the social partners' right to collective bargaining, may only take place in accordance with the principle of proportionality, as stipulated by Art. 52 CFREU. The balancing of collective bargaining rights versus the prohibition against age discrimination is therefore an issue to be assessed in the proportionality stricto sensu examination.[1626]

15.3.2 Direct age discrimination

Employment relationships of pilots that fall under collective agreements are automatically terminated when the pilot turns 60 years of age or 65, respectively.[1627] Pilots who are subject to such provisions are in a comparable situation to that of younger pilots performing the same activity for the benefit of the same airline company and/or falling under the same collective agreement.[1628] Those pilots whose employment contract terminates automatically when having reached the age of 60 or 65 years, respectively, are treated in a less favourable manner, on the grounds of their age, than the younger pilots are.[1629] The mandatory retirement provisions therefore operate through a difference in treatment based directly on the grounds of age for the purposes of Art. 1 in conjunction with Art. 2 No. 2 (a) Dir. 2000/78/EC.[1630]

By contrast, as regards dismissals of pilots due to seniority lists, it is questionable as to whether the measure of using seniority as a criterion in dismissals constitutes a direct or indirect discrimination on the grounds of age.[1631] By operating with seniority lists, that is, the employee's length of service and the criterion that the employee has reached an age where he is entitled to a pension, the dismissal decision is directly tied up with the employee's age. In particular, the criterion of pension entitlement is not an apparently neutral criterion, as stipulated in the case of indirect age discrimination in the sense of Art. 2 (b) Dir. 2000/78/EC, but rather, is directly related to the employee's age, so that direct age discrimination in the sense of Art. 2 (a) is in play.[1632] However,

---

1626 see in detail chap. 15.3.3.5.
1627 see C-447/09 (*Prigge*), para. 43.
1628 C-447/09 (*Prigge*), para. 44.
1629 ibid., para. 44.
1630 ibid., para. 45; see also BAG, Urteil vom 15. Februar 2012 – 7 AZR 946/07 –, juris, para. 24.
1631 see e.g. *Rieble* (2010), p. 1122.
1632 similar *Københavns Byret*, sag nr. BS 32C-1356/2010, judgement of 4. April 2011, p. 17; the Norwegian *Høyesterett* Rt. 2011 s. 609 (SAS), para 66ff., does not make a stand on the question of whether direct or indirect age discrimination is at hand.

when it comes to the justification analysis, seniority lists – being regarded as either indirect or direct age discrimination – have to pursue a legitimate objective; they must be necessary in terms of achieving this aim and must do so in a proportional manner.

15.3.3 Justification of direct age discrimination

The justification provisions that have, in principle, to be considered when examining the justification of the age limit of 60 or 65, respectively, for pilots, as manifested in collective agreements in Norway and Germany, are Art. 2 No. 5, Art. 4 No. 1 and Art. 6 No. 1 s. 1 Dir. 2000/78/EC.[1633] As a necessary previous step to the justification analysis, first the legitimate aim underlying the age limit for pilots has to be identified.

15.3.3.1 Legitimate aim

The potential legitimate aims that come into play when discussing mandatory retirement for pilots are first, the aim of ensuring air safety, second, the generational equity argument of enabling a turnover of employees by providing younger employees with the opportunity to get a job and finally, the aim of maintaining the pilot's dignity by sparing the employee the degrading situation of having to discuss his physical and mental capabilities after having reached the age limit in question.[1634] As neither the respective collective agreements in *Prigge* and *CHC* nor other documents explicitly mention such aims, a context analysis is necessary.[1635]

1633 similar referring court in C-447/09 (*Prigge*), para. 29-30.

1634 similar the aims referred to in C-447/09 (*Prigge*), para. 51; Rt. 2012 s. 219 (*CHC*), para. 62- 64.

1635 see in this regard Rt. 2012 s. 219 (*CHC*), para. 61 referring to C-411/05 (*Palacios de la Villa*), para. 56-57 see also Rt. 2011 s. 964 (*Gjensidige*), para. 51.

15.3.3.1.1 Security: Ensuring air safety as a legitimate aim

The key aim that may be identified as underlying both the Norwegian as well as the German provisions on mandatory retirement for pilots is that of ensuring air safety.[1636] The age limit shall thereby serve the safety of passengers, the pilots and their crew as well as residents of areas over which the aircraft might fly; that is, under the flight path.[1637] Identifying this aim as legitimate needs to be distinguished from the question as to how this aim might best be achieved. Inherent to this evaluation is the examination of the pilot's aptitude, as his physical and mental capabilities to operate the aircraft are decisive for ensuring the aim of air safety. Whether mandatory retirement is legitimate in this regard is analysed in detail when it comes to the applicable justification provisions.

The aim of ensuring air safety by using mandatory retirement is strongly built upon the assumption that there is a certain correlation between the pilot's age, his flight experience and his potential involvement in a crash. As with the other examined mandatory retirement provisions, what is inherent to this is that of the supposed capability decline of the ageing pilot. Whether this assumption is substantiated needs to be further evaluated.

Any generalised assumptions concerning the decline of pilots' capabilities with age may only be referred to as long as no medical findings exist that prove this argumentation wrong.[1638] In general, medical arguments are employed in the legal discussion in an attempt to justify mandatory retirement for pilots. Strikingly, in the judicial arena, scientific data are seldom – if at all – precisely referred to that may or may not support this view. Due to this lack of scientific substantiation in the normative argumentation, it is essential to take a closer look at scientific studies concerning the correlation between age, flight experience and crash involvement. Three hypotheses may be identified that are commonly referred to when it comes to discussing the employment of older pilots under reference to medical aspects: first, the hypothesis that older pilots may have a 'greater

---

1636 C-447/09 (*Prigge*), para. 51; see Rt. 2012 s. 219 (*CHC*), para. 62, 64, even though the Norwegian *Høyesterett* is somewhat unclear on the question whether air safety is also to be considered a legitimate aim, para. 66.

1637 see for an overview of the case law of the BAG in this regard *Falke* (2007), § 8, para. 44.

1638 *Over* (2009), pp. 215-217.

likelihood of experiencing incapacitation, either sudden or subtle, which would place the aircraft and passengers at risk'.[1639] Second, the hypothesis that is bulit upon the argument that older pilots might experience a decline in cognitive abilities that result in dangerous judgement errors that might put safety at risk.[1640] And finally, the hypothesis is made that older pilots who may be at risk for adverse health events, may not be identified via medical and psychological assessments.[1641]

One of the reasons that is referred to for operating with mandatory retirement for airline pilots has been that the risk of acute and incapacitating medical conditions such as heart attacks and strokes would increase with advancing age and that such age-related medical conditions cannot be accurately predicted at the individual level.[1642] Opponents of compulsory retirement for pilots argue that pilots, compared to the general population, feature a considerably lower overall mortality rate and lower mortality from cardiovascular diseases, and that the risk of a crash resulting from acute incapacitation of the pilot-in-command is negligible, notably when in the presence of other crew members in the cockpit.[1643] Rather than the feared age-related inflight incapacitations, the most common cause for such sudden incapacitations are not age-related cardiovascular diseases, but gastrointestinal illnesses such as gastrointestinal upset and diarrhoea that are completely unrelated to age.[1644]

1639 *Wilkening* (2002), p. 197.

1640 ibid.

1641 ibid.

1642 see to the discussion in the US: ibid.; *Li* et al. (2003) p. 874 who refer as regards the proponents of imposing mandatory retirement on pilots to Institute of Medicine, National Academy of Sciences (1981), Airline pilot age, health and performance, Washington DC.

1643 *Li* et al. (2003) p. 874; similar already *Mohler*, Stanley R. (1981), Reasons for eliminating the 'age 60' regulation for airline pilots, Aviation, space, and environmental medicine, 2002 1981, Vol. 52 No. 8, pp. 445-454, p. 451; *Wilkening* (2002), pp. 194-202, p. 197; see in detail to sudden cardiac-related flight incapacitation. *Chapman*, Peter, J. (1984), The consequences of in-flight incapacitation in civil aviation, Aviation, space, and environmental medicine, June 1984, pp. 497-500.

1644 see in detail to this aspect: *Mohler* (1981), p. 451; *Wilkening* (2002), p. 197; similar *Chapman* (1984), p. 499.

A study based on longitudinal data published in 2003 investigated the correlation between age, experience and crash involvement in a birth cohort of professional pilots.[1645] To overcome limitations in the previous studies that were cross-sectionally designed and, moreover, limited by lack of individual-level data on exposure to flights, the study by *Li* et al. was based on longitudinal data.[1646] The study's fundamental question – as regards the (at that time in the US) applicable and highly debated mandatory retirement for pilots at the age of 60 (the age-60 rule) – was whether pilots' risk of crash involvement changed significantly due to the ageing process.[1647] In essence, the study found that the crash risk was not significantly associated with advancing age. Rather, the study demonstrated that the pilot's flight experience was a more significant determinant of crash risk than ageing.[1648] The study found that the crash risk remained fairly stable as the pilots aged from their late forties to their late fifties.[1649] Scientific data for pilots above the age of sixty were, according to the authors, too scarce to enable any conclusions to be drawn.[1650] One of the reasons for this is that, at that time, on the international level, the age limit for pilots was still set at 60 as a maximum. What turned out to be more relevant than age was the pilot's flight experience, as measured by total flight time at baseline, which demonstrated a significant protective effect against the risk of crash involvement.[1651]

1645 *Li*, Guohua/*Baker*, Susan P./*Grabowski*, Jurek G./*Qiang*, Yandong/*McCarthy*, Melissa L./*Rebok*, George W. (2003), Age, flight experience, and risk of crash involvement in a cohort of professional pilots, American Journal of Epidemiology 2003, Vol. 157 no. 10, pp. 875-880, p. 875, to material and methods used see pp. 875ff.

1646 *Li* et al. (2003), p. 875; see also *Mohler* (1981), p. 448 f., see to the limitations of cross-sectional studies in gerontology already chap. 6.3.1.

1647 *Li* et al. (2003), p. 875.

1648 *Li* et al. (2003), p. 878; similar already *Haldorsen*, Tor/*Reitan*, Jon B./*Tveten*, Ulf (2002), Aircraft accidents and other causes of death among comercial pilots, Aviation, space, and environmental medicine, 2002 June Vol. 73 No. 6, pp. 587-92, p. 589, 591.

1649 *Li* et al. (2003), p. 878 f.

1650 ibid., p. 879.

1651 ibid., p. 874, 878; similar already *Haldorsen* et al. (2002), p. 589, 591; *Mohler* (1981), p. 451.

Due to the study, pilots - with adjustments for age - who had 5,000–9,999 hours of total flight time at baseline had a 57% lower risk of crashing than their less experienced colleagues did. However, the protective effect of flight experience levelled off after a total flight time of 10,000 hours had been reached.[1652]

According to the authors, the lack of a correlation between the pilot's age and crash risk may reflect a strong so-called healthy worker effect, which stems from the rigorous medical standards and periodic physical examinations that are required for professional pilots.[1653] A lack of significant ageing impact on crash risk does not necessarily mean that safety performance cannot be affected by ageing. Rather, it might be an indication that medical standards and the physical examination system for professional pilots that are currently available are adequate in ensuring air safety. If those pilots who were screened out in the process of ageing were to have remained on active duty, 'the adverse effect of aging on crash risk might well have emerged as significant'.[1654] In contrast to the argumentation of the proponents of mandatory retirement for pilots, scientific studies could thus not prove a significant correlation between the ageing process and risks for crash involvement.[1655] Quite the contrary, it has been estimated that the risk that an airline crash will result from cardiac incapacitation is less than 1 per 8 billion pilot flight hours or, in other words, 1 accident every 400 years.[1656] In sum, age is a rather poor indicator of potential crash risk. The pilot's flight experience thus turns out to be far more relevant than his age.[1657] As emphasised by *Mohler*, the increasing age of the pilot and his experience is repeatedly correlated with a decrease in accidents.[1658] To get to the point, one may thus conclude with *Wilkening* that

---

1652 *Li* et al. (2003), p. 877.

1653 ibid., p. 874, 878; see to the 'healthy worker effect' in detail *Haldorsen* et al. (2002), p. 591.

1654 *Li* et al. (2003), p. 878.

1655 e.g. *Lüderitz* (2005), p. 85, 86 mentions generally scientific findings of age-related capabilities decline of older pilots without giving any references in this regard.

1656 see in detail *Chapman* (1984), pp. 497-500, in particular p. 499 Table II; *Wilkening* (2002), p. 198, *Li* et al. (2003), p. 874.

1657 see to this aspect *Haldorsen* et al. (2002), p. 591; *Mohler* (1981), p. 451.

1658 *Mohler* (1981), p. 451 with further extensive references to studies demonstrating the decline of flight accidents by experciened pilots with increasing age.

> Some 30 yr of accident-free air carrier experience demonstrate convincingly in very real terms that no justification exists for maintaining the Age 60 Rule based on the fear that a pilot of a multicrew aircraft will compromise passenger safety due to his or her sudden or subtle incapacitation regardless of age.[1659]

As stressed by *Li* et al. in their review of several studies as regards the effects of ageing on cognitive functions and piloting, the findings, in essence, demonstrate that whereas domain-independent cognitive functions like sensory perception and psychomotor skills decrease progressively with age, performance in most flight-related tasks such as decision-making, tracking, take-off and landing exhibits no significant difference between older pilots and their younger colleagues.[1660] When examining scientific longitudinal studies, the hypothesis that there is a general, progressive loss of cognitive functions with increasing age cannot be supported by these findings.[1661]

One of the few flight-related tasks where ageing had a noticeable impact concerned the ability to respond to communications.[1662] Older pilots are, in particular, found to be less accurate than younger pilots are in reading back and executing tape-recorded air traffic control commands, especially long and fast speech commands.[1663] The age-related decline concerning the performance of communication tasks is ascribed to a deteriorated working memory capacity in the older employees.[1664] However, one cannot ignore the fact that flight experience may eliminate age-related deficits in the performance of certain communication tasks and attenuate the adverse effects of ageing on the performance of less domain-relevant tasks.[1665] As criticised by *Li* et al., most of these studies were conducted under controlled laboratory conditions using flight simulators and were, moreover, cross-sectional in design, so that in sum, their value for examining age-related differences in terms of the risk of crash involvement is rather limited.[1666]

1659 *Wilkening* (2002), p. 198.

1660 *Li* et al. (2003), p. 875; already *Mohler* (1981), p. 448 f. could not find a support in his review of scientific findings for the hypthesis of age-based capability decline.

1661 *Mohler* (1981), p. 448 f; *Li* et al. (2003), p. 877ff.; similar as regards the US 'age-60 rule also *Wilkening* (2002), p. 196 who quotes the landmark 1981 Report of the US National Institute of Aging Panel on the Experienced Pilot Study according to which '*the Age 60 Rule appears indefensible on medical grounds*' and which stated that '*age 60 represents no medical "breakpoint" in the progressive deterioation that comes with age.*' The panel finally concluded that '*there is no convincing medical evidence to support age 60, or any other specific age, for mandatory pilot retirement*'.

1662 see in detail *Lie*, p. 875.

1663 ibid.

1664 ibid.

1665 ibid.

1666 ibid.

To conclude, protecting the life and health of third parties, other crew members, passengers and generally, human beings in the areas the pilot is flying over from potential air traffic hazards constitutes, beyond doubt, a legitimate aim.[1667] To avoid any risk situation, restrictions in the pilot's right to work therefore might even be justified. However, in view of the scientific findings that were not able to prove a definite correlation between age, flight experience and crash involvement, it is questionable as to whether an absolute mandatory retirement age should be set at the age of 60 and might not better be replaced by alternative measures. However, this is part of a necessity assessment.[1668]

15.3.3.1.2 Promotion of younger employees

In principle, the aim of promoting younger employees and opening up career opportunities for the younger generation of employees has to be considered as a potential legitimate aim.[1669] Both in *Prigge* as well as in *CHC* this has been referred to as an aim underlying the respective mandatory retirement provisions.[1670] However, as already ascertained in the compatibility of mandatory retirement for physicians and professors, it is rather questionable if this aim may be regarded as a public interest aim, as foe example is needed for the social-policy objective requirement in Art. 6 No. 1 Dir. 2000/78/EC. An aim that solely focuses on career options for the group of younger employees is, quite the contrary, to be viewed as primarily serving the individual employer's interests.

The aspect of creating career opportunities for younger pilots cannot per se be regarded as sufficient to force the older pilots to retire at the age of 60, as in the cases of *Prigge* and *CHC*.[1671] As rightly stressed by the *Høyesterettt*, such argumentation could be referred to by any employer, so that the prohibition of age discrimination might become eroded (*det ville*

1667 similar also *Over* (2009), pp. 215-217; *Groß* (2010), p. 123.

1668 see chap. 15.3.3.2.1.

1669 see in this regard Rt. 2012 s. 219 (*CHC-saken*), para. 66 under reference to the CJEU cases *Rosenbladt*, *Petersen*, *Fuchs and Köhler* and *Georgiev*.

1670 see Rt. 2012 s. 219 (*CHC*), para. 63; The argument of opening up of employment opportunities for younger pilots by terminating the employment relationship of older pilots who already had achieved the age of getting pension entitlements, was inter alia highly debated in Rt. 2011 s. 609 (*SAS*).

1671 see Rt. 2012 s. 219 (*CHC*), para. 72.

være lite igjen).[1672] Rather, it has to be proven that the age limit de facto serves the enhancement of the career opportunities of the younger pilots.[1673] This could be proven neither in *Prigge* nor in *CHC*.[1674] Moreover, the collective bargaining partners that have agreed upon the mandatory retirement provision do not enjoy more freedom than the individual employer does in setting aside the prohibition against age discrimination in favour of the faster career advancement of the younger generation of pilots.[1675]

The argument of ensuring promotion opportunities for all pilots before retirement was also pivotal in a case before the Dutch Supreme Court.[1676] In this case, the mandatory retirement age of 56 for pilots of *Martinair* was regarded as justified, as it was viewed as being necessary for the promotion of all employees who were younger than the retirees were and thus was necessary to establish a needed turnover of the pilots. The underlying rationale for the compulsory retirement of pilots at the age of 56 was to guarantee 'circulation', based upon the argumentation that any pilot's career, which generally starts with a very expensive education and ends with early retirement, is structured in terms of the expectation that it will be possible for all pilots to reach the highest seniority level before retirement.[1677] The Dutch Supreme Court finally ruled in accordance with previous instances that this rational formed an 'objective justification'.[1678] Thus, the age limit of 56 could be maintained. Interestingly enough, the Dutch age limit for pilots was not challenged based on a breach of Dir. 2000/78/EC – as the case predated the Directive, which, in consequence, was not yet implemented in the Netherlands – but based on a breach of Art. 1 of the Constitution and of Art. 26 ICCPR.[1679] Moreover, the case illustrates the potential cross-border effects that are inherent if one state, such as the Netherlands, operates with a mandatory retirement age for pilots that is lower than the international standards allow for.

1672 ibid.

1673 ibid.

1674 ibid.

1675 ibid.

1676 *Martinair Holland NV v. Vereniging van Nedelandse Verkeervliegers*, NR. C03/077HR, Dutch Supreme Court, 8 October 2004, see to a discussion of the case *O'Cinneide* (2005), p. 38, in particular fn. 94.

1677 *O'Cinneide* (2005), p. 38, fn. 94.

1678 ibid.

1679 see also *O'Cinneide* (2005), p. 38, fn. 94; see also to Art. 26 ICCPR already chap. 9.4.

15.3.3.1.3 Dignity of the employee

Moreover, the argument has been brought forward that operating with a mandatory retirement provision would guarantee the pilots who are subject to retirement an exit from working life with dignity.[1680] The underlying argumentation is that alternatives to such an age limit such as individual capability assessments might negatively affect the employee's dignity, who might then be exposed to a degrading situation at the end of his working career. The employee's Association of Pilots in *CHC* argued that the mandatory retirement would give the employees the option to retire from a job, which is inter alia coined by high physical pressure.[1681] If one were to allow the fittest employees to extend their working life, this might negatively impact the other employees, who might then also be forced to stay in employment rather than to retire.[1682] According to this line of reasoning, the employees would be spared from the fact that they are no longer performing as required, and both employees and employers would be saved from stressful court procedures.[1683] Here it has to be considered that pilots, who might fear no longer fulfilling the needed professional requirements, may consider making use of early retirement options.[1684] As long as the age limit is absolute and mandatory, the dignity argumentation runs counter to the employee's interest in exercising his right to work, as it is rather degrading to be forced to exit working life without having had the chance to prove that one is still in the possession of the required mental and physical capabilities. Furthermore, it has to be kept in mind that during their entire employment life pilots are already subject to regular assessments and are forced to terminate the employment relationship if they do not pass the tests, so that they are used to this kind of situation.[1685] It is therefore difficult to understand why the obligation to be subject to such testing should be more degrading after having reached for example

---

1680 see to this aspect Rt. 2012 s. 219 (*CHC*), para. 63 and in general to the dignity argument para. 66 and in particular para. 71ff.; see to the dignity argument in general already chap. 12.3.2.1 above.

1681 Rt. 2012 s. 219 (*CHC*), para. 63.

1682 ibid.

1683 ibid. para. 71 referring to Ot.prp. nr. 54 (2008-2009).

1684 similar ibid. para. 71, where the *Høyesterett* refers to the fact that pilots might retire with full pension entitlements according to the collective agreement already at the age of 58, see to the respective applicable provisions para. 4.

1685 similar argumentation *Høyesterett* in Rt-2012-219 (*CHC-saken*), para. 71.

the age of 60.[1686] The argument of protecting the pilot's dignity can thus according to the view held in this thesis not be referred to as a legitimate aim.

15.3.3.2 Exception according to Art. 2 No. 5 Dir. 2000/78/EC

The Norwegian and German mandatory retirement provisions for pilots might be exempted from the Directive's scope according to Art. 2 No. 5 Dir. 2000/78/EC. If this were to be the case, the Directive's further justification provisions would not be examined. However, according to the understanding laid down in this thesis, this is only the case if a strict proportionality standard is also applied in the assessment of Art. 2 No. 5. Otherwise, any proportionality requirements in for example Art. 4 No. 1 and Art. 6 No. 1 could simply be avoided by exempting a provision via Art. 2 No. 5 from the Directive's scope and thus from any further proportionality assessment.[1687]

In any case, Art. 2 No. 5 has to be interpreted strictly, as it establishes an exception to the prohibition against age discrimination.[1688] Thus, first, it has to be examined whether the aim of ensuring air safety is included in the objectives laid down in Art. 2 No. 5 and second, whether age limits for pilots manifested in collective agreements constitute a measure provided for by national legislation within the meaning of that provision.[1689] In terms of the aim of ensuring air traffic safety, it is apparent, as stressed by the CJEU in *Prigge*, that measures which aim at avoiding aeronautical accidents by monitoring pilots' aptitude and their physical capabilities with the objective of ensuring that human failure does not cause accidents, are, beyond doubt, to be regarded as measures of a nature that is meant to ensure public security within the meaning of Art. 2 No. 5.[1690] As regards the age limits laid down in a collective agreement, being the result of collective bargaining, strictly speaking they do not constitute 'measures laid

1686 Rt. 2012 s. 219 (*CHC*), para. 71.

1687 see to the justification requirements of Art. 2 No. 5 already chap. 10.3.1.

1688 C-447/09 (*Prigge*), para. 56 referring in this regard to C-341/09 (*Petersen*), para. 60; agreeing *Wachter*, Gustav (2012), Piloten: Mit 60 Jahren ist noch nicht Schluss, in: Altersdiskriminierung, Wachter, Gustav (ed.), pp. 149-157, p. 152; see generally chap. 10.3.1 above.

1689 see to this aspect, C-447/09 (*Prigge*), para. 57.

1690 C-447/09 (*Prigge*), para. 58.

down by national law', as stipulated by Art. 2 No. 5.[1691] Neither Art. 4 No. 1 nor Art. 6 No. 1 use such a restrictive terminology and rather refer to any specific legal instrument.[1692] Moreover, it has to be generally considered that social partners are not bodies that are governed by public law.[1693]

AG *Villalon* stressed e.g. in *Prigge* that the wording of Art. 2 No. 5 may be interpreted to the extent that measures that may result in a derogation from the Directive must, in any event, at least originate from a public authority.[1694] In view of this requirement, measures such as the age limit for pilots adopted by social partners, acting, in principle, independently, and laid down in a collective agreement, would not comply with the requirements stipulated in Art. 2 No. 5.[1695] According to *Villalon*'s understanding, the reference in Art. 2 No. 5 to the fact that the measure in question has to be 'necessary' to achieve the aim being pursued does not only refer to the proportionality examination of the measure in question, but also implies the essential nature that the measure must have to achieve this purpose.[1696] Given the provision's character as an exception to the prohibition against age discrimination, the provision may not simply refer to any measures that are merely instrumental in contributing to the aim of public safety or public health, but must rather refer to provisions that are especially established for such purposes. The power to take decisions e.g. concerning public security or public health, belongs inherently, by its very nature, to public authorities and thus falls basically outside the realm of collective bargaining, so his argumentation goes.[1697] Therefore, *Villalon* stresses that matters addressed by Art. 2 No. 5 may not be left to the free choice of the collective bargaining parties, so that they, in consequence, fall outside the legitimate field of intervention of the social partners.[1698] According to his point of view, the objectives set out in Art. 2 No. 5 demand action that is virtually uniform and that, in consequence, is inconsistent with collective bargaining which, according to *Villalon*, 'by definition, results in uneven regulation'.[1699] In light of these aspects, *Villalon* finally concludes that Art. 2 No. 5 may not be referred to as a justification provision for rules in collective agreements such as mandatory retirement for pilots set at the age of 60 for the purpose of ensuring air safety.[1700]

1691 see in general to this justification provision chap. 10.3.1.

1692 ibid.

1693 see C-447/09 (*Prigge*), para. 60, 61 referring in this context to Art. 3 No. 10 Dir. 96/71/EC of the European Parliament and of the Council of 16 December 1996 concerning the posting of workers in the framework of the provision of services (OJ 1997 L 18, p. 1) and C-341/05 (*Laval un Partneri*), para. 84; see also BAG, Urteil vom 15. Februar 2012 – 7 AZR 946/07 –, juris, para. 28.

1694 so the argumentation of AG *Villalón* in C-447/09 (*Prigge*), para. 51.

1695 ibid.

1696 ibid., para. 52 f.

1697 ibid., para. 53.

1698 ibid., para. 53.

1699 ibid., para. 53.

1700 ibid., para. 54; in this regard also *Wachter* (2012), p. 153.

In view of these aspects and the provision's wording, proponents of a strict understanding therefore argue that provisions in collective agreements cannot be subsumed under this provision.[1701] However, mandatory retirement age limits that are adopted by way of collective agreements may nevertheless be regarded as a measure provided for by national law, as required in Art. 2 No. 5.[1702] According to a wider understanding of Art. 2 No. 5 and its formulation, 'measures laid down by national law' may also be interpreted to the extent that member states may authorise (through rules to that effect) social partners to adopt measures, within the meaning of Art. 2 No. 5, in areas such as public security or the protection of health, as referred to in that provision, that fall within collective agreements, provided that these rules of authorisation are sufficiently precise so as to ensure that those measures fulfil the requirements stipulated by Art. 2 No. 5.[1703] This wider understanding is also advocated in this thesis, provided that a strict proportionality assessment is also applied in the case of Art. 2 No. 5.

If one thus argues that the social partners may be authorised to lay down such measures such as the mandatory age limits, which limits the pilots' exercise of their profession to the age of 60 or 65, respectively, the measure needs to pass as a further step a necessity examination, as explicitly stipulated by Art. 2 No. 5. This entails assessing whether alternative, less harmful measures to the mandatory retirement age limit are available that likewise ensure the aim of air safety. Here it has to be kept in mind that proponents of a stricter understanding, who would not deny an applicability of Art. 2 No. 5 but rather examine the mandatory retirement provsion under Art. 4 No. 1 and Art. 6 No. 1, would also ultimately need to assess the necessity of the age limit. The reason for this is that a necessity evaluation constitutes an inherent part of all these provisions. In terms of assessing the age limit's necessity, it therefore makes no difference as to which of the provisions is applied.

1701 similar as regards the situation in *Prigge Temming/Rothermund* (2010), p. 110ff.; see also discussion in *Lüderitz* (2005), p. 55; arguing for a strict understanding also *Kaiser* (2012), p. 191.

1702 see C-447/09 (*Prigge*), para. 59; see also AG *Villalón* in: C-447/09 (*Prigge*), para. 51; see to this question also *Schlachter* (2014), p. 30.

1703 C-447/09 (*Prigge*), para. 61.

15.3.3.2.1 Necessity

15.3.3.2.1.1 Medical and psychological testing as an alternative to mandatory retirement

The legitimacy of operating with age as the decisive proxy depends decisively on whether alternatives (a necessity assessment) are available that might replace the age limit and thus age as the crucial factor. This entails examining whether other options are available to achieve and guarantee the appropriate health and safety protections.[1704] Instead of using compulsory retirement, pilots could, for example, be subject to regular individual assessments that increase in frequency after a certain age.[1705] However, increasing medical scrutiny with age has been met with doubt, as the medical literature is at present without documentation that shorter intervals of control might detect any of the health deteriorations relevant for the pilot profession more efficiently or that assessments that are more frequent are better at predicting sudden onset pathologies.[1706] Moreover, the central counterargument that has been brought forward by critics – the previously mentioned third hypothesis – is that the hazard for life and health might not be totally excluded and that the remaining risk factor is still too high to rely on this as a true alternative to mandatory retirement, as it is not similarly efficient in safeguarding the aim of air safety.[1707] Mandatory retirement for pilots is, according to this reasoning, necessary, as an element of risk of sudden capability deficiency remains.[1708] Consequently, according to the critics, referring generally to age as a GOR in the sense of Art. 4 No. 1 Dir. 2000/78/EC by making use of age limits instead of opening up for individual assessments is legitimate in view of the potential hazards for the life and limb of others.[1709] However, it has to be taken into consideration that individual assessments are an integral part of the pilot profession. This is, for example, explicitly required in the international regulations. Pilots who might experience age-related declines in health and cognitive function are therefore already likely to be screened

---

1704 *Fredman* (2003), p. 52.
1705 ibid.; critical *Wilkening* (2002), p. 200 f.
1706 *Wilkening* (2002), p. 201.
1707 similar *Lüderitz* (2005), p. 85, 86.
1708 ibid.; in this regard also *Groß* (2010), p. 123 with further references.
1709 similar *Lüderitz* (2005), p. 85, 86.

out by the respective medical examination and medical certification processes, so that only the more physically and mentally fit remain in the workforce – the so-called healthy worker effect.[1710] As emphasised by *Li* et al., the overwhelming majority of nondisqualifying medical conditions are minor health problems that are unlikely to have any discernible impact on the pilot's safety performance.[1711] With regard to the relationship between ageing and safety performance, one may, in addition, take into consideration that this may be further attenuated by the so-called safe worker effect.[1712] This means that those pilots who continue to fly at advanced ages in addition to being healthy are also likely to have maintained a favourable safety record.[1713] It has thus to be borne in mind that those pilots with an excess risk of crash involvement and violations are more likely to end their careers at younger ages due to disabling injuries and licence terminations than their counterparts are: their healthy and safe colleagues.[1714]

15.3.3.2.1.2 Engagement of '60+' pilots in a multi-person cockpit crew as an alternative to mandatory retirement

Even if one were still – despite the scientific findings – to place the emphasis on a remaining risk factor, one could argue that pilots above a certain age should only be allowed to fly in multi-person cockpit crews to minimise the risk of age-related sudden and incapacitating medical conditions as far as possible. A further alternative to an absolute age limit set at the age of 60 might therefore be the engagement of '60+' pilots in a multi-person cockpit crew, as is provided for in international regulations and on the EU level.[1715] Provided that two conditions are fulfilled (first, that the older pilot – being above the age of 60 – can prove via health checks, medical certification etc. that he is still physically and mentally capable in exercising his profession and second, that he will only be engaged as a

1710 ee to this aspect *Haldorsen* et al. (2002), p. 591; *Li* et.al. (2003), p. 878.

1711 *Li* et.al. (2003), p. 878.

1712 ibid.; already *Mohler* stresses that the older and experienced pilots are the safer pilots, see *Mohler* (1981), p. 451 f.

1713 *Li* et.al. (2003), p. 878; *Wilkening* (2002), p. 201.

1714 *Li* et.al. (2003), p. 878; *Wilkening* (2002), p. 198; see already *Mohler* (1981), p. 452.

1715 see in detail to the international legal framework 15.2.1.

part of such a multi-pilot crew, where the other pilots are younger than 60), then nothing militates against an engagement of pilots above the age of 60. As long as these requirements are met, then the aim of air safety of sufficiently protecting and even engaging the older pilots beyond the age of 65 might be justifiable. Even if not recommended, it has to be kept in mind that the international regulations explicitly allow for such an option, as long as the flight is only operated over national territory.[1716]

When strictly applied, even the restrictions above the age of 60 might lack a certain argumentative coherence: if current scientific medical findings, in principle, allow for the engagement of the pilot at least until the age of 65, the question might then be raised as to whether the restrictions concerning the engagement of pilots above the age of 60 might even legitimately be based on air safety aspects.[1717] It has to be kept in mind that such provisions also apply to two-pilot cockpit settings (cockpit crews consisting of just two pilots), provided that one of the pilots is below 60 years of age in cases where the other pilot is already older than 60. Arguing that pilots above the age of 60 constitute a safety risk then lacks consistency. The reason for this is if merely two pilots are in the cockpit and one of them should suddenly be unable to work, the entire responsibility for the passengers, crew members and the flight would need to be borne by the remaining pilot. As no such rule exists that it is always the eldest pilot who will fail, the age limit may hardly be justified by primarily referring to security aspects.[1718] Rather, the provision's initial point is that in the case of an emergency, each of the pilots – be it the younger or the older pilot – could bear full responsibility.[1719] Both age limits therefore stand argumentatively on shaky ground. One might perhaps then raise a further question: if medical findings will even allow for raising *de lege ferenda* the age limit of 65 years, for example in line with the general applicable pension age in Germany, stepwise up to the age of 67.[1720] However, if one state should open up for also allowing pilots beyond the age of 65 to fly under certain restrictions, the above-mentioned cross-border problematic would still need to be solved.

1716 see. Annex I, Amendment 167 to the Chicago Convention.
1717 *Temming/Rothermund* (2010), p. 110ff.
1718 ibid.
1719 ibid.
1720 ibid.; see as regards *de lege ferenda* considerations chap. 16.3.4.

The question arises as to whether these aspects are also an issue as regards other mandatory retirement provisions such as for example for flight attendants or air traffic controllers. While as regards job demands and risk potential the profession of air traffic controllers might be comparable to the situation of pilots, the situation as regards flight attendants is of a different character. In contrast to the cockpit crew, age does not actually constitute a GOR in the case of flight attendants.[1721] This is due to the fact that flight attendants are confronted with job-related physical burdens to a lesser extent.[1722] Moreover, the risk from sudden performance deterioration is not as high.[1723] The profession of a flight attendant may be exercised by employees of any age group, as it is not characterised by an occupational requirement related to age.[1724] As rightly stressed by *Lüderitz* as regards the BFOQ defence, when assessing the age limit's proportionality, the higher the job-related safety hazard for third persons, the stricter the justification test that has to be applied.[1725] This is particularly true for the necessity test, where mandatory retirement might only be justified in cases where alternative measures such as individual health tests are unavailable or are related to disproportionate effort. For most of the professions where risks for third parties might occur, these risks might be avoided by making use of individual health and capability tests and options to prolong the employment relationship instead of making use of absolute mandatory retirement provisions.[1726] Due to the risks for third parties, the respective employee would have to prove his capabilities after having passed a certain age.[1727] Provided that the risk for third persons might then be excluded after e.g. a health and capability assessment, nothing might militate against extending the employment contract.[1728] In general, even if a member of the cabin crew should fail in exercising his work due to a sudden age-related capability decline during a flight, the potential hazard caused by this for the life and limb of third persons, in contrast to the case of cockpit-crew members, is more of a theoretical rather than a practical nature.[1729] This has also been emphasised through the scenario where if one cabin-crew member should be incapacitated, the other members of the cabin crew might compensate for the loss.[1730] A safety risk for the public that is above average is thus not present.[1731] In consequence, there is no need to operate with mandatory retirement in the case of cabin-crew members to differentiate between those employees who are capable of exercising their work and those whose capabilities might be limited, and in doing so, deprive the last group from exercising their profession.[1732] Interestingly enough – as stressed by the German BAG – the employer's interests in the young appearance of the cabin

---

1721 see to this example also *Lüderitz* (2005), p. 86; *Groß* (2010), p. 124; see also BAG, Urteil vom 31. Juli 2002 – 7 AZR 140/01 –, BAGE 102, 65-73, para. 27ff.; similar *Falke* (2007), 8, para. 47.

1722 similar *Lüderitz* (2005), p. 86.

1723 ibid.

1724 see to this aspect also *Groß* (2010), p. 124.

1725 similar *Lüderitz* (2005), p. 86.

1726 ibid.

1727 ibid.

1728 ibid.

1729 This as similarly been stressed by the CJEU in C-109/09 (*Kumpan*), Judgement of the Court of 10 March 2011, ECR 2011, I-01309, para. 21, 22.

1730 see to this aspect with further references *Groß* (2010), p. 124.

1731 ibid.

1732 ibid.

crew is, moreover, not capable of justifying mandatory retirement for cabin-crew members.[1733] Thus, mandatory retirement for members of the cabin crew may not be justified under reference to Art. 4 No. 1 Dir. 2000/78/EC.[1734]

15.3.3.2.2 Intermediate conclusion

To conclude, in view of the aim of ensuring air safety, an age limit of 60 years does not constitute a necessary measure provided that regular health tests combined with the restriction to be allowed to fly above the age of 60 only with co-pilots that are younger than 60 are likewise available. Based upon medical arguments, an absolute mandatory retirement age for pilots set at the age of 60 cannot be justified.[1735] However, if these requirements should not be fulfilled, such as for example in flights with a single pilot, a mandatory retirement age limit would still be necessary. In any case, the differentiation according to chronological age as a proxy for mental and physical fitness has to be applied by the employer in a consistent manner. Operating for example with a mandatory retirement age for cabin-crew members set at the age of 55, while at the same allowing cockpit-crew members to fly until the age of 60 is not consistent.[1736]

Mandatory retirement age limits set at the age of 60 cannot be regarded as necessary for public security and the protection of health in the sense of Art. 2 No. 5, given the fact that relevant international and European regulations fix that age limit at a higher age; namely, at the age of 65.[1737] The higher age limit set at the age of 65 corresponds to the European and international standard and thus constitutes a necessary measure.[1738]

1733 BAG v. 31.7.2002- 7 AZR 140/01, II 3.

1734 in this regard also e.g. *Groß* (2010), p. 124; whether e.g. the mandatory retirement age of 68 for *flugmedizinische Sachverständige* (aero-medical appraisers) constitutes a GOR has been left open by Niedersächsisches Oberverwaltungsgericht (OVG), who regarded the age limit as proportional, see OVG Lüneburg, Beschluss vom 13. September 2006 – 12 ME 275/06 –, juris.

1735 see to this conclusion also *Mohler* (1981), p. 450, 452.

1736 see examples given at *Beitze*, Editha (2009), in: Kommentar zum AGG, Hey, Thomas (edt.), § 8, para. 39, p. 184 f.

1737 see in this regard the conclusion CJEU C-447/09 (*Prigge*), para. 63, 64, 83; Rt. 2012 s. 219 (*CHC*), para. 52; see also BAG, Urteil vom 15. Februar 2012 – 7 AZR 946/07 –, juris, para. 29.

1738 see to the proportionality of the age limit chap. 15.3.3.5.

15.3.3.3 Justification according to Art. 4 No. 1 Dir. 2000/78/EC

However, the age limit for pilots set at the age of 60 or 65 might be justified according to Art. 4 No. 1 Dir. 2000/78/EC. After having identified the aim of ensuring air safety as a legitimate aim, as a further step, age therefore has to be examined in terms of whether age is a necessary GOR in the sense of Art. 4 No. 1 for the profession of pilots.[1739] The key question in this regard is whether age constitutes a proxy for safety-related job demands that are inherent to the profession of pilots. Even if it is generally rather questionable to use age as a proxy for characteristics such as e.g. incapacity or ill health, there may nevertheless be circumstances where an assessment of the individual employee is not feasible and where the employee's age may in some way be linked to the possession of a GOR or a characteristic that is of relevance for the particular position in question.[1740] One example in this regard is the mandatory retirement of pilots that might be deemed necessary and proportionate to achieve the legitimate objective of protecting air safety, provided that there is sufficient evidence of a decline of capabilities (e.g. eyesight and reaction-level deterioration with age) that are pivotal for the exercise of the profession as a pilot and provided that it is impossible to conduct individual tests to determine which pilots are negatively affected by the ageing process.[1741] Inherent to this assessment is to demonstrate that mandatory retirement for pilots is clearly necessary to achieve the aim of air safety or as *O'Cinneide* put it, 'even a pressing legitimate aim such as public safety cannot justify the sweeping use of age limits where individual assessment is possible'.[1742] As analysed as regards Art. 2 No. 5, the necessity of a 60-year age limit has to be denied, while the 65-year age limit may be considered necessary to ensure the aim of air safety.

That the age-limit necessity and the impossibility of conducting individual assessments has to be proven even in cases where public safety is concerned – as in the case of flight engineers – has e.g. also been emphasised by the US Supreme Court.[1743] It has to be noted that the scope of the ADEA's general prohibition against age discrimination is not generally provided in an unlimited

---

1739 see in general to this justification provision, chap. 10.3.2.

1740 *O'Cinneide* (2005), p. 34 f.

1741 similar *O'Cinneide* (2005), p. 35; see also *Over* (2009), pp. 215-217; *Temming/ Rothermund* (2010), p. 61 f., 74 f.

1742 *O'Cinneide* (2005), p. 35.

1743 ibid., p. 35; see US Supreme Court, Western Air Lines v. Criswell, 472 U.S. 400 (1985).

sense. Quite the contrary, some professions such as fire fighters or police officers are explicitly exempted from it.[1744] In addition, pilots in the USA are confronted with mandatory retirement.[1745] Interestingly enough, this professional category is not explicitly exempted from the ADEA's scope. The age limit for pilots is one of the few examples in the US, where it is referred to Art. 623 (f) (1) alt. 1 ADEA, according to which a differential treatment based on age may be justified provided that age is a BFOQ.[1746] This provision has, in principle, been interpreted narrowly and has so far only been recognised as a justification provision in cases that were directly related to the protection of public security.[1747] One example constitutes the case of *Western Airlines v. Criswell,*[1748] which concerned a mandatory age limit for pilots laid down in a federal administration regulation due to which persons serving as a pilot or co-pilot had to retire at the age of 60 (the so-called age-60 rule).[1749] The claimant, who was forced to retire due to this provision, applied after having reached the age limit for a job as a flight engineer, a position that in principle was not encompassed by the mandatory retirement regulation. However, the airline company also applied the 60-year age limit to its flight engineers, who were members of the cockpit crews, to retire at the age of 60. The employer argued that the age limit constituted a BFOQ that was reasonably necessary for the safe operation of the airline and thus for the safety of its passengers.[1750] What was decisive was the aspect that in cases where the pilots were unable to fly, which de facto only occurs in very rare cases, the flight engineer would be forced to fly the aircraft instead.[1751] The airline could finally not prove that age and the duties of a flight engineer might negatively impact the employer's safety interest.[1752] The criterion of age has not been recognised as a BFOQ defence.[1753] The judgement generally illustrates how narrowly the BFOQ defence is interpreted.[1754] Until 13 December 2007, the US – being an ICAO member state – limited its pilots operating under Title 14 of the Code of Federal Regulations (14 CFR) part 121 to the age 60. As the ICAO revised the maximum age for certain pilots engaged in international operations from 60 to 65, the US enacted the Fair Treatment for Experienced Pilots Act (the

---

1744 see in detail *Groß* (2010), p. 34.
1745 see in general *Meenan* (2005), p. 23 f.
1746 *Groß* (2010), p. 35; see for a general discussion of the BFOQ-defense, chap. 10.3.2 above; *Temming/Rothermund* (2010), p. 74 f.
1747 see for an overview *Groß* (2010), p. 35.
1748 see US Supreme Court, Western Air Lines v. Criswell, 472 U.S. 400 (1985), available at: https://supreme.justia.com/cases/federal/us/472/400/ (last accessed: 17.12.2014).
1749 see to the historical background of the 'age-60 rule', *Wilkening*, Robin (2002), The age 60 rule: age discrimination in commerical aviation, Aviation, space, and environmental medicine 2002, Vol. 73 No. 73, pp. 194-202, p. 194ff.
1750 US Supreme Court, Western Air Lines v. Criswell, 472 U.S. 400 (1985).
1751 *Rasnic*, Carol D./*Resch*, Reinhard (2010/2011), Altersdiskriminierung nach amerikanischem Recht, Zeitschrift für Ausländisches und Internationales Arbeits- und Sozialrecht (ZIAS), 2010 Issue 3, Vol. 24/25, pp. 274-292, p. 280 f.
1752 ibid.
1753 ibid.
1754 ibid.

age-65 law), according to which pilots are in principle allowed to continue working until the age of 65.[1755] Thus, in the US *de lege lata* pilots may continue until the age of 65, as specified in the Act.

15.3.3.4 Justification according to Art. 6 No. 1 Dir. 2000/78/EC

As the examined age limits for pilots (set at the age of 60 or 65) are based on the legitimate aim of guaranteeing air traffic safety,[1756] it has to be examined whether such an objective constitutes a legitimate aim within the meaning of Art. 6 No. 1 Dir. 2000/78/EC.[1757] Some have argued that in principle, any aspect of public interest may be regarded as a legitimate social-policy objective.[1758] Due to this reasoning, such objectives also encompass the protection of citizens against hazards of life and health.[1759] However, as stressed by the CJEU in its settled case law, aims that are considered as legitimate in the sense of this justification provision have to be social-policy objectives, such as those related to employment policy, the labour market or vocational training.[1760] In accordance with such a narrow interpretation, the aim of ensuring air safety cannot be subsumed under the category of social-policy objectives, as referred to by Art. 6 No. 1.[1761] Relying on Art. 6 No. 1 as a justification provision is thus not possible.[1762]

1755 see Fair Treatment for Experienced Pilots Act, 49 U.S.C: section 44729(g)(2) recorded as Public Law 110, 135 of December 13, 2007, available at: http://www.gpo.gov/fdsys/pkg/PLAW-110publ135/pdf/PLAW-110publ135.pdf (last accessed: 17.12.2014).

1756 see in this regard C-447/09 (*Prigge*), para. 51, 68, 78.

1757 C-447/09 (*Prigge*), para. 79.

1758 see in this regard *Mohr* (2013), p. 40 building his argumentation upon jurisdiction of the BVerfG and the BAG by referring to BVerfG 12 1, 1982 – 2 BvR 113/81, BVerfGE 59, 216, 229; BVerfG 12.051992 – 2BvR 470/90, BVerfGE 86, 90, 108; BAG 22.1.2009 – 8AZR 906/07, NZA 2009, 945, para. 45ff.

1759 see in this regard *Mohr* (2013), p. 40 referring to Maunz/Dürig/DiFabio, Grundgesetz, 65. Ergänzungslieferung 2012, Art. 2, para. 61.

1760 C-447/09 (*Prigge*), para. 81 referring to C-388/07 (*Age Concern*), para. 46, C-88/08 (*Hütter*), para. 41.

1761 see in this regard C-447/09 (*Prigge*), para. 82.

1762 similar as regards *Prigge Temming/Rothermund* (2010), p. 110ff.; *Wachter* (2012), p. 155 similar also as regards mandatory retirement for cabin crew members: *Groß* (2010), p. 124; arguing on the contrary pro a justification according to Art. 6 No. 1 Dir. 2000/78/EC: ArbG Frankfurt, Urteil vom

However, it has been brought forward that – given the fact that the mandatory retirement provision for pilots is laid down in a collective agreement – the protection of autonomy in collective bargaining and the preservation of scope for the operation of collective bargaining might constitute a legitimate aim of social policy within the meaning of Art. 6 No. 1 Dir. 2000/78/EC.[1763] However, if one follows this line of argumentation, then any measure, such as compulsory retirement provisions for pilots that are the result of a collective bargaining process, may thus be regarded as being built upon the general social-policy objective of preserving a certain degree of scope for collective bargaining for the social partners. One might, in particular, criticise that this involves the risk that such a generalised aim might per se be allocated to any measure that is based on a collective agreement, which would easier open up for a justification according to Art. 6 No. 1, without the necessity of having to prove a concrete relationship between the aim and the age limit in question. In a way, this would open up for recognising a legitimate aim as a social-policy objective 'through the back door' and might make any thorough assessment of potential social-policy objectives obsolete. In any case, even if one were to recognise a social-policy objective in the sense of Art. 6 No. 1, this does not mean, as rightly stressed by Advocate *Villalon* in *Prigge*, that

> … the social partners cannot operate with absolute freedom, since, once the legitimacy of the objective which opens the way for Article 6(1) to apply has been established, the measure is still subject to the test of proportionality imposed by this provision. This means that, in the case of the profession of pilot, the concept of an age-band below the age of 65 which can be the subject of collective bargaining is not, in principle, incompatible with Directive 2000/78, provided, of course, that it satisfies a proportionality test.[1764]

---

14. März 2007 – 6 Ca 7405/06 –, juris, para. 29ff., which examines the age limits on the basis of § 10 AGG and thus implicit by means of Art. 6 No. 1 Dir. 2000/78/EG.

1763 AG *Villalón* in: C-447/09 (*Prigge*), para. 77 (b), para. 84 f.; In this regard also Rt-2012-219 (*CHC-saken*), para. 65.

1764 AG *Villalón*, in: C-447/09 (*Prigge*), para. 85, see also para. 91.

15.3.3.5 Proportionality test: Balancing of interests

Even though the age limit of 60 years has not been considered as necessary, which would make any further proportionality stricto sensu assessment superfluous, it shall nevertheless be used to shed light on the balancing of interests involved here. This is important for two reasons: first, if one regards the higher age limit of 65 as necessary, the next step would thus be a proportionality analysis in the narrow sense. Second, mandatory retirement for pilots manifested in collective agreements primarily affects three fundamental rights of the CFREU: on the one side, the employee's right not to be discriminated against on the grounds of age (Art. 21 No. 1) and his right to work (Art. 15 No. 1), and on the other side, the right of the social partners to collective bargaining (Art. 28). As stipulated in Art. 52 No. 1 CFREU, any limitations of the Charter's basic rights have to be in accordance with the principle of proportionality.

Common to the Norwegian and German mandatory retirement age limits for pilots is that by manifesting compulsory retirement, social partners exclude pilots above the age of 60 from exercising their profession as a pilot with the key aim of ensuring air safety by avoiding an age-based capability decline. In order for the age limit to be proportional, a significant decrease in capability at the age of 60 (or 65) has to be sufficiently proven.[1765] In general, as already ascertained the scientific substantiation of an age-related capability decline in pilots has to be met with criticism. At this point, it is decisive as to how rigorously the capability decline has to be proven.[1766] It has to be kept in mind that mere generalisations do not constitute sufficient evidence that the chosen means are suitable for achieving the aim in question.[1767] By contrast, both the German BAG and BVerfG stressed in their justification analyses that it is sufficient that a capability decline in pilots corresponds to the general experience of life (*allgemeine Lebenserfahrung*).[1768] Such generalised assumptions may,

---

1765 *Kaiser* (2012), p. 193.

1766 ibid., p. 193.

1767 see to this aspect C-388/07 (*Age Concern*), para. 51, see already in general chap. 10.3.5 above.

1768 see BAG, Urteil vom 21. Juli 2004 – 7 AZR 589/03 –, juris, para. 24; BAG, Urteil vom 27. November 2002 – 7 AZR 655/01 –, juris, para. 37 f.; BVerfG, Nichtannahmebeschluss vom 25. November 2004 – 1 BvR 2459/04 –, juris, (*Altersgrenze für Piloten*), para. 19.

however, after the implementation of Dir. 2000/78/EC and the coming into force of the prohibition against age discrimination, no longer be maintained.[1769] Given a strict proportionality assessment, the situation of the individual pilot has to be considered, and either individual capability assessments have to be conducted or recent scientific findings have to be consulted.[1770] In this context, it is interesting to know that the age limit that was subject to the *Prigge* case, for instance, was based on a collective agreement from 1956.[1771] This concerns the question as to what the parameters are that are used by the social partners when determining mandatory retirement for pilots. In essence, in terms of utilising collective bargaining rights, the underlying key question is how much 'legislative' leeway is granted to the social partners in determining mandatory retirement in cases where mandatory retirement based on the legitimate aim of air safety and securing the health and life of human beings is concerned.[1772]

On the one hand, the pilot is strongly affected by the age limit in terms of his right to work and his right not to be discriminated against on the grounds of age. On the other hand, the employer is responsible for the air safety and thus pursues an objective that is of a public interest nature.[1773] The strong intervention in the employee's rights requires that the social partners establish an explicit relationship to the profession or sector, which is generally complied with, provided that a reference is made to the empirical and medical data available for this aviation sector.[1774] Given the research findings on ageing and crash involvement, maintaining an absolute 60-year age limit without, at the same time, providing for alternatives, may hardly be justified. However, the question arises as to whether the social partners, as a consequence, have to raise the age limit to the maximum of 65 years, which is basically permitted in line with the international requirements.[1775] Again, this is about how much leeway is granted to the social partners in setting the age limit. The BAG for example denies

1769 *Kaiser* (2012), p. 193.

1770 see similar in general *Brors* (2008), § 8, para. 30 and elaborately *Temming* (20008), p. 614 f.

1771 This aspect has been stressed by *Kaiser* (2012), p. 193.

1772 see to the relationship of protection against discrimination and the right to collective bargaining in general *Mohr* (2013), p. 43.

1773 *Kaiser* (2012), p. 194.

1774 ibid., p. 194.

1775 similar *Temming* (2008), p. 615; *Kaiser* (2012), p. 194.

such an obligation by the social partners and rather emphasises their freedom in terms of collective bargaining (*Tarifautonomie*).[1776] The CJEU, interestingly enough, did not address the issue of how much leeway should be given to the social partners in determining the age limit.[1777] The key question in a proportionality assessment is whether the social partners go beyond the limits of their freedom in collective bargaining at the expense of the employee's right not to be discriminated against on the grounds of age.[1778] It thus has to be assessed after a balancing of interests has taken place as to whether an age limit of 60 (or 65, respectively) constitutes an unproportional intervention in the employee's rights.[1779] In general, one might argue that the mandatory retirement provision is already the result of a balancing of interests; namely, that of employer and employees, insofar as the age limit might be considered as proportional. Against this argument, it has to be brought forward that the age limit is the result of a generalised assumption rather than of considering the individual's interests. However, in this regard, it has to be kept in mind that a pilot, as with any other employee, shall be protected in terms of his right to work and his individual self-esteem. However, in contrast to general age limits, the pilot's interests have to be weighed up against a considerable public interest; namely, that of ensuring air safety. This encompasses security interests as regards air traffic in general and especially the interests of protecting the life and limb of third persons. The safety interests of employers, passengers and any other potentially affected human beings have to be weighed up against the pilot's interests in continuing his working life and exercising his right to work. Public safety thereby constitutes the overriding interest. The airline must be able to conduct its flights with the highest possible degree of safety. The employee's right to work and freedom to exercise the profession is basically sufficiently accounted for if

---

1776 see reference for the premilimary ruling Prigge in BAG, EuGH-Vorlage vom 17. Juni 2009 – 7 AZR 112/08 (A) –, BAGE 131, 113-144, para. 18ff; see to this aspect in detail *Kaiser* (2012), p. 194; critical to use the term '*Tarifautonomie'* in an analysis of Art. 28 CFREU and rather advocating the use of 'broad discretion' of the social partners: *Forst*, Gerrit (2012), Kollektivvertragsfreiheit versus Verbot der Altersdiskriminierung, EuZA 2012/5, pp. 225-235, p. 227.

1777 see to this aspect *Schlachter* (2014), p. 31; also the *Høyesterett* did not go into this question, see Rt. 2012 s. 219 (*CHC*), para. 65.

1778 *Kaiser* (2012), p. 194.

1779 similar ibid., p. 194.

the social partners base the risk of capability decline in their assessment on scientifically reliable research findings that also are reflected in the international regulations.[1780] By contrast, any generalised assumptions about the employee's capability do not incorporate the employee's interests.[1781] The previous argumentation of e.g. the BAG, referring in this regard to general experience in life, can thus no longer be maintained.[1782] As regards the remaining scope in which the social partners may determine the age limit – that is, in the age range of 60 to 65 years of age –, some have argued that the social partners in view of their European and constitutional law guaranteed margin of discretion are allowed to choose an age limit at the lower end of this range in order to ensure air safety.[1783] According to this view, operating with an age limit of 60 would be legitimate.[1784] Prescribing alternative measures to an age limit such as individual capability assessments would constitute an unproportional intervention into the collective bargaining rights of the social partners, according to the argument.[1785] However, operating with an absolute mandatory retirement age that is considerably below the internationally applicable standard and not providing alternative measures is, on the other hand, a measure that is very punitive for the individual employee.[1786] In this balancing of interests, it has to be kept in mind that the principle of non-discrimination on the grounds of age now takes a sufficiently secure enough position in EU law to take priority over the aspect of collective bargaining in this regard.[1787] Furthermore, the pilot's right to work is affected by terminating the employment relationship via compulsory retirement.[1788] In general, it is about balancing the right of collective bargaining as proclaimed in Art. 28 CFREU versus the right not to be discriminated against on the grounds of age as laid down in Art. 21 No. 1 CFREU and the right to work in Art. 15 No. 1 CFREU. As repeatedly clarified by the CJEU, in this regard, the right of collective bargaining goes only as far as, and as long as it complies with EU law; that is, in this example, Dir. 2000/78/EC and the

---

1780 *Kaiser* (2012), p. 195.
1781 ibid., p. 195.
1782 ibid., p. 195.
1783 ibid., p. 195 referring in this regard to BAG 17.6.2009, para. 24.
1784 ibid., p. 195, 197.
1785 ibid., p. 195.
1786 AG *Villalón*, in: C-447/09 (*Prigge*), para. 92.
1787 ibid., para. 92.
1788 ibid., para. 92; agreeing also *Temming* (2012), p. 213 f.; *Wachter* (2012), p. 156.

prohibition against age discrimination as concretised therein.[1789] Thus, Art. 28 CFREU has to step back beyond Art. 21 No. 1 CFREU.[1790] On behalf of the pilots, two fundamental rights are involved – the right not to be discriminated against on the grounds of age plus the right to work – that considerably outweigh the social bargaining rights of the social partners. The social partners' discretion in setting the mandatory retirement age limit is thus limited by the employee's rights. Rather, the age limit has to be set at the upper end of the age range – that is, closer to the age of 65 – in order to cope with the pilot's rights and the international standards. Otherwise, the age limit has to be considered as unproportional. In view of these aspects, one might therefore conclude that by terminating the employment contract at the age of 60, the respective collective agreements go beyond the operational margin that they, in principle, might enjoy.[1791] In consequence, absolute mandatory retirement provisions for pilots agreed upon in a process of collective bargaining and set at the age of 60 are not proportional and thus not justifiable.[1792]

15.4 Final conclusion

Pilots are a highly selected group and they have an exceptional position compared to other professions. As the occupational field of pilots is coined by a high degree of security risk for air safety that, even after assessments of the employee's capabilities, may not entirely be eliminated, the individual interest of the pilot in realising his occupational interests has to take a back seat compared to the public interest of ensuring air traffic safety, which outweighs the pilot's interests. Given that, the profession of pilot seems at first glance to be one of the last bastions where compulsory retirement age limits may be justifiably maintained. However, as taking a closer look at the scientific studies on the relationship between the pilots' age and their alleged capability decline and crash involvement

1789 see for further references C-447/09 (*Prigge*), para. 47ff.; this is also referred to by the *Høyesterett* in Rt. 2012 s. 219 (*CHC*), para. 49.

1790 in this regard also *Temming* (2012), p. 213; *Wachter* (2012), p. 156.

1791 in this regard also AG *Villalón* in: C-447/09 (*Prigge*), para. 93; critical to the judgement and rather stressing the social partners' margin of discretion: *Kaiser* (2012), p. 197: *Kaiser* regards mandatory retirement age limits for pilots set at the age of 60 as proportionate and justified, see p, 195, 197.

1792 similar ibid. under reference to Art. 6 No. 1 Dir. 2000/78/EC.

has demonstrated, age constitutes a rather poor indicator for the pilot's job performance. Operating with mandatory retirement to ensure air safety has thus no scientifically reliable underpinning. As long as no scientific data are available that claim the contrary, using the age limit of 60 rather than 65 is rather questionable. Or, in the words of *Wilkening*,

> Some 40 yr of scientific research refute the notion that the chronological age of 60 heralds a universal, inevitable, and precipitous decline in commercial airline pilots' physical health and mental proficiency, or even an age beyond which health and proficiency cannot be either measured or monitored. Some 40 yr of pilot performance data underscore the excellent safety record of older, more experienced pilots.[1793]

The mandatory age limit of 60 years for pilots in Norway and Germany, as it was subject to in the cases of *Prigge* and *CHC*, is not in conformity with Dir. 2000/78/EC and is, in particular, not justifiable in view of the internationally applicable higher age limit set at 65 years of age in the relevant international and EU regulations. Even conformity to a higher age limit for pilots – for example set at the age of 65 in line with the international requirements – with the prohibition against age discrimination may be viewed with scepticism. It is necessary thus to differentiate between two situations in this regard: first, the situation where the respective pilot, being above the age of 60, is working alone and second, where he is engaged as part of a multi-pilot crew. In the first example, operating with mandatory retirement is necessary and proportional in the strict sense, as in case this pilot should unexpectedly fail to exercise his job, alternative measures that contribute similarly to effectively safeguard air safety are not available. However, as long as there is no scientific evidence that underpins the maintenance of an absolute 60-year age limit for pilots, abolishing such compulsory retirement in favour of alternative measures may only contribute to enhancing air safety, as employers will be able to continue utilising the advanced skills and experience of the older healthy pilots.[1794]

As regards the second situation – engagement of a '60+' pilot in a multi-pilot crew –, an age limit may not be justified to ensure the aim of air safety as long as the pilot has successfully passed the relevant health and capability tests and as long as the other cockpit members are under the

---

1793 *Wilkening* (2002), p. 201.

1794 see conclusion by *Mohler* (1981), p. 452.

age of 60. However, as rightly argued by *Temming* and *Rothermund*, the requirement that the co-members also have to be younger than 60 meets with doubt. As long as no medical findings are available that contradict an engagement of older pilots, mandatory retirement may hardly be justified in the multi-pilot constellation. *De lege ferenda* one might therefore even evaluate an increase of the age limit for pilots in multi-member situations.[1795] In sum, one may conclude that in professions where a high risk for other persons is involved and where no other measures than a mandatory retirement age are available to safeguard the aim of protecting the life and health of others, mandatory retirement provisions might be justifiable, such as in the case of single-pilot assignments.

1795 see to *de lege ferenda* evaluations chap. 16.3.4.

Part IV

16 De lege ferenda considerations

16.1 Introduction

De lege lata it may be ascertained that several of the existing mandatory retirement provisions, if viewed in light of the prohibition against age discrimination and following a rigorous proportionality analysis, may hardly be justified. This finding implies that alternatives to the instrument of the compulsory termination of an employment contract upon having reached a certain age have to be considered. Finding the 'best' solution for the transition from work to retirement in terms of its conformity with the prohibition against age discrimination and the aim to take age equality seriously as a starting point, involves addressing several questions such as: how long are employees able and willing to work? What should the pathway from working life to retirement preferably look like? Should the mandatory retirement provisions for example be entirely abolished or should one keep mandatory retirement but offer solutions to postpone it? How should employment beyond compulsory retirement look like?[1796] Several solutions to create flexible pathways from working life to retirement might be possible. No matter what this pathway to retirement might ultimately look like, what is inherent in any of these alternatives is that those employees who are willing to extend their working life should be enabled to do so. It is beyond doubt that extending working life might not only serve the employee's interests but might also contribute to society by fighting the consequences of demographic change.[1797] Ultimately, it is high time that employment law also acknowledged that ageing as a mere process of decline has been unmasked as a myth. What is required instead of still

---

1796 see similar research challenges referred to by *Ilmarinen*, Juhani (2011), Research challenges for older workers, in: Older workers in a sustainable society, Ennals, Richards/Salomon, Robert H. (eds.), pp. 15-18, in particular p. 16.

1797 see already to the demographic change and recent pension reforms in Norway and Germany to tackle this challenge: chap. 1.4.

relying on absolute mandatory retirement age limits is to dignify the potential of older employees and the valuable contributions they can make.

16.2 General considerations

16.2.1 Enabling employees to extend their working life: Workability, employability and flexicurity

What is essential for any extension of working life is that the employees really feel physically and mentally able to carry on. Any extension of working life must therefore go hand in hand with providing the requirements to enable the older employee to postpone retirement.[1798] This, in turn, requires a holistic perspective that inter alia focuses on measures such as lifelong learning and/or health promotion that are applied throughout the whole work cycle. Three approaches thereby play a central role: first the workability approach, second the employability approach and finally the flexicurity approach.

Discussing alternatives to absolute age limits involves shedding light on measures that enable the employee to make full use of the opportunity to remain in working life. A key to this might be the application of the workability approach. This approach aims at improving the working situation of employees via proactive, preventive and holistic measures throughout their entire working life.[1799] In doing so, the employee's workability would be improved, which in turn may contribute to increased productivity and the retention of older workers in later life.[1800] The key focus of the approach rests on the individual employee and the dynamic relationship between work demands, on the one hand, and the employee's capacity to

---

1798 see in general for an overview *Swedish National Institute of Public Health* (2006), Healthy ageing, A challenge for Europe, p. 65ff.

1799 see in detail *Ilmarinen*, Juhani (2005), Towards a longer worklife!, Ageing and the quality of worklife in the European Union, Finnish Institute of Occupational Health; such as for an overview *Maltby*, Tony (2011), Extending working lives? Employability, work ability and better quality working lives, Social Policy & Society Vol. 10:3, pp. 299-308, p. 302.

1800 *Maltby* (2011), p. 302.

meet them on the other.[1801] Moreover, it encourages a cooperative relationship between employers and employees with the objective being to find a balance between work demands and employee capacities and to find mutually acceptable solutions to maintain this balance in the long run.[1802] Central to the concept is that it aims at encouraging employers to tailor work to the individuals as they age and similarly to improve their health, skills and/or knowledge that are of relevance for the job in question.[1803] According to Finish empirical studies – the approach was originally developed in Finland – applying the concept contributed significantly to improved quality of work, the employees felt able to extend their working career and seemed to have better quality retirements.[1804] Thus, they could provide benefits for the economy, the employer, the employee and the society as such.[1805] The approach's success may be seen as stemming from the fact that it considers a multitude of factors, how they interplay and how a balance might be built up between them. These are all aspects that play a central role when it comes to enabling an employee to function well in his job.[1806]

Ilmarinen illustrates the interplay of multiple factors by depicting a house with several floors – the so-called workability house model.[1807] The workability as such is the roof. It thus depends on the following four floors: located on the top or fourth floor are 'work, work community and leadership', followed by 'values, attitudes and motivation' on the third, 'competences', encompassing knowledge and skills on the second and finally, as its fundamental basis on the ground floor of the house, 'health and functional capacities'.[1808] Moreover, the 'house' is pictured in its environment, meaning that so-called non-work-based factors that have an impact on the employee's working performance and productivity are also considered. Family, relatives and friends, such as the society as a whole, are considered as external factors.[1809] When it comes to health and functional

1801 *Ilmarinen* (2005), p. 132ff.; *Paullin*, Cheryl/*Whetzel*, Deborah L. (2012), Rentention strategies and older workers, pp. 392-418, p. 399.
1802 *Paullin*/*Whetzel* (2012), p. 399.
1803 *Maltby* (2011), p. 302 who in turn refers to *Ilmarinen*, Juhani/*Tuomi*, K. (2004), 'Past present and future of workability', People and Work Research Reports, 65, 1–25 and *Ilmarinen* (2005).
1804 *Maltby* (2011) referring to *Ilmarinen* (2005).To scientifically measure current and predict future workability of the employee in question the concept uses the so-called the Work Ability index (WAI), see in detail *Ilmarinen*, Juhani (2007), The Workability Index (WAI), Occupational Medicine 2007, Vol. 57, Issue 2, p. 160.
1805 *Maltby* (2011), referring to *Ilmarinen* (2005).
1806 similar *Maltby* (2011), p. 302.
1807 *Ilmarinen* (2005), p. 132ff, p. 133 Figure 12; *Ilmarinen* (2011), p. 15.
1808 *Ilmarinen* (2011), p. 15.
1809 *Ilmarinen* (2005), p. 134; *Ilmarinen* (2011), p. 15.

capacities, for example 'age suitable' – e.g. ergonomic – workplaces and working conditions that are adapted to meet the health and safety needs of older employees play a role.[1810] With regard to the aspect of competence, the individual's cognitive capacities and the ability to learn new skills, which is affected by the differences in crystalline and fluid intelligence, come into play. On the third floor, the question is whether values, attitudes and motivation change with age and how these changes can be met. When it comes to work and management issues on the top floor, the question of flexibility becomes important. Here, flexible options have to be discussed such as decreasing the workload, in particular, with physically demanding work.[1811] Moreover, the possibilities of regulating one's own work, which involves addressing the question of what kind of autonomy is needed at work, have to be considered. Here, best practices in managing older workers have to be identified. Following a life course approach, the pivotal element in applying the workability concept is age or generation management.[1812] According to *Ilmarinen,* age management means that the employee's age and age-related factors have to be taken into account in daily work management, planning and organisation, so that every employee – irrespective of their age – may achieve personal and organisational targets healthily and safely.[1813]

As stressed by *Ilmarinen,* making working life better and thus enabling older employees to extend their working life by making use of the workability model is an indispensable prerequisite before reducing early retirement incentives and increasing retirement age.[1814] This necessary preliminary step will thus contribute to the fact that employees can, will and may work longer.

Taking into consideration the workability of employees, it has to start at an early stage in their working lives. It is a continuous process, which is important for the whole work cycle, from its very beginning to the end. Promoting workability and guaranteeing a good work–life balance encompasses creating the conditions that also enable older employees to have the real capacities to perform work, which in the end benefits both the employer as well as the individual employee. This necessarily also implies that the labour market situation really opens up for the participation of older workers. Sustainable employability and workability that follows a broad, preventive, proactive and holistic approach, enables the older employee to de facto make use of the opportunity to remain in working life and thus contributes to substantive age equality.[1815] What is crucial to

---

1810 similar *Meenan* (2007 a), p. 283.

1811 *Ilmarinen* (2011), p. 18.

1812 *Ilmarinen* (2005), p. 119, 120.

1813 *Ilmarinen* (2005), p. 120.

1814 *Ilmarinen* (2011), p. 18; The necessity to strengthen the employability of older employees in Norway has also been emphasised by the OECD in *OECD* (2013), p. 11.

1815 similar *Maltby* (2011), p. 300.

this are individual or tailor-made solutions rather than rigid age limits.[1816] The need for workers to stay fit and healthy and maintain their workability in the long run also constitutes a necessity with regard to the increasing pressure on social security systems.

Being aware of the demographic change, the EU dedicated the year 2012 to 'Active Ageing and Solidarity between the Generations'.[1817] The year was intended to raise awareness as regards the contribution that older people make to society, including the employment sphere. It aimed to encourage policymakers and relevant stakeholders at all levels to take action to create better opportunities for active ageing and strengthen solidarity between generations. Active ageing may, in short, be described as a 'process of optimizing opportunities for health, participation and security in order to enhance quality of life as people age'.[1818] At a societal level, active ageing should contribute to higher growth, lower dependency burdens and substantial cost savings in pensions and health.[1819] In doing so, active ageing policies may 'represent win–win strategies for people of all ages'.[1820]

The decision to extend or not to extend working life should, in principle, be a question of real and fair choice. As it depends on a multitude of individual, organisational, economic and societal factors, the prolongation might fit for some and not for others. The driving forces behind the political and legal debate on extending working life have to be critically examined and dismantled. Several questions arise here: first, for whom is the extension intended, second, how long should the extension period be,

---

1816 *Meenan* (2007 a), p. 282 f., who also refers in this regard to Ilmarinen, Juani (2001) Ageing Workers in Finland and in the European Union: their situation and the Promotion of Their Working Ability, Employability and Employment, Vol. 2, No. 4, Geneva Papers on Risk and Insurance, pp. 623-641; see also *European Commission*, Communication Increasing the employment of older workers and delaying the exit from the labour market, COM(2004) 146 final, p. 11.

1817 see http://europa.eu/ey2012/ey2012main.jsp?catId=971&langId=en (last accessed 17.12.2014); see also Council Declaration on the European Year for Active Ageing and Solidarity between Generations (2012): The Way Forward, 16592/12 SOC 948 SAN 289, available at: http://register.consilium.europa.eu/doc/srv?l=EN&f=ST%2017468%202012%20INIT (last accessed 17.12.2014).

1818 *World Health Organization* (2002), Active ageing, a policy framework, p. 12; see also COM(2002) 143 final, Europe's Response to World Ageing, Promoting Economic and Social Progress in an Ageing World: A Contribution of the European Commission to the Second World Assembly on Ageing, in particular p. 6.

1819 COM(2002) 143 final, p. 6 f.

1820 ibid., p. 6.

third, by what means does it take place, fourth, what is its underlying purpose and finally, in whose interests is the extension?[1821] Addressing these questions when discussing opportunities to extend older workers' working life implies that one should also be aware of the fact that extending working life might not only contribute to the realisation of age equality, but might also be at the employee's expense. From the employee's perspective, the central issue therefore is whether extending working life is possible[1822] and how a better and longer working life might be realisable. One has to – literally speaking – also be aware of the 'two sides of the coin': the older worker also has to be protected against 'exploitation', against working conditions that are not adapted to the particular needs of an ageing workforce. One has to take into further consideration the fact that under-pensioned groups may be 'forced' to remain in the labour market, despite health problems, for them to be able to afford a living in their old age and to secure pension entitlements, which might especially be the case for manual workers, ethnic minorities or women with an interrupted work career.[1823] Here again, an issue that might come into play is that of multiple discrimination.[1824] The prolongation of working life under precarious working conditions is not what is intended by taking age equality seriously. Otherwise, retirement as being (since *Bismarck*) 'the' achievement of the 20th century might be replaced by insecure employment and uncertain transitions in the 21st century.[1825] While so far the welfare state has assumed responsibility as regards protection against risks in old age, the future risk is that ageing might become an individual risk to an increasing extent.

1821 see questions raised by *Phillipson*, Chris (2011), Extending working life and redefining retirement: Problems and challenges for social policy, in: Older workers in a sustainable society, Ennals, Richards/Salomon, Robert H. (eds.), pp. 233-243, p. 233.

1822 *Phillipson* (2011) p. 235.

1823 similar among others *Taylor*, Philip (2011), Is early retirement history?, in: Older workers in a sustainable society, Ennals, Richards/Salomon, Robert H. (eds.), pp. 225-232, p. 229 f. who inter alia stresses that security and choice should be placed at the centre of any efforts to extend working life; see also *Phillipson* (2011), p. 237.

1824 see to the problem of multiple discrimination already chap. 10.2.2.3.

1825 similar *Phillipson* (2011), p. 233.

The workability approach has to be distinguished from that of employability. Employability may be described as the individual's ability to become employed and to be able to sustain that employment or alternatively find a new job.[1826] In short, employability is about 'access, retention and progression of people in paid work across their lifecourse'.[1827]

To address the difficulties related to the achievement and maintenance of employability, the so-called flexicurity approach has been developed, which inter alia aims at promoting 'flexibility' in the phase of transition between jobs by constantly up-grading employees' skills and providing the necessary social protection in transition periods.[1828] The European Commission defines flexicurity as a strategy that simultaneously enhances flexibility and security in the labour market.[1829] As *Rönnmar* put it: 'flexicurity is partly about deregulation of permanent employment combined with the equal treatment of various forms of employment, and partly about a 'tenure track approach' and a ladder of legal protections'.[1830] When applied to the situation of older employees, this approach might include, amongst others, flexible contractual agreements such as the creation of an inclusive labour market for older employees, which helps to reintroduce inactive older employees into employment.[1831] With its focus on flexible and contractual work arrangements, it might lead to an increase in the

1826 *Maltby* (2011), p. 301; see to the aspect of employability of older workers *Kadefors/Hanse* (2012) p. 30.

1827 *Maltby* (2011), p. 301.

1828 see for further detailsCOM (2007), 359 final, Towards Common Principles of Flexicurity: More and better jobs through flexibility and security available at: http://eur-lex.europa.eu/LexUriServ/LexUriServ.do?uri=COM:2007:0359:FIN:EN:PDF (last accessed: 17.12.2014).

1829 see ibid.; see in general for definition and overview of the concept of flexicurity: *European Foundation for the improvement of living and working conditions* (2010), Foundation Findings – Flexicurity: perspectives and practice, available at: http://eurofound.europa.eu/sites/default/files/ef_files/pubdocs/2011/87/en/1/EF1187EN.pdf (last accessed: 17.12.2014)

1830 *Rönnmar*, Mia (2013), Flexicurity and the legal position of the elderly, in: Introduction to the Norma Elder Law Research Environment, Numhauser-Henning, Ann (ed.), pp. 51-60, p. 52.

1831 see in general the eight principles on flexicurity adopted by the EU Council on 23 November 2007, Towards Common Principles of Flexicurity - Draft Council Conclusions SOC 476 ECOFIN 483, for an overview see http://www.eurofound.europa.eu/areas/industrialrelations/dictionary/definitions/flexicurity.htm (last accessed: 17.12.2014).

number of vulnerable workers, in particular, older employees.[1832] Important legal instruments for achieving the inclusion of older employees and facilitating their access to employment are therefore principles of equal treatment and non-discrimination, which are (besides Dir. 2000/78/EC) manifested on EU level in the directives on part-time work, fixed-term work and temporary agency work.[1833]

In sum, irrespective of age, it has to be acknowledged that individuals can still play their part in society and enjoy a better quality of life.[1834] As stressed by the EU, the challenge is to make the most of the enormous potential that individuals harbour even at a more advanced age.[1835] One central dimension in policies on active ageing is therefore to maintain functional capacity over an individual's lifetime, which is crucial in particular for older employees to de facto be able to remain in employment and to feel more fulfilled in their job. It is not only simply about realising one's right to work or being protected against age discrimination, it is also a question of dignity to remain in working life.

16.2.2 Attitudes towards extending working life

Moreover, what is central to the process of reviewing existing mandatory retirement is to shed light on the employee's and employer's attitudes towards extending working life. From the employee's perspective, the key question is whether there is any interest in remaining in working life. This has, amongst others, been subject to the Norwegian Senior Policy Barometer of 2012 and 2013. In general it can be asceratined, that there has been

---

1832 see *Rönnmar* (2013), p. 53; see moreover to the critics of this approach in general *Burroni*, Luigi/*Keune*, Maarten (2011), 'Flexicurity: a conceptual critique', European Journal of Industrial Relations, 17, 1, 2011, pp. 75-91.

1833 see to this aspect *Rönnmar* (2013), p. 53 who refers in this regard to Council Dir. 97/81/EC of 15 December 1997 concerning the Framework Agreement on part-time work concluded by UNICE, CEEP and the ETUC, Council Dir. 1999/70/EC of 28 June 1999 concerning the framework agreement on fixed-term work, concluded by ETUC; UNICE And CEEP and Dir. 2008/104/EC of the European Parliament and of the Council of 19 November 2008 on temporary agency work.

1834 see policy statement regards 'European Year for Active Ageing and Solidarity between Generations in 2012': http://ec.europa.eu/archives/ey2012/ey2012main9ef0.html. (last accessed 17.12.2014).

1835 ibid.

a considerable recorded change concerning older workers and their intentions regarding their withdrawal from working life. The average age that is preferred by Norwegian employees for retirement has considerably increased and is now by 65.1 years of age, which is an increase of by 5.1 years compared to 2003.[1836] More than half of the employees (51%) reported in 2012 that they could see themselves working beyond the age where they were entitled to retirement, as opposed to 35% in 2003.[1837] In the 60+ age group, up to 64% of the in 2012 interviewed employees were positive towards extending their working career after the pension age.[1838] According to the Center for Senior Policy (CSP), this can be regarded as a strong signal that older employees wish to stay active and that this considerable potential for the Norwegian labour market should be used.[1839] Moreover, due to recent surveys, Norwegian employers in general want to extend the careers of older workers, as a significant number of them (87%) stated that if the employees were to choose to remain active at work until they were entitled to retirement, this would be an advantage for the company.[1840] Furthermore, the 2012 Barometer raised the question as to whether there should be an upper age limit for the right to remain in work – a mandatory retirement age – or whether the respondents had not yet formed an opinion about this aspect.[1841] The respondents disagreed in this regard, as 28% of the respondents advocated a mandatory retirement age, while 51% answered in the negative.[1842] In line with previous questionnaires, it is interesting to see that the percentage of those who are in favour of an upper age limit is highest amongst the 50–59 age group and lowest amongst the youngest respondents.[1843] A further question concerned the mandatory retirement age limits in high-risk jobs such as the police, fire fighters and pilots, where the age limit is lower than the general pension

---

1836 see *Norsk Seniorpolitisk Barometer* (2012 b), Kommentarrapport yrkesaktive, written by Dalen, Erik on behalf of the Center for Senior Policy, p. 19, 20 and *Norsk Seniorpolitisk Barometer* (2013 a), Kommentarrapport yrkesaktive, written by Dalen, Erik on behalf oft he Center for Senior Policy, p. 21

1837 *Norsk Seniorpolitisk Barometer* (2012 b), p. 18, Tabell 14-17.

1838 ibid., p. 18.

1839 ibid., p. 19.

1840 *Norsk Seniorpolitisk Barometer* (2013 b), Kommentarrapport ledere i arbeidslivet, written by Dalen, Erik on behalf of the Center for Senior Policy, p. 14.

1841 Norsk Seniorpolitisk Barometer (2012 b), p. 24 f.

1842 ibid., p. 24.

1843 ibid., p. 24.

age. The question was whether there should be a common low mandatory age or regular tests of health and workability instead, so that wishing to remain in employment could work as long as the individuals were capable of doing so.[1844] Remarkably, 78% of the respondents stated that employment should be based on regular tests of health and work capability and that one should not have a common low age limit, while only 9% were in favour of common mandatory retirement.[1845]

Whether people wish to work beyond mandatory retirement in Germany has also inter alia been examined in a German study that aimed at understanding the needs of older employees in their workplaces and their willingness to continue beyond retirement age.[1846] In their survey sample, *Dittrich* et al. concluded that the majority of respondents disagreed with recent pension reforms in Germany, in particular as regards the stepwise increase of the pension age; however, 47% of respondents wished to extend their working life upon having reached the retirement age.[1847] When assessing the driving forces for the wish to extend their working life, the analysis by *Dittrich* et al. observed that the main predictive factors for the desire to continue working proved to be household income, firm size, work classification and the expected workability. In determining an individual's subjective current workability, health was the single most important factor. Furthermore, they observed that the key factors for an individual's disposition for further education were his work motivation and his job demands.[1848]

What is remarkable as regards both Norway and Germany is that in both countries, approximately half of the respondents expressed the wish to continue beyond the general pension age. However, it is beyond doubt that more should be done so that the legal and factual circumstances are at hand to make this wish come true. Not surprisingly, *Dittrich* et al. concluded:

1844 ibid., p. 25.

1845 13% had no certain opinion, p. 24, 25.

1846 *Dittrich*, Dennis/*Büsch*, Victoria/*Micheel*, Frank (2011), Working beyond retirement age in Germany: The employee's perspective, in: Older workers in a sustainable society, Ennals, Richard/Salomon, Robert (eds.), pp. 189-202, p. 191.

1847 ibid., see main conclusion at p. 198.

1848 ibid., p. 195ff.

> A better understanding of the transition into retirement helps to identify (new) potential, and develop new strategies for management to maintain qualified personnel until or even beyond, legal retirement age. For future research, retirement should not be seen as an event but as a process [...] Longitudinal data is needed to study the retirement process, and isolate cohort effects from period effects.[1849]

From a legal perspective, what is therefore essential is to review existing mandatory retirement provisions and consider positive measures to enable employees to extend working life.

16.2.3 Flexible pathways from working life to retirement

The answer to the question regarding how alternative solutions to absolute retirement age limits might look does not necessarily lead to an 'either/or decision' between working life or retirement, as smooth transitions are also possible, such as so-called flexible retirement.[1850] The need to motivate older employees to remain in working life and to encourage employers to hire and keep these employees has been emphasised both in the recent Norwegian as well as German pension reforms.[1851] The promotion of flexible solutions to form a gradual transition from work to retirement is central to the pension reforms. To cope with ageing being an individual process, such flexible solutions designed for the individual employee might therefore replace (absolute) age limits. In general, flexibility also

---

1849 ibid., p. 200.

1850 see elaborately *Temming* (2008) p. 58 f., who states. '*Dabei muss es nicht notwendigerweise auf ein striktes "Entweder-Arbeit-oder-Ruhestand" hinauslaufen. Auch gleitende Übergänge sind denkbar.*' (p. 58) and who refers in terms of felxibel solutions inter alia to Lehr (20007), Psychologie des Alterns, p. 244 f. and *Levine*, Martin L. (1988) Age Discrimination and the Mandatory Retirement Controversy, p. 32ff.

1851 see emphasis put on these aspects e.g. in the Norwegian preparatory work to the recent pension reform: Ot.prp. nr. 37 *Om lov om endringer i folketrygdloven (ny alderspensjon)*, 2008-2009, chap. 1.3.3, p. 15 referring to Innst. S. nr. 195 (2004–2005); see to the Norwegian and German pension reforms already chap. 1.4.

means reorganising working time and redesigning jobs.[1852] Flexible pathways might involve for example flexible work schedules, job-sharing, phased retirement, part-time work or telework.[1853]

Alternative work arrangements for older workers may take various forms: flextime, where the employee determines what time of the day he is willing to work; compressed work schedules such as the flexweek, which entails working extra hours each day and having more days off; and finally, extra hours, where an employee works additional hours, which are later used as time or days off. Moreover, flexible work may also include a change in the work location, which is called flexplace.[1854]

Common to such flexible options is that they encourage a soft pathway out of the workforce by building a bridge from working life to retirement in a stepwise fashion. They thus constitute smooth transitions to retirement as opposed to an absolute exit from the workforce via compulsory age limits. Nevertheless, flexibility may also be required on the demand side. One might therefore argue for individual flexibility when it comes to the employee's wages, which could for example mean taking a few financial steps down the ladder in old age. The argument has been made that the seniority element of pay could be reconsidered and pay could be more closely related to productivity as an incentive for employers to both hire and keep older employees.[1855] Despite these considerations, given the demographic trend, the situation of the senior workforce might, in principle, be getting better, as labour is bound to be a scarcer resource and, quite to the contrary, inter alia financial incentives might be needed to keep older workers in employment. Therefore, not only those employees who are close to retirement should be motivated to extend their careers but also

---

1852 see to this aspect *Meenan* (2007 a), p. 283 who refers in this regard to Reday-Mulvey, Geneviève, Working Beyond 60: Key Policies and Practices in Europe, p. 80; see also recommendations given at *Stein*, David/*Rocco*, Tonette S./*Goldenetz*, Kelly A. (2000), Age and the university workplace, Human Resource Development Quarterly, Vol. 11, No. 1, 2000, pp. 61-80, p. 77 f.

1853 see in detail to the various options: *Sharit*, Joseph/*Czaja*, Sara J. (2012), Job design and redesign for older workers, in: The Oxford Handbook of Work and Aging, Hedge Jerry W./Borman, Walter C. (eds.), pp. 454-482, p. 473 f.; see also in the same handbook: *Paullin*/*Whetzel* (2012), p. 400; *McNamara*, Tay K./*Sano*, Joelle M./*Williamson*, John B. (2012), The pros and cons of pro-work policies and programs for older workers, pp. 663-683; p. 670, 671; Remarkably, flexible work arrangements are also explicitly recommended in the recent OECD report, *OECD* (2013), Ageing and employment policies: Norway, p. 11.

1854 *Sharit*/*Czaja* (2012), p. 473.

1855 see to this aspect also already chap. 12.3.2.1. above.

older people who have already exited the work sphere due to retirement could be motivated to re-enter the labour market – so-called 'unretirement'.

However, flexible retirement needs to be seriously applied in working life. Applying de facto flexibility implies abolishing the rigid boundary between the sphere of working life and retirement in favour of part-time work, job-sharing or work-sharing.[1856] Flexible retirement solutions involve ensuring that the employment sector as such and in particular retirement schemes on the company level become more flexible, so that a truly gradual transition from work to retirement can take place.[1857] Instead of using the blunt tool of a mandatory retirement age, employers might, as stressed by *O'Cinneide*, 'achieve the same degree of certainty and planning by setting individual contractual terms, encouraging early retirement where necessary, and using good performance management'.[1858] Both the employer and employee should be actively involved in the decision about flexible retirement. Advocates for the maintenance of compulsory retirement often refer at this point to the classical counterargument that the employee would be exposed to a degrading situation where he would have to 'discuss' his actual work performance with his employer.[1859] Remarkably, this constituted one of the arguments of the CJEU in the *Hörnfeldt* case concerning the Swedish so-called '67-year rule' that allows employers to terminate an employment contract at the end of the month in which the employee reaches the age of 67.[1860] Here, the CJEU argued in favour for the maintenance of the 67-year age limit and stated:

1856 see elaborately *Temming* (2008), p. 58 with further references; see also *Leeftijd* (2009), online available at: http://leeftijd.nl/wp-content/uploads/2014/07/cao_wijzer_duurzame_participatie.pdf (last accessed 17.12.2014); see also *Sharit/Czaja* (2012), p. 473.

1857 *Leeftijd* (2009).

1858 *O'Cinneide* (2005), p. 42; similar also recommendations given by *Leeftijd* (2009).

1859 see for a legal discussion of the use of this justification pattern chap. 12.3.2.1. above.

1860 see elaborately to this case *Numhauser-Henning*, Ann/*Rönnmar*, Mia (2013), Compulsory retirement and age discrimination – the Swedish Hörnfeldt case put in perspective, in: Essays in honour of Michael Bogdan, Lindskoug, Patrik/Maunsbach, Ulf/Millqvist, Göran/Samuelsson, Per/Vogel, Hans-Heinrich (eds.), pp. 401-415 and to the controversial provision p. 405 f.

> … it can also be accepted that the 67-year rule, by authorising employers to terminate an employment contract when the employee has reached that age, makes it possible to avoid a situation in which employment contracts are terminated in situations which are humiliating for elderly workers.[1861]

However, nothing is more degrading – for those wishing to stay active in employment – than being forced to retire and exit the workforce based on an absolute age limit without having had the chance to discuss less restrictive means.[1862] As pointed out by *O'Cinneide*, depriving the employee of the opportunity to work may close off opportunities for individual self-esteem and constitutes a paternalistic intrusion into the employee's life that finally violates the principle of human dignity.[1863] Instead, one should rather focus on the employee, allow for the participation of the employee and favour tailor-made solutions for the individual employee over generalised mandatory retirement age limits.[1864] What is central to this might for example be to encourage the dialogue between employees and employers in terms of performance and employability.[1865] To address the individuality of the ageing process, measures such as the individual assessment of the employee's capabilities could therefore replace mandatory retirement.[1866] Reviewing mandatory retirement provisions and abolishing those that are not proportional might finally contribute to maximising the employee's autonomy and choice in determining the form of terminating their working life.

In addition, it has to be kept in mind that any abolishment of mandatory retirement provisions may *de lege ferenda* demand a new design of dismissal protection legislation, both in the employee's as well as the employer's interests, to determine the modus operandi at the end of working life and the transition from work to retirement. The element of senior-

1861 C-141/11 (*Hörnfeldt*), para. 34.

1862 see to the dignity aspect *Fredman* (2003), p. 45; see chap. 12.3.2.1. above.

1863 *O'Cinneide* (2005), p. 42.

1864 see e.g. recommendations given by *Leeftijd* (2009).

1865 *Leeftijd* (2009).

1866 similar *Temming* (2008), p. 58, 313 f.; Interestingly enough, *Temming* refers in fn. 258 to the opinion of AG *Jacobs* delivered on 27 October 2005 in C-227/04 P (*Lindorfer*), ECR 2007, I-06767, where *Jacobs* critically points in para. 59 f. to the use of mere generalisations in the field of sex discrimination.

ity and age in employment relations might have to be reconsidered in many ways as regards the whole work cycle, including dismissals.[1867] The protection of older employees should not be unproportionally provided at the expense of younger employees. Also, in this regard, a true balancing of interests is required. By operating with compulsory retirement, there was *de lege lata* no need to address the question of how the employment relationship might be terminated, as the contract automatically ended upon having reached a certain age. One of the central challenges that will arise if mandatory retirement were to be abolished concerns sparing the employee as much as possible from any humiliating situations when it comes to the end of his working life, while at the same time offering him the opportunity to continue working and exercising his right to work and, above all, ensuring that no discrimination on the grounds of age takes place. *Numhauser-Henning* put this problematic in a nutshell by stating:

> The general rule would then imply that you terminate your working life in terms of a disqualification – a less satisfying order.
> In addition, an abolition of the rule of compulsory retirements risks diminishing the employee's employment protection before he or she reaches retirement age. If retirement practices are to become more diffuse or individualised, there is no possibility to uphold a practice such as the one in Sweden, where as a general rule, 'normal ageing' does not constitute just cause for dis-

1867 see for the German context already extensively the *de lege ferenda* considerations as regards a potential reform of the German dismissal legislation in case of an abolishment of mandatory retirement provisions: *Preis*, Ulrich (2008), Verhandlungen des 67. Deutschen Juristentages Erfurt, 2008 Band I: Gutachten/Teil B: Alternde Arbeitswelt, B90. *Preis* is in particular critical to the use of pension entitlements and age as criteria in the selection process in dismissals; critical also to the use of pension entitlements as a criterion in dismissals moreover *Temming* (2008), p. 548 f; see as regards seniority element in pay e.g. Joined cases C-297/10 und C 298/10 (*Hennigs* and *Mai*), Sabine Hennigs v Eisenbahn-Bundesamt and Land Berlin v Alexander Mai, ECR 2011 I-7965, where the CJEU concluded that a provision laid down by a collective agreement that provides that, within each salary group, the basic pay step of a public sector contractual employee is determined on appointment by reference to the employee's age is against the prohibition of non-discrimination on grounds of age as concretisised in Art. 6 No. 1 Dir. 2000/78/EC and not justifiable, see para. 78; see also joined cases C-501/12 to C-506/12, C-540/12 and C-541/12 (*Specht* and others), Judgement of 19 June 2014 (not yet published), where the CJEU examined the German Federal Law on remuneration of civil servants and considered the basic pay for civil servants dependent upon age being unjustifiable age discrimination, see para. 52.

> missal. And, employers' incentives for age management by way of systematic work adaptation may also weaken well before retirement age. There is a risk that setting no upper limit to employment will case a decrease in people aged 55+ who work, thus undermining employment protection from 'within'.[1868]

To avoid humiliating situations, it has therefore been suggested that mandatory retirement should be maintained but that postponing the age limit via fixed-term employment contracts should be allowed.[1869] Moreover, this approach could ensure both the right to work and the 'right to retire'.[1870] Such a solution for a pathway to retirement seems to have been chosen by the German legislator with the recent reform of § 41 s. 3 SGB VI, which aims at increasing flexibility at the end of working life by allowing for the postponement of mandatory retirement age limits via fixed-term employment contracts.[1871] Even though strictly speaking one still operates with a mandatory retirement age limit, this new regulation de facto eases continued employment after having reached the age limit. The main difference to temporary employment contracts is that these agreements on extending the employment relationship do not need to be based on an objective reason, as otherwise required by § 14 (1) of the Act on Part-Time Work and Fixed-Term Employment Contracts (*Teilzeit- und Befristungsgesetz*) – TzBfG. However, such consecutive temporary employment contracts (*Kettenbefristungen*) again run the risk of being age discriminatory and thus contrary to the Directive's justification requirements.[1872] Moreover, keeping a mandatory retirement provision and not abolishing it runs the risk of just maintaining the age-discriminatory *de lege lata* status quo if the option of postponement should de facto not really have been used. If this were the case, such a regulation would be nothing more than a 'toothless tiger'. However, it may generally be ascertained that getting the opportunity to be employed beyond mandatory retirement age limits at least contributes more to age equality than any rigid and absolute compulsory retirement regimes would do.

1868 *Numhauser-Henning* (2013), p. 49 f.

1869 ibid., p. 50.

1870 ibid., p. 50.

1871 see to the recent reform already chap. 1.4.2; see in detail to the amendment *Bader*, Peter (2014), Arbeitsrechtliche Altersgrenzen weiter flexibilisiert, NZA 2014, pp. 749-753.

1872 see to the critics also ibid., pp. 749-753, in particular p. 753.

In any case, if older employees were to apply for a new job to work beyond the retirement age limit, they would likewise be protected by the prohibition against age discrimination.[1873] This has to be taken seriously – be it for example via an anonymised curriculum vitae or generally via an open company culture that encourages an age-diverse workforce.[1874] In view of demographic change, there is reason to hope that older employees will increasingly be considered as a valuable resource and not as a burden. As already ascertained, employment law should also finally allow for the status quo in gerontopsychological research, instead of remaining in the outdated mindset of ageing as a mere process of decline.[1875]

In essence, it is all about flexibility, which finally benefits both sides of the employment contract. From the perspective of the older employee, flexibility is about making use of his right to retire or, on the contrary, to prolong his working life or even to combine both. How this flexibility may best be achieved without being age discriminatory remains to be seen. Further research in this regard would therefore be useful.

16.3 De lege ferenda considerations as regards selected examples of mandatory retirement

16.3.1 Introduction

Also in terms of the selected examples of mandatory retirement, a further step involves elaborating on what kinds of solutions *de lege ferenda* are possible. Here, the key question is likewise how the possible pathways from working life to retirement might look that could replace the existing absolute mandatory retirement age limits that employees are confronted

---

1873 This argument has inter alia been brought forward by the CJEU in C-45/09 (*Rosenbladt*), para. 74.

1874 see as regards recommendations in terms of an open company culture e.g. *Leeftijd* (2009).

1875 see to this aspect also chap. 8; advocating in view of gerontopsychology research findings flexibility at the end of working life rather than mandatory retirement age limits in Germany already *Boerner*, Dietmar (1992), Altersgrenzen für die Beendigung von Arbeitsverhältnissen in Tarifverträgen und Betriebsvereinbarungen, p. 5ff, in particular p. 10, p. 132 f. and p. 316 f.; arguing for a flexible approach to retirement also already *Schröder* (1984), p. 20ff., p. 43ff., in particular p. 57 and 65.

with in all the selected examples. Central to any possible *de lege ferenda* solution is that alternatives have to be found that are in conformity with the prohibition against age discrimination and that moreover contribute to the realisation of the older employee's right to work. The essential precondition for any extension of working life, be it for employees working as physicians, university professors or pilots, may only be realised if the employees really are enabled to make use of this opportunity.

16.3.2 De lege ferenda considerations as regards mandatory retirement for physicians

While Norway still operates with an upper absolute age limit set at the age of 75 for a physician working as a *fastlege*, Germany has completely abolished its mandatory retirement provision for SHI physicians. Nevertheless, in Norway, physicians may be allowed to work beyond the age of 75 under the licence system, even though this is restricted to work outside the *fastlege* system. Given the central aim of the Norwegian regulations of protecting the health of the patients, allowing physicians to work outside the *fastlege* system, while at the same time excluding them for the very same reason from any further employment as a *fastlege,* is incongruent and needs to be re-examined. *De lege ferenda* it is worth reconsidering the absolute 75-year age limit to work as a *fastlege*. One solution could be to extend the licence system also to the work of a *fastlege*. In doing so, physicians could extend their working life beyond the age of 75 and work in- or outside the *fastlege* system. The mandatory retirement age limit for physicians working as a *fastlege* could be abolished and altered to an age limit that obliges all physicians (upon having reached a certain age) to undertake periodical health checks to avoid potential risks for the patients and to guarantee constant good quality within the health service in line with § 1 hlspl. The awarding of a licence for further employment beyond that age limit could be made dependent on having passed these regular assessments. Such a regulation could strengthen an individual and rather tailor-made approach, considering the workability of each individual physician in question, and it could thereby avoid generalised assumptions. This would inter alia be in conformity with the research results concerning the correlation between the (risk) of malpractice and the physician's age, which did not fortify the claim of a performance decline with increasing age. In any case, it is fundamental from the physician's perspective and in terms of his interest in extending his working life that the licence system is thoroughly applied based on an objective analysis of the de facto existing physician's capabilities. Moreover, critics of the *de lege lata* situation in Norway point out that one has to discuss whether it is proper and desirable that physicians without formal clinical tasks in the healthcare system only undertake sporadic clinical activities.[1876] This practice is doubtful and may constitute a risk for the patients, whether the physicians in question are 35 or 75 years of age.[1877] Therefore, the question has been raised as to whether authorisation limits should not be based more on the physician's association with organised clinical business rather than on his age.[1878] Moreover, it has been stressed that there should also be room for older physicians in the healthcare system in particular, as their expertise might constitute a fruitful resource for their younger colleagues.[1879] Some argue therefore for integration of the older physicians and cooperation in the existing system instead of creating and encouraging 'unorganized medical services outside the system', which is, in particular, true for the GP system.[1880] In doing so, hospitals might use their retired colleagues' expertise by offering, for example, various forms of part-time affiliation.[1881] The active integration of older physicians in the *fastlege* system could thus also better contribute to the original legislator's rationale for introducing the 75-year age limit, as it could ameliorate the quality of medical work done by older physicians.[1882] Therefore, some argue that the existing limitation of the authorisation should not be abolished, but that it should be maintained, and that the licence system should be changed instead to the extent that the older physician should really become integrated in the system, instead of letting him practice sporadically outside the system. [1883]

1876 *Bruusgaard* (2011), p. 1906.
1877 ibid., p. 1906.
1878 ibid., p. 1906.
1879 similar ibid., p. 1906; *Pahle/Hansen* (2008), p. 1546.
1880 *Bruusgaard* (2011), p. 1906.
1881 ibid., p. 1906, who points out that many hospitals express the wish to integrate and engage retired physicians; another opportunity could be that physicians above the age of 75 could work in palliative medicine, see *Pande/Holmsen* (2006), pp. 3283-3284.
1882 *Bruusgaard* (2011), p. 1906.
1883 ibid., p. 1906.

To conclude, maintaining an age limit, but allowing for further employment beyond this age limit – be it working as a *fastlege* or SHI physician or working in a private practice – via fixed-term employment could be a *de lege ferenda* solution not only in Norway but also in Germany. Combining a licence system with a control mechanism by requiring an individual health assessment, as in the case of Norway, could also be the way forward in Germany. That way the aim of protecting the health of the patients and the public health in general alongside protecting the physician's interests in extending his working life could both be ensured. With regard to the Norwegian situation, one may conclude that if the licence requirements were fulfilled, there would be no need to further limit the possibility of getting further employment as a *fastlege*, as this is *de lege lata* the case in Norway with the 75-year age limit.

16.3.3 De lege ferenda considerations as regards mandatory retirement for professors

Different models of flexible retirement could also be taken into consideration when it comes to the legal situation of university professors that ultimately might mutually benefit both the university staff and the demand for services from the university's side.[1884] However, as already stressed in the general considerations, any extension of working life might also, as regards university professors, only be realised if the working environment is adjusted to cope with an ageing workforce, and to really enable the employee to perform to the best of his abilities at whatever age and stage of his career and, in doing so, enable him to remain in an active role in academia and continue working beyond retirement.[1885] Here again, it has to be kept in mind that chronological age should not be the determinant when providing e.g. training opportunities.[1886]

1884 see recommendations given by *Manfredi*, Simonetta (2008), Developing good practice in managing age diversity in the higher education sector: An evidence-based approach, p. 8.

1885 see to this aspect already ibid, p. 213; see *Manfredi* (2008), p. 8.

1886 see to this aspect *Stein* et al. (2000), p. 76 who refer in this regard to Greller, M./ Stroh, L. (1995), Careers in mid-life and beyond: A fallow field in need of sustenance, Journal of Vocational Behaviour, 47 (3), pp. 232-247.

One possible form of senior academics continuing beyond the age limit could be employment on a part-time basis and/or via fixed-term employment contracts. This is, in principle, already provided both in Norway and in Germany. However, such opportunities for extending a university professor's working life are limited by an absolute age limit in both countries. This absolute boundary needs to be re-examined and flexible employment opportunities should also be provided beyond these absolute age limits. As the analysis of the current legal situation of university professors in Norway has demonstrated, in reality, the legal framework is applied with less flexibility than the regulations basically allow for. The margin of discretion that the provisions open up for in extending the professor's working life through temporary employment contracts until the age of 75 seems to be utilised only in exceptional circumstances to the full extent in favour of the professors. *De lege ferenda* taking advantage of the possibilities that rest in § 3 *aldersgrenselov* could therefore contribute to minimising the age-discriminatory character of the mandatory retirement age limit in § 2 *aldersgrenselov*, and might thus contribute to more vigorous use of § 3 and to more age equality by really giving university professors the option to work until the age of 75, as is basically provided for in § 3. However, the *de lege lata* situation in Norway might already function as a 'best-practice model' if compared to the legal situation for university professors in Germany, who are confronted with an absolute age limit that is considerably lower than in the case of Norway.[1887] An increase in the upper absolute age limit – both in Norway and in Germany – might at least contribute to an enhancement of the older professors' employment situation. Nevertheless, in view of the strict proportionality test that is required to enable the prohibition against age discrimination to be taken seriously, maintaining any upper age limit is more than questionable.[1888] In light of the pension reform's aim in Norway and in Germany to motivate and enable employees to remain in working life as long as possible, such as by considering the fact that e.g. the Norwegian *Statens personalhåndbok* explicitly encourages public employers to facilitate older employees to stay in employment, *de lege ferenda* removing the upper age limit in Norway and in Germany should be taken into consideration by the legislators.[1889] Universities should establish workplaces that embrace older fac-

1887 see already chap. 14.5; see also conclusion *Hack* (2012 b), p. 212 f.
1888 ibid., p. 212.
1889 see to the pension reforms chap. 1.4.

ulty members as 'capable, productive, and knowledgeable lifelong workers'[1890] who represent 'a rich source of experience, accumulated knowledge, and wisdom'[1891] rather than exclude them.

Part-time or fixed-term employment solutions might for example be favourable at universities where one needs to overcome challenges as regards lack of staff turnover and departmental finances.[1892] It needs e.g. to be discussed whether academic staff past the retirement age could be required to step down from any senior position that they are holding, which could free up opportunities for career progression for other (younger) members of staff.[1893] It has been argued that the advantages of such an approach are that it would enable the departments of the universities to keep senior academics past retirement age, while at the same time 'balancing the books', as in particular, senior professorship positions might be very cost-intensive.[1894] The benefits of such flexible retirement solutions are that they might positively contribute to the universities' succession planning and enable them to establish 'some overlap between retiring and new employees to ensure the flow of knowledge and expertise between different generations of employees'.[1895] However, it has to be kept in mind that such a solution might lead to the financial hardship of the individual professors if the loss of income cannot be compensated for by them starting to withdraw their pensions.[1896] Furthermore, one should be aware of the fact that facilitating a smooth transition from working life to retirement does not lead to an enhancement of early retirement patterns. This would be a step backwards in the fight for age equality and quite the opposite to any of the pension reforms' aims. It should be in the self-interest of universities to encourage older faculty staff to remain in employment, as this inter alia could address the brain drain of senior academics to jurisdictions without mandatory retirement age limits and, in doing so, one could keep valuable expertise and knowledge at the home institution.[1897] Another aspect that has been brought forward in favour of abolishing

1890 *Stein* et al. (2000), p. 77.
1891 ibid., p. 77.
1892 see e.g. options discussed at *Manfredi* (2008), p. 49 f.
1893 ibid. p. 50, 53, see also p. 58 f.
1894 ibid.
1895 ibid., p. 59.
1896 ibid., p. 50.
1897 see to this aspect already chap. 14.5.

mandatory retirement in academia concerns the relationship between age and gender. In this regard, it has been emphasised that, in particular, women are more likely to reach seniority in academia in later life than their male colleagues are, which might be due to either having entered into an academic role at a later stage or to an interrupted career for childcare reasons.[1898]

Irrespective of the pathway that should *de lege ferenda* be chosen, alternatives to absolute mandatory retirement age limits also need to be critically examined in terms of their legitimacy in light of the prohibition against age discrimination. It is beyond doubt that allowing for further flexibility rather than retaining compulsory retirement requires balancing the expectations of the university professors to work longer with staff turnover and budgetary aspects. This is not an easy task, but one that is essential if the prohibition against age discrimination is to be taken seriously. *De lege ferenda* allowing for different models of flexibility as regards the transition from working life to retirement, be it an extension via full-time or part-time temporary employment contracts or any other model of flexibility, could finally be a win–win situation for both the professors and the universities. In any event, the key element of all these options is again that of flexibility or in other words: 'The workplace becomes a dynamic space for older workers rather than a unidirectional journey leading to retirement.'[1899]

16.3.4 De lege ferenda considerations as regards mandatory retirement for pilots

Of the selected examples, the provisions on compulsory retirement for pilots are the only example where an entire abolishment of any age limits due to security aspects is *de lege ferenda* not recommended. Thus, they might in fact be the last 'bastion' for absolute mandatory retirement age limits. Here, the security interests outweigh the interests of the individual pilot in being not discriminated against on the grounds of age and exercising the right to work. However, *de lege ferenda* an adaptation of the existing – if still prevailing – mandatory retirement provisions in collective

1898 see arguments brought forward by respondents in study by *Manfredi* (2008), p. 50.

1899 *Stein* et al. (2000), p. 78.

agreements for pilots in Norway and Germany to the international standard needs to be considered. Moreover, provided that the conditions as required by international regulations – multi-pilot cockpit crew and successful completion of a capability assessment – are fulfilled, a further increase in the age limit in line with the stepwise increase of the general applicable pension age might *de lege ferenda* be considered as e.g. suggested by *Rothermund* and *Temming.*[1900] However, it remains to be seen whether the referred to existing inconsistencies as regards the international requirements could really be addressed in this way.[1901] Central to any extension of working life – as being fundamental for the profession of a pilot irrespective of the pilot's age – should be a close-meshed control mechanism in order to guarantee air safety. In addition, the further employment of pilots beyond retirement age in other areas where security aspects are less of an issue such as e.g. in consulting, teaching, administration or organisational work could be considered. In doing so, employers could make use of the pilot's know-how and expertise, while at the same time offering the pilot the opportunity to remain in working life.

17 Final remarks and key findings

The initial impetus for the thesis came from the claim that age equality needs to be taken more seriously. The central and overarching aim of this work has been to examine equality in the sense of 'equality of opportunity', which means equality in terms of the situation of older employees, in that all employees, irrespective of their age, should, in principle, be provided with the same opportunity to participate fully and equally in working life. In view of this overriding claim, selected examples of mandatory retirement provisions have been examined and these were subsequently identified as being an obstacle to any equal participation in working life for older employees. Such provisions, particularly when they relate to absolute age limits, constitute *expressis verbis* a limitation to the employee's right to work and negatively impact on the individual's dignity.

1900 see key conclusions by *Rothermund/Temming* (2010), p. 119, para. 16.
1901 see to the inconsistencies chap. 15.3.3.2.1.2.

Two approaches have been chosen for the legal analysis of mandatory retirement: first, an interdisciplinary approach and second, a legal comparative approach. In part I, I argue that in view of such an interdisciplinary and contextualised approach, and by taking into consideration demographic developments, labour-market data and gerontopschycological research, mandatory retirement provisions cannot be upheld from a legal perspective. In particular, the stereotypes on age and ageing – regarding ageing as a mere process of decline in terms of capabilities – that mandatory retirement provisions seem to be deeply founded in, were unmasked as a myth. Ageing is thus an individual process of change, which is characterised by its inter- and intra-individual variability. The ageing process is determined by a range of factors that interact and are part of a complex, reciprocal causal network of multidimensional determinants. Mandatory retirement provisions that solely rely on the employee's chronological age and are based on generalised assumptions on ageing have been identified as being contrary to these findings and, by being rooted in stereotypes on ageing, they are to be considered as a form of ageism.

The standard of comparison for the comparative legal analysis between Norway and Germany has been Dir. 2000/78/EC. Examining the selected mandatory retirement provisions in light of the prohibition against age discrimination – as concretised by Dir. 2000/78/EC – entailed elaborating on the prohibition's manifestation in both human rights and EU law. When looking at its manifestation in human rights law, it can indeed be concluded that there is no explicit protection against discrimination on the grounds of age in the reviewed treaties. However, it could be ascertained that together with the analysed soft law instruments, the examined hard law provisions on non-discrimination might at least help in contributing to the fight for age equality. It is argued that this is even truer if these non-discrimination provisions are read in conjunction with the right to work and to the free choice of employment, as both universal rights are essential for the full realisation of age equality for older employees. The argument is made that soft law might be regarded as a catalyst in strengthening protection against age discrimination and towards substantive protection *de lege ferenda* of the rights of the elderly, including older employees. As regards to more substantive protection for the group of older people, a treaty that is designed specifically for this group and that enshrines obligatory legal validity is needed.

In contrast to human rights law, age discrimination is explicitly prohibited in EU law. Fundamental to the process of reinforcing the prohibition against age discrimination has been the enactment of the Lisbon Treaty, which led to the principle's explicit manifestation in EU primary law. It has been concluded that *de lege lata*, the CFREU gives more impetus to the assertion of the prohibition of age discrimination in secondary law and ultimately contributes, together with Dir. 2000/78/EC, to a strengthening of the prohibition. If this prohibition is de facto to be effective and in order to take it seriously, it is imperative that the justification requirements for the prohibition against age discrimination, as concretised in Dir. 2000/78/EC, are interpreted in the narrow sense. This requires a strict application of the proportionality test. Mandatory retirement provisions that are directly age-discriminatory are therefore only justifiable when three steps are fulfilled; that is, the measure needs to be suitable, necessary and finally, proportional *stricto sensu*. Only the application of such a strict standard of proof is rigorous enough when the aim is to take the prohibition against age discrimination seriously; this is the central argument in the thesis when it comes to the chosen standard of comparison.

As both Germany and the non-EU member Norway have implemented Dir. 2000/78/EC into national law, consequently, as shown in part II, such a strict justification standard is also required on the national level. Given that, it has been emphasised that for the understanding of both the Norwegian and German law on age discrimination, a thorough analysis of the underlying Dir. 2000/78/EC and its interpretation through the CJEU is pivotal. Analysing Dir. 2000/78/EC and the relevant case law is a *sine qua non* for any comprehensive analysis of the law on age discrimination on the national level. From the Norwegian perspective, the need for a strict proportionality assessment is even more apparent if one considers the recent explicit manifestation and constitutional underpinning of the general prohibition against discrimination in the Constitution.

In part III, three selected examples on mandatory retirement provisions for physicians, university professors and pilots have been examined in terms of their compatibility with the prohibition against age discrimination as concretised in Dir. 2000/78/EC and the justification requirements manifested therein. All examples constituted direct age discrimination and the key question was whether they could be justified according to Dir. 2000/78/EC or not. In view of a strict standard of proof, I have argued that the selected examples of the absolute mandatory retirement provisions for physicians in Norway and for university professors in Norway and Germany proved to be a violation of the prohibition against age discrimination: the provisions did not pass the proportionality test and thus are not justifiable. However, *de lege lata* there is a margin of discretion already provided for in the existing regulations for physicians and professors when deciding on extending the employment contract beyond the mandatory retirement age limit. Making de facto use of this discretionary margin would at least contribute to enhanced age equality. The only example where a justification was considered possible – in line with international requirements – concerned mandatory retirement for pilots, even though, strictly speaking, from a gerontological perspective, the often referred to correlation between ageing, a decline in capabilities and crash involvement as regards to older pilots could not be proven based on scientific findings. Of the analysed examples, the pilot profession might therefore be considered as the last 'bastion' where it is legitimate to operate with absolute age limits.

In general, using capability procedures rather than rigid statutory procedures such as absolute compulsory retirement should be the preferred route, which is the argument in this thesis. It has therefore been concluded (in part IV, concerning *de lege ferenda* considerations) that flexibility is the key when designing a smooth transition from working life to retirement, which is in conformity with the prohibition against age discrimination. Restructuring and reorganising work by, for example, postponing retirement and generally encouraging flexible work arrangements is essential when coping with an ageing society. This would, as emphasised also in view of the selected examples of mandatory retirement, be a win–win situation for all parties involved: employees – be it a *fastlege*, a university professor or a pilot – employers or the society as such. In view of the challenges of an ageing society that both Norway and Germany are, beyond a doubt, confronted with, it should be the order of the day to embrace those employees who are willing to extend, and who are capable of extending, their working life. However, as further stressed in the thesis, extending working lives may only be realised if the employees are de facto enabled (through provisions) to make use of the opportunity to extend their working life and exercise their right to work even beyond mandatory retirement.

List of laws, preparatory work, official documents etc.

International treaties

Charter of the United Nations 26 June 1945

Universal Declaration of Human Rights (UDHR) 10 December 1948

International Convention on the Elimination of All Forms of Racial Discrimination (ICEAFRD) 21 December 1965

International Covenant on Civil and Political Rights (ICCPR) 16 December 1966

International Covenant on Economic, Social and Cultural Rights (ICESCR) 16 December 1966

Convention on the Elimination of All Forms of Discrimination against Women (CEDAW) 18 December 1979

Convention on the Rights of Persons with Disabilities (CRPD) 13 December 2006

Convention on International Civil Aviation (Chicago Convention)

Annex I (Personnel Licensing) Amendment 167, 7. December 1944

United Nation documents

General Assembly Resolution A/RES/37/51 (The Vienna Plan) International plan of action on aging, 6 August 1982

General Assembly meeting, A/RES/46/91 (UN Principles for Older Persons) Implementation of the International plan of action on ageing and related activities, 16 December 1991

General Assembly Resolution A/RES/47/5 Proclamation on Ageing, 16 October 1992

Report of second world assembly on ageing, Madrid 6-12 April 2002

Political Declaration to UN Second World Assembly on Ageing and

International Plan of Action on Ageing (The Madrid Plan), 12 April 2002

General Comment No. 18 E/C.12/GC/18, Committee on Economic, Social and Cultural Rights (CESCR), 6 February 2006

General Assembly Recommendation 1796 (2007), The situation of elderly persons in Europe

General Comment No. 18 Human Rights Committee (HRC) Non-discrimination (Thirty-seventh session, 1989)

General Comment No. 6 Committee on Economic, Social and Cultural Rights (CESCR) The economic, social and cultural rights of older persons (Thirteenth session, 1995)

General Comment No. 20 Committee on Economic, Social and Cultural Rights (CESCR) Non-discrimination in economic, social and cultural rights, 2 July 2009

International Labour Organization (ILO)

ILO Convention No. 111 concerning Discrimination in Respect of Employment and Occupation, 1958

ILO Convention No. 122 concerning Employment Policy, 1964

ILO Convention No. 156 concerning Workers with Family Responsibilities Convention, 1981

ILO Convention No. 158 concerning Termination of Employment at the Inititative of the Employer, 1982

ILO Recommendation No. 162 Older Workers Recommendation (OWR), 1980

ILO Recommendation No. 166 Termination of Employment Recommendation, 1982

Council of Europe

European Convention on Human Rights (Convention for the Protection of Human Rights and Fundamental Freedoms, ECHR) 1950, CETS No. 5

European Social Charter (ESC) 1961, CETS No. 35

European Social Charter (revised – RESC) 1996, CETS No. 163

Explanatory Report: European Social Charter (revised) 1996, CETS No. 163

Protocol No. 12 to the Convention for the Protection of Human Rights and Fundamental Freedoms, 2000, CETS No. 177

Explanatory Report: Protocol No. 12 to the Convention for the Protection of Human Rights and Fundamental Freedoms 2000, ETS No. 177

Parliamentary Assembly Resolution 1502: Demographic challenges for social cohesion, 2006

Parliamentary Assembly Recommendation 1796: The situation of elderly persons in Europe, 2007

Parliamentary Assembly Resolution 1793 (2011): Promoting active ageing – capitalising on older people's working potential, 2011

European Economic Area

Agreement on the European Economic Area (EEA), OJ No L 1, 3.1.1994

Annex XVIII Health and Safety at Work, Labour Law, and Equal Treatment for Men and Women, List provided for in Articles 67 to 70

European Union

Treaty Establishing the European Community (TEC); Consolidated version 2002, OJ C 325, 24.12.2002

Treaty on European Union (TEU), 2009, OJ C 83/13; Consolidated version, 2012, OJ C 326/13

Treaty on the Functioning of the Union (TFEU), 2009, OJ C 83/47

Charter of Fundamental Rights of the European Union (CFREU), 2000, OJ C 364/01

Commission Regulations

Commission Regulation (EU) No 1178/2011 of 3 November 2011 laying down technical requirements and administrative procedures related to civil aviation aircrew, OJ L 074

Commission Regulation (EU) No 290/2012 of 30 March 2012 amending Regulation (EU) No 1178/2011 laying down technical requirements and administrative procedures related to civil aviation aircrew pursuant to Regulation (EC) No 216/2008 of the European Parliament and of the Council, OJ L 100

Commission Regulation (EU) No 6/2013 of 8 January 2013 amending Regulation (EC) No 216/2008 of the European Parliament and of the Council on common rules in the field of civil aviation and establishing a European Aviation Safety Agency, and repealing Council Directive 91/670/EEC, Regulation (EC) No 1592/2002 and Directive 2004/36/EC, OJ L 4

Council Directives

Council Directive 2000/43/EC of 29 June 2000 implementing the principle of equal treatment between persons irrespective of racial or ethnic origin, OJ L 180

Council Directive 2000/78/EC of 27 November 2000 establishing a general framework for equal treatment in employment and occupation, OJ L 303

Directive Dir. 2002/73/EC of the European Parliament and of the Council of 23 September 2002 amending Council Dir. 76/207/EEC on the implementation of the principle of equal treatment for men and women as regards access to employment, vocational training and promotion, and working conditions, OJ L 269/15

Council Directive 2004/113/EC of 13 December 2004 implementing the principle of equal treatment between men and women in the access to and supply of goods and services, OJ L 373

European Commission and European Council documents

COM (1999) 565 final, Proposal for a Council Directive (2000/C 177 E/07) establishing a general framework for equal treatment in employment and occupation, OJ C 177 E/42

COM(2002) 143 final, Communication from the Commission to the Council and the European Parliament - Europe's response to World Ageing - Promoting Economic and Social progress in an ageing world A contribution of the European Commission to the 2nd World Assembly on Ageing

COM (2004) 146 final, Increasing the employment of older workers and delaying the exit from the labour market, OJ L 146

COM (2007) 359 final, Towards Common Principles of Flexicurity: More and better jobs through flexibility and security

COM (2008) 426 final, Proposal for a Council Directive on implementing the principle of equal treatment between persons irrespective of religion or belief, disability, age or sexual orientation, 2008/0140 (CNS)

COM (2010) 2020 final, A strategy for smart, sustainable and inclusive growth

COM (2010) 2020, Conclusions by the European Council EUCO 13/10

SEC (2010) 114 final, Lisbon Strategy evaluation document

Norwegian laws and regulations

1814	Kongeriket Norges Grunnlov av 17. mai 1814
1949	Lov 28. juli 1949 nr. 26 om Statens pensjonskasse
1953	Lov 26. juni 1953 nr. 11 om pensjonsordning for apotekvirksomhet mv.
1956	Lov 21. desember 1956 nr. 1 om aldersgrenser for offentlige tjenestemenn m.fl. (aldersgrenselov)
1962	Lov 22. juni 1962 nr. 12 om pensjonsordning for sykepleiere (sykepleierpensjonsloven)
1975	Lov 5. mai 1975 nr. 18 Sjømannslov (Opphevet)
1983	Lov 4. april 1983 nr. 3 om statens tjenestemenn m.m. (tjenestemannsloven –tjml)
1992	Lov 27. november 1992 nr. 109 om gjennomføring i norsk rett av hoveddelen i avtale om Det europeiske økonomiske samarbeidsområde (EØS) m.v. (EØS-loven)
1997	Lov 28. februar 1997 nr. 19 om folketrygd (folketrygdloven eller ftrl)
1997	Lov 23. mai 1997 nr. 31 om eierseksjoner (eierseksjonsloven)
1998	Lov 21. august 1998 nr. 65 om pensjonsordning for ballettdansere, sangsolister og korsangere ved Den Norske Opera & Ballett (operapensjonsloven)

1999	Lov 26. mars 1999 nr. 17 om husleieavtaler (husleieloven)
1999	Lov 2. juli 1999 nr. 63 om pasient- og brukerrettigheter (pasient- og brukerrettighetsloven)
1999	Lov 7. juli 1999 nr. 64 om helsepersonell m.v. (helsepersonelloven eller hlspl)
2003	Lov 6. juni 2003 nr. 38 om bustadbyggjelag (bustadbyggjelagslova)
2003	Lov 6. juni 2003 nr. 39 om burettslag (burettslagslova)
2005	Lov 1. april 2005 om universiteter og høyskoler (universitets- og høyskoleloven)
2005	Lov 17. juni 2005 nr. 62 om arbeidsmiljø, arbeidstid og stillingsvern mv.(arbeidsmiljøloven)
2005	Lov 21. desember 2005 nr. 124 om obligatorisk tjenestepensjon [OTP-loven]
2013	Lov 21. juni 2013 nr. 58 om forbud mot diskriminering på grunn av seksuell orientering, kjønnsidentitet og kjønnsuttrykk (diskrimineringsloven om seksuell orientering)
2013	Lov 21. juni 2013 nr. 59 om likestilling mellom kjønnene (likestillingsloven)
2013	Lov 21. juni 2013 nr. 60 om forbud mot diskriminering på grunn av etnisitet, religion og livssyn (diskrimineringsloven om etnisitet)
2013	Lov 21. juni 2013 nr. 61 om forbud mot diskriminering på grunn av nedsatt funksjonsevne (diskriminerings- og tilgjengelighetsloven)
2013	Lov 21. juni 2013 nr. 102 om stillingsvern mv. for arbeidstakere på skip (skipsarbeidsloven)
FOR-1997-04-22-374	Forskrift om pensjonsordninger for kommunalt eller fylkeskommunalt ansatte
FOR-2000-12-21-1379	Forskrift om lisens til helsepersonell
FOR-2000-12-21-1384	Forskrift om spesialistgodkjenning av helsepersonell og turnusstillinger for leger
FOR-2004-08-30-1224	Forskrift om endring i forskrift om lisens til helsepersonell
FOR-2005-12-19-1653	Forskrift om veiledet tjeneste for å få adgang til å praktisere som allmennlege med rett til trygderefusjon
FOR-2008-06-19-617	Forskrift om gjennomføring av felleseuropeiske bestemmelser om medisinske krav for tjenestegjørende på luftfartøy, BSL JAR-FCL 3 (Flight Crew Licencing) endring 5
FOR-2012-08-29-842	Forskrift om fastlegeordning i kommunene
FOR-2013-07-16-916	Forskrift om sertifisering av besetningsmedlemmer

German laws

Allgemeines Gleichbehandlungsgesetz (AGG)

Arbeitsgerichtsgesetz (ArbGG)

Beamtenstatusgesetz (BeamtSTG)

Betriebsverfassungsgesetz (BetrVG)

Bundesbeamtengesetz (BBG)

Bundesnotarordnung (BNotO)

Grundgesetz (GG)

Kündigungsschutzgesetz (KSchG)

Schornsteinfegergesetz

Sozialgesetzbuch (SGB) V

Sozialgesetzbuch (SGB) VI

Gesetz über die Gleichbehandlung der Soldatinnen und Soldaten (SoldGG)

Gesetz zur Anpassung der Regelaltersgrenze an die demografische Entwicklung und zur Stärkung der Finanzierungsgrundlagen der gesetzlichen Rentenversicherung (RV-Altersanpassungsgesetz vom 20.04.2007, BGBl. 2007, I, p. 554ff

Gesetz zur Weiterentwicklung der Organisationsstrukturen in der gesetzlichen Krankenversicherung (GKV-OrgWG) vom 15. 12. 2008, BGBl. I

Gesetz zur Veränderung des Vertragsarztrechts und anderer Gesetze (Vertragsarztrechtsänderungsgesetz) vom 22.12.2006 (enacted on 01.01.2007, BGBl. 2006, I, S. 3439)

Gesetz zur Anpassung des Luftverkehrsrechts an die Verordnung (EU) Nr. 1178/2011 der Kommission vom 3. November 2011 zur Festlegung technischer Vorschriften und von Verwaltungsverfahren in Bezug auf das fliegende Personal in der Zivilluftfahrt gemäß der Verordnung (EG) Nr. 216/2008 des Europäischen Parlaments und des Rates vom 20. Februar 2008 vom 07. August 2013, BGBl I 2013, 3123

Laws on Länder level

Bayerisches Beamtengesetz (BayBG)

Bayerisches Hochschulpersonalgesetz (BayHSchPG)

Landesbeamtengesetz (LBG) Berlin

LBG in Brandenburg

Bremisches Beamtengesetz (BremBG)

Hamburgisches Beamtengesetz (HmbBG)

Hessisches Beamtengesetz (HBG)

Hessisches Hochschulgesetz

Beamtengesetz für das Land Mecklenburg-Vorpommern (LBG M-V)

LBG in Rheinland-Pfalz

Saarländisches Beamtengesetz (SBG)
Sächsisches Beamtengesetz (SächsBG)
Beamtengesetz des Landes Sachsen-Anhalt (LBG LSA)
LBG Schleswig-Holstein
Thüringer Beamtengesetz (ThürBG)

Foreign laws

United States of America

1967	Age Discrimination in Employment Act (ADEA)

Norwegian preparatory work (forarbeider)

Innst. O. nr. 55. (1979-80)	Innstilling fra sosialkomitéen om lov om leger og om lov om tannleger
Innst. S. nr. 77 (1995-1996)	Innstilling fra familie-, kultur- og administrasjonskomiteen om aldersgrenser for offentlige tjenestemenn m.fl.
Innst. S. nr. 76 (2002-2003)	Innstilling fra sosialkomiteen om forslag om en endring i FOR 2000-12-21 nr. 1379
Innst. O.nr. 52 (2003-2004)	Innstilling fra kommunalkomiteen om lov om endringer i lov 4. februar 1977 nr. 4 om arbeidervern og arbeidsmiljø mv. (likebehandling i arbeidslivet) m.m.
Innst. S.nr. 195 (2004-2005)	Innstilling fra finanskomiteen om pensjonsreform - trygghet for pensjonene
NOU 1972:21	Oppsigelse ved nådd pensjonsalder etter Lov om folketrygd; Om revisjon av reglene i Arbeidervernloven om vern mot usaklig oppsigelse
NOU 1976:1	Legers og tannlegers rettigheter og plikter
NOU 1993:33	Helsepersonells rettigheter og plikter
NOU 1998:19	Fleksibel pensjonering
NOU 2000:27	Sykefravær og uførepensjonering. Et inkluderende arbeidsliv
NOU 2003:2	Skjerpet vern mot diskriminering i arbeidslivet
NOU 2009:14	Et helhetlig diskrimineringsvern: Diskrimineringslovutvalgets utredning om en samlet diskrimineringslov, grunnlovsvern og ratifikasjon av tilleggsprotokoll nr. 12 til EMK
NOU 2011:18	Struktur for likestilling

NOU 2012:18	Rett om bord - Ny skipsarbeidslov
Ot.prp. nr. 4 (1917)	Aldersgrenseloven
Ot.prp. nr. 8 (1956)	Om lov om arbeidervern
Ot.prp. nr. 60 (1956)	Om lov om aldersgrenser for offentlige tjenestemenn m.fl.
Ot.prp. nr. 17 (1972-73)	Om lov om endringer i lov av 7. desember 1956 nr. 2 om arbeidervern
Ot.prp. nr. 41 (1975-76)	Om arbeidstid, oppsigelsesvern, arbeidstilsyn m.v. i lov om arbeidervern og arbeidsmiljø
Ot.prp. nr. 1 (1979-80)	Om lov om leger og om lov om tannleger
Ot.prp. nr. 4 (1998-99)	Om lov om endringer i folketrygdloven og i enkelte andre lover (samleproposisjon høsten 1998)
Ot.prp. nr. 13 (1998-99)	Om lov om helsepersonell m v (helsepersonelloven)
Ot.prp. nr. 104 (2002-2003)	Om lov om endringer i lov 4. februar 1977 nr. 4 om arbeidervern og arbeidsmiljø mv. (likebehandling i arbeidslivet) m.m.
Ot.prp. nr. 49 (2004-2005)	Om lov om arbeidsmiljø, arbeidstid og stillingsvern mv. (arbeidsmiljøloven)
Ot.prp. nr. 37 (2008-2009)	Om lov om endringer i folketrygdloven (ny alderspensjon)
Ot.prp. nr. 54 (2008-2009)	Om lov om endringer i arbeidsmiljøloven (likestilling av arbeidstiden for skift- og turnusarbeidere mv)
Meld. St. 6 (2012–2013)	Melding til Stortinget En helhetlig integreringspolitikk
Prop. 115 L (2012-2013)	Lov om stillingsvern mv. for arbeidstakere på skip (skipsarbeiderloven)
Prop. 48 L (2014–2015)	Endringer i arbeidsmiljøloven og Allmenngjøringsloven (arbeidstid, aldersgrenser, straff mv.)
Grunnlovsforslag 30 (2011-2012), Dok.nr. 12:30 (2011-2012)	Grunnlovsforslag fra Per-Kristian Foss, Martin Kolberg, Marit Nybakk, Jette F. Christensen, Anders Anundsen, Hallgeir H Langeland, Per Olaf Lundteigen, Geir Jørgen Bekkevold og Trine Skei Grande om grunnlovfesting av sivile og politiske menneskerettigheter
St.prp. nr. 11 (2003-2004)	Om samtykke til godkjenning av ei avgjerd i EØS-komiteen om innlemming i EØS-avtala av fellesskapshandlingsprogrammet om motkjemping av diskriminering (2001-2006)
St.meld.nr.12 (2004-2005)	Pensjonsreform – trygghet for pensjonene

German preparatory work (Bundestagsdrucksachen)

Bundestagsdrucksachen

Bt-Drs. 16/10609, Beschlussempfehlung und Bericht, des Ausschusses für Gesundheit (14. Ausschuss), zu dem Gesetzentwurf der Bundesregierung – Drucksachen 16/9559, 16/10070 – Entwurf eines Gesetzes zur Weiterentwicklung der Organisationsstrukturen in der gesetzlichen Krankenversicherung (GKV-OrgWG)

Bt-Drs. 16/1780, Entwurf eines Gesetzes zur Umsetzung europäischer Richtlinien zur Verwirklichung des Grundsatzes der Gleichbehandlung

Bt-Dr. 16/4027, Entwurf eines Gesetzes zur Regelung des Statusrechts der Beamtinnen und Beamten in den Ländern (Beamtenstatusgesetz – BeamtStG)

Bt-Drs. 12/3608, Entwurf eines Gesetzes zur Sicherung und Strukturverbesserung der gesetzlichen Krankenversicherung (Gesundheits-Strukturgesetz)

Sessions of the German Reichstag

Stenographische Berichte über die Verhandlungen des Reichstags, Session 1884, V, IV, Bd. I, p. 481

Table of Cases

Norway

Norwegian Supreme Court (Høyesterett)

Rt. 2000 s. 1811	Finanger I
Rt. 2010 s. 202	Kystlink-dommen
Rt. 2010 s. 944	kjennelse CHC-saken
Rt. 2011 s. 609	SAS-saken
Rt. 2011 s. 964	Gjensidige-saken
Rt. 2012 s. 219	CHC-saken

Lower Courts

LB-2010-99486 (Borgarting Court of Appeal)	Gjensidige-saken (Rt. 2011 s. 964)
LE-2009-47936 (Eidsivating Court of Appeal)	
TSTVG-2005-75777 (Stavanger District Court)	Statoil-saken
TOSLO-2009-143503 (Oslo District Court)	Gjensidige-saken (Rt. 2011 s. 964)

Administrative law bodies (not including decisions by Norwegian Appeal Board for Health Personnel)

Equality and Anti-Discrimination Ombudsman – Likestillings- og diskrimineringsombudet (LDO)

LDO case 09/1839, statement 11 February 2011

LDO case 10/142, statement 11 April 2011

The Equality and Anti-discrimination Tribunal - Likestillings- og diskrimineringsnemnda (LDN)

LDN case 36/2009, statement 14 December 2009

LDN case 24/2011, statement 22 November 2011

Germany

Bundesverfassungsgericht (German Supreme Court - BVerfG)

BVerfG, Beschluss vom 30 April 1952 – 1 BvR 14/52, 1 BvR 25/52, 1 BvR 167/52 –, BVerfGE 1, 264-28 (Bezirksschornsteinfeger)

BVerfG, Beschluss vom 16. Juni 1959 – 1 BvR 71/57 –, BVerfGE 9, 338-354 (Altersgrenze für Hebammen)

BVerfG, Entscheidung vom 17. Juli 1961 – 1 BvL 44/55 –, BVerfGE 13, 97 (Befähigungsnachweis für Handwerker)

BVerfG, Beschluss vom 04. Mai 1983 – 1 BvL 46/80, 1 BvL 47/80 –, BVerfGE 64, 72-86 (Prüfingenieur)

BVerfG, Beschluss vom 10. April 1984 – 2 BvL 19/82 –, BVerfGE 67, 1-25 (Emeritierungsalter)

BVerfG, Beschluss vom 21. Juni 1989 – 1 BvR 32/87 –, BVerfGE 80, 257-268

BVerfG, Kammerbeschluss vom 16. November 1990 – 1 BvR 1280/90 –, juris

BVerfG, Kammerbeschluss vom 29. Oktober 1992 – 1 BvR 1581/91 –, (Nichtannahmebeschluß: Verfassungsmäßigkeit der Höchstaltersgrenze von 70 Jahren für die Ausübung des Notarberufs)

BVerfG, Kammerbeschluss vom 31. März 1998 – 1 BvR 2167/93, 1 BvR 2198/93 –, juris

BVerfG, Nichtannahmebeschluss vom 07. August 2007 – 1 BvR 1941/07 –, juris (Altersgrenze für Vertragszahnärzte)

BVerfG, Stattgebender Kammerbeschluss vom 24. Oktober 2011 – 1 BvR 1103/11 –, juris

BVerfG, Kammerbeschluss vom 20. Dezember 1996 – 1 BvL 10/96 –, juris

BVerfG, Beschluss vom 20. März 2001 – 1 BvR 491/96 –, BVerfGE 103, 172-195

BVerfG, Nichtannahmebeschluss vom 04. Oktober 2001 – 1 BvR 1435/01 –, juris

BVerfG, Nichtannahmebeschluss vom 04. Oktober 2001 – 1 BvR 1418/01 –, juris

BVerfG, Nichtannahmebeschluss vom 30. Juni 2008 – 1 BvR 1159/08 –, juris

BVerfG, Nichtannahmebeschluss vom 26. Januar 2007 – 2 BvR 2408/06 –, juris

BVerfG, Nichtannahmebeschluss vom 25. November 2004 – 1 BvR 2459/04 –, juris (Altersgrenze für Piloten)

Bundesverwaltungsgericht (BVerwG)

BVerwG, Urteil vom 01. Februar 2012 – 8 C 24/11 –, BVerwGE 141, 385-393

Bundesarbeitsgericht (BAG)

BAG, Urteil vom 28. 9. 1961 - 2 AZR 428/60, NJW 1962, pp. 73-74
BAG, Urteil vom 31. Juli 2002 – 7 AZR 140/01 –, BAGE 102, 65-73
BAG, Urteil vom 27. November 2002 – 7 AZR 655/01 –, juris
BAG, Urteil vom 21. Juli 2004 – 7 AZR 589/03 –, juris
BAG, EuGH-Vorlage vom 17. Juni 2009 – 7 AZR 112/08 (A) –, BAGE 131, 113-144
BAG, Urteil vom 15. Februar 2012 – 7 AZR 946/07 –, juris

Bundessozialgericht (BSG)

BSG, Urteil vom 25. November 1998 – B 6 KA 4/98 R –, SozR 3-2500 § 95 Nr 18, BSGE 83, 135-145
BSG, Beschluss vom 18. August 2010 – B 6 KA 18/10 B –, SozR 4-2500 § 95 Nr 17

Hessischer Verwaltungsgerichtshof (VGH)

Hessischer VGH, Urteil vom 28. September 2009 – 1 B 2487/09 –, juris
Hessischer VGH, Beschluss vom 28. Oktober 2013 – 1 B 1638/13 –, juris

Oberverwaltungsgericht (OVG) Lüneburg

OVG Lüneburg, Beschluss vom 13. September 2006 – 12 ME 275/06 –, juris

Reichsgericht (RG)

RG, 3. Zivilsenat, Urteil vom 14.03.1922, Akz. III 689/21104, RGZ 58 (63)

Lower courts

Verwaltungsgericht (VG) Frankfurt a.M., Beschluss vom 29. März 2010 – 9 K 3854/09.F – , juris
ArbG Frankfurt, Urteil vom 14. März 2007 – 6 Ca 7405/06 –, juris

European Union

Court of Justice of the European Union (CJEU, previously European Court of Justice (ECJ))

Case C-43/75 *Gabrielle Defrenne v Société anonyme belge de navigation aérienne Sabena*, ECR 1976, 455

Case 96/80 *Mrs J. P. Jenkins v Kingsgate (Clothing Productions) Ltd*, ECR 1981, 911

Case 152/84, *M. H. Marshall v Southampton and South-West Hampshire Area Health Authority*, ECR 1986, 723

Case 170/84, *Bilka - Kaufhaus GmbH v Karin Weber von Hartz*, ECR 1986, 1607

Case C-91/92 *Paola Faccini Dori v Recreb Srl.*, ECR 1994 I-3325

Case C-273/97, *Angela M. Sirdar v The Army Board/Secretary of State for Defence*, ECR 1999 I-7403

Case C-285/98, *Tanja Kreil v Bundesrepublik Deutschland*, ECR 2000 I-69

Case C-476/99, *H. Lommers v Minister van Landbouw, Natuurbeheer en Visserij*, ECR 2002 I-02891

Joined cases C-397/01 to C-403/01, *Bernhard Pfeiffer and others v Deutsches Rotes Kreuz, Kreisverband Waldshut eV*, ECR 2004 I-8835

Case C-144/04, *Werner Mangold v Rüdiger Helm*, ECR 2005 I-9981

Case C-227/04 P, *Maria-Luise Lindorfer v Council of the European Union*, ECR 2007 I-6767

Case C-411/05, *Félix Palacios de la Villa v Cortefiel Servicios SA*, ECR 2007 I-8531

Case C-427/06, *Birgit Bartsch v Bosch und Siemens Hausgeräte (BSH) Altersfürsorge GmbH*, ECR 2008 I-7245

Case C-388/07 *The Queen, on the application of The Incorporated Trustees of the National Council for Ageing (Age Concern England) v Secretary of State for Business, Enterprise and Regulatory Reform*, ECR 2009 I-1569

Case C-555/07, *Seda Kücükdeveci v Swedex GmbH & Co. KG*, ECR 2010 I-365

Case C-88/08, *David Hütter v Technische Universität Graz*, ECR 2009 I-5325

Case C-499/08, *Ingeniørforeningen i Danmark v Region Syddanmark*, ECR 2010 I-9343

Case C-341/08, *Domnica Petersen v Berufungsausschuss für Zahnärzte für den Bezirk Westfalen-Lippe*, ECR 2010 I-47

Case C-45/09, *Gisela Rosenbladt v Oellerking Gebäudereinigungsges*, ECR 2010 I-9391

Joined cases C-250/09 and C-268/09, *Vasil Ivanov Georgiev v Tehnicheski universitet - Sofia, filial Plovdiv*, ECR 2010 I-11869

Cases C-159/10 and C-160/10, *Gerhard Fuchs and Peter Köhler v Land Hessen*, ECR 2011 I-06919

Joined cases C-297/10 and (C-298/10), *Sabine Hennigs v Eisenbahn-Bundesamt and Land Berlin v Alexander Mai,* ECR 2011 I-7965

Case C-447/09, *Reinhard Prigge and Others v Deutsche Lufthansa AG*, ECR 2011 I-8003

Case C-109/09, *Deutsche Lufthansa AG v Gertraud Kumpan*, ECR 2011, I-1309

Case C-286/12, *European Commission v Hungary*, ECR 2012 -00000

Case C-152/11, *Johann Odar v Baxter Deutschland GmbH*, ECR 2012 -00000

Case C-141/11, *Torsten Hörnfeldt v Posten Meddelande AB*, ECR 2012 -00000

Case C-476/11, *HK Danmark (Kristensen) v Experian A/S*, ECR 2013 -00000

Joined cases C-501/12 to C-506/12, C-540/12 and C-541/12, *Thomas Specht and others v Bundesrepublik Deutschland*, (not yet published)

Case C-416/13 (Vital Pérez), *Mario Vital* Pérez v Ayuntamiento de Oviedo (not yet published)

Opinions of the Advocate General

AG Sharpston, in: C-227/04 P (Lindorfer)

AG Mazák, in: C- 411/05 (Palacios de la Villa)

AG Sharpston, in: C-427/06 (Bartsch)

AG Bot, in: C-555/07 (Kücükdeveci)

AG Bot, in: C-341/08 (Petersen)

AG Bot in: joined cases C-250/09 and C-268/09 (Georgiev)

AG Trstenjak, in: C-45/09 (Rosenbladt)

AG Villalón, in: C-447/09 (Prigge)

UN Human Rights Committee (UN HRC)

UN HRC, Communication No. 895/1999, *Alejandro Marín Gómez v Spain UN*, 20 July 1998

UN HRC, Communication No. 855/1999, *M. Schmitz-de-Jong v The Netherlands,* 25 November 1998 (initial submission)

UN HRC, Communication No. 1016/2001, *Rubén S. Hinostroza Solís v. Peru*, 19 July 1999

UN HRC, Communication No 983/2001, *Love et al v. Australia*, 28 April 2003

European Committee for Social Rights (ECSR)

Complaint No. 74 (2011) *Fellesforbundet for Sjøfolk (FFFS) v. Norway*; Decision on the merits, 20 October 2011

Foreign case law

Denmark

Københavns Byret, sag nr. BS 32C-1356/2010, judgement of 4 April 2011

Sweden

Arbetsdomstolens dom, nr 37/11, judgement of 4 May 2011

The Netherlands

Dutch Supreme Court, NR. C03/077HR Martinair Holland NV v. Vereniging van Nedelandse Verkeervliegers, judgement of 8 October 2004

United States of America

U.S. Supreme Court, 472 U.S. 400, Western Air Lines v. Criswell, (1985)

Bibliography

A

Aarbakke, Magnus/Helgesen, Jan 1982, 'Sources of law in Norway' in: The sources of law. A comparative empirical study. National systems of sources of law, Kourilsky, Chantal /Rácz, Attila/Schäffer, Heinz (eds.), pp. 189-225.

Aasland, Olaf G./Bringedal, Berit/Ronge, Kari 2010, 'Aldersgrense for legers autorisasjon og lisens' Tidsskrift for Den norske legeforening. Nr. 19, 2010, 130, pp. 1917-1920.

Aasland, Olaf G./Førde, Reidun. 2005, 'Impact of feeling responsible for adverse events on doctors' personal and professional lives: the importance of being open to criticism from colleagues' Quality and Safety in Health Care. 2005:14, pp. 13–17.

Age reference Group on Equality and Human Rights 2005, 'Age and multiple discrimination in older people' A Discussion Paper. online available at: http://www.ageuk.org.uk/documents/en-gb/for-professionals/research/age%20and%20multiple%20discrimination%20(2005)_pro.pdf?dtrk=true (last accessed: 17.12.2014).

Andersen, Kristen 1967, Fra arbeidslivets rett, 1967.

Andenæs, Mads H. 1997, Rettskildelære.

Annan, Kofi A. 2002, Foreword to UN Madrid Plan and the Political Declaration, 2002.

Arber, Sara/Ginn, Jay 1991, Gender and Later Life.

Atchley, Robert C. 1971, 'Retirement and leisure participation: Continuity or crisis?' The Gerontologist 11(1), 1971, pp. 13–17.

Atchley, Robert C. 1989, 'A continuity theory of normal aging' The Gerontologist (1989) 29 (2), 1989, pp. 183-190.

B

Bagger, Tuk 2013, 'Alder som diskriminationgrund' in: Liber Amicarum et Amicorum in Honour of Ruth Nielsen, Festskrift. Fejø, Jens/Neergard, Ulla/Tvarnø, Christina D./Ølykke, Grith Skovgaard (eds.), pp. 61-79.

Bader, Peter 2014, 'Arbeitsrechtliche Altersgrenzen weiter flexibilisiert' Neue Zeitschrift für Arbeitsrecht. 2014, pp. 749-753.

Baker, Aaron 2008, 'Proportionality and Employment Discrimination in the UK' Industrial Law journal. Vol. 37 (4), 2008, pp. 305-328.

Bamforth, Nicolas/Malik, Maleiha/O'Cinneide, Colm 2008, Discrimination Law: Theory and Context.

Barnard, Catherine/Hepple, Bob 2000, 'Substantive Equality' The Cambridge Law Journal. Vol. 59 Issue 03, 2000, pp. 562-585.

Baßlsperger, Maximilian 2008, 'Altersdiskriminierung durch Beamtenrecht' Zeitschrift für Beamtenrecht. 10/2008, pp. 339-350.

Bauer, Jobst-Hubertus/Arnold, Christian 2006, 'Auf Junk folgt Mangold - Europarecht verdrängt deutsches Arbeitsrecht' Neue Juristische Wochenschrift. 2006, pp. 6-12.

Bauer, Jobst-Hubertus/Arnold, Christian 2008, 'Verbot der Altersdiskriminierung, Die Bartsch-Entscheidung des EuGH und ihre Folgen' Neue Juristische Wochenschrift. 2008, pp. 3377-3383.

Bauer, Jobst-Hubertus 2009, 'Der Professorenentwurf zum ArbVG - Kein Danaergeschenk, sondern sinnvolle Diskussionsgrundlage!' Arbeitsrechtliche Entscheidungen. 2009, pp. 14-15.

Bauckhage-Hoffer, Florian/Umnuß, Karsten 2011, 'Die 'Mangold'-Entscheidung des EuGH und das deutsche Arbeitsrecht - der vorerst letzte Akt' Europäisches Wirtschafts- und Steuerrecht. 2011, pp. 38-44.

Bayefsky, Anne 1990, 'The Principle of Equality or Non-Discrimination in International Law' Human Rights Quarterly Vol. 11 No.1-2 (1990), pp. 1-34.

Becker, Ulrich 1999, 'Zur verfassungsrechtlichen Stellung der Vertragsärzte am Beispiel der zulassungsbezogenen Altersgrenzen' Neue Zeitschrift für Sozialrecht. 1999, pp. 521-530.

Befring, Anne K./Grytten, Nils J./Ohnstad, Bente 2002, Jus for leger.

Beitze, Editha 2009, § 8, in: Kommentar zum AGG, Thomas Hey (ed.).

Belling, Detlev W. 2011, § 10 AGG, in: Erman BGB, Kommentar, Westermann, Harm P. (ed.), 13.edt.

Benda-Beckmann, Keebet 1979, 'Einige Bemerkungen über die Beziehung zwischen Rechtssoziologie und Rechtsvergleichung' Zeitschrift für vergleichende Rechtswissenschaften 78, 1979, pp. 51-67.

Berg, Peter 2014, § 75, in: BetrVG, Däubler, Wolfgang/Kittner, Michael/Klebe, Thomas/Wedde, Peter (eds.), 14.edt.

Bertelsmann, Klaus 2007, § 10 AGG in: AGG, Rust, Ursula/Falke, Josef (eds.).

Bertnes, Pål A. 1993, 'Sources to legal information in Norway' International Journal of Legal Information. Vol. 21, 1993, pp. 154-166.

Beschorner, Jürgen 2010, 'Zulässigkeit von Altersgrenzen für Vertragszahnärzte nach der Richtlinie 2000/78/EG' Zeitschrift für ausländisches und internationales Arbeits- und Sozialrecht. 3/2010, pp. 252-265.

Birren, James E./Cunningham, W. 1985 , 'Research on the psychology of aging: principles, concepts and theory', in: Handbook of the Psychology of Ageing. James E. Birren/Schaie, K. Warner (eds.), pp. 3–34.

BIS 2011, Phasing out the Default Retirement Age - Government Response to Consultation, January 2011, available at: https://www.gov.uk/government/consultations/phasing-out-the-default-retirement-age *(last accessed: 17.12.2014)*

Bjørgen, Ivar A. 2010, 'Aldersgrenser som diskriminering' adressa.no 18.2.2010.

Blanpain, Roger 2011, 'Discrimination on the basis of age, The EU: Only a beginning', in: Labour law between change and tradition, Blanpain, Roger/Hendrickx, Frank (eds.), pp. 1-9.

Boecken, Winfried 2005, 'Die Altersgrenze von 68 Jahren für Vertragsärzte aus EG-rechtlicher Sicht' Neue Zeitschrift für Sozialrecht. 2005, pp. 393-400.

Boecken, Winfried 2008, 'Höchstaltersgrenze für Vertragsärzte' ArztRecht. 2008, pp. 299-302.

Boerner, Dietmar 1992, Altersgrenzen für die Beendigung von Arbeitsverhältnissen in Tarifverträgen und Betriebsvereinbarungen.

Brand, Oliver 2003, 'Grundfragen der Rechtsvergleichung' Juristische Schulung. 2003, pp. 1082-1091.

Brand, Oliver 2007, 'Conceptual Comparisons: Towards a Coherent Methodology of Comparative Legal Studies' Brooklyn Journal of international law, Vol. 32 Issue 2, 2007, pp. 405-466.

Brors Christiane 2008, § 8, § 10 in: Allgemeines Gleichbehandlungsgesetz. Däubler, Wolfgang/Bertzbach, Martin (eds.).

Brors, Christiane 2012, 'Wann ist eine Altersdiskriminierung nach der Rechtsprechung des EuGH gerechtfertigt?' Recht der Arbeit. 2012, pp. 346-353.

Brock-Utne, Birgit 2010, 'Det er arbeidet som gir livet mitt innhold' Morgenbladet 30. April 2010.

Brox, Hans/Rüthers, Bernd/Henssler, Martin 2007, Arbeitsrecht. 17. ed.

Bruusgaard, Dag 2010, 'Forsvarlighet og autorisasjon' Tidsskrift for Den norske legeforening. Nr. 19 2010, 130, p. 1906.

Burroni, L./Keune, M. 2011, 'Flexicurity: a conceptual critique', European Journal of Industrial Relations. No. 17, 1 (2011), pp. 75–91.

Busse, E.W./Maddox, G. L. (eds.) 1985, The Duke longitudinal studies on normal aging: 1955-1980.

Butler, Robert N. 1969, 'Age-ism: Another form of bigotry' The Gerontologist. Vol. 9 (4), 1969, pp. 243-246.

Butler, Robert N. 2002, 'Declaration of the Rights of Older Persons' The Gerontologist. Vol. 42, 2002, pp. 152-153.

Bytheway, Bill 1995, Ageism.

Bytheway, Bill 2005, 'Ageism' in: The Cambridge Handbook on age and ageing. Johnson, Malcom L. et al. (eds.) pp. 338-345.

C

Calasanti, Toni/Slevin, Kathleen 2006, 'Introduction: Age Matters' in: Age Matters: Re-aligning Feminist Thinking. Calasanti, Toni/Slevin, Kathleen (eds.) pp. 1-20.

Calasanti, Toni M./Slevin, Kathleen F./King, Neal 2006 , 'Ageism and Feminism: From 'Et Cetera' to Center' National Women's Studies Association Journal. (now: Feminist Formations), Vol. 18, No. 1, 2006, pp. 13-30.

Calasanti, Toni M. 2008, 'A feminist confronts ageism' Journal of Ageing Studies. Vol. 22 (2), 2008, pp. 157-162.

Chapman, Peter, J. 1984, 'The consequences of in-flight incapacitation in civil aviation' Aviation, space, and environmental medicine. June 1984, pp. 497-500

Chen, Lung-Chu 1987, 'Aging: A new human rights concern – A policy-oriented perspective, Proceedings of the American Society of International Law' American Society of International Law. Vol. 81, 1987, pp. 169–175.

Christensen, Anna 2000, 'Normativa grundmönster i pensjonssystemen' in: Lovens liv, Festskrift Jörgen Dalberg-Larsen. Olsen, Henrik P.(ed.), pp. 171-193.

Cicero 106 B.C.–43 B.C., On Old Age The Harvard Classics, 1909–1914.

Collier, Roger 2008, 'Diagnosing the aging physician' Canadian Medical Association Journal. April 22, 2008, pp. 1121-1123.

Cotter, Anne-Marie 2008, Just a Number, An international legal analysis to age discrimination.

Cumming, Elaine/Dean, Lois R./Newell, David S./McCaffrey, Isabel 1960, 'Disengagement-A Tentative Theory of Aging' Sociometry. Vol. 23, No. 1, 1960, pp. 23-35.

Cumming, Elaine/Henry, W.E. (eds.) 1961, Growing old: The process of disengagement.

D

Danisi, Carmelo 2011, 'How far can the European Court of Human Rights go in the fight against discrimination? Defining new standards in its nondiscrimination jurisprudence' International Journal of Constitutional Law. 2011: 9, pp. 793-807.

Däubler, Wolfgang 2008, Einleitung, in: Allgemeines Gleichbehandlungsgesetz. Däubler, Wolfgang/Bertzbach, Martin (eds.) 2. edt.

de Beauvoir, Simone 1972, Coming of Age. translated by Patrick O' Brian, ed. 1996.

de Cruz, Peter 2007, Comparative law in a changing world. 3. edt.

De Coninck, Julie 2010, 'The functional method of comparative law, Quo vadis?' Zeitschrift für ausländisches und internationales Privatrecht. 74 2010, pp. 351-359.

Deflem, Mathieu 2008, Sociology of law: Visions of scholarly tradition.

De Hert, Paul/Mantovani, Eugenio 2011, 'Specific Human Rights of older persons?' European Human Rights Law Review. Issue 4, 2011, pp. 398-418.

De Schutter, Olivier 2005, The prohibition of discrimination under European human rights law.

Dittrich, Dennis/Büsch, Victoria/Micheel, Frank 2011, 'Working beyond retirement age in Germany: The Employee's perspective' in: Older Workers in a sustainable society. Ennals, Richard/Salomon, Robert (eds.), pp. 189-202.

Doron, Israel 2005, 'From National to International Elder Law' The Journal of International Aging, Law & policy. Vol. I, 2005, pp. 43-67.

Doron, Israel 2007, 'Demographic, social change and equality' in: Equality Law in an Enlarged European Union. Meenan, Helen (ed.), pp. 117-141.

Doron, Israel/Itai Apter 2010, 'The debate around the need for an international convention on the rights of older persons' The Gerontologist. Vol. 50 Issue 4, 2010, pp. 586-593.

Duncan, Colin/Loretto, Wendy 2004, 'Never the right age? Gender and age-based discrimination in employment' Gender, Work & Organization. Vol. 11, Issue 1, 2004, pp. 95–115.

Dunkel-Benz, Friederike 2008, 'Altern aus medizinischer Sicht – Vermeidbares und Unvermeidliches' Neue Zeitschrift für Arbeitsrecht. Beilage 2008, pp. 25-26.

Dybendal, Kirsten Enger/Skiri, Halvard 2005, 'Klare geografiske forskjeller i levealder mellom bydeler i Oslo' in: samfunnspeilet. Vol. 6, 2005, pp. 18-27.

E

European Commission 2010, Developing Anti-Discrimination Law in Europe.

European Union Agency for Fundamental Rights/European Court of Human Rights – Council of Europe (2011), Handbook on European non-discrimination law.

Eckhoff, Torstein/Helgesen, Jan E. 2001, Rettskildelære. 5.edt.

Econ Pöyry 2010, 'Sammfunnsøkonomisk gevinst ved økt pensjoneringsalder, utarbeidet for Senter for seniorpolitikk' Notat 2010-020.

Eichenhofer, Eberhard 1997, 'Einführung in die Sozialrechtsvergleichung' Neue Zeitschrift für Sozialrecht. 1997, pp. 97-102.

Eichenhofer, Eberhard 2007, 'Gesetzliche Altersgrenze im Vertrags(zahn)arztrecht: Kann nach dem AGG alles beim Alten bleiben?' Die Sozialgerichtsbarkeit. 2007, pp. 580-585.

Ekroll, Torbjørn 2009, 'Når de yngste får bestemme' Tidsskrift for Den norske legeforening. Nr. 9, 2009, 129, pp. 892-893.

Ellis, Evelyn 1999, The Principle of Proportionality in the Laws of Europe.

Ellis, Evelyn/Watson, Philippa 2012, EU anti-discrimination law. 2. edt.

Enehaug, Heidi/Hilsen, Anne I./Steinum, Trude 2008, 'Særaldersgrenser og virksomhetens handlingsrom' AFI-notat 2008/5.

Eurostat (2013), Average exit age from the labour force –annual data, available at: http://appsso.eurostat.ec.europa.eu/nui/show.do?dataset=lfsi_exi_a&lang=en (last accessed 17.12.2014).

Evans, John G. 2003, 'Age discrimination: Implications of the ageing process' in: Age as an equality issue. Fredman, Sandra/Spencer, Sarah (eds.) pp. 11-20.

Evju, Stein 1979, 'Om kontraktsvern, arbeidstilsyn og straff' in: Arbeidsrettslige emner. Stein Evju, and Henning Jakhelln (eds.) pp. 215-376.

Evju, Stein 2006, 'Aldersdiskriminering, likebehandling og pensjonsalder' Arbeidsrett. Vol. 3 Nr. 3, 2006, pp. 137–161.

Evju, Stein 2009, Proposisjon om "70-årsregelen" i arbeidsmiljølovens § 15-7, Nytt i privatretten, p. 4.

Evju, Stein 2013, Saklighet og saklighetsprøvelse, en rettgenetisk studie, Arbeidsrett Vol. 10 Nr. I, 2013, pp. 82-111.

F

Fafo 2012, Seniorpolitiske framtidsbilder, available at: http://www.fafo.no/pub/rapp/20229/20229.pdf (last accessed: 17.12.2014).

Fahlbeck, Reinhold 2003, 'Comparative labor law – Quo vadis?' Comparative Labour Law & Policy Journal. Vol. 25:7, 2003-2004, pp. 7-20.

Falke, Josef 2007, § 8 AGG, in: AGG Rust, Ursula/Falke, Josef (eds.).

Fanebust, Arne 2013, Innføring i arbeidsrett. 3. edt.

Feldman, David 1999, Human dignity as a legal value: Part 1, Public Law (1999), pp. 682-702.

Fenske, Antje 1998, Das Verbot der Altersdiskriminierung im US-amerikanischen Arbeitsrecht.

Fornyings- og administrasjons-departementet 2009, Aldersgrensene i staten og aldersgrensene for øvrige medlemmer i statens pensjonskasse.

Fornyings-, administrasjons- og kirkedepartementet 2013 , Statens Personalhåndbook.

Forshaw, Simon/Pilgerstorfer, Marcus 2008, 'Direct and Indirect Discrimination: Is There Something in between?' Industrial Law Journal. Vol. 37, 2008, pp. 347-364.

Forst, Gerrit 2012, 'Kollektivvertragsfreiheit versus Verbot der Altersdiskriminierung' Europäische Zeitschrift für Arbeitsrecht. 2012, pp. 225-235.

Foster, Nigel/Sule, Satish 2002, German legal system and laws. 3. edt.

Foster, Nigel/Sule, Satish 2010, German legal system and laws. 4. edt.

Frankenberg, Günter 1985, 'Critical comparisons: Re-thinking comparative law' Harvard International Law Journal. Vol. 26 No .2, 1985, pp. 411-455.

Fredman, Sandra 1999, 'A critical review of the concept of equality in U.K. anti-discrimination law, Independent review of the enforcement of U.K. anti-discrimination legislation' Working Paper No. 3, Cambridge Centre for Public Law and Judge Institute of Management Studies 1999.

Fredman, Sandra 2003, 'The age of equality' in: Age as an equality issue. Fredman, Sandra/Spencer, Sarah (eds.), pp. 21-69.

Fredman, Sandra 2005, 'Double trouble: multiple discrimination and EU law' in: European Anti-Discrimination Law Review. Issue No. 2, 2005, pp. 13-18.

Fredman, Sandra 2011, Discrimination Law. 2. edt.

Fredriksen Haukeland, Halvard 2007, 'Domstolenes prøving av EØS-avtalens proporsjonalitetsgrunnsetning – En kommentar til Høyesteretts dom i spilleautomatsaken' Jussens Venner. Nr. 5, 2007, pp. 295-305.

Frenz, Walter 2010, 'Unmittelbare Arbeitnehmerrechte aus Richtlinien mit Anwendungsstopp durch das BVerfG? Die Verfassungsbeschwerde Honeywell' Recht der Arbeit. 2010, pp. 229-234.

Fuchs, Maximilian 2011, 'Mangold – Kein ausbrechender Rechtsakt' Zeitschrift für europäisches Sozial- und Arbeitsrecht. 2011, pp. 3-9.

G

Gamillscheg, Franz 1964, 'Die Grundrechte im Arbeitsrecht' Archiv für civilistische Praxis. vol. 164, 1964, pp. 385-445.

Gerards, Janneke 2004, 'The Application of Article 14 ECHR by the European Court of Human Rights' in: The development of Legal Instruments to Combat Racism in a Diverse Europe. Niessen, Jan/Chopin, Isabelle (eds.), pp. 3-60.

Gerards, Janneke 2007, 'Multiple Discrimination', in: Cases, materials and text on national, supranational and international non-discrimination law. Schiek, Dagmar/Waddington, Lisa/Bell, Mark (eds.), chap. 1.5, pp. 170-179.

Gerhardt, Michael 2010, 'Europa als Rechtsgemeinschaft: Der Beitrag des Bundesverfassungsgerichts' Zeitschrift für Rechstpolitik. 2010, pp. 161-165.

Gerken, Lüder/Rieble, Volker/Roth, Günter H./Stein, Torsten/Streinz, Rudolf 2009, 'Mangold' als ausbrechender Rechtsakt.

Ghosheh, Naj 2008, 'Age discrimination and older workers: Theory and legislation in comparative context' Conditions of work and employment. Series, No. 20, 2008.

Giegerich, Thomas 2007, Einleitung, in: AGG. Rust, Ursula/Falke, Josef (eds.).

Gislerud, G./Claussen, B./Bruusgaard, D. 2000, 'Lisens for leger' Tidsskrift for Den norske legeforening. 2000, 120, pp. 2446-2447.

Gogstad Anders/Aasland Olaf G. 1998, 'Hvordan har de pensjonerte legene det?' Tidsskrift for Den norske legeforening. 1998, 118, pp. 1378-1382.

Gomien, Donna/Harris, David/Zwaak, Leo 1996, Law and Practice of the European Convention on Human Rights and the European Social Charter.

Gosepath, Stefan 2007, 'Equality' in: Stanford Encyclopedia of Philosophy, available at: http://plato.stanford.edu/entries/equality/ (last accessed 17.12.2014).

Groß, Daniela 2010, Die Rechtfertigung einer Altersdiskriminierung auf der Grundlage der Richtlinie 2000/78/EG.

Grossfeld, Bernhard 1990, The strength and weakness of comparative law.

Gärditz, Ferdinand K. 2010, 'Zur Vereinbarkeit beamtenrechtlicher Altersgrenzen mit der EG-Gleichbehandlungsrichtlinie 2000/78/EG' Zeitschrift für das Privatrecht der Europäischen Union. 2010, pp. 17-19.

H

Haak, Sabine 2009, 'Das Ende der Zwangspensionierung, Gesetzliche Altersregelung für Ärzte' in: Hartmannbund Magazin. Nr. 1, 10, 2009

Haave, Per 2007, 'Da legene skulle autoriseres' Tidsskrift for Den norske legeforening. Nr. 24, 2007, 127, pp. 3267-3271.

Hack, Melanie R. 2010 a, 'Impact or potential of anti-discrimination legislation in light of the demographic change – Comparisons between Norway and Germany' Europäische Zeitschrift für Arbeitsrecht. 2010, pp. 347-359.

Hack Melanie R., 2010 b, 'Arbeidsrett. Lek med ilden - djevelen stikker i detaljene: Aldersdiskriminering, maksimalalder for ansettelse i brannvesen - EU-domstolens dom 12. januar 2010, sak C-229/08 Colin Wolf mot Stadt Frankfurt am Main' in: Nytt i privatretten. (1), 2010, pp. 7-8.

Hack, Melanie R. 2010 c, 'Etter lek med ild, nå lek med vann: Aldersgrense, pensjonsalder, sjømenn Høyesterettsdom 18. februar 2010 (HR-2010-00303-A)' Nytt i privatretten. (2), 2010, pp. 2-3.

Hack, Melanie R. 2011, 'Gamle professorer, bedriftsfastsatte aldersgrenser og eldrebølgen' Nytt i privatretten. (2), 2011, pp. 5-6.

Hack, Melanie R. 2012 a, 'To be or not be be? – The Norwegian dilemma of being just politically bound to Framework Directive 2000/78/EC' Europäische Zeitschrift für Arbeitsrecht. 2012, pp. 357-367.

Hack, Melanie R. 2012 b, 'Should I stay or should I go? Altersgrenzenregelungen für Professoren in Norwegen' in: Altersdiskriminierung, Jahrbuch 2012. Wachter, Gustav (ed.), pp. 193 –214.

Hagen, Steinar 2009, 'Samfunnets hån mot eldre leger' Tidsskrift for Den norske legeforening. nr. 4, 2009, 129, pp. 311-312.

Hagestad, Gunhild O./Uhlenberg, Peter 2005, 'The Social Separation of Old and Young: A Root of Ageism' Journal of Social Issues. Vol. 61 Issue 2, 2005, pp. 343-360.

Hahn, Oliver 2006, Auswirkungen der europäischen Regelungen zur Altersdiskriminierung im deutschen Arbeitsrecht: Mit rechtsvergleichenden Hinweisen zum U.S.-amerikanischen Recht.

Haldorsen, Tor/Reitan, Jon B./Tveten, Ulf 2002, 'Aircraft accidents and other causes of death among comercial pilots' Aviation space and environmental medicine. Vol. 73 No. 6, June 2002, pp. 587-592.

Hanau, Peter 2010, 'Die Europäische Grundrechtscharta - Schein und Wirklichkeit im Arbeitsrecht' Neue Zeitschrift für Arbeitsrecht. 2010, pp. 1-6.

Hannett, Sarah 2003, 'Equality at the intersections: The legislative and judicial failure to tackle multiple discrimination' Oxford Journal of Legal Studies. Vol. 23 No. 1, 2003, pp. 65-86.

Hartmer, Michael 2009, 'Prof. em. oder Prof. a.D.? Zur Titelführung von pensionierten und emeritierten Hochschullehrern' Forschung & Lehre. 10. October 2009, available at: http://www.forschung-und-lehre.de/wordpress/?p=2888 (last accessed 17.12.2014).

Haugum, Per 2008, 'Eldre leger diskrimineres ikke' Tidskrift for Den norske legeforening. Nr. 13-14, 2008, 128, pp. 1545-1546.

Havighurst, Robert J. 1961, 'Successful Aging' The Gerontologist. 1 (1), March 1961 pp. 8-13.

Heemskerk, Mark 2009, De arbeidsdeelname van oudere werknemers.

Heikkinnen, Satu/Krekula, Clary 2008, 'Ålderism ett fruktbart begrepp?' Sociologisk Forskning. 2008, pp. 19-34.

Helsedirektoratet 2012, Ny turnusordning for leger, Informasjon og veiledningsmateriell. 1. edt., available at: http://helsedirektoratet.no/helsepersonell/turnusordning-for-leger/Documents/Ny_turnusordning_veiledningsmateriell_1.pdf (last accessed 17.12.2014).

Henrÿ, Hagen 1997, 'Kulturfremdes Recht erkennen. Warum? Wie?' Zeitschrift für Rechtsvergleichung. Vol. 38 H 2, 1997, pp. 45-55.

Hensrud, Anne/Kristiansen, Ivar S. 1994, 'Yrkesaktivet og pensjonering blant norske leger over 55 år' Tidsskrift for Den norske legeforening. Nr. 26, 1994, 114, pp. 3093-3096.

Hepple, Bob 2003, 'Age discrimination in employment: Implementing the Framework Directive 2000/78/EC' in: Age as an equality issue. Fredman, Sandra/Spencer, Sarah (eds.), pp. 71-96.

Herlofsen, Erik R. 2008, 'Diskriminerende aldersgrenser for leger, "Autorisasjonen er inndratt"' Vi Over 60. Nov. 2008, pp. 68-69.

Herlofsen, Erik R. 2013, 'Særaldersgrenser på gyngende juridisk grunn?' in: seniorpolitikken.no 2013, available at: www.seniorpolitikken.no (last accessed: 17.12.2014).

Hesral, Harald 2013, 'chap. 3, B. Anspruch auf Wiederzulassung zur vertragsärztlichen Versorgung' in: Disziplinarrecht für Ärzte und Zahnärzte. Ehlers, Alexander (ed.) 2. edt.

Hippe, Jon M./Midtsundstad, Tove/Arup Seip, Åsmund/Bogen, Hanne/Hernes, Gudmund 2012, 'When I'm Sixty-Four – seniorpolitiske framtidsbilder' Fafo-rapport 2012:02.

Hochschild, Arlie R. 1975, 'Disengagement Theory: A Critique and Proposal' American Sociological Review. Vol. 40, No. 5, October 1975, pp. 553-569.

Holgersen, Gudrun 2013, 'Aldersdiskriminering' in: Undring og erkjennelse, Festskrift til Jan Fridthof Bernt 70 år. Søvig, Karl H/Schütz, Sigrid Eskeleand/Rasmussen, Ørnulf (eds), pp. 207-219.

Hotvedt, Marianne, Jenum/Ulseth, Terese Smith 2013, 'Arbeidsavtalen og styringsrett: Harmoni i en domsoktett' Arbeidsrett. Vol. 10 Nr. 1, 2013, pp. 112-138.

Howard, Erica 2010, The EU race directive: Developing the protection against racial discrimination within the EU.

Hug, Walther 1932, 'History of comparative law' Harvard Law Review. Vol. 45 Issue 6, 1932, pp. 1027-1070.

Hunstad, Nils 2009, 'Opphør av autorisajon ved fylte 75 år' Tidsskrift for Den norske legeforening. Nr. 9, 2009, 129, p. 892.

Husa, Jaakko 2003, 'Farewell to functionalism of methodological tolerance?' Zeitschrift für ausländisches und internationales Privatrecht. 419, Bd. 67 H. 3, 2003, pp. 419-447.

Husmann, Manfred 2005, 'Die EG-Gleichbehandlungs-Richtlinien 2000/2002 und ihre Umsetzung in das deutsche, englische und französische Recht' Zeitschrift für europäisches Sozial- und Arbeitsrecht 2005, pp. 167-175.

Hustad-Johansen, Finn E. 2009, 'Tanker omkring 70-årseregelen for fastlegehjemmel' Tidsskrift for Den norske legeforening. Nr. 9, 2009, 129, p. 892.

Hyggen, Christer 2008, 'Slitne kvinner og farlige menn, Om grunnlaget for særaldersgrenser i Norge' Fafo-rapport 2008:16, available at: http://www.fafo.no/pub/rapp/20058/20058.pdf (28.03.2012) (last accessed 17.12.2014).

Högenauer, Nikolaus 2002, Die europäischen Richtlinien gegen Diskriminierung im Arbeitsrecht.

I

Iannone, Enrico 2009, Die Kodifizierung des Arbeitsvertragsrechts - ein Jahrhundertprojekt ohne Erfolgsaussicht?.

Ilmarinen, Juhani/Tuomi, K. 2004, 'Past present and future of workability', People and Work Research Reports. 65, 2004, pp. 1–25.

Ilmarinen, Juhani 2006, 'Towards a longer worklife, Aging and the quality of worklife in the European Union' Finnish Institute of Occupational Health. 2006.

Ilmarinen, Juhani 2007, 'The Workability Index (WAI)', Occupational Medicine. Vol. 57, 2007, p. 160.

Ilmarinen, Juhani 2011, 'Research challenges for older workers' in: Older workers in a sustainable society. Ennals, Richard/Salomon, Robert (eds.), pp. 15-18.

ILO 2007, Equality at work, 2007.

ILO 2008, Conditions of work and employment: Issues for older workers, Information Sheet No. OW-1.

Issacharoff, Samuel/Harris Worth, Erica 1997, 'Is age discrimination really age discrimination?: The ADEA's unnatural solution' in: New York University Law Review. 1997, pp 780-840.

Itzin, Chaterine/Phillipson, Chris 1995, 'Gendered ageism: A double jeopardy for women in organizations' in: Gender, Culture and Organizational Change. Itzin, Catherine/Newman, Janet (eds.), pp. 84-94.

Iversen, Thomas N./Larsen, Lars/Solem, Per E. 2009, 'A conceptual analysis of ageism' Nordic Psychology. Vol. 61 (3), 2009, pp. 4-22.

J

Jaeger, Berit 2008, '68-Jahres-Altersgrenze für Vertragsärzte mit deutschem und europäischem Recht vereinbar' Medizinrecht. 2008, pp. 456-458.

Jakhelln, Henning 1989, 'Embetsmenn eller tjenestemenn' in: Institutt for offentlig retts skriftserie. Nr. 2/1989.

Jakhelln, Henning 2000, 'Åremålskontrakter, særskilte aldersgrenser og retrettstillinger' in: Arbeidsrettslige studier bind II. (originally published in Institutt for offentlig retts skriftserie Nr. 5/1986) pp. 756-828.

Jakhelln, Henning 2007, Oversikt over arbeidsretten. 4. edt.

Janbu, Torunn 2011, 'Eldre leger og lisens' Tidsskrift for Den norske legeforening. Nr. 2, 2011, 131, p. 111.

Johnsen, Jan R. 2006, Health systems in transition, Norway, European observatory on health systems and policies.

Joseph, Sarah/Schultz, Jenny/Castan, Melissa 2004, The International Covenant on Civil and Political rights: Cases, materials, and commentary. 2. edt.

Joseph, Sarah 2010, 'UN Covenants and Labour Rights', in: Fenwick, Colin/Novitz, Tonia (eds.), Human Rights at work: Perspectives on Law and Regulation, pp. 331ff.

Joseph, Sarah/Castan, Melissa 2013, The International Covenant on Civil and Political rights. 3. edt.

Joussen, Jacob 2012, '§ 95 Teilnahme an der vertragsärztlichen Versorgung' in: SGB V, Gesetzliche Krankenversicherung, 3. edt. Becker, Ulrich/Kingreen, Thorsten (eds.).

K

Kadefors, Roland/Hanse, Jan J. 2012, 'Employers' attitudes toward older workers and obstacles and opportunities for the older unemployed to reenter working life' in: Nordic journal of working life studies. Vol. 2, No. 3, August 2012, pp. 29-47.

Kasprzyk, Izabela 2014, Altersdiskriminierung im deutschen Arbeitsrecht.

Kazemi, Robert/Leopold, Anders 2007, 'Ist die Altersgrenze von 68 Jahren in § 95 SGB V noch verfassungsgemäß?' Arzt Zahnarzt Recht. 2007, pp. 118-122.

Kilpatrick, Claire 2011, 'The Court of Justice and labour law in 2010: A new EU discrimination law architecture' Industrial Law Journal. Vol. 40 No. 3, 2011, pp. 280-301.

Kjønstad, Asbjørn 2012, 'Folketrygdens alderspensjoner' Jussens Venner. 47(2), 2012, pp. 85-157.

Knapp, Kenneth A. 2007, 'The Fallacy of the Lump of Labor: Adding to the Costs of Ageism' ILC Issue Brief. December 2007, pp. 1-8, available at: http://www.aging-society.org/agingsociety/links/ilcusaageism.pdf (last accessed 17.12.2014).

Knill, Christoph/Becker, Florian 2003, 'Divergenz trotz Diffusion? Rechtsvergleichende Aspekte des Verhältnismäßigkeitsprinzips in Deutschland, Großbritannien und der Europäischen Union' Die Verwaltung. 36 (4), 2003, pp. 447-481.

Kohte, Wolfhard 2011, 'Altersdiskriminierung von Universitätsprofessoren ("Georgiev")' jurisPraxisReport-ArbeitsRecht. 2/2011, Anm. 7, Kohte.

Kreikebohm, Ralf 2013 a, Einleitung, IV. Die Rentenreform 2001, E. Hinzuverdienstgrenzen (§ 34), § 35, in: Sozialgesetzbuch VI, Kreikebohm, Ralf (ed.), 4. edt.

Kreikebohm, Ralf 2013 b, 'E. Hinzuverdienstgrenzen (§ 34), § 35', in: Beck'scher Online-Kommentar Sozialrecht, BeckOK SGB VI, Rolfs, Christian/Giesen, Richard/Kreikebohm, Ralf/Udsching, Peter (eds.), Stand: 1.9.2013.

Krekula, Clary/Närvänen, Anna-Liisa/Näsman, Elisabet 2005, 'Ålder i intersektionell analys' Kvinnovetenskaplig tidskrift. 2-3, 2005, pp. 81-94.

Krois, Christopher 2011, 'Altersgrenzen für Universitätsprofessoren' Europäische Zeitschrift für Arbeitsrecht. 2011, pp. 351-361.

Kruge, Geir J. 2007, Diskriminering på grunn av alder – særlig om aldersgrenser, Status og kommentar, Arbeidsrett 2007, pp. 237-252.

Kummer, Pierre 2003, Umsetzungsanforderungen der neuen arbeitsrechtlichen Antidiskriminierungsrichtlinie (RL 2000/78/EG).

Kyvik, Svein/Olsen,Terje B. 2008, 'Does the Aging of Tenured Academic Staff Affect the Research Performance of Universities?' Scientometrics. Vol. 76 No. 3, 2008, pp. 439-455.

Kämmerer, Jörg A. 2008, 'Deutsches Beamtenrecht und Verbot der Altersdiskriminierung' Zeitschrift für Beamtenrecht 10/2008, pp. 325-339.

König, Doris/Peters, Anne 2006, 'Das Diskriminierungsverbot' in: EMRK/GG Konkordanzkommentar zum europäischen und deutschen Grundrechtsschutz, Grote, Rainer/Marauhn, Thilo (eds.), chap. 21.

Kötz, Hein 1999, 'Comparative law in Germany today' Revue internationale de droit comparé. Vol. 51 No. 4, 1999, pp. 753-758.

L

Landsverk, Johanne 2010, 'Ingen propp i systemet' Forskerforum. 1, 2010, pp. 13-17.

Lassmann, Andreas 2007, Kündigung und Kündigungsschutz im norwegischen Arbeitsrecht.

Lee, Luke T. 1987, 'Remark to "Aging: A new human rights concern"' in: American Society of International Law. Vol. 81, 1987, pp. 169-175.

Leeftijd 2009, http://leeftijd.nl/wp-content/uploads/2014/07/cao_wijzer_duurzame_participatie.pdf (last accessed: 17.12.2014).

Lehr, Ursula 1982, 'Socio-psychological correlates of longevity' Annual Review of gerontology and geriatrics. 3, 1982, pp. 102-147.

Lehr, Ursula 2007, Psychologie des Alterns, 11. edt.

Lehr, Ursula 2008, 'Living in an aging world: a challenge for the individual and the society' HUM ONTOGENET 2(2), 2008, pp. 41-49.

Lehr, Ursula 2009, Population ageing, in: Online-handbook demography, Berlin Institute for Population and Development (ed.), available at: http://www.berlin-institut.org/?id=573 (last accessed: 17.12.2014).

Lehr, Ursula/Minnemann, Elisabeth 1987, 'Veränderung von Quantität und Qualität sozialer Kontakte vom 7. zum 9. Lebensjahrzehnt' in: Formen seelischen Alterns. Lehr, Ursula/Thomae, Hans (eds.), pp. 80-91.

Li, Guohua/Baker, Susan P./Grabowski, Jurek G./Qiang, Yandong/McCarthy, Melissa L./Rebok, George W. 2003, 'Age, flight experience, and risk of crash involvement in a cohort of professional pilots' American Journal of Epidemiology. Vol. 157 No. 10, 2003, pp. 875-880.

Lilli, Marco (1999), 'Forholdsmessighetsprinsippet i EU-retten og dets betydning i norsk rett' Lov og Rett. 1999, pp. 515-536.

Linsenmaier, Wolfgang 2003, 'Das Verbot der Diskriminierung wegen des Alters' Recht der Arbeit. Sonderbeilage zu Heft 5, 2003, pp. 22-33.

Linz, Kathrin/Stula, Sabrina 2010, 'Demographic change in Europe' Working paper no. 4 of Observatory for Sociopolitical Developments in Europe.

Lohne, Ylva L./Næsheim, Helge N. 2006, Eldre i arbeidslivet, available at: https://www.ssb.no/a/publikasjoner/pdf/rapp_200609/rapp_200609.pdf (last accessed 17.13.2014).

Lowzow, Andreas H. 2010, 'Ny alderspensjon' Institutt for offentlig retts skriftserie. Nr. 4, 2010.

Lykke, Nina 2005, 'Nya perspektiv på intersektionalitet. Problem och möjligheter' Kvinnovetenskaplig tidskrift. 2-3, 2005, pp. 7-17.

Lüderitz, Martin 2005, Altersdiskriminierung durch Altersgrenzen.

Löwisch, Manfred 2006, 'Kollektivverträge und Allgemeines Gleichbehandlungsgesetz' Der Betrieb. 2006, pp. 1729-1732.

M

Macnicol, John 2006, Age discrimination, An historical and contemporary analysis.

Makkonen, Timo 2002, 'Multiple, Compound and Intersectional Discrimination, Bringing the experience of the most marginalized to the fore' available at: http://cilvektiesibas.org.lv/site/attachments/01/02/2012/timo.pdf (last accessed 17.12.2014).

Maltby, Tony 2011, 'Extending working lives? Employability, work ability and better quality working lives', Social Policy & Society. Vol. 10:3, 2011, pp. 299-308.

Manfredi, Simonetta 2008, Developing good practice in managing age diversity in the higher education sector: An evidence-based approach. available at: https://wiki.brookes.ac.uk/download/attachments/21430381/adreportv 3.pdf?version=1&modificationDate=1228180173000 (last accessed 17.12.2014).

Manfredi, Simonetta/Vickers, Lucy 2009, 'Retirement and Age Discrimination: Managing Retirement in Higher Education', Industrial Law Journal. Vol. 38, 2009, pp. 343-364.

Martin, Brian 1984, 'Age discrimination in academia' ANU reporter. Vol.15, No. 11, 27 July 1984, available at: http://www.bmartin.cc/pubs/84agediscrimination.html (last accessed 17.12.2014).

Materstvedt, Lars J. 2010, 'En "propp" snakker ut- om aldersgrenser for professorer' in: universitetsavisa.no. 18.02.2010, online available at: http://www.universitetsavisa.no/leserbrev/article3245.ece (last accessed 17.12.2014).

Mathisen, Gjermund 2007, 'Om proporsjonalitet som skranke for tiltak som gjør inngrep i EØS-avtalens fire friheter' Jussens Venner. 2007, pp. 80-92.

McColgan, Aileen 2003, 'Principles of equality and protection from discrimination in international human rights law', European Human Rights Law Review. 2, 2003, pp. 157-175.

McColgan, Aileen 2014, 'Discrimination, equality and the law, 2014.

McCrudden, Christopher 2003, 'Theorising European equality law, in: Equality in diversity, The new equality directives, Costello, Cathryn/Barry, Ellis (eds.), 2003, pp. 1-38.

McCrudden, Christopher/Prechal, Sacha 2009, The concepts of equality and non-discrimination in Europe: A practical approach. European Network of Legal Experts in the field of Gender Equality.

McNamara, Tay K./Sano, Joelle M./John B. Williamson 2012, 'The pros and cons of pro-work policies and programs for older workers' The Oxford Handbook of Work and Aging. Borman Walter C./Hedge, Jerry W. (eds.) pp. 663-683.

Meenan, Helen 2005, 'The future of ageing and the role of age discrimination in the global debate' Journal of international aging, law & policy. pp. 1-4.

Meenan, Helen 2006, 'Thinking outside the box: age and other grounds', Contemporary Issues in Law. 8 (1), 2006, pp. 80-96.

Meenan, Helen 2007a, 'Age discrimination: Cinderella & The golden bough' in: Equality Law in an Enlarged European Union. Meenan, Helen (ed.), pp. 278-312.

Meenan, Helen 2007b, 'Reflecting on Age Discrimination and rights of the elderly in the European Union and the Council of Europe' 14 MJ 1, 2007, pp. 39-82.

Meenan, Helen 2007c, 'Age discrimination in Europe: Late bloomer or wall-flower?' Nordic journal of Human Rights. No. 02, 2007, pp. 97-118.

Meenan, Helen 2009, 'Reflecting on age discrimination in the European Union – the search for clarity and food for thought' ERA Forum 10, 2009, pp. 107-124.

Mégret, Frédéric 2011, 'The Human Rights of Older Persons: A Growing Challenge' in: Human Rights Law Review. 11:1, 2011, pp. 37-66.

Meixner, Rüdiger 2009, 'Betroffene gehen rechtlich gegen Altersdiskriminierung vor, Trotz Ende der 68er-Altersgrenze' Niedergelassene Arzt. Nr. 3, 2009, p. 31.

Mellbye, Fredrik 1996, 'Aldersgrense for licentia practicandi' Tidsskrift for Den norske legeforening. 1996, 116, p. 1137.

Merten, Sonja 2008, 'Das Arbeitsvertragsgesetz und das AGG' Fachanwalt Arbeitsrecht. 2008, pp. 173-176.

Michaels, Ralf 2006, 'The Functional Method of comparative Law' in: The Oxford Handbook of Comparative Law. pp. 339-382.

Mikkola, Matti 2010, Social human rights of Europe.

Mohler, Stanley R. 1981, 'Reasons for eliminating the "age 60" regulation for airline pilots' Aviation, space, and environmental medicine. Vol. 52 No. 8, 1981, pp. 445-454.

Mohr, Joachim 2007, 'Die Vertreibung der Weisen' Der Spiegel. available at: http://www.spiegel.de/unispiegel/jobundberuf/0,1518,458419,00.html (last accessed 17.12.2014).

Mohr, Jochen 2009, 'Die Rechtsstellung pensionierter und emeritierter Hochschullehrer bei vertraglicher Verpflichtung zur Vertretung ihres Lehrstuhls in Lehre, Forschung und Prüfung bis zur Wiederbesetzung' Neue Zeitschrift für Arbeitsrecht. 2009, pp. 1-6.

Mohr, Jochen 2013, 'Unwirksamkeit tariflicher Altersgrenzen für das Cockpitpersonal von Fluggesellschaften' Sammlung Arbeitsrechtlicher Entscheidungen. 02/2013, pp. 36-44.

Monaghan, Karon 2011, 'Multiple and intersectional discrimination' European Anti-Discrimination Law Review. No. 13, 2011, pp. 20-32.

Mowbray, Alastair 2004, European Convention on Human Rights, Article 14 prohibition of discrimination.

Müller, Thomas 2011, Alter und Recht, Das menschliche Alter und seine Bedeutung für das Recht unter besonderer Berücksichtigung des europäischen und nationalen Antidiskriminierungsrecht.

N

Nelson, Todd D. 2005, 'Ageism: Prejudice against our feared future self' Journal of Social Issues. Vol. 61, No. 2, 2005 pp. 207-221.

Neumann, A. 2011, § 95, in: Beck'scher Online-Kommentar Sozialrecht, BeckOK SGB V, Rolfs, Christian/Giesen, Richard/Kreikebohm, Ralf/Udsching, Peter (eds.), edt. 30, Stand: 01.03.2011.

Ng, Thomas, W. H./Feldman, Daniel C. 2008, 'The relationship of age to ten dimensions of job performance' Journal of Applied Psychology. Vol. 93(2), 2008, pp. 392-423.

Nielsen, Ruth 2009, 'Is European Union equality law capable of addressing multiple and intersectional discrimination yet? Precautions against, neglecting intersectional cases' in: European Union Non-Discrimination Law. Schiek, Dagmar/Chege, Victoria (eds.) pp. 31-51.

Norsk Seniorpolitisk Barometer 2012 a, Yrkesaktiv befolking, 13-23 august 2012.

Norsk Seniorpolitisk Barometer 2012 b, Kommentarrapport yrkesaktive, written by Dalen, Erik on behalf of the Center for Senior Policy.

Norsk Seniorpolitisk Barometer 2013 a, Kommentarrapport yrkesaktive, written by Dalen, Erik on behalf oft he Center for Senior Policy.

Norsk Seniorpolitisk Barometer 2013 b , Kommentarrapport ledere i arbeidslivet, written by Dalen, Erik on behalf of the Center for Senior Policy.

NOSOCO 2008, 'Old-age pensions in Norway' in: Old-age pension systems in the Nordic countries. pp. 95-104.

Novitz, Tonia/Syrpris, Philip 2010, 'Giving with the one hand and taking with the other: Protection of worker's human rights in the European Union' in: Human rights at work. Fenwick, Colin/Novitz, Tonia (eds.), pp. 463-483.

Nowak, Manfred 2005, U.N. Covenant on Civil and Political Rights: CCPR Commentary.

Numhauser-Henning, Ann 2010, 'Åldersdiskriminering og några antsällningsskydssrelaterade frågar' in: Vänbok til Ronnie Eklund. Ahlberg, Kerstin (ed.), pp. 439-473.

Numhauser-Henning, Ann 2011, 'Var står diskrimineringsretten i dag?' in: Festkrift till Boel Flodgren. Lindell-Frantz, Eva/Moberg, Krister/Nyström, Birgitta/Olsson, Katarina (eds.), pp. 289-307.

Numhauser-Henning, Ann 2013, 'Age Discrimination and compulsory retirement' in: Introduction to the Norma Elder Law Research Environment. Numhauser-Henning, Ann (ed.) pp. 41-50.

Numhauser-Henning, Ann/Rönnmar, Mia 2013, 'Compulsory retirement and age discrimination – the Swedish Hörnfeldt case put in perspective' in: Essays in honour of Michael Bogdan. Lindskoug, Patrik/Maunsbach, Ulf/Millqvist, Göran/Samuelsson, Per/Vogel, Hans-Heinrich (eds.), pp. 401-415.

Nussberger, Angelika 2002, 'Altersgrenzen als Problem des Verfassungsrechts' Juristen Zeitung. 2002, pp. 524-532.

O

Obermann, Konrad/Müller, Peter/Müller, Hans-Heiko /Schmidt, Burkhard/Glazinski, Bernd 2013, Understanding the German Health Care System.

Obwexer, Walter 2012, 'Auswirkungen des Beitritts der EU zur EMRK auf das Verbot der Altersdiskriminierung' in: Altersdiskriminierung. Gustav Wachter (ed.), pp. 13-28.

O'Cinneide, Colm 2005, Age discrimination and European Law.

O'Cinneide, Colm 2008, 'Age Discrimination', in: Bamforth, et al. 2008, Discrimination law: Theory and context

O'Cinneide, Colm/Tobler, Christina 2012 , The Evolution and Impact of the case-law of the Court of Justice of the European Union on Directives 2000/43/EC and 2000/78/EC.

OECD 1996, Employment Outlook 1996.

OECD 2009, Employment Outlook 2009.

OECD 2011 a, Pensions at a glance 2011: Retirement-income systems in OECD countries, Germany.

OECD 2011 b, Trends in retirement and in working at older ages, in: Pensions at a glance. 2011: Retirement-income systems in OECD and G20 countries.

OECD 2012, Employment Outlook 2012.

OECD 2013, Ageing and Employment Policies: Norway 2013, Working Better with Age.

Oksholen, Tore 2010, 'Hvor gammel får en professor bli?' Universitetsavisa. 18.01.2010.

Oswick, Cliff/Rosenthal, Patrice 2001, 'Towards a relevant theory of age discrimination in employment' in: Equality, Diversity and Disadvantage in Employment. Noon, Mike/Ogbonna, Emmanuel (eds) pp. 156-171.

Over, Henrik 2009, Das Verbot Der Altersdiskriminierung im Arbeitsrecht nach dem Allgemeinen Gleichbehandlungsgesetz.

P

Pahle, Egill/Hansen, Jan A. 2008, 'Diskriminerende aldersgrense for leger' Tidsskrift for Den norske legeforening. Nr. 13-14, 2008, 128, p. 1075.

Pande, Helene/Holmsen, Eva 2006, 'Palliativ medisin – en oppgave for pensjonerte leger?' Tidsskrift for Den norske legeforening. Nr. 24, 2006, 126, pp. 3283–3284.

Pande, Helene/Noreik, Kjell 2008, 'Eldre legers syn på tap av autorisasjon ved 75 år' Tidsskrift for Den norske legeforening. Nr. 24, 2008, 128, p. 2843.

Paullin, Cheryl/Whetzel, Deborah L. 2012, 'Rentention strategies and older workers', The Oxford Handbook of Work and Aging. Hedge, Jerry W./Borman, Walter, C. (eds.), pp. 392-418.

Plato, Republic, book I, 328 e, translation G.M.A. Grube, 1992.

Poguntke, David 2011, 'Das Hinausschieben der Altersgrenze auf Initiative des Beamten' Die Öffentliche Verwaltung. 2011, pp. 561-568.

Polloczek, Tobias 2008, Altersdiskriminierung im Licht des Europarechts.

Posner, Richard. A. 1995, Aging and Old Age.

Pound, Roscoe 1910, 'Law in the books and law in action' American Law Review. Vol. 44, 1910.

Pound, Roscoe 1954, 'Some thoughts about comparative law' in: Festschrift Ernst Rabel I. Dölle, Hans/Rheinstein Max/Zweigert Konrad (eds.) pp. 7-16.

Preis, Ulrich 2008, Verhandlungen des 67. Deutschen Juristentages Erfurt, 2008 Band I: Gutachten/Teil B: Alternde Arbeitswelt.

Preis, Ulrich/Temming, Felipe 2010 a, 'Der EuGH, das BVerfG und der Gesetzgeber – Lehren aus Mangold II' Neue Zeitschrift für Arbeitsrecht. 2010, pp. 185-19.

Preis, Ulrich/Temming, Felipe 2010 b, 'Schlangenlinien in der Rechtsprechung des EuGH zur Altersdiskriminierung' Neue Zeitschrift für Arbeitsrecht. 2010, pp. 1323-1328.

Pötters, Stephan/Traut, Johannes 2010, 'Eskalation oder Burgfrieden: Mangold vor dem BVerfG' Zeitschrift für europäisches Sozial- und Arbeitsrecht. 2010, pp. 267-276.

R

Rabel, Ernst, 1951, 'Deutsches und Amerikanisches Recht' Rabels Zeitschrift für ausländisches und internationals Privatrecht. Vol. 16 H. 3, 1951, pp. 340-359.

Rasnic, Carol D./Resch, Reinhard 2010, 'Altersdiskriminierung nach amerikanischem Recht' Zeitschrift für Ausländisches und Internationales Arbeits- und Sozialrecht. Issue 3, Vol. 24/25, 2010, pp. 274-292.

Rawls, John 1971, A theory of justice.

Rehm, Johannes 2013, Ungleichbehandlungen aufgrund des Alters im Kündigungsrecht, Eine Untersuchung anhand deutscher und europarechtlicher Diskriminierungsverbote.

Rehman, Javaid 2010, International human rights law. 2. edt.

Rengier, Bernhard 2012, Teil H. Betriebliche Altersversorgung, § 36 Grundlagen, § 38 Ansprüche nach dem Betriebsrentengesetz, in: Moll, Wilhelm (ed.) Münchener Anwaltshandbuch Arbeitsrecht, 3. edt. 2012.

Richter, Claudia 2011, Benachteiligung wegen des Alters im Erwerbsleben, Eine Analyse der gesetzlichen Regelungen - unter besonderer Berücksichtigung des AGG und des KSchG - und ihre Handhabung in der betrieblichen Praxis.

Rieble, Volker 2010, 'Seniorität in der Luftfahrt' in: Festschrift für Eduard Picker zum 70. Geburtstag. Lobinger, Thomas (ed.), pp. 1117-1130.

Riedel, Daniel 2009, 'Das Teilhabegrundrecht auf Zulassung zur vertragsärztlichen Versorgung' Neue Zeitschrift für Sozialrecht. 2009, pp. 260-264.

Riesenhuber, Karl 2007, 'Case ECJ – Mangold' European Review of Contract Law. Band 3, Heft 1, 2007, pp. 62–71.

Rische, Herbert/Thiede, Rheinhold 2013, 'Die Zukunft der gesetzlichen Rentenversicherung' Neue Zeitschrift für Sozialrecht. 2013, pp. 601-605.

Rivlin, Michael M. 2000, 'Why the fair innings argument is not persuasive' BMC Medical Ethics 1:1, 2000, available at: http://www.biomedcentral.com/1472-6939/1/1 (last accessed 17.14.2014).

Rixen, Stephan 2007, 'Rettung für den altersdiskriminierten Vertragsarzt durch den EuGH' Zeitschrift für europäisches Sozial- und Arbeitsrecht. 2007, pp. 345-353.

Robbers, Gerhard 1998, An Introduction to German Law.

Rodriguez-Pinzon, Diego/Martin, Claudia 2003, 'The international status of the rights of Elderly Persons' American University International Law Review. 18, no. 4, 2003, pp. 915-1008.

Rombach, Annett 2010, "Age Concern Germany": Zur gemeinschaftsrechtlichen (Un-) Zulässigkeit von Altershöchstgrenzen im öffentlichen Dienst' Neue Zeitschrift für Verwaltungsrecht. 2010, pp. 102-104.

Roseth, Kai O./Kvalvik, Christel 2012, 'Aldersgrenser og aldersdiskriminering – er det lenger rom for å fastsette eller avtale særskilte aldersgrenser I norsk arbeidsliv?' Arbeidsrett. Vol. 9 Nr. 1, 2012, pp. 142-165.

Rott, Christoph/Thomae, Hans 1991, 'Coping in longitudinal perspective: Findings from the Bonn longitudinal study on aging' Journal of Cross-Cultural Gerontology. Vol. 6, Issue 1, 1991, pp. 23-40.

Rothermund, Klaus/Temming, Felipe 2010, Diskriminierung aufgrund des Alters.

Rudolf, Beate 2007, § 2, in: Gleichbehandlungsrecht. Rudolf, Beate/Mahlmann, Matthias (eds.).

Rönnmar, Mia 2004, Arbetsledningsrätt och arbetsskyldighet.

Rönnmar, Mia 2013, 'Flexicurity and the legal position of the elderly' in: Introduction to the Norma Elder Law Research Environment. Ann Numhauser-Henning (ed.), pp. 51-60.

S

Salthouse, T. A. 1986, Functional age: Examination of a concept, in: Birren, J. E./ Robinson, P. K./Livingston, J. (eds.), Age, Health, & Employment, pp. 78-92.

Samuel, Lenia 2002, Fundamental social rights, case law of the European Social Charter. 2 edt.

Sargeant, Malcolm 2005, 'Disability and age-multiple potential for discrimination', International Journal of the Sociology of Law. Vol. 33, Issue 1, March 2005, pp. 17-33.

Sargeant, Malcolm 2006, Age discrimination in employment.

Schaie, K. Warner 2005, 'What can we learn from longitudinal studies of adult development?' Research in Human Development. 2 (2005), pp. 133-158.

Scheinin, Martin/Krause, Catarina 2000, 'The right not to be discriminated against: The case of social security' in: The jurisprudence of human rights law: A comparative interpretive approach. Orlin, Theodore S./Scheinin, Martin (eds.), pp. 253-286

Schiek, Dagmar 2005, Europäisches Arbeitsrecht. 2. edt.

Schiek, Dagmar 2009, Part I executive summary, in: Multiple discrimination in EU law opportunities for legal responses to intersectional gender discrimination?, European Network of Legal Experts in the field of Gender Equality. pp. 1-26.

Schiek, Dagmar/Waddington, Lisa/Bell, Mark 2007, 'Introductory chapter, A comparative perspective on non-discrimination law' in: Cases, materials and text on national, supranational and international non-discrimination law, Schiek, Dagmar/ Waddington, Lisa/Bell, Mark (eds.), pp. 25-32.

Schlachter, Monika 2003, 'Altersgrenzen angesichts des gemeinschaftsrechtlichen Verbots der Altersdiskriminierung' in: Altersgrenzen und Alterssicherung im Arbeitsrecht, Gedenkschrift für Wolfgang Blomeyer. Rheinhard Richardi, and Hermann Reichold (eds.), pp. 355-373.

Schlachter, Monika 2011, 'Mandatory retirement and age discrimination under EU law' International Journal of Comparative Labour Law and Industrial Relations. Vol. 27 Issue 3, 2011, pp. 287-299 .

Schlachter, Monika 2014, 'Gutachten, Das Verbot der Altersdiskriminierung und der Gestaltungsspielraum der Tarifvertragsvertragsparteien', Hugo Sinzheimer Institut (HIS)-Schriftenreihe, Band 10, 2014.

Schmidt, Folke 1981, 'The need for a multi-axial method in comparative law' Festschrift für Konrad Zweigert zum siebzigsten Geburtstag. Bernstein, Herbert/ Drobnig, Ulrich/Kötz, Hein (eds.) pp. 525-536.

Schmidt, Marlene/Senne, Daniela 2002, 'Das gemeinschaftsrechtliche Verbot der Altersdiskriminierung und seine Bedeutung für das deutsche Arbeitsrecht' Recht der Arbeit. 2002, pp. 80-89.

Schmidt, Marlene 2005, 'The principle of non-discrimination in respect of age: Dimensions of the ECJ's Mangold judgment' German Law Journal. Vol. 07 No. 05, 2005, pp. 505-524.

Schmidt, Marlene 2008, 'Germany' in: The law on age discrimination in the EU. Sargeant, Macolm (ed.), pp. 29-54.

Smith, Nicholas 2007, 'A critique of recent approaches to discrimination law', New Zealand Law Review, 2007, pp. 499-525.

Schäfer, Hauke 2009, 'Hat der Beamte ein subjektives Recht auf Dienstzeitverlängerung?' Zeitschrift für Beamtenrecht. 2009, pp. 301-305.

Schokkenbroek, Jeroen 2004, 'A new European standard against discrimination: Negotiating Protocol No. 12 to the European Convention on Human Rights' in: The development of legal instruments to combat racism in a diverse Europe. Niessen, Jan/Isabelle Chopin (eds.), 2004, pp. 61-80.

Schraepler, Ernst 1985, 'Die Entwicklung nach dem Zweiten Weltkrieg bis 1970', in: Die Entwicklung der Menschen- und Bürgerrechte von 1776 bis zur Gegenwart. 5. edt. Hartung, Fritz/Commichau, Gerhard (eds.), pp. 33-40.

Schroots, Johannes J. F. 1996, 'Theoretical developments in the psychology of aging' The Gerontologist. Vol. 36 No. 6, 1996, pp. 742-748.

Schroots Johannes J. F./Birren, James E. 1988, 'The nature of time: implications for research on aging' Comprehensive Gerontology. C, 2, 1988, pp. 1–29.

Schröder, Ulrich 1984, Altersbedingte Kündigungen und Altersgrenzen im Individualarbeitsrecht.

Schwall, Alexander R. 2012, 'Defining age and using age-relevant constructs' in: The Oxford Handbook of Work and Aging, Hedge, Jerry W./Borman, Walter, C. (eds.), chap. 10, pp. 169-186.

Schwintowski, Hans-Peter 2009, '§ 43 Betriebliche Altersvorsorge' in: Versicherungsrechts-Handbuch. 2. edt. Beckmann, Roland M./Matusche-Beckmann, Annemarie (eds.)

Seitsamo, Jorma/Ilmarinen, Juhani 1997, 'Life style, aging and work ability among active Finnish workers in 1981-1992' Scandinavian Journal of Work and Environmental Health. 23, Suppl.1, 1997, pp. 20-26.

Sharit, Joseph/Czaja, Sara J. 2012, 'Job design and redesign for older workers', in: The Oxford Handbook of Work and Aging. Hedge, Jerry W./Borman, Walter, C. (eds.), pp. 454-482.

Shoben, Elaine W. 1980, 'Compound Discrimination: The Interaction of Race and Sex in employment Discrimination' New York University Law Review. Vol. 55, Issue 5, 1990, pp. 793-837.

Shock, Nathan W./Greulich, Richard C./Costa, Paul T, Jr./Andres, Reubin/Lakatta, Edward G./Arenberg, David/Tobin, Jordan D. 1984, Normal human aging, the Baltimore Longitudinal Study of Aging.

Simitis, Spiros 1994 a, 'Denationalizing labour law: The case of age discrimination' Comparative Labor Law & Policy Journal. 15, 1994, pp. 321-339.

Simitis, Spiros 1994 b, 'Altersdiskriminierung - die verdrängte Benachteiligung' Neue Juristische Wochenschrift. 1994, pp. 1453-1454.

Solanke, Iyiola 2009, 'Stigma: A limiting principle allowing multiple-consciousness in anti-discrimination law?' in: European Non-Discrimination Law, Schiek, Dagmar/ Chege, Victoria (eds.) pp. 115-130.

Solem, Per E. 2007, 'Aldring og social deltagelse' in: Gerontopsykologi, Larsen, Lars (ed.), pp. 95-120.

Sprenger, Markus 2006, Das arbeitsrechtliche Verbot der Altersdiskriminierung nach der Richtlinie 2000/78/EG.

Statistisches Bundesamt 2009, Bevölkerung Deutschlands bis 2060, 12. koordinierte Bevölkerungsvorausberechnung.

Statistisk sentralbyrå 2014, Arbeidskraftundersøkelsen, 3. kvartal 2014.

Statistics Norway 2009, Population projections, National and regional figures, 2009-2060, available at: https://www.statistics.no/en/befolkning/statistikker/folkfram/aar/2009-06-11 (last accessed: 17.12.2014).

Steen, B./Djurfeldt, H. 1993, 'The gerontological and geriatric population studies in Gothenburg/Sweden' Zeitschrift für Gerontologie 26, pp. 163-169

Stuart-Hamilton, Ian 2006, The psychology of ageing.

Streinz, Rudolf/Herrmann, Christoph 2007, 'Der Fall Mangold - eine "kopernikanische Wende im Europarecht"?' Recht der Arbeit. 2007, pp. 165-169.

Sembdner, Friedrich 2007, 'Zur Verlängerung der aktiven Dienstzeit des Beamten bis zur Vollendung des 67. Lebensjahres' Die Personalvertretung. 6/7, 2007, pp. 312-316.

Sen, Amartya 1992, Inequality reexamnied, third printing 1995.

Senne, Daniela 2006, Auswirkungen des europäischen Verbots der Altersdiskriminierung auf das deutsche Arbeitsrecht.

Settersten, Richard A. Jr./Mayer, Karl U. 1997, 'The Measurement of Age, Age Structuring, and the Life Course' Annual Review of Sociology. Vol. 23, August 1997, pp. 233-261.

Sheehan, Myles N. 2003, 'Disabilities and ageing' Theoretical Medicine and Bioethics. Vol. 24: 6, 2003, pp. 525-533.

Sodan, Helge 2009, Vertrags(zahn)ärzte und ihre Patienten im Spannungsfeld von Sozial-, Verfassungsrecht und Europarecht, Eine kritische Analyse unter besonderer Berücksichtigung der Arztwahlfreiheit der Versicherten.

Soellner, Alfred 1985, 'Zur Verfassungs- und Gesetzestreue im Arbeitsrecht', Recht der Arbeit. 1985, pp. 328-337.

Statistics Norway 2009, Population projections, National and regional figures, 2009-2060, available at: https://www.statistics.no/en/befolkning/statistikker/folkfram/aar/2009-06-11 (last accessed 17.12.2014).

Stein, David/Rocco, Tonette S./Goldenetz, Kelly A. 2000, 'Age and the University workplace' Human Resource Development Quarterly. Vol. 11, No. 1, 2000, pp. 61-80.

Strand, Vibeke Blaker 2007, 'Vern mot direkte og indirekte diskriminering etter norsk rett- et ensartet vern?' Lov og rett. 2007, pp. 131-153.

Stroebe, Wolfgang 2010, 'The graying of academia' American Psychologist. Vol. 65 No. 7, 2010, pp. 660-673.

Steinsvoll, Steinar, P. 2009, 'Diskriminering av eldre leger', Tidsskrift for Den norske legeforening. Nr. 7, 2009, 129, p. 650.

Summer, Rudolf 2007, 'Die Altersgrenze für den Eintritt in den Ruhestand – Probleme durch Europarecht', Zeitschrift für Beamtenrecht. 11/2007, pp. 368-371.

Summer, Rudolf 2009, 'Die Altersgrenze für den Wechsel aus dem aktiven Beamtenverhältnis in den Ruhestand und die individuellen Abweichungen' Die Personalvertretung. 5 2009, pp. 164-168.

Summers, Clyde W. 1982, 'Employee Participation in Sweden and the United States: Some Comparisons from an American Perspective' 1 Arbetsrättsliga Uppsatser. 49, 1982, pp. 49-80.

Svabø, Harry M. 1996, 'Eldre legers kår' Tidsskrift for Den norske legeforening. 1996, 116, p. 1064.

Swedish National Institute of Public Health 2006 , Healthy ageing, A challenge for Europe.

Schüffner, Marc/Schnall, Laura 2009, Hypertrophie des ärztlichen Sozialrechts, Verfassungs- und europarechtliche Regelungen des (zahn-)ärztlichen Berufsrechts anhand ausgewählter Beispiele.

Søndergaard, Dorte M. 2005, 'Making Sense of Gender, Age, Power and Disciplinary Position: Intersecting Discourses in the Academy' Feminism and Psychology. Vol. 15 No. (2), 2005, pp. 189-208.

T

Kwong-Leung, Tang/Jik-Joen, Lee 2006, 'Global social justice for older people: The case for an international convention on the rights of older people', British Journal of Social Work. Vol. 36, 2006, pp. 1135–1150.

Tangen, Erik 2011, 'Diagnose: For gammel' nyhet Bærum. 12. February 2011, p. 12.

Taylor, Philip 2011, 'Is early retirement history?', in: Older workers in a sustainable society. Richards Ennals, and Robert H. Salomon (eds.), pp. 225-232.

Temming, Felipe 2008, Altersdiskriminierung im Arbeitsleben: Eine rechtsmethodische Analyse.

Temming, Felipe 2012 a, 'Labour and the role of law' Kölner Schrift zum Wirtschaftsrecht 2012, pp. 122-128.

Temming, Felipe 2012 b; Compulsory retirement and the fixing of a maximum age for recruitment - lawful or unlawful age discrimination, available at:, http://www.equineteurope.org/IMG/pdf/felipe_temming___presentation-2.pdf (last accessed: 17.12.2014).

Temming, Felipe 2012 c, 'Diskriminierende Beendigung der Arbeitsverträge von Piloten bei Vollendung des 60. Lebensjahres', Europäische Zeitschrift für Arbeitsrecht 2012, pp. 205-224.

Tempelmann, Achim/Stenslik, Bastian-Peter 2011, 'Altersgrenzenregelungen im Arbeitsrecht' Deutsches Steuerrecht. 2011, pp. 577-581.

Thieme, Werner 1956, Deutsches Hochschulrecht.

Thüsing, Gregor 2014, Vor § 611, in: Arbeitsrecht Kommentar. 6. edt. Martin Henssler, Heinz J. Willemsen, Heinz-Jürgen Kalb (eds.).

Tobler, *Christa 2005*, Indirect Discrimination.

Toft, Martin 2010, 'Snart 70 – nektar å pensjonera seg' UNIFORM 04, 11.03.2010.

Tornstam, Lars 1989, 'Gero-transcendence: A reformulation of the disengagement theory' Aging 1, 1989, pp. 55-63.

Tornstam, Lars 2005, Gerotranscendence: A developmental theory of positive ageing.

Torp, Kå Hå 1996, 'Må en lege alltid være lege?' Tidsskrift for Den norske legeforening. Nr 9, 1996, p. 1120.

Trasch, Timo 2008, Der Prüfungsmaßstab des § 10 Satz 1 AGG bei der Rechfertigung der unmittelbaren Diskriminierung wegen des Alters.

Tridimas, Takis 2006, The General principles of EU Law.

U

United Nations 2002, Report of Second World Assembly on Ageing, Madrid 6.12 April 2002.

United Nations 2002, Gender dimensions of ageing.

UN Expert Group (2009), Report of the expert group meeting "Rights of older persons".

UN Human Rights Council, The necessity of a human rights approach and effective United Nations mechanism for the human rights of the older person', see Working Paper, A/HRC/AC/4/CRP.,

V

Van Bueren, Geraldine 2009, 'The Protection of the Human Rights of Older Persons in Europe: A legal perspective, background briefing paper' International Symposium on the Rights of Older People Hosted by Age Concern England in collaboration with HelpAge International and the International Federation on Ageing, available at: http://www.globalaging.org/elderrights/world/2009/humanrightseurope.pdf (last accessed 17.12.2014)

van Dijk, Pieter/van Hoof, Fried/van Rijn, Arjen/Zwaak, Leo (eds.) 2006, Theory and Practice of the European Convention on Human Rights, 4 edt.

van Hoof, Fried 2006, chap. 3 in: Theory and Practice of the European Convention on Human Rights, 4 edt., van Dijk et al. (eds.)

Vigen, Terje 1999, 'Legemangelmysteriet - kan det løses?' Tidsskrift for Den norske legeforening. 1999, 119, p. 487.

von Benda-Beckmann, Keebet 1979, 'Einige Bemerkungen über die Beziehung zwischen Rechtssoziologie und Rechtsvergleichung', Zeitschrift für vergleichende Rechtswissenschaften. 1979, pp. 51-67.

von Hoff, Konrad 2009, Das Verbot der Altersdiskriminierung aus Sicht der Rechtsvergleichung und der ökonomischen Analyse des Rechts.

von Lübtow, Ulrich 1967, Die Rechtsstellung des entpflichteten Professors.

von Steinau-Steinrück, Robert/Schneider, Volker/Wagner, Tobias 2005, 'Der Entwurf eines Antidiskriminierungsgesetzes: Ein Beitrag zur Kultur der Antidiskriminierung?' Neue Zeitschrift für Arbeitsrecht. 2005, pp. 28-32.

von Steinau-Steinrück, Robert/Schneider, Volker 2010, § 2 AGG, in: AnwaltKommentar Arbeitsrecht.

von Roetteken, Thorsten/Rothländer, Christian/Burkholz, Bernhard/Kohde, Jens 2013, § 25 Ruhestand wegen Erreichens der Altersgrenze, IV. Ergänzung durch Landesrecht, in: v. Roetteken, Thorsten/Rothländer, Christian (eds.), BeamtStG Kommentar zum Beamtenstatusgesetz, 16. Update 12/13.

von Roetteken, Thorsten 2014, § 10, in: AGG, 36. Update 07/14

W

Wachter, Gustav 2010, ''Sprachverwirrung' bei der Altersdiskriminierung', Zeitschrift für europäisches Sozial- und Arbeitsrecht. 2010, pp. 49-54.

Wachter, Gustav 2012, 'Piloten: Mit 60 Jahren ist noch nicht Schluss' in: Altersdiskriminierung. Wachter, Gustav (ed.), pp. 149-157.

Wachter, Gustav 2013, 'Altersdiskriminierung, Diskriminierung/Höhe der Altersrente', Zeitschrift für europäisches Sozial- und Arbeitsrecht 2013, pp. 125-133.

Wank, Rolf 2012, 'Altersgrenzen in Tarifverträgen nach der EuGH-Rechtsprechung' in: Arbeitsgerichtsbarkeit und Rechtsprechung, Festschrift für Klaus Bepler zu, 65. Geburtstag, pp. 585-603.

Weiss, Manfred/Schmidt, Marlene 2008, Labour Law and Industrial Relations in Germany.

Wenner, Ulrich 2009, 'Neue Rollenanforderungen an den Vertragsarzt, Freiberuflicher Unternehmer, Funktionsträger im Gesundheitskonzern, Restverwalter oder Vollzugsakteur staatlicher Gesundheitspolitik?' GesundheitsRecht. 2009, pp. 505-518.

Wilkening Robin 2002, 'The age 60 rule: age discrimination in commerical aviation' Aviation, space, and environmental medicine. Vol. 73 No. 73, 2002, pp. 194-202.

Woodruff, Bryan B. 1997-1998, 'Unprotected until forty: The Limited Scope of the Age Discrimination in Employment Act of 1967' Indiana Law Journal. Vol. 73, 1997-1998, pp. 1295-1312.

Wulfers, Christian/Hecht, Diana 2007, 'Altersdiskriminierung durch Tarifbestimmungen – Eine Analyse des TvöD und TV-L' Zeitschrift für Tarifrecht 2007, pp. 475-483.

Y

Yntema, Hessel E. 1956, 'Comparative legal research: some remarks on „looking out of the cave"' Michigan Law Review. Vol. 54, No. 7, May, 1956, pp. 899-928.

Young, Iris 1990, Justice and the politics of difference.

Z

Zweigert, Konrad F./Kötz, Heinz 1998, Comparative Law. 3 edt.